Cabling: The Complete Guide to Network Wiring

Cabling: The Complete Guide to Network Wiring

David Groth
Jim McBee
David Barnett

SYBEX®

San Francisco • Paris • Düsseldorf • Soest • London

Associate Publisher: Richard Staron
Acquisitions & Developmental Editor: Maureen Adams
Editor: Joseph A. Webb
Production Editor: Liz Burke
Technical Editor: Art Brieva
Book Designer: Kris Warrenburg
Graphic Illustrators: Eric Houts, Tony Jonick
Electronic Publishing Specialist: Franz Baumhackl
Proofreaders: Laurie O'Connell, Nancy Riddiough, Emily Hsuan, Yariv Rabinovitch, Suzanne Stein
Indexer: Ted Laux
Cover Designer: Calyx Design
Cover Illustrator: Richard Miller, Calyx Design
Color Insert: Owen Wolfson, Gareth Hopson Photography

Library of Congress Card Number: 2001090464

ISBN: 0-7821-2958-7

For my wife, my daughter, my family,
and my friends.
—D.G.

This book is dedicated to my family
(Mom, Dad, sisters, cousins, and aunts).
Over a distance of thousands of miles and many
years, you still influence my actions every day.
We are all products of our environment;
mine was great!
—J.M.

For Shan, Jordan, and Cameron.
—D.B.

ACKNOWLEDGMENTS

This book has been a long time in the making. First and foremost, I would like to acknowledge my coauthor, Jim McBee, for his excellent work on this project. He should be proud of his efforts, and it shows in the quality of this book. Also, we would like to acknowledge the other behind-the-scenes people that helped to make this book, starting with Dan Whiting of Border States Electric Supply in Fargo, ND, for all the reference material and pictures he and his company provided. His expertise was invaluable in the making of this book. Thanks, Dan! We would also like to thank photographer Steve Sillers for taking many of the pictures throughout this book.

This book would not exist without Sybex Acquisitions and Developmental Editor Maureen Adams. Thanks for bringing Jim and me together and for managing this project. Additionally, I would like to thank Editor Joe Webb for editing this book and Production Editor Liz Burke for managing its production. Also, I would like to recognize the rest of the Sybex staff for all their hard work on this book, including (but not limited to) Eric Houts and Tony Jonick, the graphic illustrators; Owen Wolfson and Amy Changar, for their work on the color insert; all of the proofreaders (Laurie O'Connell, Nancy Riddiough, Suzanne Stein, Emily Hsuan, and Yariv Rabinovitch); the indexer Ted Laux; and electronic publishing specialist Franz Baumhackl, who spent time and effort making the book look good.

Finally, I would like to recognize my wife, daughter, family, and friends, without whom I couldn't do any of this and for whom I do this.

—David Groth

At the Spring 1999 Networld+InterOp, David Groth, Maureen Adams from Sybex, and I talked about the need for a book about network cabling that was targeted toward IT professionals and people just starting out with cabling. The first edition was a resounding success, and now you hold a brand-new second edition in your hands!

Special thanks also goes to Janice Boothe, RCDD (and her awesome www.wiring .com Web site) and Mike Holt for their knowledge of codes. Paul Lucas, RCDD, of Paul's Cabling tolerated my nonstop questions and provided many great stories and experiences. Kudos to Matt Bridges for his assistance with components. Jeff Deckman gave his vital insight and input to the Request for Proposal (RFP) chapter; his cooperative approach to working with vendors will help many people successfully deploy telecommunications infrastructures. Charles Perkins drew from his years of field experience to help with the case studies.

Others who reviewed portions of the book and provided feedback include Maureen McFerrin, Randy Williams, RD Clyde, John Poehler, and David Trachsel. Jeff Bloom and the folks at Computer Training Academy (where I teach Windows NT, TCP/IP, and Exchange courses) are always outstandingly patient when I take on a project like this.

Finally, the consummate professionals at Sybex always leave me in awe of their skills, patience, and insight.

—*Jim McBee*

I originally got involved with this book by assisting Jim McBee with the initial writing of the first edition. Based on his recommendation, Sybex asked me to revise the book for the second edition. I'm grateful to Jim and everyone at Sybex for entrusting me with the project. Thanks to all.

Much of my cable knowledge was accumulated under the supervision of Dr. James S. Tyler, and I would be remiss if I didn't acknowledge his significant contribution to my experience. Also, I would like to thank Jeanie Baer, RCDD, for her help and advice over the years and most recently for keeping me up-to-date on what's happening in the TIA standards' workgroups. Ron Hayes, practitioner of the black art of transmission engineering, deserves thanks and credit for suffering me as his occasional sorcerer's apprentice. I would like to thank Rob Jewson, RCDD, friend and business partner, for his advice and assistance.

My wife, Shan, deserves special thanks for encouraging me to take on this project in addition to a "real" job plus a residential installation business, and then putting up with the consequences. What were you thinking, dear?

—*David Barnett*

CONTENTS AT A GLANCE

Appendices

CONTENTS

INTRODUCTION

Welcome to the incredibly complex world of premises data-communications cabling. This introduction will tell you a little about how this book came about and how you can use it to your best advantage.

Not only does cabling carry the data across your network, it can also carry voice, serial communications, alarm signals, video, and audio transmissions. In the past, people took their cabling systems for granted. However, over the last few years, the Information Technology world has begun to understand the importance of a reliable and well-designed structured cabling system. The past five years have witnessed an explosion in the number of registered structured-cabling installers. The number of people who need to know the basics of cabling has increased dramatically.

We had a great time writing this book. In the yearlong process of researching, writing, and editing it, we met many consummate professionals in the cabling business. Many distributors, manufacturers, and cabling contractors provided us with feedback, tips, and in-the-field experiences.

During the research phase of the book, we continually reviewed newsgroups, cabling FAQs, and other Internet resources, besides polling Information Technology managers, help-desk staff, network designers, cable installers, and system managers, to find out what people want to know about their cabling system. The answers we received helped us write this book.

About This Book

This book's topics run the gamut of cabling; they include the following:

- An introduction to data cabling
- Information on cabling standards and how to choose the correct ones
- Cable system and infrastructure constraints

- Cabling-system components

- Tools of the trade

- Copper, fiber-optic, and unbounded media

- Wall plates and cable connectors

- Cabling-system design and installation

- Cable-connector installation

- Cabling-system testing and troubleshooting

- Creating Request for Proposals (RFPs)

- Cabling case studies

A cabling dictionary is included at the end of the book so you can look up unfamiliar terms. Five other appendixes include resources for cabling information, tips on how to get your Registered Communications and Distribution Designer (RCDD) certification, information for the home cabler, a discussion of USB/1394 cabling, and information about ETA's line of cabling certifications. Finally, a 24-page color insert shows you what various cabling products look like in their "natural environment."

Who Is This Book For?

If you are standing in your neighborhood bookstore browsing through this book, you may be asking yourself if you should buy it. The procedures in this book are illustrated and written in English rather than "technospeak." That's because we, the authors, designed this book specifically to help unlock the mysteries of the wiring closet, cable in the ceiling, wall jacks, and other components of a cabling system. Cabling can be a confusing topic; it has its own language, acronyms, and standards. We designed this book with the following types of people in mind:

- Information Technology (IT) professionals who can use this book to gain a better understanding and appreciation of a structured cabling system

- IT managers who are preparing to install a new computer system

- Do-it-yourselfers who need to install a few new cabling runs in their facility and want to get it right the first time

- New cable installers who want to learn more than just what it takes to pull a cable through the ceiling and terminate it to the patch panel

How to Use This Book

To understand the way this book is put together, you must learn about a few of the special conventions we used. Following are some of the items you will commonly see.

Italicized words indicate new terms. After each italicized term, you will find a definition.

TIP   *Tips* will be formatted like this. A tip is a special bit of information that can either make your work easier or make an installation go more smoothly.

NOTE   *Notes* are formatted like this. When you see a note, it usually indicates some special circumstance to make note of. Notes often include out-of-the-ordinary information about working with a telecommunications infrastructure.

WARNING   *Warnings* are found within the text whenever a technical situation arises that may cause damage to a component or cause a system failure of some kind. Additionally, warnings are placed in the text to call particular attention to a potentially dangerous situation.

KEY TERMS   *Key Terms* are used to introduce a new word or term that you should be aware of. Just as in the worlds of networking, software, and programming, the world of cabling and telecommunications has its own language.

Sidebars

This special formatting indicates a sidebar. *Sidebars* are entire paragraphs of information that, although related to the topic being discussed, fit better into a standalone discussion. They are just what their name suggests: a sidebar discussion.

Cabling @ Work Sidebars

These special sidebars are used to give real-life examples of situations that actually occurred in the cabling world.

Appendix A is a glossary of the terms used throughout this book. Additionally, a 32-page color insert will show you certain items in color.

Keep an eye out for these special items as you read.

Enjoy!

Have fun reading this book—we've had fun writing it. We hope that it will be a valuable resource to you and will answer at least some of your questions on LAN cabling. As always, we love to hear from our readers; you can reach David Groth at dgroth@corpcomm.net. Jim McBee can be reached at jmcbee@somorita.com. David Barnett can be contacted at david@wiring.com.

part I

Cabling Technology and Components

Introduction to Data Cabling

"**D**ata cabling! It's just wire. What is there to plan?" the newly promoted programmer-turned-MIS-director commented to Jim. The MIS director had been contracted to help the company move its 750-node network to a new location. During the initial conversation, the director had a couple of other "insights":

- He said that the walls were not even up in the new location, so it was too early to be talking about data cabling.

- To save money, he wanted to pull the old Category 3 cabling and move it to the new location. ("We can run 100Base-TX on the old cable.")

- He said not to worry about the voice cabling and the cabling for the photo-copier tracking system; someone else would coordinate that.

Jim shouldn't have been too surprised by the ridiculous nature of these comments. Too few people understand the importance of a reliable, standards-based, flexible cabling system. Fewer still understand the challenges of building a high-speed network. Some of the technical problems associated with building a cabling system to support a high-speed network are comprehended only by electrical engineers. And many believe that a separate type of cable should be in the wall for each application (PCs, printers, terminals, copiers, etc.).

Data cabling has come a long way in the past 15 years. This chapter discusses some of the basics of data cabling, including topics such as:

- The golden rules of data cabling

- The importance of reliable cabling

- The legacy of proprietary cabling systems

- The increasing demands on data cabling to support higher speeds

- Cable design and materials used to make cables

- Types of communications media

- Limitations that cabling imposes on higher-speed communications

- The future of cabling performance

You are probably thinking right now that all you really want to know is how to install cable to support a few 10Base-T workstations. Words and phrases such as *attenuation*, *crosstalk*, *twisted pair*, *modular connectors*, and *multimode optical-fiber cable* may be completely foreign to you. Just as the world of PC LANs and WANs has its own industry buzzwords, so does the cabling business. In fact, you may hear such an endless stream of buzzwords and foreign terminology that you'll wish you had majored in electrical engineering in college. But it's not really that mysterious, and, armed with the background and information we'll provide, you'll soon be using cablespeak like a cabling professional.

The Golden Rules of Data Cabling

Listing our own golden rules of data cabling is a great way to start this chapter and the book. If your cabling is not designed and installed properly, you will have problems that you can't even imagine. From our experience, we've become cabling evangelists, spreading the good news of proper cabling. What follows is our list of rules to consider when planning structured-cabling systems:

- Networks never get smaller or less complicated.

- Build one cabling system that will accommodate voice and data.

- Always install more cabling than you currently require. Those extra outlets will come in handy someday.

- Use structured-cabling standards when building a new cabling system. Avoid anything proprietary!

- Quality counts! Use high-quality cabling and cabling components. Cabling is the foundation of your network; if the cabling fails, nothing else will matter. For a given grade or category of cabling, you'll see a range of pricing, but the highest prices don't necessarily mean the highest quality. Buy based on the manufacturer's reputation and proven performance, not the price.

- Don't scrimp on installation costs. Even quality components and cable must be installed correctly; poor workmanship has trashed more than one cabling installation.

- Plan for higher speed technologies than are commonly available today. Just because 1000Base-T Ethernet seems unnecessary today does not mean it won't be a requirement in five years.

- Documentation, although dull, is a necessary evil that should be taken care of while you're setting up the cabling system. If you wait, more pressing concerns may cause you to ignore it.

The Importance of Reliable Cabling

We cannot stress enough the importance of reliable cabling. Two recent studies vindicated our evangelical approach to data cabling. The studies showed:

- Data cabling typically accounts for less than 10 percent of the total cost of the network infrastructure.

- The life span of the typical cabling system is upwards of 16 years. Cabling is likely the second most long-lived asset you have (the first being the shell of the building).

- Nearly 70 percent of all network-related problems are due to poor cabling techniques and cable-component problems.

TIP If you have installed the proper Category or grade of cable, the majority of cabling problems will usually be related to patch cables, connectors, and termination techniques. The permanent portion of the cable (the part in the wall) will not likely be a problem unless it was damaged during installation.

Of course, these were facts that we already knew from our own experiences. We have spent countless hours troubleshooting cabling systems that were non-standard, badly designed, poorly documented, and shoddily installed. We have seen many dollars wasted on the installation of additional cabling and cabling infrastructure support that should have been part of the original installation.

Regardless of how you look at it, cabling is the foundation of your network. It must be reliable!

The Cost of Poor Cabling

The costs that result from poorly planned and poorly implemented cabling systems can be staggering. One company that had recently moved into a new office space used the existing cabling, which was supposed to be Category 5 cable. Almost immediately, 100Mbps Ethernet network users reported intermittent problems.

These problems included exceptionally slow access times when reading e-mail, saving documents, and using the sales database. Other users reported that applications running under Windows 98 and Windows NT were locking up, which often caused them to have to reboot their PC.

After many months of network annoyances, the company finally had the cable runs tested. Many cables did not even meet the minimum requirements of a Category 5 installation, and other cabling runs were installed and terminated poorly.

WARNING   Often, network managers mistakenly assume that data cabling either works or it does not, with no in-between. Cabling *can* cause intermittent problems.

Is the Cabling to Blame?

Can faulty cabling cause the type of intermittent problems that the aforementioned company experienced? Contrary to popular opinion, it certainly can. In addition to being vulnerable to outside interference from electric motors, fluorescent lighting, elevators, cellular phones, copiers, and microwave ovens, faulty cabling can lead to intermittent problems for other reasons.

These reasons usually pertain to substandard components (patch panels, connectors, and cable) and poor installation techniques, and they can subtly cause dropped or incomplete packets. These lost packets cause the network adapters to have to time-out and retransmit the data.

Robert Metcalfe (inventor of Ethernet, founder of 3Com, columnist for *InfoWorld*, industry pundit, and Jim's hero) helped coin the term *drop-rate magnification*. Drop-rate magnification describes the high degree of network problems caused by dropping a few packets. Metcalfe estimates that a 1-percent drop in Ethernet packets can correlate to an 80 percent drop in throughput. Modern network protocols that send multiple packets and expect only a single acknowledgement (such as TCP/IP and Novell's IPX/SPX) are especially susceptible to drop-rate magnification, as a single dropped packet may cause an entire stream of packets to be retransmitted.

Dropped packets (as opposed to packet collisions) are more difficult to detect because they are "lost" on the wire. When data is lost on the wire, the data is transmitted properly but, due to problems with the cabling, the data never arrives at the destination or it arrives in an incomplete format.

You've Come a Long Way, Baby:
The Legacy of Proprietary Cabling Systems

Early cabling systems were unstructured, proprietary, and often worked only with a specific vendor's equipment. They were designed and installed for mainframes and were a combination of thicknet cable, twinax cable, and terminal cable (RS-232). Because no cabling standards existed, an MIS director simply had to ask the vendor which cable type should be run for a specific type of host or terminal. Frequently, though, vendor-specific cabling caused problems due to lack of flexibility. Unfortunately, the legacy of early cabling still lingers in many places.

PC LANs came on the scene in the mid-1980s; these systems usually consisted of thicknet cable, thinnet cable, or some combination of the two. These cabling systems were also limited to only certain types of hosts and network nodes.

As PC LANs became popular, some companies demonstrated the very extremes of data cabling. Looking back, it's surprising to think that the ceilings, walls, and floor trenches could hold all the cable necessary to provide connectivity to each system. As one company prepared to install a 1,000-node PC LAN, they were shocked to find all the different types of cabling systems needed. Each system was wired to a different wiring closet or computer room and included the following:

- Wang dual coaxial cable for Wang word-processing terminals

- IBM twinax cable for IBM 5250 terminals

- Twisted-pair cable containing one or two pairs, used by the digital phone system

- Thick Ethernet from the DEC VAX to terminal servers

- RS-232 cable to wiring closets connecting to DEC VAX terminal servers

- RS-232 cable from certain secretarial workstations to a proprietary NBI word-processing system

- Coaxial cables connecting a handful of PCs to a single NetWare server

Some users had two or three different types of terminals sitting on their desks and, consequently, two or three different types of wall plates in their offices or cubicles. Due to the cost of cabling each location, the locations that needed certain terminal types were the only ones that had cables that supported those terminals. If users moved—and they frequently did—new cables often had to be pulled.

The new LAN was based on a twisted-pair Ethernet system that used unshielded twisted-pair cabling called Synoptics Lattisnet, which was a precursor to the 10Base-T standards. Due to budget considerations, when the LAN cabling was installed, this company often used spare pairs in the existing phone cables. When extra pairs were not available, additional cable was installed. Networking standards such as 10Base-T were but a twinkle in the IEEE's (Institute of Electrical and Electronic Engineers) eye, and guidelines such as the ANSI/TIA/EIA-568-A Cabling Standard were not yet formulated (see the next section for more information on TIA/EIA-568-A). Companies deploying twisted-pair LANs had little guidance, to say the least.

Much of the cable that was used at this company was sub–Category 3, meaning that it did not meet the minimum Category 3 performance requirements. Unfortunately, because the cabling was not even Category 3, once the 10Base-T specification was approved, many of the installed cables would not support 10Base-T cards on most of the network. So three years into this company's network deployments, it had to rewire much of its building.

KEY TERM   **Application**   Often, you will see the term *application* used when referring to cabling. If you are like me, you think of an application as a software program that runs on your computer. However, when discussing cabling infrastructures, an application is the technology that will take advantage of the cabling system. Applications include telephone systems (analog voice and digital voice), Ethernet, Token Ring, ATM, ISDN, and RS-232.

Proprietary Cabling Is a Thing of the Past

The company discussed in the last section had at least seven different types of cables running through the walls, floors, and ceilings. Each cable met only the standards dictated by the vendor that required that particular cable type.

As early as 1988, the computer and telecommunications industry yearned for a versatile standard that would define cabling systems and make the practices used to build these cable systems consistent. Many vendors defined their own standards for various components of a cabling system. Communications product distributor Anixter (www.anixter.com) codeveloped and published a document called *Cable Performance Levels* in 1990, which provided a purchasing specification for communication cables. It was an attempt to create a standard by which cabling performance could be measured. Veterans in the networking industry will remember cables often being referred to as Level 1, Level 2, or Level 3 cables. Anixter continues to maintain the Anixter levels program; it is currently called Anixter Levels XP.

The Need for a Comprehensive Standard

Twisted-pair cabling in the late 1980s and early 1990s was often installed to support digital or analog telephone systems. Early twisted-pair cabling (Level 1 or Level 2) often proved marginal or insufficient for supporting the higher frequencies and data rates required for network applications such as Ethernet and Token Ring. Even when the cabling did marginally support higher speeds of data transfer (10Mbps), the connecting hardware and installation methods were often still stuck in the "voice" age, which meant that connectors, wall plates, and patch panels were designed to support voice applications only.

The Anixter Cables Performance Levels document only described performance standards for cables. A more comprehensive standard had to be developed to outline not only the types of cables that should be used but also the standards for deployment, connectors, patch panels, and more.

A consortium of telecommunications vendors and consultants worked in conjunction with the American National Standards Institute (ANSI), Electronic Industries Association (EIA), and the Telecommunications Industry Association (TIA) to create a standard originally known as the Commercial Building Telecommunications Cabling Standard or ANSI/EIA/TIA-568-1991. This Standard has been revised and updated several times and is now known as ANSI/TIA/EIA-568-A or just TIA/EIA-568-A; it is discussed at length in Chapter 2. In subsequent years, TIA/EIA-568-A has been updated with a series of addenda. The latest addendum, TIA/EIA-568-A-5, covers requirements for enhanced Category 5 (Category 5e). A completely updated version of this standard is currently being authored by a working committee of the TIA and will be released as ANSI/TIA/EIA-568-B.

Cabling and the Need for Speed

The past few years have seen some tremendous advances not only in networking technologies but also in the demands placed on them. In the past 15 years, we have seen the emergence of standards for 10Mb Ethernet, 16Mb Token Ring, 100Mb FDDI, 100Mb Ethernet, 155Mb ATM (Asynchronous Transfer Mode), 655Mb ATM, 1Gb Ethernet, and 2.5Gb ATM. Network-technology designers are already planning technologies that may support data rates of up to 10Gbps, such as 10Gbps ATM and 10Gbps Ethernet.

The average number of nodes on a network segment has decreased dramatically, while the number of applications and the size of the data transferred has increased dramatically. Applications are becoming more complex and the amount of network bandwidth required by the typical user is increasing. Is the bandwidth provided by some of the new ultra-high-speed network applications (such as 1Gb Ethernet) required today? Maybe not, but networks and applications will no doubt require such throughput in the future.

Cabling @ Work: The Increasing Demands of Modern Applications

A perfect example of the increasing demands put on networks by applications is a law firm that eight years ago was running typical office-automation software applications on its LAN. The average document worked on was about four pages in length and 12KB in size. This firm also used electronic mail; a typical e-mail size was no more than 500 bytes. Other applications included dBase III and a couple small corresponding databases, a terminal-emulation application that connected to the firm's IBM minicomputer, and a few Lotus 1-2-3 programs. The size of transferred data files was relatively small, and the average 10Base-T network-segment size was about 100 nodes per segment.

Today, the same law firm is still using its 10Base-T and finding it increasingly insufficient for their ever-growing data processing and office-automation needs. The average document length is still around four pages, but, thanks to the increasing complexity of modern word-processing software and templates, the average document is nearly 50KB in size!

Even simple e-mail messages have grown in size and complexity. An average, simple e-mail message size is now about 1.5KB, and, with the new message technologies that allow the integration of inbound/outbound faxing, an e-mail message with a six-page fax attached has an average size of 550KB. Further, the firm integrated the voice-mail system with the e-mail system so that inbound voice mail is automatically routed to the user's mailbox. The average 30-second voice mail message is about 150KB.

The firm also implemented an imaging system that scans and stores many documents that previously would have taken up physical file space. Included in this imaging system are litigation support documents, accounting information, and older client documentation. A single-page TIF file can vary in size (depending on the complexity of the image) from 40 to 125KB.

Continued on next page

Additional software applications include a client/server document-management system, a client/server accounting system, and several other networked programs that the firm only dreamed about eight years before. Most of the firm's attorneys make heavy use of the Internet, often visiting sites that provide streaming audio and video.

Today, the firm's average switched segment size is less than 36 nodes per segment, and the segments are switched to a 100Mbps backbone. Even with these small segment sizes, many segments are congested. Although the firm would like to begin running 100Base-TX Ethernet to the desktop, it is finding that its Category 3 cabling does not support 100Base-TX networking.

When this firm installs its new cabling system to support the next-generation network applications, you can be sure that it will want to choose the cabling infrastructure and network application carefully to ensure that its needs for the next 10 to 15 years will be accommodated.

Does the fact that software applications and data are putting more and more of a demand on the network have anything to do with data cabling? You might think that the issue is more related to network-interface cards, hubs, switches, and routers, but, as data rates increase, the need for higher levels of performance on the cable also increases.

Types of Communications Media

Four major types of communications media (cabling) are available for data networking today: unshielded twisted pair, shielded twisted pair, coaxial, and fiber optic. An additional variety of twisted-pair cable called *screened twisted pair* has recently appeared; it is a hybrid of shielded and unshielded twisted pair.

It is important to distinguish between backbone cables and horizontal cables. Backbone cables connect network equipment such as servers, switches, and routers and connect equipment rooms and communication closets. Horizontal cables run from the communication closets to the wall outlets. For new installations, multi-strand fiber-optic cable is essentially universal as backbone cable. For the horizontal, UTP reigns supreme. Much of the focus of this book is on UTP cable.

Twisted-Pair Cable

By far the most economical and widely installed cabling today is twisted-pair wiring. Not only is twisted-pair wiring less expensive than other media, installation is also simpler, and the tools required to install it are not as costly. Unshielded twisted pair (UTP) and shielded twisted pair (STP) are the two primary varieties of twisted pair on the market today, but screened twisted pair (ScTP) is emerging and may become more common.

Unshielded Twisted Pair (UTP)   Though it has been used for many years for telephone systems, unshielded twisted pair (UTP) for LANs first became common in the late 1980s with the advent of Ethernet over twisted-pair wiring and the 10Base-T standard. UTP is cost effective and simple to install, and its bandwidth capabilities are continually being improved.

NOTE   An interesting historical note: Alexander Graham Bell invented and patented twisted-pair cabling and an optical telephone in the 1880s. During that time, Bell offered to sell his company to Western Union for $100,000, but it refused to buy.

UTP cabling typically has only an outer covering (jacket) consisting of some type of nonconducting material. This jacket covers one or more pairs of wire that are twisted together. In this chapter, as well as throughout much of the rest of the book, assume unless specified otherwise that UTP cable is a four-pair cable. Four-pair cable is the most commonly used cable in network installations today. The characteristic impedance of UTP cable is 100 ohms plus or minus 15 percent, though 120-ohm UTP cable is sometimes used in Europe and is allowed by the ISO/IEC 11801 cabling standard.

A typical UTP cable is shown in Figure 1.1. This simple cable consists of a jacket that surrounds four twisted pairs. Each wire is covered by an insulation material with good *dielectric* properties. For data cables, this means that in addition to being electrically nonconductive, it must also have certain properties that allow good signal propagation.

UTP cabling seems to generate the lowest expectations of twisted-pair cable. Its great popularity is mostly due to the cost and ease of installation. With every new generation of UTP cable, network engineers think they have reached the limits of the UTP cable's bandwidth and capabilities. However, cable manufacturers continue to extend its capabilities. During the development of 10Base-T and a number of pre-10Base-T proprietary UTP Ethernet systems, critics said that UTP would never support data speeds of 10Mbps. Later, the skeptics said that UTP would never support data rates at 100Mbps. In July 1999, the IEEE approved the 1000Base-T standard, which allows Gigabit Ethernet to run over Category 5 cable!

FIGURE 1.1:

UTP cable

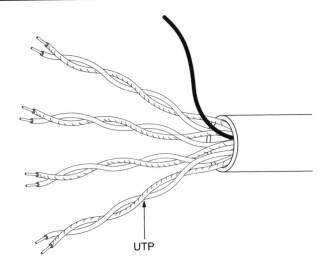

UTP

Not All UTP Is Created Equal!

Though two cables may look identical, their supported data rates can be dramatically different. Older UTP cables that were installed to support telephone systems may not even support 10Base-T Ethernet. The ANSI/TIA/EIA-568-A Standard helps consumers choose the right cable (and components) for the right application. The Standard has been updated over the years and contains addenda 1 through 5. It currently defines several categories of UTP cable: Categories 3, 4, 5, and 5e. Categories 1 and 2 are de facto definitions commonly held by the industry:

Category 1 (not defined by ANSI/EIA/TIA-568-A)   This type of cable usually supports frequencies of less than 1MHz. Common applications include analog voice telephone systems.

Category 2 (not defined by ANSI/EIA/TIA-568-A)   This cable type supports frequencies of up to 4MHz. It's not commonly installed, except in installations that use twisted-pair ArcNet and Apple LocalTalk networks. Its requirements are based on the original, proprietary IBM Cabling System.

Continued on next page

Category 3   This type of cable supports data rates up to 16MHz. The cable was the most common variety of UTP for a number of years starting in the late 1980s. Common applications include 4Mbps UTP Token Ring, 10Base-T Ethernet, 100Base-T4, and digital and analog telephone systems.

Category 4   Cable belonging to Category 4 was designed to support frequencies of up to 20MHz, specifically in response to a need for a UTP solution for 16Mbps Token Ring LANs. It was quickly replaced in the market when Category 5 was developed, as Category 5 gives five times the bandwidth with only a small increment in price.

Category 5   Currently, Category 5 is the most common cable installed, although most new installations use an enhanced version. It is designed to support frequencies of up to 100MHz. Applications include 100Base-TX TP-PMD (FDDI over copper), 155Mbps ATM over UTP, and, thanks to sophisticated encoding techniques, 1000Base-T Ethernet. To support 1000Base-T applications, the installed cabling system must pass performance tests specified by TSB-95 (TSB-95 is a Technical Service Bulletin issued in support of ANSI/TIA/EIA-568-A, which defines additional test parameters.)

Category 5e (enhanced Category 5)   Category 5e was introduced with the TIA/EIA-568-A-5 addendum of the cabling standard. Even though it has the same rated bandwidth as Category 5, i.e., 100MHz, additional performance criteria and a tighter transmission test requirement make it more suitable for high-speed applications such as Gigabit Ethernet. Applications are the same as those for Category 5 cabling.

Other TIA/EIA categories are in development that will support even higher frequencies than 100MHz; among these are Category 6 and Category 7 cabling.

The cabling standards are discussed in more detail in Chapter 2. Additional information on copper media can be found in Chapters 7 and 9.

Shielded Twisted Pair (STP)   Shielded twisted-pair (STP) cabling was first made popular by IBM when it introduced Type classification for data cabling. Though more expensive to purchase and install than UTP, STP offers some distinct advantages. The current ANSI/TIA/EIA-568-A cabling Standard permits IBM Type 1A horizontal cable, which supports frequency rates of up to 300MHz. STP cable is also much less susceptible to outside electromagnetic interference (EMI) than UTP cabling because all cable pairs are well shielded.

Some STP cabling, such as IBM Types 1 and 1A cable, uses a woven copper-braided shield, which provides considerable protection against electromagnetic interference (EMI.) Inside the woven copper shield, STP consists of twisted pairs of wire (usually two pairs) wrapped in a foil shield. Some STP cables have only the foil shield around the wire pairs. Figure 1.2 shows a typical STP cable. In the IBM design, the wire used in STP cable is 22 AWG (just a little larger than the 24 AWG wire used by typical UTP LAN cables) and has a nominal impedance of 150 ohms.

FIGURE 1.2:

STP cable

Constructions of STP in 24 AWG, identical in copper conductor size to UTP cables, are more commonly used today.

Simply installing STP cabling does not guarantee you will improve a cable's immunity to EMI or reduce the emissions from the cable. Several critical conditions must be met to achieve good shield performance:

- The shield must be electrically continuous along the whole link.

- All components in the link must be shielded. No UTP patch cords can be used.

- The shield must full enclose the pair and the overall shield must fully enclose the core. Any gap in the shield covering is a source of EMI leakage.

- The shield must be grounded at both ends of the link, and the building grounding system must conform to grounding standards (such as TIA/EIA-607).

If one of these conditions is not satisfied, shield performance will be badly degraded. For example, tests have shown that if the shield continuity is broken, the emissions from a shielded cabling system increase by 20dB on the average.

Screened Twisted Pair (ScTP)   One of the interesting developments over the past few years is screened twisted-pair (ScTP) cabling, a hybrid of STP and UTP cable. ScTP cable contains four pairs of 24 AWG, 100-ohm wire (see Figure 1.3) surrounded by a foil shield or wrapper and a drain wire for bonding purposes. ScTP is also sometimes called foil twisted-pair (FTP) cable because the foil shield surrounds all four conductors. This foil shield is not as large as the woven copper-braided jacket used by some STP cabling systems such as IBM Types 1 and 1A. ScTP cable is essentially STP cabling that does not shield the individual pairs; the shield may also be smaller than some varieties of STP cabling.

FIGURE 1.3:

ScTP cable

Foil shield or screen

Cable jacket

Wire pairs

The foil shield is the reason ScTP is less susceptible to noise. In order to implement a completely effective ScTP system, however, the shield continuity must be maintained throughout the entire channel—including patch panels, wall plates, and patch cords. Yes, you read this correctly; the continuity of not only the wires but also the shield must be maintained through connections. Like STP cabling, the entire system must be bonded to ground at both ends of each cable run, or you will have created a massive antenna.

Standard eight-position modular jacks (commonly called RJ-45s) do not have the ability to insure a proper ground through the cable shield. So special mating hardware, jacks, patch panels, and even tools must be used to install an ScTP cabling system. Many manufacturers of ScTP cable and components exist—just make sure to follow all installation guidelines.

ScTP is recommended for use in environments that have abnormally high ambient electromagnetic interference, such as hospitals, airports, or government/military communications centers. The value of an ScTP system in relation to its additional cost is sometimes questioned, as some tests indicate that UTP noise immunity and emissions characteristics are comparable with ScTP cabling systems. Often, the decision to use ScTP simply boils down to whether you want the warm and fuzzy feeling of knowing an extra shield is in place.

No standard exists on the use of ScTP, though the TIA is currently working on one. So a number of vendors have introduced their own ScTP products. They are proprietary and often don't work with other vendor's components. If you choose an ScTP solution prior to the standards being developed for it, you should use a single vendor's cable and components.

Should You Choose Unshielded, Shielded, Screened, or Optical-Fiber Cable for Your Horizontal Wiring?

Many network managers and cabling-infrastructure systems designers face the question of which cabling to choose. Often the decision is very cut and dried, but sometimes it is not.

For typical office environments, UTP cable will be always be the best choice (at least until fiber-network components drop in price). Most offices don't experience anywhere near the amount of electromagnetic interference necessary to justify the additional expense of installing shielded twisted-pair cabling.

Environments such as hospitals and airports may benefit from a shielded or screened cabling system. The deciding factor seems to be the external field strength. If the external field strength does not exceed three volts per meter (V/m), good-quality UTP cabling should work fine. If the field strength exceeds threeV/m, shielded cable will be a better choice.

However, many cabling designers think that if the field strength exceeds three V/m, fiber-optic cable is a better choice. Further, these designers will point out the additional bandwidth and security of fiber-optic cable.

Continued on next page

Although everyone has an opinion on the type of cable you should install, it is true that the only cable type that won't be outgrown quickly is optical fiber. Fiber-optic cables are already the media of choice for the backbone. As hubs, routers, and workstation network-interface cards for fiber-optic cables come down in price, fiber will move more quickly in to the horizontal cabling space.

Optical-Fiber Cable

As late as 1993, it seemed that in order to move toward the future of desktop computing, businesses would have to install fiber-optic cabling directly to the desktop. Copper cable (UTP) performance continues to be surprising, however. Fiber-optic cable is discussed in more detail in Chapter 10.

NOTE   *Fiber* versus *fibre*: Are these the same? Yes, just as *color* (U.S. spelling) and *colour* (British spelling) are the same. Your spell checker will probably question your use of *fibre*, however.

Although, for most of us, fiber to the desktop is not yet a practical reality, fiber-optic cable is touted as the ultimate answer to all our voice, video, and data transmission needs and continues to make inroads in the LAN market. Some distinct advantages of fiber-optic cable include:

- Transmission distances can be much greater than with copper cable.

- Potential bandwidth is dramatically higher than with copper.

- Fiber optic is not susceptible to outside EMI or crosstalk interference, nor does it generate EMI or crosstalk.

- Fiber-optic cable is much more secure than copper cable because it is extremely difficult to monitor, "eavesdrop," or tap a fiber cable.

NOTE   Fiber-optic cable can easily handle data at speeds above 1Gbps; in fact, it has been demonstrated to handle data rates exceeding 200Gbps!

Since the late 1980s, LAN solutions have used fiber-optic cable in some capacity. Recently, a number of ingenious solutions that allow both voice and data to use the same fiber-optic cable have emerged.

Fiber Optics Comes of Age (Affordably)

Fiber-optic cable used to be much harder to install than copper cable, requiring precise installation practices. However, in the past few years, the cost of an installed fiber-optic link has dropped and is now often only 10 to 15 percent more than the cost of a UTP link. Better fiber-optic connectors and installation techniques have made fiber-optic systems easier to install. In fact, installers experienced with both fiber-optic systems and copper systems will tell you that with the newest fiber-optic connectors and installation techniques, fiber-optic cable is easier to install than UTP.

The main hindrance to using fiber optics all the way to the desktop in lieu of UTP or STP is that the electronics (workstation network-interface cards and hubs) are still significantly more expensive.

Fiber-optic cable uses a strand of glass or plastic to transmit data signals using light; the data is carried in light pulses. Unlike the transmission techniques used by its copper cousins, optical fibers are not electrical in nature.

Plastic-core cable is easier to install and slightly cheaper than glass core, but plastic cannot carry data as far as glass. In addition, graded-index plastic optical fiber (POF) has yet to make a widespread appearance on the market, and the cost-to-bandwidth value proposition for POF is poor and may doom it to obscurity.

NOTE   Light is transmitted through a fiber-optic cable by light-emitting diodes (LEDs) or lasers. With newer LAN equipment designed to operate over longer distances, such as with 1000Base-LX, lasers are commonly being used.

A fiber-optic cable (shown in Figure 1.4) consists of a jacket (sheath), protective material, and the optical-fiber portion of the cable. The optical fiber consists of a core (typically 62.5 microns in diameter, but it can also be 8.3 or 50 microns) that is smaller than a human hair, which is surrounded by a cladding. The cladding (typically 125 micrometers in diameter) is surrounded by a coating, buffering material, and, finally, a jacket. The cladding provides a lower refractive index to cause reflection within the core so that light waves can be transmitted through the fiber.

A dual fiber-optic cable

Two varieties of fiber-optic cable are commonly used in LANs and WANs today: single-mode and multimode. The mode can be thought of as bundles of light rays entering the fiber; these light rays enter at certain angles.

KEY TERM   **Dark Fiber**   No, *dark fiber* is not a special, new type of fiber cable. When telecommunications companies and private businesses run fiber-optic cable, they never run the exact number of strands of fiber they need. That would be foolish. Instead, they run two or three times the amount of fiber they require. The spare strands of fiber are often called *dark fiber* because they are not then in use, i.e., they don't have light passing through them. Telecommunications companies often lease out these extra strands to other companies.

Single-Mode Fiber-Optic Cable   *Single-mode fiber* (SMF, sometimes called monomode) optic cable is most commonly used by telephone companies and in data installations as backbone cable. Single-mode fiber-optic cable is *not* used as horizontal cable to connect computers to hubs. The light in a single-mode cable travels straight down the fiber (as shown in Figure 1.5) and does not bounce off the surrounding cladding as it travels. Typical single-mode wavelengths are 1,310 and 1,550 nanometers.

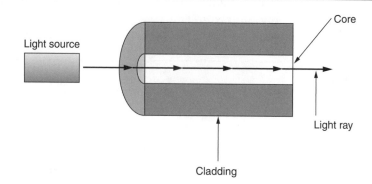

Before you install single-mode fiber-optic cable, make sure the equipment you are using supports it. The equipment that uses single-mode fiber typically uses lasers to transmit light through the cable because a laser is the only light source capable of inserting light into the very small (8 to 10 micron) core of a single-mode fiber.

Multimode Fiber-Optic Cable   *Multimode fiber* (MMF) optic cable is usually the fiber-optic cable used with networking applications such as 10Base-FL, 100Base-F, FDDI, ATM, and others that require fiber optics for both horizontal and backbone cable. Multimode cable allows more than one mode of light to propagate through the cable. Typical wavelengths of light used in multimode cable are 850 and 1,300 nanometers.

There are two types of multimode fiber-optic cable: step index or graded index. Step-index multimode fiber-optic cable indicates that the refractive index between the core and the cladding is very distinctive. The graded-index fiber-optic cable is the most common type of multimode fiber. The core of a graded-index fiber contains many layers of glass; each has a lower index of refraction going outward from the core of the fiber. Both types of multimode fiber permit multiple modes of light to travel through the fiber simultaneously (see Figure 1.6). Graded-index fiber is preferred because less light is lost as the signal travels around bends in the cable.

The typical multimode fiber-optic cable used for horizontal cabling consists of two strands of fiber (duplex); the core is 62.5 microns (micrometers) in diameter, and the cladding is 125 microns in diameter (the measurement is often simply referred to as 62.5/125-micron). The newest version of the ANSI/TIA/EIA-568-B Standard also recognizes the use of 50/125-micron multimode fiber-optic cable.

FIGURE 1.6:

Multimode fiber-optic cable
(graded-index multimode)

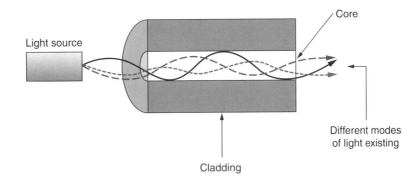

Coaxial Cable

At one time, *coaxial cable* was the most widely used cable type in the networking business. However, it is falling by the wayside in the data-networking arena, except for those lucky enough to have cable-modem Internet service. Coaxial (or just coax) cable is difficult to run and is generally more expensive than twisted-pair cable. In defense of coaxial cable, however, it provides a tremendous amount of bandwidth and is not as susceptible to outside interference as is UTP. Overall installation costs might also be lower than for other cable types because the connectors take less time to apply. Although we commonly use it to connect our televisions to our VCRs, we will probably soon see fiber-optic or twisted-pair interfaces to televisions and VCRs.

Coaxial cable comes in many different flavors, but the basic design is the same for all types. Figure 1.7 shows a typical coaxial cable; at the center is a solid (or sometimes stranded) copper core. Some type of insulation material, such as TFE or PVC, surrounds the core. Either a sleeve or braided-wire mesh shields the insulation, and a jacket covers the entire cable.

The shielding shown in Figure 1.7 protects the data transmitted through the core from outside electrical noise and keeps the data from generating significant amounts of interference. Coaxial cable works well in environments where high amounts of interference are common. For example, some years ago, Jim installed coaxial cable in a power plant because in some areas the Category 3 cable was not reliable.

A number of varieties of coaxial cable are available on the market. You pick the coaxial cable required for the application; unfortunately, coaxial cable installed for Ethernet cannot be used for an application such an ArcNet. Some common types of coaxial cable are listed in Table 1.1.

TABLE 1.1:   Common Coaxial-Cable Types

Cable	Description
RG-58 /U	A 50-ohm coaxial cable with a solid core. Commonly called thinnet and used with 10Base-2 Ethernet and some cable-TV applications.
RG-58 A/U	A 50-ohm coaxial cable with a stranded core. Also known as thinnet. Used by 10Base-2 Ethernet and some cable-TV applications.
RG-58 C/U	A military-specification version of RG-58 A/U.
RG-59U	A 75-ohm coaxial cable. Used with Wang systems and some cable-TV applications.
RG-6U	A 75-ohm coaxial cable. The current minimum grade to install in residences because it will handle the full frequency range of satellite service, plus high-definition TV and cable-modem service.
RG-6 Quad Shield	Same as RG-6U, but with additional shielding for enhanced noise immunity. Currently the recommended cable to use in residences.
RG-62U	A 93-ohm coaxial cable. Used with IBM cabling systems and ArcNet.

Cable Design

Whether you are a network engineer, cable installer, or network manager, a good understanding of the design and components of data cabling is important. Do you know what types of cable can be run above the ceiling? What do all those markings on the cable mean? Can you safely untwist a twisted-pair cable? What is the difference between shielded and unshielded twisted-pair cable? What is the difference between single-mode and multimode fiber-optic cable?

You need to know the answer to these questions—not only when designing or installing a cabling system but also when working with an existing cabling system. All cable types must satisfy some fundamental fire-safety requirements before any other design elements are considered. The U.S. National Electrical Code (NEC) defines five levels of cable for use with LAN cabling and telecommunications, shown in Table 1.2. Cables are rated on their flammability, heat resistance, and how much visible smoke (in the case of plenum cable) they generate when exposed to a flame. The ratings are a hierarchy, with Plenum-rated cables at the top. In other words, a cable with a higher rating can be used instead of any lesser-rated (lower down in the table) cable. For example, a Riser cable can be used in place of General Purpose and Limited Use cables but cannot be used in place of a Plenum cable. A Plenum cable can substitute for all those below it.

TABLE 1.2: NEC Flame Ratings

Optical Fiber Article 770	Twisted Pair Article 800	Coaxial Cable Article 820	Common Term	Notes
OFNP[1] OFCP[2]	CMP[3] MPP[4]	CAVTP	Plenum	Most stringent rating. Must limit the spread of flame and the generation of visible smoke. Intended for use in HVAC (heating ventilation and air conditioning) plenum areas; can be substituted for all subsequent lesser ratings.
OFNR OFCR	CMR MPR	CATVR	Riser	When placed vertically in a building riser shaft going from floor to floor, cable must not transmit flame between floors.
OFNG OFCG	CMG MPG	CATVG	General Purpose	Flame spread limited to 4 ft., 11 in. during test. Cable may not penetrate floors or ceilings, i.e., may only be used within a single floor. This designation was added as a part of the harmonization efforts between U.S. and Canadian standards.

Continued on next page

TABLE 1.2 CONTINUED: NEC Flame Ratings

Optical Fiber Article 770	Twisted Pair Article 800	Coaxial Cable Article 820	Common Term	Notes
OFN OFC	CM	CATV	General Purpose	Flame spread limited to 4 ft, 11 in during test. Cable may not penetrate floors or ceilings, i.e., may only be used within a single floor.
Not applicable	CMX	CATVX	Limited Use	For residential use, but can only be installed in one- and two-family (duplex) housing units. Often co-rated with optional UL requirements for limited outdoor use.

[1] OFN = Optical Fiber, Nonconductive (no metallic elements in the cable)

[2] OFC = Optical Fiber, Conductive (contains a metallic shield for mechanical protection)

[3] CM = Communications cable

[4] MP = Multipurpose cable (can be used as a communication cable or a low-voltage signaling cable per NEC Article 725)

NOTE   More details on the National Electrical Code are given in Chapter 4.

Plenum

According to building engineers, construction contractors, and air-conditioning people, the *plenum* (shown in Figure 1.8) is the space between the false ceiling (a.k.a. drop-down ceiling) and the structural ceiling, *when that space is used for air circulation, heating ventilation, and air conditioning (HVAC)*. Occasionally, the space between a false floor (such as a raised computer-room floor) and the structural floor is referred to as the plenum. Typically, the plenum is used for returning air to the HVAC equipment.

Raised ceilings and floors are convenient spaces in which to run data and voice cable, but national code requires that plenum cable be used in plenum spaces. Be aware that some people use the word *plenum* too casually, referring to all ceiling and floor spaces, whether or not they are plenums. This can be expensive because plenum cables can cost more than twice their nonplenum equivalent. (See the sidebar "Plenum Cables: Debunking the Myths.")

Cable-design engineers refer to *plenum* as a type of cable that is rated for use in the plenum spaces of a building. Those of us who have to work with building engineers, cabling professionals, and contractors must be aware of when the term applies to the air space and when it applies to cable.

Some local authorities and building management may also require plenum-rated cable in nonplenum spaces. Know the requirements in your locale.

FIGURE 1.8:

The ceiling space and a riser

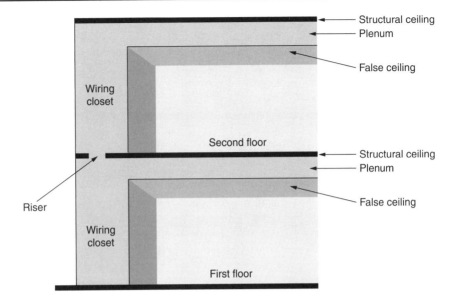

Plenum Cables: Debunking the Myths

It's time to set the record straight about several commonly held, but incorrect, beliefs about plenum-rated cable. These misconceptions get in the way of most discussions about LAN cabling, but are especially bothersome in relation to UTP.

Myth #1: Any false or drop-ceiling area or space beneath a raised floor is a plenum, and I must use plenum-rated cables there.   Not true. Although many people call all such spaces the plenum, they aren't necessarily. A plenum has a very specific definition. It is a duct, raceway, or air space that is part of the HVAC air-handling system. *Sometimes*, or even *often*, the drop-ceiling or raised-floor spaces are used as return air passageways in commercial buildings, but not always. Your building-maintenance folks should know for sure, as will the company that installed the HVAC. If it isn't a plenum space, then you don't have to spend the extra for plenum-rated cable.

Continued on next page

Myth #2: There are plenum cables and PVC cables.   The wording here is nothing but sloppy use of terminology, but it results in the widespread notion that plenum cables don't use PVC in their construction and that nonplenum cables are all PVC. In fact, virtually all four-pair UTP cables in the United States use a PVC jacket, plenum cables included. And guess what? Virtually none of the Category 5 or better cables on the market use any PVC as an insulation material for the conductors, no matter what the flame rating. So a plenum-rated cable actually has just as much PVC in it as does a so-called PVC nonplenum cable. Unless you have to be specific about one of the lesser flame ratings, you are more accurate when you generalize about cable flame ratings if you say *plenum* and *nonplenum* instead of *plenum* and *PVC*.

Myth #3: Plenum cables don't produce toxic or corrosive gasses when they burn.   In Europe and in the United States (regarding specialized installations), much emphasis is placed on "clean" smoke. Many tests, therefore, measure the levels of toxic or corrosive elements in the smoke. But for general commercial and residential use, the U.S. philosophy toward fire safety as it relates to cables is based on two fundamentals: First, give people time to evacuate a building and, second, don't obscure exits and signs that direct people to exits. NEC flame-test requirements relate to tests that measure resistance to spreading a fire, to varying degrees and under varying conditions based on intended use of the cable. The requirements satisfy part one of the philosophy—it delays the spread of the fire. Because all but plenum cables are intended for installation behind walls or in areas inaccessible to the public, the second part doesn't apply. However, because a plenum cable is installed in an air-handling space where smoke from the burning cable could spread via HVAC fans to the populated part of the building, the plenum test measures the generation of *visible* smoke. Visible smoke can keep people from recognizing exits or suffocate them (which actually happened in some major hotel fires before plenum cables were defined in the code).

Myth #4: I should buy plenum cable if I want good transmission performance. If you've got money to burn (ha!), believe this. Although FEP (fluorinated ethylene-propylene, the conductor insulation material used in plenum-rated Category 5 and higher cables) has excellent transmission properties, its use in plenum cables is due more to its equally superb resistance to flame propagation and relatively low level of visible-smoke generation. In Category 5 and higher nonplenum cables, HDPE (high-density polyethylene) is commonly used as conductor insulation. It has almost as good transmission properties as does FEP and has the added benefit of being several times lower than FEP in cost (and thus explains the primary difference in price between plenum and nonplenum UTP cables). HDPE does, however, burn like a candle and generate copious visible smoke. Cable manufacturers can adjust the PVC jacket of a four-pair construction to allow an HDPE-insulated cable to pass all flame tests except

Continued on next page

the plenum test. They also compensate for differences in transmission properties between FEP and HDPE (or whatever materials they select) by altering the dimensions of the insulated conductor. End result: No matter what the flame rating, if the cable jacket says Category 5 or better, you get Category 5 or better.

Myth #5: To really protect my family, I should specify plenum cable to be installed in my home.   The lack of logic and understanding here stuns us. First, communication cables are almost never the source of ignition or flame spread in a residential fire. It's not impossible, but it's extremely rare. Secondly, to what should the "fireproof" cable be attached? It is going to be fastened to wooden studs, most likely—wooden studs that burn fast, hot, and with much black, poisonous smoke. While the studs are burning, the flooring, roofing, electrical wiring, plastic water pipes, carpets, curtains, furniture, cabinets, and woodwork are also blazing away merrily, also generating much smoke. A plenum cable's potential to mitigate such a conflagration is essentially nil. Install a CMX-rated cable, and you'll comply with the National Electric Code. Install CM, CMG, or CMR, and you'll be exceeding NEC requirements. Leave the CMP cable to the commercial environments for which it's intended and don't worry about needing it at home.

Riser

The *riser* is a vertical shaft used to route cable between two floors. Often, it is nothing more complicated than a hole (core) that is drilled in the floor and allows cables to pass through. However, a hole between two floors with cable in it introduces a new problem. Remember the fire-disaster movie *The Towering Inferno*? In it, the fire spread from floor to floor through the building cabling. That should not happen nowadays because building codes require that riser cable be rated properly. So the riser cable must have certain fire-resistant qualities.

TIP   The National Electrical Code permits plenum cable to be used in the riser, but it does not allow riser cable to be used in the plenum.

The Towering Inferno had a basis in reality, not only because cables at the time burned relatively easily but also because of the chimney effect. A chimney works by drawing air upward, through the fire, invigorating the flames with oxygen flow. In a multistory building, the riser shafts can act as chimneys, accelerating the spread and intensity of the fire. Therefore, building codes usually require that the riser be firestopped in some way. That's accomplished by placing special blocking material in the riser at each penetration of walls or ceilings after the cables have been put in place. Techniques for firestopping are discussed in Chapter 12.

General Purpose

The general-purpose rating is for the classic horizontal cable for runs from the wiring closet to the wall outlet. It is rated for use within a floor and cannot penetrate a structural floor or ceiling. It is also the rating most commonly used for patch cords because, in theory, a patch cord will never go through a floor or ceiling. You should be aware that riser-rated cable is most commonly used for horizontal runs, simply because the price difference between riser and general-purpose cables is typically small and contractors don't want to haul more cable types than they have to.

Limited Use

The limited-use rating is for single and duplex (two-family) residences only. Some exceptions in the code allow its use in other environments, as in multi-tenant spaces such as apartments. However, the exceptions impose requirements that are typically either impractical or aesthetically unpleasant, and so it is better to consider limited-use cables as just for single and two-family residences.

Cable Jackets

Because UTP is virtually ubiquitous in the LAN environment, the rest of this chapter will focus on design criteria and transmission-performance characteristics related to UTP cable.

The best place to start looking at cable design is on the outside. Each type of cable (twisted pair, fiber optic, or coaxial) will have different designs with respect to the cable covering or the jacket.

KEY TERMS   **Jacket and Sheath**   The cable's jacket is the plastic outer covering of the cable. Sheath is sometimes synonymous with jacket but not always. The sheath includes not only the jacket of the cable but also any outside shielding (such as braided copper or foil) that may surround the inner wire pairs. With UTP and most fiber-optic cables, the sheath and the jacket are the same. With ScTP and STP cables, the sheath includes the outer layer of shielding on the inner wires.

One of the most common materials used for the cable jacket is *polyvinyl chloride* (PVC); UTP cables in the United States are almost exclusively jacketed with PVC, regardless of the flame rating of the cable. PVC was commonly used in early LAN cables (Category 3 and lower) as an insulation and as material for jackets, but the dielectric properties of PVC are not as desirable as that of other substances, such as FEP, HDPE, or PP (polypropylene), that can be used for higher-frequency transmission. Figure 1.9 shows a cutaway drawing of a UTP cable.

FIGURE 1.9:

Cutaway drawing of a UTP cable showing insulated wire pairs, slitting cord, and jacket

Slitting cord made of nylon or other polymer

Jacket

Twisted pairs—
each wire's insulation
is color coded.

Other substances commonly used in cable jackets of indoor cables include ECTFE (HALAR), PVDF (KYNAR) and FEP (Teflon or NeoFlon.) These materials have enhanced flame-retardant qualities as compared to PVC but are much more costly. Where PVC can do the job, it's the jacket material of choice.

KEY TERM   **Slitting Cord**   Inside some UTP cable jackets is a polyester or nylon string called the *slitting cord or slitting string*. The purpose of this cord is to assist with slicing the jacket open when more than an inch or two of jacket needs to be removed. Some cable installers love them; many find them a nuisance, as they get in the way during termination.

NOTE   No standard exists for the jacket color, so manufacturers can make the jacket any color they care to. You can order Category 5 cable in at least a dozen different colors, including hot pink. Colors like hot pink and bright yellow don't function any differently than plain gray cables, but they sure are easier to spot when you are in the ceiling! Many cable installers will pick a different color cable based on the jack position or patch panel the cable is going to so that it is easier to identify quickly.

Cable Markings

Have you examined the outside jacket of a twisted-pair or fiber-optic cable? If so, you noticed many markings on the cable that may have made sense. Unfortunately, no standard exists for cable markings, so understanding them is hit or miss. For cables manufactured for use in the United States and Canada, these markings may identify the following:

- Cable manufacturer and manufacturer part number.
- Category of cable (e.g., UTP).
- NEC/UL flame tests and ratings.
- CSA flame tests.
- Footage indicators. Sometimes these are "length-remaining markers" that count down from the package length to zero so you can see how many feet of cable remains on a spool or in a box. Superior Essex (www.superioressex.com) is one cable manufacturer that imprints footage indicators.

For a list of definitions of some marking acronyms, see the section "Common Abbreviations."

Here is an example of one cable's markings:

```
000750 FT 4/24 (UL) c(UL) CMP/MPP VERIFIED (UL) CAT 5
    SUPERIOR ESSEX COBRA 2319 H
```

These markings identify the following information about the cable:

- The 000750 FT is the footage indicator.
- The 4/24 identifies the cable as having four pairs of 24 AWG wire.

- The (UL) symbol indicates that the cable is UL listed. Listing is a legal requirement of the NEC.

- The symbol c(UL) indicates that the cable is UL listed to Canadian requirements in addition to U.S. requirements. Listing is a legal requirement of the CSA.

- The CMP/MPP code stands for communications plenum (CMP) and multipurpose plenum (MPP) and indicates that the cable can be used in plenum spaces. This is the NEC flame/smoke rating.

- The term VERIFIED CAT 5 means that the cable has been verified by the UL as being Category 5 compliant (and TIA/EIA-568-A compliant). Verification to transmission properties is optional.

- SUPERIOR ESSEX is the manufacturer of the cable.

- COBRA is the cable brand (in this case, a Category 5e–plus cable, which means it exceeds the requirements for Category 5e).

- The numbers 2319 indicate the date of manufacture in Julian format. In this case, it is the 231st day of 1999.

- H indicates the Superior Essex manufacturing plant.

Some manufacturers may also include their "E-file" number instead of the company name. This number can be used when calling the listing agency (such as the UL) to trace the manufacturer of a cable. In the case of UL, you can look up the E-file numbers online at www.ul.com.

WARNING   Note that cables marked with *CMR* (communications riser) and *CMG* (communications general) must *not* be used in the plenum spaces.

Common Abbreviations   So that you can better decipher the markings on cables, here is a list of common acronyms and what they mean:

NFPA   The National Fire Protection Association

NEC   The National Electrical Code that is published by the NFPA once every three years

UL   The Underwriters Laboratories

CSA The Canadian Standards Association

PCC The Premises Communications Cord standards for physical wire tests defined by the CSA

Often, you will see cables marked with UL-910, FT-4, or FT-6. The UL-910 is a specific UL flame test, and the FT-4 and FT-6 are CSA flame tests.

Wire Insulation

Inside the cable jacket are the wire pairs. The material used to insulate these wires must have excellent dielectric and transmission properties. Refer back to Figure 1.9 for a diagram of the wire insulation.

KEY TERM   **Dielectric**   A material that has good dielectric properties is a poor conductor of electricity. Dielectric materials are insulators. In the case of LAN cables, a good dielectric material also has characteristics conducive to the transmission of high-frequency signals along the conductors.

A variety of insulating materials exists, including polyolefin (polyethylene and polypropylene), fluorocarbon polymers, and even PVC.

The manufacturer chooses the materials based on the material cost, flame-test ratings, and desired transmission properties. Materials such as polyolefin are cheap and have great transmission properties, but they burn like crazy, so they must be used in combination with material that has better flame ratings. That's an important point to keep in mind: Don't focus on a particular material. It is the material *system* selected by the manufacturer that counts. A manufacturer will choose insulating and jacketing material that work together according to the delicate balance of fire resistance, transmission performance, and economics.

The most common materials used to insulate the wire pairs in Category 5 and greater plenum-rated cables are fluorocarbon polymers. The two varieties of fluorocarbon polymers are fluorinated ethylene-propylene (FEP) and Polytetrafluoroethylene (PTFE or TFE).

These polymers were developed by DuPont and are also sometimes called by their trademark, Teflon. The most commonly used and most desirable of these materials is FEP. Over the past few years, the demand for plenum-grade cables exceeded the supply of available FEP. During periods of FEP shortage, Category 5 plenum designs emerged that substituted another material for one or more of the pairs of wire. The substitution raised concerns about the transmission capabilities of such designs, specifically related to a property called *delay skew*. In addition, some instances of marginal performance occurred in the UL-910 burn test for plenum cables. These concerns, coupled with increases in the supply of FEP, have driven these designs away.

TIP

When purchasing Category 5 and higher plenum cables, ask whether other insulation material has been used in combination with FEP for wire insulation.

In nonplenum Category 5 and higher and in the lower categories of cable, much less expensive and more readily available materials, such as HDPE (high-density polyethylene), are used. You won't sacrifice transmission performance; the less stringent flame tests just allow less expensive materials.

Insulation Colors

The insulation around each wire in a UTP cable is color-coded. The standardized color codes help the cable installer make sure each wire is connected correctly with the hardware. In the United States, the color code is based on 10 colors. Five of these are used on the *tip* conductors, and five are used on the *ring* conductors. Combining the tip colors with the ring colors results in 25 possible unique pair combinations. Thus, 25 pair groups have been used for telephone cables for decades.

NOTE

The words *tip* and *ring* hark back to the days of manual switchboards. Phono-type plugs (like the ones on your stereo headset cord) were plugged into a socket to connect one extension or number to another. The plug had a tip, then an insulating disk, and then the shaft of the plug. One conductor of a pair was soldered into the tip and the other soldered to the shaft, or ring. Remnants of 100-year-old technology are still with us today.

Table 1.3 lists the color codes found in a binder group (a group of 25 pairs of wires) in larger-capacity cables. The 25-pair cable is not often used in data cabling, but it is frequently used for voice cabling for backbone and cross-connect cable.

TABLE 1.3:   Color Codes for 25-Pair UTP Binder Groups

Pair Number	Tip Color	Ring Color
1	White	Blue
2	White	Orange
3	White	Green
4	White	Brown
5	White	Slate
6	Red	Blue
7	Red	Orange
8	Red	Green
9	Red	Brown
10	Red	Slate
11	Black	Blue
12	Black	Orange
13	Black	Green
14	Black	Brown
15	Black	Slate
16	Yellow	Blue
17	Yellow	Orange
18	Yellow	Green
19	Yellow	Brown
20	Yellow	Slate
21	Violet	Blue
22	Violet	Orange
23	Violet	Green
24	Violet	Brown
25	Violet	Slate

With LAN cables, it is common to use a modification to this system known as *positive identification*. PI, as it is sometimes called, involves putting either a longitudinal stripe or circumferential band on the conductor in the color of its pair mate. In the case of most four-pair UTP cables, this is usually done only to the tip conductor because each tip conductor is white, whereas the ring conductors are each a unique color.

Table 1.4 lists the color codes for a four-pair UTP cable. The PI color is indicated after the tip color.

TABLE 1.4:   Color Codes for Four-Pair UTP Cable

Pair Number	Tip Color	Ring Color
1	White/Blue	Blue
2	White/Orange	Orange
3	White/Green	Green
4	White/Brown	Brown

Waiter! There's Halogen in My Cable!

Much of the cable currently in use in the United States and elsewhere in the world contains halogens. A *halogen* is a nonmetallic element, such as fluorine, chlorine, iodine, or bromine. When exposed to flames, substances made with halogens give off toxic fumes that quickly harm the eyes, nose, lungs, and throat. Did you notice that fluorine and chlorine are commonly found in cable insulation and jackets? Even when cables are designed to be flame-resistant, any cable, when exposed to high enough temperatures, will melt and burn. PVC cables contain chlorine, which emits toxic fumes when burned.

Many different manufacturers are now making low-smoke, zero-halogen (LSZH or LSOH) cables. These cables are designed to emit no toxic fumes and produce little or no smoke when exposed to flames. Tunnels, enclosed rooms, aircraft, and other minimum-ventilation areas are prime spots for the use of LSOH cables, because those areas are more difficult to escape from quickly.

Continued on next page

LSOH cables are popular outside the United States. Some safety advocates are calling for the use of LSOH cables in the United States, specifically for the plenum space. Review your local building codes to determine if you must use LSOH cable. Non-LSOH cables will produce corrosive acids if they are exposed to water (such as from a sprinkler system) when burned; such acids may theoretically further endanger equipment. But many opponents of LSOH cable reason that if an area of the building is on fire, the equipment will be damaged by flames before it is damaged by corrosives from a burning cable.

Why, you might ask, would anyone in his or her right mind argue against the installation of LSOH cables everywhere? First, reducing toxic fumes doesn't necessarily mean the cable is more fireproof. The flame-spread properties may even be worse than for cables in use today. Second, consider practicality. LSOH is an expensive solution to a problem that doesn't seem to really exist in the United States. When was the last time you heard of a major commercial fire where inhalation of the fumes from burning cables was a cause of death? If it ain't broke…

We don't expect that LSOH cables will take over anytime soon, but a movement is underway to define a *smoke-limited* cable in the next version of the NEC (Article 800).

Twists

When you slice open a UTP communications cable, you will notice that the individual conductors of a pair of wire are twisted around one another. At first, you may not realize how important these twists are.

TIP   Did you know that in Category 5 cables a wire pair untwisted more than half of an inch can adversely affect the performance of the entire cable?

Twisted-pair cable is any cable that contains a pair of wires that are wrapped or twisted around one another between 2 and 12 times per foot—and sometimes even greater than 12 times per foot (as with Category 5 and higher). The twists help to cancel out the electromagnetic interference (EMI) generated by voltage used to send a signal over the wire. The interference can cause problems, called crosstalk, for adjacent wire pairs. Crosstalk and its effects are discussed in the "Speed Bumps" section later in this chapter.

Cables commonly used for patch cables and for horizontal cabling (patch panel to wall plate) typically contain four pairs of wire. The order in which the wires are crimped or punched down can be very important.

TIP

Companies such as Panduit (`www.panduit.com`) have developed termination tools and patch cables that all but eliminate the need to untwist cables more than a tiny amount.

Wire Gauge

Copper-wire diameter is most often measured by a unit called AWG (American Wire Gauge). Contrary to what logic may tell you, as the AWG number gets smaller, the wire diameter actually gets larger; thus, AWG 24 wire is smaller than AWG 22 wire. Larger wires are useful because they have more physical strength and lower resistance. However, the larger the wire diameter, the more copper is required to make the cable. This makes the cable heavier, harder to install, and more expensive.

NOTE

The reason the AWG number increases as the wire diameter decreases has to do with how wire is made. You don't dump copper ore into a machine at one end and get 24 AWG wire out the other end. A multistep process is involved—converting the ore to metal, the metal to ingots, the ingots to large bars or rods. Rods are then fed into a machine that makes them into smaller-diameter rods. To reach a final diameter, the rod is pulled through a series of holes, or dies, of decreasing size. Going through each die causes the wire to stretch out a little bit, reducing its diameter. The AWG number represents the number of dies the wire had to go through to get to its finished size. So, the smaller the wire, the more dies involved and the higher the AWG number.

The cable designer's challenge is to use the lowest possible diameter wire (reducing costs and installation complexity) while at the same time maximizing the wire's capabilities to support the necessary power levels and frequencies.

Category 5 UTP is always 24 AWG; IBM Type 1A is typically 22 AWG. Patch cords may be 26 AWG, especially Category 3 patch cords. The evolution of higher-performance cables such as Category 5e and Category 6 has resulted in 23 AWG often being substituted for 24 AWG. Table 1.5 shows 22, 23, 24, and 26 AWG sizes along with the corresponding diameter, area, and weight per kilometer.

TABLE 1.5: American Wire Gauge Diameter, Area, and Weight Values

AWG	Nominal Diameter		Circular-Mil Area[1]	Area sq. mm	Weight kg/km
	Inches	Mm			
22	0.0253	0.643	640.4	0.3256	2.895
23	0.0226	0.574	511.5	0.2581	2.295
24	0.0201	0.511	404.0	0.2047	1.820
26	0.0159	0.404	253.0	0.1288	1.145

[1] A circular mil is the area of a circle 1/1000 inches in diameter.

The dimensions in Table 1.5 were developed more than 100 years ago. Since then, the purity and, therefore, the conductive properties of copper have improved due to better copper-processing techniques. Specifications that cover the design of communications cables have a waiver on the actual dimensions of a wire. The real concern is not the dimensions of the wire, but how it performs, specifically with regard to resistance in ohms. The AWG standard indicates that a 24 AWG wire will have a diameter of 0.0201 inches, but based on the performance of the material, the actual diameter of the wire may be slightly less or slightly more (but usually less).

Solid Conductors versus Stranded Conductors

Category 5 cable used as horizontal cable (permanent cable or cable in the walls) has a solid conductor, as opposed to patch cable and cable that is run over short distances, which usually have a stranded conductor. Stranded-conductor wire consists of many smaller wires interwoven together to form a single conductor.

TIP   Connector types (such as patch panels and modular jacks) for solid-conductor cable are different than those for stranded-conductor cable. Stranded-conductor cables will *not* work with IDC-style connectors found on patch panels and 66-style punch-down blocks.

Though stranded-conductor wire is more flexible, solid-conductor cable has much better electrical properties than stranded-conductor cable because stranded-conductor wire is subject to as much as 20 percent more attenuation (loss of signal)

due to a phenomenon called *skin effect*. At higher frequencies (the frequencies used in LAN cables), the signal current concentrates on the outer circumference of the overall conductor. Since stranded-conductor wire has a less-defined overall circumference (due to the multiple strands involved), attenuation is increased.

KEY TERM   **Core**   The core of the cable is anything found inside the sheath. The core is usually just the insulated twisted pairs, but it may also include a slitting cord and the shielding over individual twisted pairs in an STP cable. People incorrectly refer to the *core* of the cable when they mean the *conductor*.

Most cabling standards recommend using solid-conductor wire in the horizontal or permanent portion of the link, but the standards allow for stranded-conductor wire in patch cables where flexibility is more important. We know of several Category 5 installations that have used stranded-conductor wires for their horizontal links. Although we consider this a poor practice, here are some important points to keep in mind if you choose to use a mixture of these cables:

- Stranded-conductor wire requires different connectors.

- Stranded-conductor wires don't work as well in punch-down blocks designed for solid-conductor cables.

- You must account for reduced horizontal-link distances.

Cable Length

The longer the cable, the less likely the signal will be carried completely to the end of the cable, because of noise and signal attenuation. Realize, though, that for LAN systems the time it takes for a signal to get to the end is also critical. Cable design engineers are now measuring two additional performance parameters of cable: the propagation delay and the delay skew. Both parameters are related to the speed at which the electrons can pass through the cable and the length of the wire pairs in cable. The variables are discussed in the "Speed Bumps" section later in this chapter.

Cable Length versus Conductor Length   A Category 5 cable has four pairs of conductors. By design, each of the four pairs is twisted in such a fashion so that the pairs are slightly different lengths. (Varying twist lengths from pair to pair improves crosstalk performance.) Therefore, signals transmitted simultaneously on two different pairs of wire will arrive at slightly different times. The *conductor length* is the length of the individual pair of conductors, whereas the *cable length* is the length of the cable jacket.

Part of a modern cable tester's feature set is the ability to perform conductor-length tests. Here is a list of the conductor lengths of a cable whose cable length is 139 feet from the wall plate to the patch panel. As you can see, the actual conductor length is longer due to the twists in the wire.

Pair	Distance
1-2	145 ft
3-6	143 ft
4-5	141 ft
7-8	142 ft

Warp Factor One, Please

Light travels almost 300,000,000 meters per second in a perfect vacuum, faster than non-physicists can imagine. If traveling at the speed of light were possible, it would take a mere 8.5 seconds to reach the sun from Earth. In a fiber-optic cable one kilometer long, data can travel from start to finish in about 3.3 microseconds (0.0000033 seconds).

Data does not travel through copper cabling quite as fast. One of the ways that the speed of data through a copper cable is measured is by how fast electricity can travel through the cable. This value is called the Nominal Velocity of Propagation (NVP) and is expressed as a percentage of the speed of light. The value for most cables is between 60 and 90 percent. The cable manufacturer specifies NVP as part of the cable's design.

Take, for example, a cable that Jim recently measured using a hand-held cable tester. The NVP for this cable was 67 percent and the cable was 90 meters long. Electricity will travel through this cable at a speed of about 200,000,000 meters per second; it travels from one end of the cable to another in 450 nanoseconds (0.00000045 seconds).

Data Communications 101

Before we discuss more of the limitations involved with data communications and network cabling, some basic terms must be defined. Unfortunately, vendors, engineers, and network managers serve up high-tech and communications terms like balls in a tennis match. Worse, they often misuse the terms or don't even fully understand what they mean.

One common term is *bandwidth*. Does it mean maximum frequency or maximum data rate? Other terms are thrown at you as if you have a Ph.D. in Electrical Engineering, including *impedance*, *resistance*, and *capacitance*.

Our favorite misunderstood term is *decibels*. We always thought decibels were used to measure sound, but that's not necessarily true when it comes to data communications. Over the next few pages, we will take you through a crash course in Data Communications 101 and get you up to speed on certain terms pertaining to cabling.

Bandwidth, Frequency, and Data Rate

One initially confusing aspect about cabling is that cables are rated in hertz rather than bits per second. Network engineers (and you, presumably) are more concerned with how much data can be pushed through the cable than with the frequency at which that data is traveling.

Frequency is the number of cycles completed per unit of time and is generally expressed in *hertz* (cycles per second). Figure 1.10 shows a cycle that took one second to complete; this is one hertz. Data cabling is typically rated in kilohertz (kHz) or Megahertz (MHz). For a cable rated at 100MHz, the cycle would have to complete 100,000,000 times in a single second! The more cycles per second, the more noise the cable generates and the more susceptible the cable is to signal-level loss.

The bandwidth of a cable is the maximum frequency at which data can be effectively transmitted and received. The bit rate is dependent upon the network electronics, not the cable, provided the operating frequency of the network is within the cable's usable bandwidth. Put another way, the cable is just a pipe. Think of the bandwidth as the pipe's diameter. Network electronics provide the water pressure. Either a trickle comes through or a gusher, but the pipe diameter doesn't change.

FIGURE 1.10:

One cycle every second or one hertz

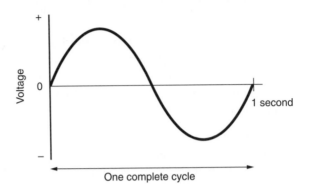

Cable bandwidth is a difficult animal to corral. It is a function of three inter-related, major elements: distance, frequency, and signal-level-to-noise-level ratio (SNR). Changing any one element alters the maximum bandwidth available. As you increase the frequency, SNR gets worse, and the maximum bandwidth is decreased. As you increase distance, SNR worsens, thereby decreasing the maximum bandwidth. Conversely, reducing frequency or distance increases the maximum bandwidth because SNR improves.

To keep the same maximum bandwidth, increasing the frequency means you must either decrease distance or improve the signal level at the receiver. If you increase the distance, either the frequency must decrease, or, again, the signal level at the receiver must improve. If you improve signal level at the receiving end, you can either increase frequency or leave the frequency alone and increase distance. It's a tough bronc to ride.

With all this variability, how do you get anywhere with cable and network design? It helps to lasso one or more of the variables.

This is done for you via the IEEE network specifications and implemented through ANSI/TIA/EIA 568-A. A maximum horizontal-run length of 100 meters (308 feet), including workstation and communication closet patch cords, is speci-fied. This figure arises from some timing limitations of some Ethernet implemen-tations. So distance is fixed.

The standards also define the maximum operating frequency. In the case of Cat-egory 3 cables, it is 16MHz. In the case of Category 5 and 5e, it is 100MHz.

Now that two of the three elements are firmly tied to the fence, you can rope in the last. Cable design focuses on improving the signal level and reducing the noise in the cable to achieve optimum transmission performance for given frequencies at a fixed length.

"Huh?" you may be saying to yourself. "That implies I could have horizontal run lengths greater than 100 meters if I'm willing to lower my bandwidth expectations or put up with a lower signal level. I thought 100 meters was the most a Category 5 cable could run." According to the Standard, 100 meters is the maximum. But technically, the cabling might be able to run longer. Figure 1.11 unhitches length and instead ties down frequency and SNR. In the graph, the frequency at which the signal and noise level coincides (the "ACR=0" point) is plotted against distance. You can see that if the signal frequency is 10MHz, a Category 5 cable is capable of carrying that signal almost 2,500 feet, well beyond the 100-meter (308-foot) length specified.

FIGURE 1.11:

ACR=0

So why not do so? Because you'd be undermining the principal of structured wiring, which requires parameters that will work with many LAN technologies, not just the one you've got in mind for today. Some network architectures wouldn't tolerate it, and future upgrades might be impossible. Stick to the 100-meter maximum length specified.

The *data rate* (throughput or information capacity) is defined as the number of bits per second that move through a transmission medium. With some older LAN technologies, the data rate has a one-to-one relationship with the transmission frequency. For example, 4Mbps Token Ring operates at 4MHz.

It's tough to keep pushing the bandwidth of copper cables higher and higher. There are the laws of physics to consider, after all. So techniques have been developed to allow more than one bit per hertz to move through the cable. Table 1.6 compares the operating frequency of transmission with the throughput rate of various LAN technologies available today.

TABLE 1.6: LAN Throughput vs. Operating Frequency

LAN System	Data Rate	Operating Frequency
Token Ring	4Mbps	4MHz
10BaseT Ethernet	10Mbps	10MHz
Token Ring	16Mbps	16MHz
100BaseT Ethernet	100Mbps	31.25MHz
ATM 155	155Mbps	38.75MHz
1000BaseT (Gigabit) Ethernet	1,000Mbps	Approximately 65MHz

All the systems listed in the table will work with Category 5 cable. So how do techniques manage to deliver data at 1Gbps across a Category 5 cable whose maximum bandwidth is 100MHz? The next section gives you the answer.

The Secret Ingredient: Encoding and Multipair Simultaneous Send and Receive

Consider the example illustrated in Figure 1.12. A street permits one car to pass a certain stretch of road each second. The cars are spaced a certain distance apart, and their speeds are limited so that only one is on the stretch of road at a time.

But suppose as in Figure 1.13 that the desired capacity for this particular part of the street is three cars per second. The cars can drive faster, and they can be spaced so that three at a time fit on the stretch of road. This is bit encoding. It is a technology for packing multiple data bits in each hertz to increase throughput.

FIGURE 1.12:

A street that allows one car to pass each second

Only a single car can pass through each second.

FIGURE 1.13:

A street that allows multiple cars through during each cycle

Allows three cars to pass through each second. That's encoding!

Add a lane in each direction, and you can see how most LAN technologies work today. They use two of the four pairs of cable, one to transmit and one to receive—effectively, a two-lane highway.

At some point, though, a limit will be reached as to how fast the cars can travel. Plus, eventually the cars will be packed end-to-end in a lane and we just won't be able to fit any more cars (data bits) through that stretch in the available time.

What to do? How about building multiple lanes? Instead of using two lanes, one in each direction, four lanes (four pairs of cable) would ease the congestion.

Four lanes still might not be enough capacity to get all the cars needed down the highway. So all four lanes will be used, but instead of two being dedicated to send and two to receive, the cars will drive both directions in every lane. It takes accurate timing and nerves of steel, but it can be done. This is, in fact, how Gigabit Ethernet is implemented on Category 5. Transmitting at an operating frequency of about 65MHz, data is simultaneously sent and received on all four pairs at a rate of 250Mbps each. Voila! That's 1,000Mbps in less than 100MHz of bandwidth!

TIP   For Gigabit Ethernet to work over Category 5 cabling, all four pairs must be used.

What a Difference a dB Makes!

Suppose you are comparing cable performance. A manufacturer states that the attenuation (power loss) for a cable with a length of 90 meters, operating at 100MHz, is 20dB. What does the measurement mean? Would you be surprised to learn that the signal strength has dropped by a factor of 100? That's right, if you apply an input power level of five watts, the output level will be 0.05 watts! For every 3dB of attenuation, it's a 50 percent loss of power!

To summarize: Low decibel values of attenuation are desirable because then less of the signal is lost on its way to the receiver. Higher decibel values of crosstalk (NEXT, ELFEXT, etc.) and return loss are actually desirable because that means less signal has been measured on adjacent wires. (For more on NEXT and ELFEXT, see "Noise" later in this chapter.)

This section may be all you ever wanted to know about decibels. If you want to know more and get the technical details, read on!

Digging a Little Deeper into Decibels

You may think of a decibel in terms of audible noise. When referring to the domain of sound, a decibel is not actually a specific unit of measurement but rather is used to express a ratio of sound pressure.

However, the decibel is also commonly used when defining attenuation, crosstalk, and return loss. Just as with sound, when referring to communications and electrical transmission performance, the decibel is a ratio rather than a specific measurement. Because analog and digital communication signals are just electrical energy instead of sound pressure, the dB unit is a ratio of input power to output power. The decibel value is independent of the actual input and output voltage or power and is thus considered a generic performance specification. Understanding what the decibel numbers mean is important when comparing one cabling media or performance measurement with another.

Decibels 101 The *bel* part of decibel was named after Alexander Graham Bell, the inventor of the telephone. A *decibel* is a tenfold logarithmic ratio of power (or voltage) output to power (or voltage) input. Keep in mind that the decibel is indicating a power ratio, not a specific measurement. The decibel is a convenient way to reflect the power loss or gain, regardless of the actual values.

NOTE   For measurements such as attenuation, NEXT, ELFEXT, ACR, and return loss, the decibel value is always negative because it represents a loss, but often the negative sign is ignored when the measurement is written. The fact that the number represents a loss is assumed.

Cable testers as well as performance specifications describe attenuation in decibels. Let's say, for example, that you measure two cables of identical length and determine that the attenuation is 15dB for one cable and 21dB for the other. Naturally, you know that because lower attenuation is better, the cable with an attenuation of 15dB is better than the one with a 21dB value. But how much better? Would you be surprised to learn that even though the difference between the two cables is only 6dB, there is 50 percent more attenuation of voltage or amperage (power is calculated differently) on the cable whose attenuation was measured at 21dB?

Knowing how a decibel is calculated is vital to appreciating the performance specifications that the decibel measures.

Decibels and Power   When referring to power (watts), decibels are calculated in this fashion:

    dB = 10*log10(P1/P2)

P1 indicates the measured power, and P2 is the reference power (or input power).

To expand on this formula, consider this example. The reference power level (P2) is 1.0 watts. The measured power level (P1) on the opposite side of the cable is 0.5 watts. Therefore, through this cable, 50 percent of the signal was lost due to attenuation. Now, plug these values into the power formula for decibels. Doing so yields a value of3dB. What does the calculation mean? It means that:

- Every 3dB of attenuation translates into 50 percent of the signal power being lost through the cable. Lower attenuation values are desirable, as a higher power level will then arrive at the destination.

- Every 3dB of return loss translates into 50 percent of the signal power being reflected back to the source. Higher decibel values for return loss are desirable, as *less* power will then be returned to the sender.

- Every 3dB of NEXT translates into 50 percent of the signal power being allowed to couple to adjacent pairs. Higher decibel values for NEXT (and other crosstalk values) are desirable, as higher values indicate that less power will then couple with adjacent pairs.

An increase of 10dB means a tenfold increase in the actual measured parameter. Table 1.7 shows the logarithmic progression of decibels with respect to power measurements.

TABLE 1.7: Logarithmic Progression of Decibels

Decibel Value	Actual Increase in Measured Parameter
3dB	2
10dB	10
20dB	100
30dB	1,000
40dB	10,000
50dB	100,000
60dB	1,000,000

Decibels and Voltage   Most performance specifications and cable testers typically reference voltage ratios, not power ratios. When referring to voltage (or amperage), decibels are calculated slightly differently than for power. The formula is as follows:

dB = 20*log10(P1/P2)

P1 indicates the measured voltage or amperage, and P2 is the reference (or output) voltage (amperage). Substituting a reference value of 1.0 volt for P2 and 0.5 volts for P1 (the measured output), you get a value of –6dB. What does the calculation mean? It means that:

- Every 6dB of attenuation translates into 50 percent of the voltage being lost to attenuation. Lower decibel attenuation values are desirable, as a higher voltage level will then arrive at the destination.

- Every 6dB of return loss translates into 50 percent of the voltage being reflected back to the source. Higher decibel values for return loss are desirable, as *less* voltage will then be returned to the sender.

- Every 6dB of NEXT translates into 50 percent of the voltage coupling to adjacent wire pairs. Higher decibel values for NEXT (and other crosstalk values) are desirable, as higher values indicate that less power will then couple with adjacent pairs.

Table 1.8 shows various decibel levels and the corresponding voltage and power ratios. Notice that (for the power ratio) if a cable's attenuation is measured at 10dB, only one-tenth of the signal transmitted will be received on the other side.

TABLE 1.8:   Decibel Levels and Corresponding Power and Voltage Ratios

dB	Voltage Ratio	Power Ratio
1	1	1
-1	0.891	0.794
-2	0.794	0.631
-3	0.707	0.500
-4	0.631	0.398
-5	0.562	0.316
-6	0.500	0.250
-7	0.447	0.224
-8	0.398	0.158
-9	0.355	0.125
-10	0.316	0.100
-12	0.250	0.063
-15	0.178	0.031
-20	0.100	0.010
-25	0.056	0.003
-30	0.032	0.001
-40	0.010	0.000
-50	0.003	0.000

Applying Knowledge of Decibels

Now that you have a background on decibels, look at the specified channel performance for Category 5 versus the proposed channel performance for Category 6 cable at 100Mhz.

Media Type	Attenuation	NEXT	Return Loss
Category 5	24	27.1	8.0
Category 6	20.9	39.9	12.0

For the values to be meaningful, you need to look at them with respect to the actual percentage of loss. For this example, use voltage. If you take each decibel value and solve for the P1/P2 ratio using this formula, you would arrive at the following values:

```
Ratio = 1 / (Inverse log10(dB/20))
```

Media	Remaining Signal Due to Attenuation	Allowed to Couple (NEXT)	Signal Returned (NEXT)
Category 5	6.3%	4.4%	39.8%
Category 6	9.0%	1%	25.1%

Existing cable standards allow a transmission to lose 99 percent of its signal but still be received properly. In the Category 5 cable example, only 6.3 percent of the voltage is received at the destination. For an Ethernet application operating at 2.5 volts of output voltage, the measured voltage at the receiver would be about 0.16 volts for Category 5 cable and 0.23 volts for Category 6 cable.

Using such techniques for reversing the decibel calculation, you can better compare the performance of any media.

Speed Bumps: What Slows Down Your Data

The amount of data that even simple unshielded twisted-pair cabling can transfer has come a long way over the past dozen or so years. In the late 1980s, many experts felt that UTP cabling would never support data rates greater than 10Mbps.

Today, data rates of 1.2Gbps and higher are supported over cable lengths approaching 100 meters! And UTP may be able to support even greater data rates in the future.

Think back to the MIS director who mistakenly assumed that "it is just wire." Could he be right? What is the big deal? Shouldn't data cabling be able to support even higher data rates?

Have you tried to purchase data-grade cable recently? Have you ever tested a cable run with an even mildly sophisticated cable tester? A typical cabling catalog can have over 2,000 different types of cables! You may have come away from the experience wondering if you needed a degree in electrical engineering in order to understand all the terms and acronyms. The world of modern cabling has become a mind-boggling array of communications buzzwords and engineering terms.

As the requirements for faster data rates emerges, the complexity of the cable design increases. As the data rates increase, the magic that happens inside a cable becomes increasingly mysterious, and the likelihood that data signals will become corrupt while traveling at those speeds also increases.

Ah! So it is not that simple after all! As data rates increase, electrical properties of the cable change, signals become more distorted, and the distance that a signal can travel decreases. Designers of both 1000Base-T (Gigabit Ethernet) and the cables that can support frequencies greater than 100Mhz have found electrical problems that they did not have to contend with at lower frequencies and data rates. These additional electrical problems are different types of crosstalk and arrival delay of electrons on different pairs of wires.

Hindrances to High-Speed Data Transfer

Electricity flowing through a cable is nothing more than electrons moving inside the cable and bumping into each other—sort of like dominoes falling. For a signal to be received properly by the receiver, enough electrons must make contact all the way through the cable from the sender to the receiver. As the frequency on a cable (and consequently the potential data rate) increases, a number of phenomena hinder the signal's travel through the cable (and, consequently, the transfer of data). These phenomena are important not only to the person who has to authorize cable purchase but also to the person who tests and certifies the cable.

The current specifications for Category 5 cabling outline a number of these phenomena and the maximum (or minimum) acceptable values that a cable can meet and still be certified as Category 5 compliant.

Due to the complex modulation technology used by 1000Base-T Ethernet, the TIA has recently specified cabling performance specifications beyond what was included in the original testing specification (TSB-67). These performance characteristics include power-sum and pair-to-pair crosstalk measurements, delay skew, return loss, and ELFEXT. Some of these newer performance characteristics are important as they relate to crosstalk. Although crosstalk is important in all technologies, faster technologies such as 1000Base-T are more sensitive to it because they use all four pairs in parallel for transmission.

The TIA/EIA has released an updated specification called TSB-95 that specifies additional testing and performance parameters required to certify a cable to support higher-speed installations such as 1000Base-T. All those requirements are also built into the addendum that covers Category 5e, ANSI/TIA/EIA-568-A-5.

Many transmission requirements are expressed as mathematical formulae. For the convenience of humans who can't do complex log functions in their heads (virtually everyone!), values are precomputed and listed in the specification according to selected frequencies. But, the actual requirement is that the characteristic must pass the "sweep test" across the full bandwidth specified for the cable category. So performance must be consistent and in accordance with the formula, at any given frequency level from the lowest to the highest frequency specified.

The major test parameters for communication cables, and the general groupings they fall into, are as follows:

- Attenuation (signal-loss) related
    - Conductor resistance
    - Mutual capacitance
    - Return loss
    - Impedance
- Noise related
    - Resistance unbalance
    - Capacitance unbalance
    - Near-end crosstalk (NEXT)
    - Far-end crosstalk (FEXT)
    - Power-sum NEXT
    - Power-sum FEXT

- Other

  - Attenuation-to-crosstalk ratio (ACR)

  - Propagation delay

  - Delay skew

Attenuation (Loss of Signal)

As noted earlier, attenuation is loss of signal. That loss happens because as a signal travels through a cable, some of it doesn't make it all the way to the end of the cable. The longer the cable, the more signal loss there will be. In fact, past a certain point, the data will no longer be transmitted properly because the signal loss will be too great.

Attenuation is measured in decibels (dB), and the measurement is taken on the receiver end of the conductor. So if 10dB of signal were inserted on the transmitter end and 3dB of signal were measured at the receiver end, the attenuation would be calculated as 3 - 10 = -7dB. The negative sign is usually ignored, so the attenuation is stated as 7dB *of signal loss*. If 10dB were inserted at the transmitter and 6dB measured at the receiver, then the attenuation would be only 4dB. So, the lower the attenuation value, the more of the original signal is received (in other words, lower the better).

Figure 1.14 illustrates the problem that attenuation causes in LAN cabling.

FIGURE 1.14:

The signal deteriorates as it travels between a node on a LAN and the hub.

UTP cable

Transmitted signal

PC

Hub

Signal is weaker on the receiving side due to attenuation.

Attenuation on a cable will increase as the frequency used increases. A 100-meter cable may have a measured attenuation of less than 2dB at 1MHz but greater than 20dB at 100MHz!

Higher temperatures increase the effect of attenuation. For each higher degree Celsius, attenuation is typically increased 1.5 percent for Category 3 cables and 0.4 percent for Category 5 cables. Attenuation values can also increase by 2 to 3 percent if the cable is installed in metal conduit.

When the signal arrives at the receiver, it must still be recognizable to the receiver. Attenuation values for cables are very important.

Attenuation values are different for the categories of cables and the frequencies employed. As the bandwidth of the cable increases, the allowed attenuation values get lower (less loss), although the differences between Category 5, 5e, and 6 are negligible at the common frequency of 100MHz.

Characteristics that contribute to attenuation are detailed as follows:

Conductor resistance   Conductor resistance acts as a hindrance to the signal because it restricts the flow of electricity through the cable conductors. This causes some of the signal energy to be dissipated as heat, but the amount of heat generated by LAN cabling is negligible due to the low current and voltage levels. The longer the cable or the smaller the conductor diameters (actually, the cross-sectional area), the more resistance. After allowing for dimensional factors, resistance is more or less a fixed property of the conductor material. Copper, gold, and silver offer low resistance and are used as conductors.

Mutual capacitance   This characteristic is an electrical occurrence experienced when a cable has more than one wire and the wires are placed close together. The insulation material will steal and store some of the signal energy, acting as a capacitor between two conductors in the cable. A property of the insulating material called *dielectric constant* has a great influence over the mutual capacitance. Different materials have different dielectric constants. The lower the dielectric constant, the less signal loss. FEP and HDPE have low dielectric constants, along with other properties, that make them well suited for use in high-frequency cables.

Impedance   Impedance is a combination of resistance, capacitance, and inductance and is expressed in ohms; a typical UTP cable is rated at between 85 and 115 ohms. All Category 3, 4, 5, and 5e cables used in the United States are rated at 100 ± 15 ohms. Impedance values are useful when testing the cable for problems, shorts, and mismatches. A cable tester could show three possible impedance readings that indicate a problem:

- An impedance value not between 85 and 115 ohms indicates a mismatch in the type of cables or components. This might mean that an incorrect connector type has been installed or an incorrect cable type has been cross-connected into the circuit.

- An impedance value of zero indicates that the cable is open or cut.

- An impedance value of infinity indicates that the cable has been short-circuited.

Some electrons sent through a cable may hit an impedance mismatch or imperfection in the wire and be reflected back to the sender. Such an occurrence is known as *return loss*. If the electrons travel a great distance through the wire before being bounced back to the sender, the return loss may not be noticeable because the returning signal may have dissipated (due to attenuation) before reaching the sender. If the signal echo from the bounced signal is strong enough, it can interfere with ultra-high-speed technologies such as 1000Base-T.

Noise (Signal Interference)

Everything electrical in the cable that isn't the signal itself is noise and constitutes a threat to the integrity of the signal. Many sources of noise exist, from within and outside the cable. Controlling noise is of major importance to cable and connector designers because uncontrolled noise will overwhelm the data signal and bring a network to its knees.

Twisted-pair cables utilize balanced signal transmission. The signal traveling on one conductor of a pair should have essentially the same path as the signal traveling the opposite direction on the other conductor. (That's as opposed to coaxial cable, in which the center conductor provides a very easy path for the signal but the braid and foil shield that make up the other conductor is less efficient and therefore a more difficult pathway for the signal.)

As signals travel along a pair, an electrical field is created. When the two conductors are perfectly symmetrical, everything flows smoothly. However, minute changes in the diameter of the copper, the thickness of the insulating layer, or the centering of conductors within that insulation cause disturbances in the electrical field called *unbalances*. Electrical unbalance means noise.

Resistance unbalance occurs when the dimensions of the two conductors of the pair are not identical. Mismatched conductors, poorly manufactured conductors, or one conductor that got stretched during installation will result in resistance unbalance.

Capacitance unbalance is also related to dimensions, but to the insulation surrounding the conductor. If the insulation is thicker on one conductor than on the other, then capacitance unbalance occurs. Or, if the manufacturing process is not well controlled and the conductor is not perfectly centered (like a bull's-eye) in the insulation, then capacitance unbalance will exist.

Both these noise sources are usually kept well under control by the manufacturer and are relatively minor compared to *crosstalk*.

You've likely experienced crosstalk on a telephone. When you hear another's conversation through the telephone, that is crosstalk. Crosstalk occurs when some of the signal being transmitted on one pair leaks over to another pair.

When a pair is in use, an electrical field is created. This electrical field induces voltage in adjacent pairs, with an accompanying transfer of signal. The more the conductors are parallel, the worse this phenomena is, and the higher the frequency, the more likely crosstalk will happen. Twisting the two conductors of a pair around each other couples the energy out of phase (that's electrical-engineer talk) and cancels the electrical field. The result is reduced transfer of signal. *But the twists must be symmetrical*; i.e., both conductors must twist around each other, not one wrapping around another that's straight, *and two adjacent pairs shouldn't have the same interval of twists*. Why? Because those twist points become convenient signal-transfer points, sort of like stepping stones in a stream. In general, the shorter the twist intervals, the better the cancellation and the less crosstalk. That's why Category 5 and higher cables are characterized by their very short twist intervals.

Crosstalk is measured in decibels; the higher the crosstalk value, the less crosstalk noise in the cabling. See Figure 1.15.

FIGURE 1.15:

Crosstalk

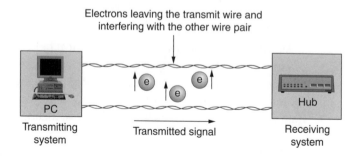

Wait a Minute! Higher Crosstalk Values Are Better?

Yep, illogical as it seems at first, higher crosstalk values are better. Unlike attenuation, where you measure output signal at the receiving end of a single pair, crosstalk coupling is measured between two separate pairs. The way the testing is done, you measure how much signal energy *did not* transfer to the other pair. A pair (or pairs, in the case of power-sum measurements) is energized with a signal. This is the *disturber*. You "listen" on another pair called the *disturbed pair*. Subtracting what you inserted on the disturber from what you measure on the disturbed tells you how much signal stayed with the disturber. For example, a 10dB signal is placed on the disturber, but 6dB is detected on the disturbed pair. So -4dB of signal did not transfer (6 – 10). The sign is ignored, so the crosstalk is recorded as 4dB. If 2dB were measured on the disturbed pair, then 2 – 10 = -8dB of signal did not transfer, and the crosstalk value is recorded as 8dB. Higher crosstalk numbers represent less loss to adjacent pairs.

Near-End Crosstalk (NEXT)   When the crosstalk is detected on the same end of the cable that generated the signal, then near-end crosstalk has occurred. NEXT is most common within 20 to 30 meters (60 to 90 feet) of the transmitter. Figure 1.16 illustrates near-end crosstalk.

FIGURE 1.16:

Near-end crosstalk (NEXT)

Crosstalk on poorly designed or poorly installed cables is a major problem with technologies such as 10Base-T and 100Base-TX. However, as long as the cable is installed correctly, NEXT is less of an issue when using 1000Base-T because the designers implemented technologies to facilitate NEXT cancellation.

NEXT-cancellation techniques with 1000Base-T are necessary because all four pairs are employed for both transmitting and receiving data.

NOTE   Cables that have had their twists undone (untwisted) can be problematic because the twists help cancel crosstalk. Twists are normally untwisted at the ends near the patch panels or connectors when the cable is connected. On the receiving pair of wires in a cable, the signal received at the end of the cable will be the weakest. So the signal there can be more easily interfered with. If the wires on adjacent transmit pairs are untwisted, this will cause a greater amount of crosstalk than normal. A cable should never have the wire pairs untwisted more than 0.5 inches for Category 5 and 5e, and 0.375 inches maximum will be the requirement for Category 6 cables.

Far End Crosstalk (FEXT)   *Far-end crosstalk* (FEXT) is similar to NEXT except that it is detected at the opposite end of the wire from where the signal was sent. Due to attenuation, the signals at the far end of the transmitting wire pair are much weaker than the signals at the near end.

The measure of FEXT is used to calculate equal-level far-end crosstalk (ELFEXT) (discussed in the next section). More FEXT will be seen on a shorter cable than a longer one because the signal at the receiving side will have less distance over which to attenuate.

Equal-Level Far-End Crosstalk (ELFEXT)

Equal-level far-end crosstalk (ELFEXT) is the crosstalk coupling between cabling pairs measured at the end of the cable opposite to the end of the signal source, taking into account signal loss. ELFEXT is calculated, not measured, by subtracting the attenuation of the disturber pair from the far-end crosstalk (FEXT) on the disturbed pair. The calculation describes the ratio of disturbance to the level of the desired signal; it is another indication of signal-to-noise ratio. Another way of looking at it is that the value represents the ratio between the strength of the noise due to crosstalk from end signals compared to the strength of the received data signal. You could also think of ELFEXT as far-end ACR (attenuation-to-crosstalk ratio, described later in this chapter).

Each pair-to-pair combination is measured, as the attenuation on each pair will be slightly different. If the ELFEXT value is very high, it may indicate that either excessive attenuation has occurred or that the far-end crosstalk is higher than expected.

Pair-to-Pair Crosstalk

For both near-end crosstalk and far-end crosstalk, one way of measuring crosstalk is the *pair-to-pair* method. In pair-to-pair measurement, one pair, the disturber, is energized with a signal, and another pair, the disturbed, is measured to see how much signal transfer occurs. The following six combinations are tested in a four-pair cable:

- Pair 1 to pair 2
- Pair 1 to pair 3
- Pair 1 to pair 4
- Pair 2 to pair 3
- Pair 2 to pair 4
- Pair 3 to pair 4

The test is repeated from the opposite end of the cable, resulting in 12 pair-to-pair combinations tested. The worst combination is what is recorded as the cable's crosstalk value. See Figure 1.17.

FIGURE 1.17:

Cutaway of a UTP cable, showing pair-to-pair crosstalk

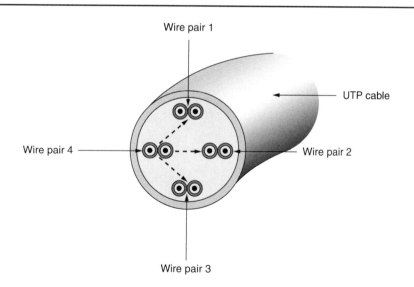

Wire pair 4 will generate crosstalk that will affect the other three pairs of wire in the cable.

Power-Sum Crosstalk

Power-sum crosstalk also applies to both NEXT and FEXT and must be taken into consideration for cables that will support technologies using more than one wire pair at the same time. When testing power-sum crosstalk, all pairs except one are energized as disturbing pairs, and the remaining pair, the disturbed pair, is measured for transferred signal energy. Figure 1.18 shows a cutaway of a four-pair cable. Notice that the energy from pairs 2, 3, and 4 can all affect pair 1. The sum of this crosstalk must be within specified limits. Because each pair affects each other pair, this measurement will have to be made four separate times, once for each wire pair against the others. Again, testing is done from both ends, raising the number of tested combinations to eight. As with pair-to-pair measurements, the worst combination is recorded as the cable crosstalk.

FIGURE 1.18:

Power-sum crosstalk

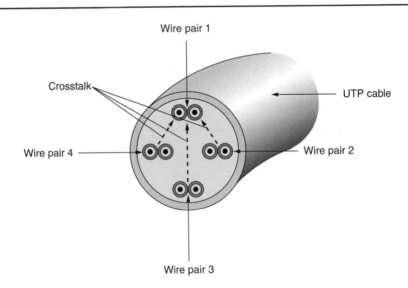

Crosstalk from pairs 2, 3, and 4 will affect pair 1.

External Interference

One hindrance to transmitting data at high speed is the possibility that the signals traveling through the cable will be acted upon by some outside force. Though the designer of any cable, whether it's twisted pair or coaxial, attempts to compensate for this, external forces are beyond the cable designer's control. All electrical devices, including cables with data flowing through them, generate electromagnetic interference (EMI). Low-power devices and cables supporting low-bandwidth applications do not generate enough of an electromagnetic field to make a difference. Some equipment generates radio-frequency interference; you may notice this if you live near a TV or radio antenna and you own a cordless phone.

Set Your Cell Phones to Stun

At the beginning of each Microsoft technical class that Jim teaches, he asks his students to set their cell phones and pages on stun (silent ring or vibrate mode). Even so, in almost every class, at least one student complains that his or her computer monitor is sometimes unreadable or "jumping around." The cause: the cell phone was placed under the monitor and is ringing. Anytime the phone is ringing, it interferes with a nearby electrical device.

Devices and cables that use much electricity can generate EMI that can interfere with data transmission. Consequently, cables should be placed in areas away from these devices. Some common sources of EMI in a typical office environment include the following:

- Motors
- Heating and air-conditioning equipment
- Fluorescent lights
- Laser printers
- Elevators
- Electrical wiring
- Televisions
- Some medical equipment

NOTE   Talk about electromagnetic interference! An MRI (magnetic-resonance-imaging) machine, which is used to look inside the body without surgery or x-rays, can erase a credit card from 10 feet away.

When running cabling in a building, do so a few feet away from these devices. Never install data cabling in the same conduit as electrical wiring.

In some cases, even certain types of businesses and environments have high levels of interference, including airports, hospitals, military installations, and power plants. If you install cabling in such an environment, consider using cables that are properly shielded or use fiber-optic cable.

Cabling and Standards

Maximum acceptable values of attenuation, minimum acceptable values of crosstalk, and even cabling-design issues—who is responsible for making sure standards are published? The group varies from country to country; in the United States, the predominant standards organization supervising data cabling standards is the TIA/EIA (Telecommunications Industries Association/Electronic Industries Association). The standard that covers Category 5 cabling, for example, is ANSI/TIA/EIA-568-A, which is part of the guideline for building structured cabling systems. These standards are not rigid like an Internet RFC but are refined as needed via addenda. The ANSI/TIA/EIA-568-A document dictates the performance specifications for cables and connecting hardware. Chapter 2 discusses common cabling standards in more detail.

Attenuation-to-Crosstalk Ratio (ACR)

Attenuation-to-crosstalk ratio (ACR) is an indication of how much larger the received signal is when compared to the NEXT (crosstalk or noise) on the same pair. ACR is also sometimes referred to as the *signal-to-noise ratio* (SNR). It is a calculated value; you can't "measure" ACR. Also, it's not really a ratio. It is the mathematical difference you get when you subtract the crosstalk value from the attenuation value at a given frequency. Technically, SNR also incorporates not only noise generated by the data transmission but also outside interference. For practical purposes, the ACR and true SNR are functionally identical, except in environments with high levels of EMI.

Headroom   Because ACR represents the minimum gap between attenuation and crosstalk, the *headroom* represents the difference between the minimum ACR and the actual ACR performance values. Greater headroom is desirable because it provides additional performance margin that can compensate for the sins of cheap connectors or sloppy termination practices. It also results in a slight increase in the maximum bandwidth of the cable.

The differential between the crosstalk (noise) and the attenuation (loss of signal) is important because it assures that the signal being sent down a wire is stronger at the receiving end than any interference that may be imposed by crosstalk or other noise.

Figure 1.19 shows the relationship between attenuation and NEXT and graphically illustrates ACR for Category 5. Notice that as the frequency increases, the NEXT values get lower while the attenuation values get higher. The difference between the attenuation and NEXT lines is the ACR. Note that for all cables, a theoretical maximum bandwidth exists greater than the specified maximum in the standards. This is appropriate conservative engineering.

FIGURE 1.19:

Attenuation-to-crosstalk ratio for a Category 5 channel link

Solving problems relating to ACR usually means troubleshooting NEXT because, short of replacing the cable, the only way to reduce attenuation is to use shorter cables.

Propagation Delay

Electricity travels through a cable at a constant speed, expressed as a percentage-of-light speed called NVP (Nominal Velocity of Propagation). For UTP cables, NVP is usually between 60 and 90 percent. The manufacturer of the cable controls the NVP value because it is largely a function of the dielectric constant of the insulation material. The difference between the time at which a signal starts down a pair and the time at which it arrives on the other end is the *propagation delay*.

Delay Skew

Delay skew is a phenomenon that occurs as a result of each set of wires being different lengths (as shown in Figure 1.20). Twisting the conductors of a pair around each other to aid in canceling crosstalk increases the actual length of the conductors relative to the cable length. Because the pairs each have a unique twist interval, the conductor lengths are unique as well. Signals transmitted on two or more separate pairs of wire will arrive at slightly different times, as the wire pairs are slightly different lengths. Cables that are part of a Category 5, 5e, or 6 installation cannot have more than a 50ns delay skew.

FIGURE 1.20:

Delay skew for four-pair operation

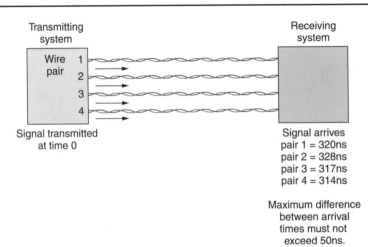

Transmitting system

Wire pair 1
          2
          3
          4

Signal transmitted
at time 0

Receiving system

Signal arrives
pair 1 = 320ns
pair 2 = 328ns
pair 3 = 317ns
pair 4 = 314ns

Maximum difference
between arrival
times must not
exceed 50ns.

Excessive delay or delay skew may cause timing problems with network transceivers. These timing issues can either slow a link dramatically because the electronics are constantly requesting that the data be resent or can choke it off completely.

The Future of Cabling Performance

In the near future, Category 6 will be ratified, and the initial Category 7 standards will be developed. The draft of Category 6 cabling already includes some additional performance characteristics not found in Category 5 or TSB-95, including ELFEXT loss and FEXT loss.

It is conceivable that 10Gbps Ethernet will soon run to the desktop over twisted-pair cable. Some pundits claim it will never happen, but some of them were the ones who claimed that 10Mbps Ethernet would never operate over twisted pair. As materials and manufacturing techniques improve, who knows what types of performance future twisted-pair cabling may offer?

chapter **2**

Cabling Specifications and Standards

- Structured Cabling and Standardization

- The ANSI/TIA/EIA-568-A Commercial Building Telecommunications Cabling Standard

- The ISO/IEC 11801 Generic Cabling for Customer Premises Standard

- The Anixter Cable Performance Levels Program

- Other Cabling Technologies

In the past, companies often had several cabling infrastructures because no single cabling system would support all of a company's applications. A standardized cabling system is important not only for consumers but also for vendors and cabling installers. Vendors must clearly understand how to design and build products that will operate on a universal cabling system. Cable installers need to understand what products can be used, proper installation techniques and practices, and how to test installed systems.

This chapter covers some of the important topics related to cabling Standards.

Structured Cabling and Standardization

Typical business environments and requirements change quickly. Companies restructure and reorganize at alarming rates. In some companies, the average employee changes work locations once every two years. During a two-year tenure, Jim changed offices at a particular company five times. Each time, his telephone, both networked computers, a VAX VT-100 terminal, and a networked printer had to be moved. The data and voice cabling system had to support these reconfigurations quickly and easily. Earlier cabling designs would not have easily supported this business environment.

Until the early 1990s, cabling systems were proprietary, vendor-specific, and lacked flexibility. Some of the downsides of pre-1990 cabling systems included the following:

- Vendor-specific cabling locked the customer into a proprietary system.

- Upgrades or new systems often required a completely new cabling infrastructure.

- Moves and changes often necessitated major cabling plant reconfigurations. Some coaxial and twinax cabling systems required that entire areas (or the entire system) be brought down in order to make changes.

- Companies often had several cabling infrastructures that had to be maintained for their various applications.

- Troubleshooting proprietary systems was time consuming and difficult unless you were intimately familiar with that system.

Cabling has changed quite a bit over the years. Cabling installations have evolved from proprietary systems to flexible, open solutions that can be used by many vendors and applications. This change is the result of the adaptation of standards-based, structured cabling systems. The driving force behind this acceptance is due not only to customers but also to the cooperation between many telecommunications vendors and international standards organizations.

A properly designed *structured cabling* system is based around components or wiring units. An example of a wiring unit is a story of an office building, as shown in Figure 2.1. All the work locations on that floor are connected to a single wiring closet. Each of the wiring units (stories of the office building) can be combined together using backbone cables as part of a larger system.

FIGURE 2.1:

A typical small office with horizontal cabling running to a single wiring closet

Workstation outlets (phone and data)

Telecommunications (wiring) closet

Horizontal cabling to wiring closet

TIP

This point bears repeating: A structured cabling system is not designed around any specific application but rather is designed to be generic. This permits many applications to take advantage of the cabling system.

The components used to design a structured cabling system should be based on a widely accepted specification and should allow many applications (analog voice, digital voice, 10Base-T, 100Base-TX, 16Mbps Token Ring, RS-232, etc.) to use the cabling system. The components should also adhere to certain performance specifications so that the installer or customer will know exactly what types of applications will be supported.

A number of documents are related to data cabling. In the United States, the Standard is ANSI/TIA/EIA-568-A 1995, also known as the Commercial Building Telecommunications Cabling Standard. The ANSI/TIA/EIA-568-A Standard is a specification adopted by ANSI (American National Standards Institute), but the ANSI portion of the document name is commonly left out. In Europe, the predominant Standard is the ISO/IEC 11801 Standard, also known as the International Standard on Information Technology Generic Cabling for Customer Premises.

NOTE   When is a standard not a Standard? In the United States, a document is not officially a national Standard until it is sanctioned by ANSI. In Canada, the CSA is the sanctioning body, and in Europe, it is ISO. Until sanctioned by these organizations, a requirements document is merely a specification. However, many people use the words *specification* and *standard* interchangeably. (In Europe, the word *norm* also comes into play.) Just be aware that a standard can be created by anyone with a word processor, whereas a Standard carries the weight of governmental recognition as a comprehensive, fair, and objective document.

These two documents are quite similar, although their terminology is different, and the ISO/IEC 11801 Standard permits an additional type of UTP cabling. Throughout much of the rest of the world, countries and specifications organizations have adopted one of these Standards as their own. Both of these documents are discussed in more detail later in this chapter.

Cabling Standards: A Moving Target

This chapter briefly introduces the ANSI/TIA/EIA-568-A and the ISO/IEC 11801 Standards, but it is not intended to be a comprehensive guide to either. Even as you read this book, networking vendors and specifications committees are figuring out ways to transmit larger quantities of data, voice, and video over copper and fiber-optic cable. Therefore, the requirements and performance specifications for the Standards are continually being updated. If you are responsible for large cabling-systems design and implementation, you should own a copy of the relevant documents.

Continued on next page

Most of the TIA/EIA documents mentioned in this chapter are available for purchase through Global Engineering Documents at (800) 854-7179 or on the Web at `http://global.ihs.com`. Global Engineering Documents sells printed versions of the TIA, EIA, and ETSI specifications, as well as others The ISO/EIC Standards and ITU recommendations are available for purchase from the ITU's Web site at `www.itu.int/publications/bookstore.html`. CSA International Standards documents are available from the CSA at (416) 747-4000 or on the Web at `www.csa.ca`.

Standards and Specifying Organizations

If you pick up any document or catalog on data cabling, you will see acronyms and abbreviations for the names of specifications organizations. If you want to know more about a particular specification, you should be familiar with the organization that publishes that particular document. These U.S.-based and international organizations publish hardware, software, and physical-infrastructure specifications to ensure interoperability between electrical, communications, and other technology systems. Your customers and coworkers may laugh at the elation you express when you get even simple networked devices to work, but you are not alone. In fact, the simple act of getting two stations communicating with one another on a 10Base-T network, for example, is a monumental achievement considering the number of components and vendors involved. Just think: Computers from two different vendors that use Ethernet adapters may also be from different manufacturers. These Ethernet adapters may also be connected by cable and connectors provided by another manufacturer, which in turn may be connected to a hub built by still another manufacturer. Even the software that the two computers are running may come from different companies. Dozens of other components must work together.

That anything is interoperable at all is amazing. Thankfully, a number of organizations around the world are devoted to the development of specifications that encourage interoperability. These organizations are often nonprofit, and the people that devote much of their time to the development of these specifications are usually volunteers. These specifications not only include cabling specifications and performance and installation practices but also the development of networking equipment like Ethernet cards. As long as the manufacturer follows the appropriate specifications, their devices should be interoperable with other networking devices.

The number of organizations that provide specifications is still more amazing. It might be simpler if a single international organization were responsible for all Standards. However, if that were the case, probably nothing would ever get accomplished. Hence the number of specifications organizations. The following sections describe these organizations, but the list is by no means exhaustive.

American National Standards Institute (ANSI)

Five engineering societies and three U.S. government agencies founded the American National Standards Institute (ANSI) in 1918 as a private, nonprofit membership organization sustained by its membership. ANSI's mission is to encourage voluntary compliance with Standards and methods. ANSI's membership includes almost 1,400 private companies and government organizations in the United States as well as international members.

ANSI does not develop the American National Standards (ANS) documents, but it facilitates their development by establishing a consensus between the members interested in developing a particular Standard.

To gain ANSI approval, a document must be developed by a representative cross section of interested industry participants. The cross section must include both manufacturers and end users. In addition, a rigorous balloting and revision process must be adhered to so that a single powerful member does not drive proprietary requirements through and establish a particular market advantage.

Through membership in various international organizations such as the International Organization for Standardizations (ISO) and the International Electrotechnical Commission (IEC), ANSI promotes standards developed in the United States. ANSI was a founding member of the ISO and is one of the five permanent members of the ISO governing council and one of four permanent members on the ISO's Technical Management Board.

ANSI Standards include a wide range of information-technology specifications, such as SCSI interface specifications, programming-language specifications, and specifications for character sets. ANSI helped to coordinate the efforts of the Electronic Industries Alliance (EIA) and the Telecommunications Industry Association (TIA) to develop ANSI/TIA/EIA-568-A, *the* cabling specification in the United States. TIA/EIA-568 is discussed in more detail later in this chapter. You can find information on it and links to purchase the documents on ANSI's Web site at www.ansi.org.

Electronic Industries Alliance (EIA)

The Electronic Industries Alliance (EIA) was established in 1924 and was originally known as the Radio Manufacturers Association. Since then, the EIA has evolved into an organization that represents a wide variety of electronics manufacturers in the United States and abroad; these manufacturers make products for a wide range of markets. The EIA is organized along specific product and market lines that allow each EIA sector to be responsive to its specific needs. These sectors include components, consumer electronics, electronic information, industrial electronics, government, and telecommunications.

The EIA (along with the TIA) was the driving force behind the ANSI/TIA/EIA-568-A Commercial Building Telecommunications Cabling Standard. More information is available on the Web at www.eia.org.

Telecommunications Industry Association (TIA)

The Telecommunications Industry Association (TIA) is a trade organization that consists of a membership of over 1,100 telecommunications and electronics companies that provide services, materials, and products throughout the world. The TIA membership manufacturers and distributes virtually all the telecommunication products used in the world today. TIA's mission is to represent its membership on issues relating to Standards, public policy, and market development. The 1988 merger of the United States Telecommunications Suppliers Association (USTSA) and the EIA's Information and Telecommunications Technologies Group formed the TIA.

The TIA (along with the EIA) was instrumental in the development of the ANSI/TIA/ EIA-568-A Commercial Building Telecommunications Cabling Standard. TIA can be found on the Web at www.tiaonline.org.

TIA Committees

In the United States (and much of the world), the TIA is ultimately responsible for the Standards related to structured cabling as well as many other technological devices used every day. If you visit the TIA Web site (www.tiaonline.org), you will find that committees develop the specifications. Often, a number of committees will contribute to a single specification. You may find a number of abbreviations that you are not familiar with. These include the following:

SFG   Standards Formulation Groups is a committee responsible for developing specifications.

Continued on next page

FO   Fiber Optics is a committee dedicated to fiber-optic technology.

TR   Technical Review is an engineering committee.

WG   Working Group is a general title for a subcommittee.

UPED   The User Premises Equipment Division centers its activities on FCC (Federal Communications Commission) regulatory changes.

Some of the TIA committees and their responsibilities are as follows:

FO-2   Optical Communications is responsible for developing specifications related to fiber-optic communications and fiber-optic devices.

FO-6   Fiber Optics is responsible for developing specifications for fiber-optic tooling and testing, connecting devices, and reliability of fiber-optic connectors.

TR-29   Facsimile Systems and Equipment is responsible for the development of specifications relating to faxing.

TR-30   Data Transmission Systems and Equipment develops specifications related to data transmission as well as faxing.

TR-32   Personal Radio Equipment is responsible for the development of consumer-oriented products such as cordless telephones.

TR-41   User Premises Telecommunications Requirements is responsible for the specifications relating to technologies such as IP (Internet Protocol), telephony (VoIP or Voiceover IP), wireless telephones, caller ID, multimedia building distribution, and wireless user-premises equipment.

TR-42   User Premises Telecommunications Infrastructure is responsible for specifications such as the Commercial Building Telecommunications Cabling (TIA/EIA-568-B.1 or subcommittee TR-42.1), Residential Telecommunications Infrastructure (TIA/EIA-570-A or subcommittee TR-42.2), Commercial Building Telecommunications Pathways and Spaces (TIA/EIA-569-A or subcommittee TR-42.3), Telecommunications Copper Cabling Systems (TIA/EIA-568-B.2 and B.4 or subcommittee TR-42.7), Workgroup on Copper Connecting Hardware (subcommittee TR 42.2.1), and Telecommunications Optical Fiber Cabling Systems (TIA/EIA-568-B.3 or subcommittee TR-42.8). The subcommittees of TR-42 formed the TIA/EIA-568-B specification that is expected to be ratified sometime in 2001.

Insulated Cable Engineers Association (ICEA)

The ICEA is a nonprofit professional organization sponsored by leading cable manufacturers in the United States. It was established in 1925 with the goal of producing cable specifications for telecommunication, electrical power, and control cables. The organization draws from the technical expertise of the representative engineer members to create documents that reflect the most current cable-design, material-content, and performance criteria. The group is organized in four sections: Power Cable, Control & Instrumentation Cable, Portable Cable, and Communications Cable.

The ICEA has an important role in relation to the ANSI/TIA/EIA Standards for network-cabling infrastructure. ICEA cable specifications for both indoor and outdoor cables, copper and fiber optic, are referenced by the TIA documents to specify the design, construction, and physical performance requirements for cables.

ICEA specifications are issued as national Standards. In the Communications section, ANSI requirements for participation by an appropriate cross section of industry representatives in a document's development is accomplished through TWCSTAC (pronounced *twix-tak*), the Telecommunications Wire and Cable Standards Technical Advisory Committee. The TWCSTAC committee consists of ICEA members, along with other manufacturers, material suppliers, and end users. The ICEA maintains a Web site at www.icea.net.

National Fire Protection Association (NFPA)

The National Fire Protection Association (NFPA) was founded in 1896 as a nonprofit organization to help protect people, property, and the environment from fire damage. NFPA is now an international organization with more than 65,000 members representing over 100 countries. The organization is a world leader on fire prevention and safety. The NFPA's mission is to help reduce the risk of fire through codes, safety requirements, research, and fire-related education. The Internet home for NFPA is at www.nfpa.org.

Though not directly related to data cabling, the NFPA is responsible for the development and publication of the National Electrical Code (NEC). The NEC is published every three years (the next NEC will be published in 2002) and covers issues related to electrical safety requirements; it is not used as a design specification or an instruction manual.

Two sections of the NEC are relevant to data cabling, Articles 725 and 800. Many municipalities have adopted the NEC as part of their building codes, and, consequently, electrical construction and wiring must meet the specifications in the NEC. Although the NEC is not a legal document, portions of the NEC become laws if municipalities adopt them as part of their local building codes. In Chapter 4, we will discuss the use of the NEC when considering the restrictions that may be placed on cabling design.

National Electrical Manufacturers Association (NEMA)

The National Electrical Manufacturers Association (NEMA) is a U.S.-based industry association that helps promote standardization of electrical components, power wires, and cables. The specifications put out by NEMA help to encourage interoperability between products built by different manufacturers. The specifications often form the basis for ANSI Standards. NEMA can be found on the Internet at www.nema.org.

Federal Communications Commission

The Federal Communications Commission (FCC) was founded in 1934 as part of the U.S. government. The FCC consists of a board of seven commissioners appointed by the President; this board has the power to regulate electrical-communications systems originating in the United States. These communications systems include television, radio, telegraph, telephone, and cable TV systems. Regulations relating to premises cabling and equipment are covered in FCC Part 68 rules. The FCC Web site is at www.fcc.gov.

Underwriters Laboratories (UL)

Founded in 1894, Underwriters Laboratories, Inc. (UL) is a nonprofit, independent organization dedicated to product safety testing and certification. Although not involved directly with cabling specifications, UL works with cabling and other manufacturers to ensure that electrical devices are safe. UL tests products for paying customers; if the product passes the specification for which the product is submitted, the UL listing or verification is granted. The UL mark of approval is applied to cabling and electrical devices worldwide. UL can be found on the Web at www.ul.com.

International Organization for Standardizations (ISO)

The International Organization for Standardizations (ISO) is an international organization of national specifications bodies and is based in Geneva, Switzerland.

The specifications bodies that are members of the ISO represent over 130 countries from around the world; the United States representative to the ISO is the American National Standards Institute (ANSI). The ISO was established in 1947 as a nongovernmental organization to promote the development of standardization in intellectual, scientific, technological, and economic activities. You can find the ISO Web site at www.iso.ch.

NOTE   If the name is the International Organization for Standardizations, shouldn't the acronym be IOS instead of ISO? It should be, if ISO were an acronym—but ISO is taken from the Greek word *isos*, meaning equal.

ISO Standards include specifications for film-speed codes, telephone and banking-card formats, standardized freight containers, the universal system of measurements known as SI, paper sizes, and metric screw threads, just to name a few. One of the common Standards that you may hear about is the ISO 9000 Standard, which provides a framework for quality management and quality assurance.

ISO frequently collaborates with the IEC (International Electrotechnical Commission) and the ITU (International Telecommunications Union). One such result of collaboration is the ISO/IEC 11801:1995 Standard titled Generic Cabling for Customer Premises. ISO/IEC 11801 is the ISO/IEC equivalent of the ANSI/TIA/EIA-568-A Standard.

International Electrotechnical Commission (IEC)

The International Electrotechnical Commission (IEC) is an international specifications and conformity-assessment body founded in 1906 to publish international specifications relating to electrical, electronic, and related technologies. Membership in the IEC includes more than 50 countries.

A full member has voting rights in the international Standards process. The second type of member, an associate member, has observer status and can attend all IEC meetings.

The mission of the IEC is to promote international Standards and cooperation on all matters relating to electricity, electronics, and related technologies. The IEC and the ISO cooperate on the creation of Standards such as the Generic Cabling for Customer Premises (ISO/IEC 11801:1995). The IEC Web site is www.iec.ch.

Institute of Electrical and Electronic Engineers (IEEE)

The Institute of Electrical and Electronic Engineers (IEEE, pronounced *I triple-E*) is an international, nonprofit association consisting of more than 330,000 members in 150 countries. The IEEE was formed in 1963 when the American Institute of Electrical Engineers (AIEE, founded in 1884) merged with the Institute of Radio Engineers (IRE, founded in 1912). The IEEE is responsible for 30 percent of the electrical-engineering, computer, and control-technology literature published in the world today. They are also responsible for the development of over 800 active specifications and have many more under development. These specifications include the 10Base-*x* specifications (such as 10Base-T, 100Base-TX, etc.) and the 802.*x* specifications (such as 802.2, 802.3, etc.). You can get more information about the IEEE on the Web at `www.ieee.org`.

National Institute of Standards and Technology (NIST)

The United States Congress established the National Institute of Standards and Technology (NIST) with several major goals in mind, including assisting in the improvement and development of manufacturing technology, improving product quality and reliability, and encouraging scientific discovery. NIST is an agency of the United States Department of Commerce and works with major industries to achieve its goals.

NIST has four major programs through which it carries out its mission:

- Measurement and Standards Laboratories
- Advanced Technology Program
- Manufacturing Extension Partnership
- A quality outreach program associated with the Malcolm Baldrige National Quality Award called the Baldrige National Quality Program

Though not directly related to most cabling and data specifications, NIST's efforts contribute to the specifications and the development of the technology based on them. You can locate NIST on the Internet at `www.nist.gov`.

International Telecommunications Union (ITU)

The International Telecommunications Union (ITU), based in Geneva, Switzerland, is the specifications organization formerly known as the International

Telephone and Telegraph Consultative Committee (CCITT). The origins of the CCITT can be traced back over 100 years; the ITU was formed to replace it in 1993. The ITU does not publish specifications per se, but it does publish recommendations. These recommendations are nonbinding specifications agreed to by consensus of 1 of 14 technical study groups. The mission of the ITU is to study the technical and operations issues relating to telecommunications and to make recommendations on implementing standardized approaches to telecommunications.

The ITU currently publishes more than 2,500 recommendations, including specifications relating to telecommunications, electronic messaging, television transmission, and data communications. The ITU's Web address is www.itu.int.

CSA International (CSA)

CSA International originated as the Canadian Standards Association but changed its name to reflect its growing work and influence on international Standards. Founded in 1919, CSA International is a nonprofit, independent organization with more than 8,000 members worldwide; it is the functional equivalent of the UL. CSA International's mission is to develop Standards, represent Canada on various ISO committees, and work with the IEC when developing the Standards. Some of the common Standards published by CSA International include:

- CAN/CSA-T524 Residential Wiring

- CAN/CSA-T527 Bonding and Grounding for Telecommunications

- CAN/CSA-T528 Telecommunications Administration Standard for Commercial Buildings

- CAN/CSA-T529 Design Guidelines for Telecommunications Wiring Systems in Commercial Buildings

- CAN/CSA-T530 Building Facilities Design Guidelines for Telecommunications

Many cabling and data products certified by the United States National Electrical Code (NEC) and Underwriters Laboratories (UL) are also certified by the CSA. Cables manufactured for use in the United States are often marked with the CSA electrical and flame-test ratings as well as the U.S. ratings, if they can be used in Canada. CSA International is on the Internet at www.csa.ca.

ATM Forum

Started in 1991, the ATM Forum (Asynchronous Transfer Mode) is an international, nonprofit organization whose mission is to promote the use of ATM products and services.

Specifications developed and published by the ATM Forum include LAN Emulation (LANE) over ATM (af-lane-0021.000) and ATM Physical Medium Dependent Interface Specification for 155Mbps over Twisted-Pair Cable (af-phy-0015.000). These documents are available free of charge on the ATM Forum's Web site at www.atmforum.org.

European Telecommunications Standards Institute (ETSI)

The European Telecommunications Standards Institute (ETSI) is a nonprofit organization based in Sophia Antipolis, France. The ETSI currently consists of almost 696 members from 50 countries and represents manufacturers, service providers, and consumers. The ETSI's mission is to determine and produce telecommunications specifications and to encourage worldwide standardization. The ETSI coordinates its activities with international Standards bodies such as the ITU. You can find the organization at www.etsi.org.

Building Industry Consulting Services International (BICSI)

Though not specifically a specifications organization, the Building Industry Consulting Services International (BICSI) deserves a special mention. BICSI is a nonprofit, professional organization founded in 1974 to support telephone-company building-industry consultants (BICs) who are responsible for design and implementation of communications-distribution systems in commercial and multifamily buildings. Currently, the BICSI serves nearly 20,000 members from 85 countries around the world.

BICSI supports a professional certification program called the RCDD (Registered Communications Distribution Designer). Over 5,500 people with the RCDD certification have demonstrated competence and expertise in the design, implementation, and integration of telecommunications systems and infrastructure. For more information on the RCDD program or becoming a member of the BICSI, check out its Web site at www.bicsi.org. Information on becoming a BICSI accredited RCDD is detailed in Appendix C.

Occupational Safety and Health Administration (OSHA)

A division of the United States Department of Labor, the Occupational Safety and Health Administration (OSHA) was formed in 1970 with the goal of making workplaces in the United States the safest in the world. To this end, it passes laws designed to protect employees from many types of job hazards. OSHA adopted many parts of the National Electrical Code (NEC), which was not a law unto itself, giving those adopted portions of the NEC legal status. For more information on OSHA, look on the Web at www.osha.gov.

ANSI/TIA/EIA-568-A Cabling Standard

In the mid-1980s, consumers, contractors, vendors, and manufacturers became concerned about the lack of specifications relating to telecommunications cabling. Before then, all communications cabling was proprietary and often suited only to a single-purpose use. The Computer Communications Industry Association (CCIA) asked the EIA to develop a specification that would encourage structured, standardized cabling.

Under the guidance of the TIA TR-41 committee and associated subcommittees, the TIA and EIA in 1991 published the first version of the Commercial Building Telecommunications Cabling Standard, better known as ANSI/TIA/EIA-568 or sometimes simply as TIA/EIA-568.

NOTE   Sometimes you will see the Commercial Building Telecommunications Cabling Standard referred to as ANSI/TIA/EIA-568 and sometimes just as TIA/EIA-568. You will also sometimes see the EIA and TIA transposed. The original name of the specification was ANSI/EIA/TIA-568-1991, but over the years it has been changed. The official name of the specification today is ANSI/TIA/EIA-568-A. Addenda to the Standard are designated as ANSI/TIA/EIA-568-A-1, ANSI/TIA/EIA-568-A-2, and so on. Five of these addenda currently exist.

Over the next few years, the EIA released a number of Telecommunications Systems Bulletins (TSB) covering specifications for higher grades of cabling (TSB-36), connecting hardware (TSB-40), patch cables (TSB-40A), testing requirements for modular jacks (TSB-40A), and additional specifications for shielded twisted-pair cabling (TSB-53). The contents of these TSBs, along with other improvements, were used to revise TIA/EIA-568; this revision was released in 1995 and is called ANSI/TIA/EIA-568-A. As published, the ANSI/TIA/EIA-568-A takes precedence over TIA/EIA-568, TSB-36, TSB-40, TSB-40A, and TSB-53.

Progress marches on, and communication technologies advance faster than entire specifications can be revised, balloted, and published as Standards. But it is relatively easy to create ad hoc addenda to a Standard as the need arises. Consequently, five official additions to the ANSI/TIA/EIA-568-A base Standard have been written since its publication in 1995:

ANSI/TIA/EIA-568-A-1, the Propagation Delay and Delay Skew Specifications for 100Ohm Four-pair Cable   Approved in August and published in September of 1997, this addendum was created to add additional requirements to those in the base Standard in support of high-performance networking, such as 100BaseT (100Mbps Ethernet).

ANSI/TIA/EIA-568-A-2, Corrections and Addition to ANSI/TIA/EIA-568-A   Approved in July and published in August 1998, this document contains corrections to the base document.

ANSI/TIA/EIA-568-A-3, Addendum No. 3 to TIA/EIA-568-A   Approved and published in December 1998, the third addendum defines bundled, hybrid, and composite cables and clarifies their requirements.

ANSI/TIA/EIA-568-A-4, Production Modular Cord NEXT Loss Test Method for Unshielded Twisted-Pair Cabling   Approved in November and published in December 1999, this addendum provides a nondestructive methodology for NEXT loss testing of modular-plug (patch) cords.

ANSI/TIA/EIA-568-A-5, Transmission Performance Specifications for Four-Pair 100-Ohm Category 5e Cabling   Approved in January and published in February 2000, the latest addendum specifies additional performance requirements for the *cabling* (not just the *cable*) for Enhanced Category 5 installations. Additional requirements include minimum-return-loss, propagation-delay, delay-skew, NEXT, PSNEXT, FEXT, ELFEXT, and PSELFEXT parameters. Also included are laboratory measurement methods, component and field-test methods, and computation algorithms over the specified frequency range. In ANSI/TIA/EIA-568-A-5, performance requirements for Category 5e cabling do not exceed 100MHz, even though some testing is done beyond this frequency limit.

NOTE   A new revision of the entire specification is expected in 2001 and will incorporate all addenda and many TSBs that affect the current Standard. Among other changes, Category 4 and Category 5 cable will no longer be recommended. In fact, Category 4 will cease to exist; Category 5e will replace Categories 4 and 5 as the recommended Category of cable. Focus will shift from requirements for individual components, e.g., the cable, to performance of the cabling link and channel—in other words, the cable, connection points, and patch cords. The new specification will be known as TIA/EIA-568-B.

NOTE   The Canadian equivalent of TIA/EIA-568-A is CSA T529, which will undoubtedly be updated to reflect the updated B version when it is ratified and published as an ANSI Standard.

Should I Use ANSI/TIA/EIA-568-A or ISO/IEC 11801?

This chapter describes both the ANSI/TIA/EIA-568-A and ISO/IEC 11801 cabling Standards. You may wonder which Standard you should follow. Though these two Standards are quite similar (ISO/IEC 11801 was based on ANSI/TIA/EIA-568-A), the ISO/IEC 11801 Standard was developed with cable commonly used in Europe and consequently contains some references more specific to European applications. Also, some terminology in the two documents is different.

If you are designing a cabling system to be used in the United States or Canada, you should follow the ANSI/TIA/EIA-568-A Standard (Or its replacement, when approved.) You should know, however, that the ISO is taking the lead (with assistance from TIA, EIA, CSA, and others) in developing new cabling specifications, so maybe in the future you will see only a single Standard implemented worldwide that will be a combination of both specifications.

ANSI/TIA/EIA-568-A Purpose and Scope

The ANSI/TIA/EIA-568 Standard was developed and has evolved into its current form for several reasons:

- To establish a cabling specification that would support more than a single vendor application

- To provide direction of the design of telecommunications equipment and cabling products that are intended to serve commercial organizations

- To specify a cabling system generic enough to support both voice and data

- To establish technical and performance guidelines and provide guidelines for the planning and installation of structured cabling systems

The ANSI/TIA/EIA-568-A Standard specifies as its scope cabling that is "office oriented." The specifications address the following:

- Subsystems of structured cabling

- Minimum requirements for telecommunications cabling

- Installation methods and practices

- Connector and pin assignments

- The life span of a telecommunications cabling system (which should exceed 10 years)

- Media types and performance specifications for horizontal and backbone cabling

- Connecting hardware performance specifications

- Recommended topology and distances

- The definitions of cabling elements (horizontal cable, cross-connects, telecommunication outlets, etc.)

WARNING   Welcome to the Nomenclature Twilight Zone. The ANSI/TIA/EIA-568-A Standard contains two wiring patterns for use with UTP jacks and plugs. They indicate the order in which the wire conductors should be connected to the pins in modular jacks and plugs and are known as T568A and T568B. Do not confuse these with the documents TIA/EIA-568-A and the forthcoming TIA/EIA-568-B. The wiring schemes are both covered in TIA/EIA-568-A and will both be covered in TIA/EIA-568-B. To learn more about the wiring patterns, see Chapter 9.

Subsystems of a Structured Cabling System

The ANSI/TIA/EIA-568-A Standard breaks structured cabling into six areas. They are the entrance facility (building entrance), equipment room, backbone cabling, telecommunications closet, horizontal cabling, and the work area.

TIP
This chapter provides an overview of the ANSI/TIA/EIA-568-A Standard and is not meant as a substitute for the official document. Cabling professionals should purchase a full copy; you can do so at the Global Engineering Documents Web site (`http://global.ihs.com`).

Interpreting Standards and Specifications

Standards and specification documents are worded with precise language designed to spell out exactly what is expected of an implementation using that specification. If you read carefully, you may notice that slightly different words are used when stating requirements.

If you see the word *shall* or *must* used when stating a requirement, it signifies a *mandatory* requirement. Words such as *should*, *may*, and *desirable* are *advisory* in nature and indicate *recommended* requirements.

Entrance Facility

The entrance facility (building entrance) defined by ANSI/TIA/EIA-568-A specifies the point in the building where cabling interfaces with the outside world. All external cabling (campus backbone, interbuilding, antennae pathways, and telecommunications provider) should enter the building and terminate in a single point. Telecommunications carriers are usually required to terminate within 50 feet of a building entrance. The physical requirements of the interface equipment are defined in ANSI/TIA/EIA-569, the Commercial Building Standard for Telecommunications Pathways. The specification covers telecommunications-closet design and cable pathways.

ANSI/TIA/EIA-569 recommends a dedicated entrance facility for buildings with more than 20,000 usable square feet. If the building has more than 70,000 usable square feet, ANSI/TIA/EIA-569 requires a dedicated, locked room with plywood termination fields on two walls. The ANSI/TIA/EIA-569 Standard also specifies recommendations for the amount of plywood termination fields, based on the building's square footage.

Demarcation Point   The *demarcation point* (also called the *demarc*, pronounced *dee-mark*) is the point within a facility, property, or campus where a circuit provided by an outside vendor, such as the phone company, terminates. Past this point, the customer provides the equipment and cabling. Maintenance and operation of equipment past the demarc is the customer's responsibility.

The entrance facility may share space with the equipment room, if necessary or possible. Telephone companies often refer to the entrance facility as the demarcation point. Some entrance facilities also house telephone or PBX (private branch exchange) equipment. Figure 2.2 shows an example of an entrance facility.

FIGURE 2.2:

Entrance facility for campus and telecommunications wiring

TIP	To improve data and voice security, the entrance facility should be located in an area that can be physically secured, e.g., a locked room.

Equipment Room

The next subsystem of structured cabling defined by ANSI/TIA/EIA-568-A is the equipment room, which is a centralized space specified to house more sophisticated equipment than the entrance facility or the telecommunications closets. Often, telephone equipment or data-networking equipment such as routers, switches, and hubs are located there. Computer equipment may possibly be stored there. Backbone cabling is specified to terminate in the equipment room.

In smaller organizations, it is desirable to have the equipment room located in the same area as the computer room, which houses network servers and possibly phone equipment. Figure 2.3 shows the equipment room.

FIGURE 2.3:

Equipment room, backbone cabling, and telecommunications closets

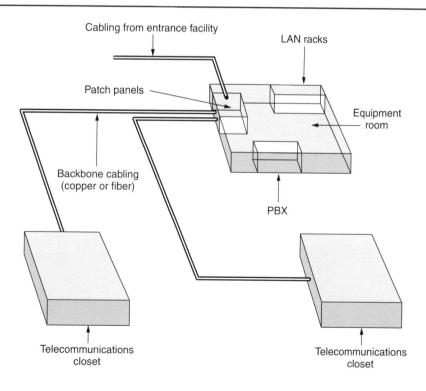

TIP   For information on the proper design of an equipment room, refer to ANSI/TIA/EIA-569.

Any room that houses telecommunications equipment, whether it's a telecommunications closet or equipment room, should be physically secured. Many data and voice systems have had security breaches because anyone could walk in off the street and gain physical access to the voice/data network cabling and equipment. Some companies go so far as to put alarm and electronic access systems on their telecommunication closets and equipment rooms.

Backbone Cabling

The third subsystem of structured cabling is called backbone cabling. (Backbone cabling is also sometimes called vertical cabling, cross-connect cabling, riser cabling, or intercloset cabling.) Backbone cabling is necessary to connect entrance facilities, equipment rooms, and telecommunications closets. Refer back to Figure 2.3 to see backbone cabling that connects an equipment room with telecommunications closets. Backbone cabling consists of not only the cables that connect the telecommunication closets, equipment rooms, and building entrance but also the cross-connect cables, mechanical terminations, or patch cords used for backbone-to-backbone cross-connection.

KEY TERM   **Cross-connect**   A *cross-connect* is a facility or location within the cabling system that permits the termination of cable elements and the reconnection of those elements by jumpers, termination blocks, and/or cables to another cabling element (another cable or patch panel).

Backbone cabling includes:

- Cabling between equipment rooms and building-entrance facilities

- In a campus environment, cabling between buildings' entrance facilities

- Vertical connections between floors

ANSI/TIA/EIA-568-A specifies additional design requirements for backbone cabling, some of which carry specific stipulations, as follows:

- Grounding should meet the requirements as defined in ANSI/TIA/EIA-607, the Commercial Building Grounding and Bonding Requirements for Telecommunications.

- Care must be taken when running backbone cables to avoid sources of electromagnetic interference or radio-frequency interference.

- No more than two hierarchical levels of cross-connects are allowed, and the topology of backbone cable will be a star topology. (A star topology is one in which all cables lead from their termination points back to a central location. Star topology is explained in more detail in Chapter 3.) Each horizontal cross-connect should be connected directly to a main cross-connect or to an intermediate cross-connect that then connects to a main cross-connect. No more than one cross-connect can exist between a main cross-connect and a horizontal cross-connect. Figure 2.4 shows multiple levels of equipment closets and telecommunications closets.

FIGURE 2.4:

Star topology of equipment room and telecommunication closets connected via backbone cabling

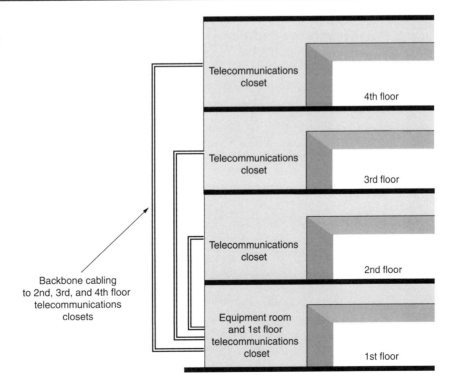

Backbone cabling to 2nd, 3rd, and 4th floor telecommunications closets

Telecommunications closet — 4th floor

Telecommunications closet — 3rd floor

Telecommunications closet — 2nd floor

Equipment room and 1st floor telecommunications closet — 1st floor

- Equipment connections to the backbone should be made with cable lengths of less than 30 meters (98 feet).

- For high-speed data applications, the total maximum backbone distance should not exceed 90 meters (295 feet) over copper wiring. This distance is for uninterrupted lengths of cable (cross-connects are not allowed).

- Bridge taps or splices are not allowed.

- Multi-pair (greater than four-pair) cable may be used as long as it meets additional performance requirements such as for power-sum crosstalk. These requirements are specified in the Standard.

KEY TERM   **Shared Sheath**   *Shared sheath*—a single cable that supports more than one application—is permitted in ANSI/TIA/EIA-568-A, with guidelines specified in Annex D of the Standard. A shared sheath may occur, for example, when Ethernet data transmission and voice transmission both are placed in a cable with more than four pairs. However, a shared sheath is not advisable, as separate applications often have incompatible signal levels, and the signal of one application will interfere as noise with the signal of the other application(s).

Recognized Backbone Media   ANSI/TIA/EIA-568-A recognizes several types of media (cable) for backbone cabling. These media types can be used in combination as required by the installation. The application and the area being served will determine the quantity and number of pairs required. Table 2.1 lists the media types, applications, and maximum distances permitted.

TABLE 2.1:   Media Types, Applications, and Maximum Distances Permitted

Media	Application	Distance
100-ohm UTP (22 or 24 AWG)	Data	90 meters (295 feet)
100-ohm UTP (22 or 24 AWG)	Voice	800 meters (2,625 feet)
150-ohm STP-A	Data	90 meters (295 feet)
Single-mode 8.3/125-micron optical fiber	Data	3,000 meters (9,840 feet)
Multimode 62.5/125-micron optical fiber	Data	2,000 meters (6,650 feet)

WARNING   ANSI/TIA/EIA-568-A specifies a maximum bend radius for backbone cabling: A backbone cable should never be bent more than 10 times its outer diameter. Tight bends can damage the cable or affect the cable's performance characteristics.

KEY TERM   **Media**   The term *media* is used in the cabling business to denote the type of cabling used. Media can include fiber-optic cable, twisted-pair cable, or coaxial cable. The definition of *media* can be broadened to include wireless networking.

Coaxial (50-ohm) cabling is recognized by the ANSI/TIA/EIA-568-A version of the Standard, but it is not recommended for new installations. With the release of TIA/EIA-568-B, coaxial cable will no longer be recognized as valid data-cabling media.

Backbone Distances

Backbone distances are dependent in part on the application. High-speed data applications over UTP (Ethernet, Token Ring, ATM, FDDI, and CDDI) are much more limited in distance than lower-speed applications. Thus, low-speed applications such as voice, RS232, and IBM 3270 can travel much farther over UTP or STP cable. In addition to the application, the distance will depend on equipment, manufacturer's specifications, and data speed.

Telecommunications Closets

The telecommunications closet is the location within a building where cabling components such as cross-connects and patch panels are located. These rooms are where the horizontal structured cabling originates. Horizontal cabling is terminated in patch panels or termination blocks and then uses horizontal pathways to reach work areas. The telecommunications closet may also contain networking equipment such as LAN hubs, switches, routers, and repeaters. Backbone-cabling equipment rooms terminate in the telecommunications closet. Figures 2.3 and 2.4 illustrate the relationship of a telecommunications closet to the backbone cabling and equipment rooms.

ANSI/TIA/EIA-569 discusses telecommunications-closet design and specifications, and a further discussion of this subsystem can be found in Chapter 5, "Cabling System Components." ANSI/TIA/EIA 569 recommends that telecommunications closets be stacked vertically between one floor and another. ANSI/TIA/EIA-568-A further dictates the following specifications relating to telecommunications closets:

- Care must be taken to avoid cable stress, tight bends, staples, wrapping the cable too tightly, and excessive tension. You can avoid these pitfalls with good cable-management techniques.

- Use only connecting hardware that is in compliance with the specifications you want to achieve.

- Patch cables, cords, equipment cables, and work-area cables are outside the scope of ANSI/TIA/EIA-568-A; these items are application (voice or data) specific.

- Horizontal cabling should not terminate directly to an application-specific device but rather to a telecommunications outlet. Patch cables or equipment cords should be used to connect the device to the cabling. For example, horizontal cabling should never come directly out of the wall and plug in to a phone or network adapter.

NOTE The entrance facility, equipment room, and telecommunications closet may be located in the same room. That room may also house telephone or data equipment.

Horizontal Cabling

Horizontal cabling, as specified by ANSI/TIA/EIA-568-A, is the cabling that extends from telecommunications closets to the work area and terminates in telecommunications outlets (information outlets or wall plates). Horizontal cabling includes the following:

- Cable from the patch panel to the work area

- Telecommunications outlets

- Cable terminations

- Cross-connections (where permitted)

- A maximum of one transition point

Figure 2.5 shows a typical horizontal-cabling infrastructure spanning out in a star topology from a telecommunications closet. The star topology is required.

FIGURE 2.5:

Horizontal cabling in a star topology from the telecommunications closet

Telecommunications outlets

Horizontal cabling

Telecommunications closet

Transition point (such as for modular furniture)

Backbone cabling to equipment room

Patch panels and LAN equipment

Application-specific components (baluns, repeaters) should not be installed as part of the horizontal-cabling system (inside the walls). These should be installed in the telecommunication closets or work areas.

Transition Point   ANSI/TIA/EIA-568-A allows for one *transition point* in horizontal cabling. The transition point is where one type of cable connects to another, such as where round cable connects to under-carpet cable. A transition point can also be a point where cabling is distributed out to modular furniture.

Recognized Media   ANSI/TIA/EIA-568-A recognizes several types of media (cables) that can be used as horizontal cabling. More than one media type may be run to a single work-area telecommunications outlet; thus, a UTP cable can be used for voice and a fiber-optic cable can be used for data. The maximum distance for horizontal cable from the telecommunications closet to the telecommunications outlet is 90 meters (295 feet) regardless of the cable media used. Horizontal cables recognized by the ANSI/TIA/EIA-568-A Standard include the following:

- Four-pair, 100-ohm, 24 AWG, solid-conductor UTP cable

- Two-pair, 150-ohm STP cable

- Two-fiber, 62.5/125-micron optical fiber

Cabling @ Work: Maximum Horizontal Cabling Distance

If you ask someone what the maximum distance of cable is between a network hub (such as 10Base-T) and the computer, you are likely to hear "100 meters." But many people ignore the fact that patch cords are required and assume the distance is from the patch panel to the telecommunication outlet (wall plate). Such is not the case.

The ANSI/TIA/EIA-568-A Standard states that the maximum distance between the telecommunications outlet and the patch panel is 90 meters. The Standard further allows for a patch cord in the workstation area that is up to 3 meters in length and a patch cord in the telecommunications closet that is up to 6 meters in length. (If you did the math, you figured out that the actual maximum length is 99 meters, but what's one meter between friends?) The total distance is the maximum distance for a structured cabling system, based on ANSI/TIA/EIA-568-A, regardless of the media type (twisted-pair copper or optical fiber).

The *100-meter* maximum distance is not a random number; it was chosen for a number of reasons, including the following:

- The number defines transmissions distances for communications-equipment designers. This distance limitation assures them that they can base their equipment designs on the maximum distance of 100 meters between the terminal and the hub in the closet.

- It provides building architects a specification that states they should place telecommunications closets so that no telecommunications outlet will be farther than 90 meters from the nearest wall outlet (that's in cable distance, which is not necessarily a straight line).

- The maximum ensures that common technologies (such as 10Base-T Ethernet) will be able to achieve reasonable signal quality and maintain data integrity. Much of the reasoning for the maximum was based on the timing required for a 10Base-T Ethernet workstation to transmit a minimum packet (64 bytes) to the farthest station on an Ethernet segment. The propagation of that signal through the cable had to be taken into account.

Continued on next page

Can a structured cabling system exceed the 100-meter distance? Sure. Good-quality Category 5 or 5e cable will allow 10Base-T Ethernet to be transmitted farther than Category 3. When using 10Base-FL (10Mbps Ethernet over fiber-optic cable), multimode optical-fiber cable has a maximum distance of 2,000 meters; so a structured cabling system that will support exclusively 10Base-FL applications could have much longer horizontal cabling runs.

But (you knew there was a *but*, didn't you?) your cabling infrastructure will no longer be based on a Standard. It will support the application it was designed to support, but it may not support others.

Further, for unshielded twisted-pair cabling, the combined effects of attenuation, crosstalk, and other noise elements increase as the length of the cable increases. Although attenuation and crosstalk do not drastically worsen immediately above the 100-meter mark, the signal-to-noise ratio begins to approach zero. When SNR equals zero, the signal is indistinguishable from the noise in the cabling. (That's analogous to a screen full of snow on a TV.) Then your cabling system will exceed the limits that your application hardware was designed to expect. Your results will be inconsistent, if the system works at all.

The moral of this story is not to exceed the specifications for a structured cabling system and still expect the system to meet the needs of specifications-based applications.

Is There a Minimum Distance for UTP Horizontal Cable?

The ANSI/TIA/EIA-568-A does not specify a minimum length for UTP cabling. However, a *short-link phenomenon* occurs in cabling links usually less than 20 meters (60 feet) long that usually support 100Base-TX applications. The first 20 to 30 meters of a cable is where near-end crosstalk (NEXT) has the most effect. In higher-speed networks such as 100Base-TX, short cables may cause the signal generated by crosstalk or return loss reflections to be returned back to the transmitter. The transmitter may interpret these returns as collisions and cause the network not to function correctly at high speeds. To correct this problem, try extending problematic cable runs with extra-long patch cords.

Telecommunications Outlets   ANSI/TIA/EIA-568-A specifies that each work area shall have a minimum of two information-outlet ports. Typically, one is used for voice and another for data. Figure 2.6 shows a possible telecommunications-outlet configuration. The outlets go by a number of names, including *information* *outlets*, *wall jacks*, and *wall plates*. However, an information outlet is officially considered to be one jack on a telecommunications outlet; the telecommunications outlet is considered to be part of the horizontal-cabling system. Chapters 9 and 10 have additional information on telecommunications outlets.

FIGURE 2.6:

A telecommunications outlet with a UTP for voice and a UTP/STP/fiber for data

Telecommunications rack in closet

The information outlets wired for UTP should follow one of two conventions for wire-pair assignments or wiring patterns: T568A or T568B. They are nearly identical, except that pairs 2 and 3 are interchanged. Neither of the two is *the* correct choice, as long as the same convention is always used throughout the cabling system. T568B is much more common in commercial installations, but T568A is now the recommended configuration. (T568A is the *required* configuration for residential installations, in accordance with ANSI/TIA/EIA-570-A.) The T568A configuration is partially compatible with an older wiring scheme called USOC, which is commonly used for voice systems.

Be consistent at both ends of the horizontal cable. When you purchase patch panels and jacks, you may be required to specify which pattern you are using, as the equipment may be color-coded to make installation of the wire pairs easier. However, many manufacturers now include options that allow either configuration to be punched down on the patch panel or jack.

Figure 2.7 shows the T568A and T568B pinout assignments. For more information on wiring patterns, modular plugs, and modular jacks, see Chapter 9.

FIGURE 2.7:

Modular jack wire pattern assignments for T568A and T568B

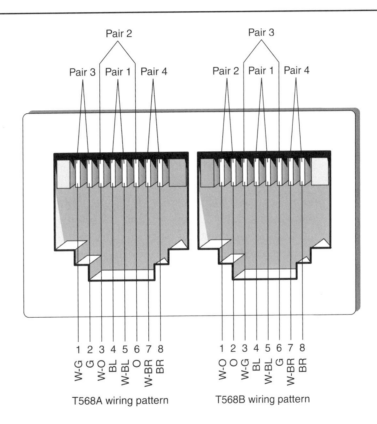

The wire/pin assignments in Figure 2.7 are designated by wire color. The standard wire colors are shown in Table 2.2.

TABLE 2.2: Wire-Color Abbreviations

Wire Abbreviation	Wire Color
W/G	White/green
G	Green
W/O	White/orange
O	Orange
W/Bl	White/blue
Bl	Blue
W/Br	White/brown
Br	Brown

Though your application may not require all the pins in the information outlet, you should make sure that all wires are terminated to the appropriate pins if for no other reason than to ensure interoperability with future applications on the same media. Table 2.3 shows some common applications and the pins that they use and clearly illustrates why all pairs should be terminated in order to make the structured-wiring installation application-generic.

TABLE 2.3: Application-Specific Pair Assignments for UTP Cabling*

Application	Pins 1-2	Pins 3-6	Pins 4-5	Pins 7-8
Analog voice	-	-	Tx/Rx	-
ISDN	Power	Tx	Rx	Power
10Base-T (802.3)	Tx	Rx	-	-
Token Ring (802.5)	-	Tx	Rx	-
100Base-TX (802.3u)	Tx	Rx	-	-
100Base-T4 (802.3u)	Tx	Rx	Bi	Bi
100Base-VG (802.12)	Bi	Bi	Bi	Bi
FDDI (TP-PMD)	Tx	Optional	Optional	Rx

Continued on next page

TABLE 2.3 CONTINUED: Application-Specific Pair Assignments for UTP Cabling*

Application	Pins 1-2	Pins 3-6	Pins 4-5	Pins 7-8
ATM User Device	Tx	Optional	Optional	Rx
ATM Network Equipment	Rx	Optional	Optional	Tx
1000Base-T (802.3ab)	Bi	Bi	Bi	Bi

Bi = Bi-directional, Optional = May be required by some vendors
*Table courtesy of The Siemon Company (www.siemon.com)

TIP

A good structured-wiring system will include documentation printed and placed on each of the telecommunications outlets.

Pair Numbers and Color Coding   The conductors in a UTP cable are twisted in pairs and color coded so that each pair of wires can be easily identified and quickly terminated to the appropriate pin on the connecting hardware (patch panels or telecommunication outlets). With four-pair UTP cables, each pair of wire is coded with two colors, the tip color and the ring color (see also "Insulation Colors" in Chapter 1). In a four-pair cable, the tip color of every pair is white. To keep the tip conductors associated with the correct ring conductors, often the tip conductor has bands in the color of the ring conductor. Such positive identification (PI) color coding is not necessary in some cases, such as with Category 5 and higher cables—the intervals between twists in the pair are very close together, making separation unlikely.

You identify the conductors by their color codes, such as white-blue and blue. With premises (indoor) cables, it is common to read the tip color first (including its PI color), then the ring color. Table 2.4 lists the pair numbers, color codes, and pin assignments for T568A and T568B.

TABLE 2.4: Four-Pair UTP Color Codes, Pair Numbers, and Pin Assignments for T568A and T568B

Pair Number	Color Code	T568A Pins	T568B Pins
1	White-Blue (W-Bl)/Blue (Bl)	W-Bl=5/Bl=4	W-Bl=5/ Bl=4
2	White-Orange (W-O)/Orange (O)	W-O=3/O=6	W-O=1/O=2

Continued on next page

TABLE 2.4 CONTINUED: Four-Pair UTP Color Codes, Pair Numbers, and Pin Assignments for T568A and T568B

Pair Number	Color Code	T568A Pins	T568B Pins
3	White-Green (W-G)/Green (G)	W-G=1/G=2	W-G=3/G=6
4	White-Brown (W-Br)/Brown (Br)	W-Br=7/Br=8	W-Br=7/Br=8

Basic Link versus Channel Link

TIA Technical Systems Bulletin (TSB) 67 specifies parameters for testing installed cabling. TIA/EIA-568 requirements as currently written only define performance criteria for individual components, not for an installed cabling system. TSB-67 defines two basic link types commonly used in the cabling industry with respect to testing: the basic link and the channel link.

The *basic link* contains only the cabling found in the walls (horizontal cabling), one transition point, the telecommunications outlet, and one cross-connect or patch panel. It is assumed to be the permanent portion of the cabling infrastructure. The basic link is illustrated below.

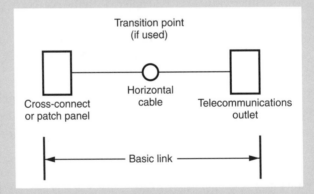

The *channel link* includes the basic link, as well as installed equipment, patch cords, and the cross-connect jumper cable; however, the channel does *not* include phones, PBX equipment, hubs, or network-interface cards. Two possible channel link configurations are shown below; one is the channel link for a 10Base-T Ethernet workstation, and one is for a telephone.

Continued on next page

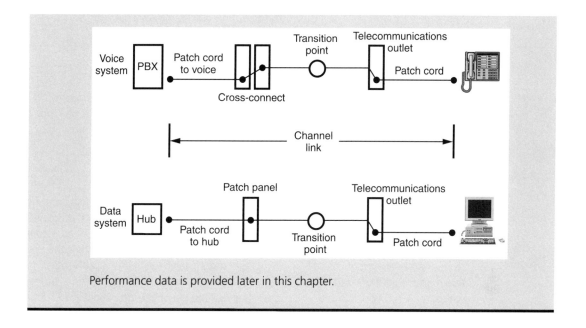

Performance data is provided later in this chapter.

Work Area

The work area is where the horizontal cable terminates at the wall outlet (telecommunications outlet). In the work area, the users and telecommunications equipment connect to the structured-cabling infrastructure. The work area begins at the telecommunications area and includes components such as the following:

- Patch cables, modular cords, fiber jumpers, and adapter cables
- Adapters such as baluns and other devices that modify the signal or impedance of the cable (these devices must be external to the information outlet)
- Station equipment such as computers, telephones, fax machines, data terminals, and modems

The work-area wiring should be simple and easy to manipulate. In today's business environments, moves, additions, and removal of equipment are frequent. Consequently, the cabling system needs to be easily adaptable to these changes.

Cabling @ Work: Planning for Sufficient Outlets and Horizontal Cable

Do you have enough horizontal cabling? Company XYZ (name changed to protect the innocent) recently moved to a new location. In its old location, the company continually suffered from a lack of data and voice outlets. Users wanted phones, modems, and fax machines located in areas that no one ever imagined would have that equipment. The explosion of users with multiple computers in their offices and networked printers only compounded the problem.

XYZ's director of information services vowed that the situation would never happen to her again. Each work area was wired with a four-port telecommunications outlet. Each of these outlets could be used for either voice or data. In the larger offices, she had telecommunications outlets located on opposite walls. Even the lunchrooms and photocopier rooms had telecommunications outlets. This foresight gave Company XYZ the ability to add many more workstations, printers, phones, and other devices that require cabling, without the additional cost of running new cables. The per-cable cost to install additional cables later is far higher than installing additional cables during the initial installation.

Media and Connecting Hardware Performance

ANSI/TIA/EIA-568-A specifies performance requirements for unshielded twisted-pair (UTP) cabling, shielded twisted-pair (STP) cabling, and fiber-optic cabling. Further, specifications are laid out for length of cable and conductor types for horizontal, backbone, and patch cables.

100-Ohm Unshielded Twisted-Pair Cabling

ANSI/TIA/EIA-568-A specifies three categories of UTP cable to be used with structured cabling systems. These are commonly referred to by their category number and are rated based on the maximum frequency bandwidth. The categories are found in Table 2.5, along with the ISO/IEC application class that each category of cable will support.

TABLE 2.5:   ANSI/TIA/EIA-568-A Cable Categories

568A Category	ISO/IEC Class	Maximum Bandwidth
Not defined	Class A	100KHz
Not defined	Class B	4MHz
Category 3	Class C	16MHz
Category 4	Not defined	20MHz
Category 5	Class D	100MHz
Category 5e[1]	Class E	100MHz
Category 6[2]	Class F	250MHz

[1] Per addendum 5 of the ANSI/TIA/EIA-568-A Standard
[2] Under development

Ensuring a Specific Level of Cabling Performance

UTP cabling systems cannot be considered Category 3–, 4–, 5–, or 5e–compliant (and consequently certified) unless all components of the cabling system satisfy the specific performance requirements of the particular category. The components include the following:

- All backbone and horizontal cabling

- Telecommunications outlets

- Patch panels

- Cross-connect wires and cross-connect blocks

All patch panel terminations, wall-plate terminations, crimping, and cross-connect punchdowns also must follow the specific recommendations for the respective category.

Horizontal and Backbone UTP Cabling   Characteristic impedance of horizontal and backbone UTP cables should be 100 ohms plus or minus 15 percent from 1MHz up to the maximum bandwidth supported by the cable. Table 2.6 lists the attenuation (highest permissible value) and near-end crosstalk (lowest permissible value) for various frequencies between 1MHz and the maximum bandwidth supported by the category of cable.

TABLE 2.6: Horizontal Cable Attenuation and NEXT Loss Per 100 Meters (328 Feet) at 20 Degrees Celsius (68 Degrees Fahrenheit)

Frequency (MHz)	CATEGORY 3 ATTN/NEXT (dB)	Category 4 Attn/NEXT (dB)	Category 5 Attn/NEXT (dB)	Category 5e Attn/NEXT (dB)
1.0	2.6/41	2.2/56	2.0/62	2.0/65.3
4.0	5.6/32	4.3/47	4.1/53	4.1/56.3
8.0	8.5/27	6.2/42	5.8/48	5.8/51.8
10.0	9.7/26	6.9/41	6.5/47	6.5/50.3
16.0	13.1/23	8.9/38	8.2/44	8.2/47.3
20.0	-	10.0/36	9.3/42	9.3/45.8
25.0	-	-	10.4/41	10.4/44.3
31.25	-	-	11.7/39	11.7/42.9
62.5	-	-	17.0/35	17.0/38.4
100	-	-	22.0/32	22.0/35.3

The values represented for NEXT in Table 2.6 represent worst pair-to-pair crosstalk in horizontal cables. These values do not include loss and crosstalk values resulting from connections such as telecommunications outlets, cross-connects, and patch panels. ANSI/TIA/EIA-568-A only specifies performance values for components. For backbone cables, the NEXT value represents the power-sum NEXT. Values are shown at the discrete frequencies for convenience only. The actual requirements are based on formulae that provide for smooth performance along the entire frequency band.

NOTE
You may recall from Chapter 1 that lower attenuation numbers and higher crosstalk numbers (NEXT) are better. Pair-to-pair crosstalk and power-sum NEXT are discussed in more detail in Chapter 1.

Connecting Hardware: Performance Loss   Part of the ANSI/TIA/EIA-568-A Standard is intended to ensure that connecting hardware (cross-connects, patch panels, patch cables, telecommunications outlets, and connectors) does not have an adverse effect on attenuation and NEXT. To this end, the Standard specifies attenuation and NEXT loss for connecting hardware; the specified values are in Table 2.7.

TABLE 2.7: Attenuation and NEXT Limits for UTP Connecting Hardware

Frequency (MHz)	CATEGORY 3 ATTN/NEXT (dB)	Category 4 Attn/NEXT (dB)	Category 5 Attn/NEXT (dB)	Category 5e Attn/NEXT (dB)
1.0	0.4/58	0.1/65	0.1/65	0.1/65.0
4.0	0.4/46	0.1/58	0.1/65	0.1/65.0
8.0	0.4/40	0.1/52	0.1/62	0.1/64.9
10.0	0.4/38	0.1/50	0.1/60	0.1/63.0
16.0	0.4/34	0.2/46	0.2/56	0.2/58.9
20.0	-	0.2/44	0.2/54	0.2/57.0
25.0	-	-	0.2/52	0.2/55.0
31.25	-	-	0.2/50	0.2/53.1
62.5	-	-	0.3/44	0.3/47.1
100	-	-	0.4/40	0.4/43.0

Tables 2.6 and 2.7 are intended to give you an idea of the performance requirements and their difference between category. Additional characteristics and parameters for cable and connection components are included in the ANSI/TIA/EIA-568-A and its five addenda. Please consult those documents if you want full details of performance requirements or are a hopeless insomniac.

TIP

It is highly recommended that you familiarize yourself with cabling requirements to specify performance to a cabling contractor. You should only have to reference the Standard for purposes of the Request for Quotation, but your knowledge will help in your discussions with the contractor.

Patch Cables and Cross-Connect Jumpers   ANSI/TIA/EIA-568-A also specifies requirements that apply to cables used for patch cables and cross-connect jumpers. The requirements include recommendations for maximum-distance limitations for patch cables and cross-connects, as shown here:

Cable Type	Maximum Distance
Main cross-connect*	20 meters (66 feet)
Intermediate cross-connect*	20 meters (66 feet)
Telecommunications closet	6 meters (20 feet)
Work area	3 meters (10 feet)

*Main and intermediate cross-connects will only be used with voice and other low-bandwidth applications.

The total maximum distance of the channel should not exceed the maximum distance recommended for the application being used. For example, the channel distance for 100Base-TX Ethernet should not exceed 100 meters.

> **TIP**   Patch cables should use stranded conductors rather than solid conductors so that the cable is more flexible. Solid-conductor cables are easily damaged if they are bent too tightly or too often.

Patch cables usually have a slightly higher attenuation than horizontal cables because they are stranded rather than solid conductors. Though stranded conductors increase patch-cable flexibility, they also increase attenuation. Table 2.8 lists the maximum attenuation for patch cables.

TABLE 2.8:   Maximum Attenuation for Patch Cables

Frequency (MHz)	Category 3 (dB)	Category 4 (dB)	Category 5 (dB)
1.0	3.1	2.6	2.4
4.0	6.7	5.2	4.9
8.0	10.2	7.4	6.9
10.0	11.7	8.3	7.8

Continued on next page

TABLE 2.8 CONTINUED: Maximum Attenuation for Patch Cables

Frequency (MHz)	Category 3 (dB)	Category 4 (dB)	Category 5 (dB)
16.0	15.7	10.7	9.9
20.0	-	12.0	11.1
25.0	-	-	12.5
31.25	-	-	14.1
62.5	-	-	20.4
100	-	-	26.4

NOTE   ANSI/TIA/EIA-568-A-5 does not specify separate requirements for Category 5e patch cables. Instead, channel performance is specified, and the patch-cable influence is measured as part of the composite performance of cables, connecting hardware, and patch cables.

150-Ohm Shielded Twisted-Pair Cabling

Shielded twisted-pair cabling (STP) may sometimes be desirable for data communications because of the shield of metallic foil around all pairs of the cable and the shield on individual pairs of wire. *If the shield is properly grounded,* STP cable performs extremely well in areas where electromagnetic interference (EMI) and/or radio-frequency interference are concerns.

WARNING   Shielded cables, when improperly grounded, can actually perform worse than their UTP counterparts from an electrical-noise standpoint. Instead of creating a barrier to electromagnetic noise, a poorly installed shielded cable becomes a nice long antenna that is both receptive to noise from external sources and a source of noise emission in itself.

Because the Standard requirements for STP are based on IBM Type 1A cable and IBM Type 1A cable has 22 AWG instead of 24 AWG conductors, specified attenuation loss is lower for STP cable than it is for 24 AWG UTP horizontal cable. NEXT performance is also much better (due to the shielding). However, STP is not used as often as UTP in most environments because the cost of the cable is higher, it is more difficult to terminate correctly, and the hardware that takes advantage of it is often more expensive.

STP Backbone and Horizontal Cable IBM type 1A cabling (STP-A) is recognized for use as backbone and horizontal cabling; IBM type 6A is recognized for use as patch cable. The IBM type 6A cable is two-pair, 22 AWG solid-conductor cable with characteristic impedance of 150 ohms (plus or minus 10 percent) and is rated for frequency usage between 3MHz and 300MHz. Table 2.9 shows the performance characteristics for attenuation and NEXT for STP-A cabling.

NOTE   STP cable does not have to be the IBM Type 1A design with 22 AWG conductors. There are 24 AWG versions of STP (fully shielded twisted pair) in which each pair has a foil and/or braid shield enclosing it and has a wrapping of foil and/or braid that encloses all the shielded pairs, just like the IBM Type 1A design. Variants called ScTP (screened core twisted pair) or FTP (foil shielded twisted pair), are cables in which the pairs do not have individual shields, but there is an overall shield enclosing the pairs as a group. Many systems use 24 AWG shielded cables that terminate in shielded jacks fitting the RJ45 type jack footprint. From an installation standpoint, these cabling systems are very similar to their UTP counterparts.

TABLE 2.9: Horizontal and Backbone STP-A Performance Characteristics

Frequency (MHz)	Attenuation (dB)*	NEXT (dB)
4.0	2.2	58.0
8.0	3.1	54.9
10.0	3.6	53.5
16.0	4.4	50.4
20	4.9	49.0
25	6.2	47.5
31.25	6.9	46.1
62.5	9.8	41.5
100	12.3	38.5
300	21.4	31.3

*Attenuation is per 100 meters (328 feet) at 25 degrees Celsius.

150-Ohm STP-A Data Connectors   ANSI/TIA/EIA-568-A specifies a 150-ohm STP-A data connector for connections. This unique hermaphroditic connector was originally developed by IBM and is also sometimes called the IBM data connector.

TIA/EIA specifies worst-case attenuation and NEXT-loss performance parameters for 150-ohm STP-A connectors, as seen in Table 2.10.

TABLE 2.10:   Attenuation and NEXT Loss for 150-Ohm STP-A Data Connectors

Frequency (MHz)	Attenuation (dB)	NEXT (dB)
4.0	.05	65.0
8.0	.10	65.0
10.0	.10	65.0
16.0	.15	62.4
20.0	.15	60.5
25	.15	58.5
31.25	.15	56.6
62.5	.20	50.6
100	.25	46.5
300	.45	36.9

TIP   Studies and demonstrations have shown repeatedly that a well-made Category 5 (or better) UTP cable with quality connectivity components will perform very well in electrically noisy environments. Geometrically symmetrical conductors and pairs, connected to impedance-matched components, are able to effectively cancel electromagnetic noise. You should discuss your electrical-noise concerns with a professional before undertaking the expense of installing STP. It may be unnecessary.

Optical-Fiber Cabling

The ANSI/TIA/EIA-568-A Standard permits both single-mode and multimode fiber-optic cables. Horizontal cabling systems are specified to use 62.5/125 micron multimode cable, whereas backbone cabling may use either multimode or single-mode optical-fiber cable.

Two connectors are widely used with fiber-optic cabling systems, the ST and SC connectors. Currently installed applications that require the ST connector type are allowed, but future applications and deployments should use the 568SC-type connector. This specification was changed so that the fiber-optic specifications in the ANSI/TIA/EIA-568-A could agree with the IEC 11801 Standard used in Europe. The ANSI/TIA/EIA-568-A Standard does not currently recognize the new small-form factor connectors such as the MT-RJ connector.

KEY TERM   **Fiber Modes**   Fiber-optic cable is referred to as either single-mode or multimode fiber. The term *mode* refers to the bundles of light that enter the fiber-optic cable. Single-mode fiber-optic cable uses only a single mode of light to propagate through the fiber cable, whereas multimode fiber allows multiple modes of light to propagate. In multimode fiber-optic cable, the light bounces off the core "walls" formed by the cladding as it travels through the fiber, which causes the signal to weaken more quickly.

NOTE   What do those numbers mean: 62.5/125, 8.7/125, 50/125? Is this Math class? Fiber-optic strands consist of two primary layers. In the center is the core, where the light is actually transmitted. Surrounding the core is a layer known as the cladding. The cladding material has a different optical index than the core, acting as a reflective barrier so the light stays in the center. The numbers are the diameters of the layers, measured in microns, or one-thousandth of a millimeter. So, a 62.5/125 fiber-optic strand has a core diameter of 62.5 microns with a cladding layer 125 microns in diameter. Why are all the cladding diameters the same when the core diameters are different? That's so stripping and termination devices can be used with all types of fiber strands. Genius, huh?

Multimode Optical-Fiber Cable   Multimode fiber optic is most often used as horizontal cable. Multimode cable permits multiple modes of light to propagate through the cable and thus lowers cable distances and has a lower available bandwidth. Devices that use multimode fiber-optic cable typically use light-emitting diodes (LEDs) to generate the light that travels through the cable; however, higher-bandwidth network devices such as Gigabit Ethernet are now using lasers with multimode fiber-optic cable. ANSI/TIA/EIA-568-A recognizes two-fiber (duplex) 62.5/125-micron multimode fiber; it also recognizes 50/125-micron multimode fiber-optic cable. Table 2.11 shows the maximum permitted attenuation at the commonly used wavelengths.

TABLE 2.11: Performance of Multimode Optical-Fiber Cable Used for Horizontal or Backbone Cabling

Wavelength (Nm)	Maximum Attenuation (dB/Km)	Minimum Bandwidth M(Hz-Km)
850	3.75	160
1300	1.5	500

Single-Mode Optical-Fiber Cable   Single-mode optical-fiber cable is commonly used as backbone cabling and is also usually the cable type for long-distance phone systems. Light travels through single-mode fiber-optic cable using only a single mode, meaning it travels straight down the fiber and does not "bounce" off the cable walls. Because only a single mode of light travels through the cable, single-mode fiber-optic cable supports higher bandwidth and longer distances than multimode fiber-optic cable. Devices that use single-mode fiber-optic cable typically use lasers to generate the light that travels through the cable.

ANSI/TIA/EIA-568-A recognizes 8.7/125-micron single-mode optical fiber cables. It states that the maximum backbone distance using single-mode fiber-optic cable is 3,000 meters (9,840 feet), and the maximum backbone distance using multimode fiber is 2,000 meters (6,560 feet). Table 2.12 shows the maximum attenuation for single-mode fiber at common wavelengths.

TABLE 2.12: Performance of Single-Mode Optical-Fiber Cable Used for Backbone Cabling

Wavelength (Nm)	Maximum Attenuation Outdoor Cable (dB/Km)	Maximum Attenuation Indoor Cable (dB/Km)
1310	0.5	1.0
1550	0.5	1.0

Optical Fiber and Telecommunications Closets   The ANSI/TIA/EIA-568-A Standard specifies that certain features of telecommunications must be adhered to in order for the installation to be specifications-compliant:

- The telecommunications outlet(s) must have the ability to terminate a minimum of two fibers into 568SC couplings.

- To prevent damage to the fiber, the telecommunications outlet(s) must provide a means of securing fiber and maintaining a minimum bend radius of 30 millimeters.

- The telecommunications outlet(s) must be able to store at least one meter of two-fiber (duplex) cable.

- The telecommunications outlet(s) supporting fiber cable must be a surface-mount box that attaches on top of a standard 4" x 4" electrical box.

The *B* Version Is Coming

Sometime in 2001, the TIA TR42.1 committee (with help from other subcommittees) will ratify the TIA/EIA-568-B version of the Commercial Building Telecommunications Cabling Standard. Much has changed since the *A* version of the specification was developed. Even though addenda and Telecommunications Systems Bulletins have been issued to keep the specification current, the specification needs to be updated to reflect the changing world. The new *B* version has been broken into three sections:

TIA/EIA-568-B.1: General Requirements   Part 1 addresses issues such as cabling distances (horizontal and backbone), media selection, open-office cabling, installation practices, field-test practices, work-area connections, and telecommunication and equipment rooms. This section will incorporate the content from the *A* version of the specification as well as all addenda to the *A* version, TSB-67, TSB-72, TSB-75, and TSB-95.

TIA/EIA-568-B.2: Twisted-Pair Media   Part 2 covers the electrical and mechanical requirements for twisted-pair cables, patch cables, connectors, component testing, field-tester requirements, and testing methods. It will draw from the previous version of the specification as well as from TSB-67 and TSB-95.

Continued on next page

Expect Category 4 and Category 5 cable to disappear from the recommended media list (they will be recognized, but not recommended); Category 5e cable will take the place of Category 5 cable. Category 5e cable has been a standard media type since fall 1999 when the fifth addendum was added to the *A* version of the specification. Do not expect Category 6 cable to appear in the specification until sometime in 2001. Category 7 cabling is being worked on by the ISO and will probably be adopted by the EIA once the ISO has the kinks worked out.

TIA/EIA-568-B.3: Optical-Fiber Media   This portion of the specification is already issued under ANSI sanction under the title *Optical Fiber Cabling Components Standard*. It was approved in March 2000. The Standard covers the use of optical-fiber cables, including fiber-optic testing, field-performance testing, cable types, patch cables, and connectors. The small form factor war was not settled with this specification, as the committee did not feel that these connectors are mature enough to be incorporated into the document.

Telecommunications Systems Bulletins

Periodically, the TIA publishes Telecommunications Systems Bulletins (TSBs) to make recommendations or provide information or guidance relating to a particular host specification. TSBs are not considered standards, as they specify no mandatory requirements. Some of the TSBs are later incorporated into updated versions of the specifications.

The TIA has released a number of TSBs relating to the ANSI/TIA/EIA-568-A version of the Standard. Two key TSBs are TSB-67 and TSB-95, which relate to field testing of cabling.

TSB-67

TIA published TSB-67 to provide guidelines for testing UTP cabling systems. TSB-67 (a.k.a. "Transmission Performance Specifications for Field Testing UTP Cabling Systems") defines a number of performance parameters, along with their minimum or maximum values. TSB-67 also defines basic link and channel link.

Table 2.13 shows the maximum attenuation and minimum NEXT loss performance parameters for the basic link.

TABLE 2.13: Basic Link Attenuation and NEXT Loss in dB

Frequency (MHz)	Attenuation (Maximum)			NEXT Loss (Minimum)		
	Cat 3	Cat 4	Cat 5	Cat 3	Cat 4	Cat 5
1	3.2	2.2	2.1	40.1	54.7	60.0
4	6.1	4.3	4.0	30.7	45.1	51.8
8	8.8	6.0	5.7	25.9	40.2	47.1
10	10.0	6.8	6.3	24.3	38.6	45.0
16	13.2	8.8	8.2	21.0	35.3	42.3
20	-	9.9	9.2	-	33.7	40.7
25	-	-	10.3	-	-	39.1
31.25	-	-	11.5	-	-	37.6
62.5	-	-	16.7	-	-	32.7
100	-	-	21.6	-	-	29.3

Table 2.14 shows the maximum attenuation and the minimum NEXT loss for the channel link. The channel-link numbers include losses as a result of cross-connects and patch cables.

TABLE 2.14: Channel Link Attenuation and NEXT Loss in dB

Frequency (MHz)	Attenuation (Maximum)			NEXT Loss (Minimum)		
	Cat 3	Cat 4	Cat 5	Cat 3	Cat 4	Cat 5
1	4.2	2.6	2.5	39.1	53.3	60.0
4	7.3	4.8	4.5	29.3	43.3	50.6
8	10.2	6.7	6.3	24.3	38.2	45.6
10	11.5	7.5	7.0	22.7	36.6	44.0
16	14.9	9.9	9.2	19.3	33.1	40.6

Continued on next page

TABLE 2.14 CONTINUED: Channel Link Attenuation and NEXT Loss in dB

Frequency (MHz)	Attenuation (Maximum)			NEXT Loss (Minimum)		
	Cat 3	Cat 4	Cat 5	Cat 3	Cat 4	Cat 5
20	-	11.0	10.3	-	31.4	39.0
25	-	-	11.4	-	-	37.4
31.25	-	-	12.8	-	-	35.7
62.5	-	-	18.5	-	-	30.6
100	-	-	24.0	-	-	27.1

TSB-95

The TIA subsequently published TSB-95 (a.k.a. "Additional Transmission Performance Guidelines for 100-Ohm Four-Pair Category 5 Cabling") to guide in testing existing cabling systems for support of high-speed, duplex applications such as Gigabit Ethernet. TSB-95 is considered a complement to TSB-67; it provides additional performance characteristics for equal-level far-end crosstalk (ELFEXT), return loss (RL), delay, and delay skew. Chapter 1 describes these performance parameters in detail.

TSB-95 is targeted toward installed cabling systems. It does not provide performance parameters for connectors and cable, only for the basic link and the channel link. If you plan to install a new cabling system, be aware that the performance characteristics in TSB-95 are included in the latest version of the TIA specifications.

TSB-75

The TIA published TSB-75 (a.k.a. "Open Office Cabling Index") to provide additional specifications for horizontal cabling in office environments that use modular furniture and moveable partitions. ANSI/TIA/EIA-568-A provides no allowances for offices that can be "rearranged"; it assumes that once a cable is placed, it is stationary. In modern office areas, such an assumption is not necessarily practical because work areas often consist of cubicles and moveable walls.

TSB-75 defines horizontal cabling methodologies that permit the use of multiuser telecommunication outlets and/or consolidation points. TSB-75 uses two terms relating to open-office cabling that may be of interest:

MuTOA   This acronym stands for multiuser telecommunications outlet assembly, which is an outlet that consolidates telecommunications jacks for many users into one area.

CP   CP stands for consolidation point, which is an intermediate interconnection scheme that allows horizontal cables that are part of the building pathways to extend to telecommunication outlets in open-office pathways such as those in modular furniture. The ISO/IEC 11801 refers to the CP as a transition point (TP).

If you plan to use modular furniture or moveable partitions, check with the vendor of the furniture or partitions to see if it provides data-cabling pathways within its furniture. Then ask what type of interface it may provide or require for your existing cabling system. You will have to plan for connectivity to the furniture in your wiring scheme.

Cabling vendor The Siemon Company and modular-furniture manufacturer DRG have teamed up to build innovative modular furniture with built-in cable management compliant with TSB-75 and the TIA/EIA-568 specifications. The furniture system is called MACsys; you can find more information about the MACsys family of products on the Web at `www.siemon.com/macsys/`.

ANSI/TIA/EIA-569-A

Though the ANSI/TIA/EIA-568-A Standard describes the subsystems of a structured cabling system, the TIA has published a more thorough document called ANSI/TIA/EIA-569-A Commercial Building Standard for Telecommunications Pathways and Spaces. The purpose of the ANSI/TIA/EIA-569-A Standard is to provide a flexible and standardized support system for a structured cabling system, along with the detail necessary to design and build these facilities. The detail pertains to both single and multitenant buildings.

NOTE   This 569-A document is especially important because network managers, architects, and even cable installers often don't give enough forethought to the spaces and infrastructure that will support structured-cabling systems or data-communications equipment.

Though repetitive to large degree with respect to ANSI/TIA/EIA-568-A, ANSI/TIA/EIA-569-A does define and detail pathways and spaces used by a commercial cabling system. The elements defined include:

- Entrance facility

- Equipment room

- Main terminal space

- Telecommunications closets

- Horizontal pathways

- Backbone pathways

- Work areas

WARNING   When planning telecommunications pathways and spaces, make sure you allow for future growth.

ANSI/TIA/EIA-569-A provides some common design considerations for the entrance facility, equipment room, and telecommunications closets with respect to construction, environmental considerations, and environmental controls:

- The door (without sill) should open outward, slide sideways, or be removable. It should be fitted with a lock and be a minimum of 36 inches (.91 meters) wide by 80 inches (2 meters) high.

- Electrical power should be supplied by a minimum of two dedicated 120V-20A nominal, nonswitched, AC-duplex electrical outlets. Each outlet should be on separate branch circuits. The equipment room may have additional electrical requirements based on the telecommunications equipment that will be supported there (such as LAN servers, hubs, PBXs, or UPS systems).

- Sufficient lighting should be provided (500 lx or 50-foot candles). The light switches should be located near the entrance door.

- Grounding should be provided and used per ANSI/TIA/EIA-607 (the Commercial Building Grounding and Bonding Requirements for Telecommunications Standard) and either the NEC or local code, whichever takes precedence.

- These areas should not have false (drop) ceilings.

- Slots and sleeves that penetrate firewalls or that are used for riser cables should be firestopped per the applicable codes.

- Separation of horizontal and backbone pathways from sources of electromagnetic interference (EMI) must be maintained per NEC Article 800.52.

- Metallic raceways and conduits should be grounded.

Based on our own experiences, we recommend the following:

- Equip all telecommunications closets, the entrance facility, and the equipment room with electrical surge suppression and a UPS (uninterruptible power supply) that will supply that area with at least 15 minutes of standby AC power in the event of a commercial power failure.

- Equip these areas with standby lighting that will last for at least an hour if the commercial power fails.

- Make sure that these areas are sufficiently separated from sources of EMI such as antennas, medical equipment, elevators, motors, and generators.

- Keep a flashlight or chargeable light in an easy-to-find place in each of these areas in case the commercial power fails and the battery-operated lights run down.

NOTE   For full information, consult the ANSI/TIA/EIA-569 Standard, which may be purchased through Global Engineering Documents on the Web at `http://global.ihs.com`.

Entrance Facility

The location of the entrance facility is usually either on the first floor or in the basement of a building and must take into consideration the requirements of the telecommunications services required and other utilities (such as CATV, water, and electrical power).

ANSI/TIA/EIA-569-A specifies the following design considerations for an entrance facility:

- When security, continuity, or other needs dictate, an alternate entrance facility may need to be provided.

- One wall at a minimum should have 3/4" (20 mm) A-C plywood.

- It should be a dry area not subject to flooding.

- It should be as close to the actual entrance pathways (where the cables enter the building) as possible.

- Equipment not relating to the support of the entrance facility should not be installed there.

WARNING   The entrance facility should not double as a storage room or janitor's closet.

Main-Terminal Space

The main-terminal space is a facility that is commonly a shared space in a multi-tenant building. The main cross-connects are in this room. This room is generally a combination of an equipment room and a telecommunications closet, though the TIA/EIA specifies that the design for a main-terminal space should follow the design considerations laid out for an equipment room. Customer equipment may or may not be located here. However, our opinion is that it is not desirable to locate your own equipment in a room shared with other tenants. One reason is that you may have to get permission from the building manager to gain access to this facility.

Equipment Room

Considerations to think about when designing an equipment room include the following:

- Environmental controls must be present to provide HVAC at all times. A temperature range of 64–75 degrees Fahrenheit (or 18–24 degrees Celsius) should be maintained, along with 30–55 percent relative humidity. An air-filtering system should be installed to protect against pollution and contaminants such as dust.

- Seismic and vibration precautions should be taken.

- The ceiling should be at least 8.0 feet (2.4 meters) high.

- A double door is recommended. (See also door-design considerations at the beginning of section "ANSI/TIA/EIA-569-A .")

- The entrance area to the equipment room should be large enough to allow delivery of large equipment.

- The room should be above water level to minimize danger of flooding.

- The backbone pathways should terminate in the equipment room.

- In a smaller building, the entrance facility and equipment room may be combined into a single room.

Cabling @ Work: Bad Equipment-Room Design

One company we are familiar with spent nearly a million dollars designing and building a high-tech equipment room, complete with raised floors, cabling facilities, power conditioning, backup power, and HVAC. The room was designed to be a showcase for its voice and computer systems. On the delivery day, much of the HVAC equipment could not be moved into the room because of lack of clearance in the outside hallway. Several walls had to be torn out (including the wall of an adjacent tenant) to move the equipment into the room.

Another company located its equipment room in a space that used to be part of a telecommunications closet. The space had core holes drilled to the floor above, but the holes had not been filled in after the previous tenant vacated. The company installed its computer equipment but did not have the core holes filled. A few months later, a new tenant on the second floor had a contractor fill the holes. The contractor's workers poured nearly a ton of concrete down the core and on top of the computer equipment in the room below before someone realized the hole was not filling up.

Many organizations have experienced the pain of flooding from above. One company's computer room was directly below bathrooms. An overflowing toilet caused hundreds of gallons of water to spill down into the computer room. Don't let this kind of disaster occur in your equipment rooms!

Telecommunications Closets

Here are some design considerations for telecommunications closets, suggested by the ANSI/TIA/EIA-569-A:

- Each floor of a building should have at least one telecommunications closet, depending on the distance to the work areas. The closets should be close enough to the areas being served so that the horizontal cable does not exceed a maximum of 90 meters (as specified by the ANSI/TIA/EIA-568-A Standard).

- Environmental controls are required to maintain a temperature that is the same as adjacent office areas. Positive pressure should be maintained in the telecommunications closets, with a minimum of one air change per hour (or per local code).

- Ideally, closets should "stack" on top of one another in a multifloor building. Then, backbone cabling (sometimes called vertical or riser cable) between the closets merely goes straight up or down.

- Two walls of the telecommunications closet must have ¾" (20 mm) A-C plywood mounted on the walls, and the plywood should be 8.0 feet (2.4 meters) high.

- Vibration and seismic requirements should be taken into consideration for the room and equipment installed there.

- Two closets on the same floor must be interconnected with a minimum of one 78(3) trade-size conduit or equivalent pathway. The 78(3) trade-size conduit has a sleeve size of 78 mm or 3 inches.

Shake, Rattle, and Roll

A company that Jim worked for was using metal racks and shelving in the equipment rooms and telecommunications closets. The metal racks were not bolted to the floors or supported from the ceiling. During the 1989 San Francisco earthquake, these racks all collapsed forward, taking with them hubs, LAN servers, tape units, UPSs, and disk subsystems. Had the racks been secured to the wall and ceilings, some or all of the equipment would have been saved. If you live in an area prone to earthquakes, be sure to take seismic precautions.

Horizontal Pathways

The horizontal pathways are the paths that horizontal cable takes between the wiring closet and the work area. The most common place in which horizontal cable is routed is in the space between the structural ceiling and the false (or drop) ceiling. Hanging devices such as J hooks should be secured to the structural ceiling to hold the cable. The cable should be supported at intervals not greater than 60 inches. For long runs, this interval should be varied slightly so that structural harmonics (regular physical anomalies that may coincide with transmission frequency intervals) are not created in the cable, which could affect transmission performance.

NOTE Cable installers often install cable directly on the upper portion of false ceiling. This is a poor installation practice because cable could then also be draped across fluorescent lights, power conduits, and air-conditioning ducts. In addition, the weight of cables could collapse the false ceiling. Some local codes may not permit communications cable to be installed without conduit, hangers, trays, or some other type of pathway.

WARNING In buildings where the ceiling space is also used as part of the environmental air-handling system (i.e., as an air return), plenum-rated cable must be installed in accordance with Article 800 of the NEC.

Other common types of horizontal pathways include conduit and trays (or wireways). *Trays* are metal or plastic structures that the cable is laid into when it is installed. The trays can be rigid or flexible. *Conduit* can be metal or plastic tubing and is usually rigid but can also be flexible (in the case of fiber-optic cable, the flexible tubing is sometimes called *inner duct*). Both conduit and trays are designed to keep the cable from resting on top of the false ceiling or being exposed if the ceiling is open.

Other types of horizontal pathways include the following:

- Access floor, which is found in raised-floor computer rooms. The floor tile rests on pedestals, and each tile can be removed with a special tool. Some manufacturers make cable-management systems that can be used in conjunction with access floors.

- Under floor or trenches, which are in concrete floors. They are usually covered with metal and can be accessed by pulling the metal covers off.

- Perimeter pathways, which are usually made of plastic or metal and are designed to mount on walls, floors, or ceilings. A pathway contains one or more cables. Many vendors make pathway equipment (see Chapter 5 for more information).

When designing or installing horizontal pathways, keep the following considerations in mind:

- Horizontal pathways are not allowed in elevator shafts.

- Make sure that the pathways will support the weight of the cable you plan to run and that they meet seismic requirements.

- Horizontal pathways should be grounded.

- Horizontal pathways should not be routed through areas that may collect moisture.

KEY TERMS   **Drawstring**   A *drawstring* is a small nylon cord inserted into a conduit when the conduit is installed; it assists with pulling cable through. Larger conduits will have multiple drawstrings.

Backbone Pathways

Backbone pathways provide paths for backbone cabling between the equipment room, telecommunications closets, main-terminal space, and entrance facility. The TIA suggests in ANSI/TIA/EIA-569-A that the telecommunications closets be stacked on top of one another from floor to floor so that cables can be routed straight up through a riser. ANSI/TIA/EIA-568-A defines a few types of backbone pathways:

Ceiling pathways   These pathways allow the cable to be run loosely though the ceiling space.

Conduit pathways   Conduit pathways have the cable installed in a metallic or plastic conduit.

Tray pathways   These are the same types of trays used for horizontal cabling.

KEY TERMS   **Sleeves, Slots, and Cores**   *Sleeves* are circular openings that are cut in walls, ceilings, and floors; a *slot* is the same but rectangular in shape. A *core* is a circular hole that is cut in a floor or ceiling and is used to access the floor above or below. Cores, slots, and sleeves cut through a floor, ceiling, or wall designed as a firestopping wall must have firestopping material inserted in the hole after the cable is installed through it.

Some points to consider when designing backbone pathways include the following:

- Intercloset conduit must be 78(3) trade size (3-inch or 78 mm sleeve).

- Backbone conduit must be 103(4) trade size (4-inch or 103 mm sleeve).

- Firestopping material must be installed where a backbone cable penetrates a firewall (a wall designed to stop or hinder fire).

- Trays, conduits, sleeves, and slots need to penetrate at least 1 inch (25 mm) into telecommunication closets and equipment rooms.

- Backbone cables should be grounded per local code, the NEC, and ANSI/TIA/EIA-607.

- Backbone pathways should be dry and not susceptible to water penetration.

WARNING Devices such as cable trays, conduit, and hangers must meet requirements of the NEC with regard to their placement. For example, flexible-metal conduit is not allowed in plenum spaces except under restricted circumstances.

Work Areas

ANSI/TIA/EIA-569-A recommendations for work areas include the following:

- A power outlet should be nearby but should maintain minimum power/telecommunications separation requirements (see NEC Article 800-52 for specific information).

- Each work area should have at least one telecommunications outlet box. ANSI/TIA/EIA-568-A recommends that each telecommunications outlet box should have a minimum of two outlets (one for voice and one for data).

- For voice applications, the PBX control-center, attendant, and reception areas should have independent pathways to the appropriate telecommunications closets.

- The minimum bend radius of cable should not be compromised at the opening in the wall.

ANSI/TIA/EIA-569 also makes recommendations for wall openings for furniture pathways.

ANSI/TIA/EIA-607

The ANSI/TIA/EIA-607 Commercial Building Grounding and Bonding Requirements for Telecommunications Standard covers grounding and bonding to support a telecommunications system. This document should be used in concert with Article 250 and Article 800 of the NEC. ANSI/TIA/EIA-607 does *not* cover building grounding; it only covers the grounding of telecommunications systems.

ANSI/TIA/EIA-607 specifies that the telecommunications ground must tie in with the building ground. Each telecommunications closet must have a telecommunications grounding system, which commonly consists of a *telecommunications bus bar* tied back to the building grounding system. All shielded cables, racks, and other metallic components should be tied into this bus bar.

ANSI/TIA/EIA-607 specifies that the minimum ground-wire size must 6 AWG, but, depending on the distance that the ground wire must cover, it may be up to 3/0 AWG (a pretty large copper wire!). Ground-wire sizing is based on the distance that the ground wire must travel; the further the distance, the larger the wire must be. ANSI/TIA/EIA-607-A supplements (and is supplemented by) the NEC. For example, Article 800-33 specifies that telecommunications cables *entering* a building must be grounded as near as possible to the point at which it enters the building.

WARNING When protecting a system with building ground, don't overlook the need for lightning protection. Network and telephone components are often destroyed by a lightning strike. See NEC Article 780 for more information.

Grounding is one of the most commonly overlooked components during the installation of a structured cabling system. An improperly grounded communications system, although supporting low-voltage applications, can result in, well, a shocking experience. Time after time we have heard stories of improperly grounded (or ungrounded) telecommunications-cabling systems that have generated mild electrical or throw-you-off-your-feet shocks; they have even resulted in some deaths.

Grounding is not to be undertaken by the do-it-yourselfer or an occasional cable installer. A professional electrician *must* be involved. He or she will know the best practices to follow, where to ground components, which components to ground, and the correct equipment to be used. Further, electricians must be involved when a telecommunications bus bar is tied into the main building-ground system.

WARNING   Grounding to a water pipe may not provide you with sufficient grounding, as many water systems now tie in to PVC-based (plastic) pipes. It may also violate NEC and local-code requirements.

Cabling @ Work: An Example of Poor Grounding

One of the best examples we can think of that illustrates poor grounding practices was a very large building that accidentally had two main grounds installed. A building should only have one main ground, yet in this building each side had a ground. A telecommunications backbone cable was then grounded to each main ground.

Under some circumstances, a ground loop formed that caused this cable to emit electromagnetic interference at specific frequencies. This frequency just so happened to be used by air-traffic-control beacons. When the building cable emitted signals on this frequency, it caused pilots to think they were closer to the airport than they really were. One plane almost crashed as a result of this poorly grounded building. The FAA (Federal Aviation Administration) and the FCC (Federal Communications Commission) closed the building and shut down all electrical systems for weeks until the problem was eventually found.

ANSI/TIA/EIA-570-A

ANSI, EIA, and TIA published ANSI/TIA/EIA-570-A, or the Residential and Light Commercial Telecommunications Cabling Standard, to address the growing need for "data-ready" homes. Just a few years ago, only the most serious geeks would have admitted to having a network in their homes. Today, more and more homes have small networks consisting of two or more home computers, a cable modem, and a shared printer. Even apartment buildings and condominiums are being built or remodeled to include data outlets; some apartment buildings and condos even provide direct Internet access.

The ANSI/TIA/EIA-570-A Standard provides standardized requirements for residential telecommunications cabling for two grades of information outlets: basic and multimedia cabling. This cabling is intended to support applications such as voice, data, video, home automation, alarm systems, environmental controls, and intercoms. The two grades are as follows:

Grade 1 This grade supports basic telephone and video services. The Standard recommends using one four-pair Category 3 or 5 UTP cable (Category 5 preferred) and one RG-6 coaxial cable.

Grade 2 Grade 2 supports enhanced voice, video, and data service. The Standard recommends using two four-pair Category 5 cables and two RG-6 coaxial cables. One Category 5 cable is used for voice and the other for data. One RG-6 cable is for satellite service, and the other is for a local antenna or cable-TV connection.

The Standard further dictates that a central location within a home or multitenant building be chosen at which to install a central cabinet or wall-mounted rack to support the wiring. This location should be close to the telephone-company demarcation point and near the entry point of cable-TV connections. Once the cabling system is installed, you can use it to connect phones, televisions, computers, cable modems, and EIA-6000-compliant home-automation devices.

Other TIA/EIA Standards and Bulletins

The TIA/EIA alliance published additional specifications and bulletins relating to data and voice cabling as well as performance testing. Table 2.15 shows many of these documents and bulletins, as well as some new specifications that were developed and then incorporated into the TIA/EIA-568 specifications.

TABLE 2.15: TIA/EIA Standards and Bulletins (and Standards Incorporated into TIA/EIA-568)

Standard	Description
ANSI/TIA/EIA-569-A	*Commercial Building Standards for Telecommunications Pathways and Spaces* This Standard specifies design and construction practices within and between buildings to support telecommunications media and equipment. Specific requirements are included for areas through which telecommunications equipment media are installed.
ANSI/TIA/EIA-606	*Administration Standard for the Telecommunications Infrastructure of Commercial Buildings* Specifies methods for labeling telecommunications infrastructure equipment such as pathways, spaces, and media-dependent applications. The document includes specifications for labels, color coding, and data recording. It was incorporated into ANSI/TIA/EIA-568-A in 1995.

Continued on next page

TABLE 2.15 CONTINUED: TIA/EIA Standards and Bulletins (and Standards Incorporated into TIA/EIA-568)

Standard	Description
ANSI/TIA/EIA-607	*Commercial Building Grounding and Bonding Requirements for Telecommunications* This Standard covers planning, design, and implementation of grounding systems to support multivendor and multiproduct environments.
TIA/EIA TSB-36	*Additional Cable Specifications for Unshielded Twisted-Pair Cables* This document was incorporated into ANSI/TIA/EIA-568-A in 1995 and is included in the "B" version as well. It provides performance characteristics for high-performance UTP cabling and is primarily targeted toward cable manufacturers.
TIA/EIA TSB-40A	*Additional Transmission Specifications for Unshielded Twisted-Pair Connecting Hardware* This document was incorporated into ANSI/TIA/EIA-568-A in 1995 and is included in the "B" version as well. It provides transmission-performance requirements for UTP connecting hardware for Category 3, 4, and 5 cable. Connecting hardware includes outlets, patch panels, transition connectors, and cross-connect blocks.
TIA/EIA TSB-53A	*Additional Specifications for Shielded Twisted-Pair (STP) Connecting Hardware* Provides transmission-performance characteristics for STP connecting hardware. In 1995, this TSB was incorporated into ANSI/TIA/EIA-568-A and is included in the "B" version as well.
TIA/EIA TSB-67A	*Transmission Performance Specifications for Field Testing of UTP Cabling Systems* This bulletin provides test methods, performance parameters, and minimum requirements for testing of Category 3, 4, and 5 cabling and related connecting hardware.
TIA/EIA TSB-72	*Centralized Optical Fiber Cabling Guidelines* Specifies guidelines and connecting hardware requirements for fiber-optic cabling systems supporting centralized equipment located within a telecommunications closet or equipment room. This bulletin was incorporated into ANSI/TIA/EIA-568-A and is included in the "B" version as well.
TIA/EIA TSB-95	*Additional Transmission Performance Guidelines for 100-Ohm Four-Pair Category 5 Cabling* This document defines additional performance-testing characteristics above and beyond the parameters specified in TSB-67. The characteristics are to be used with existing Category 5 cabling systems to ensure they will support Gigabit Ethernet systems.

As requirements and cabling change, specifications are updated, and new TSBs are issued. Table 2.16 shows some of the emerging specifications and TSBs.

TABLE 2.16:   Emerging Standards and Bulletins

Standard	Description
TSB-96	*Field Certification of Installed Category 5 Channels and Level II-E Test Equipment* Specifies additional performance categories for field testing of Category 5 and 5e cabling required to support Gigabit Ethernet (1000Base-T). It introduces new testing parameters such as ELFEXT, return loss, propagation delay, and delay skew. This bulletin will also specify tighter requirements for a new level of field test equipment (Level II-E).
TIA/EIA 526-14	*Optical Power Loss Measurements of Installed Multimode Fiber Cable Plant* Specifies guidelines and procedures for measuring optical loss between two passively connected points of a multimode fiber-optic cabling plant. This document specifies light sources, test jumpers, calibration, accuracy, interpretation of results, and documentation.
TIA/EIA 526-7	*Measurement of Optical Power Loss of Installed Single-Mode Fiber Cable Plant* Specifies guidelines and procedures for measuring optical loss between two passively connected points of a single-mode fiber-optic cabling plant.
Category 6	*Transmission Performance Specifications for Four-Pair 100-Ohm Category 6 Cabling* Specifies components such as cabling and connecting hardware and defines basic link and channel link for Category 6 channels and Level III field tester requirements. Ratification is expected later in 2001.
Category 7	*Transmission Performance Specifications for Four-Pair 100-Ohm Cabling at Bandwidth up to 600Mhz* Work has just begun creating a specification for Category 7 cabling running at 600Mhz. This specification will require different connecting hardware and a different cable design, probably STP. Interestingly, TIA is not directly involved in this specification but will probably adopt whatever specification the ISO comes up with. No realistic time frame can be established for ratification because so much work needs to be done on this cable specification.

If you want to keep up on the latest TIA/EIA specifications and the work of the various committees, visit the TIA Web site at www.tiaonline.org/standard/sfg and go to the TR-42 page.

ISO/IEC 11801

The International Organization Standards (ISO) and the International Electrotechnical Commission (IEC) publish the ISO/IEC 11801 Standard predominantly used in Europe. This Standard was released in 1995 and is similar in many ways to the ANSI/TIA/EIA-568-A Standard upon which it is based. However, the Standard has a number of differences in terminology and some slightly different specifications. Table 2.17 shows the common codes and elements of an ISO/IEC 11801 structured cabling system.

TABLE 2.17: Common Codes and Elements Defined by ISO/IEC 11801

Element	Code	Description
Building distributor	BD	A distributor in which building-to-building backbone cabling terminates and where connections to interbuilding or campus backbone cables are made.
Building entrance facilities	BEF	Location provided for the electrical and mechanical services necessary to support telecommunications cabling entering a building.
Campus distributor	CD	Distributor location from which campus backbone cabling originates.
Equipment room	ER	Location within a building dedicated to housing distributors and specific equipment.
Floor distributor	FD	A distributor used to connect horizontal cable to other cabling subsystems or equipment.
Horizontal cable	HC	Cable from the floor distributor to the telecommunications outlet.
Telecommunications closet	TC	Cross-connection point between backbone cabling and horizontal cabling. May house telecommunications equipment, cable terminations, cross-connect cabling, and data-networking equipment.
Telecommunications outlet	TO	The point where the horizontal cabling terminates on a wall plate or other permanent fixture. The point is an interface to the work-area cabling.
Transition point	TP	The location in horizontal cabling of a change of cable form, such as from round to under-carpet cable.
Work-area cable		Connects equipment in the work area (phones, computers, etc.) to the telecommunications outlet.

Differences between ANSI/TIA/EIA-568-A and ISO/IEC 11801 include the following:

- ISO/IEC 11801 allows for two additional media types for use with backbone and horizontal cabling, 120-ohm UTP cable and 50/125-micron multimode optical fiber.

- The term *transition point* is much broader in ISO/IEC 11801; it includes not only transition points for under-carpet cable to round cable (as defined by ANSI/TIA/EIA-568-A) but also consolidation-point connections.

- ISO/IEC 11801 specifies a maximum patch cable and cross-connect length of 5.0 meters (16.4 feet).

Terminology differences between ANSI/TIA/EIA-568-A and ISO/IEC 11801 include the following:

- The ISO/IEC 11801 definition of the campus distributor (CD) is similar to the ANSI/TIA/EIA-568-A definition of a main cross-connect (MC).

- The ISO/IEC 11801 definition of a building distributor (BD) is equal to the ANSI/TIA/EIA-568-A definition of an intermediate cross-connect (IC).

- The ISO/IEC 11801 definition of a floor distributor (FD) is defined by ANSI/TIA/EIA-568-A as the horizontal cross-connect (HC).

Classification of Applications and Links

ISO/IEC 11801 defines classes of applications and links based on the type of media used and the frequency requirements. The original 11801 specification defines four classes of applications for copper and one for fiber-optic cabling. The ISO/IEC 11801 specifies the following classes of applications and links:

Class A   This class is for voice and low-frequency applications up to 100kHz.

Class B   Class B is for low-speed data applications operating at frequencies up to 1MHz.

Class C   This class is for medium-speed data applications operating at frequencies up to 16MHz.

Class D   Class D concerns high-speed applications operating at frequencies up to 100MHz.

Optical Class   An optional class is for applications where bandwidth is not a limiting factor.

These applications are then cross-referenced against the category of cabling that will support them and the maximum permissible distances. Table 2.18 illustrates the categories, classes, and permissible distances.

TABLE 2.18: Maximum Distances for Classes of Application and Categories of Cable

Media	Class A	Class B	Class C	Class D	Optical
Category 3	2km	200m	100m	-	-
Category 4	3km	260m	150m	-	-
Category 5	3km	260m	260m	100m	-
150-ohm shielded cable	3km	400m	250m	150m	-
Multimode optical fiber	-	-	-	-	2km
Single-mode optical fiber	-	-	-	-	3km

Distances include allowances for patch cables, jumpers, and equipment connections. The basic-link specification for Class C applications on Category 3 cable and Class D applications on Category 5 cable is 90 meters.

Anixter Cable Performance Levels Program

The networking industry is rapidly changing; new technologies are released every few months, and updates to existing technologies occur almost constantly. Such rapid change in the industry is not conducive to clear, sweeping standards. Standards can take years to ratify; often by the time a Standard can be agreed upon and published, it is dated for those who are already deploying leading-edge technologies.

If you have picked up a cabling-component catalog recently, you probably saw twisted-pair cabling products promising performance (lower attenuation values and higher crosstalk and return-loss values) better than Category 5 cabling. Some of these cable products call themselves category 5-plus, category 6, category 7, or other such names—note that *category* is in lowercase. The TIA has working groups continually revising the TIA/EIA specifications, and many of these "better-than-Category 5" cable types will eventually become Standards, as recently occurred with the publication of ANSI/TIA/EIA-568-A-5 for Category 5e.

The problem is that they are not currently Standards. A vendor that advertises category 6 or category 7 performance specifications is really not giving you any further data to compare other types of cables from other vendors. Differentiating these products becomes nearly impossible.

NOTE   Don't confuse the TIA/EIA Categories (with a capital *C*) with Anixter Cable Performance Levels. Though they are quite similar, cabling products that are classified for a specified Anixter Level may either meet or exceed requirements put forth by specifications organizations.

For this reason, Anixter (www.anixter.com), a worldwide distributor of communications products and cable, developed the Anixter Cable Performance Levels program (now called Anixter Levels XP). The initial document was published in 1989 and defined three levels of cable performance for twisted-pair cabling. Anixter tested and categorized the products that they sold, regardless of the manufacturer, so that customers could properly choose products and compare products between vendors. The requirements for the three levels were as follows:

Level 1   Minimum-quality cable in Level 1 was that which could support telephone voice-grade applications.

Level 2   Minimum-quality cable here had to support low-speed (less than 1.2Mbps) data communications, such as to mainframe and minicomputer terminals.

Level 3   Minimum-quality cable in this level had to support 10Mbps Ethernet and 4/16Mbps Token Ring.

These cable types were defined three years prior to the first ANSI/TIA/EIA-568 Standard, which defined Category 1, 2, and 3 cabling. When the first iteration of TIA/EIA-568 was released in 1991, vendors were already making promises of higher performance and better cabling. To meet these needs, Anixter added two new levels:

Level 4   Minimum-quality cable was required to support applications operating at a frequency of up to 20MHz, which would include passive 16Mbps Token Ring.

Level 5   Minimum-quality cable was required to support applications operating at frequencies up to 100MHz. The original intent of Level 5 was to provide a copper version of Fiber Distributed Data Interface (FDDI).

Anixter no longer maintains Levels 1 through 4, as the performance requirements for those levels are either considered obsolete or are specified by the ANSI/TIA/EIA-568-A Categories and ISO/IEC 11801 Standards. However, Anixter's Level 5 specification exceeds the new Category 5e performance specifications.

Anixter Levels: Looking Forward

By 1997, newer networking technologies were on the horizon. At that time, the need for better twisted-pair cable performance was becoming evident. To complicate matters even further, over 150 different constructions of Category 5 cabling existed. Some of these Category 5 cables performed half as well as others.

To further help customers compare cable technologies that would exceed Category 5 requirements, two additional levels of performance were specified in the Anixter Levels 97 program. The Level 5 specification was also updated. The performance levels specified by the ALC 97 program included the following:

Level 5   Minimum cable performance had to be acceptable for handling frequencies up to 200MHz.

Level 6   Minimum cable performance had to be acceptable for handling frequencies up to 350MHz.

Level 7   Minimum cable performance had to be acceptable for handling frequencies up to 400MHz.

NOTE   For a vendor's cables or components to be categorized as part of the Anixter Levels Program, Anixter must test the components in its own lab, the manufacturer must use only virgin materials, and the manufacturer must be ISO 9000 registered.

What About Components?

We would like to put forth a word of caution here that will be reiterated throughout this book. If you require Level 5, 6, or 7 performance from your cabling infrastructure, choosing the correct level of cable is only a small part of the decision. Anixter further tests and certifies components (patch panels, wall plates, patch cables, connectors, etc.) to be used with the cabling.

The components used must be certified to the same level as the cable. Further, we recommend that you use components from the same manufacturer as the cable you are purchasing, or from a combination of manufacturers whose cable and connecting components are proven to work well together. Finally, solid installation practices must be followed to get the performance you expect.

Other Cabling Technologies

Over the years, a number of vendor-specific systems were widely adopted and came to be considered de facto standards. Some of these are still widely used today. One attractive feature of proprietary systems is that only one company need be named in the lawsuit. (That was a poor attempt at humor.) Seriously, when a single company is responsible for the components and installation as well as the cable, you can be assured that the cabling infrastructure should function as promised. Complications arise when vendors and competing technologies need to be integrated together.

Though some of these systems may lock the customer into a single-vendor solution, the advantages of that single vendor solution may be attractive. Some of the more popular vendor solutions include:

- The IBM Cabling System
- Lucent Technologies SYSTIMAX
- Digital Equipment Corporation's DECconnect
- NORDX/CDT Integrated Building Distribution System

The focus of this book is centered on the ANSI/TIA/EIA-568-A Standards, but the foregoing specifications deserve mentioning and are briefly discussed in the following pages.

The IBM Cabling System

In the early 1980s, specifications for cabling and structure were even more rare than they were in the late 1980s. In an attempt to encourage a single specification for cabling, IBM in 1984 developed its own cabling system called the IBM Cabling System. Though we personally disliked working with the IBM Cabling System, we do respect that IBM was way ahead of the rest of the industry in promoting a standard cabling system. IBM cabling is still in wide enough use to deserve a mention.

The original IBM Cabling System defined a number of different components, including:

- Cable types
- Data connectors
- Face plates
- Distribution panels

IBM Cable Types

The IBM Cabling System defines cables as Types rather than Categories or Levels. Seven types of cable are defined by the IBM Cabling System:

Type 1A   Type 1A cabling (originally known simply as Type 1) is the only cable type adopted as part of the ANSI/TIA/EIA-568-A Standard. Type 1A cable was designed to support 4- and 16Mbps Token Ring but has been improved to support FDDI over copper and video applications operating at frequency rates of up to 300MHz. The ISO is currently working on a specification that will allow STP cable to operate at frequencies up to 600MHz.

Type 1A (shown in Figure 2.8) cabling consists of two pairs of twisted-pair wire (22 AWG). The wire impedance is 150 ohms, plus or minus 10 percent. Each wire is insulated, and the wire pair is twisted; each pair is then encased in additional shielding. Both pairs are then encased in a jacket. This design results in less attenuation and significantly better NEXT performance. The same type of cable can be used for horizontal cabling as well as patch cabling.

FIGURE 2.8:

IBM Cabling System Type 1A and Type 2A cabling

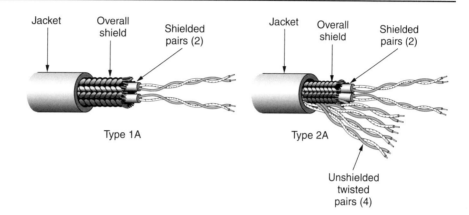

Type 1A   Type 2A

Unshielded twisted pairs (4)

Type 2A   Type 2A cabling (originally known simply as Type 2) is essentially the same cable as IBM Type 1A. Type 2A is also shown in Figure 2.8; the difference is that in addition to the shielded twisted pair of Type 1A, four pairs of unshielded twisted-pair cable are outside the main shield. These additional pairs are Category 3–compliant and can be used for applications that do not require shielded twisted cable, such as voice applications.

Type 3   Type 3 cable is voice grade, unshielded twisted-pair cable. It consists of four solid, unshielded twisted-pair 22 AWG or 24 AWG pairs. The twisted pairs have a minimum of two twists per foot and impedance of 100 ohms through a frequency range of 256KHz to 2.3MHz. Do not confuse Type 3 with Category 3, because the performance specifications are different.

Type 5   Type 5 cable consists of two 62.5/125-micron multimode fibers in an optical cable. IBM has also used 50/125- and 100/140-micron fiber-optic cable, but because 62.5/125-micron is the de facto standard for FDDI and is included in both the ANSI/TIA/EIA-568-A and ISO/IEC 11801 Standards, it is more desirable. Three connector types are specified: SMA, ST, and SC connectors.

Type 6   Type 6 cable consists of two twisted-pair cables with one shield. The wires are 26 AWG stranded cable with an impedance of 150 ohms, plus or minus 10 percent. They are designed to be used as station or patch cable up to a 30-meter maximum.

Type 8   Type 8 cable is designed for use under carpeting. The cable is housed in a flat jacket and consists of two shielded twisted-pair 22 AWG cables with an impedance of 100 ohms. Type 8 cable is limited to 50 percent of the distance that can be used with Type 1A cable.

Type 9   Type 9 cable is similar to Type 6. It consists of two 26 AWG wire pairs twisted together and then shielded. The wire core can be either stranded or solid, and the impedance is 150 ohms, plus or minus 10 percent. Type 9 offers the advantage of having a smaller diameter and accepting eight-position modular-jack connectors (a.k.a. RJ-45). Though Type 9 was designed to connect from the wall plate to the station adapter, it can be used as horizontal cabling as well.

IBM Data Connector

The most unique component of the IBM Cabling System is the IBM connector. The IBM connector (or simply data connector) is neither a male connector nor a female connector but is hermaphroditic. Two identical connectors can be connected to each other.

This data connector is used in patch panels, hubs, and wall plates. The beauty of this connector is that it eliminated the need for complementary male and female connectors. Its downfall is that it is complicated and expensive to apply to the cable. The data connector (shown in Figure 2.9) is commonly used with IBM Token Ring MAUs.

FIGURE 2.9:

IBM data connector

Four-position data connectors used for IBM Type 1 cabling system

Lucent SYSTIMAX SCS Cabling System

The Bell Labs subsidiary Lucent Technologies (formerly AT&T) developed the SYSTIMAX SCS (Structured Connectivity Solutions) Cabling System. Calling SYSTIMAX SCS Cabling System a proprietary solution would be a stretch because the SYSTIMAX is based on the ANSI/TIA/EIA-568 Standards.

Lucent has developed a number of structured connectivity solutions that include copper and fiber media. These modular solutions incorporate Lucent cabling and components as well as Lucent cable management and patch panels. Lucent has solutions that can provide up to 622Mbps over copper.

Because Lucent is providing a single-vendor solution for all components, it is much easier for them to take a holistic approach to cable performance and reliability. Rather than looking at the performance of individual components, the SYSTIMAX designers look at performance optimization for the entire channel.

For further information about the SYSTIMAX SCS Cabling System, check it out on the Web at www.lucent.com/netsys/systimax.

Digital Equipment Corporation DECconnect

Digital Equipment Corporation designed the DECconnect system to provide a structured cabling system for its customers. DECconnect consists of four different types of technologies and five different cable types (listed in Table 2.19). DECconnect never caught on as a widely used cabling system for Local Area Networking and voice applications, though we still see it at customers with VAXs.

TABLE 2.19: DECconnect Applications and Cable Types

Application	Cable Type	Connector Type
Voice	Four-pair UTP	RJ-45
Low-speed data (terminals)	Two-pair UTP	Modified, keyed RJ-45
Network	50-ohm coax	BNC
Network	62.5/125-micron fiber	ST or SMA
Video	75-ohm coax	F-Type

One of the downsides of the DECconnect system was the variety of cable types that had to be run. If you had locations that required a terminal, a PC with Ethernet, and a PBX telephone, you would possibly have to run three different types of horizontal cable to a single wall plate. With modern structured cabling systems such as those specified in the ANSI/TIA/EIA-568-A Standard, a single cable type could be used, though three cables would still be run.

NORDX/CDT Integrated Building Distribution System

The Integrated Building Distribution System (IBDN) originated with Northern Telecom (Nortel) and is now sold by NORDX/CDT. The IBDN system is similar to the Lucent SYSTIMAX SCS system and the structured systems of ANSI/TIA/EIA-568-A. When used within the guidelines of the ANSI/TIA/EIA-568-A, IBDN is Standards compliant. For more information on IBDN, see the NORDX/CDT Web site at www.nordx.com.

chapter 3

Choosing the Correct Cabling

- Network Topologies

- UTP, Optical Fiber, and Future-Proofing

- Network Architectures

- Network-Connectivity Devices

Technically, when you begin the planning stages of a new cabling installation, you should not have to worry about the types of applications used. The whole point of structured cabling Standards such as ANSI/TIAEIA-568-A and ISO/IEC 11801 is that they will support almost any networking or voice application in use today.

Still, it is a good idea to have an understanding of the networking application you are cabling for and how that can affect the use of the cabling system. Further, because cabling that's related to data also connects to various types of network devices, it is a good idea to have an understanding of the networking hardware used in common installations.

Topologies

The network's *topology* refers to the physical layout of the nodes and hubs that make up the network. Choosing the right topology is important because the topology affects the type of networking equipment, cabling, growth path, and network management.

Today's networking architectures fall into one of three categories:

- Star

- Bus

- Ring

Topologies are tricky because some networking architectures appear to be one type of technology but are in reality another. Token Ring is a good example of this because Token Ring uses hubs (MAUs). All stations are connected to a central hub, so physically it is a star topology; logically, though, it is a ring topology. Often two topology types will be used together to expand a network.

Whereas *topology* refers to the physical layout of the wiring and nodes of a network, it also refers to its method of transmitting data and to its *logical*, or *virtual*, layout of the nodes. Before the advent of structured wiring, physical and logical topology were often the same. For example, a network that had a ring topology actually had the wiring running from node to node in a ring. This can be confusing these days. The implementation of structured wiring standardized a star configuration as the physical topology for modern networks, and network electronics takes care of the logical topologies.

Topology and *architecture* are often used interchangeably. They are not exactly synonymous but are close enough for purposes of this book.

Star Topology

When implementing a *star topology*, all computers are connected to a single, centrally located point. This central point is usually a hub. All cabling used in a star topology is run from the point where the network nodes are located back to a central location. Figure 3.1 shows a simple star topology.

FIGURE 3.1:

Star topology with a central hub

> **NOTE**
>
> A hub by any other name would still be a hub. In the early days of UTP Ethernet, the Ethernet equipment manufacturer Synoptics called their hubs *concentrators*. IBM still refers to their STP hubs sometimes as *MAUs* or *MSAUs* (multistation access units) and their UTP hubs as *CAUs* (controlled access units). Still other manufacturers and users refer to a hub as a *repeater* because it repeats the signal it receives to all nodes.

From the perspective of cabling, the star topology is now almost universal. It is also the easiest to cable. The ANSI/TIAEIA-568-A and ISO/IEC 11801 Standards assume that the network architecture uses a star topology as its physical configuration. If a single node on the star fails or the cable to that node fails, then only that single node fails. However, if the hub fails, then the entire star fails. Regardless, identifying and troubleshooting the failed component is much easier than with other configurations because every node can be isolated and checked from the central distribution point.

From this point on in the chapter, we will assume you understand that the physical layout of a modern network is a star topology and that when we discuss bus and ring topologies we're referring to the logical layout of the network.

Killing an Entire Star Topology

Although a single node failure cannot usually take down an entire star topology, sometimes it can. In some circumstances, a node fails and causes interference for the entire star. In other cases, shorts in a single cable can send disruptive electrical signals back to the hub and cause the entire star to cease functioning. Of course, failure of the hub will also affect all nodes in a star topology.

Bus Topology

The *bus topology* is the simplest network topology. Also known as a *linear bus*, all computers are connected to a contiguous cable or a cable joined together to make it contiguous. Figure 3.2 illustrates a bus topology.

FIGURE 3.2:

Bus topology

FIGURE 3.2:

Bus topology

Ethernet is a common example of a bus topology. Each computer determines when the network is not busy and transmits data as needed. Computers in a bus topology only listen for transmissions from other computers; they do not repeat or forward the transmission on to other computers.

The signal in a bus topology travels to both ends of the cable. To keep the signal from bouncing back and forth on the cable, both ends of the cable in a bus topology must be terminated. A component called a *terminator*, essentially nothing more than a resistor, is placed on both ends of the cable. The terminator absorbs the signal and keeps it from bouncing; this is referred to as *maximum impedance*. If either terminator is removed or if the cable is cut anywhere along its length, all computers on the bus will fail to communicate.

Coaxial cabling is most commonly used in true bus-topology networks such as thin/thick Ethernet. However, 10Base-T Ethernet still functions as if it were a bus topology even though it is wired as a star topology.

Ring Topology

A *ring topology* requires that all computers be connected in a contiguous circle, as shown in Figure 3.3. The ring has no ends or hub. Each computer in the ring receives signals (data) from its neighbor, repeats the signal, and passes it along to the next node in the ring. Because the signal has to pass through each computer on the ring, a single node or cable failure can take the entire ring down.

FIGURE 3.3:

Ring topology

A true ring topology is a pain in the neck to install cable for because the circular nature of the ring makes it difficult to expand a ring over a large physical area. Token Ring is a ring topology. Even though Token Ring stations may be connected to a central MAU (and thus appear to be a star topology), the data on the Token Ring travels from one node to another. It passes though the MAU each time.

UTP, Optical Fiber, and Future-Proofing

The common networking technologies today (Ethernet, Token Ring, FDDI, and ATM) can all use either UTP or optical-fiber cabling, and IT professionals are faced with the choice. MIS managers and network administrators hear much about "future-proofing" their cabling infrastructures. If you believe the hype from some cabling vendors, installing their particular cable and components will guarantee that you won't have to ever update your cabling system again. However, you should keep in mind that in the early 1990s network managers thought they were future-proofing their cabling system when they installed Category 4 rather than Category 3 cabling.

Today, decision-makers who must choose between Category 5, 5e, and 6 cabling and components are thinking about future-proofing. Each category is an improvement in potential data throughput and therefore a measure of "future-proofing." Deciding whether to use optical fiber adds to the complexity. Here are some of the advantages of using optical fiber:

- It has higher potential bandwidth.

- It's not susceptible to electromagnetic interference.

- It can transmit over longer distance (although distance is set at 100 meters for horizontal cabling, regardless of media, according to ANSI/TIA/EIA-568-A.).

- Improved termination techniques and equipment make it easier to install and implement.

- Cable, connectors, and patch panels are now cheaper than before.

- It's valuable in situations where EMI is especially high.

- It offers better security (because the cable cannot be easily tapped or monitored).

Though optical fiber cable has come of age, UTP cabling still reigns, and you may want to consider remaining with UTP cabling for the following reasons:

- Fiber-optic cable installation is 10 to 15 percent more expensive than an equivalent Category 5e installation.

- Networking hardware (network-interface cards and hubs) is two to three times more expensive than UTP-based hardware.

- If higher bandwidth (more than a gigabit per second) requirements are not an issue for you, you may not need optical fiber.

- Fiber optics is the medium of choice for security only if security concerns are unusually critical.

- EMI interference is only an issue if it is extreme.

When considering optical-fiber cable, remember that you are trying to guarantee that the cabling system will not have to be replaced for a very long time, regardless of future networking technologies. Some questions you should ask yourself when deciding if fiber optic is right for you include the following:

- Do you rent or own your current location?

- If you rent, how long is your lease, and will you be renewing your lease when it is up?

- Are there major renovations planned that would cause walls to be torn out and rebuilt?

If you will occupy your present space for longer than five years and you want to future-proof your cabling infrastructure, optical fiber may be the right choice for your horizontal cabling. (Don't forget to take into consideration the higher cost of networking hardware.)

Network Architectures

The ANSI/TIAEIA-568-A cabling Standard covers almost any possible combination of cable necessary to take advantage of the current network architectures found in the business environment. These network architectures include Ethernet, Token Ring, Fiber Distributed Data Interface (FDDI), Asynchronous Transfer Mode (ATM), and 100VG-AnyLAN. Although the predominant cabling infrastructure is UTP, many of these architectures are capable of operating on other media as well. Understanding the different types of cable that these architectures utilize is important.

Ethernet

Ethernet is the most mature and common of the network architectures. According to technology analysts IDC (International Data Corporation), Ethernet is used in over 80 percent of all network installations.

In some form, Ethernet has been around for over 30 years. A predecessor to Ethernet was developed by the University of Hawaii (called, appropriately, the Alohanet) to connect geographically dispersed computers. This radio-based network operated at 9,600Kbps and used an access method called CSMA/CD

(Carrier Sense Multiple Access/Collision Detection), in which computers "listened" to the cable and transmitted data if there was no traffic. If two computers transmitted data at exactly the same time, the nodes needed to detect a collision and retransmit the data. Extremely busy CSMA/CD-based networks became very slow when collisions were excessive.

In the early 1970s, Robert Metcalfe and David Boggs, scientists at Xerox's Palo Alto Research Center (PARC), developed a cabling and signaling scheme that used CSMA/CD and was loosely based on the Alohanet. This early version of Ethernet used coaxial cable and operated at 2.94Mbps. Even early on, Ethernet was so successful that Xerox (along with Digital Equipment Corporation and Intel) updated it to support 10Mbps. Ethernet was the basis for the IEEE 802.3 specification for CSMA/CD networks.

NOTE   Ever seen the term *DIX*? Or *DIX connector*? DIX is an abbreviation for Digital, Intel, and Xerox. The DIX connector is also known as the AUI (attachment unit interface), which is the 15-pin connector that you see on older Ethernet cards and transceivers.

Over the past 25 years, despite stiff competition from more modern network architectures, Ethernet has flourished. In the past 10 years alone, Ethernet has been updated to support speeds of 100Mbps and 1000Mbps; currently, researchers are planning 10Gbps Ethernet!

Ethernet has evolved to the point that it can be used on a number of different cabling systems. Table 3.1 lists some of the Ethernet technologies. The first number in an Ethernet designator indicates the speed of the network, the second portion (the *base* portion) indicates baseband, and the third indicates the maximum distance or the media type.

TABLE 3.1:   Cracking the Ethernet Designation Codes

Designation	Description
10Base-2	10Mbps Ethernet over thinnet coaxial cable (RG-58) with a maximum segment distance of 185 meters (it was rounded up as 10Base-2 instead of 10Base185).
10Base-5	10Mbps Ethernet over thick (50-ohm) coaxial cable with a maximum segment distance of 500 meters.

Continued on next page

TABLE 3.1 CONTINUED: Cracking the Ethernet Designation Codes

Designation	Description
10Base-36	A 10Mbps broadband implementation of Ethernet with a maximum segment length of 3,600 meters.
10Base-T	10Mbps Ethernet over unshielded twisted-pair cable. Maximum cable length (hub to network card) is 100 meters.
10Base-FL	10Mbps Ethernet over multimode optical-fiber cable. Designed for connectivity between network-interface cards on the desktop and a fiber-optic Ethernet hub. Maximum cable length (hub to network card) is 2,000 meters.
10Base-FB	10Mbps Ethernet over multimode optical-fiber cable. Designed to use a signaling technique that allows a 10Base-FB backbone to exceed the maximum number of repeaters permitted by Ethernet. Maximum cable length is 2,000 meters.
10Base-FP	10Mbps Ethernet over multimode optical-fiber cable designed to allow linking multiple computers without a repeater. Not commonly used. Maximum of 33 computers per segment, and the maximum cable length is 500 meters.
100Base-TX	100Mbps Ethernet over Category 5 or better UTP cabling using two wire pairs. Maximum cable distance is 100 meters.
100Base-T4	100Mbps Ethernet over Category 3 or better UTP cabling using all four wire pairs. Maximum distance using Category 3 cable is 100 meters.
100Base-FX	100Mbps Ethernet over multimode optical-fiber cable. Maximum cable distance is 400 meters.
100Base-VG	More of a first cousin of Ethernet. This is actually 100VG-AnyLAN, which is described later in this chapter.
1000Base-SX	Gigabit Ethernet over multimode optical-fiber cable, designed for workstation-to-hub implementations.
1000Base-LX	Gigabit Ethernet over single-mode optical-fiber cable, designed for backbone implementations.
1000Base-CX	Gigabit Ethernet over STP Type 1 cabling, designed for equipment interconnection such as clusters. Maximum distance is 25 meters.
1000Base-T	Gigabit Ethernet over Category 5 or better UTP cable where the installation has passed performance tests specified by TSB-95. Maximum distance is 100 meters from network-interface card to hub.

10Mbps Ethernet Systems

Why is Ethernet so popular? On a properly designed and cabled network, Ethernet is fast, easy to install, reliable, and cheap. Ethernet can be installed on almost any type of structured cabling system, including unshielded twisted-pair and fiber-optic cable.

10Base-5: "Standard Ethernet Cable"

The earliest version of Ethernet ran on a rigid coaxial cable that was called Standard Ethernet cable but was more commonly referred to as *thicknet*. To connect a node to the thicknet cable, a specially designed connector was attached to the cable (called a *vampire tap* or *piercing tap*).

When the connector was tightened down on to the cable, the tap pierced the jacket, shielding, and insulation to make contact with the inner core of the cable. This connector had a transceiver attached, to which a transceiver cable (or drop cable) was linked. The transceiver cable connected to the network node.

Though thicknet was difficult to work with (because it was not very flexible and was hard to install and connect nodes to), it was reliable and had a usable cable length of 500 meters (about 1,640 feet). That is where the *10* and *5* in 10Base-5 come from: *10Mbps, baseband, 500 meters.*

Though we never see new installations of 10Base-5 systems anymore, it can still be found in older installations, typically used as backbone cable. The 10Base-T hubs and coaxial (thinnet) cabling are attached at various places along the length of the cable. Given the wide availability of fiber-optic equipment and inexpensive hubs and UTP cabling, virtually no reason exists for you to install a new 10Base-5 system today.

10Base-T Ethernet   For over 10 years, 10Base-T (the T stands for twisted pair) Ethernet reigned as king of the network architectures. There is a good reason for this: 10Base-T Ethernet will work over any regular Category 3 or better UTP cabling, and UTP cabling is cheap to install, reliable, and easy to manage.

If you are cabling a facility for 10Base-T, plan to use, at a minimum, Category 5 cable and components. The incremental price is only slightly higher than Category 3, and you will provide a growth path to faster network technologies. In the last few years, 100Base-T has begun to overtake 10Base-T in popularity due to the widespread deployment of Category 5 installations, coupled with falling prices of 100Base-T network components. If you've got the cabling in place to handle it, it's hard to say no to 10 times your current bandwidth when the only obstacle in the way is inexpensive hubs and NICs (network-interface cards).

Here are some important facts about 10Base-T:

- The maximum cable length of a 10Base-T segment is 100 meters (328 feet) when using Category 3 cabling. Somewhat longer distances may be achieved with higher grades of equipment, but remember that you are no longer following the Standard if you attempt to stretch the distance.

- The minimum length of a 10Base-T cable (node to hub) is 2.5 meters (about 8 feet).

- A 10Base-T network can have a maximum of 1,024 computers on it; however, performance may be extremely poor on large networks.

- For older network devices that have only AUI-type connectors, transceivers can be purchased to convert to 10Base-T.

- Though a 10Base-T network appears to operate like a star topology, internally it is a bus architecture. Unless a technology like switching or bridging is employed, a signal on a single network segment will be repeated to all nodes on the network.

- 10Base-T requires only two wire pairs of an eight-pin modular jack. Figure 3.4 shows the pin layout and usage.

Even though 10Base-T uses only two pairs of a four-pair cable, all eight pins should be connected properly in anticipation of future upgrades or other network architectures.

FIGURE 3.4:

An eight-pin modular jack
used with 10Base-T

10Base-F Ethernet   Specifications for using Ethernet over fiber-optic cable existed back in the early 1980s. Originally, fiber-optic cable was simply used to connect repeaters whose separation exceeded the distance limitations of thicknet cable. The original specification was called Fiber Optic Inter Repeater Link (FOIRL), which described linking two repeaters together with fiber-optic cable up to 1,000 meters (3,280 feet) in length.

NOTE   Unless stated otherwise, all fiber-optic devices are assumed here to use multimode optical-fiber cable.

The cost of fiber-optic repeaters and fiber-optic cabling dropped greatly during the 1980s, and connecting individual computers directly to the hub via fiber-optic cable became more common. Originally, the FOIRL specification was not designed with individual computers in mind, so the IEEE developed a series of fiber-optic media specifications. These specifications are collectively known as 10Base-F. The individual specifications for (and methods for implementing) 10Base-F Ethernet include the following:

10Base-FL   This specification is an updated version of the FOIRL specification and is designed to interoperate with existing FOIRL equipment. Maximum distance used between 10Base-FL and an FOIRL device is 1,000 meters, but it is 2,000 meters (6,561 feet) between two 10Base-FL devices. The 10Base-FL is most commonly used to connect network nodes to hubs and to interconnect hubs. Most modern Ethernet equipment supports 10Base-FL; it is the most common of the 10Base-F specifications.

10Base-FB The 10Base-FB specification describes a synchronous signaling backbone segment. This specification allows the development of a backbone segment that exceeds the maximum number of repeaters that may be used in a 10Mbps Ethernet system. The 10Base-FB is available only from a limited number of manufacturers and supports distances of up to 2,000 meters.

10Base-FP This specification provides the capability for a fiber-optic mixing segment that links multiple computers on a fiber-optic system without repeaters. The 10Base-FP segments may be up to 500 meters (1,640 feet), and a single 10Base-FP segment (passive star coupler) can link up to 33 computers. This specification has not been adopted by many vendors and is not widely available.

Why Use 10Base-FL?

In the past, fiber-optic cable was considered expensive, but it is becoming more and more affordable. In fact, fiber-optic installations are becoming nearly as inexpensive as UTP copper installations. The major point that causes some network managers to cringe is that the network equipment is more expensive. A recent price comparison found one popular 10Base-F network-interface card was more than 2.5 times more expensive than the 10Base-T equivalent.

However, fiber-optic cable, regardless of the network architecture, has key benefits for many businesses:

- Fiber-optic cable will make it easy to incorporate newer and faster technologies in the future.

- Fiber-optic cable is not subject to electromagnetic interference, nor does it generate interference.

- Fiber-optic cable is difficult to tap or monitor for signal leakage, so it is more secure.

- Potential data throughput of fiber-optic cable is greater than any current or forecast copper technologies.

So fiber-optic cable more desirable for customers who are concerned about security, growth, or electromagnetic interference. Fiber is commonly used in hospitals and military environments.

Getting the Fiber-Optic Cable Right   A number of manufacturers make equipment that supports Ethernet over fiber-optic cabling. One of the most important elements of the planning of a 10Base-F installation is to pick the right cable and connecting hardware. Here are some pointers:

- Use 62.5/125-micron multimode fiber-optic cable. (Note: as 50/125 micron multimode fiber becomes more accepted as a cable medium, it should be given consideration as well.)

- Each horizontal run should have at least two strands of multimode fiber.

- Make sure that the connector type for your patch panels and patch cables matches the hardware you choose. Some older equipment uses exclusively the ST connector, whereas newer equipment uses the more common SC connector. Follow the current Standard requirements when selecting a connector type.

10Base-2 Ethernet   Though not as common as it once was, 10Base-2 is still an excellent way to connect a small number of computers together in a small physical area such as a home office, classroom, or lab. The 10Base-2 Ethernet uses thin coaxial (RG-58 /U or RG-58 A/U) to connect computers together. This thin coaxial cable is also called *thinnet*.

Coaxial cable and network-interface cards use a special connector called a *BNC connector*. This male connector (on the network-interface card) is inserted into the female, and the female connector (called a T-connector) is then twisted 90 degrees to lock it into place. The T-connector allows two cables to be connected on each side of it, and the middle of the T-connector plugs into the network-interface card. The thinnet cable never connects directly to the network-interface card. This arrangement is shown in Figure 3.5.

NOTE   *BNC* is an abbreviation for Bayonet-Neill-Concelman. The *B* indicates that the connector is a bayonet-type connection, and Neill and Concelman are the inventors of the connector. You may also hear this connector called a British Naval Connector.

FIGURE 3.5:

The 10Base-2 network

The ANSI/TIAEIA-568-A Standard does not recommend the use of coaxial cabling, though it recognizes that it still exists. The next revision of the ANSI/TIAEIA-568 Standard will probably remove any mention of coaxial cable. From our own experience, here are some reasons *not* to use 10Base-2:

- The 10Base-2 network isn't suited for connecting more than 10 computers on a single segment.

- Ethernet cards with thinnet (BNC) connections are not as common as they once were. Usually you have to pay extra for network-interface cards with thinnet connectors.

- The network may not be the best choice if you want to use Ethernet switching technologies. Although switching technologies are available for thin Ethernet, they are less common and more expensive than they are for thick Ethernet.

- If your network spans more than one or two rooms or building floors, 10Base-2 isn't for you.

- If you are building a home network and plan to connect to the Internet using a cable modem or DSL, investing in a simple 10Base-T hub is a better choice.

- UTP cabling, 10Base-T hubs, and 10Base-T network-interface cards are plentiful and inexpensive.

Though 10Base-2 is simple to install, you should keep a number of points in mind if you choose to implement it:

- Both ends of the cable must be terminated.

- A cable break anywhere along the length of the cable will cause the entire segment to fail.

- The maximum cable length is 185 meters and the minimum is 0.5 meters.

- T-connectors must always be used for any network node; cables should never be connected directly to a network-interface card.

- A thinnet network can have as many as five segments connected by four repeaters. However, only three of these segments can have network nodes attached. The other two segments will only connect to repeaters; these segments are sometimes called *interrepeater links*.

WARNING   Coaxial cables should be grounded properly (the shield on one end of the cable should be grounded, but not both ends). If they aren't, possibly lethal electrical shocks can be generated. Refer to ANSI/TIAEIA-607 for more information on building grounding or talk to your electrical contractor. We know of one network manager who was thrown flat on his back when he touched a rack because the cable and its associated racks had not been properly grounded.

100Mbps Ethernet Systems

Though some critics said that Ethernet would never achieve speeds of 100Mbps, designers of Fast Ethernet proved them wrong. Two approaches were presented to the IEEE 802.3 committee. The first approach was to simply speed up current Ethernet and use the existing CSMA/CD access-control mechanism. The second was to implement an entirely new access-control mechanism called *demand priority*. In the end, the IEEE decided to create specifications for both approaches. The 100Mbps version of 802.3 Ethernet is called 100Base-T Fast Ethernet, and the demand-priority approach is called 100VG-AnyLAN (described later in this chapter).

Three different approaches exist for cabling a Fast Ethernet system, standardized as 100Base-TX, 100Base-T4, and 100Base-FX.

100Base-TX Ethernet   The 100Base-TX specification uses physical-media specifications developed by ANSI that were originally defined for FDDI (ANSI specification X3T9.5). The 100Base-TX requires Category 5 or better cabling but uses only two of the four pairs. The eight-position modular jack (RJ-45) uses the same pin numbers as 10Base-T Ethernet.

Though a typical installation requires hubs or switches, two 100Base-TX nodes can be connected together "back-to-back" with a crossover cable made exactly the same way as a 10Base-T crossover cable. (See Chapter 9, "Cable Connectors," for more information on making a 10Base-T or 100Base-TX crossover cable.) Understand the following when planning a 100Base-TX Fast Ethernet network:

- All components must be Category 5 certified, including cables, patch panels, and connectors. Proper installation practices must be followed.

- The cabling system must be able to pass tests specified by TIA TSB-67. If you plan to move to faster networking technologies (1000Base-T), make sure that the cable tester checks for compliance with TSB-95.

- The maximum segment cable length is 100 meters. With higher-grade cables, longer lengths of cable may work, but proper signal timing cannot be guaranteed.

- The network uses the same pins as 10Base-T, as shown previously in Figure 3.4.

100Base-T4 Ethernet   The 100Base-T4 specification was developed as part of the 100Base-T specification so that existing Category 3–compliant systems could also support Fast Ethernet. The designers accomplish 100Mbps throughput on Category 3 cabling by using all four pairs of wire; 100Base-T4 requires a minimum of Category 3 cable. The requirement can ease the migration path to 100Mbps technology.

The 100Base-T4 is not used as frequently as 100Base-TX, partially due to the cost of the network-interface cards and network equipment. The 100Base-T4 network-interface cards are generally 50 to 70 percent more expensive than 100Base-TX cards. Also, 100Base-T4 cards do not automatically negotiate and connect to 10Base-T hubs, as most 100Base-TX cards do. Therefore, 100Base-TX cards are more popular. However, 100Base-TX does require Category 5 cabling.

If you plan to use 100Base-T4, understand the following:

- Maximum cable distance is 100 meters using Category 3, although distances of up to 150 meters can be achieved if Category 5 or better cable is used.

Distances greater than 100 meters are not recommended, however, because round-trip signal timing cannot be ensured even on Category 5 cables.

- All eight pins of an eight-pin modular jack must be wired. Older Category 3 systems often wired only the exact number of pairs (two) necessary for 10Base-T Ethernet. Figure 3.6 shows the pins used, and Table 3.2 shows the usage of each of the pins in a 100Base-T4 connector. Either the T568A or T568B pinout configurations can be used, but you must be consistent.

FIGURE 3.6:

The eight-pin modular-jack wiring pattern for 100Base-T4

- The 100Base-T4 specification recommends using Category 5 patch cables, panels, and connecting hardware wherever possible.

TABLE 3.2: Pin Usage in an Eight-Pin Modular Jack Used by 100Base-T4

Pin	Name	Usage	Abbreviation
1	Data 1 +	Transmit +	Tx_D1+
2	Data 1 −	Transmit −	Tx_D1−
3	Data 2 +	Receive +	Rx_D2+
4	Data 3 +	Bidirectional Data 3 +	Bi_D3+
5	Data 3 −	Bidirectional Data 3 −	Bi_D3−
6	Data 2 −	Receive −	Rx_D2−
7	Data 4 +	Bidirectional Data 4 +	Bi_D4+
8	Data 4 −	Bidirectional Data 4 −	Bi_D4−

100Base-FX Ethernet   Like its 100Base-TX copper cousin, 100Base-FX uses a physical-media specification developed by ANSI for FDDI. The 100Base-FX specification was developed to allow 100Mbps Ethernet to be used over fiber-optic cable. Though the cabling plant is wired in a star topology, 100Base-FX is a bus architecture.

If you choose to use 100Base-FX Ethernet, consider the following:

- Cabling-plant topology should be a star topology and should follow ANSI/TIAEIA-568-A or ISO 11801 recommendations.

- Each network node location should have a minimum of two strands of multimode fiber (MMF).

- Maximum link distance is 400 meters; though fiber-optic cable can transmit over much farther distances, proper signal timing cannot be guaranteed. If you follow ANSI/TIAEIA-568-A or ISO 11801 recommendations, the maximum horizontal-cable distance should not exceed 100 meters.

- The most common fiber connector type used for 100Base-FX is the SC connector, but the ST connector and the FDDI MIC connector may also be used. Make sure you know which type of connector(s) your hardware vendor will require.

Gigabit Ethernet (1000Mbps)

The IEEE approved the first Gigabit Ethernet specification in June 1998—IEEE 802.3z. The purpose of IEEE 802.3z was to enhance the existing 802.3 specification to include 1000Mbps operation (802.3 supported 10Mbps and 100Mbps). The new specification covers media access control, topology rules, and the gigabit media-independent interface. IEEE 802.3z specifies three physical layer interfaces: 1000BASE-SX, 1000BASE-LX, and 1000BASE-CX.

In July 1999, the IEEE approved an additional specification known as IEEE 802.3ab, which adds an additional Gigabit Ethernet physical layer for 1000Mbps over UTP cabling. The UTP cabling, all components, and installation practices must be Category 5 or greater. The only caveat is that the Category 5 installation must meet the performance requirements outlined in TSB-95.

Gigabit Ethernet deployment is still in the early stages, and we don't expect to see it extended directly to the desktop in most organizations. The cost of Gigabit Ethernet hubs and network-interface cards is too high to permit this in most environments. Only applications that demand the highest performance will actually see Gigabit Ethernet to the desktop in the next few years.

Initially, the most common uses for Gigabit Ethernet will be for intrabuilding or campus backbones. Figure 3.7 shows a before-and-after illustration of a simple network with Gigabit Ethernet deployed. Prior to deployment, the network had a single 100Mbps switch as a backbone for several 10Mbps and 100Mbps segments. All servers were connected to the 100Mbps backbone switch, which was sometimes a bottleneck.

FIGURE 3.7:

Moving to a Gigabit Ethernet backbone

During deployment of Gigabit Ethernet, the 100Mbps backbone switch is replaced with a Gigabit Ethernet switch. The network-interface cards in the servers are replaced with Gigabit network-interface cards. The 10Mbps and 100Mbps hubs connect to ports on the Gigabit switch that will accommodate 10- or 100Mbps segments. In this simple example, the bottleneck on the backbone has been relieved. The hubs and the computers did not have to be disturbed.

TIP   To take full advantage of Gigabit Ethernet, computers that have Gigabit Ethernet cards installed should have a 64-bit PCI bus. The 32-bit PCI bus will work with Gigabit Ethernet, but it is not nearly as fast as Gigabit Ethernet.

Gigabit Ethernet and Fiber-Optic Cables   Initially, 1000Mbps Ethernet was only supported on fiber-optic cable. The IEEE 802.3z specification included support for three physical-media options (PHYs), each designed to support different distances and types of communications:

> **1000Base-SX**   Targeted to horizontal cabling applications such as to workstations and other network nodes, 1000Base-SX is designed to work with multimode fiber-optic cable.

> **1000Base-LX**   Designed to support backbone-type cabling such as intra-building and campus backbones, 1000Base-LX is for single-mode fiber-optic cable, though in some cases multimode fiber can be used. Check with the equipment vendor.

> **1000Base-CX**   Designed to support interconnection of equipment clusters, this specification uses 150-ohm STP cabling similar to IBM Type 1 cabling over distances no greater than 25 meters.

When cabling for Gigabit Ethernet using fiber, you should follow the ANSI/TIAEIA-568-A Standards for 62.5/125-micron multimode fiber for horizontal cabling and 8.3/125-micron single-mode fiber for backbone cabling.

1000Base-T Ethernet   The IEEE designed 1000Base-T with the intention of supporting Gigabit Ethernet to the desktop. One of the primary design goals was to support the existing base of Category 5 cabling. Except for a few early adopters, most organizations have not quickly adopted 1000Base-T to the desktop. However, as 1000Base-T network equipment becomes more cost effective, this will change.

In July 1999, the IEEE 802.3ab task force approved IEEE specification 802.3ab, which defines using 1000Mbps Ethernet over Category 5 unshielded twisted-pair cable. Unlike 10Base-T and 100Base-TX, all four pairs must be used with 1000Base-T. Network electronics simultaneously send and receive 250Mbps over each pair using a transmission frequency of about 65MHz. These special modulation techniques are employed to "stuff" 1000Mbps through a cable that is only rated to 100MHz.

In 1999, the TIA issued TSB-95 to define additional performance parameters (above and beyond those specified in TSB-67) that should be performed in order to certify an existing Category-5 cabling installation for use with 1000Base-T. The additional criteria cover far-end crosstalk, delay skew, and return loss. For more information on these performance criteria, see Chapter 1.

If you plan to deploy 1000Base-T in the future, make sure that you use a minimum of Category 5 cable, that solid installation practices are used, and that all links are tested and certified using TSB-67 and TSB-95 performance criteria. Using Category 5e or higher cable and components is even better assurance of future performance.

Token Ring

Developed by IBM, *Token Ring* uses a ring architecture to pass data from one computer to another. A former teacher of Jim's referred to Token Ring as the Fahrenheit network architecture because more people with Ph.D. degrees worked on it than there are degrees in the Fahrenheit scale.

NOTE   Token Ring is perhaps a superior technology compared to Ethernet, but Token Ring has not enjoyed widespread success since the early 1990s. IBM was slow to embrace structured wiring using UTP and eight-position (RJ-45 type) plugs and jacks, so cabling and components were relatively expensive and difficult to implement. When IBM finally acknowledged UTP as a valid media, 4Mbps Token Ring would run on Category 3 UTP, but 16Mbps Token Ring required a minimum of Category 4. In the meantime, a pretty quick and robust 10Mbps Ethernet network could be put in place over Category 3 cables that many offices already had installed. So, while Token Ring was lumbering, Ethernet zoomed by, capturing market share with the ease and economy of its deployment.

Token Ring employs a sophisticated scheme to control the flow of data. If no network node needs to transmit data, a small packet, called the *free token*, continually circles the ring. If a node needs to transmit data, it must have possession of the free token before it can create a new Token Ring data frame. Once the data arrives at its destination, a new free token is placed on the original network by the *transmitting* station. Then the next node on the ring can transmit data if necessary.

This scheme, called *token passing*, guarantees equal access to the ring and that no two computers will transmit at the same time. Token passing is the basis for IEEE specification 802.5. This scheme might seem pretty slow since the free token must circle the ring continually, but keep in mind that the free token is circling at speeds approaching 70 percent of the speed of light. A smaller Token Ring network may see a free token circle the ring up to 10,000 times per second!

On 4Mbps Token Ring, one free token always circles the ring. With 16Mbps Token Ring, four free tokens circle the ring.

Because a ring topology is difficult to cable, IBM employs a hybrid star/ring topology. All nodes in the network are connected centrally to a hub (MAU or MSAU, in IBM jargon), as shown in Figure 3.8. The transmitted data still behaves like a ring topology, traveling down each cable (called a *lobe*) to the node and then returning to the hub, where it starts down the next cable on the MAU.

FIGURE 3.8:

A Token Ring hybrid star/ring topology

Even a single node failure or lobe cable can take down a Token Ring. The designers of Token Ring realized this and designed the MAU with a simple electromechanical switch (a relay switch) that adds a new node to the ring when it is powered on. If the node is powered off or if the lobe cable fails, the electromechanical switch disengages, and the node is removed from the ring. The ring continues to operate as if the node were not there.

Token Ring operates at either 4Mbps or 16Mbps; however, a ring only operates at a single speed. (That's unlike Ethernet, where 10Mbps and 100Mbps nodes can coexist on the same network.) Care must be taken on older Token Ring hardware that a network adapter operating at the wrong speed is not inserted into a ring because doing so can shut down the entire network.

Token Ring and Shielded Twisted Pair (STP)

Token Ring originally operated on shielded twisted-pair (STP) cabling. IBM designed a cabling system that included a couple of types of shielded twisted-pair cables; the most common of these was IBM Type 1 cabling (later called IBM Type 1A). IBM Type 1A cabling is now specified as a valid cable type in the ANSI/TIAEIA-568-A specification.

The IBM cabling system used a unique, hermaphroditic connector that is commonly called an *IBM data connector*. The IBM data connector has no male and female components, so two IBM patch cables can be connected together to form one long patch cable.

Unless your cabling needs specifically require an STP cabling solution for Token Ring, we recommend against STP cabling. Excellent throughput is available today over UTP cabling; the only reason to implement STP is if electromagnetic interference is too great to use UTP.

Token Ring and Unshielded Twisted Pair (UTP)

Around 1990, vendors started releasing unshielded twisted-pair solutions for Token Ring. The first of these solutions was simply to use media filters or baluns on the Token Ring network-interface cards, which connected to the card's nine-pin interface and allowed a UTP cable to connect to the media filter. The balun matches the impedance between the 100-ohm UTP and the network device, which is expecting 150 ohms.

KEY TERMS   **Baluns and Media Filters**   *Baluns* and *media filters* are designed to match impedance between two differing types of cabling, usually unbalanced coaxial cable and balanced two-wire twisted pair. Although baluns can come in handy, they can also be problematic and should be avoided if possible.

The second UTP solution for Token Ring was network-interface cards equipped with eight-pin modular jacks (RJ-45) that supported 100-ohm cables, rather than a DB9 connector.

Any cabling plant certified Category 3 or better should support 4Mbps Token Ring. However, for growth and future expansion, a minimum of Category 5 cabling and components should be used.

NOTE   A number of vendors make Token Ring network-interface cards that support fiber-optic cable. Although using Token Ring over fiber-optic cables is uncommon, it is possible.

Fiber Distributed Data Interface (FDDI)

Fiber Distributed Data Interface (FDDI) is a networking specification that was produced by the ANSI X3T9.5 committee in 1986. It defines a high-speed (100Mbps), token-passing network using fiber-optic cable. In 1994, the specification was updated to include copper cable (called CDDI or *Copper Distributed Data Interface*). FDDI was slow to be widely adopted, but it has found a niche as a reliable, high-speed technology for backbones and applications that demand reliable connectivity.

Though at first glance FDDI appears to be similar to Token Ring, it is different from both Token Ring and Ethernet. A Token Ring node can transmit only a single frame when it gets the free token; it must wait for the token to transmit again. An FDDI node, once it possesses the free token, can transmit as many frames as it can generate within a predetermined time before it has to give up the free token.

FDDI can operate as a true ring topology, or it can be physically wired like a star topology. Figure 3.9 shows an FDDI ring that consists of *dual-attached stations* (DAS); this is a true ring topology. A dual-attached station has two FDDI interfaces. The first is called an A port, which is used to connect the input of the primary ring and the output of the secondary ring. The second is called a B port, which is used to connect the output of the primary ring and the input of the secondary ring. Each node on the network in Figure 3.9 has an FDDI network-interface card that has two FDDI attachments. The card creates both the primary and secondary rings. Cabling for such a network is a royal pain because the cables have to form a complete circle.

FDDI networks can also be cabled as a star topology, though they would still behave like a ring topology. FDDI network-interface cards may be purchased with either a single FDDI interface (*single-attached station* or SAS) or with two FDDI interfaces (DAS). Single-attached stations must connect to an FDDI concentrator or hub. A network can also be mixed and matched, with network nodes such as workstations using only a single-attached station connection and servers or other critical devices having dual-attached station connections. That configuration would allow the critical devices to have a primary and secondary ring.

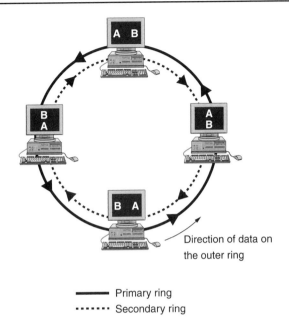

Direction of data on
the outer ring

——— Primary ring
······· Secondary ring

FDDI has new terminology and acronyms, including the following:

MAC   The media access control is responsible for addressing, scheduling, and routing data.

PHY   The physical protocol layer is responsible for coding and timing of signals, such as clock synchronization of the ring. The actual data speed on an FDDI ring is 125Mbps; an additional control bit is added for every four bits.

PMD   The physical layer medium is responsible for the transmission between nodes. FDDI includes two PMDs: Fiber-PMD for fiber-optic networks and TP-PMD for twisted-pair networks.

SMT   The station management is responsible for handling FDDI management, including ring management (RMT), configuration management (CFM), connection management (CMT), physical-connection management (PCM), and entity-coordination management (ECM). SMT coordinates neighbor identification, insertion to and removal from the ring, fault detection, traffic monitoring, and fault detection.

Cabling and FDDI

When planning cabling for an FDDI network, practices recommended in ANSI/TIAEIA-568-A or ISO 11801 should be followed. FDDI using fiber-optic cable for the horizontal links uses FDDI MIC connectors. Care must be taken to ensure that the connectors are keyed properly for the device they will connect to.

FDDI using copper cabling (CDDI) requires Category 5 cable and associated devices. Horizontal links should at a minimum pass performance tests specified in TSB-67, though it is also a good idea to use the performance criteria specified by TSB-95. Of course, a Category 5e or better installation is a better way to go.

Asynchronous Transfer Mode (ATM)

ATM (*asynchronous transfer mode*, not to be confused with automated teller machines) first emerged in the early 1990s. If networking has an equivalent to rocket science, then ATM is it. ATM was designed to be a high-speed communications protocol that does not depend on any specific LAN topology. It uses a high-speed cell-switching technology that can handle data as well as real-time voice and video. The ATM protocol breaks transmitted data up in to 53-byte cells. A cell is analogous to a packet or frame, except that an ATM cell does not always contain source or destination addressing information; the ATM cell also contains no higher-level addressing and packet-control information.

ATM is designed to "switch" these small cells through an ATM network very quickly. It does this by setting up a virtual connection between the source and destination nodes; the cells may go through multiple switching points before ultimately arriving at their final destination. The cells may also arrive out of order, so the receiving system may have to correctly order the arriving cells. ATM is a connection-oriented service in contrast to most network architectures, which are broadcast based.

Data rates are scalable and start as low as 1.5Mbps, with other speeds of 25-, 51-, 100-, and 155Mbps and higher. The most common speeds of ATM networks today are 51.84Mbps and 155.52Mbps. Both of these speeds can be used over either copper or fiber-optic cabling. A 622.08Mbps ATM is also becoming common but is currently used exclusively over fiber-optic cable, mostly as a network backbone architecture. ATM supports very high speeds because it is designed to be implemented by hardware rather than software. Soon, fiber-based ATM networks will be operating at data rates of 10Gbps.

In the United States, the specification for synchronous data transmission on optical media is SONET (Synchronous Optical Network); the international equivalent of SONET is SDH (Synchronous Digital Hierarchy). SONET defines a base data rate of 51.84Mbps; multiples of this rate are known as optical carrier (OC) levels, such as OC-3, OC-12, etc. Table 3.3 shows common OC levels and their associated data rate.

TABLE 3.3: Common Optical Carrier Levels (OC-*X*)

Level	Data Rate
OC-1	51.84Mbps
OC-3	155.52Mbps
OC-12	622.08Mbps
OC-48	2.488Gbps

ATM was designed as a WAN protocol. However, due to the high speeds it can support, many organizations are using it to attach servers (and often workstations) directly to the ATM network. To do this, a set of services, functional groups, and protocols was developed to provide *LAN emulation* (called *LANE* by the ATM folks). LANE also provides communication between network nodes attached to a LAN (such as Ethernet) and ATM-attached nodes. Figure 3.10 shows an ATM network connecting to LANs using LANE. Note that the ATM network does not have to be in a single physical location and can span geographic areas.

NOTE   For more information on ATM, check out the ATM Forum's Web site at www. atmforum.org.

Cabling and ATM

What sort of cabling should you consider for ATM networks? Fiber-optic cabling
is still the medium of choice for most ATM installations. Although ATM to the
desktop is still not terribly common, we know of at least a few organizations that
have deployed 155Mbps ATM directly to the desktop.

For fiber-optic cable, as long as you follow the ANSI/TIAEIA-568-A Standard
or the ISO 11801 Standard, you should not have problems. ATM equipment and
ATM network-interface cards use 62.5/125-micron multimode optical fiber.

If you plan on using 155Mbps ATM over copper, plan to use Category 5e cabling
at minimum.

100VG-AnyLAN

Initially developed by Hewlett Packard, AT&T, and IBM as an alternative to other
100BaseX technologies (100Base-TX and 100Base-T4), 100VG-AnyLAN was refined
and ratified by the IEEE as IEEE specification 802.12. It combines the best of both

Ethernet and Token Ring technologies and includes the following as its design goals:

- It permits the use of existing Category 3, 4, or 5 cabling.

- The 100VG-AnyLAN provides a smooth migration path from Ethernet and Token Ring LANs and frame formats.

- It eliminates the collisions associated with Ethernet.

- It supports a cascaded star topology of 2.5 km and more than three levels of cascading.

- Cable distances of 200 meters for UTP and 2,000 meters for fiber are supported.

- It provides fair access and bounded latency.

- The 100VG-AnyLAN provides two levels of priority for frames: normal and high.

- It provides a low-latency service through high priority to support multimedia applications.

NOTE What does the *VG* stand for? Voice grade. The 100VG-AnyLAN was designed to operate over a minimum of Category 3 cable.

Nodes on a 100VG-AnyLAN network can receive at any time, but they are subject to media-access rules, called *demand priority*, when they need to transmit. Other network technologies, such as Ethernet, Token Ring, and FDDI, implement media-access rules at the node. For example, a Token Ring node can transmit only when it has possession of the free token. Ethernet nodes can transmit anytime they sense that the media is not currently in use. The 100VG-AnyLAN nodes transmit only when their hub decides that they can transmit—the node requests permission. Each node thus has "equal" access, though simultaneous requests are serviced in *port order* unless the node sent a high-priority request to the hub.

Unlike Token Ring and FDDI, no token passing takes place on an 100VG-AnyLAN network. Network access is provided by the 100VG-AnyLAN hubs rather than by a free token.

Cable and 100VG-AnyLAN

The 100VG-AnyLAN design was intended to be used on UTP-based networks. Equipment that shipped for 100VG-AnyLAN was designed for use with Category 3, 4, or 5 cabling. Since 1994, additional media has been supported in the form of fiber-optic and STP cabling. Any cabling infrastructure designed using the ANSI/TIAEIA-568A Standards should be capable of supporting 100VG-AnyLAN, including those using Category 3 cables.

WARNING   The 100VG-AnyLAN design uses *all* four pairs in a Category 3, 4, or 5 cable. Therefore, all of these pairs must be connected and wired properly.

Initially, it seemed that 100VG-AnyLAN would require Category 5 cables and connecting hardware just like 100Base-T. However, this is not the case because VG uses a frequency of 30MHz and employs all four pairs in the cable. If you are wondering how 100VG-AnyLAN can use Category 3, which is rated to only 16MHz, and Category 4, which is rated to only 20MHz, give yourself a gold star. The answer is that 100VG-AnyLAN overcomes the noise through the use of sophisticated transceivers and runs Category 3 and Category 4 cables at 30MHz. However, the cables must meet Category 3 or 4 specifications exactly.

The cables that may be used and the maximum distances permitted are shown in Table 3.4; the distances specified in this table are not only for node-to-hub cables but also hub-to-hub cables. The IEEE 802.12 specification specifies the cable formats that can be used within a demand-priority network such as 100VG-AnyLAN.

TABLE 3.4: Cable Categories, Types, and Maximum Distances

Category	Cable Type	Maximum Distance
Category 3	four-pair UTP	100 meters
Category 4	four-pair UTP	100 meters
Category 5	four-pair UTP	200 meters
IBM Type 1A	two-pair STP	100 meters
Fiber Optic	Multimode	2,000 meters

What Is Multipair Cable? The 100VG-AnyLAN hubs allow a UTP cable option called multipair cable. *Multipair cable* has many twisted-pair cables within a single sheath—usually 25 pairs. Multipair cable is permitted between the nodes and the hubs but not in hub-to-hub connections. This specification allows support for older Category 3 cabling infrastructures that used multipair cable as part of their horizontal cabling.

Most new cabling installations use individual cables consisting of a single sheath that contains four pairs. The 100VG-AnyLAN hub has an option labeled with something like "Use Multipair Cable." You should use this option only if you are using multipair cable (for example, cable with 25 pairs), or it can cause a performance hit. If this option is turned on, the 100VG-AnyLAN hub ensures that only a single packet is in a sheath of cable at any given time. Although the hub has the capability to transmit over many pairs simultaneously, it will not do so if the multipair option is selected.

NOTE

Multipair was also referred to as *bundled cable*, but recent innovations in cable installation make the term a misnomer. These days, bundled cables refer to several individual cables under a common jacket or tied together with a spiral wrapping. Cables inside the jacket or wrap can be all of a single type, or several types combined, e.g., UTP, coax, and fiber optic. Depending on the configuration, the bundled cables are also called composite or hybrid cables. The third addendum to ANSI/TIA/EIA-568-A was written and adopted to define and describe bundled, composite, and hybrid constructions.

Can two 100VG-AnyLAN nodes be connected without a hub (like using a crossover cable for 10Base-T)? No, 100VG-AnyLAN cards require the hub to tell them when they can transmit.

Cascading

Multiple levels of 100VG-AnyLAN hubs can be cascaded together, provided the hub's uplink port is used to connect it to the next higher level. There is typically a root-level hub with one or more child hubs. Child hubs can have only a single parent, except for the root hub, which does not need a parent. Up to four levels of cascaded hubs can come off of a single root hub (the root hub is considered the top or fifth level). This arrangement is illustrated in Figure 3.11.

FIGURE 3.11:

The 100VG-AnyLAN
cascading

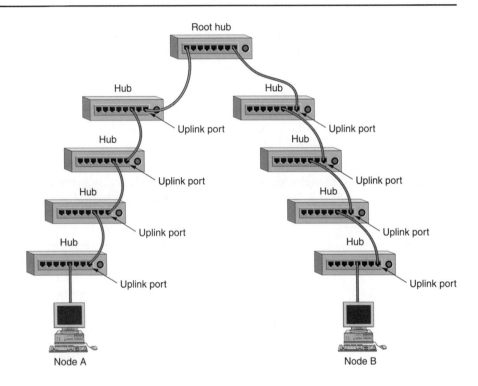

Node A   Node B

NOTE	Five levels of hubs can cascade in 100VG-AnyLAN. With 100Base-X, only two levels of hubs can be cascaded.

Cascading multiple hubs can build an exceptionally large network, especially given the extended cable distances that 100VG-AnyLAN allows. One limitation that this size network does impose is the maximum cable radius.

Maximum Cable Radius   The 100VG-AnyLAN design imposes a maximum cable radius that depends on the media being employed. The maximum cable radius is the maximum distance between two nodes on the network, such as nodes A and B in Figure 3.11. When using Category 3, 4, or 5 cable, the maximum distance between two nodes is 2,000 meters. Figure 3.11 shows 10 separate physical cable segments; assuming that each node is using the maximum Category 5 UTP cable length of 200 meters (per Table 3.4), the 2,000-meter limit will be reached.

Fiber-optic 100VG-AnyLAN networks and copper-fiber combination networks have a maximum cable radius of 2,500 meters. The limitation exists due to a restriction on the maximum delay from any node to the root repeater.

Network-Connectivity Devices

Thus far, we've talked about many of the common network architectures that you may encounter and some points you may need to know relating to providing a cabling infrastructure to support them. We've looked at the products you can use to bring your communication endpoints to a central location. But is there any communication taking place over your infrastructure? What you need now is a way to tie everything together.

This section focuses on the rest of the pieces you need to establish seamless communication across your internetwork.

Repeaters

Nowadays, the terms *repeater* and *hub* are used synonymously, but they are actually not the same. Prior to the days of twisted-pair networking, network backbones carried data across coaxial cable, similar to what is used for cable television.

Computers would connect into these either by BNC connectors, in the case of thinnet, or by vampire taps, in the case of thicknet. Everyone would be connected to the same coaxial backbone. Unfortunately, when it comes to electrical current flowing through a solid medium, you have to contend with the laws of physics. A finite distance exists in which electrical signals can travel across a wire before they become too distorted. Repeaters were used with coaxial cable to overcome this challenge.

Repeaters work at the physical layer of the OSI reference model. Their job is to simply boost an electrical signal's strength so that it can travel farther across a wire. Figure 3.12 illustrates a repeater in action.

FIGURE 3.12:

Repeaters are used to boost signal strength.

Repeater

Being passive in nature, repeaters do not look at or alter the contents of the packets flowing across the wire.

Theoretically, repeaters could be used to extend cables infinitely, but due to the underlying limitations of communication architectures like Ethernet's collision domains, repeaters were used to tie together a maximum of five coaxial-cable segments.

Hubs

Because repetition of signals is a function of repeating hubs, *hub* and *repeater* are used interchangeably when referring to twisted-pair networking. The semantic distinction between the two terms is that a repeater joins two backbone coaxial cables, whereas a hub joins two or more twisted-pair cables.

In twisted-pair networking, each network device is connected to an individual network cable. In coaxial networking, all network devices are connected to the same coaxial backbone. A hub eliminates the need for BNC connectors and vampire taps. Figure 3.13 illustrates how network devices connect to a hub versus to coaxial backbones.

FIGURE 3.13:

Twisted-pair networking versus coaxial networking

Hubs work the same way as repeaters in that incoming signals are amplified before they are retransmitted across its ports. Like repeaters, hubs operate at the OSI physical layer, which means they do not alter or look at the contents of a packet traveling across the wire. When a hub receives an incoming signal, it amplifies it and sends it out over all its ports. Figure 3.14 shows a hub at work.

FIGURE 3.14:

Hubs at work

Hub

Outgoing signals   Incoming signals

Hubs typically provide from 8 to 24 twisted-pair connections, depending on the manufacturer and model of the hub (although some hubs support several dozen ports). Hubs can also be connected to each other (cascaded) by means of BNC, AUI ports, or crossover cables to provide flexibility as networks grow. The cost of this flexibility is paid for in performance.

As a media-access architecture, Ethernet is built on carrier-sensing and collision-detection mechanisms (CSMA/CD). Prior to transmitting a signal, an Ethernet host listens to the wire to determine if any other hosts are transmitting. If the wire is clear, the host transmits. On occasion, two or more hosts will sense that the wire is free and try to transmit simultaneously or nearly simultaneously. Only one signal is free to fly across the wire at a time, and when multiple signals meet on the wire, they become corrupted by the collision. When a collision is detected, the transmitting hosts wait a random amount of time before retransmitting, in the hopes of avoiding another data collision. Figures 3.15 shows a situation where a data collision is produced, and Figure 3.16 shows how Ethernet handles these situations.

FIGURE 3.15:

An Ethernet data collision

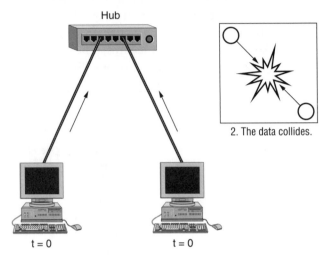

Hub

2. The data collides.

t = 0   t = 0

Two stations transmit
at exactly the same time.

FIGURE 3.16:

How Ethernet responds to
data collisions

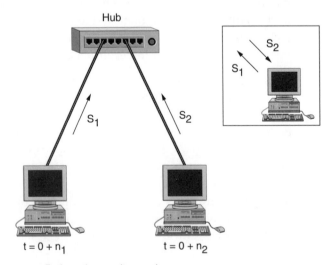

Hub

S_2

S_1

S_1 S_2

$t = 0 + n_1$ $t = 0 + n_2$

Both stations wait a random
amount of time and retransmit.

So what are the implications of collision handling on performance? If you recall from our earlier explanation of how a hub works, a hub, after it receives an incoming signal, simply passes it across all its ports. For example, with an eight-port hub, if a host attached to port 1 transmits, the hosts connected to ports 2 through 8 will all receive the signal. Consider the following: If a host attached to port 8 wants to communicate with a host attached to port 7, the hosts attached to ports 1 through 6 will be barred from transmitting when they will sense signals traveling across the wire.

NOTE   Hubs pass incoming signals across all their ports, preventing two hosts from transmitting simultaneously. All the hosts connected to a hub are therefore said to share the same amount of bandwidth.

On a small scale, such as our eight-port example, the shared-bandwidth performance implications may not be that significant. However, consider the cascading of four 24-port hubs, where 96 hosts share the same bandwidth. When one host transmits, 95 others cannot. The bandwidth that the network provides is finite (limited by the cable plant and network devices). Therefore, in shared-bandwidth configurations, the amount of bandwidth available to a connected host is inversely proportional to the number of hosts sharing that bandwidth. For example, if 96 hosts are connected to the same set of Fast Ethernet (100Mbps) hubs, they have only 1.042Mbps available each. For Ethernet (10Mbps), the situation is even worse, with only 0.104Mbps available each. All hope is not lost, however. We'll look at ways of overcoming these performance barriers through the use of switches and routers.

As a selling point, hubs are relatively inexpensive to implement.

Bridges

When we use the terms *bridge* and *bridging*, we are generally describing functionality provided by modern switches. Just like a repeater, a bridge is a network device used to connect two network segments. The main difference between them is that bridges operate at the link layer of the OSI reference model and can therefore provide translation services required to connect dissimilar media access architectures such as Ethernet and Token Ring. Therefore, bridging is an important internetworking technology.

In general, there are four types of bridging:

Transparent bridging   Typically found in Ethernet environments, the transparent bridge analyzes the incoming frames and forwards them to the appropriate segments one hop at a time (see Figure 3.17).

FIGURE 3.17:

Transparent bridging

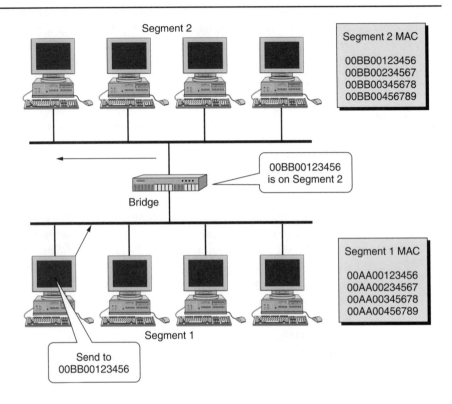

Source-route bridging Typically found in Token Ring environments, source-route bridging provides an alternative to transparent bridging for NetBIOS and SNA protocols. In source-route bridging, each ring is assigned a unique number on the source-route bridge port. Token Ring frames contain address information, including a ring number, which the bridge analyzes to forward the frame to the appropriate ring (see Figure 3.18).

FIGURE 3.18:

Source-route bridging

Source-route transparent bridging   Source-route transparent bridging is an extension of source-route bridging whereby nonroutable protocols such as NetBIOS and SNA receive the routing benefits of source-route bridging and a performance increase associated with transparent bridging.

Translation bridging   Translation bridging is used to connect network segments with different underlying media-access technologies such as Ethernet to Token Ring or Ethernet to FDDI, etc. (see Figure 3.19).

FIGURE 3.19:

Translation bridging

Compared to modern routers, bridges are not complicated devices; they consist of network-interface cards and the software required to forward packets from one interface to another. As previously mentioned, bridges operate at the link layers of the OSI reference model, so to understand how bridges work, a brief discussion of link-layer communication is in order.

How are network nodes uniquely identified? In general, OSI network-layer protocols, such as the Internet protocol (IP), are assumed. When you assign an IP address to a network node, one of the requirements is that it must be unique on the network. At first, you might think every computer in the world must have a unique IP address in order to communicate, but such is not the case. This is because of the Internet Assigned Numbers Authority's (IANA) specification for the allocation of private address spaces, in RFC 1918. For example, Company XYZ and Company WXY could both use IP network 192.168.0.0/24 to identify network devices on their private networks. However, networks that use a private IP address specified in RFC 1918 cannot communicate over the Internet without network-address translation or proxy-server software and hardware.

IP as a protocol merely provides for the logical grouping of computers as networks. Because IP addresses are logical representations of groups of computers, how does communication between two endpoints occur? IP as a protocol provides the rules governing addressing and routing. IP communication occurs at the link layers of the OSI reference model.

Every network-interface card has a unique 48-bit address, known as its *MAC address*, assigned to the adapter. For two nodes to converse, one computer must first resolve the MAC address of its destination. In IP, this is handled by a protocol known as the *Address Resolution Protocol* (ARP). Once a MAC address is resolved, the frame gets built and is transmitted on the wire as a unicast frame. (Both a source and a destination MAC address exist.) Each network adapter on that segment hears the frame and examines the destination MAC address to determine if the frame is destined for them. If the frame's destination MAC address matches the receiving system's MAC address, the frame gets passed up to the network layer; otherwise, the frame is simply discarded.

So how does the communication relate to bridging, you may ask? In transparent bridging, the bridge passively listens to all traffic coming across the wire and analyzes the source MAC addresses to build tables that associate a MAC address with a particular network segment. When a bridge receives a frame destined for a remote segment, it then forwards that frame to the appropriate segment so that the clients can communicate seamlessly.

Bridging is one technique that can solve the shared-bandwidth problem that exists with hubs. In the hub example where we cascaded four 24-port hubs through the use of bridges, we can physically isolate each segment so that only 24 hosts compete for bandwidth; throughput is therefore increased. Similarly, with the implementation of bridges, you can also increase the number of nodes that can transmit simultaneously from one (in the case of cascading hubs) to four. Another benefit is that collision domains can be extended; that is, the physical distance between two nodes can exceed the physical limits imposed if the two nodes exist on the same segment. Logically, all of these nodes will appear to be on the same network segment.

Bridging does much for meeting the challenges of internetworking, but its implementation is limited. For instance, bridges will accommodate a maximum of seven physical segments. And although you will have made more efficient use of available bandwidth through segmentation, you can still do better with switching technologies.

Switches

A *switch* is the next rung up the evolutionary ladder from bridges. In modern star-topology networking, when you need bridging functionality you often buy a switch. But bridging is not the only benefit of switch implementation. Switches also provide the benefit of micro-LAN segmentation, which means that every node connected to a switched port receives its own dedicated bandwidth. And with Layer-3 switching, you can further segment the network into virtual LANs.

Like bridges, switches also operate at the link layers of the OSI reference model and, in the case of Layer-3 switches, sometimes extend into the network layer. The same mechanisms are used to build dynamic tables that associate MAC addresses with switched ports. However, whereas bridges implement store-and-forward bridging via software, switches implement either store-and-forward or cut-through switching via hardware, with a marked improvement of speed.

Micro-LAN segmentation is the key benefit of switches, and most organizations have either completely phased out hubs or are in the process of doing so to accommodate the throughput requirements for multimedia applications. Although switches are becoming more affordable, ranging in price from $10 to slightly over $20 per port, their price may still prevent organizations from migrating to completely switched infrastructures. At a minimum, however, servers and workgroups should be linked through switched ports.

Routers

Routers are packet-forwarding devices just like switches and bridges; however, routers allow transmission of data between network segments. Unlike switches, which forward packets based on physical node addresses, routers operate at the network layer of the OSI reference model, forwarding packets based on a network ID.

If you recall from our communication digression in the discussion on bridging, we defined a network as a logical grouping of computers and network devices. A collection of interconnected networks is referred to as an *internetwork*. Routers provide the connectivity within an internetwork.

So how do routers work? In the case of the IP protocol, an IP address is 32 bits long. Those 32 bits contain both the network ID and the host ID of a network device. IP distinguishes between network and host bits by using a subnet mask. The *subnet mask* is a set of contiguous bits with values of one from left to right, which IP considers to be the address of a network. Bits used to describe a host are masked out by a value of 0, through a binary calculation process called *ANDing*. Figure 3.20 shows two examples of network IDs calculated from an ANDing process.

FIGURE 3.20:

Calculation of IP
network IDs

192.168.145.27 / 24
Address: 11000000 10101000 10010001 00011011
Mask: 11111111 11111111 11111111 00000000
Network ID: 11000000 10101000 10010001 00000000
192.168.145.0

192.168.136.147 / 29
Address: 11000000 10101000 10001000 10010011
Mask: 11111111 11111111 11111111 11111000
Network ID: 11000000 10101000 10001000 10010000
192.168.136.144

NOTE   We use IP as the basis of our examples because it is the industry standard for enterprise networking; however, TCP/IP is not the only routable protocol suite. Novell's IPX/SPX and Apple Computer's AppleTalk protocols are also routable.

Routers are simply specialized computers concerned with getting packets from point A to point B. When a router receives a packet destined for its network interface, it examines the destination address to determine the best way to get it there. It makes the decision based on information contained within its own routing tables. Routing tables are associations of network IDs and interfaces that know how to get to that network. If a router can resolve a means to get the packet from point A to point B, it forwards it to either the intended recipient or to the next router in the chain. Otherwise, the router informs the sender that it doesn't know how to reach the destination network. Figure 3.21 illustrates communication between two hosts on different networks.

Routers enabled with the TCP/IP protocol and all networking devices configured to use TCP/IP make some sort of routing decision. All decisions occur within the IP-protocol framework. IP has other responsibilities that are beyond the scope of this book, but ultimately IP is responsible for forwarding or delivering packets. Once a destination IP address has been resolved, IP will perform an AND calculation on the IP address and subnet mask, as well as on the destination IP address to the subnet mask. IP then compares the results. If they are the same, then both devices exist on the same network segment, and no routing has to take place. If the results are different, then IP checks the devices routing table for explicit instructions on how to get to the destination network and forwards the frame to that address or sends the packet along to a default gateway (router).

FIGURE 3.21:

Host communication between internetworked segments

A detailed discussion on the inner workings of routers is well beyond the scope of this book. Internetworking product vendors such as Cisco Systems offer certifications in the configuration and deployment of their products. If you are interested in becoming certified in Cisco products, Sybex also publishes excellent study guides for the CCNA and CCNP certification exams. For a more intimate look at the inner workings of the TCP/IP protocol suite, check *TCP/IP: 24seven* by Gary Govanus (Sybex 1999).

chapter **4**

Cable System and Infrastructure Constraints

- What Are Codes, and Where Did They Come From?

- The National Electrical Code

- Knowing and Following the Codes

What constrains you when building a structured cabling system? Can you install cable anywhere you please? You probably already realize some of the restrictions of your cabling activities, including installing cable too close to electrical lines and over fluorescent lights. However, many people don't realize that documents and codes help dictate how cabling systems (both electrical as well as communications) must be designed and installed to conform to your local laws.

In the United States, governing bodies issue codes for minimum safety requirements to protect life, health, and property. Once adopted by the local regulating authority, codes have the force of law. Standards, which are guidelines to ensure system functionality after installation, are issued to ensure construction quality.

The governing body with local jurisdiction will issue codes for that locality. The codes for an area are written or adopted by and under control of the jurisdiction having authority (JHA). Sometimes these codes are called *building codes* or simply *codes*. This chapter discusses codes and how they affect the installation of communications cabling.

Where Do Codes Come From?

Building, construction, and communications codes originate from a number of different sources. Usually, these codes originate nationally rather than at the local city or county level. Local municipalities usually adopt these national codes as local laws. Other national codes are issued that affect the construction of electrical and communications equipment.

Two of the predominant national code players in the United States are the Federal Communications Commission and the National Fire Protection Association. The Americans with Disabilities Act also affects the construction of cabling and communications facilities because it requires that facilities must be constructed to provide universal access.

The United States Federal Communications Commission

The United States Federal Communications Commission (FCC) issues guidelines that govern the installation of telecommunications cabling and the design of communications devices built or used in the United States. The guidelines help to prevent problems relating to communications equipment, including interference with the operation of other communications equipment. The FCC Part 68 Rule provides regulations that specifically address connecting premises cabling and customer-provided equipment to the regulated networks.

The FCC also publishes numerous Reports and Orders. These Reports and Orders deal with specific issues regarding communications cabling, electromagnetic emissions, and frequency bandwidths. The following is a list of some of the more important documents issued by the FCC:

Part 68 Rule (FCC Rules)   Rules here govern the connection of premise equipment and wiring to the national network.

Telecommunications Act 1996   The Act establishes new rules for provisioning and additional competition in telecommunications services.

CC Docket 81-216   Rules in the docket are for providing customer-owned premise wiring.

CC Docket 85-229   Here is the Computer Inquiry III review of the regulatory framework for competition in telecommunications.

CC Docket 86-9   Policies in this docket govern shared-tenant services in commercial buildings.

Part 15 (FCC Rules)   These rules address electromagnetic radiation of equipment and cables.

CC Docket 87-124   This FCC docket addresses implementing the ADA (Americans with Disabilities Act).

CC Docket 88-57   The information here defines the location of the demarcation point on a customer premise.

Fact Sheet ICB-FC-011   The fact sheet deals with connection of one- and two-line terminal equipment to the telephone network and the installation of premises wiring.

Memorandum Opinion and Order FCC 85-343   This document covers the rights of users to access embedded complex wire on customer premises.

TIP

Most of the FCC rules, orders, and reports can be viewed on the FCC Web site at www.fcc.gov.

The National Fire Protection Association

In 1897, a group of industry professionals (insurance, electrical, architectural, and other allied interests) formed the National Association of Fire Engineers with the purpose of writing and publishing the first guidelines for the safe installation of electrical systems and providing guidance to protect people, property, and the environment from fire. The guidelines are called the *National Electrical Code* (NEC). Until 1911, the group continued to meet and update the NEC. The National Fire Protection Association (NFPA), an international, nonprofit, membership organization representing over 65,000 members and 100 countries, now sponsors the National Electrical Code. The NFPA continues to publish the NEC as well as other recommendations for a variety of safety concerns.

The National Electrical Code is updated by various committees and code-making panels, each responsible for specific subarticles in the NEC. The NEC is just one article sponsored by the NFPA, Article 70.

TIP You can find information about the NFPA and many of its codes and standards at www.nfpa.org. You can purchase NFPA codes through Global Engineering Documents (http://global.ihs.com); major codes, such as the National Electrical Code, can be purchased through almost any bookstore.

The National Fire Protection Association (NFPA) also sponsors fire and safety codes relating to telecommunications. Currently, more than 600 NFPA fire codes and standards are used in the United States and throughout the world. The following are some examples of these documents:

NFPA 1 (Fire Prevention Code) The code addresses basic fire-prevention requirements to protect buildings from hazards created by fire and explosion.

NFPA 13 (Installation of Sprinkler Systems) NFPA 13 addresses proper design and installation of sprinkler systems for all types of fires.

NFPA 54 (National Fuel Gas Code) The code provides safety requirements for fuel-gas-equipment installations, piping, and venting.

NFPA 70 (National Electrical Code) This document deals with proper installation of electrical systems and equipment.

NFPA 70B (Recommended Practice for Electrical Equipment Maintenance) NFPA 70B provides guidelines for maintenance and inspection of electrical equipment such as batteries.

NFPA 70E (Standard for Electrical Safety Requirements for Employee Workplaces)   The code is a basis for evaluating and providing electrical safety-related installation requirements, maintenance requirements, requirements for special equipment, and work practices. This document is compatible with OSHA (Occupational Safety and Health Administration) requirements.

NFPA 72 (National Fire Alarm Code)   NFPA 72 provides a guide to the design, installation, testing, use, and maintenance of fire-alarm systems.

NFPA 75 (Standard for the Protection of Electronic Computer/Data Processing Equipment)   The code establishes requirements for computer-room installations that require fire protection.

NFPA 101 (Life Safety Code)   NFPA deals with minimum building-design, construction, operation, and maintenance requirements needed to protect building occupants from fire.

NFPA 262 (Standard Method of Testing for Fire and Smoke Characteristics of Wires and Cables)   The code describes techniques for testing visible smoke and fire-spreading characteristics of wires and cables.

NFPA 780 (Standard for the Installation of Lightning Protection Systems)   NFPA 780 establishes guidelines for protection of buildings, people, and special structures from lightning strikes.

NFPA 1221 (Standard for the Installation, Maintenance, and Use of Public Fire Service Communications Systems)   NFPA 1221 provides guidance for fire-service communications systems used for emergency notification. This guide incorporates NFPA 297 (Guide on Principals and Practices for Communications Systems).

These codes are updated every few years; the NEC, for example, is updated every three years. It was updated in 1999 and will be again in 2002.

You can purchase guides to the NEC that make the code easier for the layman to understand. Like the NEC, these guides may be purchased at almost any technical or large bookstore. You can instead purchase the NEC online from the NFPA's excellent Web site at www.nfpa.org.

If you are responsible for the design of a telecommunications infrastructure, a solid understanding of the NEC is essential. Otherwise, your installation may run into all sorts of red tape from your local municipality.

TIP   The best reference on the Internet for the NEC is the National Electrical Code Internet Connection maintained by Mike Holt at `www.mikeholt.com`. You'll find useful information there for both the beginner and expert. Mike Holt is also the author of the book *Understanding the 1999 National Electrical Code*, which is an excellent reference for anyone trying to make heads or tails of the NEC.

Underwriters Laboratories

Underwriters Laboratories, Inc. (UL) is a nonprofit product-safety testing and certification organization. Once an electrical product has been tested, UL allows the manufacturer to place the UL listing mark on the product or product packaging.

KEY TERMS   **UL listed and UL recognized**   The UL mark identifies whether a product is UL *listed* or UL *recognized*. If a product carries the *UL Listing Mark* (UL in a circle) followed by the word *LISTED*, an alphanumeric control number, and the product name, the complete (all components) product has been tested against the UL's nationally recognized safety standards and found to be reasonably free of electrical-shock risk, fire risk, and other related hazards. If a product carries the *UL Recognized Component Mark* (the symbol looks like a backward *R* and *J*), it means that individual components may have been tested but not the complete product. This mark may also indicate that testing or evaluation of all the components is incomplete.

You may find a number of different UL marks on a product listed by the UL (all UL listing marks contain UL inside of a circle). Some of these include the following:

UL   This is the most common of the UL marks and indicates that samples of the complete product have met UL's safety requirements.

C-UL   This UL mark is applied to products that have been tested (by Underwriters Laboratories) according to Canadian safety requirements and can be sold in the Canadian market.

C-UL-US   This is a new listing mark that indicates compliance with both Canadian and U. S. requirements.

UL-Classified   The UL-Classified mark indicates that the product has been evaluated for a limited range of hazards or is suitable for use under limited or special conditions. Specialized equipment such as fire-fighting gear, industrial trucks, and other industrial equipment carry this mark.

C-UL-Classified   This is the classification marking for products that the UL has evaluated for specific hazards or properties, according to Canadian standards.

C-UL-Classified-US   Products with this classification marking meet the classified compliance standards for both the United States and Canada.

Recognized Component Mark (backward *R* and *J*)   Products with the backward *R* and *J* have been evaluated by the UL but are designed to be part of a larger system. Examples are the power supply, circuit board, disk drives, CD-ROM drive, and other components of a computer. The Canadian designator (a *C* preceding the Recognized Component Mark) is the Canadian equivalent.

C-Recognized Component   The marking indicates a component certified by the UL according to both the U. S. and Canadian requirements.

International EMC Mark   The electromagnetic compatibility mark indicates that the product meets the electromagnetic requirements for Europe, the United States, Japan, and Australia (or any combination of the four). In the United States, this mark is required for some products, including radios, microwaves, medical equipment, and radio-controlled equipment.

Other marks on equipment include the Food Service Product Certification mark, the Field Evaluated Product mark, the Facility Registration mark, and the Marine UL mark.

The NEC requires that a Nationally Recognized Test Laboratory (NRTL) rate communications cables used in commercial and residential products as "listed for the purpose." Usually UL is used to provide listing services, but the NEC only requires that the listing be done by an NRTL; other laboratories, therefore, can provide the same services. One such alternate testing laboratory is ETL SEMKO (www.etlsemko.com).

More than 750 UL standards and standard safety tests exist; some of the ones used for evaluating cabling-related products include the following:

UL 444   The standard applies to testing multiple conductors, jacketed cables, single or multiple coaxial cables, and optical-fiber cables. This test applies to communications cables intended to be used in accordance with the NEC Article 800 or the Canadian Electrical Code (Part I) Section 60.

UL 910   The standard applies to testing the flame spread and smoke density (visible smoke) for electrical and optical-fiber cables used in spaces that handle environmental air (that's a fancy way to say the *plenum*). This test does not investigate the level of toxic or corrosive elements in the smoke produced, nor does it cover cable construction or electrical performance. NEC Article 800 specifies that cables that have passed this test can carry the NEC flame rating designation CMP (communications multipurpose plenum).

UL 1581   UL 1581 is for testing flame-spread properties of a cable designed for general-purpose or limited use. This standard contains details of the conductors, insulation, jackets, and coverings, as well as the methods for testing preparation. The measurement and calculation specifications given in UL 1581 are used in UL 44 (Standards for the Thermoset-Insulated Wires and Cables), UL 83 (Thermoplastic-Insulated Wires and Cables), UL 62 (Flexible Cord and Fixture Wire), and UL 854 Service-Entrance Cables). NEC Article 800 specifies that cables that have passed these tests can carry the NEC flame-rating designation CMG, CM, or CMX (all of which mean communications general-purpose cable).

UL 1666   The standard applies to testing flame-propagation height for electrical and optical-fiber cables installed in vertical shafts (the riser). This test only makes sure that flames will not spread from one floor to another. It does *not* test for visible smoke, toxicity, or corrosiveness of the products' combustion. It does not evaluate the construction for any cable or the cable's electrical performance. The NEC Article 800 specifies that cables that have passed this test may carry a designation of CMR (communications riser).

UL has an excellent Web site that has summaries of all the UL standards and provides access to its newsletters. The main UL Web site is www.ul.com; a separate Web site for the UL Standards Department is located at http://ulstandardsinfonet .ul.com. UL Standards may be purchased through Global Engineering Documents on the Web at http://global.ihs.com.

Codes and the Law

At the state level in the United States, many public-utility/service commissions issue their own rules governing the installation of cabling and equipment in public buildings. States also monitor tariffs on the state's service providers.

At the local level, the state, county, city, or other authoritative jurisdiction issues codes. Most local governments issue their own codes that must be adhered to when installing communications cabling or devices in the jurisdictions under their authority. Usually, the NEC is the basis for electrical codes, but often the local code will be stricter.

Over whom the jurisdiction has authority must be determined prior to any work being initiated. Most localities have a code office, a fire marshal, or a permitting office that must be consulted.

The strictness of the local codes will vary from location to location and often reflects a particular geographic region's potential for or experience with a disaster. For example:

- Some localities in California have strict earthquake codes regarding how equipment and racks must be attached to buildings.

- In Chicago, some localities require that all cables be installed in metal conduits so that cables will not catch fire easily. This is also to help prevent flame spread that some cables may cause.

- Las Vegas has strict fire-containment codes, which require firestopping of openings between floors and firewalls. These openings may be used for running horizontal or backbone cabling.

WARNING   Local codes take precedence over all other installation guidelines. Ignorance of local codes could result in fines, having to reinstall all components, or the inability to obtain a Certificate of Occupancy.

Localities may adopt any version of the NEC or write their own codes. Don't assume that a specific city, county, or state has adopted the NEC word for word. Contact the local building-codes, construction, or building-permits department to be sure that what you are doing is legal.

Historically, telecommunications cable installations were not subject to local codes or inspections. However, during several commercial building fires, the communications cables burned and produced toxic smoke and fumes, and the smoke obscured the building's exit points. This contributed to deaths. When the smoke mixed with the water vapor, hydrochloric acid was produced, resulting in significant property damage. Because of these fires, most jurisdictions having authority now issue permits and perform inspections of the communications cabling.

It is impossible to completely eliminate toxic elements in smoke. Corrosive elements, although certainly harmful to people, are more a hazard to electronic equipment and other building facilities. The NEC flame ratings for communications cables are designed to limit the spread of the fire and, in the case of plenum cables, the production of visible smoke that could obscure exits. The strategy is to allow sufficient time for people to exit the building and to minimize potential property damage. By specifying acceptable limits of toxic or corrosive elements in the smoke and fumes, the NFPA is not trying to make the burning cables "safe." Note, however, that there are exceptions to the previous statement, notably cables used in transportation tunnels, where egress points are limited.

TIP   If a municipal building inspector inspects your cabling installation and denies you a permit (such as a Certificate of Occupancy), he or she must tell you exactly which codes you are not in compliance with.

The National Electrical Code

This section summarizes the information in the National Electrical Code (NFPA 70). All information contained in this chapter is based upon the 1999 edition of the NEC; the code is reissued every three years. Prior to installing any communications cable or devices, consult your local jurisdictions having authority to determine which codes apply to your project.

Become familiar with the local codes. Verify all interpretations with local code-enforcement officials, as enforcement of the codes is their responsibility. If you are responsible for the design of a telecommunications infrastructure or if you supervise the installation of such an infrastructure, you should own the official code documents and be intimately familiar with them.

The following list of NEC articles is not meant to be all-inclusive; it is a representation of some of the articles that may impact telecommunications installations.

The NEC is divided into chapters, articles, and sections. Technical material often refers to a specific article or section. Section 90-3 explains the arrangement of the NEC chapters. The NEC currently contains nine chapters; most chapters concern the installation of electrical cabling, equipment, and protection devices. The pertinent chapter for communications is Chapter 8. The rules governing the installation of communications cable differ from those that govern the installation of electrical cables; thus, the rules for electrical cables as stated in the NEC do not generally apply to communications cables. Section 90-3 states this by saying that Chapter 8 is independent of all other chapters in the NEC except where they are specifically referenced in Chapter 8.

This section only summarizes information from the 1999 National Electrical Code relevant to communications systems. Much of this information refers to Chapter 8 of the NEC.

NOTE   If you would like more information about the NEC, you should purchase the NEC in its entirety or a guidebook.

NEC Chapter 1 General Requirements

NEC Chapter 1 includes definitions, usage information, and descriptions of spaces about electrical equipment. Its Articles are described in the following sections.

Article 100—Definitions

Article 100 contains definitions for NEC terms that relate to the proper application of the NEC.

Article 110-3 (b)—Installation and Use

Chapter 8 references this article, among others. It states that any equipment included on a list acceptable to the local jurisdiction having authority and/or any equipment labeled as having been tested and found suitable for a specific purpose shall be installed and used in accordance with any instructions included in the listing or labeling.

Article 110-26—Spaces about Electrical Equipment

This article calls for a minimum of three feet of clear working space around all electrical equipment, to permit safe operation and maintenance of the equipment. Article 110-26 is not referenced in Chapter 8, but many standards-making bodies address the need for three feet of clear working space around communications equipment.

NEC Chapter 2 Wiring and Protection

NEC Chapter 2 includes information about conductors on poles, installation requirements for bonding, and grounding.

WARNING   Grounding is important to all electrical systems because it prevents possibly fatal electrical shock. Further information about grounding can be found in TIA/EIA-607, which is the Commercial Building Grounding and Bonding Requirements for Telecommunications standard.

The grounding information in NEC Chapter 2 that affects communications infrastructures includes the following Articles.

Article 225-14 (d)—Conductors on Poles

This article is referenced in Chapter 8 and states that conductors on poles shall have a minimum separation of one foot where not placed on racks or brackets. If a power cable is on the same pole as communications cables, the power cable (over 300 volts) shall be separated from the communications cables by not less than 30 inches. Historically, power cables have always been placed above communications cables on poles because when done so communications cables cannot inflict bodily harm to personnel working around them. Power cables, though, *can* inflict bodily harm, so they are put at the top of the pole out of the communications workers' way.

Article 250—Grounding

Article 250 covers the general requirements for the bonding and grounding of electrical-service installations. Communications cables and equipment are bonded to ground using the building electrical-entrance service ground. Several subsections in Article 250 are referenced in Chapter 8; other subsections not referenced in Chapter 8 will be of interest to communications personnel both from a safety standpoint and for effective data transmission. Buildings not properly bonded to ground are a safety hazard to all personnel. Communications systems not properly bonded to ground will not function properly.

Article 250-2 (c)—Bonding of Electrically Conductive Materials and Other Equipment

Electrically conductive materials (such as communications conduits, racks, cable trays, and cable shields) likely to become energized in a transient high-voltage situation (such as a lightning strike) shall be bonded to ground in such a manner as to establish an effective path to ground for any fault current that may be imposed.

Article 250-32—Two or More Buildings or Structures Supplied from a Common Service

This article is referenced in Chapter 8. In multibuilding campus situations, the proper bonding of communications equipment and cables is governed by several different circumstances, as follows:

> **Section 250-32 (a)—Grounding Electrode** Each building shall be bonded to ground with a grounding electrode (such as a ground rod), and all grounding electrodes shall be bonded together to form the grounding-electrode system.

> **Section 250-32 (b)—Grounded Systems** In remote buildings, grounding system shall comply with either (1) or (2):

>> **(1) Equipment-Grounding Conductor** Rules here apply where the equipment-grounding conductor is run with the electrical-supply conductors and connected to the building or structure disconnecting means and to the grounding-electrode conductors.

>> **(2) Grounded Conductor** Rules here apply where the equipment-grounding conductor is not run with the electrical-supply conductors.

> **Section 250-32 (c)—Ungrounded Systems** The electrical ground shall be connected to the building disconnecting means.

> **Section 250-32 (d)—Disconnecting Means Located in Separate Building or Structure on the Same Premises** The guidelines here apply to installing grounded circuit conductors and equipment-grounding conductors and bonding the equipment-grounding conductors to the grounding-electrode conductor in separate buildings when one main electrical service feed is to one building with the service disconnecting means and branch circuits to remote buildings. The remote buildings do not have a service disconnecting means.

> **Section 250-32 (e)—Agricultural Buildings or Structures** Buildings in which livestock are housed have special rules for bonding the buildings to ground.

> **Section 250-32 (f)—Grounding Conductor** The size of the grounding conductors per NEC Table 250-122 is discussed here.

Article 250-50—Grounding-Electrode System

The Article is referenced from Chapter 8. On premises with multiple buildings, each electrode at each building shall be bonded together to form the grounding-electrode system. The bonding conductor shall be installed in accordance with the following:

Section 250-64 (a)   Aluminum or copper-clad aluminum conductors shall not be used.

Section 250-64 (b)   The section deals with grounding-conductor installation guidelines.

Section 250-64 (e)   Metallic enclosures for the grounding-electrode conductor shall be electrically continuous.

The bonding conductor shall be sized per Section 250-66; minimum sizing is listed in NEC Table 250-66. The grounding-electrode system shall be connected per Section 250-70. An unspliced (or spliced using an exothermic welding process or an irreversible compression connection) grounding-electrode conductor shall be run to any convenient grounding electrode. The grounding electrode shall be sized for the largest grounding-electrode conductor attached to it.

WARNING   Note that interior metallic water pipes shall not be used as part of the grounding-electrode system. This is a change from how communications workers historically bonded systems to ground.

The bonding conductor shall also be installed in accordance with the following:

Section 250-50 (a)—Metal Underground Water Pipe   An electrically continuous metallic water pipe, running a minimum of 10 feet in direct contact with the earth, may be used in conjunction with a grounding electrode. The grounding electrode must be bonded to the water pipe.

Section 250-50 (b)—Metal Frame of the Building or Structure   The metal frame of a building may be used as the grounding electrode, where effectively grounded.

Section 250-50 (c)—Concrete-Encased Electrode   Very specific rules govern the use of steel reinforcing rods, embedded in concrete at the base of the building, as the grounding-electrode conductor.

Section 250-50 (d)—Ground Ring   A ground ring that encircles the building may be used as the grounding-electrode conductor if the minimum rules of this section are applied.

Article 250-52—Made and Other Electrodes

Where none of the structural electrodes specified in Section 250-50 is available, one or more of the electrodes specified in Section 250-52 (b) through (d) shall be used. *Made electrodes* are electrodes that are not an integral part of the permanent building structure. *Made rods* are installed for the sole purpose for bonding the structure to ground. They are described as follows:

Section 250-52 (b)—Other Local Metal Underground Systems or Structures   Underground pipes, tanks, or other metallic systems may be used as the grounding electrode. In certain situations, vehicles have been buried and used for the grounding electrode.

Section 250-52 (c)—Rod and Pipe Electrodes   Rods and pipes of not less than eight feet in length shall be used. Rods or pipes shall be installed in the following manner (the numbers correspond to NEC subsections):

(1)   Electrodes of pipe or conduit shall not be smaller than ¾ inch trade size and shall have an outer surface coated for corrosion protection.

(2)   Electrodes of rods of iron or steel shall be at least ⅝ inch in diameter.

(3)   The electrode shall be installed so that at least eight feet of length is in contact with the soil at an angle not more than 45 degrees from the vertical. The upper end of the electrode shall be below ground level or flush with the ground. All connections to the rod shall be protected against physical damage.

Section 250-52 (d)—Plate Electrodes   Each plate shall be at least ¼ inch in thickness installed not less than 2 ½ feet below the surface of the earth.

Article 250-60—Use of Air Terminals

This section is referenced in Article 800. *Air terminals* are commonly known as lightning rods. They must be bonded directly to ground in a specific manner. The grounding electrodes used for the air terminals shall not replace a building grounding electrode. Article 250-60 does not prohibit the bonding of all systems together. FPN (fine print note) number 2: Bonding together of all separate grounding systems will limit potential differences between them and their associated wiring systems.

Article 250-70—Methods of Grounding Conductor Connection to Electrodes

This section is referenced in Article 800 of Chapter 8. All conductors must be bonded to the grounding-electrode system. Connections made to the grounding-electrode conductor shall be made by exothermic welding, listed lugs, listed pressure connectors, listed clamps, or other listed means. Not more than one conductor shall be connected to the electrode by a single clamp.

For indoor telecommunications purposes only, a listed sheet-metal strap-type ground clamp, which has a rigid metal base and is not likely to stretch, may be used.

Article 250-92 (b)—Bonding to Other Services

An accessible means for connecting intersystem bonding and grounding shall be provided at the service entrance. This section is also referenced in Article 800, as telecommunications services must have an accessible means for connecting to the building bonding and grounding system where the telecommunications cables enter the building. The three acceptable means are as follows:

(1)   Exposed inflexible metallic service raceways.

(2)   Exposed grounding-electrode conductor.

(3)   Approved means for the external connection of a copper or other corrosion-resistant bonding or grounding conductor to the service raceway or equipment. An approved external connection is the main grounding bus-bar, which should be located in the telecommunications entrance facility.

Article 250-104—Bonding of Piping Systems and Exposed Structural Steel

Article 250-104 concerns the use of metal piping and structural steel. The following section is relevant here:

Section 250-104 (a)—Metal Water Piping   The section is referenced in Article 800. Interior metal water-piping systems may be used as bonding conductors as long as the interior metal water piping is bonded to the service-entrance enclosure, the grounded conductor at the service, or the grounding-electrode conductor or conductors.

Article 250-119—Identification of Equipment-Grounding Conductors

Equipment-grounding conductors may be bare, covered, or insulated. If covered or insulated, outer finish shall be green or green with yellow stripes. The following section is relevant:

Section 250-119 (a)—Conductors Larger Than No. 6   A conductor larger than No. 6 shall be permitted. The conductor shall be permanently identified at each end and at each point where the conductor is accessible. The conductor shall have one of the following:

(1) Stripping on the insulation or covering for the entire exposed length

(2) A green coloring or covering

(3) Marking with green tape or adhesive labels

NOTE   The bonding and grounding minimum specifications listed here are for safety. Further specifications for the bonding of telecommunication systems to the building grounding electrode are in the ANSI/TIA/EIA-607 Standard, which is discussed in detail in Chapter 2.

NEC Chapter 3 Wiring Methods and Materials

NEC Chapter 3 covers wiring methods for all wiring installations. Certain articles are of special interest to telecommunication installation personnel and are described as follows.

Article 300-11—Securing and Supporting

This article covers securing and supporting electrical and communications wiring. The following section is of interest:

Section 300-11 (a)—Secured in Place   Cables and raceways shall not be supported by ceiling grids or by the ceiling support-wire assemblies. All cables and raceways shall use an independent means of secure support and shall be securely fastened in place. This section is a new addition in the 1999 code. Currently, any wires supported by the ceiling assembly are "grandfathered" and do not have to be rearranged. So if noncompliant ceiling assemblies existed before NEC 1999 was published, they can remain in place. A ceiling or the ceiling support wires cannot support new installations of cable; the cables must have their own independent means of secure support.

Ceiling support wires may be used to support cables; however, those support wires shall not be used to support the ceiling. The cable support wires must be distinguished from the ceiling support wires by color, tags, or other means. Cable support wires shall be secured to the ceiling assembly.

Article 300-21—Spread of Fire or Products of Combustion

Installations of cable in hollow spaces such as partition walls, vertical shafts, and ventilation spaces such as ceiling areas shall be made so that the spread of fire is not increased. Communications cables burn rapidly and produce poisonous smoke and gasses. If openings are created or used through walls, floors, ceilings, or fire-rated partitions, they shall be firestopped. If a cable is not properly firestopped, a fire can follow the cable (remember the movie *Towering Inferno*?). A basic rule of thumb is this: If a hole exists, firestop it. Firestop manufacturers have tested and approved design guidelines that must be followed when firestopping any opening.

WARNING   Consult with your local jurisdiction having authority prior to installing any firestop.

Article 300-22—Wiring in Ducts, Plenums, and Other Air-Handling Spaces

This Article applies to using communications and electrical cables in air ducts and the plenum. The following sections go into detail:

> **Section 300-22 (a)—Ducts for Dust, Loose Stock, or Vapor Removal**
> No wiring of any type shall be installed in ducts used to transport dust, loose stock, or flammable vapors or for ventilation of commercial cooking equipment.

> **Section 300-22 (b)—Ducts or Plenums Used for Environmental Air**   If cables will be installed in a duct used to transport environmental air, the cable must be enclosed in a metal conduit or metallic tubing. Flexible metal conduit is allowed for a maximum length of four feet.

Section 300-22 (c)—Other Space Used for Environmental Air   The space over a hung ceiling, which is used for the transport of environmental air, is an example of the type of space to which this section applies. Cables and conductors installed in environmental air-handling spaces must be listed for the use; e.g., a plenum-rated cable must be installed in a plenum-rated space. Other cables or conductors that are not listed for use in environmental air-handling spaces shall be installed in electrical metallic tubing, metal conduit, or solid-bottom metal cable tray with solid metal covers.

Section 300-22 (d)—Information Technology Equipment   Electric wiring in air-handling spaces beneath raised floors for information-technology equipment shall be permitted in accordance with Article 645.

NEC Chapter 5 Special Occupancy

NEC Chapters 1 through 3 apply to residential and commercial facilities. NEC Chapter 5 deals with areas that may need special consideration, including those that may be subject to flammable or hazardous gas and liquids and that have electrical or communications cabling.

Articles 500 through 504

Articles 500 through 504 cover the requirements for electrical and electronic equipment and wiring for all voltages in locations where fire or explosion hazards may exist. Flammable gases or vapors, flammable liquids, combustible dust, or fibers that may ignite may cause such conditions. This article also specifies that all areas designated as hazardous (classified) locations shall be properly documented. This documentation shall be available to those authorized to design, install, inspect, maintain, or operate electrical equipment at the location. This article further references other standards from the National Fire Protection Association, the American Petroleum Institute, and the Instrument Society of America.

NOTE   For more information on installing wiring and systems in hazardous locations, see Articles 501-4 (a), 501-5 (a) and (c), 501-14, 502-4 (a), 502-14, and 503-12. All of these articles are referenced in Article 800.

NEC Chapter 7 Special Conditions

NEC Chapter 7 deals with low-power systems such as signaling and fire-control systems.

Article 725-1—Scope

This article covers remote-control, signaling, and power-limited circuits that are not an integral part of a device or appliance (for example, safety-control equipment and building-management systems). The article covers the types of conductors to be used, their insulation, and conductor support.

Article 760—Fire-Alarm Systems

Fire-alarm systems are not normally considered part of the communications infrastructure, but the systems and wiring used for fire-alarm systems are becoming increasingly integrated into the rooms and spaces designated for communications. As such, all applicable codes must be followed. Codes of particular interest to communications personnel are as follows:

Section 760-61 (d)—Cable Uses and Permitted Substitutions   Multiconductor communications cables CMP, CMR, CMG, and CM are permitted substitutions for Class 2 and 3 general- and limited-use communication cable. Class 2 or 3 riser cable can be substituted for CMP or CMR cable. Class 2 or 3 plenum cable can only be substituted with CMP or MPP plenum cable. Coaxial, single-conductor cable MPP (multipurpose plenum), MPR (multipurpose riser), MPG (multipurpose general), and MP (multipurpose) are permitted substitutions for FPLP (fire-protective signal cable plenum), FPLR (fire-protective signal cable riser), and FPL (fire-protective signal cable general use) cable.

Section 760-71 (b)—Conductor Size   The size of conductors in a multiconductor cable shall not be smaller than AWG 26. Single conductors shall not be smaller than AWG 18. Standard multiconductor communications cables are AWG 24 or larger. Standard coaxial cables are AWG 16 or larger.

Article 770—Optical-Fiber Cables and Raceways

The provisions of this article apply to the installation of optical-fiber cables, which transmit light for control, signaling, and communications. This article also applies to the raceways that contain and support the optical-fiber cables. The provisions of this article are for the safety of the installation personnel and users coming in contact with the optical-fiber cables; as such, installation personnel should follow the manufacturers' guidelines and recommendations for the installation specifics on the particular fiber being installed. Three types of optical fiber are defined in the NEC:

Nonconductive   Optical-fiber cables that contain no metallic members or other conductive materials are nonconductive. It is important for personnel to know whether a cable contains metallic members. Cables containing metallic members may become energized by transient voltages or currents, which may cause harm to the personnel touching the cables.

Conductive   Cables that contain a metallic strength member or other metallic armor or sheath are conductive. The conductive metallic members in the cable are for the support and protection of the optical fiber—not for conducting electricity or signals—but they may become energized and should be tested for foreign voltages and currents prior to handling.

Composite   Cables that contain optical fibers and current-carrying electrical conductors, such as signaling copper pairs, are composite. Composite cables are classified as electrical cables and should be tested for voltages and currents prior to handling. All codes applying to copper conductors apply to composite optical-fiber cables.

Article 770-6—Raceways for Optical-Fiber Cables

Plastic raceways for optical-fiber cables, otherwise known as *innerducts*, shall be listed for the space they occupy; for example: a general listing for a general space, a riser listing for a riser space, or a plenum listing for a plenum space. The optical fiber occupying the innerduct must also be listed for the space. Unlisted-underground or outside-plant innerduct shall be terminated at the point of entrance.

Article 770-8—Mechanical Execution of Work

Optical-fiber cables shall be installed in a neat and workmanlike manner. Cables and raceways shall be supported by the building structure. The support structure for the optical fibers and raceways must be attached to the structure of the building, not attached to a ceiling, lashed to a pipe or conduit, or laid in on ductwork.

Article 770-50—Listings, Marking, and Installation of Optical-Fiber Cables

Optical-fiber cables shall be listed as suitable for the purpose; cables shall be marked in accordance with NEC Table 770-50. Most manufacturers put the marking on the optical-fiber cable jacket every two to four feet. The code does not tell you what type of cable to use (such as single-mode or multimode), just that the cable should be resistant to the spread of fire. For fire-resistance and cable markings for optical cable, see Table 4.1.

TABLE 4.1:   Optical Cable Markings from NEC Table 770-50

Marking	Description
OFNP	Nonconductive optical-fiber plenum cable
OFCP	Conductive optical-fiber plenum cable
OFNR	Nonconductive optical-fiber riser cable
OFCR	Conductive optical-fiber riser cable
OFNG	Nonconductive optical-fiber general-purpose cable
OFCG	Conductive optical-fiber general-purpose cable
OFN	Nonconductive optical-fiber general-purpose cable
OFC	Conductive optical-fiber general-purpose cable

The markings are described as follows:

Section 770-50 (a)—Types OFNP and OFCP   Cables with these markings are for use in plenums, ducts, and other spaces used for handling environmental air. These cables have adequate fire resistance and low smoke-producing characteristics.

Section 770-50 (b)—Types OFNR and OFCR   These markings indicate cable for use in a vertical shaft or from floor to floor. These cables have fire-resistant characteristics capable of preventing the spread of fire from floor to floor.

Section 770-50 (c)—Types OFNG and OFCG   Cables with these designations are for use in spaces not classified as a plenum and are for general use on one floor. These cables are fire resistant.

Section 770-50 (d)—Types OFN and OFC   These cables are for the same use as OFNG and OFCG cables. OFN and OFC have the same characteristics as OFNG and OFCG, though they must meet different flame tests.

Article 770-52—Optical-Fiber Raceways

This article defines the types of raceways that should be used in various situations. They are described as follows:

Section 770-52 (a)—Plenum raceways   These raceways have adequate fire-resistant and low smoke-producing characteristics. Plenum raceways must be used in plenum-rated areas. Plenum-rated cable is the only type cable that may occupy the plenum-rated raceway.

Section 770-52 (b)—Riser raceways   Riser raceways have fire-resistant characteristics to prevent the spread of fire from floor to floor and must be used in the riser.

Section 770-52 (c)—General-Purpose Raceways   General-purpose raceways are fire resistant and used in general nonplenum areas, or they travel from floor to floor.

Section 770-52 (d)—Cable Trays   Optical-fiber cables of the proper listing may be installed in cable trays with other low-voltage communication, remote-control, signaling, and network cables.

Article 770-53—Cable Substitutions

No substitution is permitted for an OFNP cable, but an OFNP cable may be substituted for any other listed cable.

NEC Chapter 8 Communications Systems

NEC Chapter 8 is the section of the NEC that directly affects the design and installation of a telecommunications infrastructure.

Article 800-1—Scope

This article covers telephone, telegraph, outside wiring for alarms, paging systems, building-management systems, and other central station systems.

NOTE   For the purposes of this chapter, we define *cable* as a factory assembly of two or more conductors having an overall covering.

Article 800-6—Mechanical Execution of Work

Cables and equipment shall be installed in a neat and workmanlike manner. Cables shall be supported by the building structure and installed in such a manner that they will not be damaged by normal building use.

Article 800-7—Hazardous Locations

Cables and equipment installed in hazardous locations shall be installed in accordance with Article 500.

Article 800-10—Overhead Wires and Cables

Cables entering buildings from overhead poles shall be located on the pole on different crossarms from power conductors; the crossarms for communications cables shall be located below the crossarms for power. Sufficient climbing space must be between the communications cables in order for someone to reach the power cables. A minimum distance separation of 12 inches must be maintained from power cables.

Article 800-11—Underground Circuits Entering Buildings

In a raceway system underground, such as one composed of conduits, communications raceways shall be separated from electric-cable raceways with brick, concrete, or tile partitions. The following subsection is of interest:

> **Section 800-11 (c)—Point of Entry**   New to the 1999 NEC, wiring and cables for communications shall enter a building within 20 feet of the electrical-service entry point. Separate rooms should be maintained for power and communications, but the service entry rooms shall be within 20 feet of each other for grounding purposes.

Article 800-30—Circuits Requiring Primary Protectors

A listed primary protector shall be provided on each circuit run partly or entirely in aerial wire and on each circuit that may be exposed to accidental contact with electric light or power. Primary protection shall also be installed on circuits in a multibuilding environment on premises in which the circuits run from building to building and in which a lightning exposure exists. A circuit is considered to have lightning exposure unless one of the following conditions exists:

(1)   The buildings are sufficiently high to intercept lightning (such as circuits in a large metropolitan area). Chances of lightning hitting a cable are minimal; the lightning will strike a building and be carried to ground through the lightning-protection system. Furthermore, Article 800-13 states that a separation of at least six feet shall be maintained from lightning conductors; do not attach cable to lightning conductors, run cable parallel with them, or lay your cables across them. Stay as far away from the lightning-protection systems as possible.

(2)   Direct burial or underground cable runs 140 feet or less with a continuous metallic shield or in a continuous metallic conduit where the metallic shield or conduit is bonded to the building grounding-electrode system. An underground cable with a metallic shield or in metallic conduit that has been bonded to ground will carry the lightning to ground prior to its entering the building. If the conduit or metallic shields have not been bonded to ground, the lightning will be carried into the building on the cable, which could result in personnel hazards and equipment damage.

(3)   The area has an average of five or fewer thunderstorm days per year with an earth resistance of less than 100 ohm-meters.

Very few areas in the United States meet any one of these criteria. It is required that customers in areas that do meet any one of these criteria install primary protection. Primary protection is inexpensive compared to the people and equipment it protects. When in doubt, install primary protection on all circuits entering buildings no matter where the cables originate or how they travel.

Several types of primary protectors are permitted by the National Electrical Code:

Fuseless primary protectors   Fuseless primary protectors are permitted under any of the following conditions:

- Noninsulated conductors enter the building through a cable with a grounded metallic sheath, and the conductors in the cable safely fuse on all currents greater than the current-carrying capacity of the primary protector. This protects all circuits in an overcurrent situation.

- Insulated conductors are spliced onto a noninsulated cable with a grounded metallic sheath. The insulated conductors are used to extend circuits into a building. All conductors or connections between the insulated conductors and the exposed plant must safely fuse in an overcurrent situation.

- Insulated conductors are spliced onto noninsulated conductors without a grounded metallic sheath. A fuseless primary protector is allowed in this case only if the primary protector is listed for this purpose or the connections of the insulated cable to the exposed cable or the conductors of the exposed cable safely fuse in an overcurrent situation.

- Insulated conductors are spliced onto unexposed cable.

- Insulated conductors are spliced onto noninsulated cable with a grounded metallic sheath, and the combination of the primary protector and the insulated conductors safely fuse in an overcurrent situation.

Fused primary protectors   If the requirements for fuseless primary protectors are not met, a fused type primary protector shall be used. The fused-type protector shall consist of an arrester connected between each line conductor and ground.

The primary protector shall be located in, on, or immediately adjacent to the structure or building served and as close as practical to the point at which the exposed conductors enter or attach to the building. In a residential situation, primary protectors are located on an outside wall where the drop arrives at the house. In a commercial building, the primary protector is located in the space where the outside cable enters the building. The primary-protector location should also be the one that offers the shortest practicable grounding conductor to the primary protector to limit potential differences between communications circuits and other metallic systems. The primary protector shall not be located in any hazardous location nor in the vicinity of easily ignitable material.

Article 800-32—Secondary Protector Requirements

Secondary protection shunts to ground any currents or voltages that are passed through the primary protector. Secondary protectors shall be listed for this purpose and shall be installed behind the primary protector. Secondary protectors provide a means to safely limit currents to less than the current-carrying capacity of the communications wire and cable, listed telephone-line cords, and listed communications equipment that has ports for external communications circuits.

Article 800-33—Cable Grounding

The metallic sheath of a communications cable entering a building shall be grounded as close to the point of entrance into the building as practicably possible. The sheath shall be opened to expose the metallic sheath, which shall then be grounded. In some situations, it may be necessary to remove a section of the metallic sheath to form a gap. Each section of the metallic sheath shall then be bonded to ground.

Article 800-40—Primary-Protector Grounding

Primary protectors shall be grounded in one of the following ways:

Section 800-40 (a)—Grounding Conductor Insulation   The grounding conductor shall be insulated and listed as suitable for the purpose. The following criteria apply:

Material   The grounding conductor shall be copper or other corrosion-resistant conductive material and either stranded or solid.

Size   The grounding conductor shall not be smaller than 14 AWG (American Wire Gauge).

Run in a straight line   The grounding conductor shall be run in as straight a line as possible.

Physical damage   The grounding conductor shall be guarded from physical damage. If the grounding conductor is run in a metal raceway (such as conduit), both ends of the metal raceway shall be bonded to the grounding conductor.

Section 800-40 (b)—Electrode   The grounding conductor shall be attached to the grounding electrode as follows:

- It should be attached to the nearest accessible location on the building or structure grounding-electrode system, the grounded interior metal water-pipe system, the power-service external enclosures, the metallic power raceway, or the power-service equipment enclosure.

- If a building has no grounding means from the electrical service, install the grounding conductor to an effectively grounded metal structure or a ground rod or pipe of not less than five feet in length and ½ inch in diameter, driven into permanently damp earth and separated at least six feet from lightning conductors or electrodes from other systems.

Section 800-40 (d)—Bonding of Electrodes If a separate grounding electrode is installed for communications, it must be bonded to the electrical electrode system with a conductor not smaller than AWG 6. Bonding together of all electrodes will limit potential differences between them and their associated wiring systems.

Article 800-50—Listings, Markings, and Installation of Communications Wires and Cables

Communications wires and cables installed in buildings shall be listed as suitable for the purpose and marked in accordance with NEC Table 800-50. Listings and markings shall not be required on a cable that enters from the outside and where the length of the cable within the building, measured from its point of entrance, is less than 50 feet. It is possible to install an unlisted cable more than 50 feet into a building from the outside, but it must be totally enclosed in rigid metal conduit. Outside cables may not be extended 50 feet into a building if it is feasible to place the primary protector closer than 50 feet to the entrance point. Table 4.2 refers to the contents of NEC Table 800-50.

TABLE 4.2: Copper Communications-Cable Markings from NEC Table 800-5

Marking	Description
MPP	Multipurpose plenum cable
CMP	Communications plenum cable
MPR	Multipurpose riser cable
CMR	Communications riser cable
MPG	Multipurpose general-purpose cable
CMG	Communications general-purpose cable
MP	Multipurpose general-purpose cable
CM	Communications general-purpose cable
CMX	Communications cable, limited use
CMUC	Under-carpet communications wire and cable

Article 800-50—Listing Requirements for Communications Wires and Cables and Communications Raceways

Conductors in communications cables, other than coaxial, shall be copper. The listings are described as follows:

Section 800-50 (a)—Type CMP   Type CMP cable is suitable for use in ducts, plenums, and other spaces used for environmental air. CMP cable shall have adequate fire-resistant and low smoke-producing characteristics.

Section 800-50 (b)—Type CMR   Type CMR cable is suitable for use in a vertical run from floor to floor and shall have fire-resistant characteristics capable of preventing the spreading of fire from floor to floor.

Section 800-50 (c)—Type CMG   Type CMG is for general use, not for use in plenums or risers. Type CMG is resistant to the spread of fire.

Section 800-50 (d)—Type CM   Type CM is suitable for general use, not for use in plenums or risers; it is also resistant to the spread of fire.

Section 800-50 (e)—Type CMX   Type CMX cable is used in residential dwellings. It is resistant to the spread of fire.

Section 800-50 (f)—Type CMUC   Type CMUC is a cable made specifically for under-carpet use; it may not be used in any other place, nor can any other cable be installed under carpets. It is resistant to flame spread.

Section 800-50 (g)—Multipurpose (MP) Cables   Multiconductor and coaxial cables meeting the same requirements as communications cables shall be listed and marked as MPP, MPR, MPG, and MP.

Section 800-50 (h)—Communications Wires   Wires and cables used as cross-connects or patch cables in communications rooms or spaces shall be listed as being resistant to the spread of fire.

Section 800-50 (i)—Hybrid Power and Communications Cable   Hybrid power and communications cables are permitted if they are listed and rated for 600 volts minimum and are resistant to the spread of fire. These cables are allowed only in general-purpose spaces, not in risers or plenums.

Section 800-50 (j)—Plenum Communications Raceway   Plenum-listed raceways are allowed in plenum areas; they shall have low smoke-producing characteristics and be resistant to the spread of fire.

Section 800-50 (k)—Riser Communications Raceway   Riser-listed raceways have adequate fire-resistant characteristics capable of preventing the spread of fire from floor to floor.

Section 800-50 (l)—General-Purpose Communications Raceway   General-purpose raceways have adequate fire-resistant characteristics.

Article 800-52—Installation of Communications Wires, Cables, and Equipment

This article defines the installation of communications wires, cables, and equipment with respect to electrical-power wiring. The following sections are of note:

Section 800-52 (a)   Communications wires and cables are permitted in the same raceways and enclosures with the following power-limited types: remote-control circuits, signaling circuits, fire-alarm systems, nonconductive and conductive optical-fiber cables, community antenna and radio distribution systems, and low-power network-powered broadband-communications circuits.

Section 800-52 (c) (1)   Communications cables or wires shall not be placed in any raceway, compartment, outlet box, junction box, or similar fitting with any conductors of electrical power. The following requirements also apply:

Other Applications   Communications cables and wires shall be separated from electrical conductors by at least two inches, but the more separation the better. The NEC and the ANSI standards no longer give minimum power separations from high-voltage power and equipment because it has been found that separation is generally not enough to shield communications wires and cables from the induced noise of high power. Concrete, tiles, grounded metal conduits, or some other form of insulating barrier may be necessary to shield communications from power.

Spread of Fire or Products of Combustion   Openings around penetrations through walls, floors, ceilings, or partitions shall be firestopped using approved methods.

Knowing and Following the Codes

Knowing and following electrical and building codes is of utmost importance. If you don't, at the very least you may have problems with building inspectors. But more importantly, an installation that does not meet building codes may endanger the lives of the building's occupants.

Furthermore, even if you are an information-technology director or network manager, being familiar with the codes that affect the installation of your cabling infrastructure can help you when working with cabling and electrical contractors. Knowing your local codes can also help you when working with your local, city, county, or state officials.

chapter 5

Cabling System Components

- The Cable

- Wall Plates and Connectors

- Cabling Pathways

- Wiring Closets

Pick up any cabling catalog, and you will find a plethora of components and associated buzzwords that you never dreamed existed. Terms such as *patch panel*, *wall plate*, *plenum*, *110-block*, *66-block*, *modular jacks*, *raceways*, and *patch cables* are just a few. What do they all mean, and how are these components used to create a structured cabling system?

In this chapter, we'll provide an overview and descriptions of the inner workings of a structured cabling system so that you won't feel so confused next time you pick up a cabling catalog or work with professional cabling installers. Topics in this chapter include the following:

- Picking the right type of cable

- Fire safety and cabling products

- Cabling components in workstation areas

- Concealing cables and protecting fiber-optic cable

- Telecommunications closets

- Networking components often found in a telecommunications closet

The Cable

In Chapter 2, we discussed the various cable media recommended by the ANSI/TIA/EIA-568-A Commercial Building Telecommunications Cabling Standard and some of the cables' performance characteristics. Rather than repeating the characteristics of available cable media, we'll describe the components involved in transmitting data from the work area to the wiring closet. These major cable components are horizontal cable, backbone cable, and patch cable.

Horizontal and Backbone Cables

The terms *horizontal cable* and *backbone* (sometimes called *vertical* or *riser*) *cable* have nothing to do with the cable's physical orientation toward the horizon. Horizontal cables run between a cross-connect panel in a wiring closet and a wall jack. Backbone cables run between wiring closets and the main cross-connect point of a building (usually referred to as the *equipment room*). Figure 5.1 illustrates the typical components found in a structured cabling environment, including the horizontal cable, backbone cable, telecommunication outlets, and patch cables.

FIGURE 5.1:

Typical components found in a structured cabling system

More information on horizontal and backbone cabling can be found in Chapter 2. Installing copper cabling for use with horizontal or backbone cabling is discussed in Chapter 7.

Horizontal Cables

Horizontal runs are usually implemented with 100-ohm, four-pair, unshielded twisted-pair (UTP), solid-conductor cables, as specified in the ANSI/TIA/EIA-568 Standard for commercial buildings. The Standard also provides for horizontal cabling to be implemented using 150-ohm shielded twisted-pair (STP) cable, 62.5/125-micron multimode optical fiber, and 50-ohm coaxial cable. Coaxial cable will be dropped from the recognized media in the *B* version of the 568 Standard, which is still in the revision process for copper cables.

Backbone Cables

As with horizontal cables, backbone cables can be implemented using 100-ohm UTP, 150-ohm STP, 62.5/125-micron multimode optical fiber, or 8.3/125-micron single-mode optical cable. Optical fiber is the preferred installation medium because of distance limitations associated with copper wiring. Another plus for running a fiber backbone is that glass does not conduct electricity and is thus not subject to electromagnetic interference (EMI) like copper is.

Modular Patch Cables

Modular patch cables (patch cords) are used to provide the connection between field-terminated horizontal cables and network-connectivity devices such as switches and hubs. As the saying goes, a chain is only as strong as its weakest link. Because of their role in structured cable infrastructures, modular patch cords are almost always the weakest link.

Whereas horizontal cables contain solid conductors, patch cords are made with stranded conductors because they are more flexible. The flexibility allows them to withstand the abuse of frequent flexing and reconnecting. Although you could build your own field-terminated patch cords, we strongly recommend against it.

The manufacture of patch cords is very exacting, and even under controlled factory conditions it is difficult to achieve and guarantee consistent transmission performance. The first challenge lies within the modular plugs themselves. The parallel alignment of the contact blades forms a capacitive plate, which becomes a source of signal coupling or crosstalk. Further, the untwisting and splitting of the pairs as a result of the termination process increases the cable's susceptibility to crosstalk interference. If that weren't enough, the mechanical crimping process that secures the plug to the cable could potentially disturb the cable's normal geometry by crushing the conductor pairs. This is yet another source of crosstalk interference and a source of attenuation.

TIP   Modular cords that have been factory terminated and tested are required to achieve consistent transmission performance.

At first glance, modular patch cords may seem like a no-brainer, but they may actually be the most crucial component to accurately specify. When specifying patch cables, you may also require that your patch cords be tested to ensure that they meet the proper transmission-performance standards for their category.

Pick the Right Cable for the Job

Professional cable installers and cable-plant designers are called upon to interpret and/or draft cable specifications to fulfill businesses' structured-cabling requirements. Anyone purchasing cable for business or home use may also be required to make a decision regarding what type of cable to use. Installing inappropriate cable could be very unfortunate in the event of a disaster such as a fire.

What do we mean by unfortunate? It is very conceivable that the cable-plant designer or installer could be held accountable in court and held responsible for damages incurred as a result of substandard cable installation. Cables come in a variety of different ratings, and many of these ratings have to do with how well the cable will fare in a fire.

Using the general overview information provided in Chapter 1 and the more specific information in Chapters 2 though 4, you should now have adequate information to specify the proper cable for your installation.

First, you must know the installation environment and what the applicable NEC and local fire-code requirements will allow regarding the cables' flame ratings. In a commercial building, this usually comes down to where plenum-rated cables must be installed and where a lower rating (usually CMR) is acceptable.

Your second decision on cabling must be on media type. The large majority of new installations use fiber-optic cable in the backbone and UTP cable for the horizontal.

For fiber cable, you will need to specify single-mode or multimode, and if it is multimode, you will need to specify core diameter, i.e., 62.5/125 or 50/125. For UTP cables, you need to specify the appropriate transmission-performance category. Most new installations today use Category 5e. There is somewhat of a migration to Category 6, even though a national standard does not yet exist and users must rely on vendor-specific specifications for a Category 6 cabling system. Make sure that you specify that patch cords be rated in the same category as, or higher than, the horizontal cable.

NOTE　　　See the InfraTech, Inc. white paper *Warranty Liability* for some interesting information on warranties, cable testing, and the critical issues surrounding cabling. It can be found on the Internet at `www.totalcomsolution.com`.

Wall Plates and Connectors

Wall plates and connectors serve as the work-area endpoints for horizontal cable runs. In addition to wall plates, you have the option of installing surface and/or floor-mounted boxes in your work area. Using these information outlets or telecommunications outlets helps you organize your cables and aid in protecting horizontal wiring from end users. Without the modularity provided by information outlets, you would wind up wasting a significant amount of cable trying to accommodate all the possible computer locations within a client's work area—the excess cable would most likely wind up as an unsightly coil in a corner.

NOTE   Refer to Chapter 8 for more information on wall plates.

The drawback of information outlets is that they require you to introduce another patch cable into your cabling equation, and we've already discussed the issues regarding patch-cable reliability and performance.

Wall plates and surface- and floor-mounted boxes come in a variety of colors to match your office's decor. Companies such as Ortronics, Panduit, and The Siemon Company also offer products that can be used with modular office furniture. The Siemon Company even went one step further and integrated its telecommunications cabling system into its own line of office furniture called MACsys. Figure 5.2 shows a sample faceplate from the Ortronics TracJack line of faceplates.

FIGURE 5.2:

Ortronic's TracJack faceplates

(Photo courtesy of Ortronics)

To help ensure that a cable's proper bend radius is maintained, Panduit and The Siemon Company offer angled modules to snap into their faceplates. Figure 5.3 shows The Siemon Company's CT faceplates and MAX series angled modules. Faceplates with angled modules for patch cords keep the cord from sticking straight out and becoming damaged.

FIGURE 5.3:

The Siemon Company's CT faceplates and MAX series angled modules

(Photo courtesy of The Siemon Company)

In addition to modular connectors for twisted-pair cable, connectors also exist for optical fiber, coaxial, and even audio/video cable.

Cabling Pathways

In this section, we'll look at the cabling-system components outlined by the ANSI/ TIA/ EIA-569-A Commercial Building Telecommunications Pathways and Spaces Standard for concealing, protecting, and routing your cable plant. In particular, we'll describe the components used in work areas and wiring closets and for horizontal and backbone cable runs. As you read these descriptions, you'll notice they all must be electrically grounded per the ANSI/TIA/EIA-607 Commercial Building Grounding and Bonding Requirements for Telecommunications.

Conduit

Conduit is pipe. It can be metallic or nonmetallic, rigid or flexible (as permitted by the applicable electrical code), and it runs from a work area to a wiring closet. One advantage of using conduit to hold your cables is that it may already exist in your building. Assuming the pipe has space, it shouldn't take long to pull your cables through it. A drawback to conduit is that it provides a finite amount of space to house cables. When drafting specifications for conduit, we recommend that you require that enough conduit be installed so that it would be only 40 percent full by your current cable needs. Conduit should only be filled to a maximum of 60 percent, so this margin leaves you with room for future growth.

According to the ANSI/TIA/EIA-569-A, standard conduit can be used to route horizontal and backbone cables. Firestopped conduit can also be used to connect wiring closets in multistoried buildings. Some local building codes require the use of conduit for *all* cable, both telecommunication and electrical.

In no cases should communication cables be installed in the same conduit as electrical cables without a physical barrier between them. Aside from (and because of) the obvious potential hazard, it is not allowed by the NEC.

Cable Trays

As an alternative to conduit, *cable trays* can be installed to route your cable. Cable trays are typically wire racks specially designed to support the weight of a cable infrastructure. They provide an ideal way to manage a large number of horizontal runs. Cables simply lie within the tray, so they are very accessible when it comes to maintenance and troubleshooting. The ANSI/TIA/EIA-569-A Standard provides for cable trays to be used for both horizontal and backbone cables.

Figure 5.4 shows a cable runway system. This type of runway looks like a ladder that is mounted horizontally inside the ceiling space or over the top of equipment racks in a telecommunications closet or equipment room. In the ceiling space, this type of runway keeps cables from being draped over the top of fluorescent lights,

HVAC equipment, or ceiling tiles; they are also helpful in keeping cable from crossing electrical conduit. Separating the cable is especially useful near telecommunication closets and equipment rooms where there may be much horizontal cable coming together. When used in a telecommunications or equipment room, this runway can keep cables off the floor or run from a rack of patch panels to an equipment rack.

FIGURE 5.4:

A runway system used to suspend cables overhead

J-hooks

Ladder racks for managing cables in equipment room, in telecommunications closet, or in the plenum

19" rack

Another type of cable-suspension device is the CADDY CatTrax from Erico. These cable trays are flexible, easy to install, and can be installed in the ceiling space, telecommunications closet, or equipment room. The CatTrax (shown in Figure 5.5) also keeps cables from being laid directly onto the ceiling tile of a false ceiling or across lights and electrical conduit because it provides continuous support for cables.

FIGURE 5.5:

The CADDY CatTrax flexible
cable tray from Erico

(Photo courtesy of Erico)

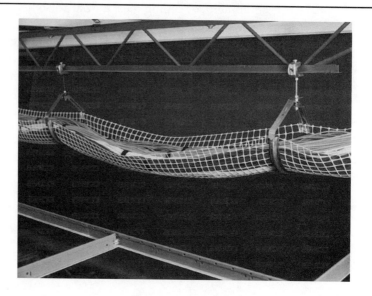

TIP   Numerous alternatives to cable-tray supports exist. One of the most common is a J hook. J hooks are metal supports in the shape of an *L* or *J* that attach to beams, columns, walls, or the structural ceiling. Cables are simply draped from hook to hook. Spacing of hooks should be from four feet to five feet maximum, and the intervals should vary slightly to avoid the creation of harmonic intervals that may affect transmission performance.

Raceways

Raceways are special types of conduits used for surface mounting horizontal cables and are usually pieced together in a modular fashion with vendors providing connectors that do not exceed the minimum bend radius. Raceways are mounted on the outside of a wall in places where cable is not easily installed inside the wall; they are commonly used on walls made of brick or concrete, where no telecommunications conduit has been installed. To provide for accessibility and modularity, raceways are manufactured in components (see Figure 5.6). Figure 5.7 shows a sample of a surface-mount raceway carrying a couple of different cables; this raceway is hinged to allow cables to be easily installed.

FIGURE 5.6:

A surface-mounted modular raceway system

(Photo courtesy of MilesTek)

FIGURE 5.7:

A sample surface-mount raceway with cables

(Photo courtesy of The Siemon Company)

One-piece systems usually provide a flexible joint for opening the raceway to access cables; after opening, the raceway can be snapped shut. To meet information-output needs, raceway vendors often produce modular connectors to integrate with their raceway systems.

Fiber-Protection Systems

As with raceways, *fiber-protection systems* (see Figure 5.8) are special types of conduits and cable-management systems designed specifically to address the special protection needs of optical-fiber cable. Although maintaining proper bend radius is important for all cable media, severe bends in optical-fiber cable will result in attenuation and eventual signal loss, which translates to lost data, troubleshooting, downed network connections, and lost productivity. Severe bends can also lead to cracking and physical failure of the fiber. To protect your fiber investment, we recommend that you consider investing in a fiber-protection system.

FIGURE 5.8:

The Siemon Company's LightWays fiber-protection system

(Photo courtesy of The Siemon Company)

KEY TERM   **Inner Duct**   *Inner duct* is a flexible, plastic conduit system often used inside a larger conduit; fiber-optic cable is run through it for an additional layer of protection.

When evaluating a prospective fiber-protection system, you should account for the total cost of the installation rather than the cost of materials. Also ensure that it will support the weight of your cable without sagging. In addition, because your network will grow with time, you should consider how flexible the solution will be for future modifications. Will you be able to add new segments or vertical drops without having to move existing cable? The most expensive part of your system will be the labor costs associated with the installation. Does the system require special tools to install, or does it snap together in a modular fashion?

Wiring Closets

The *wiring closet* is where your network begins. Up to this point, we've described the components required to bring your end users to this common ground, the foundation of the digital nervous system. In this section, we'll cover the types of wiring closets, along with suggested design elements. From there, we'll discuss the pieces of equipment found within a typical closet. We'll conclude with a brief discussion on network devices.

A Wiring Closet by Any Other Name

Wiring closets are known by a number of names and acronyms. Although some cabling professionals use the term *wiring closets*, others call them *intermediate cross-connects* (ICCs) or *intermediate distribution frames* (IDFs). The ANSI/TIA/EIA-568-A Standard refers to wiring closets as *telecommunications closets*. They are usually remote locations in a large or multistory building.

The wiring closets are all connected to a central wiring center known by the ANSI/TIA/EIA-568-A Standard as an *equipment room* (or *telecommunications room*). Other cabling professionals call this the *main distribution frame* (MDF) or the *main cross-connect* (MCC.)

Intermediate cross-connect, main distribution frame, and main cross-connect are incomplete descriptions of the rooms' purposes because modern systems require the housing of electronic gear in addition to the cross-connect frames, main or intermediate.

Horizontal cabling is run from telecommunications closets to the workstation areas. Backbone cabling runs from the telecommunications closets to the equipment rooms and between telecommunications closets.

Two types of wiring closets exist: telecommunications closets and equipment rooms. Depending on the size of your organization and size of your building, you may have one or more telecommunications closets concentrating to an equipment room. Telecommunications closets are strategically placed throughout a building to provide a single point for termination from your work areas. In a multistory building, you should have at least one telecommunications closet per floor. As the distances between your end devices and telecommunications closet approach their recommended maximum limits (90 meters in the case of Category 5 installations), you should consider implementing additional telecommunications closets.

Telecommunications closets are connected to the equipment room in a star configuration by either fiber or copper. As we mentioned in our discussion of backbone cabling, fiber is preferred because the distances from the equipment room to the last telecommunications closet can total 2,000 meters for multimode and 3,000 meters for single mode. When connecting with UTP copper, the backbone run lengths must total 800 meters or less for telephone systems and 90 meters or less for data systems.

TIA/EIA Recommendations for Wiring Closets

The TIA/EIA does not distinguish between the roles of telecommunications closets for its published standards. The following is a summary of the minimum standards for a telecommunications wiring closet per the ANSI/TIA/EIA-569-A Commercial Building Telecommunications Pathways and Spaces Standard:

- The telecommunications closet must be dedicated to telecommunications functions.

- Equipment not related to telecommunications shall not be installed in or enter the telecommunications closet.

- Multiple closets on the same floor shall be interconnected by a minimum of one 78(3) (3-inch or 78-mm opening) trade-size conduit or equivalent pathway.

- The telecommunications closet must support a minimum floor loading of 2.4 kilo-Pascals (50 $^{lb}/_{ft^2}$).

The equipment room is used to contain the main distribution frame (the main location for backbone cabling), phone systems, power protection, uninterruptible power supplies, LAN equipment (such as bridges, routers, switches, and hubs), and possible file servers and data-processing equipment. ANSI/TIA/EIA-569-A provides a recommendation of a minimum of .75 square feet of floor space in the equipment room for every 100 square feet of user workstation area. You can also estimate the requirements for square footage using Table 5.1, which shows estimated equipment-room square footage based on the number of workstations.

| TIP | Further information about the ANSI/TIA/EIA-569-A Standard can be found in Chapter 2. |

TABLE 5.1: Estimated Square-Foot Requirements Based on the Number of Workstations

Number of Workstations	Estimated Equipment-Room Floor Space
1 to 100	150 square feet
101 to 400	400 square feet
401 to 800	800 square feet
801 to 1,200	1,200 square feet

| NOTE | The floor space required in any equipment room will be dictated by the amount of equipment that must be housed there. Use Table 5.1 for a base calculation but don't forget to take into account equipment that may be in this room, such as LAN racks, phone switches, and power supplies. |

The TIA/EIA further recommends that the following conditions be met in addition to the minimum standards requirements:

- There shall be a minimum of two dedicated 120V 20A nominal, non-switched, AC duplex electrical-outlet receptacles, each on separate branch circuits.

- Additional convenience duplex outlets shall be placed at 1.8-meter (6-foot) intervals around the perimeter, 150 mm (6 inches) above the floor.

- There shall be access to the telecommunications grounding system, as specified by ANSI/TIA/EIA-607.

- HVAC requirements to maintain temperature the same as the adjacent office area shall be met. A positive pressure shall be maintained with a minimum of one air change per hour or per code.

- There shall be a minimum of one closet per floor to house telecommunications equipment/cable terminations and associated cross-connect cable and wire.

- The wiring closet shall be located near the center of the area being served.

- Horizontal pathways shall terminate in the telecommunications closet on the same floor as the area served.

- The wiring closet shall accommodate seismic requirements.

- Two walls should have 20-mm (¾-inch) A-C plywood 2.4 m (8 ft.) high.

- Lighting shall be a minimum of 500 lx (50 footcandles) and mounted 2.6 m (8.5 ft.) above the floor.

- False ceilings shall not be provided.

- There shall be a minimum door size of 910 mm (36 in.) wide and 2,000 mm (80 in.) high without sill, hinged to open outward or slide side-to-side or be removable, and it shall be fitted with a lock.

Although the items are suggestions, it is our position that you should strive to fulfill as many of these requirements as possible. If your budget only allows for a few of these suggestions, grounding, separate power, and the ventilation and cooling requirements should be at the top of your list.

WARNING   As noted in Chapter 2, telecommunications closets and equipment rooms should be locked. If your organization's data is especially sensitive, consider putting an alarm system on the rooms.

Cabling Racks and Enclosures

Racks are the pieces of hardware that help you organize cabling infrastructure. They range in height from 39 to 84 inches and come in two widths, 19 and 23 inches. Nineteen-inch widths are much more commonplace and have been in use for nearly 60 years. These racks are commonly called just 19-inch racks or, sometimes, EIA racks. Mounting holes are spaced between ⅝ and two inches apart, so you can be assured that no matter what your preferred equipment vendor is, its equipment will fit in your rack. In general, three types of racks are available for purchase: wall-mounted brackets, skeletal frames, and full equipment cabinets.

TIP
Not all racks use exactly the same type of mounting screws or mounting equipment. Make sure that you have sufficient screws or mounting gear for the types of racks you purchase.

Wall-Mounted Brackets

For small installations and areas where economy of space is a key consideration, *wall-mounted brackets* may provide the best solution. Wall-mounted racks such as MilesTek's Swing Gate wall rack in Figure 5.9 have a frame that swings out 90 degrees to provide access to the rear panels and include wire guides to help with cable management.

FIGURE 5.9:

MilesTek's Swing Gate wall rack

(Photo courtesy of MilesTek)

Racks such as the one in Figure 5.9 are ideal for small organizations that may only have a few dozen workstations or phone outlets but are still concerned about building an organized cabling infrastructure.

TIP   Prior to installing wall-mounted racks with swinging doors, be sure to allow enough room to open the front panel.

Skeletal Frames (19-Inch Racks)

Skeletal frames, often called *19-inch racks* or *EIA racks*, are probably the most common type of rack. These racks, like the one shown in Figure 5.10, are designed and built based on the EIA-310C standards. These skeletal frames come in sizes ranging from 39 to 84 inches in height with a 22-inch base plate to provide stability. Their open design makes it easy to work on both the front and back of the mounted equipment.

FIGURE 5.10:

A skeletal frame
(19-inch rack)

(Photo courtesy of MilesTek)

When installing a skeletal frame, you should leave enough space between the rack and the wall to accommodate the installed equipment (most equipment is 6 to 18 inches deep). You should also leave enough space behind the rack for an individual to work (at least 12 to 18 inches). You will also need to secure the rack to the floor so that it does not topple over.

These racks can also include cable management. If you have ever worked with a rack that has more than a few dozen patch cords connected to it with no cable-management devices, then you understand just how messy skeletal racks can be. Figure 5.11 shows an Ortronics Mighty Mo II wall-mount rack that includes cable management.

FIGURE 5.11:

The Ortronics Mighty Mo II wall-mount rack with cable management

(Photo courtesy of Ortronics)

Racks are not limited to just patch panels and network-connectivity devices. Server computers, for example, can be installed into a rack-mountable chassis. Many accessories can be mounted into rack spaces, including utility shelves, monitor shelves, and keyboard shelves. Figure 5.12 shows some of the more common types of shelves available for 19-inch racks. If you have a need for some sort of shelf not commercially available, most machine shops are equipped to manufacture it.

FIGURE 5.12:

Shelves available for
19-inch racks

(Photo courtesy of MilesTek)

Full Equipment Cabinets

The most expensive of your rack options, *full equipment cabinets*, offer the security benefits of locking cabinet doors. Full cabinets can be as simple as the ones shown in Figure 5.13, but they can also become quite elaborate, with Plexiglas doors and self-contained cooling systems. Racks such as the one in Figure 5.13 provide better physical security, cooling, and protection against electromagnetic interference than standard 19-inch rack frames. In some high-security environments, this type of rack is required for LAN equipment and servers.

FIGURE 5.13:

A full equipment cabinet

(Photo courtesy of MilesTek)

Cable-Management Accessories

If your rack equipment does not include wire management, numerous cable-management accessories, as shown in Figure 5.14, can suit your organizational requirements. Large wiring closets can quickly make a rat's nest out of your horizontal cable runs and patch cables. Cable hangers on the front of a rack can help arrange bundles of patch cables to keep them neat and orderly. Rear-mounted cable hangers provide strain-relief anchors and can help to organize horizontal cables that terminate at the back of patch panels.

FIGURE 5.14:

Cable-management accessories from MilesTek

(Photo courtesy of MilesTek)

Electrical Grounding

In our discussion on conduit, we stated that regardless of your conduit solution, you will have to make sure that it complies with the ANSI/TIA/EIA-607 Commercial Building Grounding and Bonding Requirements for Telecommunications Standard for electrical grounding. The same holds true for your cable-rack implementations. Why is this so important? Well, to put it bluntly, your network can kill you, and in this case, we're not referring to the massive coronary brought on by users' printing challenges!

For both alternating- and direct-current systems, electrons flow from a negative to a positive source, with two conductors required to complete a circuit. If a difference in resistance exists between a copper wire path and a grounding path, a voltage potential will develop between your hardware and its earth ground. In the best-case scenario, this voltage potential will form a Galvanic cell, which will simply corrode your equipment. This phenomenon is usually demonstrated in freshman chemistry classes by using a potassium-chloride salt bridge to complete the circuit between a zinc anode and a copper cathode. If the voltage potential were to become great enough, simply touching your wiring rack could complete the circuit and discharge enough electricity to kill you or one of your colleagues.

WARNING   One of the authors knows someone who was thrown to the ground when he touched an improperly grounded communications rack. Grounding is serious business and should not be undertaken by the layperson. Low voltage does not mean large shocks cannot be generated.

We recommend working with your electrical contractor and power company to get the best and shortest ground you can afford. One way to achieve this is to deploy separate breaker boxes for each office area. Doing so will shorten the grounding length for each office or group.

Cross-Connect Devices

Fortunately for us, organizations seem to like hiring consultants; however, most people are usually less than thrilled to see some types of consultants—in particular, space-utilization and efficiency experts. Why? Because they make everyone move! *Cross-connect devices* are cabling components you can implement to make changes to your network less painful.

The 66 Punch-Down Blocks

For more than 25 years, *66 punch-down blocks*, shown in Figure 5.15, have been used as telephone-system cross-connect devices. They support 50 pairs of wire. Wires are connected to the terminals of the block using a punch-down tool. When a wire is "punched down" into a terminal, the wire's insulation is pierced and the connection is established to the block. Separate jumpers then connect blocks. When the need arises, jumpers can be reconfigured to establish the appropriate connections.

FIGURE 5.15:

A 66 punch-down block

(Photo courtesy of The Siemon Company)

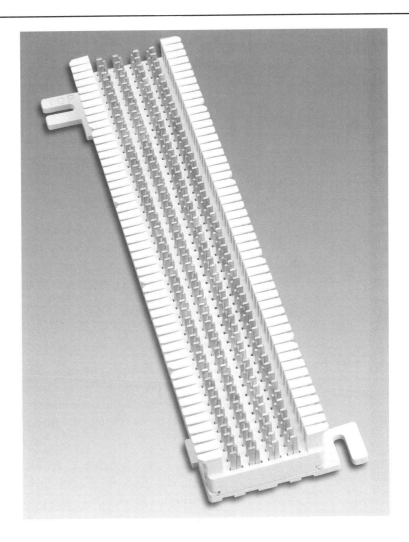

The 110 and S-210 Punch-Down Blocks

Figure 5.16 shows *110-blocks*, another flavor of punch-down media; they are better suited for use with data networks. The 110-blocks come in sizes that support anywhere from 25 to 500 wire pairs. Unlike 66-blocks, 110-blocks are not interconnected via jumpers but instead use 24 AWG cross-connect wire. The Siemon Company produces a connecting block called an S-210 that is capable of delivering the proposed performance standards for Category 6.

FIGURE 5.16:

Another type of punch-down media, 110 punch-down blocks

(Photo courtesy of MilesTek)

Some installations of data and voice systems require the use of 25-pair connectors. Some network hubs and phone systems use these 25-pair connectors, rather than modular-type plugs like the RJ-45, to interface with their hardware. You can purchase 110-style connector blocks prewired with 25-pair connector cables, such as the one seen in Figure 5.17.

TIP   If you purchase a 110- or 66-style block wired to 25-pair connectors, make sure the equipment is rated to the appropriate Category of cable performance that you intend to use it with. The 66-blocks are rarely used for data.

Modular Patch Panels

As an alternative to punch-down blocks, you can also terminate your horizontal cabling directly into RJ-45 patch panels (see Figure 5.18). This approach is becoming increasingly popular because it lends itself to exceptionally easy reconfigurations. To reassign a network client to a new port on the switch, all you have to do is move a patch cable. Another benefit is that when they're installed cleanly, they can make your wiring closet look great!

TIP When ordering any patch panel, make sure that you order one that has the correct wiring pattern (T568A or T568B). The wiring pattern is usually color-coded on the 110-block.

Patch panels normally have 110-block connectors on the back. In some environments, only a few connections are required, and a large patch panel is not needed. In other environments, it may not be possible to mount a patch panel with a 110-block on the back because of space constraints. In this case, smaller modular-jack wall-mount blocks (see Figure 5.19) may be useful. These are available in a variety of sizes and port configurations. You can also get these in either horizontal or backbone configurations.

FIGURE 5.18:

Modular patch panels

(Photo courtesy of MilesTek)

FIGURE 5.19:

The Siemon Company's S-110 modular-jack wall-mount block

(Photo courtesy of The Siemon Company)

Consolidation Points

Both the ANSI/TIA/EIA-568-A and ISO/IEC 11801 Standards allow for a single transition point or *consolidation point* in horizontal cabling. The consolidation point is usually used to transition between a 25-pair UTP cabling (or separate four-pair UTP cables) that originated in the wiring closet and cable that spreads out to a point where many networked or voice devices may be, such as with modular furniture. An example of a typical consolidation point (inside a protective cabinet) is shown in Figure 5.20.

FIGURE 5.20:

A consolidation point

(Photo courtesy of The Siemon Company)

Fiber-Optic Connector Panels

If your organization is using optical-fiber cabling (either for horizontal or backbone cabling), then you may see *fiber-optic connector panels*. These will sometimes look similar to the UTP RJ-45 panels seen earlier in this chapter, but they are commonly separate boxes that contain space for cable slack. A typical 24-port fiber-optic panel is pictured in Figure 5.21.

FIGURE 5.21:

A fiber-optic connector panel

(Photo courtesy of MilesTek)

Administration Standards

After troubleshooting a network issue and figuring out that it's a problem with the physical layer, have you ever found complete spaghetti in a wiring closet? In our consulting practices, we see this all too often. Our clients then pay two to three times the regular consulting fees because it takes so much time to sort through the mess.

NOTE   Network administrators should be judged by the neatness of their wiring closets.

To provide a standard methodology for the labeling of cables, pathways, and spaces, the TIA/EIA published the ANSI/TIA/EIA-606 Administration Standard for the Telecommunications Infrastructure of Commercial Buildings. In addition to guidelines for labeling, the Standard also recommends the color-coding scheme shown in Table 5.2. This scheme applies not only to labeling of cables and connections but also to the color of the cross-connect backboards in the telecommunication closets. It does not necessarily apply to the colors of cable jackets, although some installations may attempt to apply it.

TABLE 5.2:   Color-Coding Schemes

Color Code	Usage
Black	No termination type assigned
White	First-level backbone (MC/IC or MC/TC terminations)
Red	Reserved for future use
Gray	Second-level backbone (IC/TC terminations)
Yellow	Miscellaneous (auxiliary, security alarms, etc.)
Blue	Horizontal-cable terminations
Green	Network connections
Purple	Common equipment (PBXs, host LANs, muxes)
Orange	Demarcation point (central-office terminations)
Brown	Interbuilding backbone (campus cable terminations)

Besides labeling and color-coding, you should also consider bundling groups of related cables with plastic cable ties (tie-wraps). Plastic cable ties come in a variety of sizes for all kinds of applications. When bundling cables, however, be sure not to cinch them too tightly, as you could disturb the natural geometry of the cable. If you ever have to perform maintenance on a group of cables, all you have to do is cut the plastic ties and add new ones when you're finished. Plastic tie-wraps are sturdy and very common, but they must be cut to be removed; some companies are now making hook-and-loop (Velcro) tie-wraps.

TIP   Plastic cable ties are inexpensive, and you can never have too many of them.

Whether you implement the ANSI/TIA/EIA-606 Standard or come up with your own methodology, the most import aspect of cable administration is to have accurate documentation of your cable infrastructure.

Stocking Your Wiring Closets

The wiring equipment discussed in this chapter is commonly found in many cabling installations; larger, more complex installations may have additional components that we did not mention here. The components mentioned in this chapter can be purchased from just about any cabling or telecommunications supplier. Some of the companies that were very helpful in the production of this chapter have much more information online. You can find more information about these companies and their products by visiting them on the Web:

MilesTek   www.milestek.com

The Siemon Company   www.siemon.com

Ortronics   www.ortronics.com

Erico   www.erico.com

Tools of the Trade

This chapter discusses tools that are essential to proper installation of data and video cabling. It also describes tools, many of which you should already have, that make the job of installing cables easier.

If you're reading this book, it is likely that you're a do-it-yourselfer or you're managing people who are hands-on. So be advised: Don't start any cabling job without the proper tools. You might be able to install a data-cabling system with nothing but a knife and screwdriver, but doing so may cost you many hours of frustration and diminished quality.

If you are a hands-on person, you can probably relate to this story: A number of years ago, Jim was attempting to change the rear shock absorbers on a truck. The nuts holding the shocks were rusted in place and, working in his garage, there was nothing he could do to loosen them. After maybe an hour of frustrating effort, Jim gave up and took the truck to a local service station for help. In literally seconds, the nuts were loose. What made the difference? Tools. The mechanics at the station had access to tools that were missing from Jim's home handyman kit. Using tools like a hydraulic lift and impact wrenches made the job infinitely easier than lying on a garage floor and tugging on a Craftsman Best box-end wrench.

In addition to saving time, using the appropriate tools will save money. Knowing what the right tools are and where to use them is an important part of the job.

The Right Tool and the Right Price

Just as the right tools are important for doing a job well, so is making sure that you have high-quality equipment. Suppose you see two punch-down tools advertised in a catalog and one of them is $20 and the other is $60. Ask why one is more expensive than the other is. Compare the features of the two; if they seem to be the same, you can usually assume that more expensive tool is designed for professionals.

With all tools, there are levels of quality and a range of prices you can choose from. It's trite but true: You get what you pay for, generally speaking, so our advice is to stay away from the really cheap stuff. On the other hand, if you only anticipate light to moderate use, you needn't buy top-of-the-line equipment.

Building a Cabling Tool Kit

Throughout this chapter, a number of different of tools are discussed, and photos illustrate them. Don't believe for a minute that we've covered all the models and permutations available! This chapter should be an introduction to the types of tools you may require, and it should help you to recognize a particular tool so you can go get the one that best suits you. It is impossible for us to determine your exact tool needs. Keeping your own needs in mind, read through the descriptions that follow, and choose those tools that you anticipate using. Then, shop your list.

Myriad online catalog houses and e-commerce sites sell the tools and parts you need to complete your cabling tool kit. A few of these include:

- IDEAL DataComm at www.idealindustries.com

- MilesTek at www.milestek.com

- Jensen Tools at www.jensentools.com

- The Siemon Company at www.siemon.com

- Radio Shack at www.radioshack.com

- Labor Saving Devices, Inc. at www.lsdinc.com

If you have to scratch and sniff before buying, visit a local distributor in your area. Check your local phone book for vendors such as Anicom, Anixter, GE Supply, Graybar, and many other distributors that specialize in servicing the voice/-data market; many of these vendors have counter sale areas where you can see and handle the merchandise before purchasing.

We can't possibly describe in precise detail how each tool works or all the ways you can apply it to different projects. We'll supply a basic description of each tool's use, but because of the wide variety of manufacturers and models available, you'll have to rely on the manufacturer's instructions on exactly how to use a particular device.

Tools Can Be Expensive

Most people who are not directly involved in the installation of telecommunications cabling systems don't realize how many tools you might need to carry or the value of them. A do-it-yourselfer can get by with a few hundred dollars' worth of tools, but a professional may need to carry many thousands of dollars' worth, depending on the job that is expected.

A typical cabling team of three or four installers may carry as much as $12,000 in installation gear and tools. If this team carries sophisticated testing equipment such as a fiber-optic OTDR, the value of their tools may jump to over $50,000. A fully equipped fiber-optic team carrying an OTDR and optical-fiber fusion splicer could be responsible for over $100,000 worth of tools. And some people wonder why cabling teams insist on taking their tools home with them each night!

Common Cabling Tools

A number of tools are common to most cabling tool kits: wire strippers, wire cutters, cable crimpers, punch-down tools, fish tape, and toning tools. Most of these tools are essential for installing even the most basic of cabling systems.

Wire Strippers

What do you want to strip today? The variety of cable strippers represented in this section is a function of the many different types of cable you can work with, different costs of the cable strippers, and versatility of the tools.

Strippers for UTP and STP cables are used to remove the outer jacket and have to accommodate the wide variation in the geometry of UTP cables. Unlike coax, which is usually consistently smooth and round, twisted-pair cables can have irregular surfaces due to the jacket shrinking down around the pairs. Additionally, the jacket thickness can differ greatly depending on brand and flame rating. The trick is to aid removal of the jacket without nicking or otherwise damaging the insulation on the conductors underneath.

The wire stripper in Figure 6.1 uses an adjustable blade so that you can fix the depth, matching it to the brand of cable you are working with. Some types use spring tension to help keep the blade at the proper cutting depth.

FIGURE 6.1:

A wire stripper

(Photo courtesy of MilesTek)

In both cases, the goal is to score (cut) the jacket without penetrating it completely. Then, you flex the cable to break the jacket along the scored line. This ensures that the wire insulation is nick-free. In some models, the tool can also be used to score or slit the jacket lengthwise in the event you need to expose a significant length of conductors.

> **NOTE** When working with UTP or STP cables, you will rarely need to strip the insulation from the conductors. Termination of these cable types on patch panels, cross-connects, and most wall plates employs the use of *insulation displacement connectors* (IDCs) that make contact with the conductor by slicing through the insulation. Should you need to strip the insulation from a twisted-pair cable, keep a pair of common electrician's strippers handy. Just make sure it can handle the finer gauge wires such as 22, 24, and 26 AWG that are commonly used with LAN wiring.

Coaxial Wire Strippers

Coaxial cable strippers are designed with two or three depth settings. These settings correspond to the different layers of material in the cable. Coaxial cables are pretty standardized in terms of central-conductor diameter, thickness of the insulating and shielding layers, and thickness of the outer jacket, making this an effective approach.

In the inexpensive (but effective for the do-it-yourself folks) model shown in Figure 6.2, the depth settings are fixed. The wire stripper in Figure 6.2 can be used to strip coaxial cables (RG-59 and RG-6) to prepare them for F-type connectors.

FIGURE 6.2:

Inexpensive coaxial wire strippers

(Photo courtesy of MilesTek)

To strip the cable, you insert it in a series of openings that allows the blade to penetrate to different layers of the cable. At every step, you rotate the tool around the cable and then pull the tool toward the end of the cable, removing material down to where the blade has penetrated. To avoid nicking the conductor, the blade is notched at the position used to remove material.

One problem with the model shown in Figure 6.2 is that you end up working pretty hard to accomplish the task. For its low price, the extra work may be a good tradeoff if stripping coax isn't a day-in, day-out necessity. However, if you are going to be working with coaxial cables on a routine basis, you should consider some heftier equipment. Figure 6.3 shows a model that accomplishes the task in a more mechanically advantageous way (that means it's easier on your hands). In addition, it offers the advantage of adjustable blades so that you can optimize the cutting thickness for the exact brand of cable you're working with.

Coaxial strippers are commonly marked with settings that assist you in removing the right amount of material at each layer from the end of the cable so it will fit correctly in an F- or BNC-type connector.

Fiber-Optic Cable Strippers

Fiber-optic cables require very specialized tools. Fortunately, the dimensions of fiber coatings, claddings, and buffers are standardized and manufactured to precise tolerances. This allows tool manufactures to provide tools such as the one shown in Figure 6.4 that will remove material to the exact thickness of a particular layer without damage to the underlying layer. Typically, these look like a conventional multigauge wire stripper with a series of notches to provide the proper depth of penetration.

A fiber-optic cable stripper

(Photo courtesy of IDEAL DataComm)

Wire Cutters

You can, without feeling very guilty, use a regular set of lineman's pliers to snip through coaxial, UTP, and STP. You can even use them for fiber-optic cables, but cutting through the aramid yarns used as strength members can be difficult; you will dull your pliers quickly, not to mention what you may do to your wrist.

KEY TERM   **Aramid**   *Aramid* is the common name for the material trademarked as Kevlar that's used in bulletproof vests. It is used in optical-fiber cable to provide additional strength.

So why would you want a special tool for something as mundane as cutting through the cable? Here's the catch regarding all-purpose pliers: As they cut, they will mash the cable flat. All the strippers described previously work best if the cable is round. Specialized cutters such as the one shown in Figure 6.5 are designed for coax and twisted-pair cables to preserve the geometry of the cable as they cut. This is accomplished using curved instead of flat blades.

FIGURE 6.5:

Typical wire cutters

(Photo courtesy of MilesTek)

For fiber-optic cables, special scissors are available that cut through aramid with relative ease. Figure 6.6 shows scissors designed for cutting and trimming the Kevlar strengthening members found in fiber-optic cables.

FIGURE 6.6:

IDEAL DataComm's Kevlar scissors

(Photo courtesy of IDEAL DataComm)

Cable Crimpers

Modular plugs and coaxial connectors are attached to cable ends using crimpers. Crimpers are essentially very specialized pliers. So why can't you just use a pair of pliers? Crimpers are designed to apply force evenly and properly for the plug or connector being used. Some crimpers use a ratchet mechanism to ensure that a complete crimp cycle has been made. Without this special design, your crimp job will be inconsistent at best, and it may not work at all. In addition, you'll damage connectors and cable ends, resulting in wasted time and materials. Remember that the right tool, even if it's expensive, can save you money!

Twisted-Pair Crimpers

Crimpers for twisted-pair cable must accommodate various-sized plugs. The process of crimping involves removing the cable jacket to expose the insulated conductors, inserting the conductors in the modular plug (in the proper order!), and applying pressure to this assembly using the crimper. The contacts for the modular plug (such as the ones shown in Figure 6.7) are actually blades that cut through the insulation and make contact with the conductor. The act of crimping not only establishes this contact but also pushes the contact blades down into proper position for insertion into a jack. Finally, the crimping die compresses the plug strain-relief indentations to hold the connector on the cable.

FIGURE 6.7:

An eight-position modular plug (a.k.a. RJ-45 connector)

(Photo courtesy of The Siemon Company)

NOTE   Modular plugs for cables with solid conductors (horizontal wiring) are sometimes different from plugs for cables with stranded conductors (patch cords). The crimper fits either, and some companies market a universal plug that works with either. Make sure you select the proper type when you buy plugs and make your connections.

The crimper shown in Figure 6.8 is designed so that a specific die is inserted, depending on the modular plug being crimped. If you buy a flexible model like this, you will need dies that fit an eight-conductor position (data, a.k.a. RJ-45) and a six-position type (voice, a.k.a. RJ-11 or RJ-12) plug at a minimum. If you intend to do any work with telephone handset cords, you should also get a die for four-position plugs.

FIGURE 6.8:

A crimper with multiple dies for RJ-11, RJ-45, and MMJ modular connectors

(Photo courtesy of MilesTek)

Other twisted-pair crimpers are configured for specific plug sizes and don't offer the flexibility of changeable dies. Inexpensive models available at the local home-improvement center for less than $15 usually have two positions; these are configured to crimp eight-, six-, or four-position type plugs. These inexpensive tools often do not have the ratchet mechanism found on professional installation crimpers. Figure 6.9 shows a higher-quality crimper that has two positions, one for eight-position plugs and one for four-position plugs.

FIGURE 6.9:

An Ideal Ratchet Telemaster crimper with crimp cavities for eight- and four-position modular plugs

(Photo courtesy of IDEAL DataComm)

Less expensive crimpers are targeted at the do-it-yourself market—those who are doing a little phone-extension work around the house on a weekend or who only crimp a few cables at a time. Better-quality units targeted for the intermediate user will usually have one opening for eight-position and one opening for six-position plugs. If you work with data connectors such as the eight-position modular jack (RJ-45), your crimping tool must have a crimp cavity for eight-position plugs.

Coaxial-Cable Crimpers

Coaxial-cable crimpers also are available with either changeable dies or with fixed-size crimp openings. Models aimed strictly at the residential installer will feature dies or openings suitable for applying F-type connectors to RG-58, RG-59, and RG-6 series coax. For the commercial installer, a unit that will handle dies such as RG-11 and thinnet with BNC-type connectors is also necessary. Figure 6.10 shows IDEAL DataComm's Crimpmaster Crimp Tool, which can be configured with a variety of die sets such as RG-6, RG-9, RG-58, RG-59, RG-62, cable-TV F-type connectors, and others.

FIGURE 6.10:

An Ideal Crimpmaster Crimp Tool

(Photo courtesy of IDEAL DataComm)

There's a very functional item that is used in conjunction with your crimper to install F-type RG-59 and RG-6 connectors. Figure 6.11 shows an F-type connector installation tool. One end is used to ream space between the outer jacket and the dielectric layer of the coax. On the other end, you thread the connector and use the tool to push the connector down on the cable. This accessory speeds installation of F-type connectors and reduces wear and tear on your hands.

FIGURE 6.11:

A MilesTek F-type connector installation tool

(Photo courtesy of MilesTek)

Punch-Down Tools

Twisted-pair cables are terminated in jacks, cross-connect blocks (66-blocks), or patch panels (110-blocks) that use insulation-displacement connectors (IDCs). Essentially, IDCs are little knife blades with a V-shaped gap or slit between them. You force the conductor down into the V and the knife blades cut through the insulation and make contact with the conductor. Although you could accomplish this using a small flat-blade screwdriver, doing so very often will guarantee you infamy in the Hack Hall of Fame. It would be sort of like hammering nails with a crescent wrench. The correct device for inserting a conductor in the IDC termination slot is a punch-down tool.

NOTE   You can find more information on 66-blocks and 110-blocks in Chapter 5 and Chapter 7. Additional information about wall plates can be found in Chapter 8.

A punch-down tool is really just a handle with a special "blade" that fits a particular IDC. There are two main types of IDC terminations: the 66-block and the 110-block. The 66-block terminals have a long history rooted in voice cross-connects. The 110-block is a newer design, originally associated with AT&T but now generic in usage. In general, 110-type IDCs are used for data, and 66-type IDCs are used for voice, but neither is absolutely one or the other.

Different blades are used depending upon whether or not you are going to be terminating on 110-blocks or 66-blocks. Though the blades are very different, most punch-down tools are designed to accept either. In fact, most people purchase the tool with one and buy the other as an accessory, so that one tool serves two terminals.

Blades are designed with one end being simply for punch down. When you turn the blade and apply the other end, it punches down and cuts off excess conductor in one operation. Usually you will use the punch-and-cut end, but for daisy chaining on a cross-connect, you would use the end that just punches down.

TIP

If you are terminating cables in Krone or BIX (by Norcom) equipment, you will need special punch-down blades. These brands use proprietary IDC designs.

Punch-down tools are available as *nonimpact* in their least expensive form. Non-impact tools generally require more effort to make a good termination, but they are well suited for people who only occasionally perform punch-down termination work. Figure 6.12 shows a typical nonimpact punch-down tool.

FIGURE 6.12:

IDEAL DataComm's nonim-pact punch-down tool

(Photo courtesy of IDEAL DataComm)

The better-quality punch-down tools are spring-loaded *impact* tools. When you press down and reach a certain point of resistance, the spring gives way, providing positive feedback that the termination is made. Typically, the tool will adjust to high- and low-impact settings. Figure 6.13 shows an impact punch-down tool. Notice the dial near the center of the tool—it allows the user to adjust the impact setting. The manufacturer of the termination equipment you are using will recommend the proper impact setting.

FIGURE 6.13:

IDEAL DataComm's impact tool with adjustable impact settings

(Photo courtesy of IDEAL DataComm)

With experience, you can develop a technique and rhythm that lets you punch down patch panels and cross-connects very quickly. However, nothing is so frustrating as interrupting your sequence rhythm because the blade stayed on the

terminal instead of in the handle of the tool. The better punch-down tools have a feature that locks the blade in place, rather than just holding it in with friction. For the occasional user, a friction-held blade is okay, but for the professional, a lock-in feature is a must that will save time and, consequently, money.

TIP

You should always carry at least one extra blade for each type of termination that you are doing. Once you get the hang of punch-downs, you'll find that the blades don't break often, but they do break occasionally. Extra blades are inexpensive and can be easily ordered from the company you purchased your punch-down tool from.

Some brands of 110-block terminations support the use of special blades that will punch down multiple conductors at once, instead of one at a time.

If you are punching down IDC connectors on modular jacks from The Siemon Company that fit into modular wall plates, a tool from that company may be of use to you. Rather than trying to find a surface to hold the modular jack against, you can use the Palm Guard (see Figure 6.14) to hold the modular jack in place while you punch down the wires.

FIGURE 6.14:

The Palm Guard

(Photo courtesy of The Siemon Company)

Fish Tapes

A good fish tape is the best friend of the installer who does MACs (moves, adds, changes) or retrofit installations on existing buildings. Essentially, it is a long wire, steel tape, or fiberglass rod that is flexible enough to go around bends and corners but retains enough stiffness so that it can be pushed and worked along a pathway without kinking or buckling.

Like a plumber's snake, a fish tape is used to work blindly through an otherwise inaccessible area. For example, say you needed to run a cable from a ceiling space down inside a joist cavity in a wall to a new wall outlet. From within the ceiling space, you would thread the fish tape down into the joist cavity through a hole in the top plate of the wall. From this point, you would maneuver it in front of any insulation and around any other obstacles such as electrical cables that might also be running in the joist cavity. When the tape becomes visible through the retrofit outlet opening, you would draw the tape out. Then you would attach either a pull string or the cable itself and withdraw the fish tape.

Fish tapes (see Figure 6.15) are available in various lengths, with 50- and 100-foot lengths being common. They come in spools that allow them to be reeled in and out as necessary and are available virtually anywhere electrical supplies are sold, in addition to those sources mentioned earlier.

FIGURE 6.15:

IDEAL DataComm's fish tape

(Photo courtesy of IDEAL DataComm)

An alternative to fish tapes that is often helpful when placing cable in existing wall or ceiling spaces is the fiberglass pushrod, as shown in Figure 6.16. These devices are more rigid than fish tapes but are still able to flex when necessary. Their advantage is that they will always return to a straight orientation, making it easier to probe for "hidden" holes and passageways. The rigidity also lets you push a cable or pull string across a space. Some types are fluorescent or reflective so that you can easily see their position in a dark cavity. They typically come in 48-inch sections that connect together as you extend them into the space. A number of accessories (see Figure 6.17) are available to place on the tip, which make it easier to push the rod over obstructions, to aid in retrieval through a hole at the other end, or to attach a pull string or cable for pull back through the space.

FIGURE 6.16:

Fiberglass pushrods

(Photo courtesy of Labor Saving Devices, Inc.)

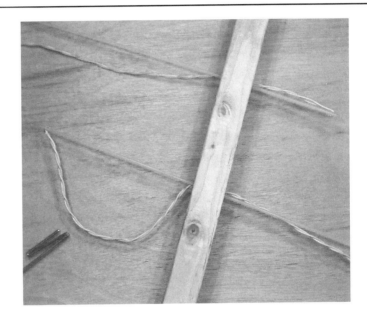

FIGURE 6.17:

Pushrod accessories

(Photo courtesy of Labor Saving Devices, Inc.)

Voltage Meter

There is a right way and a wrong way to determine if an electrical circuit has a live voltage on it. Touching it is the wrong way. A simple voltage meter such as the one pictured in Figure 6.18 is a much better solution, and it won't put your health plan to work. Though not absolutely necessary in the average data-cabling tool kit, a voltage meter is rather handy.

FIGURE 6.18:

A voltage/continuity tester

(Photo courtesy of IDEAL DataComm)

Cable Testing

Dozens of cable testers are available on the market. Some of them sell for less than $100; full-featured ones sell for over $5,000. High-end fiber-optic testers can sell for over $30,000! Chapter 14 discusses cable testing and certification, so we won't steal any thunder from that chapter here. However, in your tool kit you should include some basic tools that you don't need to get a second mortgage on your house to purchase.

Cable testers can be as simple as a cable-toning tool that helps you to identify a specific cable; they can also be continuity testers or the cable testers that cost thousands of dollars.

A Cable-Toning Tool

A cable toner is a device for determining if the fundamental cable installation has been done properly. It should be noted that we are not discussing the sophisticated type of test set required to certify a particular level of performance, such as a Category 5 link or channel. These are discussed in detail in Chapter 14.

In its simplest form, the toner is a simple continuity tester that confirms that what is connected at one end is electrically continuous to the other end. An electrical signal, or tone, is injected on the circuit being tested and is either received and verified on the other end or looped back for verification on the sending end. Some tools provide visual feedback (with a meter), whereas others utilize audio feedback. Testing may require that you have a partner (or a lot of scurrying back and forth on your part) at the far end of the cable to administer the inductive probe or loop-back device. Figure 6.19 shows a tone generator and Figure 6.20 shows the corresponding amplifier probe.

More sophisticated testers will report, in addition to continuity, length of run and check for shorts and crosses (accidental contact of one conductor with another), reversed pairs, transposed pairs, and split pairs.

FIGURE 6.19:

A tone generator

(Photo courtesy of IDEAL DataComm)

Twisted-Pair Continuity Tester

Many of the common problems of getting cables to work are simple ones. The $5,000 cable testers are nice, but for simple installations they are overkill. If the cable installer is not careful during installation, the cable's wire pairs may be reversed, split, or otherwise incorrectly wired. A simple continuity tester can help you solve many of the common problems of data and voice twisted-pair cabling, including testing for open circuits and shorts.

Figure 6.21 shows a simple continuity tester from IDEAL DataComm; this tester (the LinkMaster Tester) consists of the main testing unit and a remote tester. The remote unit is patched into one side of the cable, and the main unit is patched into the other side. It can quickly and accurately detect common cabling problems such as opens, shorts, reversed pairs, or split pairs. Cable testers such as the one shown in Figure 6.19 are available from many vendors and sell for under $100. Testers such as these can save you many hours of frustration as well as the hundreds or even thousands of dollars that you might spend on a more sophisticated tester.

FIGURE 6.21:

Ideal's LinkMaster Tester

(Photo courtesy of IDEAL DataComm)

Coaxial Tester

Though coaxial cable is a little less complicated to install and terminate, problems can still arise during installation. The tester shown in Figure 6.22 is the IDEAL DataComm Mini Coax Tester. This inexpensive, compact tester is designed to test coax-cable runs terminated with BNC-style connectors. It can test two modes of operation: standard and Hi-Z for long runs. Coaxial-cable testers will quickly help you identify opens and shorts.

FIGURE 6.22:

Ideal's Mini Coax Tester

(Photo courtesy of IDEAL DataComm)

Optical-Fiber Testers

Optical fiber requires a whole new class of cable testers. Just like copper-cable testers, optical-fiber testers are specialized. Figure 6.23 shows a simple continuity tester that verifies that light transmits through the cable.

FIGURE 6.23:

An optical-fiber continuity tester

(Photo courtesy of Jensen Tools)

Another type of optical-fiber test device is the attenuation tester, such as the one shown in Figure 6.24. Like the continuity tester, the attenuation tester tests whether or not light is making its way through the cable; but it also tests how much of the light signal is being lost. Anyone installing much fiber-optic cable should have an attenuation tester. Most problems with optical-fiber cables can be detected with this tool. Good optical-fiber attenuation testers can be purchased for less than $1,000.

FIGURE 6.24:

An optical-fiber attenuation tester

(Photo courtesy of Jensen Tools)

NOTE   An attenuation tester checks for how much signal is lost on the cable, whereas a continuity tester only measures whether light is passing through the cable.

Many high-end cable testers, such as those available from Hewlett-Packard, Microtest, and others, can test both optical fiber and copper (provided you have purchased the correct add-on modules). You need to know a few points when you purchase any type of optical-fiber tester:

- The tester should include the correct fiber connectors (ST, SC, FDDI, LC, MT-RJ, etc.) for the types of connectors you will be using.

- The tester should support the type of fiber-optic cable you need to test (single mode or multimode).

- The tester should test the bandwidth (for attenuation testers) at which you require the cable to be used (usually 850 or 1300nm).

Professional fiber-optic-cable installers usually carry tools such as an optical time domain reflectometer (OTDR) that perform more advanced tests on optical-fiber cable. OTDRs are not for everyone, as they can easily cost in excess of $30,000.

Cabling Supplies and Tools

When you think of cabling supplies, you probably envision boxes of cables, wall plates, modular connectors, and patch panels. True, those are all necessary parts of a cabling installation, but you should have other key consumable items in your cabling tool kit that will make your life a little easier.

Some of the consumable items you may carry are fairly generic. A well-equipped cabling technician carries a number of miscellaneous items essential to a cabling install, including the following:

- Electrician's tape—multiple colors are often desirable

- Duct tape

- Plastic cable ties (tie-wraps) for permanent bundling and tie-offs

- Hook and loop cable ties for temporarily segregating and bundling cables

- Adhesive labels or a specialized cable-labeling system

- Sharpies or other type of permanent markers

- Wire nuts or crimp-type wire connectors

An item that most cable installers use all the time is the tie-wrap. Tie-wraps help to make the cable installation neater and more organized. However, most tie-wraps are permanent; you have to cut them to release them. Hook-and-loop (Velcro-type) cable wraps (shown in Figure 6.25) give you the ability to quickly wrap a bundle of cable together (or attach it to something else) and then to remove it just as easily. These come in a variety of colors and sizes and can be ordered from most cable-equipment and wire-management suppliers.

FIGURE 6.25:

Reusable cable wraps

(Photo courtesy of MilesTek)

Cable-Pulling Tools

One of the most tedious tasks that a person pulling cables will face is the process of getting the cables through the area between the false or drop-ceiling tiles and the structural ceiling. This is where most horizontal cabling is installed. One method is to pull out every ceiling tile, pull the cable a few feet, move your stepladder to the next open ceiling tile, and pull the cable a few more feet. Some products that are helpful in the cabling-pulling process are telescoping pull tools and pulleys that cable can be threaded through so that more cable can be pulled without exceeding the maximum pull tension.

Figure 6.26 shows the Gopher Pole, which is a telescoping pole that compresses to a minimum length of less than 5 feet and extends to a maximum length of 22 feet. This tool can help when pulling or pushing cable through hard-to-reach places.

FIGURE 6.26:

The Gopher Pole

(Photo courtesy of MilesTek)

Another useful set of items to carry are cable pulleys (shown in Figure 6.27); these pulleys help a single person to do the work of two people when pulling cable. We recommend carrying a set of four pulleys if you are pulling a lot of cable.

FIGURE 6.27:

Cable pulleys

(Photo courtesy of MilesTek)

Though not specifically in the cable-pulling category, equipment to measure distance is especially important. A simple tape measure will suffice for most of you, but devices that can record long distances quickly may also be useful if you measure often. Sophisticated laser-based tools measure distances at the click of a button; however, a more reasonable tool would be something like one of the rolling measure tools pictured in Figure 6.28. This tool has a measuring wheel that records the distance as you walk.

FIGURE 6.28:

Professional rolling measure tools

(Photo courtesy of MilesTek)

Necessity Is the Mother of Invention

The need to get a pull string across extended distances of inaccessible area—for example, in a drop-ceiling space—is a common one faced by cable installers. Devices like the Gopher Pole described previously are certainly one solution. Left to their own devices, however, inventive cable installers have come up with a number of clever methods for getting their pull string from one point to another. We know of cases where the string was taped to a tennis ball and thrown or attached to an arrow and shot across the space with a bow. One company markets a toy dart gun that carries the pull string with the dart. Trained ferrets have been used. Our favorite though, is the one used by a guy who brought his kid's 4 x 4 radio-controlled toy truck and off-roaded his way across the ceiling tiles, trailing the pull string behind.

If you do much work fishing cable through tight, enclosed spaces, such as stud or joist cavities in walls and ceilings, the Walleye, shown in Figure 6.29, can be an indispensable tool. This device is a periscope with a flashlight attachment that fits through small openings (like a single-gang outlet cutout) and lets you view the inside of the cavity. You can look for obstructions, locate fish-tapes, or spot errant cables that have gotten away during the pulling process.

FIGURE 6.29:

The Walleye

(Photo courtesy of Labor Saving Devices, Inc.)

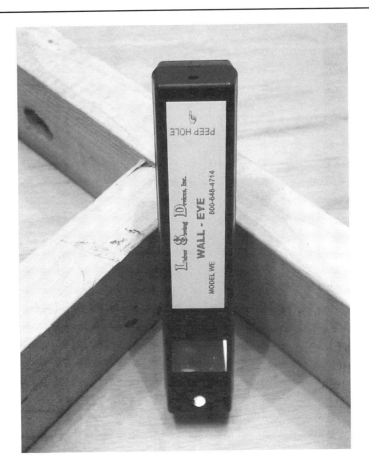

Another great tool for working in cavities and enclosed spaces is a length of bead chain and a magnet. When you drop the chain into a cavity from above (holding on to one end, of course), the extremely flexible links will "pour" over any obstructions and eventually end up in the bottom of the cavity. You insert the magnet into an opening near the bottom of the cavity and snag and extract the chain. Attach a pull-string, retract the chain, and you're ready to make the cable pull. One model of such a device is the Wet Noodle, marketed by Labor Saving Devices Inc., and shown in Figure 6.30.

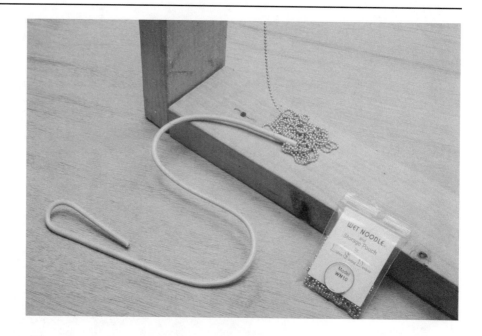

Retrofit installations in residences require specialized drill bits. These bits come on long, flexible shafts that let you feed them through restricted openings in order to drill holes in studs, joists, and sole and top plates. Attachable extensions let you reach otherwise inaccessible locations. Examples of these bits and extensions are shown in Figure 6.31. Because of their flexibility, they can bend or curve, even during the drilling process. You can almost literally drill around corners! Most models have holes in the ends of the bit for attaching a pull string so that when you retract the bit, you can pull cable back through. The bits can be purchased in lengths up to 72 inches, with extensions typically 48 inches each.

Controlling flexible drill bits requires an additional specialized tool, the bit directional tool as shown in Figure 6.32. It has loops that hook around the shaft of the drill bit and a handle you use to flex the bit to its proper path—simple in design, essential in function.

FIGURE 6.31:

Specialized drill bits and extensions

(Photos courtesy of Labor Saving Devices, Inc.)

A bit directional tool

(Photo courtesy of Labor Saving Devices, Inc.)

Wire-Pulling Lubricant

Wire- or cable-pulling lubricant is a slippery, viscous liquid goop that you apply to the cable jacket to allow it to slide more easily over surfaces encountered during the cable pull. Wire lubricant (see Figure 6.33) is available in a variety of quantities, from less than a gallon to five-gallon buckets.

The vast majority of cable jackets for premises cables in the U.S. are some form of PVC. One characteristic of PVC is that, depending on the specific compound, it has a relatively high coefficient of friction. This means that at the microscopic level, the material is rough, and the rough surface results in drag resistance when the cable jacket passes over another surface. Where two PVC-jacketed cables are in contact, or where PVC conduit is used, the problem is made worse. Imagine two sandpaper blocks rubbing against each other.

FIGURE 6.33:

Wire-pulling lubricant

(Photo courtesy of IDEAL DataComm)

In many cases, the use of pulling lubricant is not necessary. However, for long runs through conduit or in crowded cable trays or raceways, you may find that you either cannot complete the pull or you will exceed the cable's maximum allowable pulling tension unless a lubricant is used.

The lubricant is applied either by continuously pouring it over the jacket near the start of the run, or by wiping it on by hand as the cable is pulled. Where conduit is used, the lubricant can be poured in the conduit as the cable is pulled.

Lubricant has some drawbacks. Obviously, it can be messy; some types also congeal or harden over time, which makes adjustment or removal of cables difficult because they are effectively glued in place. Lubricant can also create a blockage in conduit and raceways that prevents new cables from being installed in the future.

TIP
Make sure the lubricant you are using is compatible with the insulation and jacket material of which the cables are made (hint: Don't use 10W30). The last thing you need is a call back because the pulling lubricant you used dissolved or otherwise degraded the plastics in the cable, leaving a bunch of bare conductors or fibers.

Cable-Marking Supplies

One of our biggest beefs with installed cabling systems (and those yet to be installed) is a profound lack of documentation. If you observe a professional data-cable installer in action, you will notice that the cabling system is well documented. Though some professionals will even use color coding on cables, the best start for cable documentation is assigning each cable a number.

The easiest way to number cables is to use a simple numbering system consisting of strips of numbers. These strips are numbered *0* through *9* and come in a variety of colors. Colors include black, white, gray, brown, red, orange, yellow, green, blue, and violet. You can use these strips to create your own numbering system. The cable is labeled at each end (the patch panel and the wall plate), and the cable number is recorded in whatever type of documentation is being used.

The numbered strips are often made of Tyvek, a material invented by DuPont that is well suited for making strong, durable products of high-density polyethylene fibers. Tyvek is nontoxic and chemically inert, so it will not adversely affect cables that it is applied to.

These wire-marking labels are available in two flavors: rolls and sheets. The rolls can be used without dispensers. Figure 6.34 shows a 3M dispenser that holds rolls of wire markers; the dispenser also provides a tear-off cutting blade.

FIGURE 6.34:

A 3M dispenser for rolls of wire-marking strips

(Photo courtesy of MilesTek)

Figure 6.35 shows a booklet of wire-marker sheets that allow you to pull off individual numbers.

FIGURE 6.35:

A booklet of wire-marker sheets

(Photo courtesy of IDEAL DataComm)

Wall-Plate Marking Supplies

Some wall-plate and patch-panel systems provide their own documentation tools, but others don't. A well-documented system includes identifying labels on the wall plates. Figure 6.36 shows self-adhesive letters, numbers, and icons that can be used with wall plates and patch panels. Check with the manufacturer of your wall plates and patch panels to see if these are part of the system you are using; if they are not, you should use some such labeling system.

FIGURE 6.36:

Letters, numbers, and icons on self-adhesive strips

(Photo courtesy of MilesTek)

1	2	3	4	5	6	7	8	9	10
11	12	13	14	15	16	17	18	19	20
A	B	C	D	E	F	G	H	J	K
5	5	5	5	5	FIBER	FIBER	FIBER	FIBER	FIBER
☎	☎	☎	☎	☎	💻	💻	💻	💻	💻
10 BASE-T	10 BASE-T	TOKEN RING	TOKEN RING		ETHERNET	ETHERNET	ISDN	ISDN	

Tools That a Smart Data-Cable Technician Carries

Up to this point, all the tools we've described are specific to the wire-and-cable installation industry. But you'll also need everyday tools in the course of the average install. Even if you don't carry all of these (you'd clank like a knight in armor and your tool belt would hang around your knees if you did), you should at least have them handy in your arsenal of tools:

- A flat blade and number 1 and number 2 Phillips screwdrivers (power screwdrivers are great time-and-effort savers, but you'll still occasionally need the hand types).

- A hammer.

- Nut drivers.

- Wrenches.

- A flashlight (a no-hands or headband model is especially handy).

- A drill and bits up to 1.5 inches.

- A saw that can be used to cut rectangular holes in drywall for electrical boxes.

- A good pocket, electrician's, or utility knife.

- Electrician's scissors.

- A tape measure.

- Face masks to keep your lungs from getting filled with dust when working in dusty areas.

- A stud finder to locate wooden or steel studs in the walls.

- A simple continuity tester or multitester.

- A comfortable pair of work gloves.

- A sturdy stepladder, nonconductive recommended.

- A tool belt with appropriate loops and pouches for the tools you use most.

- Two-way radios or walkie-talkies. They are indispensable for pulling or testing over even moderate distances or between floors. Invest in the hands-free models that have a headset, and you'll be glad you did.

- Extra batteries (or recharging stands) for your flashlights, radios, and cable testers.

TIP

Installation Tip: Wall-outlet boxes are often placed one hammer length from the floor, especially in residences (this is based on a standard hammer, not the heavier and longer framing hammers). It's a real time saver, but check the boxes installed by the electricians before you use this quick measuring technique for installing the datacom boxes, so that they'll all be the same height.

A multipurpose tool is also very handy. One popular choice is a Leatherman model with a coax crimper opening in the jaws of the pliers. It's just the thing for those times when you're on the ladder looking down at the exact tool you need lying on the floor where you just dropped it.

One of the neatest ideas for carrying tools is something that IDEAL DataComm calls the Bucket Bag (pictured in Figure 6.37). This bag sits over a five-gallon bucket and allows you to easily organize your tools.

FIGURE 6.37:

IDEAL DataComm's
Bucket Bag

(Photo courtesy of IDEAL DataComm)

A Preassembled Kit Could Be It

Finally, don't ignore the possibility that a preassembled kit might be just right for you. It may be more economical and less troublesome than buying the individual components. IDEAL DataComm, Jensen Tools, and MilesTek all offer a range of tool kits for the voice and data installer. These are targeted for the professional installer, and they come in a variety of configurations customized for the type of installation you'll do most often. They are especially suitable for the intermediate to expert user. Figure 6.38 shows a tool kit from MilesTek, and Figure 6.39 shows a toolkit from Jensen Tools.

FIGURE 6.38:

MilesTek tool kit

(Photo courtesy of MilesTek)

FIGURE 6.39:

Jensen Tools Master Cable Installer's Kit

(Photo courtesy of Jensen Tools)

part II

Network Media and Connectors

chapter 7

Copper Cable Media

- Types of Copper Cabling

- Best Practices for Copper Installation

- Copper Cable for Data Applications

- Copper Cable for Voice Applications

- Testing

Though optical-fiber cabling has made some impressive inroads toward becoming the cabling medium of choice for horizontal cable (cable to the desktop), copper-based cabling, specifically UTP, remains king of the hill. This is, in part, due to the fact that it is inexpensive, well understood, and easy to install; further, the networking devices required to support copper cabling are inexpensive compared with their fiber-optic counterparts. Cost is almost always the determining factor when deciding whether to install copper or optical-fiber cable—unless you have a high-security or really high-bandwidth requirement, in which case optical fiber becomes more desirable.

A variety of copper cabling types is available for telecommunications infrastructures today, but this chapter will focus on the use of Category 5 (and Category 5e) unshielded twisted-pair (UTP) cable. When installing a copper-based cabling infrastructure, one of your principal concerns should be adhering to whichever Standard you have decided to use, either the ANSI/TIA/EIA-568-A Commercial Building Telecommunications Cabling Standard or the ISO/IEC 11801 Generic Cabling for Customer Premises Standard. In North America, the ANSI/TIA/EIA-568-A Standard is preferred. Both these documents are discussed in more detail in Chapter 2.

Because this book is designed as a reference, much of the material found in this chapter is repeated in other chapters.

Types of Copper Cabling

Pick up any larger cabling catalog, and you will find thousands of types of copper cables. However, many of these cables are unsuitable for data and voice communications. Often, cable is manufactured with specific purposes in mind, such as audio, doorbell, remote equipment control, or other low-speed, low-voltage applications. Cable used for data communications must support high-speed and high-bandwidth applications. Even for digital telephones, the cable must be chosen correctly.

Many types of cable are used for data and telecommunications. The application you are using must be taken into consideration when choosing the type of cable you will install. Table 7.1 lists some of the common copper cables and common applications run on them. With the UTP cabling types found in Table 7.1, applications that run on lower-grade cable will also run on higher grades of cable (for example, digital telephones can be used with Category 3, 4, 5, 5e, or 6 cabling).

TABLE 7.1: Common Types of Copper Cabling and the Applications That Run on Them

Cable Type	Common Applications
UTP Category 1	Signaling, door bells, alarm systems
UTP Category 2	Digital phone systems, Apple LocalTalk
UTP Category 3	10Base-T, 4Mbps Token Ring
UTP Category 4	16Mbps Token Ring
UTP Category 5	100Base-TX, 1000Base-T
UTP Category 5e	100Base-TX, 1000Base-T
UTP Category 6*	100Base-TX, 1000Base-T
UTP Category 7*	100Base-TX, 1000Base-T
Backbone UTP cable	Analog and digital voice applications
Shielded twisted-pair (STP)	4Mbps and 16Mbps Token Ring
Screened twisted-pair (ScTP)	100Base-TX, 1000Base-T
Coaxial RG-8	Thick Ethernet (10Base-5), video
Coaxial RG-58	Thin Ethernet (10Base-2)
Coaxial RG-59	CATV
Coaxial RG-6U	CATV, satellite, HDTV, cable modem
Coaxial RG-6U Quad Shield	Same as RG-6 with extra shielding
Coaxial RG-62	ARCnet, video, IBM 3270

*Category 6 and 7 requirements are under development and are not ratified Standards.

Major Cable Types Found Today

When you plan to purchase cable for a new installation, the decisions you have to make are mind-boggling. What cable will support 100Base-TX or 1000BaseT? Will this cable support even faster applications in the future? Do you choose stranded-conductor cable or solid-conductor cable? Should you use different cable for voice and data? Do you buy a cable that only supports present standards or one that is designed to support future standards? The list of questions goes on and on.

NOTE Solid-conductor cable is used for horizontal cabling. The entire conductor is one single piece of copper. Stranded-conductor cable is used for patch cords and shorter cabling runs; the conductor consists of strands of smaller wire. These smaller strands make the cable more flexible but also cause it to have higher attenuation. Any cable that will be used for horizontal cabling (in the walls) should be solid conductor.

We'll review the different types of cable listed in Table 7.1 and expand on their performance characteristics and some of their possible uses.

UTP cables are 100-ohm plus or minus 15 percent, 24 AWG (American Wire Gauge), twisted-pair cables. Horizontal cabling uses unshielded, four-pair cables (as shown in Figure 7.1), but voice applications can use cables with 25, 50, 100, or more pairs bundled together. UTP cables may contain a slitting cord or rip cord that makes it easier to strip back the jacket. Each of the wires is color-coded to make it easier for the cable installer to identify and correctly terminate the wire.

FIGURE 7.1:

Common UTP cable

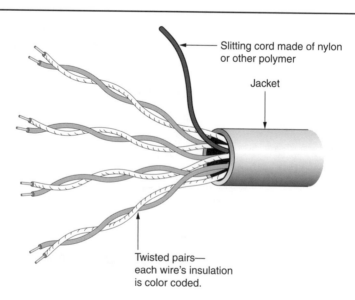

Slitting cord made of nylon or other polymer

Jacket

Twisted pairs—
each wire's insulation
is color coded.

Color Codes for UTP Cables

The individual wires in a UTP cable are color-coded for ease of identification and termination. A four-pair cable has four tip colors: blue, orange, green, and brown. Each of these is either predominantly that color with a stripe or splash of white, or it is predominantly white with a stripe or splash of the tip color. The tip color is also known as the band color, and the stripe is known as the base color. This becomes more relevant when working with 25-pair or larger cables. A four-pair UTP cable with the base and band colors labeled is shown here.

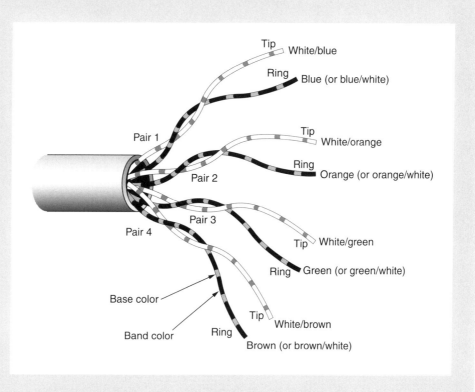

Tip and Ring Colors

The primary color is also known as the tip color and the secondary color is known as the ring color. In a four-pair cable, the cable pairs are coded in a standard color-coding; this color-coding is on the insulation of the individual wires. These colors are as follows:

Pair	Tip	Ring
Pair 1	White/blue	Blue (or blue/white)
Pair 2	White/orange	Orange (or orange/white)
Pair 3	White/green	Green (or green/white)
Pair 4	White/brown	Brown (or brown/white)

White is the common color in all four-pair cables and is always numbered or inserted into a punch-down block first. For example, in pair 1 (the blue pair), the two wires are white/blue and blue. The white (or white/blue) wire has a small blue stripe running down the length of the wire; this wire is the tip. The blue (or blue/white) wire has a small white stripe running down the length of the wire; this wire is the ring. Sometimes, the white wire will just have a smudge of blue every inch or so, and the blue wire will be solid. This depends on the cable manufacturer.

Depending on whom you ask, you may get different answers as to which wire is considered primary and which is considered secondary. In the United States and much of the world, premises-cabling people consider the tip wire to be primary because thatwire that is connected to a connecting block first. Others consider the ring wire to be the primary. However, as long as they are wired correctly, it does not matter what you call the tip and ring wires.

Category 1 UTP Cable

Category 1 cable is UTP cable designed to support applications operating at 100kHz or less. Applications operating at less than 100kHz are very low-speed applications, such as analog voice, doorbells, alarm systems, RS-232, and RS-422. Category 1 cable is not used very often due to its limited use with data and voice applications and, although it is cheap to install, it will not be possible to use it for anything other than low-speed applications.

Category 2 UTP Cable

Category 2 UTP cable is designed to support applications that operate at a frequency rate of less than 4MHz. This cable can be used for low-speed applications such as digital voice, Apple LocalTalk, serial applications, ARCnet, ISDN, some DSL applications, and T-1. Category 2 cable is not used often for anything except digital voice applications because it has limited expansion capabilities. Most telecommunications designers choose a minimum of Category 3 cable for digital voice.

Category 3 UTP Cable

Category 3 UTP cable was the workhorse of the networking industry for a few years after it was approved as a standard. It is designed to support applications requiring bandwidth up to 16MHz, including digital and analog voice, 10Base-T Ethernet, 4Mbps Token Ring, 100Base-T4 Fast Ethernet, 100VG-AnyLAN, ISDN, and DSL applications. Most digital-voice applications use a minimum of Category 3 cabling.

Category 3 cable is usually four-pair twisted-pair cable, but some backbone (bundled) cables (25-pair, 50-pair, etc.) are certified for use with Category 3 applications. Those backbone cables are sometimes used with 10Base-T Ethernet applications; they are not recommended.

NOTE   The industry trend is toward installing Category 5e cabling instead of a combination of Category 3 cabling for voice and Category 5 for data.

Category 4 UTP Cable

Category 4 cable had a short life in the marketplace and is now a thing of the past. It was designed to support applications operating at frequencies up to 20MHz. The price of Category 4 and Category 5 cable is almost identical, so most people choose Category 5 cable because it has five times the bandwidth of Category 4 and therefore the capability of supporting much higher-speed applications. The intent of Category 4 cabling was to support Ethernet, 4Mbps Token Ring, and 16Mbps Token Ring, as well as digital voice applications. The next revision of the ANSI/TIA/EIA-568-A Standard will remove Category 4 cable as a recommended medium.

Category 5/5e UTP Cable

Category 5 cable currently reigns as king in existing installations of UTP cabling for data applications. Category 5 cable was designed to support applications requiring bandwidth up to 100MHz. In addition to applications supported by Category 4 and earlier cables, Category 5 supports 100Base-TX, TP-PMD (FDDI over copper), ATM (155Mbps), and 1000Base-T (Gigabit Ethernet).

In the fall of 1999, the ANSI/TIA/EIA ratified an addendum to the ANSI/TIA/EIA-568-A Standard to approve additional performance requirements for Category 5e cabling. Category 5e has surpassed Category 5 as the preferred cable for new installations, and we recommend installing it as the minimum Category cable for new UTP installations that will support both data and voice applications.

Some manufacturers make 25-pair backbone (bundled or feeder) cable that support Category 5 installations, but we are a little uncomfortable with using these cables for high-speed applications such as 100Base-TX or 1000Base-T.

NOTE   Category 5 cable will support 1000Base-T, provided the installed cabling system passes the performance specifications outlined in TSB-95.

Category 6 UTP Cable

This cable category is currently in development and is not ratified as a Standard. Vendors are advertising Category 6–level performance, but you have no guarantee that the product will be Category 6–compliant when the Standard is ratified. With bandwidth up to 250MHz, this cable category will support any application that Category 5e and lower cables will support. Category 6 cabling is currently about 35 percent more expensive than good-quality Category 5e.

Category 7 UTP Cable

Category 7 cable specifications are currently in development by the ISO/IEC. The cable will support applications requiring bandwidth up to 600MHz. The style of connector used with previous cable categories will have to be updated to support Category 7 installations for the full supported bandwidth.

Shielded Twisted-Pair Cable (IBM Type 1A)

Originally developed by IBM to support applications such as Token Ring and the IBM Systems Network Architecture, shielded twisted-pair (STP) cable can currently support applications requiring bandwidth up to 600MHz. Though many types of shielded cable are on the market, the Type 1A cable is the most shielded. An IBM Type 1A (STP-A) cable, shown in Figure 7.2, has an outer shield that consists of braided copper; this shield surrounds the 150-ohm, 22 AWG, two-pair conductors. Each conductor is insulated and then each twisted pair is individually shielded.

FIGURE 7.2:

An STP-A cable and an ScTP cable

All the shielding in an STP-A cable provides better protection against external sources of EMI than UTP cable does, but the shielding makes the cable thicker and more bulky. Typical applications are 4Mbps and 16Mbps Token Ring and IBM terminal applications (3270 and 5250 terminals). STP cabling is expensive to install, and many people think that it provides only marginally better EMI protection than a well-made Category 5 or higher UTP. If you are considering STP cabling solely because it provides better EMI protection and higher potential bandwidth, you should consider using fiber-optic cable instead.

Other types of IBM cabling are not discussed here. See Chapter 2 for more detail on the additional IBM cabling types.

NOTE   IBM now recommends Category 5 cabling for Token Ring users.

Backbone UTP Cable

Backbone cable is cable that has more than four pairs. Often called *multipair, bundled,* or *feeder cable*, backbone usually comes in 25-, 50-, or 100-pair increments, though higher pair counts are available. Though it is called *backbone cabling*, this term can be misleading if you are looking at cabling from a data-cabling perspective. High-pair-count backbone cabling is typically used with voice applications only.

Some vendors sell 25- and 50-pair cable that is certified for use with Category 5 applications, but that many pairs of cable all supporting data in the same sheath makes us nervous. All those individual wire pairs generate crosstalk that affects all the other pairs; the factor that becomes important in higher pair counts is called *power-sum NEXT* (see Chapter 1 for more details on cable performance). The ANSI/TIA/EIA-568-A Standard recognizes this and requires power-sum crosstalk testing for all cables greater than four pair.

We have also seen applications with voice and 10Base-T Ethernet data in the same backbone cable. Sharing the same sheath with two different applications is not recommended either.

NOTE   Many manufacturers make 25-pair and 50-pair cables rated to Category 5–level performance, but we recommend using individual four-pair cables when trying to achieve Category 5 performance levels.

Color Codes and Backbone Cables   Color codes for 25-pair cables are a bit more sophisticated than for four-pair cables due to the many additional wire pairs. In the case of 25-pair cables, there is one additional ring color (slate) and four additional tip colors (red, black, yellow, and violet). Table 7.2 lists the color coding for 25-pair cables.

TABLE 7.2:   Color Coding for 25-Pair Cables

Pair Number	Tip Color	Ring Color
1	White	Blue
2	White	Orange
3	White	Green
4	White	Brown
5	White	Slate
6	Red	Blue
7	Red	Orange
8	Red	Green
9	Red	Brown
10	Red	Slate
11	Black	Blue
12	Black	Orange
13	Black	Green
14	Black	Brown
15	Black	Slate
16	Yellow	Blue
17	Yellow	Orange
18	Yellow	Green
19	Yellow	Brown
20	Yellow	Slate
21	Violet	Blue
22	Violet	Orange
23	Violet	Green
24	Violet	Brown
25	Violet	Slate

As with four-pair UTP cable, the tip color is always connected first. For example, when terminating 25-pair cable to a 66-block, white/blue would be connected to pin 1, then blue/white would be connected to pin 2, and so forth.

When cable pair counts exceed 25 pairs, the cable is broken up into *binder groups* consisting of 25 pairs of wire. A binder group is marked within the larger bundle with a uniquely colored plastic binder wrapped around the 25-pair bundle. The binder colors follow the same color-code sequence as the pairs, so installers don't have to learn two color systems.

Coaxial Cable

Coaxial cable has been around since local area networking was in its infancy. The original designers of Ethernet picked coaxial cable as their "ether" because coaxial cable is well shielded, has high bandwidth capabilities and low attenuation, and is easy to install. Coaxial cables are identified by their *RG* designation. Coaxial cable can have a solid or stranded core and impedance of 50, 75, or 92 ohms. Coaxial such as the one shown in Figure 7.3 is called coaxial cable because it has one wire that carries the signal surrounded by a layer of insulation and another concentric shield; both the shield and the inner conductor run along the same axis. The outer shield also serves as a ground and should be grounded to be effective.

FIGURE 7.3:

Coaxial cable

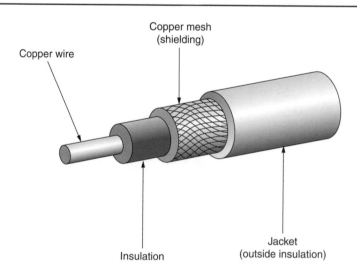

Copper mesh (shielding)

Copper wire

Insulation

Jacket (outside insulation)

NOTE	Coaxial cable is still widely used for video applications, but it is not recommended for data installations.

A number of different types of coaxial cable are used for data; these are shown in Table 7.3.

TABLE 7.3: Common Coaxial-Cable Types

RG Number	Center Wire Gauge	Impedance	Conductor
RG-6U	18 AWG	75 ohms	Solid
RG-6U QS	18 AWG	75 ohms	Solid
RG-8U	10 AWG	50 ohms	Solid
RG-58U	20 AWG	53.5 ohms	Solid
RG-58CU	20 AWG	50 ohms	Solid
RG-58AU	20 AWG	50 ohms	Stranded
RG-59U	20 AWG	75 ohms	Solid
RG-62U	22 AWG	93 ohms	Solid

NOTE Sometimes you will see coaxial cable labeled as 802.3 Ethernet Thinnet or 802.3 Ethernet Thicknet. Thin Ethernet cable is RG-58 and is used for 10-Base-2 Ethernet; thick Ethernet cable is RG-8 and is used for 10Base-5 Ethernet.

Hybrid or Composite Cable

You may hear the term *hybrid* or *composite cable* used. The cable is not really a special type of cable but is one that contains multiple smaller cables within a common cable jacket or spiral wrap. The smaller cables can either be the same type or a mixture of cable types. For example, a common cable that is manufactured now contains four-pair Category 5 UTP cable and two strands of multimode fiber-optic cable. What is nice about these cable types is that you get two different types of media to a single location by pulling only one cable. Manufacturer CommScope builds hybrid cables. For more information, check out CommScope's Web site at www.commscope.com. Requirements for these cables are clarified in ANSI/TIA/EIA-568-A-3 (addendum 3 to the Standard.)

Picking the Right Patch Cables

Though not really part of a discussion on picking cable types for horizontal cable, the subject of patch cords should be addressed. *Patch cables* (or *patch cords*) are the cables that are used to connect 110-type connecting blocks, patch-panel ports, or telecommunication outlets (wall-plate outlets) to network equipment or telephones.

We have stated this elsewhere in the book, but it deserves repeating: You should purchase factory-made patch cables. Patch cables are a critical part of the link between a network device (such as a PC) and the network equipment (such as a hub). Determining appropriate transmission requirements and testing methodology for patch codes is one of the holdups in completing the TIA/EIA Category 6 specification. Low-quality, poorly made, and damaged patch cables very frequently contribute to network problems. Often the patch cable is considered the weakest link in the structured cabling system. Poorly made patch cables will contribute to attenuation loss and increased crosstalk.

Factory-made patch cables are constructed using exacting and controlled circumstances to assure reliable and consistent transmission-performance parameters. These patch cables are tested and guaranteed to perform correctly.

Patch cables are made of stranded-conductor cable to give them additional flexibility. However, stranded cable has up to 20 percent higher attenuation values than solid-conductor cable, so lengths should be kept to a minimum. The ANSI/TIA/EIA-568-A Standard allows for a 6-meter (20-foot) patch cable in the wiring closet and a 3-meter (10-foot) patch cable at the workstation area. In our experience, the 6-meter patch cable is more useful in the workstation location, but your actual mileage may vary. Here are some suggestions to consider when purchasing patch cables:

- Don't make them yourself. Many problems result from bad patch cables.

- Choose the correct category for the performance level you want to achieve.

- Make sure the patch cables you purchase use stranded conductors for increased flexibility.

- Purchase a variety of lengths and make sure you have a few extra of each length.

- Consider color-coding your patch cords in the telecommunication closet. An example of this would be:
  - Blue cords for workstations
  - Gray cords for voice

- Red cords for servers

- Green cords for hub-to-hub connections

- Yellow for other types of connections

NOTE   The suggested color coding for patch cords loosely follows the documentation guidelines described in Chapter 5.

Why Pick Copper Cabling?

Copper cabling has been around and in use since electricity was invented. Despite its antiquity, it is much more popular than optical-fiber cabling. And the quality of copper wire has continued to improve. Over the past 100 years, copper manufacturers have developed the refining and drawing processes so that copper is even more high quality.

High-speed technologies, such as 155Mbps ATM and Gigabit Ethernet, that experts said would never run over copper wire as recently as five years ago are running over copper wiring today.

Network managers pick copper cabling for a variety of reasons: Copper cable (especially UTP cable) is inexpensive and easy to install, the installation methods are well understood, and the components (patch panels, wall-plate outlets, connecting blocks, etc.) are inexpensive. Further, UTP-based equipment (voice systems, 10Base-T Ethernet hubs, etc.) that uses the copper cabling is much more affordable than comparable fiber equipment.

NOTE   The main downsides to using copper cable are that copper cable can be susceptible to outside interference (EMI), optical fiber provides much greater bandwidth, and the data on copper wire is not as secure as data traveling through an optical fiber.

Table 7.5 lists some of the common technologies that currently use unshielded twisted-pair Ethernet. With the advances in networking technology and twisted-pair cable, it makes you wonder what applications you will see on UTP cables in the future.

TABLE 7.5: Applications That Use Unshielded Twisted-Pair Cables

Application	Data Rate	Encoding Scheme*	Pairs Required
10Base-T Ethernet	10Mbps	Manchester	2
100Base-TX Ethernet	100Mbps	4B5B/NRZI/MLT3	2
100Base-T4 Ethernet	100Mbps	8B6T	4
1000Base-T Gigabit Ethernet	1000Mbps	PAM5	4
100Base-VG AnyLAN	100Mbps	5B6B/NRZ	4
4Mbps Token Ring	4Mbps	Manchester	2
16Mbps Token Ring	16Mbps	Manchester	2
ATM-25	25Mbps	NRZ	2
ATM-155	155Mbps	NRZ	2
TP-PMD (FDDI over copper)	100Mbps	MLT-3	2

* Encoding is a technology that allows more than one bit to be passed through a wire during a single cycle (hertz).

Best Practices for Copper Installation

We used our own installations of copper cabling, as well as the tips and techniques of many others, to create guidelines for you to follow to ensure that your UTP cabling system will support all the applications you intend it to. These guidelines include the following:

- Following standards
- Making sure you do not exceed distance limits
- Good installation techniques

Following Standards

One of the most important elements to planning and deploying a new telecommunications infrastructure is to make sure you are following a Standard. In the United States, this Standard is the ANSI/TIA/EIA-568-A Commercial Building Telecommunications Cabling Standard. It may be purchased from Global Engineering

Documents on the Internet at http://global.ihs.com. We highly recommend that anyone designing a cabling infrastructure own this document.

TIP

Have you purchased or do you plan to purchase the ANSI/TIA/EIA-568-A Standard? Check to see if the ANSI/TIA/EIA-568-B version of the standard is available, as this version will be the most up-to-date. Actually, we recommend that you buy the TIA/EIA Telecommunications Building Wiring Standards collection on CD from Global. This is a terrific resource (especially from which to cut and paste sections into an RFP) and can be purchased with a subscription that lets you receive updates as they are published.

Following the ANSI/TIA/EIA-568-A Standard will ensure that your cabling system is interoperable with any networking or voice applications that have been designed to work with that Standard.

The current version of the ANSI/TIA/EIA-568-A Standard has components and performance specifications that were developed as many as 10 years ago. Getting the latest innovations incorporated into a standard is difficult because these technologies are often not tested and deployed widely enough for the standards committees to feel comfortable approving them. Some vendors (such as Avaya, with SYSTIMAX Structured Connectivity Solutions) install cabling systems that will provide much greater performance than the current Standards require and will still remain compatible with existing Standards. If a vendor proposes a solution to you that has a vendor-specific performance spin on it, make sure it is backward compatible with the current Standards.

Cable Distances

One of the most important things that the ANSI/TIA/EIA-568-A Standard defines is the maximum distance that a horizontal cable should traverse. The maximum distance between the patch panel (or cross-connect, in the case of voice) and the wall plate (the horizontal portion of the cable) *must* not exceed 90 meters (285 feet). Further, the patch cord used in the telecommunications closet (patch panel to hub or cross-connect) cannot exceed 6 meters (20 feet), and the patch cord used on the workstation side must not exceed 3 meters (10 feet).

You may find that higher-quality cables will allow you to exceed this distance limit for technologies such as 10Base-T Ethernet or 100VG-AnyLAN. However, you are not guaranteed that those horizontal cable runs that exceed 90 meters will work with future technologies designed to work with TIA/EIA Standards, so it is best to follow the Standard and not "customize" your installation.

Some tips relating to distance and the installation of copper cabling include:

- Never exceed the 90-meter maximum distance for horizontal cables.

- Don't forget to account for the fact that horizontal cable may be routed up through walls, around corners, and through conduit.

- Account for any additional cable distance that may be required as a result of trays, hooks, and cable management.

- Horizontal cable rarely goes in a straight line from the patch panel to the wall plate. Account for all distances that the cable may have to traverse in the ceiling.

- Leave some slack in the ceiling above the wiring rack in case retermination is required or the patch panel must be moved; cabling professionals call this a *service loop*. Some professional cable installers leave as much as an extra 10 feet in the ceiling bundled together or looped around a hook (as seen in Figure 7.4).

FIGURE 7.4:

Leaving some cable slack in the ceiling

Wiring Patterns

The ANSI/TIA/EIA-568-A Standard recommends one of two wiring patterns for modular jacks and plugs: T568A and T568B. The only difference between these wiring patterns is that pin assignments for pairs 2 and 3 are reversed. However, these two wiring patterns are constantly causing problems for end users and weekend cable installers. What is the problem? Patch panels and modular wall-plate outlets come in either the T568A or T568B wiring patterns. The actual construction of these devices is exactly the same, but they are color coded according to either the T568A wiring standard or the T568B wiring standard. The confusion comes from people wondering which one to use. It doesn't matter. They both work the same way. But you have to be consistent at each end of the cable. If you use T568A at one end, you must use it at the other; likewise with T568B.

The cable pairs are assigned to specific pin numbers. The pin numbers are numbered from left to right if you are looking into the modular jack or down on the top of the modular plug. Figure 7.5 shows the pin numbers for the eight-position modular jack (RJ-45) and plug.

FIGURE 7.5:

Pin positions for the eight-position modular plug and jack

Modular eight-position plug   Modular eight-position jack

Which Wiring Pattern Should You Choose?   The T568A wiring pattern is most prevalent outside of the United States and in U.S. government installations. T568B is more prevalent in private installations in the United States. This is changing, however. The recommended pattern to use for new installations is T568A. It is the only pattern recognized by ANSI/TIA/EIA-570, the residential wiring Standard. The reason for recommending T568A is that pairs 1 and 2 are configured the same as a wiring pattern called USOC, which is prevalent in voice installations.

The wiring pattern chosen makes no difference to the applications used. The signal does not care what color wire it is running through.

The most important factor is to choose one wiring configuration and stick with it. This means when purchasing patch panels, 110-blocks, and wall plates, they should all use the same wiring pattern.

NOTE More information about the T568A and T568B wiring configurations can be found in Chapter 9.

Planning

Planning plays an essential role in any successful implementation of a technology; structured cabling systems are no exception. If you are planning to install a larger structured cabling system (more than a few hundred cable runs), consider hiring a professional consultant to assist you with the planning phases.

NOTE Chapter 15 has information on planning and preparing a request for proposal for a structured cabling system. Chapter 12 covers the essential design issues you must consider when building a structured cabling system.

Some questions you should ask when planning a cabling infrastructure that includes copper cabling include:

- How many cables should be run to each location?
- Should you use cable trays, J hooks, or conduit where the cable is in the ceiling space?
- Will the voice system use patch panels, or will the voice cable be cross-connected via 66-blocks directly to the phone-system blocks?
- Is there a danger of cable damage from water, rodents, or chemicals?
- Has proper grounding been taken care of for equipment racks and cable terminations requiring grounding?
- Will you use the same category of cable for voice and data?
- Will new holes be required between floors for backbone cable or through firewalls for horizontal or backbone cable?
- Will any of the cables be exposed to the elements or outdoors?

Cabling @ Work: Critter Damage

Cabling folklore is full of stories of cabling being damaged by termites, rats, and other vermin. This might have been hard for us to believe if we had not seen such damage ourselves. One such instance of this type of damage occurred because rats were using a metal conduit to run on the cable between walls. Additional cable was installed, which blocked the rats' pathway, so they chewed holes in the cable.

We have heard numerous stories of cable damage as a result of creatures with sharp teeth. In fact, the U.S. Department of Wildlife has a facility to administer a gopher test to cables intended for outdoor use in gopher-infested areas. Outside Plant (OSP) cables typically have metal tapes surrounding the jacket. Some are thick and strong enough to resist chew-through by rodents. They test the cable by—you guessed it—letting gophers in a cage gnaw on the cable. After a predetermined duration, the cable is examined to see if the gopher was able to penetrate through the jacket and shields to the conductors.

Consider any area that cable may be run through and take into consideration what you may need to do to protect the cable.

Cable Management

Good cable management starts with the design of the cabling infrastructure. When installing horizontal cable, consider using cable trays or J hooks in the ceiling to run the cable. They will prevent the cable from resting on ceiling tiles, power conduits, or air-conditioning ducts.

Further, make sure that you plan to purchase and install cable-management guides and equipment near patch panels and on racks so that when patch cables are installed, cable management will be available.

Installing Copper Cable

When you start installing copper cabling, much can go wrong. Even if you have adequately planned your installation, situations can still arise that will cause you problems either immediately or in the long term. Here are some tips to keep in mind for installing copper cabling:

- Do not untwist the twisted pairs at the cable connector or anywhere along the cable length any more than necessary (less than 0.5 inches for Category 5 and 5e, less than 0.375 inches for Category 6).

- Taps (bridged taps) are not allowed.

- Use connectors, patch panels, and wall plates that are compatible with the cable.

- When tie-wrapping cables, do not overtighten cable bundles.

- Staples are not recommended for fastening cables to supports. If they are used, don't staple the cables too tightly. Use a staple gun and staples (plastic staples, if possible) that are designed to be used with data cables. Do not use a generic staple gun; you will be on the express train to cable damage.

- Never splice a data cable if it has a problem at some point through its length; run a new cable instead.

- When terminating, remove as little of the cable's jacket as possible, preferably less than three inches. When finally terminated, the jacket should be as close as possible to where the conductors are punched down.

- Don't lay data cables directly across ceiling tiles or grids. Use a cable tray, J hook, horizontal ladder, or other method to support the cables. Avoid any sort of cable-suspension device that appears as if it will crush the cables.

- Follow proper grounding procedures for all equipment to reduce the likelihood of electrical shock and reduce the effects of EMI.

- All voice runs should be home-run, not daisy-chained. When wiring jacks for home telephone use, the great temptation is to daisy-chain cables together from one jack to the next. Each connection causes attenuation and crosstalk, which can degrade the signal even at voice frequencies. Enough noise could occur to drop your modem speed a few Kbps.

- If you have a cable with damaged pairs, replace it. You will be glad you did. Don't use another unused pair from the same cable because other pairs may be damaged to the point where they only cause intermittent problems, which are difficult to solve. Substituting pairs also prevents any future upgrades that require the use of all four pairs in the cable.

Pulling Cable

If you are just starting out in the cabling business or if you have never been around cable when it is installed, the term *pulling cable* is probably not significant. However, any veteran installer will tell you that *pulling* is exactly what you do. Cable is pulled from boxes or spools, passed up into the ceiling, and then, every few feet, the installers climb into the ceiling and pull the cable along a few more feet. In the case of cable in conduit, the cable is attached to a drawstring and pulled through.

While the cable is pulled, a number of circumstances can happen that will cause irreparable harm to the cable. But you can take steps to make sure that damage is avoided. Here is a list of copper-cabling installation tips:

- Do not exceed the cable's minimum bend radius by making sharp bends. The bend radius for four-pair UTP cables should not exceed 4 times the cable diameter and 10 times the cable diameter for backbone (25-pair and greater cable). Avoid making too many 90-degree bends.

- Do not exceed maximum cable pulling tension (110N or 25 pounds of force for four-pair UTP cable).

- When pulling a bundle of cables, do not pull cables unevenly.

- When building a system that supports both voice and data, run the intended voice lines to a patch panel separate from the data lines.

- Be careful not to twist the cable too tightly; doing so can damage the conductors and the conductor insulation.

- Avoid sources of heat such as hot-water pipes, steam pipes, or warm-air ducts.

- Be aware that damage can be caused by all sorts of other evil entities such as drywall screws, wiring-box edges, and other sharp objects found in ceilings and walls.

New cable is shipped in reels or coils. Often the reels are in boxes and the cable easily unspools from the boxes as you pull on it. Other times, the cable reels are not in a box, and you must use some type of device to allow the reel to turn freely while you pull the cable. In these cases, a device similar to the one pictured in Figure 7.6 may be just the ticket. These are often called *wire-spool trees*.

When the coils are inside a box, you dispense the cable directly from the box by pulling on it. You should never take these coils from the box and try to use them. The package is a special design and without the box, the cable will tangle hopelessly.

FIGURE 7.6:

A reel for holding spools of cable to make cable pulling easier

| TIP | When troubleshooting any wiring system, disconnect the data or voice application from *both* sides (the phone, PC, hub, and PBX). This goes for home telephone wiring, too! |

Separating Voice and Data Patch Panels

Some installations of voice and data cabling will terminate the cabling on the same patch panel. Although this is not entirely frowned upon by cabling professionals, many will tell you that it is more desirable to have a separate patch panel dedicated to voice applications. This is essential if you use a different category of cable for voice than for data (such as if you use Category 5 cable for data but Category 3 cable for voice).

In the example in Figure 7.7, the wall plate has two eight-position modular outlets (one for voice and one for data). The outlets are labeled V1 for voice and D1 for data. In the telecommunications closet, these two cables terminate on different patch panels, but each cable goes to position 1 on the patch panel. This makes the cabling installation much easier to document and to understand. The assumption in Figure 7.7 is that the voice system is terminating to a patch panel rather than a 66-block. The voice system is then patched to another patch panel that has the extensions from the company's PBX, and the data port is patched to a network hub.

FIGURE 7.7:

Using separate patch panels for voice and data

Sheath Sharing

The ANSI/TIA/EIA-568-A Standard does not specifically prohibit sheath sharing—that is, when two applications share the same sheath. For example, someone may decide that he or she cannot afford to run two separate cables to a single location and may use different pairs of cable for different applications. Table 7.6 shows the pin arrangement that might be used if a splitter (such as the one described in Chapter 9) were employed. Some installations may split the cable at the wall outlet and patch panel rather than using a splitter.

TABLE 7.6: Shared-Sheath Pin Assignments

Pin number	Usage	T568A Wire Color	T568B Wire Color
Pin 1	Ethernet transmit +	White/green	White/orange
Pin 2	Ethernet transmit –	Green	Orange

Continued on next page

TABLE 7.6 CONTINUED: Shared-Sheath Pin Assignments

Pin number	Usage	T568A Wire Color	T568B Wire Color
Pin 3	Ethernet receive +	White/orange	White/green
Pin 4	Phone inner wire 1	Blue	Blue
Pin 5	Phone inner wire 2	White/blue	White/blue
Pin 6	Ethernet receive −	Orange	Green
Pin 7	Phone inner wire 3	White/brown	White/brown
Pin 8	Phone inner wire 4	Brown	Brown

When two applications share the same cable sheath, performance problems can occur. Two applications (voice and data or data and data) running inside the same sheath may interfere with one another. Applications operating at lower frequencies such as 10Base-T may work perfectly well, but higher-frequency applications such as 100Base-TX will operate with unpredictable results. Also, as previously noted, two applications sharing the same cable sheath will prevent future upgrades to faster LAN technologies such as Gigabit Ethernet.

Because results can be unpredictable, and to future-proof your installation, we do not recommend using a single cable for multiple applications. Even for home applications where you may want to share voice and data applications (such as Ethernet, DSL, or ISDN), we recommend separate cables. The ringer voltage on a home telephone can disrupt data transmission on adjacent pairs of wire.

Avoiding Electromagnetic Interference

All electrical devices generate electromagnetic fields in the radio frequency (RF) spectrum. These electromagnetic fields produce electromagnetic interference (EMI) and interfere with the operation of other electric devices and the transmission of voice and data. You will notice EMI if you have a cordless or cellular phone and you walk near a microwave oven or other source of high EMI.

Data transmission is especially susceptible to disruption from EMI, so it is essential that cabling installed with the intent of supporting data (or voice) transmissions be separated from EMI sources. Here are some tips that may be helpful when planning pathways for data and voice cabling:

- Data cabling must never be installed in the same conduit with power cables. Aside from the EMI issue, it is not allowed by the NEC.

- If data cables must cross power cables, they should do so at right angles.

- Power and data cables should never share holes bored through concrete, wood, or steel. Again, it is an NEC violation as well as an EMI concern.

- Telecommunication outlets should be placed at the same height from the floor as power outlets, but they should not share stud space.

- Maintain at least two inches of separation from open electrical cables up to 300 volts. Six inches is a preferred minimum separation.

- Maintain at least six inches of separation from lighting sources or fluorescent-light power supplies.

- Maintain at least four inches of separation from antenna leads and ground wires without grounded shields.

- Maintain at least six inches of separation from neon signs and transformers.

- Maintain at least six feet of separation from lightning rods and wires.

- Other sources of EMI include photocopiers, microwave ovens, laser printers, electrical motors, elevator shafts, generators, fans, air conditioners, and heaters.

Copper Cable for Data Applications

In this section of the book, we will discuss using the cable you have run for data applications, and we will give some samples of ways that these applications can be wired. An important part of any telecommunications cabling system that supports data is the 110-block, which is a great place to start.

110-Blocks

The telecommunications industry has been using the 66-style block for many years, and it is considered the mainstay of the industry. The 66-blocks are traditionally used only for voice applications; though we have seen them used to cross-connect data circuits, this is not recommended. The 110-blocks are newer than 66-blocks and have been designed to overcome some of the problems associated with 66-blocks. The 110-blocks were designed to support higher-frequency applications, accommodate higher-density wiring arrangements, and better separate the input and output wires.

The standard 66-block enabled you to connect 25 pairs of wires to it, but the 110-blocks are available in many different configurations supporting not only 25 pairs of wire but 50, 100, 200, and 300 pairs of wires as well. The 110-block has two primary components: the 110 wiring block on which the wires are placed and the 110-connecting block (shown in Figure 7.8), which is used to terminate the wires. A 110-wiring block will consists of multiple 110-connector blocks; there will be one 110-connector block for each four-pair cable that must be terminated.

FIGURE 7.8:

The 110-connector block

Wires are inserted into these slots and terminated.

The 110-wiring block will consist of a few or many rows of 110-connector blocks. The wires are inserted into the connecting block and terminated by a punch-down tool or vendor-specific tool. These blocks are a type of IDC (insulation displacement connector); as the wires make contact with the metal on the blocks, the insulation is sliced, and the metal makes contact with the conductor. Remember, to prevent excessive crosstalk, don't untwist the pairs more than 0.5 inches for Category 5 and 5e, and 0.375 inches for Category 6 cable, when terminating onto a 110-connecting block.

The 110-blocks come in a wide variety of configurations. Some simply allow the connection of 110-block jumper cables. Figure 7.9 shows a 110-block jumper cable; one side of the cable is connected to the 110-block, and the other side is a modular eight-pin plug (RJ-45).

Other 110-blocks have RJ-45 connectors adjacent to the 110-blocks, such as the one shown in Figure 7.10. If the application uses the 50-pin telco connectors such as some Ethernet equipment and many voice applications do, 110-blocks such as the one shown in Figure 7.11 can be purchased that terminate cables to the 110-connecting blocks but then connect to 50-pin telco connectors.

You will also find 110-blocks on the back of patch panels; each 110-connecting block has a corresponding port on the patch panel. Figure 7.12 shows the 110-block on the back of a patch panel. The front side of the patch panel shown in Figure 7.13 shows a 96-port patch panel; each port will have a corresponding 110-connecting block.

FIGURE 7.11:

A 110-block with 50-pin
telco connectors

(Photo courtesy of The Siemon
Company)

FIGURE 7.12:

A 110-block on the back
side of a patch panel

(Photo courtesy of Computer Training
Academy)

NOTE	The patch panel with the 110-block on the back is the most common configuration in modern data telecommunication infrastructures.

FIGURE 7.13:

A 96-port patch panel

(Photo courtesy of MilesTek)

> **NOTE**
>
> When purchasing patch panels and 110-blocks, make sure you purchase one that has the correct wiring pattern. Most 110-blocks are color-coded for either the T568A or T568B wiring pattern.
>
> The 110-connecting blocks are almost always designed for solid-conductor wire. Make sure that you use solid-conductor wire for your horizontal cabling.

Sample Data Installations

As long as you follow the ANSI/TIA/EIA-568-A Standard, most of your communications infrastructure will be pretty similar and will not vary based on whether it is supporting voice or a specific data application. The horizontal cables will all follow the same structure and rules. However, when you start using the cabling for data applications, you'll notice some differences. We will now take a look at a couple of possible scenarios for the usage of a structured cabling system.

The first scenario, shown in Figure 7.14, shows the typical horizontal cabling terminated to a patch panel. The horizontal cable terminates to the 110-block on the back of the patch panel. When a workstation is connected to the network, it is connected to the network hub by means of a RJ-45 patch cable that connects the appropriate port on the patch panel to a port on the hub.

The use of a generic patch panel in Figure 7.14 allows this cabling system to be the most versatile and expandable. Further, the system can also be used for voice applications if the voice system is also terminated to patch panels.

Another scenario involves the use of 110-blocks with 50-pin telco connectors. These 50-pin telco connectors are used to connect to phone systems or to hubs that are equipped with the appropriate 50-pin telco interface. These are less versatile than patch panels because each connection must be terminated directly to a connection that connects to a hub.

In past years, we have worked with these types of connections, and network administrators have reported to us that these are more difficult to work with. Further, these 50-pin telco connectors may not be interchangeable with equipment you purchase in the future. Figure 7.15 shows the use of a 110-block connecting to network equipment using a 50-pin telco connector.

FIGURE 7.15:

A structured cabling system terminated into 110-connecting blocks with 50-pin telco connectors

A final scenario that is a combination of the patch-panel approach and the 110-block approach is the use of a 110-block and 110-block patch cables (such as the one shown previously in Figure 7.9). This is almost identical to the patch-panel approach, except that the patch cables used in the telecommunications closet have a 110-block connector on one side and an RJ-45 on the other. This configuration is shown in Figure 7.16.

FIGURE 7.16:

Structured cabling using 110-blocks and 110-block patch cords

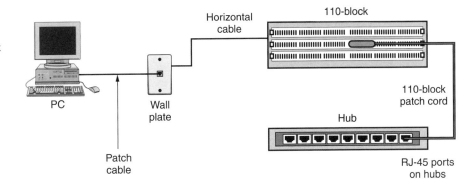

The previous examples are fairly simple and involve only one wiring closet. Any installation that requires more than one telecommunications closet and also one equipment room will require the service of a data backbone. Figure 7.17 shows an example where data backbone cabling is required. Due to distance limitations on horizontal cable when it is handling data applications, all horizontal cable is terminated to network equipment (hubs) in the telecommunications closet. The hub is then linked to other hubs via the data backbone cable.

FIGURE 7.17:

Structured cabling that includes data backbone cabling

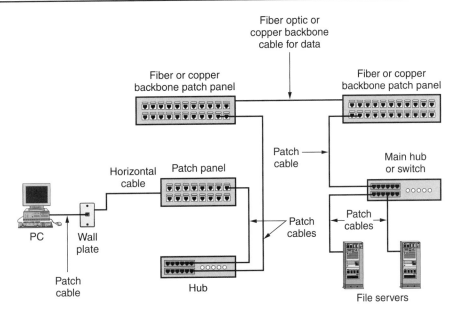

Copper Cable for Voice Applications

Unless you have an extraordinarily expensive phone system, it probably uses copper cabling to connect the desktop telephones to the phone switch or PBX (private branch exchange). Twisted-pair, copper cables have been the foundation of phone systems since the invention of the telephone. The mainstay of copper-based voice cross-connect systems was the 66-block, but it is now being surpassed by 110-block and patch-panel cross-connects.

66-Blocks

The 66-block is the most common of the punch-down blocks. It has been used with telephone cabling for many years, and its use continues to be widespread. A number of different types of 66-blocks exist, but the most common is the 66M1-50 pictured in Figure 7.18.

FIGURE 7.18:

A 66-block

(Photo courtesy of The Siemon Company)

The 66M1-50 has 50 horizontal rows of IDC connectors; each row consists of four prongs called *bifurcated contact prongs*. A side view of a row of contact prongs is shown in Figure 7.19. They are called bifurcated contact prongs because they are split in two pieces. The wire is inserted between one of the clips, and then the punch-down (impact) tool applies pressure to insert the wire between the two parts of the clip.

FIGURE 7.19:

The 66-block contact prongs

Clips

The clips are labeled *1*, *2*, *3*, and *4*. The 66-block clips in Figure 7.19 show that the two clips on the left (clips 1 and 2) are electrically connected together, as are the two clips (clips 3 and 4) on the right. However, the two sets of clips are not electrically connected to one another. Wires can be terminated on both sides of the 66-block, and a metal "bridging" clip is inserted between clips 1 and 2 and clips 3 and 4. This bridging clip mechanically and electrically joins the two sides together. The advantage to this is that the sides can be disconnected easily if you need to troubleshoot a problem.

NOTE   Some 66-blocks have a 50-pin telco connector on one side of the 66-block.

Figure 7.20 shows a common use of the 66-block; in this diagram, the phone lines from the phone company are connected to one side of the block. The lines into the PBX are connected on the other side. When the company is ready to turn the phone service on, the bridge clips are inserted, which makes the connection.

NOTE   The 66-blocks are typically designed for solid-conductor cable. Stranded-conductor cables will easily come loose from the IDC-style connectors. Stranded-conductor 66-blocks are available, however.

Figure 7.21 shows a 66-block in use for a voice system. In this picture, you can see that part of the 66-block connectors have bridging clips connecting them. This block also has a door that can be closed to protect the front of the block and prevent the bridging clips from being knocked off.

FIGURE 7.20:

A 66-block separating
phone-company lines from
the phone system

Bridging clips

Phone lines
from phone
company

Phone
system

66-block

FIGURE 7.21:

A 66-block used for voice
applications

(Photo courtesy of Computer Training
Center)

25-Pair Wire Assignments

The most typical type of cable connected to a 66-block is the 25-pair cable. The wiring pattern used with the 66-block is shown in Figure 7.22. If you look at a 66-block, you will notice notches in the plastic clips on the left and right side. These notches indicate the beginning of the next binder group.

FIGURE 7.22:

The 66-block wire-color/pin assignments for 25-pair cables

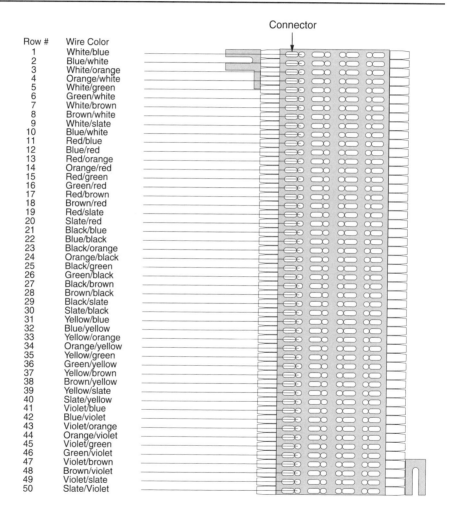

Row #	Wire Color
1	White/blue
2	Blue/white
3	White/orange
4	Orange/white
5	White/green
6	Green/white
7	White/brown
8	Brown/white
9	White/slate
10	Blue/white
11	Red/blue
12	Blue/red
13	Red/orange
14	Orange/red
15	Red/green
16	Green/red
17	Red/brown
18	Brown/red
19	Red/slate
20	Slate/red
21	Black/blue
22	Blue/black
23	Black/orange
24	Orange/black
25	Black/green
26	Green/black
27	Black/brown
28	Brown/black
29	Black/slate
30	Slate/black
31	Yellow/blue
32	Blue/yellow
33	Yellow/orange
34	Orange/yellow
35	Yellow/green
36	Green/yellow
37	Yellow/brown
38	Brown/yellow
39	Yellow/slate
40	Slate/yellow
41	Violet/blue
42	Blue/violet
43	Violet/orange
44	Orange/violet
45	Violet/green
46	Green/violet
47	Violet/brown
48	Brown/violet
49	Violet/slate
50	Slate/Violet

Connector

NOTE   The T568A and T568B wiring patterns do *not* apply to 66-blocks.

If you use 66-blocks and four-pair UTP cables instead of 25-pair cables, then the wire color/pin assignments are as shown in Figure 7.23.

FIGURE 7.23:

The 66-block wire color/pin assignments for four-pair cables

Row #	Wire Color
1	White/blue
2	Blue/white
3	White/orange
4	Orange/white
5	White/green
6	Green/white
7	White/brown
8	Brown/white
9	White/blue
10	Blue/white
11	White/orange
12	Orange/white
13	White/green
14	Green/white
15	White/brown
16	Brown/white
17	White/blue
18	Blue/white
19	White/orange
20	Orange/white
21	White/green
22	Green/white
23	White/brown
24	Brown/white
25	White/blue
26	Blue/white
27	White/orange
28	Orange/white
29	White/green
30	Green/white
31	White/brown
32	Brown/white
33	White/blue
34	Blue/white
35	White/orange
36	Orange/white
37	White/green
38	Green/white
39	White/brown
40	Brown/white
41	White/blue
42	Blue/white
43	White/orange
44	Orange/white
45	White/green
46	Green/white
47	White/brown
48	Brown/white
49	No wire on row 49 when using four-pair wire
50	No wire on row 50 when using four-pair wire

Connector

Sample Voice Installations

In many ways, voice installations are quite similar to data installations. The differences are the type of equipment that each end of the link is plugged into and, sometimes, the type of patch cables used. The ANSI/TIA/EIA-568-A Standard requires at least one four-pair, unshielded twisted-pair cable to be run to each workstation outlet installed. This cable is to be used for voice applications. We recommend using a minimum of Category 3 cable for voice applications; however, if you will purchase Category 5 or Category 5e cable for data, we advise using the same category of cable for voice.

Some sample cabling installations follow; we have seen them installed to support voice and data. Because so many possible combinations exist, we will only be able to show you a few. The first one (shown in Figure 7.24) is common in small- to medium-sized installations. In this example, each horizontal cable designated for voice terminates to an RJ-45 patch panel. A second patch panel has RJ-45 blocks terminated to the extensions on the phone switch or PBX. This makes moving a phone extension from one location to another as simple as moving the patch cable. If this type of flexibility is required, this configuration is an excellent choice.

FIGURE 7.24:

A voice application using RJ-45 patch panels

The next example illustrates a more complex wiring environment, which includes backbone cabling for the voice applications. This example could employ patch panels in the telecommunications closet or 66-blocks, depending on the flexibility desired. The telecommunications closet is connected to the equipment room via twisted-pair backbone cabling. Figure 7.25 illustrates the use of patch panels, 66-blocks, and backbone cabling.

FIGURE 7.25:

A voice application with a voice backbone, patch panels, and 66-blocks

The final example is the most common for voice installations; it uses 66-blocks exclusively. Note that in Figure 7.26 two 66-blocks are connected by cross-connected cable. Cross-connect cable is simple single-pair, twisted-pair wire that has no jacket. You can purchase cross-connect wire, so don't worry about stripping a bunch of existing cables to get it. The example shown in Figure 7.26 is not as versatile as it would be if you used patch panels because 66-blocks require either reconnecting the cross-connect or reprogramming the PBX.

FIGURE 7.26:

Voice applications using
66-blocks exclusively

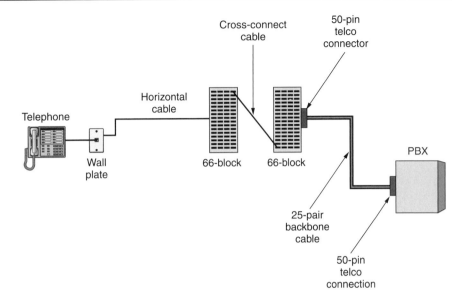

FIGURE 7.27:

A 66-block with
cross-connect wires

(Photo courtesy of The Siemon
Company)

Figure 7.27 shows a 66-block with cross-connect wires connected to it. Though you cannot tell it from the figure, cross-connect wires are often red and white.

The examples of 66-blocks and 110-blocks in this chapter are fairly common, but we could not possibly cover every possible permutation and usage of these types of blocks. We hope we have given you a representative view of some possible configurations.

Testing

Every cable run must receive a minimum level of testing. You can purchase $5,000 cable testers that will provide you with many statistics on performance, but the most important test is simply determining that the pairs are connected properly.

The $5,000 testers provide you with much more performance data than the simple cable testers and will also certify that each cable run will operate at a specific performance level. Some customers will insist on viewing results on the $5,000 cable tester, but the minimum tests you should run will determine continuity and that the wire map is correct. You can perform a couple different levels of testing. The cable testers that you can use include the following:

- Tone generators and amplifier probes
- Continuity testers
- Wire-map testers
- Cable-certification testers

Tone Generators and Amplifier Probes

If you have a bundle of cable and you need to locate a single cable within the bundle, using a tone generator and amplifier is the answer. Often, cable installers will pull more than one cable (sometimes dozens) to a single location, but they will not document the ends of the cables. The tone generator is used to send an electrical signal through the cable. On the other side of the cable, the amplifier (a.k.a. the inductive amplifier) is placed near each cable until a sound from the amplifier is heard, indicating that the cable is found. Figure 7.28 shows a tone generator and amplifier probe from IDEAL DataComm.

A tone generator and
amplifier probe

(Photo courtesy of IDEAL DataComm)

Continuity Testing

The simplest test you can perform on a cable is the continuity test. It ensures that electrical signals are traveling from the point of origin to the receiving side. Simple continuity testers only guarantee that a signal is being received; they do not test attenuation or crosstalk.

Wire-Map Testers

A wire-map tester is capable of examining the pairs of wires and indicating whether or not they are connected correctly through the link. These testers will also indicate if the continuity of each wire is good. As long as good installation techniques are used and the correct category of cables, connectors, and patch panels are used, many of the problems with cabling can be solved by a simple wire-map tester. Figure 7.29 shows a simple tester from IDEAL DataComm that performs both wire-map testing and continuity testing.

FIGURE 7.29:

A simple cable-testing tool

(Photo courtesy of IDEAL DataComm)

Cable Certification

If you are a professional cable installer, you may be required to certify that the cabling system you have installed will perform at the required levels. Testing tools more sophisticated than a simple continuity tester or wire-map tester perform these tests. The tools have two components, one for each side of the cable link. Tools such as the Microtest PentaScanner or Hewlett Packard WireScope perform many sophisticated tests that the less expensive scanners cannot. Cable testing and certification is covered in more detail in Chapter 14.

Common Problems with Copper Cabling

Sophisticated testers may provide a reason for a failed test. Some of the problems you may encounter include:

- Length problems
- Wire-map problems
- NEXT and FEXT (crosstalk) problems
- Attenuation problems

Length Problems

If a cable tester indicates that you have length problems, the most likely cause is that the cable you have installed exceeds the maximum length. Length problems may also occur if the cable has an open or short. Another possible problem is that the cable tester's NVP (nominal velocity of propagation) setting is configured incorrectly. To correct it, run the tester's NVP diagnostics or setup to make sure that the NVP value is set properly.

Wire-Map Problems

When the cable tester indicates a wire-map problem, pairs are usually transposed in the wire. This is often a problem when mixing equipment that supports the T568A and T568B wiring patterns; it can also occur if the installer has split the pairs (individual wires are terminated on incorrect pins). A wire-map problem may also indicate an open or short in the cable.

NEXT and FEXT (Crosstalk) Problems

If the cable tester indicates crosstalk problems, the signal in one pair of wires is "bleeding" over into another pair of wires; when the crosstalk values are strong enough, this can interfere with data transmission. NEXT problems indicate that the cable tester has measured too much crosstalk on the near end of the connection. FEXT problems indicate too much crosstalk on the opposite side of the cable. Crosstalk is often caused by the pairs of the cable being split too much when they are terminated. Crosstalk problems can also be caused by external interference from EMI sources and cable damage or when components (patch panels and connectors) that are only supported for lower categories of cabling are used.

NEXT failures reported on very short cable runs, 15 meters (50 feet) and less, require special consideration. Such failures are a function of signal harmonics, resulting from imbalance in either the cable or the connecting hardware or induced by poor-quality installation techniques. The hardware or installation (punch-down) technique is usually the culprit, and you can fix the problem by either reterminating (taking care not to untwist the pairs) or by replacing the connecting hardware with a product that is better electrically balanced. It should be noted that most quality NICs are constructed to ignore the "short-link" phenomenon and may function just fine under these conditions.

Attenuation Problems

When the cable tester reports attenuation problems, the cable is losing too much signal across its length. This can be a result of the cabling being too long. Also check to make sure the cable is terminated properly. When running horizontal cable, make sure that you use solid-conductor cable; stranded cable has higher attenuation than solid cable and can contribute to attenuation problems over longer lengths. Other causes of attenuation problems include high temperatures, cable damage (stretching the conductors), and the wrong category of components (patch panels and connectors).

chapter 8

Wall Plates

- Wall-Plate Design and Installation Issues

- Fixed-Design Wall Plates

- Modular Wall Plates

- Biscuit Jacks

In Chapter 5, you learned about the basic components of a structured cabling system. One of the most visible of these components is the wall plate (also called a *workstation* or *station outlet* because it is usually placed near a workstation). As its name suggests, a wall plate is a flat plastic or metal plate that usually mounts in or on a wall (although some "wall" plates actually are mounted in floors and ceilings). Wall plates include one or more *jacks*. A jack is the connector in the wall plate that allows a workstation to make a physical and electrical connection to the network cabling system.

Wall plates come in many different styles, types, brands, and yes, even colors (in case you want to color-coordinate your wiring system). In this chapter, you will learn about the different types of wall plates available and their associated installation issues.

WARNING   The National Electrical Code dictates how various types of wiring (including power and telecommunications wiring) must be installed, but be aware that NEC compliance varies from state to state. The NEC code requirements given in this chapter should be verified against your local code requirements before you do any structured cable-system design or installation.

Wall-Plate Design and Installation Issues

When you plan your cabling-system installation, you must be aware of a few wall-plate installation issues to make the most efficient installation. The majority of these installation issues come from compliance with the ANSI/TIA/EIA-570-A (for residential) and ANSI/TIA/EIA-568-A (for commercial installations) telecommunications Standards. You'll have to make certain choices about how best to conform to these Standards based on the type of installation you are doing. These choices will dictate the different steps you'll need to take during the installation of the different kinds of wall plates.

The main design and installation issues you must deal with for wall plates are as follows:

- Manufacturer system
- Wall-plate location

- Wall-plate mounting system
- Fixed-design or modular plate

In this section, you will learn what each of these installation issues is and how each will affect your cabling-system installation.

Manufacturer System

There is no "universal" wall plate. Hundreds of different wall plates are available, each with its design merits and drawbacks. It would be next to impossible to detail every type of manufacturer and wall plate, so in this chapter we'll just give a few examples of the most popular types. The most important thing to remember about using a particular manufacturer's wall-plate system in your structured-cabling system is that it is a *system*. Each component in a wall-plate system is designed to work with the other components and, generally speaking, can't be used with components from other systems. A *wall-plate system* consists of a wall plate and its associated jacks. When designing your cabling system, you must choose the manufacturer and wall-plate system that best suits your needs.

Wall-Plate Location

When installing wall plates, you must decide the best location on the wall. Obviously, the wall plate should be fairly near the workstation, and, in fact, the ANSI/-TIA/EIA-568-A Standard says that the maximum length from the workstation to the wall-plate patch cable can be no longer than 3 meters (10 feet). This short distance will affect exactly where you place your wall plate in your design. If you already have your office laid out, you will have to locate the wall plates as close as possible to the workstations so that your wiring system will conform to the Standard.

Additionally, you want to keep wall plates away from any source of direct heat that could damage the connector or reduce its efficiency. In other words, don't place a wall plate directly above a floor heating register or baseboard heater.

A few guidelines exist for where to put your wall plates on a wall for code compliance and the most trouble-free installation. You must account for the vertical and horizontal positions of the wall plate. Both positions have implications, and you must understand them before you design your cabling system. We'll examine the vertical placement first.

Vertical Position

When deciding the vertical position of your wall plates, you must take into account either the residential or commercial National Electrical Code (NEC) sections. Obviously, which section you go by depends on whether you are performing a residential or commercial installation.

In residential installations, you have some flexibility. You can place a wall plate in almost any vertical position on a wall, but the NEC suggests that you place it so that the top of the plate is no more than 18 inches from the subfloor (the same distance as electrical outlets). If the wall plate is to service a countertop or a wall phone, the top of the plate should be no more than 48 inches from the subfloor. These vertical location requirements are illustrated in Figure 8.1.

FIGURE 8.1:

Wall-plate vertical location

NOTE   The vertical heights may be adjusted, if necessary, for elderly or handicapped occupants, according to the Americans with Disabilities Act (ADA) guidelines.

TIP   Remember that the vertical heights may vary from city to city and from residential to commercial electrical codes.

Horizontal Position

Wall plates should be placed horizontally so that they are as close as possible to work-area equipment (computers, phones, etc.). In fact, the ANSI/TIA/EIA-568-A Standard requires that work-area cables should not exceed 3 meters (10 feet). So you will have to know where the furniture is in a room before you can decide where to put the wall plates for the network and phone. Figure 8.2 illustrates this horizontal-position requirement.

FIGURE 8.2:

Horizontal wall-plate placement

Max distance: 6m (20 ft.)

Patch cable no more than 3m (10 ft.) long

TIP

When placing telecommunications outlets, consider adding more than one per room to accommodate for rearrangement of the furniture. It usually helps to "mirror" the opposing wall-outlet layout (i.e., north-south and east-west walls will be mirror images of each other with respect to their outlet layout).

Another horizontal-position factor to take into account is the proximity to electrical fixtures. Data-communications wall plates and wall boxes cannot be located in the same *stud cavity* as electrical wall boxes when the electrical wire is not encased in metal conduit. (A stud cavity is the space between the two vertical wood or metal studs and the drywall or wallboard attached to those studs.)

The stud-cavity rule primarily applies to residential telecommunications wiring as per the ANSI/TIA/EIA-570-A Standard. The requirement, as illustrated in Figure 8.3, keeps stray electrical signals from interfering with communications signals. Notice that even though the electrical outlets are near to the communications outlets, they are never in the same stud cavity.

FIGURE 8.3:

Placing telecommunications outlets and electrical wall boxes in different stud cavities

Notice that telecom outlet and electrical outlets are located in separate stud cavities.

Electrical outlet

Telecom outlet

Wall-Plate Mounting System

Another decision you must make regarding your wall plates is how you will mount them to the wall. Three main systems, each with their own unique applications, are used to attach wall plates to a wall:

- Outlet boxes
- Cut-in plates
- Surface-mount outlet boxes

The following sections describe each of these mounting systems and their various applications.

Outlet Boxes

The most common wall-plate mounting in commercial applications is the *outlet box*, which is simply a plastic or metal box attached to a stud in a wall cavity. Outlet boxes have screw holes in them that allow a wall plate to be attached. Additionally, they usually have some provision (either nails or screws) that allows them to be attached to a stud. These outlet boxes, as their name suggests, are primarily used for electrical outlets, but they can also be used for telecommunications wiring because the wall plates share the same dimensions and mountings.

Plastic boxes are cheaper than metal ones and are usually found in residential or light commercial installations. Metal boxes are typically found in commercial applications and usually use a conduit of some kind to carry electrical or data cabling. Which you choose depends on the type of installation you are doing. Plastic boxes are fine for simple, residential Category 3 copper installations. However, if you want to install Category 4, 5, 5e, or higher, you must be extremely careful with the wire so that you don't kink it or make any sharp bends in it. Also, if you run your network cable before the drywall is installed (and in residential wiring with plastic boxes, you almost always have to), it is likely that during the drywall installation the wires could be punctured or stripped. Open-backed boxes are often installed to avoid bend-radius problems and to allow cable to be pushed back into the cavity and out of reach of the dry-wall installers' tools. If you can't find open-backed boxes, buy plastic boxes and cut the backs off with a saw.

Metal boxes can have the same problems, but these problems are minimized if the metal boxes are used with conduit—that is, a plastic or metal pipe that attaches to the box. In commercial installations, a metal box to be used for telecommunications wiring is attached to a stud. Conduit is run from the box to a 45-degree elbow that terminates in the airspace above a dropped ceiling. This installation technique is the most common wiring method in new commercial construction and is illustrated in Figure 8.4. This method allows you to run the telecommunications wire after the wallboard and ceiling have been installed, thus minimizing the chance of damage to the cable.

FIGURE 8.4:

A common metal box with conduit, in a commercial installation

Cut-In Mounting

Outlet boxes work well as wall-plate supports when you are able to access the studs during the construction of a building. But what type of wall-plate mounting system do you use once the drywall is in place and you need to put a wall plate on that wall? Use some kind of *cut-in* mounting hardware (also called *remodeling* or *retrofit* hardware), so named because you cut a hole in the drywall and place into it some kind of mounting box or plate that will support the wall plate. This type of mounting is used when you need to run a cable into a particular stud cavity of a finished wall.

Cut-in mountings fall into two different types: *remodel boxes* and *cover-plate mounting brackets*.

Remodel Boxes   Remodel boxes are simply plastic or metal boxes that mount to the hole in the drywall using screws or special friction fasteners. The main difference between remodel boxes and regular outlet boxes is that remodel boxes are slightly smaller and can only be mounted in existing walls. Some examples of remodel boxes are shown in Figure 8.5.

FIGURE 8.5:

Examples of common remodel boxes

Installing a remodel box so that you can use it for data cabling is simple. Just follow these steps:

1. Using the guidelines discussed earlier in this chapter, determine the location of the new cabling wall plate. With a pencil, mark a line indicating the location for the top of the box.

2. Using the hole template provided with the box, trace the outline of the hole to be cut onto the wall with a pencil or marker, keeping the top of the hole aligned with the mark you made in step 1. If no template is provided, use the box as a template by flipping the box over so the face is against the wall and by tracing around the box.

3. Using a drywall keyhole saw, cut out a hole, following the lines drawn using the template.

4. Insert the remodel box into the hole you just cut. If the box won't go in easily, trim the sides of the hole with a razor blade or utility knife.

5. Secure the box by either screwing the box to the drywall or by using the friction tabs. To use the friction tabs (if your box has them), just turn the screw attached to the tabs until the tabs are secured against the drywall.

Cover-Plate Mounting Brackets   The other type of cut-in mounting device for data cabling is the cover-plate mounting bracket. Also called a *cheater bracket*, this mounting bracket allows you to mount a wall plate directly to the wallboard without installing an outlet box. Figure 8.6 shows some examples of preinstalled cover-plate mounting brackets.

FIGURE 8.6:

Cover-plate mounting
bracket examples

These brackets are usually made of steel or aluminum and contain flexible tabs that you push into a precut hole in the drywall. The tabs fold over into the hole and hold the bracket securely to the drywall. Additionally, some brackets allow you to put a screw through both the front and the tabs on the back, thus increasing the bracket's hold on the drywall. Plastic models are becoming popular as well; these use tabs or ears that you turn to grip the drywall. Some also have ratchet-type gripping devices.

Figure 8.7 shows a cover-plate mounting bracket installed in a wall ready to accept a wall plate. Once the mounting bracket is installed, the data cable(s) can be pulled through the wall and terminated at the jacks for the wall plate, and the wall plate can be mounted to the bracket.

FIGURE 8.7:

An installed cover-plate mounting bracket

Surface-Mount Outlet Boxes

The final type of wall-plate mounting system is the surface-mount outlet box, which is used where it is not easy or possible to run the cable inside the wall (in concrete, mortar, or brick walls, for example). Cable is run in a surface-mount raceway (a round or flat conduit) to an outlet box mounted (either by adhesive or screws) on the outside of the wall. This arrangement is shown in Figure 8.8.

The positive side to surface-mount outlet boxes is their flexibility—they can be placed just about anywhere. The downside is their appearance. Surface-mount installations, even when performed with the utmost care and workmanship, still look cheap and inelegant. But sometimes they are the only choice.

Fixed-Design or Modular Plate

Another design and installation decision you have to make is whether to use *fixed-design* or *modular* wall plates. Fixed-design wall plates (as shown in Figure 8.9) have multiple jacks, but the jacks are molded as part of the wall plate. You cannot remove the jack and replace it with a different type of connector.

Fixed-design plates are usually used in telephone applications rather than LAN wiring applications because, although they are cheap, they have limited flexibility. Fixed-design plates have a couple of advantages and disadvantages (as shown in Table 8.1).

TABLE 8.1: Advantages and Disadvantages of Fixed-Design Wall Plates

Advantages	Disadvantages
Inexpensive	Configuration cannot be changed
Simple to install	Usually not compatible with high-speed networking systems

Modular wall plates, on the other hand, are generic and have multiple jack locations (as shown in Figure 8.10). In a modular wall plate system, this plate is known as a *faceplate* (it's not a wall plate until it has its jacks installed). Jacks for each faceplate are purchased separately from the wall plates.

FIGURE 8.10:

Modular wall plates with multiple jack locations

Modular wall plates

TIP
When using modular wall plates, make sure to use the jacks designed for that wall-plate system. Generally speaking, jacks from different wall-plate systems are not interchangeable.

You will learn more about these types of wall plates in the next sections.

Fixed-Design Wall Plates

A fixed-design wall plate cannot have its port/jack configuration changed. In this type of wall plate, the jack configuration is determined at the factory, and the jacks are molded as part of the plate assembly.

You must understand a few issues before choosing a particular fixed-design wall plate for your cabling installation, including the following:

- Number of sockets
- Types of sockets
- Labeling

Number of Sockets

Because fixed-design wall plates have their jacks molded into the faceplate assembly, the number of jacks that can fit into the faceplate is limited. It is very unusual to find a fixed-design faceplate with more than two jacks (they are usually in an over-under configuration, with one jack above the other). Additionally, most fixed-design wall plates are for UTP or coaxial copper cable only; very few fiber-optic fixed-design wall plates are available. Figure 8.11 shows some examples of fixed-design wall plates with various numbers of sockets.

FIGURE 8.11:

Fixed-design wall plates with varying numbers of sockets

Types of Sockets

Fixed-design wall plates can accommodate many different types of sockets for different types of data-communications media. However, you cannot change a wall plate's configuration once it is in place; instead, you must install a completely new wall plate with a different configuration.

The most common configuration of a fixed-design wall plate is the single six-position (RJ-11) or eight-position (RJ-45) jack (as shown in Figure 8.12), which is most often used for home or office telephone connections. This type of wall plate can be found in your local hardware store or home center.

FIGURE 8.12:

Fixed-design plates with a single RJ-11 or RJ-45 jack

WARNING Fixed-design wall plates that have eight-position jacks must be carefully checked to see if they are data-capable. We know of retail outlets that claim their eight-position, fixed-design wall plates are "CAT 5" compliant. They're not. They use screw terminals instead of 110-type IDC connections. If it's got screws, folks, it ain't CAT 5.

Other types of fixed-design wall plates can include any combination of socket connectors, based on market demand and the whims of the manufacturer. Some of the connector combinations commonly found are as follows:

- Single RJ-11 type
- Single RJ-45 type
- Single coax (TV cable)
- Single BNC
- Dual RJ-11 type
- Dual RJ-45 type
- Single RJ-11 type, single RJ-45 type
- Single RJ-11 type, single coax (TV cable)
- Single RJ-45 type, single BNC

Labeling

Not all wall-plate connectors are labeled. Most fixed-design wall plates don't have special preparations for labeling (unlike modular plates). However, that doesn't mean it isn't important to label each connection; on the contrary, it is extremely important so that you can tell which connection is which (extremely useful when troubleshooting). Additionally, some jacks, though they look the same, may serve a completely different purpose. For example, RJ-45 jacks can be used for both PBX telephone and Ethernet networking, so it's helpful to label which is which if a fixed-design plate has two RJ-45 jacks.

For these reasons, structured-cabling manufacturers have come up with different methods of labeling fixed-design wall plates. The most popular method is using adhesive-backed stickers or labels of some kind. There are alphanumeric labels (e.g., *LAN* and *Phone*) as well as icon labels with pictures of computers for LAN ports and pictures of telephones for telephone ports. Instead of printed labels, sometimes the manufacturer will mold the labels or icons directly into the wall plate.

Modular Wall Plates

Modular wall plates have individual components that can be installed in varying configurations depending on your cabling needs. For example, when you have a cabling-design need for a wall plate that can have three RJ-45 jacks in one configuration and one RJ-45 jack and two fiber-optic jacks in another configuration, the modular wall plate fills that design need very nicely.

Just like fixed-design wall plates, modular wall plates have their own design and installation issues, including:

- Number of sockets
- Wall-plate jack considerations
- Labeling

Number of Sockets

The first decision you must make when using modular wall plates is how many sockets you want for each wall plate. Each socket can hold a different type of jack for a different type of cable media, if necessary. The ANSI/TIA/EIA-568-A Standard recommends, at minimum, two ports for each work-area wall plate. These ports can be either side by side or over and under, but they should be in the same wall plate. Additionally, each port must be served by its own cable, and at least one of those should be a four-pair, 100-ohm, UTP cable.

The number of sockets a plate can have is based on the size of the plate. Fixed-design wall plates mainly come in one size. Modular plates come in a couple of different sizes. The smallest size is single-gang, which measures 4.5 inches high and 2.75 inches wide. The next largest size is called double-gang, which measures 4.5 by 4.5 inches (the same height as single-gang plates but almost twice as wide). There are triple- and quad-gang plates, but they are not used as often as single- and double-gang plates. Figure 8.13 shows the difference between a single- and double-gang wall plate.

FIGURE 8.13:

Single- and double-gang wall plates

Single gang   Double gang

Each manufacturer has different guidelines about how many sockets for jacks fit into each type of wall plate. Most manufacturers, however, agree that six jacks are the most you can fit into a single-gang wall plate.

With the advent of new technology and applications, such as videoconferencing and fiber to the desktop, users need more ports and different types of cabling brought to the desktop. Besides using patch panels in the telecommunications closet, you can bring Category 3, Category 5, fiber-optic, and coaxial cable to the desktop for voice, data, and video with the newer 6-, 12- and 16-port multimedia outlets.

Wall-Plate Jack Considerations

Modular wall plates are the most common type of wall plate in use for data cabling because they meet the various TIA/EIA and NEC Standards and codes for quality data-communications cabling. So modular wall plates have the widest variety of jack types available. All the jacks available today differ based on a few parameters, including the following:

- Wall-plate system type
- Cable connection

- Jack orientation
- ANSI/TIA/EIA-568-A wiring pattern

Wall-Plate System Type

Remember how the type of wall plate you use dictates the type of jacks for that wall plate? Well, the same holds true for jacks. When you pick a certain brand and manufacturer for a jack, you must use the same brand and manufacturer of wall plate.

Cable Connection

Jacks differ in the way that they connect to the horizontal cable run. Although it seems as if each manufacturer has its own unique method of connecting the individual strands to the pins in a UTP connection, each of these methods works similarly. Each uses insulation displacement connectors (IDCs), which have small metal teeth or pins in the connector that press into the individual wires of a UTP cable (or the wires are pressed into the teeth). The teeth puncture the outer insulation of the individual wires and make contact with the conductor inside, thus making a connection. This process (known as *crimping* or *punching down*, depending on the method or tool used) is illustrated in Figure 8.14.

FIGURE 8.14:

Using insulation displacement connectors (IDCs)

Though they may differ in methods, any connector that uses some piece of metal to puncture through the insulation of a strand of copper cable is an IDC connector.

Jack Orientation

Yes, jack orientation. The individual wall-plate systems use many different types of jacks, and some of those systems use jacks with positions other than straight ahead (which is the "standard" configuration). These days, a popular configuration is a jack that's angled approximately 45 degrees down. There are many reasons that this jack became popular. First off, it looks cool. Second, because it's angled, the cable-connect takes up less room (which is nice when a desk is pushed up tight against the wall plate). Finally, the angled connector works well in installations with high dust content because it's harder for dust to rest inside the connector. Figure 8.15 shows an example of an angled connector.

FIGURE 8.15:

An angled RJ-45 connector

NOTE   Angled connectors are found in many different types of cabling installations, including STP, UTP, and fiber optic.

Wiring Pattern

When connecting copper 10Base-T or 100Base-T RJ-45 jacks, you must wire all jacks and patch points according to either the T568A or T568B pattern. Figure 8.16 shows both sides of a common snap-in jack with both T568A and T568B color coding. Notice that the wiring schemes are different in that the positions of pairs 2 and 3, white/orange and white/green, respectively, are switched. (You may want to see the color version of this figure in the color section.) If your company has a standard wiring pattern and you wire a single jack with the opposing standard, that particular jack will not be able to communicate with the rest of the network.

Table 8.2 shows the wiring color scheme for the T568A pattern. Notice how the wires are paired and which color goes to which pin. Table 8.3 shows the same for T568B.

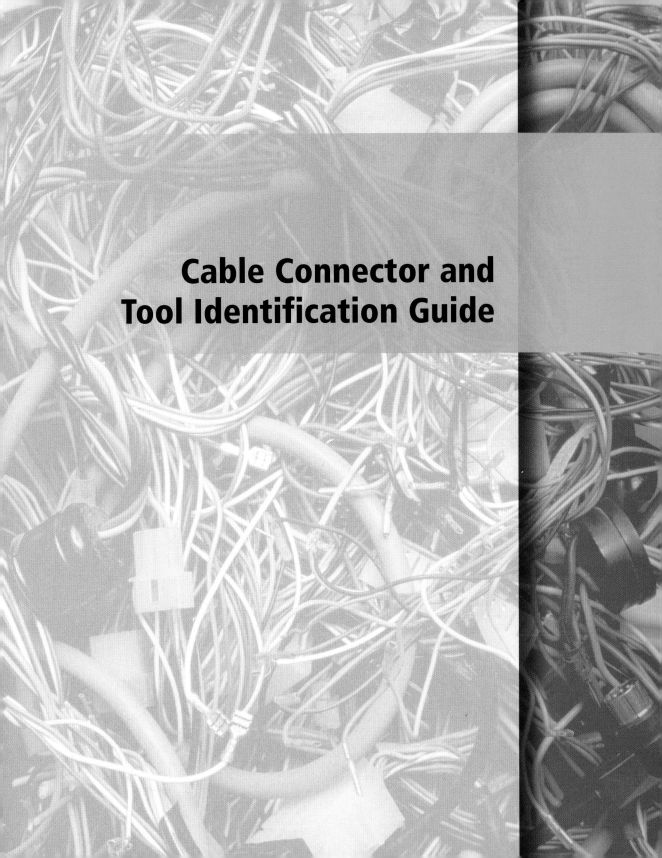

Cable Connector and
Tool Identification Guide

This Cable Connector and Tool Identification Guide will allow you to view connectors and tools in living color. Many items in the data-communications industry are color-coded; for example, orange is used to designate fiber optic cable. Some of the products shown in the following pages are:

- Connectors
- Cables
- Mount box
- Wall plates
- Jacks
- Face plates
- Cable strippers
- Connectorizing kits

- Fiber optic test scope
- Cable tester
- Punch-down block
- Fiber patch panel
- Telephone installation
- Fiber optic breakout box
- Wiring closet
- Tractor-mounted unspooler

**FIBER OPTIC PATCH
CABLE**

with MT-RJ connectors

FIBER OPTIC PATCH
CABLE
with ST connectors

A SIX-FIBER MULTIMODE FIBER OPTIC CABLE

Notice Kevlar fibers (yellow) at top.

A 25-PAIR UTP CABLE

This cable is often used for telephone applications.

TYPE 1 TOKEN RING CABLE

Notice the shielding and unique connector.

ARMORED FIBER OPTIC CABLE

TWIN-AXIAL CABLE

SILVER SATIN CABLE
with an RJ-45 connector

TWIN-AXIAL CABLE
TO RJ-11 BALUN

COLOR CODE FOR BOTH 568A AND 568B WIRING SCHEMES

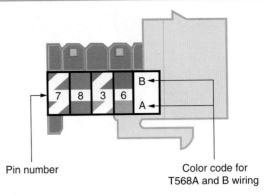

Pin number

Color code for T568A and B wiring

3M HOTMELT™ ST FIBER OPTIC CONNECTOR

RACEWAY AND SURFACE MOUNT BOX

RJ-45 CRIMP-ON CONNECTOR

(Photo courtesy of The Siemon Company)

CABLE WITH BOTH 110 AND RJ-45 ENDS

(Photo courtesy of The Siemon Company)

MODULAR WALL PLATE

with RJ-45, coaxial video, RCA, S-Video, and fiber optic connectors

SURFACE-MOUNT, MODULAR MULTIMEDIA BOX

EXAMPLE OF A SURFACE-MOUNT BISCUIT JACK

FIXED-DESIGN, DUPLEX, RJ-45 WALL PLATE THAT USES 110 PUNCH-DOWNS

FIXED DESIGN WALL PLATES

From left: Token Ring, RJ-11, and dual cable TV (coax).

MODULAR FURNITURE WITH FOUR ANGLED JACKS

(one with a dust cover)

MODULAR FURNITURE FACEPLATES

both low profile (foreground) and normal (background)

WALL PLATES

From left: Modular 3 position with three RJ-45 jacks, modular with six RJ-45 jacks, and fixed design with single RJ-45 jack.

MORE EXAMPLES OF WALL PLATES

From left to right: A 6-port wall plate filled with various types of multimedia jacks; a 4-port metal wall plate; a 4-port wall plate filled with RJ-45 jacks; a 6-port wall plate filled with various types of RJ-45 jacks.

6A FIBER OPTIC WALL PLATE SURROUND ADD-ON

HEAVILY SHIELDED 110-TO-RJ-45 PUNCH-DOWN BLOCK

SIX-GANG, MODULAR FURNITURE WALL PLATE WITH ANGLED JACKS

DUAL SC CONNECTOR FIBER PATCH PANEL

TELEPHONE WALL PLATE WITH MODULAR JACK

**66-BLOCK WITH A
50-PAIR CABLE
CONNECTOR**

SIDE VIEW OF A 110 PUNCH-DOWN BLOCK

SIDE VIEW OF A 210 PUNCH-DOWN BLOCK

Note pairs are separated from each other.

CABLE MANAGEMENT D-RINGS

ANOTHER EXAMPLE OF A 110-TO-RJ-45 PUNCH-DOWN

(Photo courtesy of The Siemon Company)

SAMPLE TELEPHONE INSTALLATION

Notice the 66- blocks, biscuit jacks, PBX, cable management rings, and 50-pair cable connections.

(Photo courtesy of Computer Training Academy)

FIBER OPTIC BREAKOUT BOX

EXAMPLE OF A WIRING CLOSET WITH RACK-MOUNTED PATCH PANELS

(Photo courtesy of Computer Training Academy)

RACK WITH COLOR-CODED PATCH CORDS

(Photo courtesy of The Siemon Company)

50-PAIR UTP TELEPHONE CABLES TERMINATED TO THE BACK OF A 110-TO-RJ-45 RACK-MOUNT PATCH PANEL

(Photo courtesy of Computer Training Academy)

THE BACK OF A 110-TO-RJ-45 RACK-MOUNTED PATCH PANEL

(Photo courtesy of Computer Training Academy)

**MODULAR JACK
PUNCH-DOWN AID
("PUCK")**

ANGLED PICK PROBE

**SIMPLE CABLE
JACKET STRIPPER**

CABLE STRIPPER WITH BOTH UTP AND COAX DIES

FIBER OPTIC TEST SCOPE

SIMPLE CABLE TESTER

FIBER OPTIC CONNECTORIZING KIT

Kevlar shears

Fiber scribing pen

Fiber strippers

Piano wire

Polishing pad

Polishing puck

Goggles

3M HOTMELT CONNECTORIZING KIT

Hotmelt™ oven

Termination test scope

Kevlar shears

No-nick fiber stripper

Scribe

Measuring calipers

Water bottle

Connector cooling stand

Polishing puck and pad

TRACTOR-MOUNTED UNSPOOLER

for optical raceway used for
outdoor installations

FIGURE 8.16:

A common snap-in jack showing both T568A and T568B wiring schemes

Color code for
T568A and B wiring

TABLE 8.2: Wiring Scheme for T568A

Pin Number	Wire Color
1	White/green
2	Green
3	White/orange
4	Blue
5	White/blue
6	Orange
7	White/brown
8	Brown

TABLE 8.3: Wiring Scheme for T568B

Pin Number	Wire Color
1	White/orange
2	Orange
3	White/green
4	Blue
5	White/blue
6	Green
7	White/brown
8	Brown

Labeling

Just like fixed-design wall plates, modular wall plates use labels to differentiate the different jacks by their purpose. In fact, modular wall plates have the widest variety of labels—every modular wall-plate manufacturer seems to pride itself on its varied colors and styles of labeling. However, as with fixed-design plates, the labels are either text (e.g., *LAN*, *Phone*) or pictures of their intended use, perhaps permanently molded in the plate or on the jack.

Biscuit Jacks

No discussion of wall plates would be complete without a discussion of *biscuit jacks*, or surface-mount jacks that look like small biscuits (see Figure 8.17). They were originally used in residential and light commercial installations for telephone applications. In fact, you may have some in your home if it was built before 1975. David's house was built in the 1920s, so when he bought it, the house was lousy with them. When he remodeled last summer, he removed all the biscuit jacks, installed wall boxes in all the rooms, ran UTP and coaxial cable to all those boxes, and installed modular wall plates, including two RJ-45s and one TV cable jack. Biscuit jacks are still used when adding phone lines in residences, especially when people can't put a hole in the wall where they want the phone jack to go.

FIGURE 8.17:

An example of a biscuit jack

Types of Biscuit Jacks

The many different types of biscuit jacks differ primarily by size and number of jacks they can support. The smaller type measures 2.25 inches wide by 2.5 inches high and is mainly used for residential-telephone applications. The smaller size can generally support up to a maximum of two jacks.

The larger-sized biscuit jacks are sometimes referred to as simply *surface-mount boxes* because they don't have the shape of the smaller biscuit jacks. These surface-mount boxes are primarily used for data-communications applications and come in a variety of sizes. They also can have any number or type of jacks and are generally modular. Figure 8.18 shows an example of a larger biscuit jack that is commonly used in surface-mount applications.

FIGURE 8.18:

Example of a larger
biscuit jack

NOTE   Generally speaking, the smaller biscuit jacks are not rated for Category 5 (or any higher categories). They must be specifically designed for a Category 5 application. Some companies offer a modular-design biscuit jack that lets you snap in high-performance, RJ-45-type jacks for Category 5 and better compliance.

Advantages of Biscuit Jacks

Biscuit jacks offer a few advantages in your structured-cabling design. First of all, they are very inexpensive compared to other types of surface-mount wiring systems, which is why many houses that had the old four-pin telephone systems now have biscuit jacks—you could buy 20 of them for around $30. Even the biscuits that support multiple jacks are still fairly inexpensive.

Another advantage of biscuit jacks is their ability to work in situations where standard modular or fixed-design wall plates won't work and other types of surface-mount wiring are too bulky. The best example of this is office cubicles (i.e., modular furniture). A biscuit jack has an adhesive tab on the back that allows it to be mounted anywhere, so you can run a telephone or data cable to a biscuit jack and mount it under the desk where it will be out of the way.

Finally, biscuit jacks are easy to install. The cover is removed with one screw. Inside many of the biscuit jacks are screw terminals (one per pin in each jack), as shown in Figure 8.19. To install the jack, strip the insulation from each conductor and wrap it clockwise around the terminal and between the washers and tighten the screw. Repeat this process for each conductor in the cable. These jacks are not high-speed data compatible and are capable of Category 3 performance at best.

FIGURE 8.19:

Screw terminals inside a biscuit jack

Screw terminals

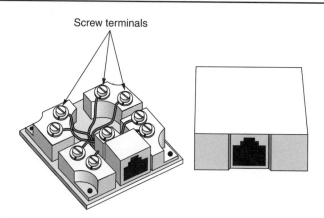

> **NOTE** Not all biscuit jacks use screw terminals. The more modern data-communications jacks use IDC connectors to attach the wire to the jack.

Disadvantages of Biscuit Jacks

The main disadvantage to biscuit jacks is that the older biscuit jacks are not rated for high-speed data communications. Notice the bunch of screw terminals in the biscuit jack shown in Figure 8.19. When a conductor is wrapped around these terminals, it is exposed to stray electromagnetic interference (EMI) and other interference, which reduces the effective ability of this type of jack to carry data. At most, the older biscuit jacks with the screw terminals can be rated as Category 3 and are not suitable for the 100Mbps communications today's wiring systems must be able to carry.

Connectors

- Twisted-Pair Cable Connectors

- Coaxial Cable Connectors

- Fiber-Optic Cable Connectors

Have you ever wired a cable directly into a piece of hardware? Some equipment in years past provided terminals or termination blocks so that cable could be wired directly into a direct component. In modern times, this is considered bad; it is fundamentally against the precepts of a structured cabling system to attach directly to active electronic components, either at the workstation or in the equipment closet. On the ends of the cable you install, something must provide access and transition for attachment to system electronics. Thus, you have connectors.

Connectors generally have a male component and a female component, except in the case of hermaphroditic connectors such as the IBM data connector. Usually jacks and plugs are symmetrically shaped, but sometimes they are *keyed*. This means that they have a unique, asymmetric shape or some system of pins, tabs, and slots that ensure that the plug can be inserted only one way in the jack. This chapter covers many of the connector types you will encounter when working with structured cabling systems.

Twisted-Pair Cable Connectors

Many people in the cabling business use twisted-pair connectors more than any other type of connector. The connectors include the modular RJ types of jacks and plugs and the hermaphroditic connector employed by IBM that is used with shielded twisted-pair cabling.

Almost as important as the cable connector is the connector used with patch panels, punch-down blocks, and wall plates; this connector is called an IDC or *insulation displacement connector*.

Patch-Panel Terminations

Most unshielded twisted-pair (UTP), screened twisted-pair (ScTP), and foil twisted-pair (FTP) cable installations use patch panels and, consequently, 110-style termination blocks. The 110-block (shown in Figure 9.1) contains rows of specially designed slots in which the cables are terminated using a punch-down tool. Patch panels and 110-blocks are described in more detail in Chapter 5 and Chapter 7.

FIGURE 9.1:

FIGURE 9.1:

An S-110-block with wire management

(Photo courtesy of The Siemon Company)

When terminating 66-blocks, 110-blocks, and, often, wall plates, both UTP and ScTP connectors use IDC (insulation displacement connector) technology to establish contact with the copper conductors. You don't strip the wire insulation off the conductor as you would with a screw-down connection. Instead, you force the conductor either between facing blades or onto points that pierce the plastic insulation and make contact with the conductor.

Solid- versus Stranded-Conductor Cables

UTP and ScTP cables have either solid copper conductors or conductors made of several tiny strands of copper. Solid conductors are very stable geometrically and, therefore, electrically superior, but they will break if flexed very often. Stranded conductors are very flexible and resistant to bend-fatigue breaks, but their cross-sectional geometry changes as they are moved, and this can contribute to electrical anomalies. Stranded cables also have a higher attenuation (signal loss) than solid-conductor cables.

NOTE   Solid-conductor cables are usually used in backbone and horizontal cabling where, once installed, there won't be much movement. Stranded-conductor cables are used in patch cords, where their flexibility is desirable and their typically short lengths mitigate transmission problems.

The differences in conductors mean a difference in IDC types. You have to be careful when you purchase plugs, wall plates, and patch panels because they won't work interchangeably with solid- and stranded-core cables because the blade designs are different.

WARNING   Using the wrong type of cable/connector combination can be a major source of flaky and intermittent connection errors after your system is running.

With a solid-conductor IDC, you are usually forcing the conductor between two blades that form a V-shaped notch. The blades slice through the plastic and into the copper conductor, gripping it and holding it in place. This makes a very reliable electrical contact. If you force a stranded conductor into this same opening, contact may still be made. But, because one of the features of a stranded design is that the individual copper filaments can move (this provides the flexibility), they will sort of mush into an elongated shape in the *V*. Electrical contact may still be made, but the grip on the conductor is not secure and often becomes loose over time.

The blade design of IDC connectors intended for stranded-core conductors is such that forcing a solid-core conductor onto the IDC connector can break the conductor or miss contact entirely. Broken conductors can be especially problematic because the two halves of the break can be close enough together that contact is made when the temperature is warm, but the conductor may contract enough to cause an open condition when cold.

Some manufacturers of plugs advertise that their IDC connectors are universal and may be used with either solid or stranded conductors. Try them if you like, but if you have problems, switch to a plug specifically for the type of cable you are using.

Jacks and termination blocks are almost exclusively solid-conductor devices. You should never punch down on a 66, 110, or modular jack with stranded conductors.

Modular Jacks and Plugs

Twisted-pair cables are most commonly available as UTP, but recent developments in screened twisted-pair cables (ScTP) are making ScTP more common. In an ScTP cable, the individual twisted pairs are not shielded, but all the pairs collectively have a thin shield around the shield of foil around them. Both UTP and

ScTP cables use modular jacks and plugs. For decades, modular jacks have been commonplace in the home for telephone wiring.

Modular connectors come in four-, six-, and eight-position configurations. The number of positions defines the width of the connector. However, many times only some of the positions have metal contacts installed. Make sure that the connectors you purchase are properly populated with contacts for your application. Commercial-grade jacks are made to snap into modular cutouts in faceplates. (More information is available on modular wall plates in Chapter 8.) This gives you the flexibility of using the faceplate for voice, data, coax, and fiber connections, or combinations thereof. Figure 9.2 shows a modular plug, and Figure 9.3 shows the modular jack used for UTP. Figure 9.4 shows a modular jack for ScTP cables. Note the metal shield around the jack; it is designed to help reduce both EMI emissions and interference from outside sources, but it must be connected properly to the cable shield to be effective.

FIGURE 9.2:

An eight-position modular plug for UTP cable

Cable

Clip

FIGURE 9.3:

An eight-position modular jack for UTP cable

FIGURE 9.4:

An eight-position modular
jack for ScTP cable

Metal shield

NOTE	The quality of plugs and jacks varies widely. Make sure that you use plugs and jacks that are rated to the category of cabling you purchase.

Though the correct name is *modular jack*, they are commonly referred to as *RJ-type connectors* (e.g., RJ-45). The RJ (registered jack) prefix is one of the most commonly (and incorrectly) used prefixes in the computer industry; nearly everyone, including people working for cabling companies, is guilty of referring to an eight-position modular jack (sometimes called an 8P8C) as an RJ-45. Bell Telephone originated the RJ prefix and the Universal Service Order Code (USOC) to indicate to telephone technicians what type of service was to be installed and the wiring pattern of the jack. Since the breakup of AT&T and the divestiture of the Regional Bell Operating Companies, *registered* has lost most of its meaning. However, the FCC has codified a number of RJ-type connectors and detailed the designations and pinout configurations in FCC Part 68, Subpart F, Section 68.502. Table 9.1 shows some of the common modular-jack configurations.

TABLE 9.1: Common Modular-Jack Designations and Their Configuration

Designation	Positions	Contacts	Used For	Wiring Pattern
RJ-11	6	2	Single-line telephones	USOC
RJ-14	6	4	Single- or dual-line telephones	USOC
RJ-22	4	4	Phone-cord handsets	USOC
RJ-25	6	6	Single-, dual-, or triple-line telephones	USOC
RJ-31	8	4	Security and fire alarm	See note
RJ-45	8	8	Data (10Base-T, 100Base-TX, etc.)	T568A or T568B

Continued on next page

TABLE 9.1 CONTINUED: Common Modular-Jack Designations and Their Configuration

Designation	Positions	Contacts	Used For	Wiring Pattern
RJ-48	8	4	1.544Mbps (T1) connections	System dependent
RJ-61	8	8	Single- through quad-line telephones	USOC

NOTE The RJ-31 connection is not specifically a LAN or phone-service jack. It's used for remote monitoring of a secured installation via the phone lines. The monitoring company needs first access to the incoming phone line in case of a security breach. (An intruder then couldn't just pick up a phone extension and interrupt the security-alert call.) USOC, T568A, or T568B wiring configuration schemes will all work with an RJ-31, but additional shorting circuitry is needed, which is built into the modules that use RJ-31 jacks.

The standard six- and eight-position modular jacks are not the only ones that you may find in use. Digital Equipment Corporation designed its own six-position modular jack called the MMJ (*modified modular jack*). The MMJ moved the clip portion of the jack to the right to reduce the likelihood that phone equipment would accidentally be connected to a data jack. The MMJ and DEC's wiring scheme for it are shown in Figure 9.5. Although the MMJ is not as common as standard six-position modular connectors (a.k.a. RJ-11) are, the displaced clip connector on the MMJ, when combined with the use of plugs called the MMP (*modified modular plug*), certainly helps reduce accidental connections by phone or non-DEC equipment.

FIGURE 9.5:

The DEC MMJ jack and wiring scheme

Pair 3

Pair Pair
1   2

1 2 3 4 5 6
T R T T R R

Note the displaced clip position.

Six-position
DEC MMJ

Another connector type that may occasionally be lumped in the category of eight-position modular-jack architecture is called the eight-position *keyed* modular jack (see Figure 9.6). This jack has a key slot on the right side of the connector. The keyed slot serves the same purpose as the DEC MMJ when used with keyed plugs; it prevents the accidental connection of equipment that should be not be connected to a particular jack.

FIGURE 9.6:

The eight-position keyed modular jack

Any wiring pattern can be used.

1 2 3 4 5 6 7 8 — Key slot

Eight-position keyed

Can a Six-Position Plug Be Used with an Eight-Position Modular Jack?

The answer is maybe. First, consider how many of the pairs of wires the application requires. If the application requires all eight pairs, or if it requires the use of pins 1 and 8 on the modular jack, then it will not work.

Further, repeated inserting and extracting of a six-position modular plug into and from an eight-position modular jack may eventually damage pins 1 and 8 in the jack.

Wiring Schemes

The *wiring scheme* (also called the *pinout scheme*, *pattern*, or *configuration*) that you choose indicates in what order the color-coded wires will be connected to the jacks. These schemes are an important part of standardization of a cabling system. Almost all UTP cabling uses the same color-coded wiring schemes for cables; the color-coding scheme uses a solid color conductor, and it has a mate that is white with a stripe or band the same color as its solid-colored mate. The orange pair, for example, is often called "orange and white/orange." Table 9.2 shows the color coding and wire-pair numbers for each color code.

TABLE 9.2: Wire Color Codes and Pair Numbers

Pair Number	Color Code
Pair 1	White/blue and blue
Pair 2	White/orange and orange
Pair 3	White/green and green
Pair 4	White/brown and brown

NOTE When working with a standardized, structured cabling system, the only wiring patterns you will need to worry about are the T568A and T568B patterns recognized in the ANSI/TIA/EIA-568-A Standard.

Determining the Pin Numbers

Which one is pin or position number 1? When you start terminating wall plates or modular jacks, you will need to know.

Wall-plate jacks usually have a printed circuit board that identifies exactly which IDC connector you should place each wire into. However, to identify the pins on a jack, hold the jack so that you are facing the side that the modular plug connects to. Make sure that the clip position is facing down. Pin 1 will be on the left-most side, and pin 8 will be on the right-most side.

View with clip side down.
Pin 1 is on the left.

1 2 3 4 5 6 7 8

Eight-position

Continued on next page

For modular jacks, hold the jack so that the portion that connects to a wall plate or network equipment is facing away from you. The clip should be facing down and you should be looking down at the connector. Pin 1 is the left-most pin, and thus pin 8 will be the right-most pin.

USOC Wiring Scheme   The Bell Telephone Universal Service Order Code (USOC) wiring scheme is simple and easy to terminate in up to an eight-position connector; this wiring scheme is shown in Figure 9.7. The first pair is always terminated on the center two positions. Pair 2 is split and terminated on each side of pair 1. Pair 3 is split and terminated on each side of pair 2. Pair 4 continues the pattern; it is split and terminated on either side of pair 3. This pattern is always the same regardless of the number of contacts you populate. You start in the center and work your way to the outside, stopping when you reach the maximum number of contacts in the connector.

Tip and Ring Colors

When looking at wiring schemes for modular plugs and jacks, you may see the letters *T* and *R* used, as in Figure 9.7. The *T* identifies the tip color, and the *R* identifies the ring color. In a four-pair cable, the cable pairs are coded in a standard color coding, which is on the insulation of the individual wires. In a four-pair cable, the tip is the wire that is predominantly white, and the ring identifies the wire that is a predominantly solid color.

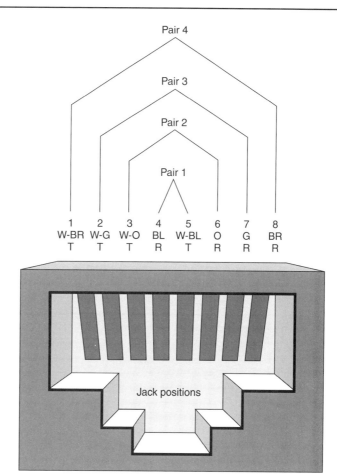

FIGURE 9.7:

The Universal Service Order Code (USOC) wiring scheme

Jack positions

WARNING Do not use the USOC wiring scheme for systems that will support data transmission.

The wire colors and associated pin assignments for USOC look like this:

Pin	Wire Color
1	White/brown
2	White/green
3	White/orange

4	Blue
5	White/blue
6	Orange
7	Green
8	Brown

USOC is used for analog and digital voice systems but should *never* be used for data installations. Splitting the pairs can cause a number of transmission problems when used at frequencies greater than those employed by voice systems. These problems include excessive crosstalk, impedance mismatches, and unacceptable signal-delay differential.

ANSI/TIA/EIA-568-A Wiring Schemes T568A and T568B   ANSI/TIA/EIA-568-A does not sanction the use of the USOC scheme. Instead, two wiring schemes are specified, both of which are suitable for either voice or high-speed LAN operation. These are designated as T568A and T568B wiring schemes.

NOTE   In the United States, the T568B wiring pattern was the most commonly used wiring scheme. This is changing, and now the current recommended pattern according to the Standard is the T568A pinout configuration. Unless a waiver is granted, the U.S. government requires all government cabling installations to use the T568A wiring pattern. ANSI/TIA/EIA-570-A Standard for home wiring requires the T568A wiring pattern. In much of the rest of the world, the T568A pattern is preferred because the T568A pattern and the USOC pattern are the same for pairs 1 and 2, making transition to and from voice systems much easier.

Both T568A and T568B are universal in that all LAN systems and most voice systems can utilize either wiring sequence without system errors. After all, the electrical signal really doesn't care if it is running on pair 2 or pair 3, as long as a wire is connected to the pin it needs to use. The TIA/EIA standard specifies eight-position, eight-contact jacks and plugs and four-pair cables, fully terminated, to facilitate this universality.

The T568B wiring configuration was the most commonly used scheme, especially for commercial installations; it is shown in Figure 9.8. The TIA/EIA adopted the T568B wiring scheme from the AT&T 258A wiring scheme. The 568A scheme (shown in Figure 9.9) is well suited to upgrades and new installations in residences because the wire-termination pattern for pairs 1 and 2 is the same as for USOC. The current recommendation is for all new installations to be wired with the T568A scheme.

FIGURE 9.8:

The T568B wiring pattern

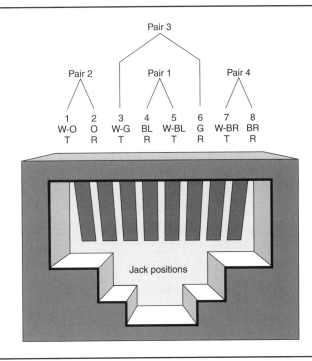

FIGURE 9.9:

The T568A wiring pattern

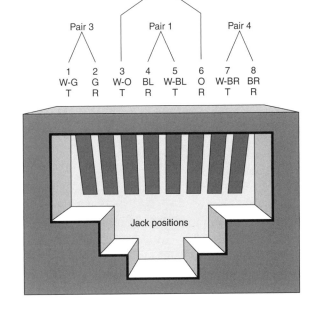

The wire colors and the associated pin assignments for the T568B wiring scheme look like this:

Pin	Wire Color
1	White/orange
2	Orange
3	White/green
4	Blue
5	White/blue
6	Green
7	White/brown
8	Brown

The pin assignments for the T568A wiring schemes are identical to the assignments for the T568B pattern except that wire pairs 2 and 3 are reversed. The T568A pattern looks like this:

Pin	Wire Color
1	White/green
2	Green
3	White/orange
4	Blue
5	White/blue
6	Orange
7	White/brown
8	Brown

Note that when you buy eight-position modular jacks, you may need to specify whether you want a T568A or T568B scheme because the jacks often have IDC connections on the back where you punch the pairs down in sequence from 1 to 4. The jacks have an internal PC board that takes care of all the pair splitting and proper alignment of the cable conductors with the pins in the jack. Most manufacturers now provide color-coded panels on the jacks that let you punch down either pinout scheme, eliminating the need for you to specify (and for them to stock) different jacks depending on which pinout you use.

<table><tr><td>**TIP**</td><td>Whichever scheme you use, T568A or T568B, you must also use that scheme for your patch panels and follow it in any cross-connect blocks you install. Consistency is the key to a successful installation.</td></tr></table>

Be aware that modular jacks pretty much look alike even though their performance may differ dramatically. Be sure you also specify the performance level (e.g., Category 3, Category 5, Category 5e, etc.) when you purchase your jacks.

When working with ScTP wiring, the drain wire makes contact with the cable shield along its entire length; this provides a ground path for EMI energy that is collected by the foil shield. When terminating ScTP, the drain wire within the cable is connected to a metal shield on the jack. This must be done at both ends of the cable. If left floating or if connected only on one end, instead of providing a barrier to EMI, the cable shield becomes a very effective antenna for both emitting and receiving stray signals.

In a cable installation that utilizes ScTP, the plugs, patch cords, and patch panels must be shielded as well.

Tips for Terminating UTP Connectors

Keep the following points in mind when terminating UTP connectors:

- When connecting to jacks and plugs, do not untwist UTP more than 0.5 inches for Category 5 and 5e and not more than 0.375 inches for Category 6.

- Always use connectors, wall plates, and patch panels that are compatible (same rating or higher) with the grade of cable used.

- To "future-proof" your installation, terminate all four pairs, even if the application requires only two of the pairs.

- Remember that the T568A wiring scheme is compatible with USOC wiring schemes that use pairs 1 and 2.

- When terminating ScTP cables, always terminate the drain wire on both ends of the connection.

372 Chapter 9 • Connectors

Other Wiring Schemes You may come across other wiring schemes, depending on the demands of the networking or voice application to be used. UTP Token Ring requires that pairs 1 and 2 be wired to the inside four pins, as shown in Figure 9.10. The T568A, T568B, and USOC wiring schemes can be used. You can also use a six-position modular jack rather than an eight-position modular jack, but we recommend against that because your cabling system would not follow the ANSI/TIA/EIA-568-A Standard.

FIGURE 9.10:

The Token Ring wiring scheme

Eight-position modular jack
wired only for Token Ring
(pairs 1 and 2)

The ANSI X3T9.5 TP-PMD Standard uses the two outer pairs of the eight-position modular jack; this wiring scheme (shown in Figure 9.11) is used with FDDI over copper and is compatible with both the T568A and T568B wiring patterns.

FIGURE 9.11:

The ANSI X3T9.5 TPPMD wiring scheme

Eight-position modular jack wired
for TP-PMD (ANSI X379.5)

If you are wiring a six-position modular jack (RJ-11) for home use, be aware that a few points are not covered by the ANSI/TIA/EIA-568-A Standard. First, the typical home-telephone cable uses a separate color-coding scheme. The wiring pattern used is the USOC wiring pattern, but the colors are different. The wiring pattern and colors for a typical home cable and RJ-11 are as follows:

Pin Number	Pair Number	Wire Color
1	Pair 3	White
2	Pair 2	Yellow
3	Pair 1	Green
4	Pair 1	Red
5	Pair 2	Black
6	Pair 3	Blue

Pins 3 and 4 carry the telephone line. Pair 3 is rarely used in home wiring for RJ-11 jacks. Splitters are available to split pins 2 and 5 into a separate jack for use with a separate phone line.

Pins Used by Specific Applications

Common networking applications require the use of specific pins in the modular connectors. The most common of these is 10Base-T and 100Base-TX. Table 9.3 shows the pin assignments and what each pin is used for.

TABLE 9.3: 10Base-T and 100Base-TX Pin Assignments

Pin	Usage
1	Transmit +
2	Transmit −
3	Receive +
4	Not used
5	Not used
6	Receive −
7	Not used
8	Not used

Using a Single Horizontal Cable Run for Two 10Base-T Connections

Let's face it, you will sometimes not run enough cable to a certain room. You will need an extra workstation in an area, and you won't have enough connections. Knowing that you have a perfectly good four-pair UTP cable in the wall and only two of those pairs are in use makes your mood even worse. Modular Y-adapters can come to your rescue.

Several companies make Y-adapters that function as splitters. They take the four pairs of wire that are wired to the jack and split them off into two separate connections. The Siemon Company makes a variety of modular Y-adapters (see Figure 9.12) for splitting 10Base-T, Token Ring, and voice applications. This splitter will split the four-pair cable so that it will support two separate applications, provided that each application requires only two of the pairs. You must specify the type of splitter you need (voice, 10Base-T, Token Ring, etc.). Don't forget, for each horizontal cable run you will be splitting, you will need two of these adapters: one for the patch-panel side and one for the wall plate.

FIGURE 9.12:

A modular Y-adapter for splitting a single four-pair cable into a cable that will support two separate applications

(Photo courtesy of The Siemon Company)

TIP

Many cabling professionals are reluctant to use Y-adapters because the high-speed applications such as 10Base-T Ethernet and Token Ring may interfere with one another if they are operating inside the same sheath. Certainly do not use Y-adapters for applications such as 100Base-TX. Furthermore, Y-adapters eliminate any chance of migrating to a faster LAN system that may utilize all four pairs.

Crossover Cables

One of the most frequently asked questions on wiring newsgroups and bulletin boards is "How do I make a crossover cable?" Computers that are equipped with 10Base-T or 100Base-TX network adapters can be connected "back-to-back"; this means they do not require a hub to be networked together. Back-to-back connections via crossover cables are really handy in a small or home office. Crossover cables are also used to link together two hubs if the hubs do not have an uplink or crossover port built-in.

A crossover cable is just a patch cord that is wired to a T568A pinout scheme on one end and a T568B pinout scheme on the other end. To make a crossover cable, you will need a crimping tool, a couple of eight-position modular plugs (a.k.a. RJ-45 plugs), and the desired length of cable. Cut and crimp one side of the cable as you would normally, following whichever wiring pattern you desire, T568A or T568B. When you crimp the other end, just use the other wiring pattern.

WARNING   As mentioned several times elsewhere in this book, we recommend that you buy your patch cords, either straight through or crossover, instead of making them yourself. Field-terminated patch cords can be time-consuming (i.e., expensive) to make and may result in poor system performance.

Table 9.4 shows the pairs that cross over. The other two pairs wire straight through.

TABLE 9.4:   Crossover Pairs

Side-One Pins	Wire Colors	Side-Two Pins
1 (Transmit +)	White/green	3 (Receive +)
2 (Transmit −)	Green	6 (Receive −)
3 (Receive +)	White/orange	1 (Transmit +)
6 (Receive −)	Orange	2 (Receive −)

Shielded Twisted-Pair Connectors

In the United States, the most common connectors for cables that have individually shielded pairs in addition to an overall shield are based on a pre-1990 proprietary cabling system specified by IBM. Designed originally to support Token Ring applications using a two-pair cable (shielded twisted-pair, or STP), the connector is hermaphroditic. In other words, the plug looks just like the jack, but in mirror image. Each side of the connection has a connector and a receptacle to accommodate it. Two hermaphroditic connectors are shown in Figure 9.13. This connector is known by a number of other names, including the STP connector, the IBM data connector, and the universal data connector.

FIGURE 9.13:

Hermaphroditic data connectors

Four-position data connectors

The original Token Ring had a maximum throughput of 4Mbps (and later 16Mbps) and was designed to run over STP cabling. The 16Mbps Token Ring used a 16MHz spectrum to achieve its throughput. Cables and connectors rated to 20MHz were required to allow the system to operate reliably, and the original STP hermaphroditic connectors were limited to a 20MHz bandwidth. Enhancements to these connectors increased the bandwidth limit to 300MHz. These higher-rated connectors (and cable) are designated as STP-A.

STP connectors are the Jeeps of the connector world. They are large, rugged, and versatile. Both the cable and connector are enormous compared to four-pair UTP and RJ-type modular plugs. They also have to be assembled and have more pieces than an Erector set. Cabling contractors used to love the STP connectors because of the premium they could charge based on the labor required to assemble and terminate them.

Darwinian theory prevailed, however, and now the STP and STP-A connectors are all but extinct—they've been crowded out by the smaller, less expensive, and easier-to-use modular jack and plug.

Coaxial Cable Connectors

Unless you have operated a 10Base-2 or 10Base-5 Ethernet network, you are probably familiar only with the coaxial connectors you have in your home for use with televisions and video equipment. Actually, a number of different types of coaxial connectors exist.

F-Series Coaxial Connectors

The coax connectors used with video equipment are referred to as *F-series connectors* (shown in Figure 9.14). The F-connector consists of a ferrule that fits over the outer jacket of the cable and is crimped in place. The center conductor is allowed to project from the connector and forms the business end of the plug. A threaded collar on the plug screws down on the jack, forming a solid connection. F-connectors are used primarily in residential installations for RG-58, RG-59, and RG-6 coaxial cables to provide CATV, security-camera, and other video service.

FIGURE 9.14:

The F-type coaxial-cable connector

F-connectors are commonly available in one-piece and two-piece designs. In the two-piece design, the ferrule that fits over the cable jacket is a separate sleeve that you slide on before you insert the collar portion on the cable. Experience has shown us that the single-piece design is superior. Fewer parts usually means less fumbling, and the final crimped connection is both more aesthetically pleasing and more durable. However, the usability and aesthetics are largely a function of the design and brand of the two-piece product. Some two-piece designs are very well received by the CATV industry.

A cheaper F-type connector available at some retail outlets attaches to the cable by screwing the outer ferrule onto the jacket instead of crimping it in place. These are very unreliable and pull off easily. Their use in residences is not recommended, and they should never be used in commercial installations.

N-Series Coaxial Connectors

The *N-connector* is very similar to the F-connector but has the addition of a pin that fits over the center conductor; the N-connector is shown in Figure 9.15. The pin is suitable for insertion in the jack and must be used if the center conductor is stranded instead of solid. The assembly is attached to the cable by crimping it in place. A screw-on collar ensures a reliable connection with the jack. The N-type connector is used with RG-8, RJ-11U, and thicknet cables for data and video backbone applications.

FIGURE 9.15:

The N-type coaxial connector

The BNC Connector

When coaxial cable distributes data in commercial environments, the *BNC connector* is often used. BNC stands for Bayonet Niell-Concelman, which describes both the method of securing the connection and its inventors. You may occasionally hear this connector referred to as the British Naval Connector. Used with RG-6, RG-58A/U thinnet, RG-59, and RG-62 coax, the BNC utilizes a center pin, as in the N-connector, to accommodate the stranded center conductors usually found in data coax.

The BNC connector (shown in Figure 9.16) can come as a crimp-on or a design that screws onto the coax jacket. As with the F-connector, the screw-on type is not considered reliable and should not be used. The rigid pin that goes over the center conductor may require crimping or soldering in place. The rest of the connector assembly is applied much like an F-connector, using a crimping die made specifically for a BNC connector.

FIGURE 9.16:

The BNC coaxial connector

Connector

To secure a connection to the jack, the BNC has a rotating collar with slots cut into it. These slots fit over combination guide and locking pins on the jack. Lining up the slots with the pins, you push as you turn the collar in the direction of the slots. The slots are shaped so that the plug is drawn into the jack, and locking notches at the end of the slot ensure positive contact with the jack. This method allows quick connection and disconnection while providing a secure match of plug and jack.

Be aware that you must buy BNC connectors that match the impedance of the coaxial cable to which they are applied. Most commonly, they are available in 75-ohm and 50-ohm types, with 93-ohm as a less-used option.

TIP   With all coaxial connectors, be sure to consider the dimensions of the cable you will be using. Coaxial cables come in a variety of diameters that are a function of their transmission properties, series rating, and number of shields and jackets. Buy connectors that fit your cable.

Fiber-Optic Cable Connectors

If you have been working with twisted-pair copper, you are in for a bit of a surprise when you start trying to figure out which fiber-optic connectors you need to use. There's a regular rogues' gallery of them, likely the result of competing proprietary systems in the early days of fiber deployment.

This section of the chapter focus on the different types of fiber connectors and discusses how they are installed onto fiber-optic cable.

Fiber-Optic Connector Types

Fiber-optic connectors use bayonet, screw-on, or "snap 'n lock" methods to attach to the jacks; a newer connector called the MT-RJ is remarkably similar to the eight-position modular connectors (a.k.a. RJ-45) that copper folks have been using for years.

To transmit data, two fibers are required: one to send and the other to receive. Fiber-optic connectors fall into one of two categories based on how the fiber is terminated:

- Simplex connectors terminate only a single fiber in the connector assembly.
- Duplex connectors terminate two fibers in the connector assembly.

The disadvantage of simplex connectors is that you have to keep careful track of polarity. In other words, you must always make sure that the plug on the "send" fiber is always connected to the "send" jack and that the "receive" plug is always connected to the "receive" jack. The real issue is when normal working folk need to move furniture around and disconnect from the jack in their work area and then get their connectors mixed up. Experience has shown us that they are not always color-coded or labeled properly. Getting these reversed means, at the least, that link of the network won't work.

Duplex plugs and jacks take care of this issue. Once terminated, color coding and keying ensures that the plug will be inserted only one way in the jack and will always achieve correct polarity.

Table 9.5 lists some common fiber-optic connectors, along with their corresponding figure numbers. These connectors can be used for either single-mode or multi-mode fibers, but make sure you order the correct model connector depending on the type of cable you are using.

TABLE 9.5:   Fiber-Optic Connectors

Designation	Connection Method	Configuration	Figure
SC	Snap-in	Simplex	Figure 9.17
Duplex SC	Snap-in	Duplex	Figure 9.18
ST	Bayonet	Simplex	Figure 9.19
Duplex ST	Snap-in	Duplex	Figure 9.20
FDDI (MIC)	Snap-in	Duplex	Figure 9.21
FC	Screw-on	Simplex	Figure 9.22

FIGURE 9.17:

An SC fiber-optic connector

FIGURE 9.18:

A duplex SC fiber-optic connector

FIGURE 9.19:

An ST connector

FIGURE 9.20:

A duplex ST fiber-optic connector

FIGURE 9.21:

An FDDI fiber-optic connector

FIGURE 9.22:

An FC fiber-optic connector

Of the four layers of a tight-buffered fiber (the core, cladding, coating, and buffer), only the core where the light is actually transmitted differs in diameter. In their infinite wisdom and foresight, the lesser gods who originally created fiber cables made the cladding, coating, and buffer diameters identical, allowing universal use of stripping tools and connectors.

Of the connectors in Table 9.5, the ST is most widely deployed and is recognized by the ANSI/TIA/EIA-568-A Standard, but the duplex SC is specified in the Standard as the connector to be used. Migration options for making the transition from ST to SC are also specified in the Standard. Other specifications, including those for ATM, FDDI, and broadband ISDN, now also specify the duplex SC.

This wide acceptance in system specifications and standards (acceptance in one begets acceptance in others), along with ease of use and positive assurance that polarity will be maintained, are all contributors to the duplex SC being the current connector of choice.

The SFF Issue

As this book is being written, so-called connector wars are being waged. The issue is the development of a *small-form-factor* (SFF) connector and jack system for fiber-optic cables. Currently, the connectors shown in Table 9.5 all take up more physical space than their RJ-45 counterparts on the copper side. This makes multimedia receptacle faceplates a little crowded and means that you get fewer terminations in closets and equipment rooms than you can get with copper in the same space. The goal is to create an optical-fiber connector with the same cross-sectional footprint as an RJ-45-style connector. For each manufacturer, the Holy Grail of this quest is to have its design win out in the marketplace and become the de facto SFF connector of choice.

SFF connectors were not included in recent revisions to the TIA Standard because the standards committees felt that none of the SFF-connector designs were mature enough. Different manufacturers were proposing different designs, all of which were new to the market. None of the designs had achieved widespread acceptance, so there was no clear de facto standard. ANSI frowns on, if not prohibits outright, adoption of single-manufacturer proprietary designs as standards because such action awards competitive advantage.

However, as this is being written, the situation is changing, and SFF fiber-optic connectors are being promoted and supported by equipment vendors. Three of the connectors are the LC, the VF-45, and the MT-RJ. The MT-RJ currently may have a slight popularity edge, but the market has not produced an overwhelming (or underwhelming) choice. The LC connector (the connector on the lower part of Figure 9.23) is also widely used and is regarded by many optical-fiber professionals as the superior connector. SFF has been taken up as a subject of consideration in TIA working group TR-48.8.1. With the recent publication of ANSI/TIA/EIA-568-B.3, "alternate" connector designs are allowed, provided they meet particular performance requirements, and small-form-factor connectors may soon be included along with the duplex SC as the recommended or recommended alternative connector for use in fiber-optic installations.

FIGURE 9.23:

Duplex SC (top), simplex ST (middle), and LC (bottom) connectors

(Photo courtesy of The Siemon Company)

Installing Fiber-Optic Connectors

With twisted-pair and coax cables, connectors are joined to the cable and conductors using some form of crimping or punch-down, forcing the components into place. With fiber-optic cables, a variety of methods can join the fiber with its connector. Each manufacturer of connectors, regardless of type, specifies the method to be used, the materials that are acceptable, and, sometimes, specialized tools required to complete the connection.

When the fiber connector is inserted into the receptacle, the fiber-optic core in the plug is placed in end-to-end contact with the fiber in the jack. Two issues are of vital importance:

- The fiber-optic cores must be properly aligned. The end-to-end contact must be perfectly flush with no change in the longitudinal axis. In other words, they can't meet at an angle.

- The surfaces must be free of defects such as scratches, pits, protrusions, and cracks.

To address the first critical issue, fiber connector systems must incorporate a method that both aligns and fixes the fiber in its proper position. The alignment is usually accomplished by inserting the fiber in a built-in sleeve or ferrule. Some technique—either gluing or crimping—is then applied to hold it in place. Three types of adhesives can glue the fiber into position:

Heat-cured adhesives　After the material is injected and the fiber is inserted into the connector assembly, it is placed in a small oven to react with the adhesive and harden it. This is time-consuming—heat-cured adhesives require as much as 20 minutes of hardening. Multiple connectors can be done at one time, but the time required to cure the adhesive still increases labor time, and the oven is, of course, extra baggage to pack to the job site.

UV-cured adhesives　Rather than hardening the material in an oven, an ultraviolet light source is used. You may have had something similar done at your dentist the last time you had a tooth filled. Only about a minute of exposure to the UV light is required to cure the adhesive, making this a more time-effective process.

Anaerobic-cured adhesives　This method relies on the chemical reaction of two elements of an epoxy to set up and harden. A resin material is injected in the ferrule. Then a hardener catalyst is applied to the fiber. When the fiber is inserted in the ferrule, the hardener reacts with the resin to cure the material. No extra equipment is required beyond the basic materials and tools. Hardening can take place as quickly as 15 seconds.

Crimp-style connector systems for fiber-optic cable are always manufacturer-specific regarding the tools and materials required. Follow the manufacturer's instructions carefully. With crimp connectors, the fiber is inserted into the connector, and the assembly is then placed in a crimping tool that holds the fiber and connector in proper position. The tool is then used to apply a very specific amount of pressure in a very controlled range of motion to crimp the connector to the buffer layer of the fiber.

To address the second critical issue, part of the connecting process usually involves a polishing step. With the fiber firmly established in the connector, the end of the fiber is rough-trimmed. A series of abrasive materials is then used to finely polish the end of the fiber.

Connector systems that do not require the polishing step are available. These rely on a clean, straight "cleave" (a guillotine-type method of cutting the fiber in two) and positive mechanical force to hold the ends of the fibers together in such a way that a polished surface is not as critical. Such connectors are used primarily, if not exclusively, with multimode fibers because of the larger core diameter of multimode fiber-optic cable.

Fiber-Optic Media

- Introduction to Fiber-Optic Transmission

- Advantages of Fiber-Optic Cabling

- Disadvantages of Fiber-Optic Cabling

- Types and Composition of Fiber-Optic Cables

- Fiber Installation Issues

- Fiber-Optic Performance Factors

Fiber-optic media (or fibers, for short) are any network-transmission media that use glass fiber to transmit network data in the form of light pulses.

Within the last five years, fiber optics has become an increasingly popular type of network transmission media. We'll begin this chapter with a brief look at how fiber-optic transmissions work.

Introduction to Fiber-Optic Transmission

Fiber-optic technology is more complex in its operation than standard copper media because the transmissions are light pulses instead of voltage transitions. Fiber-optic transmissions encode the ones and zeros of a network transmission into ons and offs of light. The light source is usually either a laser or some kind of light-emitting diode (LED). The light from the light source is flashed on and off in the pattern of the data being encoded. The light bounces inside the fiber until the light signal gets to its intended destination, as shown in Figure 10.1.

FIGURE 10.1:

Reflection of a light signal within a fiber-optic cable

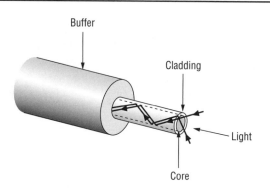

Fiber-optic cables are optimized for a specific *wavelength* of light. The wavelength of a particular light source is the length, measured in nanometers (billionths of a meter), between wave peaks in a typical light wave from that light source (as shown in Figure 10.2). Although the comparison is not exact, you can think of a wavelength as being similar to the Hertz frequency cycle discussed for copper cables.

FIGURE 10.2:

A typical light wave

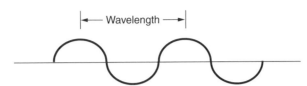

Typically, optical fibers use wavelengths between 800 and 1500nm, depending on the light source. Silica-based glass is most transparent at these wavelengths, and therefore the transmission is more efficient (less attenuation) in this range. For a reference, visible light (the light that you can see) has wavelengths in the range between 400 and 700nm. Most fiber-optic light sources operate in the infrared range (between 700 and 1100nm). You can't see infrared light, and it is a very effective fiber-optic light source.

NOTE   Most traditional light sources can only operate within the visible wavelength spectrum and over a range of wavelengths, not one specific wavelength. Lasers (light amplification by stimulated emission of radiation) and LEDs produce light in a more limited, even single-wavelength, spectrum.

When the light pulses reach the destination, a sensor picks up the presence or absence of the light signal and transforms those ons and offs back into electrical signals that represent ones and zeros.

The more the light signal bounces, the greater the likelihood of signal loss (attenuation). Additionally, every fiber-optic connector between signal source and destination presents the possibility for signal loss. Thus, the connectors must be installed perfectly at each connection.

Most LAN/WAN fiber transmission systems use one fiber for transmitting and one for reception because light only travels in one direction for fiber systems—the direction of transmission. It would be difficult (and expensive) to transform a fiber-optic transmitter into a dual-mode transmitter/receiver (one that could receive and transmit within the same connector).

Advantages of Fiber-Optic Cabling

The following advantages of fiber over other cabling systems explain why it is currently enjoying popularity as a network-cabling medium:

- Immunity to electromagnetic interference (EMI)

- Higher data rates

- Longer maximum distances

- Better security

Immunity to Electromagnetic Interference (EMI)

All copper-cable network media share one common problem: They are susceptible to electromagnetic interference (EMI). EMI is stray electromagnetism that interferes with data transmission. All electrical cables generate a magnetic field around their central axis. If you pass a metal conductor through a magnetic field, an electrical current is generated in that conductor.

When you place two copper cables next to each other, EMI will cause crosstalk (often abbreviated as *xtalk* or *xt*). See Chapter 1 for more information on crosstalk, especially the section "Speed Bumps: What Slows Down Your Data." The longer a particular copper cable is, the more chance for crosstalk.

WARNING   Never place copper cables next to AC current–carrying wires or power supplies. The wires and supplies can produce very large magnetic fields and thus may induce high levels of crosstalk noise into any copper cable placed next to them. For data cables, this will almost certainly either cause data transmissions to fail completely or become a source of intermittent network problems.

Fiber-optic cabling is immune to crosstalk because fiber uses light signals in a glass fiber, rather than electrical signals, to transmit data. So it cannot produce a magnetic field and thus is immune to EMI. Fiber-optic cables can therefore be run in areas considered to be "hostile" to regular copper cabling (e.g., elevator shafts, near transformers, in tight bundles with other electrical cables).

Higher Possible Data Rates

Because light is immune to interference and travels almost instantaneously to its destination, much higher data rates are possible with fiber-optic cabling technologies than with traditional copper systems. Data rates in the gigabit per second (Gbps) range and higher are possible. Single-mode fiber optic cables are capable of multigigabit data rates over very long distances.

Longer Maximum Distances

Typical copper data-transmission media are subject to distance limitations of maximum segment lengths no longer than one kilometer. Because they don't suffer from the EMI problems of traditional copper cabling and because they don't use electrical signals that can degrade substantially over long distances, single-mode fiber optic cables can span distances up to 70 kilometers (about 43.5 miles) without using signal-boosting repeaters.

Better Security

Copper-cable transmission media are susceptible to eavesdropping through taps. A *tap* (short for wiretap) is any device that punctures through the outer jacket of a copper cable and touches the inner conductor. The tap intercepts signals sent on a LAN and sends them to another (unwanted) location. Electromagnetic (EM) taps are similar devices; but rather than puncturing the cable, they use the cable's magnetic fields, which are similar to the pattern of electrical signals. If you'll remember, simply placing a conductor next to a copper conductor with an electrical signal in it will produce a duplicate (albeit a lower-power version) of the same signal. The EM tap then simply amplifies that signal and sends it on to the person who initiated the tap.

Because fiber-optic cabling uses light instead of electrical signals, it is immune to most types of eavesdropping. Traditional taps won't work because any intrusion on the cable will cause the light to be blocked and the connection simply won't function. EM taps won't work because no magnetic field is generated. Because of its immunity to traditional eavesdropping tactics, fiber-optic cabling is used in networks that must remain secure, such as government and research networks.

Disadvantages of Fiber-Optic Cabling

With all of its advantages, many people use fiber-optic cabling. However, fiber-optic cabling does have a couple of major disadvantages, including higher cost and a potentially more difficult installation.

Higher Cost

It's ironic, but the higher cost of fiber-optic cabling has little to do with the cable these days. Increases in available fiber-optic-cable manufacturing capacity have lowered cable prices to levels comparable to high-end UTP on a per-foot basis, and the cables are no harder to pull. Modern fiber-optic connector systems have greatly reduced the time and labor required to terminate fiber. At the same time, the cost of connectors and the time it takes to terminate UTP have increased because CAT 5e and CAT 6 require greater diligence and can be harder to work with than CAT 5. So the installed cost of the basic link, patch panel to wall outlet, is roughly the same for fiber and UTP.

Here's where the costs diverge. Ethernet hubs, switches, routers, NICS, and patch cords for UTP are very (almost obscenely) inexpensive. A good-quality 10/100 auto-sensing Ethernet NIC for a PC can be purchased for less than $20. A fiber-optic NIC for a PC costs several times as much. Hubs, routers, and switches have similar differences in price, UTP vs. fiber. For an IT manager who's got several hundred workstations to deploy and support, that translates to megabucks and keeps UTP a viable solution. The cost of network electronics keeps fiber more expensive than UTP, and ultimately it is preventing the mass stampede to fiber to the desk.

Difficult to Install

Depending on the connector system you select, the other main disadvantage of fiber-optic cabling is that it can be more difficult to install. Copper-cable ends simply need a mechanical connection, and those connections don't have to be perfect. Most often, the plug connectors for copper cables are crimped on (as discussed in Chapter 8) and are punched down in an IDC connection on the jack and patch-panel ends.

Fiber-optic cables can be much trickier to make connections for, mainly because of the nature of the glass or plastic core of the fiber cable. When you cut or cleave (in fiber-optic terms) the inner core, the end of the core consists of many very small shards of glass that diffuse the light signal and prevent it from hitting the receiver correctly. The end of the core must be polished with a special polishing tool to make it perfectly flat so that the light will shine through correctly. Figure 10.3 illustrates the difference between a polished and a nonpolished fiber-optic cable-core end. The polishing step adds extra complexity to the installation of cable ends and amounts to a longer, and thus more expensive, cabling-plant installation.

FIGURE 10.3:

The difference between a freshly cut and a polished end

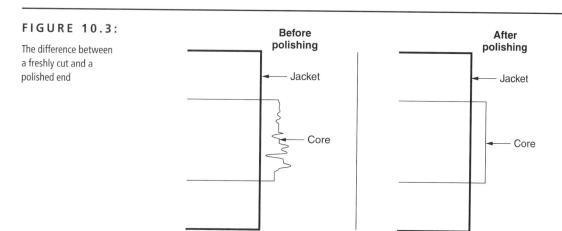

Connector systems are available for multi-mode fiber-optic cables that don't require the polishing step. Using specially designed guillotine cleavers, a clean-enough break in the fiber is made to allow a good end-to-end mate when the connector is plugged in. And, instead of using epoxy or some other method to hold the fiber in place, the fibers are positioned in the connector so that dynamic tension holds them in proper position. Such systems greatly reduce the installation time and labor required to terminate fiber cables.

Types of Fiber-Optic Cables

Fiber-optic cables come in many configurations. The fiber strands can be either single mode or multimode, step index or graded index, and tight buffered or loose-tube buffered. In addition to these options, a variety of core diameters exist for the fiber strands. Most often, the fiber strands are glass, but plastic optical fiber (POF) exists as well. Finally, the cables can be strictly for outdoor use, strictly for indoor use, or a "universal" type that works both indoors and out.

Composition of a Fiber-Optic Cable

A typical fiber-optic cable consists of several components:

- Optical-fiber strand
- Buffer
- Strength members
- Optional shield materials for mechanical protection
- Outer jacket

Each of these components has a specific function within the cable to help ensure that the data gets transmitted reliably.

Optical Fiber

An *optical-fiber strand* (also called an *optical waveguide*) is the basic element of a fiber-optic cable. All fiber strands have at least three components to their cross sections: the core, the cladding, and the coating. Figure 10.4 depicts the three layers of the strand.

FIGURE 10.4:

Elemental layers in a fiber-optic strand

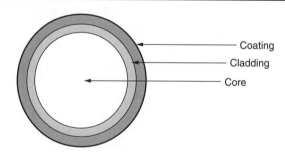

Coating

Cladding

Core

NOTE   Fiber strands have elements so small that it is hard to imagine the scale. You're just not used to dealing with such tiny elements in everyday life. The components of a fiber strand are measured in microns. A micron is one thousandth of a millimeter, or about 0.00004 inches. A typical single-mode fiber strand has a core only 8 microns, or 0.0003 inches, in diameter. A human hair is huge by comparison. The core of a commonly used multimode fiber is 62.5 microns, or 0.002 inches in diameter. For both single mode and multimode, the cladding usually has a diameter of 125 microns, or 0.005 inches. And finally, commonly used single- and multimode fiber strands have a coating layer that is 250 microns, or 0.01 inches, in diameter. Now we're getting somewhere, huh? That's all the way to one hundredth of an inch.

WARNING   The tiny diameter of fiber strands makes them extremely dangerous. When stripped of their coating layer, as must be done for some splicing and connectorizing techniques, the strands can easily penetrate the skin. Shards, or broken pieces of strand, can even be carried by blood vessels to other parts of the body (or the brain) where they could wreak serious havoc. They are especially dangerous to the eye because small pieces can pierce the eyeball, doing damage to the eye's surface and possibly getting trapped inside. Safety glasses and special shard-disposal containers are a must when connecting or splicing fibers.

The fiber core is usually made of some type of plastic or glass. As a matter of fact, several types of materials make up the core of a typical optical fiber. Each material differs in its chemical makeup and cost as well as its *index of refraction*, which is a number that indicates how much light will bend when passing through a particular material. The number also indicates how fast light will travel through a particular material.

A fiber-optic strand's *cladding* is a layer around the central core that is the first, albeit the smallest, layer of protection around the glass or plastic core. It also reflects the light inside the core because the cladding has a lower index of refraction than the core. The cladding thus permits the signal to travel in angles from source to destination—it's like shining a flashlight onto one mirror and having it reflect into another, then another, and so on.

The protective *coating* around the cladding protects the fiber core and cladding from damage. It does not participate in the transmission of light but is simply a protective material. It protects the cladding from abrasion damage, adds additional strength to the core, and builds up the diameter of the strand.

The most basic differentiation of fiber optic cables is whether the fiber strands they contain are either single mode or multimode. A mode is a path for the light to take through the cable. The wavelength of the light transmitted, the acceptance angle, and the numerical aperture interact in such a way that only certain paths are available for the light. Single-mode fibers have cores that are so small that only a single pathway for the light is possible. Multimode fibers have larger cores; the options for the angles at which the light can enter the cable are greater, and so multiple pathways are possible.

Using its single pathway, single-mode fibers can transfer light over great distances with high data-throughput rates. Concentrated (and expensive) laser light sources are required to send data down single-mode fibers, and the small core diameters make connections expensive.

Multimode fibers can accept light from less intense and less expensive sources, usually LEDs. In addition, connections are easier to align properly due to larger core diameters. Distance and bandwidth are more limited than with single-mode fibers, but multimode cabling and electronics are generally a less expensive solution.

Single-mode fibers are usually used in long-distance transmissions or in backbone cables, so you find them in both outdoor and indoor cables. These applications take advantage of the extended distance and high-bandwidth properties of single-mode fiber.

Multimode fibers are usually used in an indoor LAN environment in the horizontal cables. They are also often used in the backbone cabling where great distances are not a problem.

Single-mode and multimode fibers come in a variety of flavors. Some of the types of optical fibers, listed from highest bandwidth and distance potential to least, include the following:

- Single-mode glass

- Multimode graded-index glass

- Multimode step-index glass

- Multimode plastic-clad silica (PCS)

- Multimode plastic

Single-Mode Step-Index Glass   A *single-mode glass fiber core* is very narrow (usually less than 10 microns) and made of silica glass. To keep the cable size manageable, the cladding for a single-mode glass core is usually more than 10 times the size of the core (around 125 microns). Single-mode fibers are expensive, but because of the lack of attenuation (less than 2dB per kilometer), very high speeds are possible—in some cases, up to 50Gbps. Figure 10.5 shows a single-mode glass-fiber core.

FIGURE 10.5:

An example of a single-mode glass-fiber core

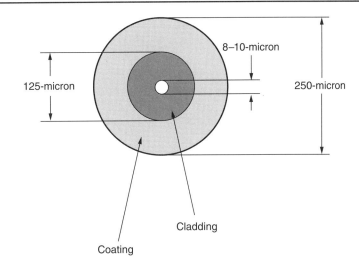

Multimode Graded-Index Glass   A *graded-index glass-fiber core*, made of sil-ica glass, has an index of refraction that changes gradually from the center out-ward to the cladding. The center of the core has the highest index of refraction. If the signals travel outside the center of the core, the lower index of refraction will bend them back toward the center, but they will travel faster. So light signals can travel in the exact center of a larger-diameter cable. The most commonly used multimode graded-index glass fibers have a core that is 62.5 microns in diameter, although multimode glass fibers with a core 50 microns in diameter are gaining in popularity. Figure 10.6 shows a graded-index glass core. Notice that the core is bigger than the single-mode core.

FIGURE 10.6:

A graded-index glass-fiber core

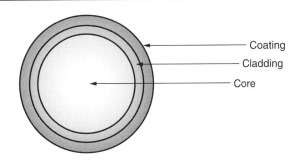

Multimode Step-Index Glass   A *step-index glass core* is similar to a single-mode glass core but with a much larger diameter (usually around 62.5 microns, although it can vary largely in size between 50 and 125 microns). It gets its name from the large and abrupt change of index of refraction from the glass core to the cladding. In fact, a step-index glass core has a uniform index of refraction. Because the signal bounces around inside the core, it is less controllable and thus suffers from larger attenuation values and, effectively, lower bandwidths. However, equipment for cables with this type of core is cheaper than other types of cable, so step-index glass cores are found in many cables.

Multimode Plastic-Clad Silica (PCS)   A *plastic-clad silica* (PCS) *fiber core* is made out of glass central core clad with a plastic coating, hence the name. PCS optical fibers are usually very large (200 microns or larger) and thus have limited bandwidth availability. However, the PCS-core optical cables are relatively cheap when compared to their glass-clad counterparts.

Multimode Plastic   Plastic optical fibers (POF) consist of a plastic core of anywhere from 50 microns on up surrounded by a plastic cladding of a different index of refraction. Generally speaking, these are the lowest-quality optical fibers and are seldom sufficient to transmit light over long distances. Plastic optical cables are used for very short-distance data transmissions or for transmission of visible light in decorations or other specialty lighting purposes not related to data transmission. Recently, POF has been promoted as a horizontal cable in LAN applications. However, the difficulty in manufacturing a graded-index POF, combined with a low bandwidth-for-dollar value, has kept POF from being widely accepted as a horizontal medium.

Buffer

The *buffer*, the second-most distinguishing characteristic of the cable, is the component that provides the most protection for the optical fibers inside the cable. The buffer does just what its name implies; it buffers, or cushions, the optical fiber from the stresses and forces of the outside world. Optical-fiber buffers are categorized as either *tight* or *loose tube*.

With tight buffers, a protective layer (usually a 900-micron thermoplastic covering) is directly over the coating of each optical fiber in the cable. Tight buffers make the entire cable more durable, easier to handle, and easier to terminate. Figure 10.7 shows tight buffering in a single-fiber (simplex) construction. Tight-buffered cables are most often used indoors because expansion and contraction caused by outdoor temperature swings can exert great force on a cable. Tight-buffered designs tend to transmit the force to the fiber strand, which can damage the strand or inhibit its transmission ability. Some specially designed tight-buffered designs are for either exclusive outdoor use or a combination of indoor/outdoor installation.

FIGURE 10.7:

A simplex fiber-optic cable
using tight buffering

A loose-tube buffer, on the other hand, is essentially a tough plastic pipe about 0.125 inches in diameter. One or several coated fibers can be placed inside the tube, depending on the cable design. The tube is then filled with a protective substance, usually a water-blocking gel, to provide cushioning, strength, and protection from the elements. Sometimes, water-blocking powders and tapes are used to waterproof the cable, either as a replacement for the gel (rare) or in addition to it (more common). A loose-tube design is very effective at absorbing forces exerted on the cable so that the fiber strands are isolated from the damaging stress. For this reason, loose-tube designs are almost always seen in outdoor installations.

Multiple tubes can be placed in a cable to accommodate a large fiber count, for high-density communication areas such as in a large city or as trunk lines for long-distance telecommunications.

Figure 10.8 shows a loose-buffered fiber-optic cable. Notice that the cable shown uses water-blocking materials.

FIGURE 10.8:

A fiber-optic cable using loose buffering with water-blocking materials

Strength Members

Fiber-optic cables require additional support to prevent breakage of the delicate optical fibers within the cable. That's where the *strength members* come in. The strength member of a fiber-optic cable is the part that provides additional tensile (pull) strength.

The most common strength member in tight-buffered cables is *aramid yarn*, a popular type of which is Kevlar, the same material found in bulletproof vests. Thousands of strands of this material are placed in a layer, called a serving, around all the tight-buffered fibers in the cable. When pulling on the cable, tensile force is transferred to the aramid yarn and not to the fibers.

TIP	Kevlar is extremely durable, so cables that use it require a special cutting tool, called Kevlar scissors. It cannot be cut with ordinary cutting tools.

Loose-tube fiber-optic cables sometimes have a strand of either fiberglass or steel wire as strength members. These can be placed around the perimeter of a bundle of optical fibers within a single cable, or the strength member can be located in the center of the cable with the individual optical fibers clustered around it. As with aramid yarn in tight-buffered cable, tensile force is borne by the strength member(s), not the buffer tubes or fiber strands.

Shield Materials

In fiber-optic cables designed for outdoor use, or for indoor environments with the potential for mechanical damage, metallic shields are often applied over the inner components but under the jacket. The shield is often referred to as *armor*. A common armoring material is 0.006-inch steel with a special coating that adheres to the cable jacket. This shield should not be confused with shielding to protect against EMI. However, when present, the shield must be properly grounded at both ends of the cable in order to avoid an electrical-shock hazard should it inadvertently come into contact with a voltage source such as a lightning strike or a power cable.

Cable Jacket

The *cable jacket* of a fiber-optic cable is the outer coating of the cable that protects all the inner components from the environment. It is usually made of a durable plastic material and comes in various colors. As with copper cables, fiber-optic cables designed for indoor applications must meet fire-resistance requirements of the NEC (See Chapter 1).

Exterior Protection of Fiber-Optic Cables

If you ever need to install fiber-optic cabling outdoors, the cable should be rated for an exterior installation. An exterior rating means that the cable is specifically designed for outdoor use. It will have features such as UV protection, superior crush and abrasion protection, protection against the extremes of temperature, and an extremely durable strength member. If you use standard indoor cable in an outdoor installation, the cables could get damaged and not function properly.

Additional Designations of Fiber-Optic Cables

Once you've determined if you need single mode or multimode, loose tube or tight-buffered, indoor or outdoor cable, fiber-optic cables still have a variety of options from which to choose. When buying fiber-optic cables, you will have to decide which fiber ratings you want for each type of cable you need. Some of these ratings include the following:

- Core/cladding sizes
- Number of optical fibers
- LAN/WAN application

Core/Cladding Size

The individual fiber-optic strands within a cable are most often rated with a ratio of *core/cladding size* (also known as the optical-fiber size), or the size of both the core and the cladding of a single optical fiber within the cable. This ratio is expressed in two numbers. The first is the diameter of the optical-fiber core, given in microns (μ). The second number is the outer diameter of the cladding for that optical fiber, also given in microns. For example, a cable with a 10-micron core with a 50-micron cladding would be designated as 10/50.

Four major core/cladding sizes are in use today:

- 8/125
- 50/125
- 62.5/125
- 100/140

We'll examine what each one looks like as well as its major use(s).

NOTE   Sometimes, you will see a third number in the ratio (e.g., 8/125/250). The third number is the outside diameter of the protective coating around the individual optical fibers.

8/125   An 8/125 optical fiber is shown in Figure 10.9. It is almost always designated as single-mode fiber because the core size is only approximately 10 times larger than the wavelength of the light it's carrying. Thus, the light doesn't have much room to bounce around. Essentially, the light is traveling in a straight line through the fiber.

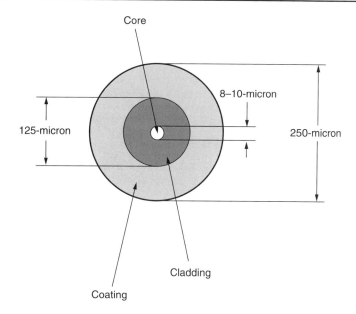

As discussed earlier, 8/125 optical fibers are used for high-speed applications, like backbone fiber architectures such as FDDI, ATM, and Gigabit Ethernet.

50/125   In recent years, Corning, as well as other fiber manufacturers, have been promoting 50/125 multimode fibers instead of the 62.5/125 fibers recognized by the ANSI/TIA/EIA-568-A Standard. It has advantages in bandwidth and distance over 62.5/125 with about the same expense for equipment and connectors. ANSI/TIA/EIA-568-B.3, the new version of the Standard, recognizes 50/125 fiber as an alternate media to 62.5/125.

62.5/125   Of all the multimode-fiber cable designations, the most common is 62.5/125 because it is specified in ANSI/TIA/EIA-568-A as the multimode media of choice for fiber installations. It has widespread acceptance in the field. A standard multimode fiber with a 62.5-micron core with 125-micron cladding is shown in Figure 10.10.

The 62.5/125 optical fibers are used mainly in LAN/WAN applications as a kind of "general-use" fiber (if there really is such a thing).

FIGURE 10.10:

A sample 62.5/125 optical fiber

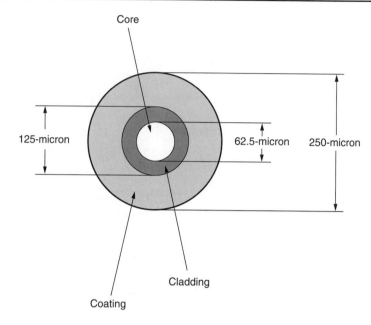

100/140 As you would expect, a 100/140 designation for an optical fiber means that it has a 100-micron core diameter with a 140-micron cladding diameter, as shown in Figure 10.11. The 100/400 fiber is not in the mainstream.

FIGURE 10.11:

A 100/140 optical fiber

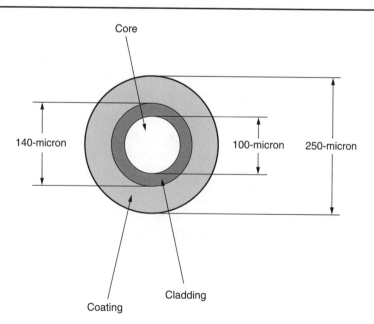

This is a rather odd combination, as you can see. However, because of its odd sizing and, therefore, very specialized application, you might be able to guess the vendor who primarily uses it. Not sure? It's the designer of such proprietary technologies as Token Ring and Micro channel: International Business Machines, or IBM. IBM uses a 100/140 optical fiber in the cables for its fiber-optic implementation of Token Ring.

Number of Optical Fibers

Yet another difference between fiber-optic cables is the number of individual optical fibers within them. The number depends on the intended use of the cable and can increase the cable's size, cost, and capacity.

Because the focus of this book is network cabling and the majority of fiber-optic cables you will encounter for networking are tight buffered, we will limit our discussions here to tight-buffered cables. These cables can be divided into three categories based on the number of optical fibers:

- Simplex cables
- Duplex cables
- Multifiber cables

A *simplex* fiber-optic cable has only one tight-buffered optical fiber inside the cable jacket. An example of a simplex cable was shown earlier in this chapter in Figure 10.7. Because simplex cables only have one fiber inside them, usually a thick strength member and a thicker jacket make the cable easier to handle.

Duplex cables, in contrast, have two tight-buffered optical fibers inside a single jacket (as shown in Figure 10.12). The most popular use for duplex fiber-optic cables is as a fiber-optic LAN backbone cable, because all LAN connections need a transmission fiber and a reception fiber. Duplex cables have both inside a single cable, and running a single cable is of course easier than running two.

TIP   One type of fiber-optic cable is called a duplex cable but technically is not one. This cable is known as *zipcord*. Zipcord is really two simplex cables bonded together into a single flat optical-fiber cable. It's called a duplex because there are two optical fibers, but it's not really duplex because the fibers aren't covered by a common jacket. Zipcord is used primarily as a duplex patch cable. It is used instead of true duplex cable because it is cheap to make and to use. Figure 10.13 shows a zipcord fiber-optic cable.

FIGURE 10.12:

A sample duplex fiber-optic cable

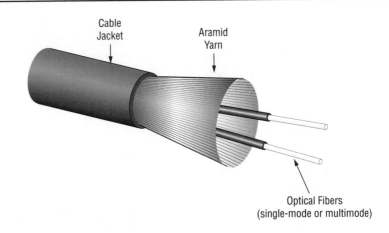

FIGURE 10.13:

A zipcord cable

Finally, *multifiber* cables contain more than two optical fibers in one jacket. Multifiber cables have anywhere from three to several hundred optical fibers in them. More often than not, however, the number of fibers in a multifiber cable will be a multiple of two because, as discussed earlier, LAN applications need a send and a receive optical fiber for each connection.

LAN/WAN Application

Different fiber cable types are used for different applications within the LAN/-WAN environment. Table 10.1 shows the relationship between the fiber network type, the wavelength, and fiber size for both single-mode and multimode fiber-optic cables.

NOTE
> The philosophy of a generic cable installation that will function with virtually any application led the industry Standard, ANSI/TIA/EIA-568-A, to cover all the applications by specifying 62.5/125 multimode as a media of choice (in addition to single-mode). The revised Standard, ANSI/TIA/EIA-568-B.3, continues to recognize single-mode and 62.5/125 multimode fiber but includes 50/125 multimode because it effectively covers all the applications as well.

TABLE 10.1:   Network-Type Fiber Applications

Network Type	Single-Mode Wavelength/Size	Multimode Wavelength/Size
Ethernet	1300nm – 8/125-micron	850nm – 62.5/125-micron
Fast Ethernet	1300nm – 8/125-micron	1300nm – 62.5/125-micron
Token Ring	Proprietary – 8/125-micron	Proprietary – 62.5/125-micron
ATM 155Mbps	1300nm – 8/125-micron	1300nm – 62.5/125-micron
FDDI	1300nm – 8/125-micron	1300nm – 62.5/125-micron

Fiber Installation Issues

Now that we've discussed details about the fiber-optic cable, we must cover the components of a typical fiber installation and fiber-optic performance factors.

We should also mention here that choosing the right fiber-optic cable for your installation is critical. If you don't, your fiber installation is doomed from the start. Remember the following:

Match the rating of the fiber you are installing to the equipment.   It may seem a bit obvious, but if you are installing fiber for a hub and workstations with single-mode connections, it is not a good idea to use multimode fiber, and vice versa.

Use fiber-optic cable appropriate for the locale.   Don't use outdoor cable in an interior application. That would be overkill. Similarly, don't use interior cable outside. The interior cable doesn't have the protection features that the exterior cable has.

Unterminated fiber is dangerous. Fiber can be dangerous in two ways: You can get glass slivers in your hands from touching the end of a glass fiber, and laser light is harmful to unprotected eyes. Many fiber-optic transmitters use laser light that can damage the cornea of the eyeball when looked at. Bottom line: Protect the end of an unterminated fiber cable.

NOTE   Installing fiber-optic cable will be covered in Part III, "Cabling Design and Installation."

Components of a Typical Installation

Just like copper-based cabling systems, fiber-optic cabling systems have a few specialized components, including enclosures and connectors.

Fiber-Optic Enclosures

Because laser light is dangerous, the ends of every fiber-optic cable must be encased in some kind of enclosure. The enclosure not only protects humans from laser light but also protects the fiber from damage. Wall plates and patch panels are the two main types of fiber enclosures. You learned about wall plates in Chapter 8, so we'll discuss patch panels here.

When most people think about a fiber enclosure, a *fiber patch panel* comes to mind. It allows connections between different devices to be made and broken at the will of the network administrator. Basically, a bunch of fiber-optic cables will terminate in a patch panel. Then, short fiber-optic patch cables are used to make connections between the various cables. Figure 10.14 shows an example of a fiber-optic patch panel. Note that dust caps are on all the fiber-optic ports; they prevent dust from getting into the connector and preventing a proper connection.

In addition to the standard fiber patch panels, a fiber-optic installation may have one or more *fiber distribution panels*, which are very similar to patch panels, in that many cables interconnect there. However, in a distribution panel (see Figure 10.15), the connections are more permanent. Distribution panels usually have a lock and key to prevent end users from making unauthorized changes. Generally speaking, a patch panel is found wherever fiber-optic equipment (i.e., hubs, switches, and routers) is found. Distribution panels are found wherever multi-fiber cables are split out into individual cables.

FIGURE 10.14:

An example of a fiber-optic patch panel

FIGURE 10.15:

A sample fiber-optic distribution panel

Fiber-Optic Connectors

Fiber-optic connectors are unique in that they must make both an optical and a mechanical connection. Connectors for copper cables, like the RJ-45 type connector used on UTP, make an electrical connection between the two cables involved. However, the pins inside the connector only need to be touching to make a sufficient electrical connection. Fiber-optic connectors, on the other hand, must have the fiber internally aligned almost perfectly in order to make a connection. The fiber-optic connectors use various methods to accomplish this.

Some of the types of optical connectors currently in use include the following:

- Subscriber connector (SC)
- 568SC (duplex SC)
- Straight-tip (ST)
- Duplex ST
- Biconic
- FDDI (MIC)
- FC
- Enterprise system connection (ESCON)
- SMA

In this subsection, we will briefly examine each connector type, starting with the SC connector. Note that each connector differs primarily in the way the connection is made, the maximum number of connections (the number of times a connector can be plugged and unplugged, also called *mating cycles*), and the size of the connector.

NOTE   Fiber-optic connector installation (called connectorizing) is covered in more detail in Chapter 13.

Subscriber Connector (SC)   The subscriber connector (SC), also sometimes known as a *square connector*, is shown in Figure 10.16. As you can see, SC connectors are latched. Unless the latch is released, usually by pressing some kind of button, the connector cannot be pulled out.

An SC connector

SC connectors work with either single- or multimode optical fibers and will last for around 1,000 matings. They are currently seeing increased use, but they still aren't as popular in the LAN environment as ST connectors are.

568SC (Duplex SC)   The 568SC connectors (also known as duplex SC connectors) are basically a pair of SC connectors in a single plastic enclosure. Figure 10.17 shows a 568SC connector. Compare the connector shown in Figure 10.17 with the one in Figure 10.16 and notice the similarities.

FIGURE 10.17:

A sample 568SC connector

Because the SC and Duplex SC connectors are basically the same, they share the same characteristics, including maximum matings and support for single- and multimode optical fibers.

Straight Tip (ST)   The straight tip (ST) fiber-optic connector, developed by AT&T, is probably the most widely used fiber-optic connector. It uses a BNC attachment mechanism, similar to the thinnet Ethernet connection mechanism, which makes connections and disconnections fairly easy. The ST's ease of use is one of the attributes that makes it so popular. Figure 10.18 shows some examples of ST connectors. Notice the BNC attachment mechanism.

FIGURE 10.18:

Some examples of ST connectors

Because it is so widely available, adapters to other fiber connector types are available for this connector type. The ST has a maximum mating cycle of around 1,000 matings.

NOTE   Some ST connectors use a plastic end; these will only survive around 250 mating cycles.

Duplex ST   Like the duplex SC connector, the duplex ST connector is simply a pairing up of the single-connector version of its namesake. It shares the same details of its singular version.

Biconic   The biconic connector was developed by AT&T; it has fallen out of favor with fiber installers. It uses a screw-together connection system, as you can see in Figure 10.19. Biconic connectors are available for both single- and multi-mode optical fibers.

FIGURE 10.19:

A biconic fiber-optic connector

FDDI (MIC)   Because the fiber-distributed data interface (FDDI) has become popular as a LAN type, the media interface connector (MIC), the main choice for FDDI, is a popular connector. Figure 10.20 shows an FDDI (MIC) connector. Notice that it is keyed (the red tab on top of the connector) to prevent it from being installed incorrectly.

FIGURE 10.20:

An FDDI (MIC) connector

NOTE   FDDI connectors work *only* with multimode fiber.

FC   The FC connector was one of the first of the smaller connectors used. It is a keyed all-metal connector with a screw-on fastening system. Along with its cousin, the D4 connector, it is quickly becoming one of the more popular small-size connectors. Figure 10.21 shows an FC connector. Note the all-metal construction that makes it durable despite its small size.

FIGURE 10.21:

An FC fiber-optic connector

The D4 connector, a variant of the FC connector, is often confused with the FC. The D4 connector is basically the same as the FC, but a "hood" is over the end of the connector to prevent damage to the fiber (as shown in Figure 10.22). Compare the D4 connector in Figure 10.22 to the FC connector in Figure 10.21.

FIGURE 10.22:

A D4 fiber-optic connector

Enterprise System Connection (ESCON)   The Enterprise System Connection (ESCON) connector is much like the FDDI (MIC) fiber-optic connector, except that the ESCON connector has a retractable cover and a lower maximum mating cycle (only 500 matings). Figure 10.23 shows an ESCON connector. Note the similarities between the ESCON connector shown here and the FDDI (MIC) connector shown earlier in Figure 10.20.

SMA   The SMA connector, developed by AMP Corporation, was designed to be a low-cost multimode fiber connector. As you can see in Figure 10.24, it's fairly simple. Therefore, and because it is made of plastic, it is only rated for a maximum of 200 mating cycles. However, it is rated for military use. That, along with its low cost, makes it very popular.

NOTE   SMA connectors are currently available for both single- and multimode optical fibers.

Fiber-Optic Performance Factors

During the course of a normal fiber installation, you must be aware of a few factors that can negatively affect performance. They are as follows:

- Attenuation
- Acceptance angle
- Numerical aperture (NA)
- Modal dispersion
- Chromatic dispersion

Attenuation

The biggest negative factor in any fiber-optic cabling installation is attenuation, or the loss or decrease in power of a data-carrying signal (in the case of fiber, the light signal). It is measured in decibels (dB or dB/km for a particular cable run). In real-world terms, a 3dB attenuation loss in a fiber connection is equal to about a 50 percent loss of signal. Figure 10.25 graphs attenuation in decibels versus percent signal loss. Notice that the relationship is exponential.

FIGURE 10.25:

Relationship of attenuation to percent signal loss of a fiber optic transmission

The more attenuation that exists in a fiber-optic cable from transmitter to receiver, the shorter the maximum distance between them. Attenuation negatively affects transmission speeds and distances of all cabling systems, but fiber-optic transmissions are particularly sensitive to attenuation.

Many different problems can cause attenuation of a light signal in an optical fiber, including the following:

- Excessive gap between fibers in a connection
- Improperly installed connectors
- Impurities in the fiber
- Excessive bending of the cable
- Excessive stretching of the cable

These problems will be covered in Chapter 14. For now, just realize that these problems cause attenuation, an undesirable effect.

Acceptance Angle

Another factor that affects the performance of a fiber-optic cabling system is the acceptance angle of the optical-fiber core. The acceptance angle (as shown in Figure 10.26) is the angle through which a particular (multimode) fiber can accept light as input.

FIGURE 10.26:

An illustration of multifiber acceptance angles

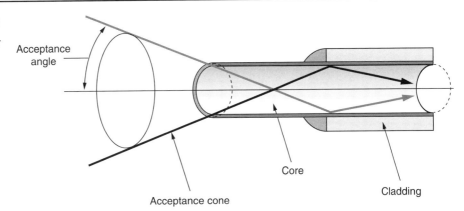

The greater the acceptance angle difference between two or more signals in a multimode fiber, the greater the effect of modal dispersion (see the following section "Modal Dispersion"). The modal-dispersion effect also has a negative effect on the total performance of a particular cable segment.

Numerical Aperture (NA)

One of the most misunderstood performance factors of fiber-optic cable is the *numerical aperture* (NA). Most people ignore this value when choosing their fiber-optic cable. However, it is a very important performance factor, especially when splicing two optical cables. NA is a decimal number between 0 and 1 that reflects the ability of a particular optical fiber to accept light. The number is the result of a mathematical equation involving the acceptance angle.

A value for NA of 0 indicates that the fiber gathers no light. A value of 1 for NA indicates that the fiber will accept all light it's exposed to. The lower the NA, the less distance the signal can travel. However, a lower NA also means more possible bandwidth is available. Conversely, a higher NA means that the signal can travel farther, but a lower bandwidth is available for that signal. Figure 10.27 illustrates the difference between high and low NA values.

FIGURE 10.27:

The difference between high and low NA values

Low NA

High NA

Modal Dispersion

Multimode cables suffer from a unique problem known *as modal dispersion*, which is similar in effect to delay skew described in Chapter 1 relative to twisted-pair cabling. Modal dispersion causes transmission delays in multimode fibers. Here's how it occurs. The modes (signals) enter the multimode fiber at varying angles. So the signals will bounce differently inside the fiber and arrive at different times (as shown in Figure 10.28). The more severe the difference between the entrance angles, the greater the arrival delay between the modes. In Figure 10.28, mode A will exit the fiber first because it has fewer bounces inside the core than mode B. Mode A has fewer bounces because its entrance angle is less severe (i.e., it's of a *lower order*) than that of mode B. The difference between the time mode A and mode B exit is the modal dispersion. Modal dispersion gets larger as the difference between the entrance angles increases.

FIGURE 10.28:

Illustration of modal
dispersion

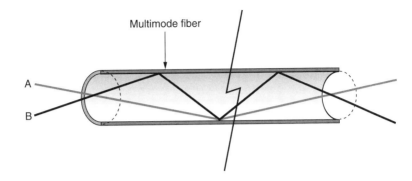

FIGURE 10.28:

Illustration of modal
dispersion

Chromatic Dispersion

The last fiber-optic performance factor is *chromatic dispersion*, which limits the
bandwidth of certain single-mode optical fibers. It occurs when the various wavelengths of light spread out as they travel through an optical fiber. This happens
because different wavelengths of light travel different speeds through the same
media. As they bounce through the fiber, the various wavelengths will reflect off
the sides of the fibers at different angles (as shown in Figure 10.29). The wavelengths will spread farther and farther apart until they arrive at the destination at
completely different times.

FIGURE 10.29:

Single-mode optical-fiber
chromatic dispersion

Unbounded (Wireless) Media

- Infrared

- Radio Frequency (RF)

- Microwave

*U*nbounded *media* have network signals that are not bound by any type of fiber or cable; hence, they are also called *wireless technologies*. Unbounded (wireless) LAN media are becoming extremely popular in modular office spaces.

You may ask, "Why talk about wireless technologies in a book about cabling?" The answer is that today's networks aren't composed of a single technology or wiring scheme—they are heterogeneous networks. Wireless technologies are just one way of solving a particular networking need in a heterogeneous cabling system. Although cabled networks are generally less expensive, more robust transmission-wise, and faster (especially in the horizontal environment), in certain situations, wireless networks can carry data where traditional cabled networks cannot. This is particularly the case in backbone or WAN implementations.

NOTE Some pretty high bandwidth numbers are detailed in the sections that follow. These are typically for interbuilding or WAN implementations. The average throughput speed of installed wireless LANs in the horizontal work environment is 1.6Mbps. (Although 10 to 11Mbps throughput is available, it is a relatively recent phenomenon.) By comparison, any properly installed Category 5 horizontal network is capable of at least 100Mbps. Wired and wireless are two different beasts, but the comparison helps to put the horizontal speed issue into perspective.

In this chapter, you will get a brief introduction to some of the wireless technologies found in both LANs and WANs and how they are used. We'll start this discussion with a look at infrared transmissions.

NOTE This chapter is only meant to introduce you to wireless networks. For more information, go to your favorite Internet search engine and type in *wireless networking*.

Infrared Transmissions

Everyone who has a television with a remote control has performed an *infrared transmission*. Infrared (IR) transmissions are signal transmissions that use infrared radiation as their transmission medium. Infrared radiation is part of the electromagnetic spectrum. It has a wavelength shorter than visible light (actually, it's shorter than the red wavelength in the visible spectrum) with more energy. Infrared is a very popular method of wireless networking. The sections that follow examine some of the details of infrared transmissions.

How Infrared Transmissions Work

Infrared transmissions are very simple. All infrared connections work similarly to LAN transmissions, except that no cable contains the signal. The infrared transmissions travel through the air and consist of infrared radiation that is modulated in order to encode the LAN data.

A *laser diode*, a small electronic device that can produce single wavelengths or frequencies of light or radiation, usually produces the infrared radiation. A laser diode differs from a regular laser in that it is much simpler, smaller, and lower powered; thus, the signals can only travel over shorter distances (usually less than 500 feet).

Besides needing an infrared transmitter, all devices that communicate via infrared need an infrared receiver. The receiver is often a photodiode, or a device that is sensitive to a particular wavelength of light or radiation and converts the infrared signals back into the digital signals that a computer will understand.

In some cases, the infrared transmitter and receiver are built into a single device known as an *infrared transceiver*, which can both transmit and receive infrared signals. Infrared transceivers are used primarily in short-distance infrared communications. For communications that must travel over longer distances (e.g., infrared WAN communications must travel over several kilometers), a separate infrared transmitter and receiver are contained in a single housing. The transmitter is usually a higher-powered infrared laser. In order to function correctly, the lasers in both devices (sender and receiver) must be aligned with the receivers on the opposite device (as shown in Figure 11.1).

Point to point and *broadcast* are the two types of infrared transmission. We'll take a brief look at each.

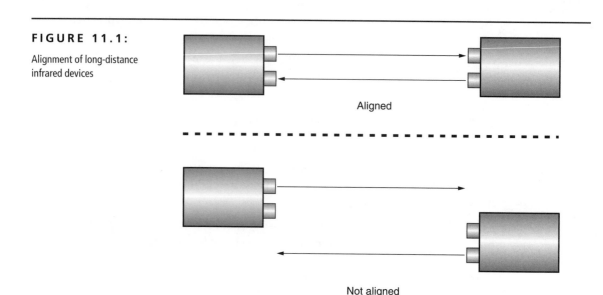

Point to Point

The most common type of infrared transmission is the point-to-point transmission, also known as *line-of-sight* transmission. Point-to-point infrared transmissions are those infrared transmissions that use tightly focused beams of infrared radiation to send information or control information over a distance (i.e., from one "point" directly to another). The aforementioned infrared remote control for your television is one example of a point-to-point infrared transmission.

LANs and WANs can use point-to-point infrared transmissions to transmit information over short or long distances. Point-to-point infrared transmissions are used in LAN applications for connecting computers in separate buildings, over short distances.

Using point-to-point infrared media reduces attenuation and makes eavesdropping difficult. Typical point-to-point infrared computer equipment is similar to that used for consumer products with remote controls, except they have much higher power. Careful alignment of the transmitter and receiver is required, as mentioned earlier. Figure 11.2 shows how a network might use point-to-point infrared transmission. Note that the two buildings are connected via a direct line of sight with infrared transmission and that the buildings are about 1,000 feet apart.

FIGURE 11.2:

Point-to-point infrared usage

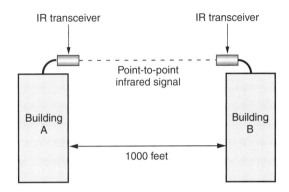

Point-to-point infrared systems have the following characteristics:

Frequency range   Infrared light usually uses the lowest range of light frequencies, between 100GHz and 1,000THz (tetrahertz).

Cost   The cost depends on the kind of equipment used. Long-distance systems, which typically use high-power lasers, can be very expensive. Equipment that is mass-produced for the consumer market and can be adapted for network use is generally inexpensive.

Installation   Infrared point-to-point requires precise alignment. Take extra care if high-powered lasers are used, because they can damage or burn eyes.

Capacity   Data rates vary from 100Kbps to 16Mbps (at one kilometer).

Attenuation   The amount of attenuation depends on the quality of emitted light and its purity, as well as general atmospheric conditions and signal obstructions.

EMI   Infrared transmission can be affected by intense visible light. Tightly focused beams are fairly immune to eavesdropping because tampering usually becomes evident by the disruption in the signal. Furthermore, the area in which the signal may be picked up is very limited.

Broadcast

Broadcast infrared systems spread the signal to a wider area and allow reception of the signal by several receivers. One of the major advantages is mobility; the workstations or other devices can be moved more easily than with point-to-point infrared media. Figure 11.3 shows how a broadcast infrared system might be used.

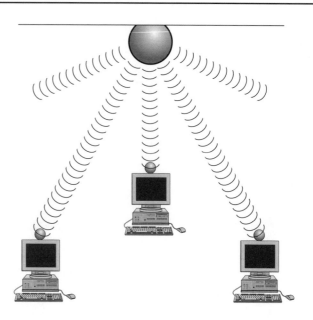

Because broadcast infrared signals (also known as *diffuse infrared*) are not as focused as point-to-point, this type of system cannot offer the same throughput. Broadcast infrared is typically limited to less than 1Mbps, making it too slow for most network needs.

Broadcast infrared systems have the following characteristics:

Frequency range   Infrared systems usually use the lowest range of light frequencies, from 100GHz to 1,000THz.

Cost   The cost of infrared equipment depends on the quality of light required. Typical equipment used for infrared systems is quite inexpensive. High-power laser equipment is much more expensive.

Installation   Installation is fairly simple. When devices have clear paths and strong signals, they can be placed anywhere the signal can reach, making reconfiguration easy. One concern should be the control of strong light sources that might affect infrared transmission.

Capacity   Although data rates are less than 1Mbps, it is theoretically possible to reach much higher throughput.

Attenuation   Broadcast infrared, like point-to-point, is affected by the quality of the emitted light and its purity and by atmospheric conditions.

Because devices can be moved easily, however, obstructions are generally not of great concern.

EMI   Intense light can dilute infrared transmissions. Because broadcast infrared transmissions cover a wide area, they are more easily intercepted for eavesdropping.

Advantages of Infrared

As a medium for LAN transmissions, infrared has many advantages that make it a logical choice for many LAN/WAN applications. These advantages include the following:

Relatively inexpensive   Infrared equipment (especially the short-distance broadcast equipment) is relatively inexpensive when compared to other wireless methods like microwave or radio frequency (RF). Because of its low cost, many laptop and portable-computing devices contain an infrared transceiver to connect to each other and transfer files. Additionally, as a WAN transmission method, you pay for the equipment once; there are no recurring line charges.

High bandwidths   Point-to-point infrared transmissions support fairly high (around 1.544Mbps) bandwidths. They are often used as WAN links because of their speed and efficiency.

No FCC license required   If a wireless transmission is available for the general (i.e., U. S.) public to listen to, the Federal Communications Commission (FCC) probably governs it. The FCC licenses certain frequency bands for use for radio and satellite transmission. Because infrared transmissions are short range and their frequencies fall outside the FCC bands, you don't need to apply for an FCC-licensed frequency (a long and costly process) to use them.

NOTE   More information on the FCC can be found at its Web site: `www.fcc.gov`.

Ease of installation   Installation of most infrared devices is very simple. Connect the transceiver to the network (or host machine) and point it at the device you want to communicate with. Broadcast infrared devices don't even need to be pointed at their host devices. Long-distance infrared devices may need a bit more alignment, but the idea is the same.

High security on point-to-point connections   Because point-to-point infrared connections are line of sight and any attempt to intercept a point-to-point infrared connection will block the signal, point-to-point infrared connections are very secure. The signal can't be intercepted without the knowledge of the sending equipment.

Portability   Short-range infrared transceivers and equipment are usually small and have lower power requirements. Thus, these devices are great choices for portable, flexible networks. Broadcast infrared systems are often set up in offices where the cubicles are rearranged often. This does *not* mean that the computers can be in motion while connected. As discussed later in this section, infrared requires a constant line of sight. If you should walk behind an object and obstruct the line-of-sight between the two communicating devices, the connection will be interrupted.

Disadvantages of Infrared

Just as with any other network technology, infrared has its disadvantages. Some of these are the following:

Line of sight needed for focused transmissions   Infrared transmissions require an unobstructed path between sender and receiver. Infrared transmissions are similar to regular light transmissions in that the signals don't "bend" around corners without help, nor can the transmissions go through walls. Some transmissions are able to bounce off surfaces, but each bounce takes away from the total signal strength (usually halving the effective strength for each bounce).

> **NOTE**   Some products achieve non-line-of-sight infrared transmissions by bouncing the signal off of walls or ceilings. You should know that for every "bounce," the signal can degrade as much as 50 percent. For that reason, we have stated here that focused infrared is primarily a line-of-sight technology.

Weather attenuation   Because infrared transmissions travel through the air, any change in the air can cause degradation of the signal over a distance. Humidity, temperature, and ambient light can all negatively affect signal strength in low-power infrared transmissions. In outdoor, higher-power infrared transmissions, fog, rain, and snow can all reduce transmission effectiveness.

Examples of Infrared Transmissions

Infrared transmissions are used for other applications in the PC world besides LAN and WAN communication. The other applications include the following:

- IrDA ports
- Infrared laser devices

We'll briefly examine these two examples of infrared technology.

IrDA Ports

More than likely, you've seen an IrDA port. IrDA ports are the small, dark windows on the backs of laptops and handheld PCs that allow two devices to communicate via infrared. IrDA is actually an abbreviation for the standards body that came up with the standard method of short-range infrared communications, the Infrared Data Association. Based out of Walnut Creek, California and founded in 1993, it is a membership organization dedicated to developing standards for wireless, infrared transmission systems between computers. With IrDA ports, a laptop or PDA (personal digital assistant) can exchange data with a desktop computer or use a printer without a cable connection.

Computing products with IrDA ports began to appear in 1995, and the Laser-Jet 5P was one of the first printers with a built-in IrDA port. You could print to the LaserJet 5P from any laptop or handheld device (as long as you had the correct driver installed) by simply pointing the IrDA port on the laptop or handheld device at the IrDA port on the 5P. This technology became known as *point and print*. Figure 11.4 shows an example of an IrDA port on a handheld PC. Notice how small it is compared to the size of the PC.

FIGURE 11.4:

An example of an IrDA port

IrDA port

NOTE

For more information about the IrDA, its membership, and the IrDA port, see its Web site at www.irda.org.

Infrared-Laser Devices

Longer-distance communications via infrared transmissions are possible, but they require the use of a special class of devices, known as infrared-laser devices. These devices have a transmitting laser, which operates in the infrared range (a wavelength from 750 to 2500nm and a frequency of around 1THz) and an infrared receiver to receive the signal. Infrared-laser devices usually connect multiple buildings within a campus or multiple sites within a city. One such example of this category of infrared devices is the TerraScope system (as shown in Figure 11.5) from Optical Access, Inc. (formerly AstroTerra). This system provides data rates from 10 to 155Mbps for distances of up to 3.75 km (2.33 miles) between sender and receiver.

FIGURE 11.5:

The TerraScope infrared laser device

NOTE

You can find out more information about the TerraScope system on Optical Access's Web site at www.opticalaccess.com.

Radio-Frequency (RF) Systems

Radio-frequency (RF) transmission systems are those network transmission systems that use radio waves to transmit data. In late 1999, RF transmission systems saw a sharp increase in use. Many companies are installing RF access points in their networks to solve certain mobility issues. The relatively low cost and ease of installation of RF systems play a part in their popularity.

In this section, we will cover RF systems and their application to LAN and WAN uses.

How RF Works

Radio waves have frequencies from 10 kilohertz (kHz) to 1 gigahertz (GHz), and RF systems use radio waves in this frequency band. The range of the electromagnetic spectrum from 10kHz to 1GHz is called radio frequency (RF).

Most radio frequencies are regulated; some are not. To use a regulated frequency, you must receive a license from the regulatory body over that area (in the United States, the FCC). Getting a license can take a long time and can be costly; for data transmission, the license also makes it more difficult to move equipment. However, licensing guarantees that, within a set area, you will have clear radio transmission.

The advantage of unregulated frequencies is that few restrictions are placed on them. One regulation, however, does limit the usefulness of unregulated frequencies: Unregulated-frequency equipment must operate at less than one watt. The point of this regulation is to limit the range of influence a device can have, thereby limiting interference with other signals. In terms of networks, this makes unregulated radio communication bandwidths of limited use.

WARNING Because unregulated frequencies are available for use by others in your area, you cannot be guaranteed a clear communications channel.

In the United States, the following frequencies are available for unregulated use:

- 902 to 928MHz
- 2.4GHz (also internationally)
- 5.72 to 5.85GHz

Radio waves can be broadcast either omnidirectionally or directionally. Various kinds of antennas can be used to broadcast radio signals. Typical antennas include the following:

- Omnidirectional towers
- Half-wave dipole
- Random-length wire
- Beam (such as the yagi)

Figure 11.6 shows these common types of radio-frequency antennas.

FIGURE 11.6:

Typical radio-frequency antennas

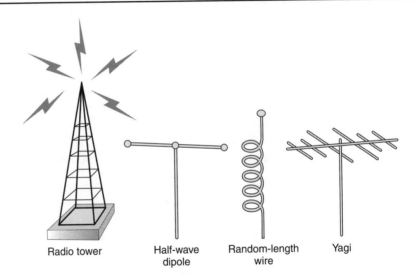

Radio tower   Half-wave dipole   Random-length wire   Yagi

The antenna and transceiver determine the power of the RF signal. Each range has characteristics that affect its use in computer networks. For computer network applications, radio waves are classified in three categories:

- Low power, single frequency
- High power, single frequency
- Spread spectrum

Table 11.1 summarizes the characteristics of the three types of radio-wave media that are described in the following sections.

TABLE 11.1: Radio-Wave Media

Factor	Low Power	High Power	Spread Spectrum
Frequency range	All radio frequencies (typically low GHz range)	All radio frequencies (typically low GHz range)	All radio frequencies (typically 902 to 928MHz, 2.4 to 2.4835GHz, and 5.725 to 5.85GHz in U.S, where 2.4 and 5.8GHz are the most popular today)
Cost	Moderate for wireless	Higher than low-power, single-frequency	Moderate
Installation	Simple	Difficult	Moderate
Capacity	From below 1 to 10Mbps	From below 1 to 10Mbps	3 to 11Mbps
Attenuation	High (25 meters)	Low	High
EMI	Poor	Poor	Fair

Low Power, Single Frequency

As the name implies, single-frequency transceivers operate at only one frequency. Typical low-power devices are limited in range to around 20 to 30 meters. Although low-frequency radio waves can penetrate some materials, the low power limits them to the shorter, open environments.

Low-power, single-frequency transceivers have the following characteristics:

Frequency range   Low-power, single-frequency products can use any radio frequency, but higher gigahertz ranges provide better throughput (data rates).

Cost   Most systems are moderately priced compared with other wireless systems.

Installation   Most systems are easy to install if the antenna and equipment are preconfigured. Some systems may require expert advice or installation. Some troubleshooting may be involved to avoid other signals.

Capacity   Data rates range from 1 to 10Mbps.

Attenuation   The radio frequency and power of the signal determine attenuation. Low-power, single-frequency transmissions use low power and consequently suffer from attenuation.

EMI   Resistance to EMI is low, especially in the lower bandwidths where electric motors and numerous devices produce noise. Susceptibility to eavesdropping is high, but with the limited transmission range, eavesdropping is generally limited to within the building where the LAN is located.

High Power, Single Frequency

High-power, single-frequency transmissions are similar to low-power, single-frequency transmissions but can cover larger distances. They can be used in long-distance outdoor environments. Transmissions can be line of sight or can extend beyond the horizon as a result of being bounced off the earth's atmosphere. High-power, single-frequency can be ideal for mobile networking, providing transmission for land-based or marine-based vehicles as well as aircraft. Transmission rates are similar to low-power rates but at much longer distances.

High-power, single-frequency transceivers have the following characteristics:

Frequency range   As with low-power transmissions, high-power transmissions can use any radio frequency, but networks favor higher gigahertz ranges for better throughput (data rates).

Cost   Radio transceivers are relatively inexpensive, but other equipment (antennas, repeaters, and so on) can make high-power, single-frequency radio moderately to very expensive.

Installation   Installations are complex. Skilled technicians must be used to install and maintain high-power equipment. The radio operators must be licensed by the FCC, and their equipment must be maintained in accordance with FCC regulations. Equipment that is improperly installed or tuned can cause low data-transmission rates, signal loss, and even interference with local radio.

Capacity   Bandwidth is typically from 1 to 10Mbps.

Attenuation   High-power rates improve the signal's resistance to attenuation, and repeaters can be used to extend signal range. Attenuation rates are fairly low.

EMI   Much like low-power, single-frequency transmission, vulnerability to EMI is high. Vulnerability to eavesdropping is also high. Because the signal is broadcast over a large area, it is more likely that signals can be intercepted.

Spread Spectrum

Spread-spectrum transmissions use the same frequencies as other radio-frequency transmissions, but they use several frequencies simultaneously rather than just one. Two modulation schemes can be used to accomplish this, *direct frequency modulation* and *frequency hopping*.

Direct frequency modulation is the most common modulation scheme. It works by breaking the original data into parts (called *chips*), which are then transmitted on separate frequencies. To confuse eavesdroppers, spurious signals can also be transmitted. The transmission is coordinated with the intended receiver, which is aware of which frequencies are valid. The receiver can then isolate the chips and reassemble the data while ignoring the decoy information. Figure 11.7 illustrates how direct frequency modulation works.

FIGURE 11.7:

Direct frequency modulation

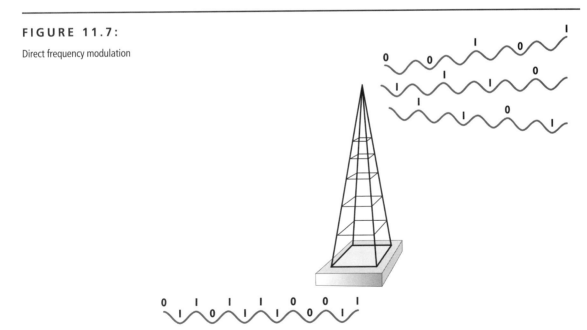

The signal can be intercepted, but it is difficult to watch the right frequencies, gather the chips, know which chips are valid data, and find the right message. This makes eavesdropping difficult.

Current 900MHz direct-sequence systems support data rates of 2 to 6Mbps. Higher frequencies offer the possibility of higher data rates.

Frequency hopping rapidly switches among several predetermined frequencies. In order for this system to work, the transmitter and receiver must be in nearly perfect synchronization. Bandwidth can be increased by simultaneously transmitting on several frequencies. Figure 11.8 shows how frequency hopping works.

FIGURE 11.8:

Frequency hopping

Spread-spectrum transceivers have the following characteristics:

Frequency range   Spread spectrum generally operates in the unlicensed-frequency ranges. In the United States, devices using the 902 to 928MHz range are most common, but 2.4GHz devices are also becoming available.

Cost   Although costs depend on what kind of equipment you choose, spread spectrum is typically fairly inexpensive when compared with other wireless media.

Installation   Depending on the type of equipment you have in your system, installation can range from simple to fairly complex.

Capacity   The most common systems, the 900MHz systems, support data rates of 2 to 6Mbps, but newer systems operating in gigahertz produce higher data rates.

Attenuation   Attenuation depends on the frequency and power of the signal. Because spread-spectrum transmission systems operate at low power, which produces a weaker signal, they usually have high attenuation.

EMI   Immunity to EMI is low, but because spread spectrum uses different frequencies, interference would need to be across multiple frequencies to destroy the signal. Vulnerability to eavesdropping is low.

Advantages of RF

As mentioned earlier, RF systems are widely used in LANs today because of many factors:

No line of sight needed   Radio waves can penetrate walls and other solid obstacles, so a direct line of sight is not required between sender and receiver.

Low cost   Radio transmitters have been around since the early twentieth century. After 100 years, high-quality radio transmitters have become extremely cheap to manufacture.

Flexible   Some RF LAN systems allow laptop computers with wireless PC NICs to roam around the room while remaining connected to the host LAN.

Disadvantages of RF

As with the other types of wireless networks, RF networks have their disadvantages:

Susceptible to jamming and eavesdropping   Because RF signals are broadcast in all directions, it is very easy for someone to intercept and interpret a LAN transmission without the permission of the sender or receiver. Those RF systems that use spread-spectrum encoding are less susceptible to this problem.

Susceptible to RF interference   All mechanical devices with electric motors produce stray RF signals, known as *RF noise*. The larger the motor, the stronger the RF noise. These stray RF signals can interfere with the proper operation of an RF-transmission LAN.

Limited range   RF systems don't have the range of satellite networks (although they can travel longer distances than infrared networks). Because of their limited range, RF systems are normally used for short-range network applications (e.g., from a PC to a hub).

Examples of RF

RF systems are being used all over corporate America. The RF networking hardware available today makes it easy for people to connect wirelessly to their corporate network as well as to the Internet.

The most popular type of RF network today is what is known as an *ad hoc RF network*, which is created when two or more entities with RF transceivers that support ad hoc networking are brought within range of each other. The two entities send out radio waves to each other and both recognize that they can communicate with another RF device close by. Ad hoc networks allow people with laptops or handheld devices to create their own networks on the fly and transfer data. Figure 11.9 shows an example of an ad hoc network between three notebooks. These three notebooks all have the some RF devices that support ad hoc and have been configured to talk to each other.

FIGURE 11.9:

An example of an ad hoc RF network

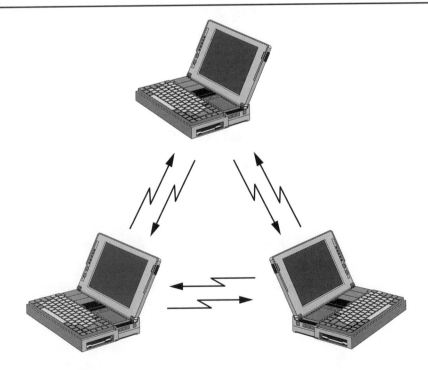

Another style of RF network is a multipoint RF network, which has many stations. Each station has an RF transmitter and receiver that communicate with a central device known as a *wireless bridge*. A wireless bridge (known as an RF access point in RF systems) is a device that provides a transparent connection to the host LAN via an Ethernet or Token Ring connection and uses some wireless method (e.g., infrared, RF, or microwave) to connect to the individual nodes. This type of network is mainly used for two applications: office "cubicle farms" and metropolitan-area wireless Internet access. Both applications require that the wireless bridge be installed at some central point and that the stations that are going to access the network be within the operating range of the bridge device. Figure 11.10 shows an example of this type of network. Note that the workstations at the top of the figure can communicate wirelessly to the server and printer connected to the same network as the bridge device.

FIGURE 11.10:

An example of an RF multipoint network

Many different brands, makes, and models of RF LAN equipment are available. The variety of equipment used to be a source of difficulty with LAN installers. In its infancy, every company used different frequencies, different encoding schemes, different antennas, and different wireless protocols. The marketplace was screaming for a standard. So the IEEE 802.11 Standard was developed. Standard 802.11 specifies various protocols for wireless networking. It does, in fact, specify that either infrared or RF can be used for the wireless network, but most RF systems are the only ones advertising IEEE 802.11 compliance.

Table 11.2 shows some examples of the available RF wireless networking products available at the time of the writing of this book. This table shows which RF technology each product uses as well as its primary application.

TABLE 11.2:   Available RF Wireless Networking Product Examples

Product	RF Technology	Application	Speed
Breezecom BreezNET	Spread spectrum	Multipoint and ad hoc	Up to 11Mbps
Agere Systems ORiNOCO	Spread spectrum	Multipoint	1 to 11Mbps
Cisco Aironet	Spread spectrum	Multipoint	Up to 11Mbps
Apple AirPort	Spread spectrum	Multipoint	11Mbps

Microwave Communications

You've seen them: the satellite dishes on the tops of buildings in larger cities. These dishes are most often used for microwave communications. Microwave communications use very powerful, focused beams of energy to send communications over very long distances.

In this section, we will cover the details of microwave communications as they apply to LAN and WAN communications.

How Microwave Communication Works

Microwave communication makes use of the lower gigahertz frequencies of the electromagnetic spectrum. These frequencies, which are higher than radio frequencies, produce better throughput and performance than other types of wireless communications. Table 11.3 shows a brief comparison of the two types of microwave datacommunications systems, terrestrial and satellite. A discussion of both follows.

TABLE 11.3: Terrestrial Microwave and Satellite Microwave

Factor	Terrestrial Microwave	Satellite Microwave
Frequency range	Low gigahertz (typically from 4 to 6GHz or 21 to 23GHz)	Low gigahertz (typically 11 to 14GHz)
Cost	Moderate to high	High
Installation	Moderately difficult	Difficult
Capacity	1 to 100Mbps	1 to 100Mbps
Attenuation	Depends on conditions (affected by atmospheric conditions)	Depends on conditions (affected by atmospheric conditions)
EMI resistance	Poor	Poor

Terrestrial

Terrestrial microwave systems typically use directional parabolic antennas to send and receive signals in the lower gigahertz frequency range. The signals are highly focused and must travel along a line-of-sight path. Relay towers extend signals. Terrestrial microwave systems are typically used when the cost of cabling is cost-prohibitive.

TIP Because they do not use cable, microwave links often connect separate buildings where cabling would be too expensive, difficult to install, or prohibited. For example, if a public road separates two buildings, you may not be able to get permission to install cable over or under the road. Microwave links would then be a good choice.

Because terrestrial microwave equipment often uses licensed frequencies, licensing commissions or government agencies (the FCC in the United States) may impose additional costs and time constraints.

Figure 11.11 shows a microwave system connecting separate buildings. Smaller terrestrial microwave systems can be used within a building as well. Microwave LANs operate at low power, using small transmitters that communicate with omnidirectional hubs. Hubs can then be connected to form an entire network.

A terrestrial microwave system connecting two buildings

Terrestrial microwave systems have the following characteristics:

Frequency range   Most terrestrial microwave systems produce signals in the low gigahertz range, usually at 4 to 6GHz and 21 to 23GHz.

Cost   Short-distance systems can be relatively inexpensive, and they are effective in the range of hundreds of meters. Long-distance systems can be very expensive. Terrestrial systems may be leased from providers to reduce startup costs, although the cost of the lease over a long term may prove more expensive than purchasing a system.

Installation   Line-of-sight requirements for microwave systems can make installation difficult. Antennas must be carefully aligned. A licensed technician may be required. Suitable transceiver sites can be a problem. If your organization does not have a clear line of sight between two antennas, you must either purchase or lease a site.

Capacity   Capacity varies depending on the frequency used, but typical data rates are from 1 to 100Mbps.

Attenuation   Frequency, signal strength, antenna size, and atmospheric conditions affect attenuation. Normally, over short distances, attenuation is not significant, but rain and fog can negatively affect higher-frequency microwaves.

EMI   Microwave signals are vulnerable to EMI, jamming, and eavesdropping (although microwave transmissions are often encrypted to reduce eavesdropping). Microwave systems are also affected by atmospheric conditions.

Satellite

Satellite microwave systems transmit signals between directional parabolic antennas. Like terrestrial microwave systems, they use low gigahertz frequencies and must be in line of sight. The main difference with satellite systems is that one antenna is on a satellite in geosynchronous orbit about 50,000 kilometers (22,300 miles) above the earth. Therefore, satellite microwave systems can reach the most remote places on earth and communicate with mobile devices.

Here's how it usually works. A LAN sends a signal through cable media to an antenna (commonly known as a *satellite dish*), which beams the signal to the satellite in orbit above the earth. The orbiting antenna then transmits the signal to another location on the earth or, if the destination is on the opposite side of the earth, to another satellite, which then transmits to a location on earth.

Figure 11.12 shows a transmission being beamed from a satellite dish on earth to an orbiting satellite and then back to earth.

FIGURE 11.12:

Satellite microwave
transmission

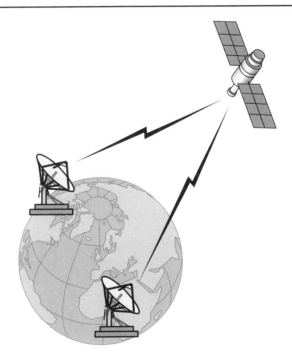

Because the signal must be transmitted 50,000 kilometers to the satellite and 50,000 kilometers back to earth, satellite microwave transmissions take about as long to reach a destination a few kilometers away on land as they do to span continents. The delay between the transmission of a satellite microwave signal and its reception, called a *propagation delay*, ranges from 0.5 to 5 seconds.

Satellite microwave systems have the following characteristics:

Frequency range   Satellite links operate in the low gigahertz range, typically from 11 to 14GHz.

Cost   The cost of building and launching a satellite is extremely expensive—as high as several hundred million dollars or more. Companies such as AT&T, Hughes Network Systems, and Scientific-Atlanta lease services, making them affordable for a number of organizations. Although satellite communications are expensive, the cost of cable to cover the same distance may be even more expensive.

Installation   Satellite microwave installation for orbiting satellites is extremely technical and difficult and certainly should be left to professionals in that field. The earth-based systems may require difficult, exact adjustments. Commercial providers can help with installation.

Capacity   Capacity depends on the frequency used. Typical data rates are 1 to 10Mbps.

Attenuation   Attenuation depends on frequency, power, antenna size, and atmospheric conditions. Higher-frequency microwaves are more affected by rain and fog.

EMI   Microwave systems are vulnerable to EMI, jamming, and eavesdropping (although the transmissions are often encrypted to reduce eavesdropping). Microwave systems are also affected by atmospheric conditions.

Advantages of Microwave Communications

Microwave communications have limited use in LAN communications. However, because of their great power, they have many advantages in WAN applications. Some of these advantages include:

Very high bandwidth   Of all the wireless technologies, microwave systems have the highest bandwidth because of the high power of the transmission systems. Speeds of 100Mbps and greater are possible.

Transmissions travel over long distances   As already mentioned, their higher power makes it possible for microwave transmissions to travel over very long distances. Transmissions can travel over distances of several miles (or several thousand miles, in the case of satellite systems).

Signals can be point to point or broadcast   As with other types of wireless communications, the signals can be focused tightly for point-to-point communications, or they can be diffused and sent to multiple locations via broadcast communications. This allows for the maximum flexibility for the most applications.

Disadvantages of Microwave Communications

Microwave communications are not an option for most users because of their many disadvantages. Specifically, a few disadvantages make microwave communications viable for only a few groups of people. Some of these disadvantages include the following:

Equipment is expensive   Microwave transmission and reception equipment is the most expensive of all the types of wireless transmission equipment discussed in this chapter. A microwave transmitter/receiver combo can cost upwards of $5,000 in the United States—and two transmitters are required for communications to take place. Cheaper microwave systems are available, but their distance and features are more limited.

Line of sight required   Microwave communications require a line of sight between sender and receiver. Generally speaking, the signal can't be bounced off any objects.

Atmospheric attenuation   As with other wireless technologies (such as infrared laser), atmospheric conditions (e.g., fog, rain, snow) can negatively affect microwave transmissions. For example, a thunderstorm between sender and receiver can prevent reliable communication between the two. Additionally, the higher the microwave frequency, the more susceptible to attenuation the communication will be.

Propagation delay   This is primarily a disadvantage of satellite microwave. When sending between two terrestrial stations using a satellite as a relay station, it can take anywhere from 0.5 to 5 seconds to send from the first terrestrial station through the satellite to the second station.

Safety   Because the microwave beam is very high powered, it can pose a danger to any human or animal that comes between transmitter and receiver. Imagine putting your hand in a microwave on low power. It may not kill you, but it will certainly not be good for you.

Examples of Microwave Communications

Microwave equipment differs from infrared and RF equipment because it is more specialized and is usually only used for WAN connections. The high power and specialization makes it a poor choice for a LAN media (you wouldn't want to put a microwave dish on top of every PC in an office!). Because microwave systems are very specialized, instead of listing a few of the common microwave products Table 11.4 lists a few microwave-product companies and their Web-site addresses so you can examine their product offerings for yourself.

TABLE 11.4:   Microwave-Product Companies and Web Sites

Company	Web Site
Adaptive Broadband	www.adaptivebroadband.com
M/A-COM	www.macom.com
Southwest Microwave	www.telspec.com/swmicro.htm

part III

Cabling Design and Installation

Cabling-System Design and Installation

- Elements of a Successful Cabling Installation

- Cabling Topologies

- Cabling-Plant Uses

- Choice of Media

- Telecommunications Closets

- Cabling Management

- Data and Cabling Security

- Cabling Installation Procedures

The previous chapters in this book were designed to teach you the basics of telecommunications cabling procedures. You learned about the various components of a typical telecommunications installation and their functions.

They're good to know, but it is more important to understand how to put the components together into a cohesive cabling-system design. That is, after all, why you bought this book, is it not? Each of the components of a cabling system can fit together in many different ways. Additionally, you must design the cabling system so that each component of that system meets or exceeds the goals of the cabling project.

In this chapter, you will learn to apply the knowledge you learned in the previous chapters to designing and installing a structured cabling system.

Elements of a Successful Cabling Installation

Before designing your system, you should understand how the following elements contribute to a successful installation:

- Using proper design
- Using quality materials
- Practicing good workmanship

Each of these aspects can drastically affect network performance.

Proper Design

A proper cabling-system design is paramount to a well-functioning cabling infrastructure. As with any other major project, the key to a successful cabling installation is that four-letter word: *p-l-a-n*. A proper cabling-system design is simply a plan for installing the cable runs and their associated devices.

So what is a *proper* design? A proper cabling-system design will take into account five primary criteria:

- Desired standards and performance characteristics
- Flexibility
- Longevity
- Ease of administration
- Economy

Failure to take these criteria into account can cause usability problems and poor network performance. We'll take a brief look at each of these factors.

Desired Standards and Performance Characteristics

Of the proper cabling-design criteria listed, standards and performance characteristics is the most critical. As discussed earlier in Chapter 1, standards ensure that products from many different vendors can communicate. When you design your cabling layout, you should decide on standards for all aspects of your cabling installation so that the various products used will interconnect. Additionally, you should choose products for your design that will meet desired performance characteristics. For example, if you will be deploying a broadcast video system over your LAN in addition to the everyday file and print traffic, it is important that the cabling system be designed with a higher-capacity network in mind (e.g., Fast Ethernet or fiber optic).

Flexibility

No network is a stagnant entity. As new technologies are introduced, companies will adopt them at different rates. When designing a cabling system, you should plan for MACs (moves, adds, and changes), so that if your network changes your cabling design will accommodate those changes. In a properly designed cabling system, a new device or technology will be able to connect to any point within the cabling system.

One aspect of flexibility that many people overlook is the number of cabling outlets or *drops* in a particular room. Many companies take a minimalist approach; that is, they put only the number of drops in each room that is currently necessary. That design is fine for the time being, but what happens when an additional device or devices are needed? It is usually easier to have an extra drop or two (or five) installed while all of the others are being installed than it is to return later to install a single drop.

Longevity

Let's face it, cabling is hard work. You must climb above ceilings and, on occasion, snake through crawlspaces to properly run the cables. Therefore, when designing a cabling system, you want to make sure that the design will stand the test of time and last for a number of years without having to be replaced. A great case in point: Many companies are currently removing their coaxial-cable-based networks in favor of the newer, cheaper, more reliable UTP cabling. Others are removing their UTP cabling in favor of fiber-optic cable's higher bandwidth. Now, wouldn't it make more sense for those companies that currently have coaxial cable to directly upgrade to fiber-optic cable (or at least to a high-quality Category 5e or Category 6 copper UTP cabling system) rather than having to "rip and replace" again in a few years? Definitely. If you have to upgrade your cabling system or are currently designing your system, it is usually best to upgrade to the most current technology you can afford.

Ease of Administration

Another element of a proper cabling design is ease of administration. This means that a network administrator should be able to access the cabling system and make additions and changes, if necessary. Some of these changes might include the following:

- Removing a station from the network

- Replacing hubs, routers, and other telecommunications equipment

- Installing new cables

- Repairing existing wires

Many elements make cabling-system administration easier, the most important of which is documentation (discussed later in this chapter). Another element is neatness. A rat's nest of cables is difficult to administrate because it is difficult to tell which cable goes where.

Economy

Finally, how much money you have to spend will play a part in your cabling-system design. If you have an unlimited budget, you'd go fiber-to-the-desktop without question. All your future-proofing worries would be over (at least until the next fiber-optic innovation.)

The reality is you probably don't have an unlimited budget, so the best cabling system for you involves compromise—taking into account the four elements listed previously and deciding how to get the most bang for the buck. You have to do some very basic value-proposition work, factoring in how long you expect to be tied to your new cabling system, what your bandwidth needs are now, and what your bandwidth needs might be in the future.

Quality Materials

Another element of a successful cabling installation is the use of quality materials. The quality of the materials used in a cabling installation will directly affect the transmission efficiency of a network. Many times, a vendor will sell many different cabling product lines, each with a different price point. The old adage that you get what you pay for really does apply to cabling supplies.

All the components that make up a cabling plant can be purchased in both high- and low-quality product lines. For example, you can buy RJ-45 connectors from one vendor that are $0.03 apiece but only rated at Category 3 (i.e., they won't work for 100Mbps networks). Another vendor's RJ-45 connectors may cost twice as much but be rated for Category 6 (155Mbps and above over copper).

That doesn't always mean that low price means low quality. Some vendors make low-price, high-quality cabling supplies. Without playing favorites to a particular vendor, we'll just say that it doesn't hurt to shop around when buying your cabling supplies. Check the Internet sites of many different cabling vendors to compare prices.

In addition to price, you should check how the product is assembled. Quality materials are sturdy and well constructed. Low-quality materials will not be durable and may actually break while you are handling them.

Good Workmanship

There is a saying that any job worth doing is worth doing correctly. When installing cabling, this saying is especially true because shoddy workmanship can cause data-transmission problems and thus lower the network's effective throughput. If you try to rush a cabling job to meet a deadline, you will usually end up doing some or the entire job over again. For example, when punching down the individual wires in a UTP installation, excessive untwisting of the individual wires can cause excessive near-end crosstalk (NEXT), thus lowering the effective data-carrying capacity of that connection. The connection must be removed and reterminated to correct the problem.

The same holds true for fiber-optic cable connections. If you rush any part of the connector installation, the effective optical transmission capacity of that connection will probably be reduced. A reduced capacity means that you may not be able to use that connection at all because the light will be refracted too far outside of the fiber and too much extraneous light will get into the connection, causing it to fail.

Cabling Topologies

As discussed in Chapter 3, a topology is basically a map of a network. The physical topology of a network describes the layout of the cables and workstations and the location of all network components. Choosing the layout of how computers will be connected in a company's network is critical. It is one of the first choices you will make during the design of the cabling system, and it is an important one because it tells you how the cables are to be run during the installation. Making a wrong decision regarding physical topology and media is costly and disruptive because it means changing an entire installation once it is in place. The typical organization changes the physical layout and physical media of a network only once every 5 to 10 years, so it is important to choose a configuration that you can live with and that allows for growth.

Chapter 3 described the basics of the star, bus, and ring topologies. Here, we'll look at some of their advantages and disadvantages and introduce a fourth seldom-used topology, the mesh topology.

Bus Topology

A bus topology has the following advantages:

- It is simple to install.
- A bus topology is relatively inexpensive.
- It uses less cable than other topologies.

On the other hand, a bus topology has the following disadvantages:

- It is difficult to move and change.
- The topology has little fault tolerance (a single fault can bring down the entire network).
- It is difficult to troubleshoot.

The Star Topology

Just as with the bus topology, the star topology has advantages and disadvantages. The increasing popularity of the star topology is mainly due to the large number of advantages, which include the following:

- It can be reconfigured quickly.
- A single cable failure won't bring down the entire network.
- It is relatively easy to troubleshoot.
- It is the only recognized topology in the industry Standard, ANSI/TIA/EIA-568-A.

The disadvantages of a star topology include the following:

- The total installation cost can be higher because of the larger number of cables.
- It has a single point of failure, the hub.

The Ring Topology

The ring topology has a few pros but many more cons, which is why it is seldom used. On the pro side, the ring topology is relatively easy to troubleshoot. A station will know when a cable fault has occurred because it will stop receiving data from its upstream neighbor.

The cons are as follows:

- It is expensive because multiple cables are needed for each workstation.
- The ring topology is difficult to reconfigure.
- It is not fault tolerant. A single cable fault can bring down the entire network.

The Mesh Topology

In a mesh topology (as shown in Figure 12.1), a path exists from each station to every other station in the network. Although not usually seen in LANs, a variation on this type of topology, the *hybrid mesh*, is used in a limited fashion on the Internet and other WANs. Hybrid mesh topology networks can have multiple connections between some locations, but this is done for redundancy. Also, it is not a true mesh because there is not a connection between each and every node; there are just a few, for backup purposes.

FIGURE 12.1:

A typical mesh topology

As you can see in Figure 12.1, a mesh topology can become quite complex as wiring and connections increase exponentially. For every n stations, you will have $\frac{n(n-1)}{2}$ connections. For example, in a network of four computers, you will have $\frac{4(4-1)}{2}$ connections, or six connections. If your network grows to only 10 computers, you will have 45 connections to manage! Given this impossible overhead, only small systems can be connected this way. The advantage to all the work this topology requires is a more fail-safe or fault-tolerant network, at least as far as cabling is concerned. On the con side, the mesh topology is expensive and, as you have seen, quickly becomes too complex. Today, the mesh topology is rarely used, and then only in a WAN environment because it is fault tolerant. Computers or network devices can switch between these multiple, redundant connections if the need arises.

Backbones and Segments

When discussing complex networks, you must be able to intelligently identify its parts. For this reason, networks are commonly broken into backbones and segments. Figure 12.2 shows a sample network with the backbone and segments identified.

Understanding the Backbone

The backbone is the part of the network to which all segments and servers connect. A backbone provides the structure for a network and is considered the main part of any network. It usually uses a high-speed communications technology of some kind (such as FDDI, ATM, or 100Mb Ethernet). All servers and all network segments typically connect directly to the backbone so that any segment is only one segment away from any server on that backbone. Having all segments close to the servers makes the network efficient. Notice in Figure 12.2 that the three servers and three segments all connect to the backbone.

Understanding Segments

Segment is a general term for any short section of the cabling infrastructure that is not part of the backbone. Just as servers connect to the backbone, workstations connect to segments. Segments are connected to the backbone to allow the workstations on them access to the rest of the network. Figure 12.2 shows three segments. Segments are more commonly referred to as the horizontal cabling.

Selecting the Right Topology

From a practical standpoint, which topology to use has been decided for you. Because of its clear-cut advantages, the star topology is the only recognized physical layout in ANSI/TIA/EIA-568-A. Unless you insist that your installation defy the Standard, this will be the topology selected by your cabling-system designer.

If you choose not to go with the star topology, the bus topology is usually the most efficient choice if you're creating a simple network for a handful of computers in a single room because it is simple and easy to install. Because MACs are managed better in a star topology, a bus topology is generally not used in a larger environment. If *uptime* is your primary definition of fault resistant (that is, 99 percent uptime, or less than eight hours total downtime per year), you should seriously consider a mesh layout. However, while you are thinking about how fault tolerant a mesh network is, let the word *maintenance* enter your thoughts. Remember, you will have $n^{(n-1)}/2$ connections to maintain, and this can quickly become a nightmare and exceed your maintenance budget.

If you decide not to automatically go with a star topology and instead consider all the topologies, be sure to keep in mind cost, ease of installation, ease of maintenance, and fault tolerance.

Cabling-Plant Uses

Another consideration to take into account when designing and installing a structured cabling system is the intended use of the various cables in the system. A few years ago, *structured cabling system* usually meant a company's data network cabling. Today, cabling systems are used to carry various kinds of information, including the following:

- Data
- Telephone
- Television
- Fire detection and security

When designing and installing your cabling system, you must keep in mind what kind of information is going to be traveling on the network and what kinds of cables are required to carry that information.

Because this book is mainly about data cabling, we'll assume you know that cables can be run for data. So, we'll start this discussion with a discussion of telephone wiring.

Telephone

The oldest (and probably most common) use for a cabling system is to carry telephone signals. In the old days, pairs of copper wires were strung throughout a building to carry the phone signal from a central telephone closet to the individual telephone handsets. In the telephone closet, the individual wires were brought together and mechanically and electrically connected to all the incoming telephone lines so that the entire building was connected to the outside world. Surprisingly, the basic layout for a telephone cabling system has changed very little. The major difference today is that telephone systems have become digital. So most require a private branch exchange (PBX), a special device that connects all the individual telephones together so the telephone calls can go out over one high-speed line (called a *trunk line*) rather than over multiple individual lines. Figure 12.3 shows how a current telephone network is arranged.

Generally speaking, today's telephone networks are run along the same cabling paths as the data cabling. Additionally, telephone systems use the same UTP cable that many networks use for carrying data. They will usually share the same wiring closets with the data and television cabling. The wires from telephone connections can be terminated almost identically to data cabling.

FIGURE 12.3:

An example of a telephone network

Television

With the increase in the use of on-demand video technology, it is now commonplace to run television cable alongside data and telephone cabling. In businesses where local cable access is possible, television cable will be run into the building and distributed to many areas to provide cable access. You may be wondering what cable TV has to do with business. The answer is plenty. News, stock updates, technology access, public-access programs, and, most importantly, Internet connections can all be delivered through television cable. Additionally, television cable is used for security cameras in buildings.

Like telephone cable, television cables can share the wiring pathways with their data counterparts. Television cable typically uses coaxial cable (usually RG-6/ U cable) along with F-type, 75-ohm coaxial connectors. The cables to the various outlets are run back to a central point where they are connected to a distribution device. This device is usually an unpowered splitter, but it can also be a powered, complex device known as a television distribution frame. Figure 12.4 shows how a typical television cabling system might look. Notice the similarities between Figures 12.4 and 12.3. The topology is basically the same.

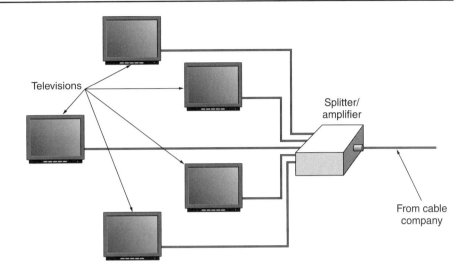

Fire-Detection and Security Cabling

One category of cabling that often gets overlooked is the cabling for fire-detection and security devices. Examples of these devices include glass-breakage sensors, smoke alarms, motion sensors, and door-opening sensors. These devices usually run on DC current anywhere from +12 to +24 volts. Cables, which are usually UTP, must be run from each of these devices back to the central security controller. Because they usually carry power, these cables should be run separately from, or at least perpendicular to, copper cables that are carrying data.

Choice of Media

A very important consideration when designing a cabling system for your company is which media to use. Different media have different specifications that make them better suited for a particular type of installation. For example, for a simple, low-cost installation, some types of copper media might be a better choice because of their ease of installation and low cost. In previous chapters, you learned about the different types of cabling media available and their different communication aspects, so we won't reiterate them here, except for the summary in Table 12.1.

TABLE 12.1: Summary of Cabling Media Types

Media	Advantages	Disadvantages
UTP	Relatively inexpensive	May be susceptible to EMI and eavesdropping
	Widely available	Only covers short (<1km) distances without additional devices
	Mature standards	
	Easy to install	
Fiber	High data rates possible	Moderately expensive electronics
	Immune to EMI and largely immune to eavesdropping	Can be difficult to install
Wireless	Few distance limitations	Atmospheric attenuation
	Relatively easy to install	More expensive than cabled media
		Some wireless frequencies require an FCC license

Telecommunications Closets

Some components and considerations that pertain to telecommunications closets must be taken into account during the design stage. In this section, we'll go over the LAN and telephone wiring found there, as well as the closets' power and HVAC requirements. For more information on the functions and requirements of telecommunications closets, see Chapters 2 and 5. Figure 12.5 shows how telecommunications closets are placed in an average building.

LAN Wiring

The first item inside a telecommunications closet that will draw your attention is the large bundle of cables coming into the closet. The bundle contains the cables that run from the closet to the individual stations and may also contain cables that run from the closet to other closets in the building. The bundle of cables is usually bound together with straps and leads the LAN cables to a patch panel, which connects the individual wires within a particular cable to network ports on the front of the panel. These ports can then be connected to the network equipment (hubs, switches, routers, and so on), or two ports can be connected together with a patch cable. Figure 12.6 shows an example of the hardware typically found in a telecommunications closet.

Placement of telecommunications closets

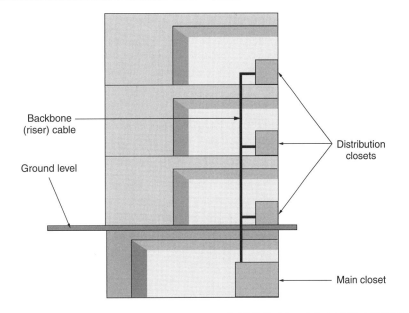

Backbone (riser) cable

Ground level

Distribution closets

Main closet

Hardware typically found in a telecommunications closet

Drop cable

Wall jack

Hub

Patch cable

Patch panel

Patch cable

Patch panels come in many different shapes and sizes (as shown in Figure 12.7). Some are mounted on a wall and are known as *surface-mount patch panels* (also called *punch-down blocks*). Others are mounted in a rack and are called *rack-mount patch panels*. Each type has its own benefits. Surface-mount panels are cheaper and easier to work with, but they can't hold as many cables and ports. Rack-mount panels are more flexible, but they are more expensive. Surface-mount patch panels make good choices for smaller (less than 50 drops) cabling installations. Rack-mount patch panels make better choices for larger installations. Patch panels are the main products used in LAN installation today because they are extremely cost-effective and allow great flexibility when connecting workstations.

FIGURE 12.7:

Patch-panel examples

Telephone Wiring

In addition to the LAN wiring components found in the telecommunications closet, you will usually also find all of the wiring for the telephone system, because the two are interrelated. In most companies, a computer and a telephone are on every desk. Software programs are even available that can connect the two technologies and allow you to receive all of your voicemails as e-mails. These programs integrate with your current e-mail system to provide integrated messaging services (a technology known as *telephony*).

The telephone cables from the individual telephones will come into the telecommunications closet in approximately the same location as the data cables. They will then be terminated in some kind of patch panel (cross-connect.) In many older installations, the individual wires will be punched down in *66-block*, a type of punch-down block that uses small "fingers" of metal to connect different UTP wires together. The wires on one side of the 66-block are from the individual wires in the cables for the telephone system. Newer installations use a type of cross-connect known as a 110-block. Although it looks different than a 66-block, it functions the same way. Instead of using punch-down blocks, it is also possible to use the same type of patch panel as is used for the UTP data cabling for the telephone cross-connect. As with the data cabling, that option enhances the flexibility of your cabling system.

The wires on the other side of the block usually come from the telephone PBX. The PBX controls all the incoming and outgoing calls as well as which pair of wires is for which telephone extension. The PBX has connectors on the back that allow 25 telephone pairs to be connected to a single 66-block at a time using a single 50-pin connector (as shown in Figure 12.8).

FIGURE 12.8:

Connecting a PBX to a 66-block

Typically, many of these 66-blocks are placed on a large piece of plywood fastened to the wall (as shown in Figure 12.9). The number of 66-blocks is as many as required to support the number of cables for the telephone system.

FIGURE 12.9:

Multiple 66-blocks in a wiring closet

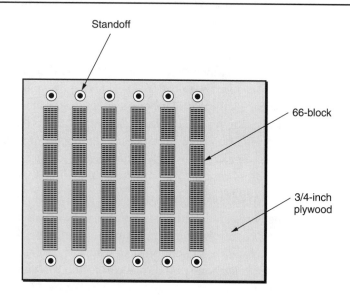

Standoff

66-block

3/4-inch plywood

Power Requirements

With all of these devices in the wiring closet, it stands to reason that you are going to need some power receptacles there. Telecommunications closets have some unique power requirements. First of all, each of the many small electronic devices will need power, and a single-duplex outlet will not have enough outlets. Additionally, these devices should all be on an electrical circuit dedicated to that wiring closet and separate from the rest of the building. The circuit should have its own *isolated ground*. An isolated ground in commercial wiring is a ground wire for the particular isolated outlet that is run in the same conduit as the electrical-supply connectors. This ground is called *isolated* because it is not tied into the grounding of the conduit at all. The wire runs from the receptacle back to the point where the grounds and neutrals are tied together in the circuit panel. You can identify isolated-ground outlets in a commercial building because they are orange with a small green triangle on them.

NOTE Most, if not all, residential outlets have an isolated ground because conduit is not used, and these outlets must have a ground wire in the cable.

The wiring closet should be equipped with a minimum of two dedicated three-wire 120-volt AC duplex outlets, each on its own 20-amp circuit, for network and system-equipment power. In addition, separate 120-volt AC duplex outlets should be provided as convenience outlets for tools, test equipment, etc. Convenience outlets should be a minimum of six inches off the floor and placed at six-foot intervals around the perimeter of the room. None of the outlets shall be switched, i.e., controlled by a wall switch or other device that might accidentally interrupt power to the system.

HVAC Considerations

Computer and networking equipment generates much heat. Place enough equipment in a telecommunications closet without ventilation, and the temperature will quickly rise to dangerous levels. As sunstroke affects the human brain, high temperatures are the downfall of electronic components. The closet temperature should match the ambient temperature of office space occupied by humans.

For this reason, telecommunications closets should be sufficiently ventilated. At the very least, some kind of fan should exchange the air in the closet. Some telecommunications closets aren't closets at all but are, in fact, pretty good-sized rooms with their own HVAC (heating, ventilation, and air conditioning) controls.

Cabling Management

Cabling management is guiding the cable to its intended destination without damaging it or its data-carrying capabilities. Many different cabling products protect cable, make it look good, and help you find the cables faster. They fall into three categories:

- Physical protection
- Electrical protection
- Fire protection

In this section, we will look at the various devices used to provide each level of protection and the concepts and procedures that go along with them.

Physical Protection

Cables can be fragile—easily cut, stretched, and broken. When performing a proper cabling installation, cables should be protected. Many items are currently used to protect cables from damage, including the following:

- Conduit
- Cable trays
- Standoffs
- D-rings

We'll take a brief look at each and the different ways they are used to protect cables from damage.

Conduit

The simplest form of cable protection is a metal or plastic conduit to protect the cable as it travels through walls and ceilings. Conduit is really nothing more than a thin-walled plastic or metal pipe. Conduit is used in many commercial installations to contain electrical wires. When electricians run conduit for electrical installation in a new building, they can also run additional conduit for network wiring. Conduit is put in place, and the individual cables are run inside it.

The main advantage to conduit is that it is the simplest and most robust protection for a network cable. Also, if you use plastic conduit, it can be a relatively cheap solution (metal conduit is more expensive).

WARNING   The flame rating of plastic conduit must match the installation environment. In other words, plastic conduit in a plenum space must have a plenum rating, just like the cable.

Rigid metal conduit (steel pipe) exceeds all flame-test requirements. Any cable can be installed in any environment if it is enclosed in rigid metal conduit. Even cable that burns like crazy can be put in a plenum space if you put it in this type of conduit.

Cable Trays

When running cable, the cable must be supported every 48 to 60 inches when hanging horizontally. Supporting the cable prevents it from sagging and putting stress on the conductors inside. For this reason, special devices known as *cable trays* (also sometimes called *ladder racks*, because of their appearance) are installed in ceilings. The horizontal cables from the telecommunications closets that run to the individual telecommunications outlets are usually placed into this tray to support them as they run horizontally. Figure 12.10 shows an example of a cable tray. This type of cable-support system hangs from the ceiling and can support hundreds of individual cables.

FIGURE 12.10:

An example of a cable tray

Standoffs

When terminating UTP wires for telephone applications in a telecommunications closet, you will often see telephone wires run from a multipair cable to the 66-punch-down block. To be neat, the individual conductors are run around the outside of the board that the punch-down blocks are mounted to (as shown in Figure 12.11). To prevent damage to the individual conductors, they are bent around devices known as standoffs. These objects look like miniature spools, are usually made of plastic, and are screwed to the mounting board every foot or so (also shown in Figure 12.11).

FIGURE 12.11:

A telecommunications board using standoffs

Telecommunications board

Side view

66-block

Standoff

Individual conductors

100-pair telephone cable

25-pair telephone cables

Telephone PBX

Telecom Board

D-Rings

For LAN installations that use racks to hold patch panels, you need some method of keeping the cables together and organized as they come out of the cable trays and enter the telecommunications closet to be terminated. On many racks, special metal rings called *D-rings* (named after their shape) are used to keep the individual cables in bundles and keep them close to the rack (as shown in Figure 12.12).

In addition to managing cable for a cabling rack, D-rings are also used on punch-down boards on the wall to manage cables, much in the same way standoffs are. D-rings are put in place to support the individual cables, and the cables are run to the individual punch-down blocks on the wall. This setup is similar to the one shown earlier in Figure 12.11.

FIGURE 12.12:

D-rings in a cabling closet
for a cabling rack

LAN equipment rack

Side view

D-rings

Electrical Protection (Spike Protection)

In addition to physical protection, you must take electrical protection into account when designing and installing your cabling system. Electricity powers the network, switches, hubs, PCs, and computer servers. Variations in power can cause problems ranging from having to reboot after a short loss of service to damaged equipment and data. Fortunately, a number of products, including surge protectors, standby power supplies, uninterruptible power supplies, and line conditioners, are available to help protect sensitive systems from the dangers of lightning strikes, dirty (uneven) power, and accidental power disconnection.

Standby Power Supply (SPS)

A standby power supply (SPS) contains a battery, a switchover circuit, and an *inverter* (a device that converts the DC voltage from the battery into the AC voltage that the computer and peripherals need). The outlets on the SPS are connected to the switching circuit, which is in turn connected to the incoming AC power (called line voltage). The switching circuit monitors the line voltage. When it drops below a factory preset threshold, the switching circuit switches from line voltage to the battery and inverter. The battery and inverter power the outlets (and, thus, the computers or devices plugged into them) until the switching circuit detects line voltage at the correct level. The switching circuit then switches the outlets back to line voltage.

NOTE   Power output from battery-powered inverters isn't exactly perfect. Normal power output alternates polarity 60 times a second (60Hz). When graphed, this output looks like a sine wave. Output from inverters is stepped to approximate this sine-wave output, but it really never duplicates it. Today's inverter technology can come extremely close, but the differences between inverter and true AC power can cause damage to computer power supplies over the long run.

Uninterruptible Power Supply (UPS)

A UPS is another type of battery backup often found on computers and network devices today. It is similar to an SPS in that it has outlets, a battery, and an inverter. The similarities end there, however.

A UPS uses an entirely different method to provide continuous AC voltage to the equipment it supports. When a UPS is used, the equipment is always running off the inverter and battery. A UPS contains a charging/monitoring circuit that charges the battery constantly. It also monitors the AC line voltage. When a power failure occurs, the charger stops charging the battery, but the equipment never senses any change in power. The monitoring part of the circuit senses the change and emits a beep to tell the user the power has failed.

Fire Protection

All buildings and their contents are subject to destruction and damage if a fire occurs. The cabling in a building is no exception. You must keep in mind a few cabling-design concerns to prevent fire, smoke, or heat from damaging your cabling system, the premises on which they are installed, and any occupants.

As discussed in Chapter 1, make sure you specify the proper flame rating for the cable according to the location in which it will be installed.

Another concern is the puncturing of fire barriers. In most residential and commercial buildings, firewalls are built specifically to stop the spread of a fire within a building. Whenever there is an opening in a floor or ceiling that could possibly conduct fire, the opening is walled over with fire-rated drywall to make a firewall that will prevent the spread of fire (or at least slow it down). In commercial buildings, cinder-block walls are often erected as firewalls between rooms.

Because firewalls prevent the spread of fire, it is important not to compromise the protection they offer by punching holes in them for network cables. If you need to run a network cable through a firewall, first try to find another route that won't compromise the integrity of the firewall. If you can't, you must use an approved firewall penetration device (see Figure 12.13). These devices form a tight seal around each cable that passes through the firewall. One type of seal is made of material that is *intumescent*; that is, it expands several times its normal size when exposed to very high heat (fire temperatures), sealing the hole in the firewall. That way, the gases and heat from a fire won't pass through.

FIGURE 12.13:

An example of a firewall penetration device

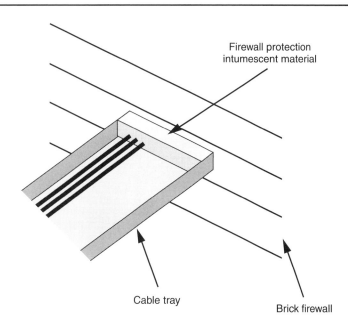

Firewall protection intumescent material

Cable tray

Brick firewall

Data and Cabling Security

Your network cables carry all the data that crosses your network. If the data your cables carry is sensitive and should not be viewed by just anyone, you may need to take extra steps when designing and installing your cabling system to ensure that the data stays where it belongs: inside the cables. The level of protection you employ depends on how sensitive the data is and how serious a security breach could be. Cabling security measures can range from the simple to the absurdly complex.

Two ways to prevent data from being intercepted are EM (electromagnetic) transmission regulation and tapping prevention.

EM (Electromagnetic) Transmission Regulation

You should know that the pattern of the magnetic field produced by any current-carrying conductor matches the pattern of the signals being transmitted. Based on this concept, devices exist that can be placed around a cable to intercept these magnetic signals and turn them back into electrical signals that can be sent to another (unwanted) location. This process is known as *EM signal interception*. Because the devices pick up the magnetic signals surrounding the cable, they are said to be noninvasive.

Susceptibility to EM signal interception can be minimized by using shielded cables or by encasing all cabling runs from source to destination in a grounded metal conduit. These shielding methods reduce the amount of stray EM signals.

Tapping Prevention

Tapping is the interception of LAN EM signals through listening devices placed around the cable. Some tapping devices are invasive and will actually puncture the outer jacket of a cable, or the insulation of individual wires, and touch the metal inner conductor to intercept all signals sent along that conductor. Of course taps can be applied at the cross-connects if security access to your equipment rooms and telecommunications closets is lax.

To prevent taps, the best course of action is to install the cables in metal conduit or to use armored cable, where practical. Grounding of the metal conduit will provide protection from both EM and invasive taps but not from taps at the cross-connect. When not practical, otherwise securing the cables can make tapping much more difficult. If the person trying to tap your communications can't get to your cables, they can't tap them. So you must install cables in secure locations and restrict access to them by locking the cabling closets. Remember: If you don't have physical security, you don't have network security.

Cabling Installation Procedures

Now that we've covered some of the factors to take into account when designing a cabling system, it's time to discuss the process of installing an entire cabling system, from start to finish. A cabling installation involves five steps:

1. Design the cabling system.

2. Schedule the installation.

3. Install the cables.

4. Terminate the cables.

5. Test the installation.

Design the Cabling System

We've already covered this part of the installation in detail in this chapter. However, it's important enough to reiterate: Following proper cabling design procedures will ensure the success of your cabling system installation. Before you pull a single cable, you should have a detailed plan of how the installation will proceed. You should also know the scope of the project (how many cable runs need to be made, what connections need to made and where, how long the project will take, and so on). Finally, you should have the design plan available to all people involved with the installation of the cable. That list of people includes the cabling installer, the electrical inspector, the building inspector, and the customer (even if you are the customer). Be sure to include anyone who needs to refer to the way the cabling is being installed. At the very least, this information should contain a blueprint of how the cables will be installed.

Schedule the Installation

In addition to having a proper cabling design, you also should know approximately how long the installation will take and pick the best time to do it. For example, the best time for a new cabling installation is while the building studs are still exposed and electrical boxes can be easily installed. From a planning standpoint, this is approximately the same time in new construction when the electrical cabling is installed. In fact, because of the obvious connection between electrical and telecommunications wiring, many electrical contractors are now learning how to do low-voltage (data) wiring so they can contract the wiring for both the electrical system and the telecommunications system.

WARNING   If you use an electrical contractor to install your communication cabling, make sure he or she is well trained in this type of installation. Many electricians are not aware of the subtleties required to properly handle network wiring. If they treat it like the electrical wire, or run it along with the electrical wire, you're going to have headaches in your network performance. We recommend that the communication wiring be installed after the electrical wiring is done so that they can be kept properly segregated.

For a postconstruction installation, you should schedule it so as to have the least impact on the building's occupants and on the existing network or existing building infrastructure.

Install the Cabling

Once you have a design and a proper schedule, you can proceed with the installation. We'll start with a discussion of the tools you will need.

Cabling Tools

Just like any other industry, cable installation has its own tools, some not so obvious, including the following:

- Pen and paper
- Hand tools
- Cable spool racks
- Fish tape
- Fish cord
- Cable-pulling lubricant
- Two-way radio
- Labeling materials
- Tennis ball

We'll briefly go over how each is used during installation.

NOTE   Tools are covered in more detail in Chapter 6.

Pen and Paper   Not every cabling installer may think of pen and paper as tools, but they are. It is a good idea to have a pen and paper handy when installing the individual cables so that you can make notes about how particular cables are routed and installed. You should also note any problems that occur during installation. Finally, during the testing phase (discussed later), you can record test data in the notebook.

These notes are invaluable when it's time to troubleshoot an installation, especially when you have to trace a particular cable. You'll know exactly where particular wires run and how they were installed.

Hand Tools   It's fairly obvious that a variety of hand tools are needed during a cabling installation. During the course of the installation, you will need to remove and assemble screws, hit and cut things, and perform various types of construction and destruction tasks. Some of the hand tools you should make sure to include in your tool kit are (but are not limited to) the following:

- Screwdrivers (Phillips, slotted, and Torx drivers)
- Hammer
- Cable cutters
- Wire strippers
- Punch-down tool
- Drywall saw

Cable Spool Racks   It is usually inefficient to pull one cable at a time during installation. Typically, more than one cable will be going from the cabling closet (usually the source of a cable run) to a workstation outlet. So a cable installer will tape several cables together and pull them as one bundle.

The tool used to assist in pulling multiple cables is the *cable spool rack* (see Figure 12.14). As you can see, the spools of cable are mounted on the rack. These racks can hold multiple spools to facilitate the pulling of multiple cables simultaneously.

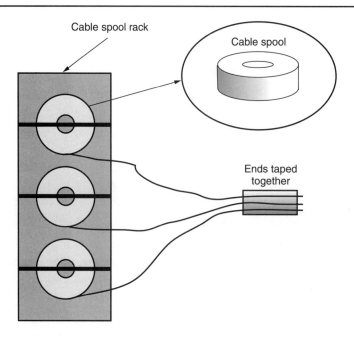

Fish Tape Many times, you will have to run cable into narrow conduits or narrow crawl spaces. Cables are flexible, much like rope. Just like rope, when you try to stuff a cable into a narrow space, it simply bunches up inside the conduit. You need a way of pulling the cable through that narrow space or providing some rigid backbone. A *fish tape* is one answer. It is really nothing more than a roll of spring steel or fiberglass with a hook on the end. A bunch of cables can be hooked and pulled through a small area, or the cables can be taped to the fish tape and pushed through the conduit or wall cavity.

Fish Cord Another way to pull cables through small spaces is with a nylon fish cord (also called a *pull string*), a heavy-duty cord strong enough to pull several cables through a conduit or wall cavity. The fish cord is either put in place before all the cables are pulled, or it is run at the same time as the cables. If it is put in place before the cables are pulled, such as when the conduit is assembled or in a wall cavity before the drywall is up, you can pull through your first cables with another string attached to the cables. The second string becomes the pull string for the next bundle, and so on. For future expansion, you leave one string in with the last bundle you pull. If the fish cord is run at the same time as the cables, it can be used to pull additional cables through the same conduit as already-installed cables.

Cable-Pulling Lubricant   It is important not to put too much stress on network cables as they are being pulled. If too much stress is put on the cable, the conductors could lose their transmission efficiency. At the worst, they could break. To prevent stress on the cable during the pulling of a cable through a conduit, a *cable-pulling lubricant* can be applied. It reduces the friction between the cable being pulled and its surroundings and is specially formulated so as not to plug up the conduit or dissolve the jackets of the other cables. It can be used any time cable needs to be pulled in tight quarters. See Chapter 6 for more details, including some drawbacks of lubricant.

Labeling Materials   With the hundreds of cables that need to be pulled in large cabling installations, it makes a great deal of sense to label both ends of each cable while it's being pulled. That way, when it's time to terminate each individual cable, you will know which cable goes where, and you can document that fact on your cabling map.

   So you will need some labeling materials. The most common are the sticky numbers sold by Panduit and other companies (check with your cabling supplier to see what it recommends). You should pick a numbering standard, stick with it, and record all the numbered cables and their uses in your cabling documentation. A good system is to number the first cable as *1*, with each subsequent cable the next higher number. You could also use combinations of letters and numbers. To label the cables, stick a number on each of the cables you are pulling and stick another of the same number on the corresponding box or spool containing the cable. When you are finished pulling the cable, you can cut the cable and stick the number from the cable spool onto the cut end of the cable. Voila! Both ends are numbered. Don't forget to record on your notepad the number of each cable and where it's going.

Two-Way Radio   Two-way radios aren't used as often as some of the other tools listed here, but they come in handy when two people are pulling or testing cable as a team. Two-way radios allow two people who are cabling within a building to communicate with each other without having to shout down a hallway or use cell phones. The radios are especially useful if they have hands-free headset microphones. Many two-way radios have maximum operating ranges of greater than several kilometers; this makes them effective for cabling even very large factories and buildings.

Tennis Ball   You may be saying, "Okay. I know why these other tools are listed here, but a tennis ball?" Think of this situation. You've got to run several cables through the airspace above a suspended ceiling. Let's say the cable run is 75 meters (around 225 feet) long. The conventional way to run this cable is to remove the ceiling tiles that run underneath the cable path, climb a ladder, and run the cable as far as you can reach (or throw). Then you would move the ladder, pull the cable a few feet farther, and repeat until you reach the end. An easier way is to tie a pull string to a tennis ball (using duct tape, nails, screws, or whatever) and throw the tennis ball from source to destination. The other end of the pull string can be tied to the bundle of cables so that it can be pulled from source to destination without going up and down ladders too many times.

TIP   You may think using a tennis ball is a makeshift tool, but cabling installers have been making their own tools for as long as there have been installers. You may find that a tool you make yourself works better that any tool you can buy.

Pulling Cable

Keep in mind the following points when pulling cable to ensure the proper operation of the network:

- Tensile strength
- Bend radius
- Protecting the cable while pulling

Tensile Strength   Contrary to popular opinion, network cables are fragile. They can be damaged in any number of ways, especially during the pulling process. The most important consideration to remember when pulling cable is the cable's *tensile strength*, a measure of how strong a cable is along its axis. The higher the tensile strength, the more resistant the cable is to stretching and, thus, breaking. Obviously, you can pull harder, without causing damage, on cables with higher tensile strength. A cable's tensile strength is normally given in either pounds, or in pounds per square inch (psi).

WARNING   When pulling cable, don't exert a pull force on the cable greater than the tensile rating of the cable. If you do, you will cause damage to the cable and its internal conductors. If a conductor break occurs, you may not know it until you terminate and test the cable. If it breaks, you will have to replace the whole cable. Standards and the manufacturer's recommendations should be reviewed for tensile-strength information.

NOTE

Four-pair UTP should not have more than 25 pounds of tension applied to it. (Note that this is 25 pounds, not 25 psi). This number is based on a calculation using the elongation properties of copper. When you are exerting pulling force on all four pairs of 24 AWG conductors in a UTP cable, 25 pounds is the maximum tensile load they can withstand before the copper starts to stretch. Once stretched, a point of high attenuation has been created that will also cause impedance and structural return-loss reflections.

Bend Radius   Most cables are designed to flex, and that makes them easy to use and install. Unfortunately, just because they can flex doesn't mean that they should be bent as far as possible around corners and other obstacles. Both copper and fiber-optic cables have a value known as the *minimum bend radius* of that cable. ANSI/TIA/EIA-568-A specifies that copper cables should be bent no tighter than the arc of a circle that has a radius four times the cables' diameter. For example, if a cable has ¼-inch diameter, it should be bent no tighter than the arc of a circle two inches in diameter. Four times a ¼ inch cable equals a 1-inch radius. The continuous arc created using a 1-inch radius creates a circle 2 inches in diameter. Figure 12.15 illustrates how bend radius is measured.

FIGURE 12.15:

The bend radius for cable installation

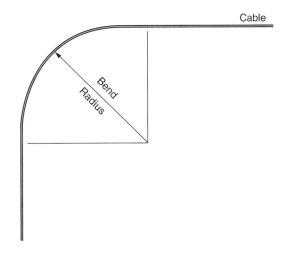

TIP

You can purchase from cabling-products vendors some devices that aid in the pulling of cable so that the minimum bend radius is not exceeded. These devices are basically plastic or metal corners with large bend radii to help guide a cable around a corner.

Protection While Pulling In addition to being careful not to exceed either the tensile strength or bend radius of a particular cable when pulling it, you should also be careful not to pull the cable over or near anything that could damage it. For example, never pull cables over sharp, metal corners, as these could cut into the outside jacket of the cable and, possibly, the interior conductors.

Many things could damage the cable during its installation. Just use common sense. If you would damage your finger (or any other body part) by running it across the surface you want to pull the cable across, chances are that it's not a good idea to run a cable over it either.

Cabling System Documentation

The most often overlooked item during cable installation is the documentation of the new cabling system. Cabling system documentation includes information about what components make up a cabling system, how it is put together, and where to find individual cables. This information is compiled in a set of documents that can be referred to by the network administrator or cabling installer any time moves, adds, or changes need to be made to the cabling system.

The most useful piece of cabling system documentation is the *cabling map*. Just as its name implies, a cabling map indicates where every cable starts and ends. It also indicates approximately where each cable runs. Additionally, a cabling map can indicate the location of workstations, segments, hubs, routers, closets, and other cabling devices.

NOTE A map can be as simple as a listing of the run numbers and where they terminate at the workstation and patch-panel ends. Or, it can be as complex as a street map, showing the exact cable routes from patch panel to workstation outlet.

To make an efficient cabling map, you need to have specific numbers for *all* parts of your cabling system. For example, a single cable run from a cabling closet to wall plate should have the same number on the patch panel port, patch cable, wall cable, and wall plate. This way, you can refer to a specific run of cable at any point in the system, and you can put numbers on the cabling map to refer to each individual cable run.

Cable Termination

Now that you've learned about installing the cable, you need to know what to do with both ends of the cable. Terminating the cables involves installing some kind of connector on each end (either a connector or a termination block) so that the cabling system can be accessed by the devices that are going to use it. This is the part of cabling-system installation that requires the most painstaking attention to detail, because the quality of the termination greatly affects the quality of the signal being transmitted. Sloppy termination will yield an installation that won't support higher-speed technologies.

Though many termination methods are used, they can be classified one of two ways: connectorizing or patch-panel termination. *Connectorizing* (putting some kind of connector directly on the end of the cable in the wall) is covered in detail in Chapter 13, so we'll briefly discuss patch-panel termination.

There are many different types of patch panels, some for copper, some for fiber. Copper-cable patch panels for UTP all have a few similar characteristics, for the most part. First off, most UTP LAN patch panels (as shown in Figure 12.16) have UTP ports on the front and punch-down blades (see Figure 12.17) in the back. During termination, the individual conductors in the UTP cable are pressed between the metal blades to make both the mechanical and electrical connection between the cable and the connector on the front of the patch panel. This type of patch panel is a 110-punch-down block (or 110-block, for short).

FIGURE 12.16:

A sample patch panel

FIGURE 12.17:

A punch-down blade on a
110-block

The procedure for connecting an individual cable is as follows:

1. Route the cable to the back of the punch-down block.

2. Strip off about ½–¾ inches of the cabling jacket. (Be careful not to strip off too much, as that can cause interference problems.)

3. Untwist each pair of UTP conductors and push each conductor onto its slot between the color-coded "finger," as shown here.

WARNING   Make sure that no more than ½ inch of each twisted-conductor pair is untwisted when terminated.

4. Using a 110-punch-down tool, push the conductor into the 110-block so that the metal fingers of the 110-block cut into the center of each conductor, thus making the connection, as shown here.

5. Repeat steps 3 and 4 for each conductor.

The process described here works only for UTP cables. Fiber-optic cables use different termination methods. For the most part, fiber-optic cables do use patch panels, but you can't punch down a fiber-optic cable because of the delicate nature of the optical fibers. Instead, the individual fiber-optic cables are simply connectorized and connected to a special "pass-through" patch panel (as shown in Figure 12.18).

NOTE   Fiber-optic connectorization is covered in Chapter 13.

FIGURE 12.18:

A fiber-optic patch panel

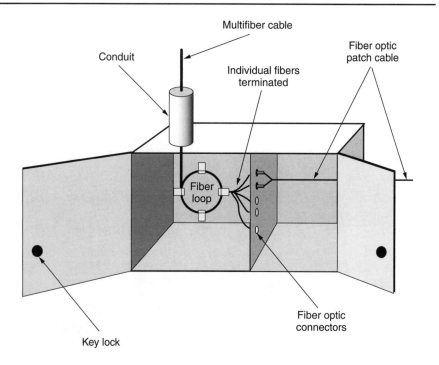

Test the Installation

Once you have a cable or cables installed and terminated, your last installation step is to test the connection. Each connection must be tested for proper operation, category rating, and possible connection problems. If the connection has problems, it must either be reterminated or, in the worst-case scenario, the entire cable must be repulled.

The method of testing individual cables is done most effectively and quickly with a LAN cable tester (as shown in Figure 12.19). This cable tester usually consists of two parts: the tester itself and a signal injector. The tester is a very complex electronic device that measures not only the presence of a signal but also the quality and characteristics of the signal. Cable testers are available for both copper and fiber-optic cables.

FIGURE 12.19:

A LAN cable tester

NOTE   Testing tools and procedures are covered in more detail in Chapter 14.

You should test the entire cabling installation before installing any other hardware (hubs, PCs, etc.). That way, you avoid having to troubleshoot cabling-related problems later (or at least you minimize possible later problems).

chapter **13**

Cable-Connector Installation

- Twisted-Pair Cable-Connector Installation

- Coaxial Cable-Connector Installation

- Fiber-Optic Cable-Connector Installation

So far, you have learned about the installation of cables and the termination process. In today's cabling installation, the cables you install into the walls and ceilings are usually terminated at either punch-down blocks or patch panels and wall outlets. In some cases (as with patch cables, for example), you may need to put a connector on the end of a piece of cable. Installing connectors, or *connectorizing*, is an important skill for the cabling installer.

This chapter will cover the basics of cable-connector installation and teach you how to install the connectors for each type of cable.

Twisted-Pair Cable-Connector Installation

For LAN installations, no cable type is currently more ubiquitous than twisted-pair copper cabling. Unshielded twisted-pair is usually used in LAN installations, although some LAN technologies, like Token Ring, require shielded twisted-pair cable. But because UTP is almost always used in Ethernet installations, twisted-pair connectorizing will apply here to UTP cable.

The main method to put connectors on twisted-pair cables (both UTP and STP) is *crimping*. You use a tool called a *crimper* to push the metal contacts inside the connector onto the individual conductors in the cable, thus making the connection.

NOTE   The topic of this chapter is *not* cable termination (which we discussed in Chapter 12). Connectorization is normally done for patch and drop cables, whereas termination is done for the horizontal cables from the patch panel in the wiring closet to the wall plate at the workstation.

Types of Connectors

Two main types of connectors (often called *plugs*) are used for connectorizing twisted-pair cable in data-communications installations: the RJ-11 and RJ-45 connectors. As discussed in Chapter 9, these are more accurately referred to as six-position and eight-position modular plugs, but the industry is comfortable with the RJ labels. Figure 13.1 shows an example of both an RJ-11 and RJ-45 connector for twisted-pair cables. Notice that these connectors are basically the same, except the RJ-45 accommodates more conductors and thus is slightly larger.

FIGURE 13.1:

RJ-11 and RJ-45 connectors

RJ-11 connectors, because of their small form factor and simplicity, are primarily used in telephone applications. RJ-45 connectors, on the other hand, because of the number of conductors they support (eight total), are used primarily in LAN applications. It should be noted, however, that many cable workers will install RJ-45 jacks for telephone applications because those jacks support both RJ-11 and RJ-45 connectors.

Both types of conductors are made of plastic with metal "fingers" inside them (as you can see in Figure 13.1). These fingers are pushed down into the individual conductors in a twisted-pair cable during the crimping process. Once these fingers are crimped and make contact with the conductors in the twisted-pair cable, they are the contact points between the conductors and the pins inside the RJ-11 or RJ-45 jack.

The different RJ connectors each come in two versions, for stranded and solid conductors. As stated elsewhere, stranded-conductor twisted-pair cables are made up of many tiny hairlike strands of copper twisted together into a larger conductor. These conductors have more surface area to make contact with but are more difficult to crimp because they change shape easily. Because of their difficulty to connectorize, they are usually used as patch cables.

Most UTP cable installed in the walls and ceilings between patch panels and wall plates is solid-conductor cable. Although they are not normally used as patch cables, solid-conductor cables are easiest to connectorize. So many people make their own patch cords out of solid-conductor UTP.

TIP

As discussed several times in this book, we do not recommend attaching your own UTP and STP plugs to make patch cords. Field-terminated modular connectors are notoriously time-consuming to apply and are unreliable. Special circumstances may require that you make your own, but whenever possible, buy your UTP and STP patch cords.

Conductor Arrangement

When making solid-conductor UTP patch cords with crimped ends, you can make many different types, determined by the order in which their color-coded wires are arranged. Inside a normal UTP cable with RJ-45 ends are four pairs of conductors (eight total). Each pair is color coded blue, orange, green, and brown. Each wire will either be the solid color or a white wire with a stripe of its pair's solid color (e.g., the orange and the white/orange pair). Table 13.1 illustrates some of the many ways the wires can be organized.

TABLE 13.1: Color-Coding Order for Various Standards

Wiring Standard	Pin #	Color Order
568A	1	White/green
	2	Green
	3	White/orange
	4	Blue
	5	White/blue
	6	Orange

Continued on next page

TABLE 13.1 CONTINUED: Color-Coding Order for Various Standards

Wiring Standard	Pin #	Color Order
	7	White/brown
	8	Brown
568B	1	White/orange
	2	Orange
	3	White/green
	4	Blue
	5	White/blue
	6	Green
	7	White/brown
	8	Brown
10Base-T only	1	White/blue
	2	Blue
	3	White/orange
	6	Orange
Generic USOC	1	White/brown
	2	White/green
	3	White/orange
	4	Blue
	5	White/blue
	6	Orange
	7	Green
	8	Brown

> **TIP**
>
> A straight-through patch cord for data applications has both ends wired the same, i.e., both ends T568A or both ends T568B. Straight-through patch cords connect PCs to wall outlets and patch panels to network equipment such as hubs, switches, and routers. A crossover patch cord is wired with one end T568A and one end T568B. Crossover cords connect two PCs directly together without any intermediate network equipment and connect one hub, router, or switch to another.

When connectorizing cables, make sure you understand which standard your cabling system uses and stick to it.

Connector Crimping Procedures

The installation procedure is pretty straightforward. The only difficult part is knowing what "hiccups" you might run into.

Prerequisites

As with any project, you must first gather all the items you will need. These items include the following:

- Cable
- Connectors
- Stripping and crimping tools

By now, you know about the cable and connectors, so we'll discuss the tools you'll need for RJ-connector installation. The first tool you're going to need is a cable-jacket stripper, as shown in Figure 13.2. It will only cut through the outer jacket of the cable, not through the conductors inside. Many different kinds of cable strippers exist, but the most common are the small, plastic ones (as in Figure 13.2) that easily fit into a shirt pocket. They are cheap to produce and purchase.

FIGURE 13.2:

A common twisted-pair cable stripper

Common strippers don't work well (if at all) on flat cables, like silver satin. But then, technically, those cables aren't twisted-pair cables and should never be used for data applications.

Another tool you're going to need when installing connectors on UTP or STP cable is a cable-connector crimper. Many different styles of crimpers can crimp connectors on UTP or STP cables. Figure 13.3 shows an example of a crimper that can crimp both RJ-11 and RJ-45 connectors. Notice the two holes for the different connectors and the cutting bar.

FIGURE 13.3:

A crimper for RJ-11 and RJ-45 connectors

The last tool you're going to use is a cable tester. This device tests not only for a continuous signal from the source connector to the destination but also the quality of that connection. We won't devote much space to it in this chapter, as it will be covered in Chapter 14.

Installing the Connector

Now we'll go over the steps for installing the connectors. Pay particular attention to the order of these steps and make sure to follow them exactly.

A manufacturer may vary from these steps slightly. Make sure you check the manufacturer's instructions before installing any connector.

1.   Measure the cable you want to put ends on and trim it to the proper length using your cable cutters (as shown here). Cut the cable about 3 inches longer than the final patch-cable length. If you want a 10-foot patch cable, cut the cable to 10 feet, 3 inches.

2.   Using your cable stripper, strip about 1.5 inches of the jacket from the end of the cable. To do this, insert the cable into the stripper so that the cutter bar in the stripper is 1.5 inches from the end of the cable (as shown in the graphic). Then, rotate the stripper around the cable twice. This will cut through the jacket. Remove the stripper from the cable and pull the trimmed jacket from the cable, exposing the inner conductors (as shown in the second graphic).

Most strippers only score the jacket to avoid cutting through and damaging the conductor insulation. The jacket is easily removed, as bending the cable at the score mark will cause the jacket to break evenly, and then it can be pulled off.

3. Untwist all the inner conductor pairs and spread them apart so that you can see each individual conductor, as shown here.

4. Line up the individual conductors so that the color code matches the color-coding standard you are using (see Table 13.1, shown previously). The alignment in the graphic shown here is for 568B, with number 1 at the top.

5.   Trim the conductors so that the ends are even with each other, making sure that the jacket of the cable will be inside the connector (as shown here). The total length of exposed connectors after trimming should be no longer than ½ " to ⅝" (as shown in the second graphic).

6.   Insert the conductors in the connector, ensuring that all conductors line up properly with the pins as they were aligned in the last step. If they don't line up, pull them out and line them up. Do this carefully, as it's the last step before crimping on the connector.

7. Carefully insert the connector and cable into the crimping tool (as shown in the following graphic). Squeeze the handle firmly as far as it will go and hold it with pressure for three seconds. As you will see in the second graphic, the crimping tool has two dies that will press into the connector and push the pins in the connector into the conductors inside the connector. A die in the crimping tool will also push a plastic divider into the cable jacket of the cable to hold it securely inside the connector.

8. Now that you've crimped the connector, remove it from the crimping tool and examine it (as shown in the next graphic). Check to ensure all conductors are making contact and that all pins have been crimped into their respective

conductors. If some of the pins did not crimp all the way into their respective conductors, reinsert the connector into the crimping tool and recrimp it. If the connector didn't crimp properly, cut off the connector and redo it.

9. To finish the patch cable, put a connector on the other end of the cable and follow these steps again, starting with step 2.

Testing

You should ensure that the connectorization was done correctly by testing the cable with a cable tester. Put the injector on one end of the cable and put the tester on the other end. Once you have the tester hooked up, you can test the cable for continuity (no breaks in the conductors), near-end crosstalk (NEXT), and Category rating (all quality-of-transmission issues). The specific procedures for testing a cable vary depending on the cable tester. Usually you select the type of cable you are testing, hook up the cable, and then press a button labeled something like *Begin Test*. If the cable does not work or meet the testing requirements, reconnectorize the cable.

NOTE   Cable testers are covered in more detail in Chapter 14.

Coaxial Cable-Connector Installation

Although less popular than either twisted-pair or fiber-optic cables, coaxial cable is still used in some installations because of its simplicity and very low cost. It is often seen in small-office installations and is used in larger installations for easy connections between hubs.

After reading this section, you should be able to install a connector on a coaxial cable.

Types of Connectors

As discussed in Chapter 9, many types of coaxial cable exist, including RG-6, RG-58, and RG-62. However, LAN applications primarily use RG-62- and RG-58-designated coaxial cables. RG-62 is used mainly for ARCNet networks, and RG-58 is mostly used for Ethernet. RG-6 is used primarily in video and television-cable installations. The preparation processes for connectorizing RG-6, RG-58, and RG-62 are basically the same; different connectors are used for different applications, either LAN or video. You can identify the cable by examining the writing on its side. The different types of cable will be labeled with their RG designation.

For LAN applications, the BNC connector (shown in Figure 13.4) is used with RG-58 or RG-62 coaxial cable. The male BNC connectors are easily identified by their knurled grip and quarter-turn locking slot. Video applications, on the other hand, use what is commonly known as a *coax cable TV connector* or *F connector* (as shown in Figure 13.5) and RG-6 cable.

FIGURE 13.4:

Male and female BNC connectors

Male

Female

FIGURE 13.5:

A coax cable-TV F connector

In addition to their physical appearance, coax connectors differ based on their installation method. Basically, two types of connectors exist: *crimp-on* and *screw-on* (also known as a *threaded*). The crimp-on connectors require that you strip the cable, insert the cable into the connector, and then crimp the connector onto the jacket of the cable to secure it. Most BNC connectors used for LAN applications use this installation method. Screw-on connectors, on the other hand, have threads inside the connector that allow the connector to be screwed onto the jacket of the coaxial cable. These threads cut into the jacket and keep the connector from coming loose. Screw-on connectors are generally unreliable because they can be pulled off with relative ease. Whenever possible, use crimp-on connectors.

Connector Crimping Procedures

Now that you understand the basic connector types, we can tell you how to install them. The basic procedural outline is similar to installing twisted-pair connectors.

Prerequisites

Make sure you have the right cable and connectors. For example, if you are making an Ethernet connection cable, you must have both RG-58 coaxial cable and BNC connectors available. Similarly, if you are making an ARCNet cable, you need to have RG-62 coaxial cable and BNC connectors.

You must also have the right tools, those being cable cutters, a cable stripper, a crimper for the type of connectors you are installing, and a cable tester. These tools were discussed in the last section and also in more detail in Chapter 6.

Installing the Connector

The connector you are going to learn how to install here is the most common crimp-on style that comes in three pieces: the center pin, the crimp sleeve, and the connector housing. Pay particular attention to the order of these steps and make sure to follow them exactly.

WARNING   A manufacturer may vary from these steps slightly. Make sure you check the manufacturer's instructions before installing any connector.

1. Measure the cable you want to put ends on and trim it to the proper length using your cable cutters. Cut the cable to exactly the length you want the cable to be.

2. Put the crimp-on sleeve on the cable jacket on the end of the cable you are going to connectorize.

3. Using your cable stripper, strip about ⅝" of the jacket from the end of the cable. To do this, insert the cable into the stripper so that the cutter bar in the stripper is one inch from the end of the cable (as shown in the graphic). Then, rotate the stripper around the cable twice. This will cut through the jacket. Remove the stripper from the cable and pull the trimmed jacket from the cable, exposing the braided shield and inner conductors.

4. Trim the braided shielding so that ⁷⁄₃₂" of braid is showing, as shown in the following graphic.

5. Strip the inner protective plastic shield around the center conductor so that ⁷⁄₁₆" of plastic is showing (thus ³⁄₁₆" of conductor is showing), as shown in the next graphic. Note that the shielding is folded back over the jacket.

6. Insert the center conductor into the center pin of the connector, as shown. Crimp the pin twice with the ratcheting crimper. After crimping (shown in the second graphic), you shouldn't be able to twist the pin around the center conductor.

7. Push the connector onto the end of the cable. The barrel of the connector should slide under the shielding. Push the connector until the center pin clicks into the connector, as shown in the following graphic.

8. Slide the crimp along the sleeve down the cable so that it pushes the braided shielding around the barrel of the connector. Crimp the barrel twice, once at the connector side and again at the jacket side, as shown in the following two graphics.

9. Now that you've crimped the connector, remove it from the crimping tool and examine it. Check to see that the connector is securely attached to the end of the cable—you should not be able to move it. If the connector didn't crimp properly, cut off the connector and redo it.

10. To finish the patch cable, put a connector on the other end of the cable and follow these steps again, starting with step 2.

Testing

Once you have a tester hooked up, you can test the cable to ensure that the cable is connectorized properly and has no breaks. See the previous subsection "Testing" under the section on twisted-pair cable-connector installation. (The procedure described there is the same as for coaxial cable.)

NOTE   Cable-testing procedures are covered in more detail in Chapter 14.

Fiber-Optic Cable-Connector Installation

In the early days of fiber-optic connections, connectorizing a single fiber-optic cable could take up to a half hour. These days, an experienced cable installer can put a connector on a fiber-optic cable in less than five minutes.

Fiber is seeing increased use in LANs, and fiber-optic connections to the desktop may soon be ubiquitous. So we need to discuss installing connectors on fiber-optic cables.

Connector Types

As discussed in Chapter 10, a number of different connector types exist for the different fiber-optic cables. Each connector type differs based on its form factor and the type(s) of fiber-optic cables it supports. Some of the most common fiber-optic connector types include the following:

- SC
- ST
- Biconic
- FDDI
- FC
- ESCON
- SMA

Each of these types of connectors is discussed in detail in Chapter 10.

Connectorizing Methods

Almost as numerous as the different types of connectors are the different methods of attaching them to the optical fiber. Optical fibers are made of glass, and, unlike copper connections, usually a mechanical connection isn't enough. The light has to come out of the end of the fiber evenly with minimal loss of signal. The optical fiber has to be aligned precisely to the optical port on the device the fiber-optical cable is connected to.

To get the best possible connection, many connectorization methods have been developed. Generally, connectors are attached with epoxy or without.

For both methods, the particulars may vary by manufacturer. When one manufacturer sees that people are using a certain connectorizing system, the manufacturer will implement its own version of that connectorizing system.

Epoxy Connectors

The epoxy system uses, obviously, the two-part glue known as *epoxy*. The optical fibers are trimmed and the epoxy is applied. Then the fiber is inserted into the connector. Some epoxy systems don't include a tube of adhesive but have the adhesive preloaded into the connector. In this case, the adhesive is only activated by some outside element. For example, 3M's HotMelt system uses a thermosetting adhesive, which means that high temperature must activate the adhesive and cause it to set. Other types of adhesive are activated by UV light.

Once the fiber is in the connector and the adhesive has been activated, the assembly is either placed aside to air dry, or the connector is inserted into a curing oven to speed the drying process.

The majority of fiber-optic connectors are installed by some type of epoxy method, mainly because of the method's simplicity and ease of installation without loss of quality.

Epoxyless Connectors

The main disadvantage to epoxy-based termination is the time and extra equipment needed to terminate a single connector—it may take up to 15 minutes. So many companies have developed connectors, called *epoxyless connectors*, that don't need any kind of adhesive to hold them together.

Instead of glue, some kind of friction method, like crimping, is used to hold the fiber in place in the connector. The 3M Cimplok is an example of an epoxyless system.

Connector Installation Procedures

In this section, you are going to learn how to connectorize a single multimode fiber-optic cable with an ST connector (the most popular type). The procedures for installing different connectors differ only slightly. Where necessary, we'll point out where other connectorizing methods differ.

Prerequisites

As with the other types of connectorization, the first step is to gather all the tools and items you are going to need. You are going to need some specialized fiber-optic tools, including epoxy syringes, a curing oven, a cable-jacket stripper, a fiber stripper, a fiber-polishing tool (including a fiber-polishing puck and abrasive pad),

Kevlar scissors, and a fiber-optic loss tester. You will also need a few consumable items, like cable, connectors, alcohol and wipes (for cleaning the fiber), epoxy (self-curing or thermosetting, depending on the application), and polishing cloths. You can buy kits that contain all of these items.

If your fiber-termination system includes an oven or UV-curing device, plug it in ahead of time so that it will be ready. If possible, make sure you have adequate space to terminate the fiber, along with an adequate light source.

TIP

If you can, work on a black surface. It makes the fiber easier to see while terminating it. It is hard to see optical fiber on a white space.

WARNING

Be extremely careful when dealing with bare fiber! Most optical fibers are made of glass. The cutting or cleaving of optical fibers produces many sharp ends. Always wear safety glasses to protect your eyes from flying shards of glass. The very fine diameter of fiber-optic strands allows them to penetrate skin easily. They can actually enter the blood vessels and be carried throughout the body, with great potential for harm. (Imagine one being carried into your brain.) Properly dispose of any cut fiber scraps.

Finally, before you start, make sure you are familiar with the connector system you are using. If possible, have the directions from the fiber connector's manufacturer available while doing the termination.

Installing the Connector

Installing the connector involves many complex steps. Unlike terminating copper, terminating fiber is a very tricky operation. You must take your time and perform the following steps correctly:

1. Cut and strip the cable.

2. Trim the aramid yarn.

3. Strip the optical-fiber buffer.

4. Prepare the epoxy.

5. Epoxy the connector.

6. Insert the fiber in the connector.

7. Dry the epoxy.

8. Scribe and remove extra fiber.

9. Polish the tip.

10. Perform a visual inspection.

11. Finish.

We have included several figures that show how to perform each operation.

Cut and Strip the Cable   Cutting the fiber is fairly simple: Simply cut through the jacket and strength members using the fiber shears included in the fiber-optic termination kit. Optical fiber cannot be cut with regular cutters, mainly because many fiber-optic cables contain aramid-yarn strength members, which are next to impossible to cut with regular cutters. Trim the cable exactly to the length that you want.

TIP   Before you get out the strippers, you should perform one operation to make the installation go smoothly. Open the fiber-optic-connector package and remove the strain-relief boot and crimp sleeve. Place them on the cable *before* you strip it. Slide them down, out of the way. That way, you don't have to try to push them over the optical fiber and aramid yarn.

Then strip one end of the cable in two steps. First, strip the outer jacket, exposing the buffered fiber and the aramid-yarn strength members. Set the jacket stripper to the size recommended by the manufacturer (3mm fiber in this case) and squeeze the handle. Figure 13.6 shows a cable jacket stripper in action. The stripper will bite through the outer jacket only. Release the handle and remove the stripper. You should then be able to pull off the outer jacket as shown in Figure 13.7.

FIGURE 13.6:

Using a cable jacket stripper

FIGURE 13.7:

Pulling off the outer jacket
of a fiber-optic cable

Second, carefully strip the buffer, exposing the optical fiber so you can insert it in the connector. A guide diagram on the back of the package containing the connector will show how much of the jacket and buffer to strip off, either with measurements or by a life-size representation. Figure 13.8 shows such a diagram.

FIGURE 13.8:

A strip guide for a fiber-optic cable

| **TIP** | If you are stripping a relatively short cable (less than 25 feet) without connectors on either end, tie a knot in the end of the cable opposite of the end you are trying to strip. That way, you can't pull the strength members out of the cable while you strip it. |

Never strip a fiber-optic cable as you would a copper cable (i.e., by twisting the stripper and pulling the stripper off with the end of the jacket). It can damage the cable.

Trim the Aramid Yarn   After removing the outer jacket, trim the aramid yarn (also called by the DuPont trademark *Kevlar*), with the aramid-yarn scissors, to the length specified by the manufacturer of the connector system. To cut the yarn, grab the bundle of fibers together and loop them around your finger. Cut the fibers so that about ¼" (more or less, depending on the connector) of yarn fiber is showing. See Figure 13.9.

FIGURE 13.9:

Cutting the aramid yarn of a fiber-optic cable

TIP   If you have trouble loosening the aramid yarn fibers from the inside of the cable, try blowing on them or shaking the cable.

Strip Optical-Fiber Buffer   Now that you've got the jacket and aramid yarn cut and stripped properly, you can strip the buffer from around the optical fiber. This step must be performed with *extreme* care. At this point, the fiber is exposed and fragile; if it is damaged or broken, you must cut off the ends you just stripped and start over.

This step is done with a different stripping tool than the stripper used to strip the cable jacket. You can choose from two types of fiber-buffer strippers: the Miller tool and the No-Nik stripper. Most first-time installers like the Miller tool, but most professionals prefer the No-Nik tool. Many fiber connectorization tool kits contain both types. For purposes here, we will show pictures of the Miller tool.

To remove the buffer, position the stripper at a 45-degree angle to the fiber (as shown in Figure 13.10) to prevent the stripper from bending, and possibly breaking, the optical fiber. Position the stripper to only remove about ⅛" to ½" of buffer. Slowly but firmly squeeze the stripper to cut through the buffer. Make sure you have cut through the entire buffer. Then, using the stripper, pull the buffer from the fiber slowly and steadily, making sure to pull straight along the fiber without bending it. You will have to exert some pressure, as the buffer will not come off easily. Repeat this process to remove additional ⅛" to ¼" "bites" of buffer until sufficient buffer has been removed from the fiber and between ½" to 1" (depending on the type of connector being used) of fiber is exposed. See Figure 13.11.

FIGURE 13.10:

Stripping buffer from the optical fiber with the Miller tool

FIGURE 13.11:

The optical fiber after stripping the buffer from the fiber

TIP
It's better to have too much fiber exposed than not enough because you will trim off excess fiber in a later step.

Prepare the Epoxy Now that the fiber-optic cable and optical fiber have been stripped and the cable is ready, set it aside and get the epoxy ready to use (assuming, of course, your connector system incorporates epoxy). Epoxy will not work unless both of its parts are mixed. The epoxy usually comes in packets with a syringe (see Figure 13.12) so that you can inject the epoxy into the connector.

FIGURE 13.12:

An epoxy packet with a syringe

Open the bag that contains the plastic epoxy envelope and the syringe. Remove the divider from the envelope and mix the epoxy by kneading it with your fingers or running the flat side of a pencil over the envelope (as shown in Figure 13.13). The epoxy is mixed when it is a uniform color and consistency. It should take a couple of minutes to fully mix the epoxy, especially if you are using your fingers.

FIGURE 13.13:

Mixing the epoxy

NOTE   Once the two chemicals that make up the epoxy are mixed, it will remain workable for only a short time (usually from 15 to 30 minutes). If you are terminating several cables, you should have them all prepared before mixing the epoxy to make the best use of your time.

Then take the new syringe out of its wrapper and remove the plunger. Hold the epoxy envelope gently (don't put a large amount of pressure on the envelope) and cut one corner so a very small opening ($\frac{1}{16}$" to $\frac{1}{8}$") is formed (see Figure 13.14).

FIGURE 13.14:

Opening the epoxy envelope

> **WARNING**   Don't use the aramid-yarn scissors to cut the epoxy envelope! Epoxy is very sticky and will ruin the scissors (and they aren't cheap!). Find a pair of cheap scissors and put these in your fiber termination kit.

Hold the envelope in one hand and the empty syringe body in the other. Slowly pour the epoxy into the syringe while being careful not to get epoxy on your hands or on the outside of the syringe (see Figure 13.15). Once the syringe is almost full (leave a ⅛" gap at the top), stop pouring and set the epoxy envelope aside (preferably on a wipe or towel, in case the epoxy spills) or throw it away if it's empty.

FIGURE 13.15:

Pouring epoxy into the syringe

Next, gently place the plunger into the end of the syringe, but *don't* push it down. Just seat it in the end of the syringe to hold it in place. Invert the syringe so that the needle is at the top and then tap the side of the syringe. The epoxy will sink to the bottom, and the air bubbles will to rise the top. Grab a wipe from your termination kit and hold it above and around the needle (as shown in Figure 13.16). Slowly squeeze the air bubbles out of the syringe until only epoxy is left in the syringe.

Removing air from the syringe

Once all the air is out of the syringe, stop pushing on the plunger. When no more epoxy comes out, pull very slightly on the plunger so a tiny bubble is at the tip of the needle. Put the cap on the needle (if there is one) and set the syringe aside, out of the way.

Epoxy the Connector   Now you have to put the connector on the fiber. Remove the rest of the components from the connector package (you already have the strain relief on the cable, remember?) and lay them out in front of you. Remove the dust cap from the end of the connector and the cap from the syringe. Push the plunger on the syringe lightly to expel the small air bubble in the needle. Insert the needle into the connector body on the cable side (the side that faces the cable, not the side that faces the equipment to be connected to).

Squeeze the plunger and expel epoxy into the inside of the connector. Continue to squeeze until a very small bead of epoxy appears at the ferrule inside the connector (as shown in Figure 13.17). The size of this bead is important, as too large of a bead means you will have spend much time polishing off the extra epoxy. On the other hand, too small of a bead may not support the optical fiber inside the connector.

TIP   The proper-size bead of epoxy to expel into the connector is approximately half the diameter of the inside of the ferrule.

Once the bead appears at the ferrule, pull the needle halfway out of the connector and continue to squeeze the plunger. Keep squeezing until the connector is filled with epoxy and the epoxy starts to come out of the backside of the connector (see Figure 13.18). Remove the needle completely from the connector and pull back slightly on the plunger to prevent the epoxy from dripping out of the needle. Then set the connector aside and clean the needle off with a wipe.

Insert the Fiber into the Connector   You will now prepare the fiber for insertion. The fiber must be free of all dirt, fingerprints, and oil to ensure the best possible adhesion to the epoxy. Most fiber termination kits come with special wipes soaked in alcohol, known as *Alco wipes*. Hold one of these wipes in one hand, between your thumb and forefinger, and run the fiber between them (see Figure 13.19).

FIGURE 13.19:

Cleaning the fiber

Pick up the connector in one hand and carefully slide the fiber into the epoxy-filled center (see Figure 13.20). While pushing the fiber in, rotate the connector back and forth. Doing so will spread the epoxy evenly around the outside of the optical fiber, and it will help to center the fiber in the connector. Don't worry if some epoxy leaks out onto the aramid yarn—that will actually help to secure the cable to the connector.

FIGURE 13.20:

Inserting the fiber into the connector

To secure the cable permanently to the connector, slide the crimp sleeve up from around the cable and over the aramid fibers so that it sits against the connector (see Figure 13.21). You must now use the crimper that comes with your fiber-optic termination kit and crimp the sleeve in two places, once at the connector and once at the fiber. The crimper has two holes for crimping, a larger and a smaller hole. Crimp the sleeve at the connector end using the larger hole and crimp the sleeve at the cable-jacket end using the smaller hole (as shown in Figure 13.22).

FIGURE 13.21:

Putting on the crimping
sleeve

FIGURE 13.22:

Crimping the sleeve

TIP While crimping, make sure to hold the connector against the jacket so that a tight connection is made.

After crimping the sleeve, slide the strain-relief boot up from the cable and over the crimp sleeve (see Figure 13.23). The connector is now secure to the cable. However, a short piece of fiber should protrude from the connector. Be careful not to break it off. It will be scribed and polished off in the next step.

FIGURE 13.23:

Installing the strain-relief boot

If you do break the piece of protruding fiber, you will have to cut off the connector and start over.

Dry the Epoxy   You must set the connector aside to dry. Most epoxies take anywhere from 12–24 hours to set completely by themselves. However, you can speed up the process either by using a curing oven (shown in Figure 13.24) or a UV setting device (depending on the type of epoxy used). To dry the epoxy using one of these devices, carefully (so that you don't break the fiber) insert the connector into the slots or holes provided in the oven or setting device. Let the connector sit as long as the manufacturer requires (usually somewhere between 5 and 15 minutes). Then, if using the oven, remove the connector and place it on a cooling rack.

FIGURE 13.24:

Drying the epoxy with an oven

While the connectors are curing in the oven, you can connectorize more fibers. Remember, you only have a short time before the epoxy is no longer usable.

Scribe and Remove Extra Fiber   After the connector has sufficiently cooled and the epoxy has dried in the connector, you are ready to remove the excess fiber. You do so with a special tool known as a *scribe*. It's impossible to get any kind of cutting tool close enough to the connector to cut off the remaining fiber and glass; instead, you remove the glass fiber by scratching one side of it and breaking off the fiber.

Hold the connector firmly in one hand and use the scribe to scratch the protruding fiber just above where it sticks out from the bead of epoxy on the connector ferrule (as shown in Figure 13.25). Use a *very* light touch. Remember, the glass is very small, and it doesn't take much to break it.

FIGURE 13.25:

Scribing the protruding fiber

To remove the fiber, grab the protruding piece of fiber and sharply pull up and away from the connector (see Figure 13.26). The glass should break completely (it will still have a rough edge, although you may not be able to see it). Dispose of the fiber remnant properly in a specially designed fiber-optic trash bag.

FIGURE 13.26:

Removing the fiber

Polish the Tip   After scribing the fiber, the end will look similar to the one shown at the left side of Figure 13.27. To make a proper connection, you must polish the end to a perfectly flat surface with varying grits of polishing films (basically the same idea as sandpaper, except that films are much, much finer). The idea is to use the polishing cloth to remove a little bit of the protruding fiber at a time until the fiber is perfectly flat and level.

FIGURE 13.27:

Fiber before and after polishing

Coarse polishing, the first polishing step, removes the burrs and sharp ends present after you've broken off the fiber. Grab a sheet of 12-micron film and hold it as shown in Figure 13.28. Bring the connector into contact with the polishing film and move the connector in a figure-eight motion. Polish the connector for about 15 seconds or until you hear a change in the sound made as the fiber scrapes along the polishing cloth. This process is known as *air polishing* because you aren't using a backing for the polishing film.

FIGURE 13.28:

Air polishing the fiber after scribing

WARNING Air polishing will take some practice. Do not overpolish the fiber! If you do, the fiber will not transmit light correctly and will have to be cut off and reterminated.

When you are done, a small amount of epoxy should be left, and the glass will not be completely smooth (as seen in Figure 13.29). Don't worry, this will be taken care of in the next part of the polishing procedure. Before proceeding, clean the end of the fiber with an Alco pad to remove any loose glass shards or epoxy bits that might scratch the fiber during the next polishing step.

Next, with the polishing puck in one hand, insert the connector into the puck (as shown in Figure 13.30). Then, very gently place the puck with the connector in it on some 3-micron polishing film placed on the polishing pad. Move the puck in a figure-eight motion four or five times (see Figure 13.31). Stop polishing when the connector fiber doesn't scrape along the polishing cloth and feels somewhat slick.

WARNING	Don't overpolish the conductor with the 3-micron polishing film. Overpolishing will cause the glass-fiber end to be undercut and cause light loss at the optic connection.

Then clean the connector with an Alco wipe to remove any debris before polishing again. Once clean, gently place the puck on some 0.3-micron film and give it five or six quick figure-eights with little or no pressure to fine-polish the fiber. Remove the connector from the polishing puck and wipe it with an Alco pad. You're done. It's time to test the connector to see how you did.

Inspect the Connector   At this stage, you should check the connector with a fiber-optic microscope for any flaws that might cause problems. A fiber-optic microscope allows you to look very closely at the end of the fiber you just terminated (usually magnifying the tip 100 times or more). Different microscopes work somewhat differently, but the basic procedure is the same.

Insert the connector into the fiber microscope (as shown in Figure 13.32). Look into the eyepiece and focus the microscope using the thumb wheel or slider so that you can see the tip of the fiber. Under 100-times magnification, the fiber should look like the image shown in Figure 13.33. What you see is the light center (the core) and the darker ring around it (the cladding). Any cracks or imperfections will show up as very dark blotches. If you see any cracks or imperfections in the cladding, it's no problem because the cladding doesn't carry a signal. However, if you see cracks in the core, first try repolishing the fiber on the 0.3-micron polishing film. If the crack still appears, you may have to cut the connector off and reterminate it.

FIGURE 13.32:

Insert the fiber into the fiber microscope

FIGURE 13.33:

A sample fiber-tip image in a fiber-optic microscope

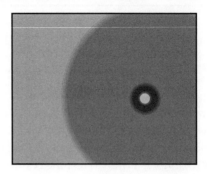

Finish   You can now terminate the other end of the cable. Then you can use a standard fiber-cable tester or optical time domain reflectometer (OTDR) to test the cable. You will learn more about optical-fiber testing in Chapter 14.

Cable-System Testing and Troubleshooting

- Installation Testing

- Cable-Plant Certification

- Cable Testing Tools

- Troubleshooting Cabling Problems

Testing a cable installation is an essential part of both installing and maintaining a data network. This chapter will examine the cable testing procedures that you should integrate into the installation process and that you are likely to need afterward to troubleshoot network communication problems. We will also examine the Standards with respect to cable testing

Installation Testing

As you've learned in earlier chapters, installing the cable plant for a data network incorporates a large number of variables. Not only must you select the appropriate cable and other hardware for your applications and your environment, but you must also install the cable so that environmental factors have as little effect on the performance of the network as possible. Part of the installation process should include an individual test of each cable run to eliminate the cables as a possible cause of any problems that might occur later when you connect the computers to the network and try to get them to communicate. Even if you are not going to be installing or testing the cabling yourself, you should be familiar with the tests that the installers perform and the types of results that they receive.

Incorporating a cable test into the installation will help to answer several questions:

> **Connections**   Have the connectors been attached to the cable properly? Have the wires been connected to the correct pins at both ends?
>
> **Cable performance**   Is the cable free from defects that can affect performance?
>
> **Environment**   Has the cable been properly routed around possible sources of interference, such as light fixtures and electrical equipment?
>
> **Certification**   Does the entire end-to-end cable run, including connectors, wall plates, and other hardware, conform to the desired Standard?

The following sections examine the tests that you can perform on copper and fiber-optic cables, the principles involved, and the tools needed. Realize, though, that you needn't perform every one of these tests on every cable installation. To determine which tests you need to perform and what results you should expect, see the section "Creating a Testing Regimen" later in this chapter.

Copper-Cable Tests

Most of the copper cable installed today is twisted-pair of one form or another, and the number of individual wire connections involved makes the installation and testing process more complicated than for other cable, particularly in light of the various standards available for the connector pinouts. The following sections list the tests for copper cables and how they work.

NOTE   For more information on the equipment used to perform these tests, see the section "Cable-Testing Tools" later in this chapter. For more information on correcting the problems detected by these tests, see the section "Troubleshooting Cabling Problems," also later in this chapter.

Wire Mapping

Wire mapping is the most basic and obvious test for any copper-cable installation, particularly those that use twisted-pair cable. Because the coaxial cable used in data networks has only two physically different conductors, a wire-mapping test is usually not needed, unless you are pulling several cables at once. In that case, you want to make sure that each cable is connected to the proper terminus. To test the continuity of a coaxial cable, you can use a digital multimeter (DMM), an inexpensive, dedicated coaxial tester, or a multifunction tester that supports coaxial cable.

For twisted-pair cables, however, you must test each cable run to make sure that the individual wires within the cable are connected properly, as shown in Figure 14.1. As mentioned earlier in this book, you can select either the T568A or T568B pinout configurations for a twisted-pair installation. Because all of the pairs are wired straight through and the difference between the two configurations is minimal, there is no functional difference between them. However, in the interest of consistency, you should select one pinout and stick to it throughout your entire installation, including patch cables. This way you can perform end-to-end tests as needed without being confused by mixed wire-pair colors. That doesn't mean you shouldn't follow some kind of wiring color-code mapping, however. It is important that you follow a standard throughout your entire network so that you—and others—can always tell what color is for what.

FIGURE 14.1:

A properly connected four-pair cable, using the T568A pinout

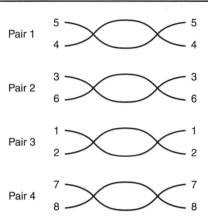

A perfunctory wire-mapping test can be performed visually by simply checking the pinouts at both ends of the cable. However, problems can occur that are not visible to the naked eye. A proper wire-mapping tester can detect any of the following faults:

Open pair   An open occurs when one or more of the wires in a cable are not connected to any pin at either end.

Shorted pair   A short occurs when the conductors of a wire pair are connected at any location in the cable.

Short between pairs   A short between pairs occurs when the conductors of two wires in different pairs are connected at any location in the cable.

Reversed pair   A reversed pair (sometimes called a *tip/ring reversal*) occurs when the two wires in a single pair are connected to the opposite pins of the same color.

Crossed pairs   Crossed (or transposed) pairs occur when both wires of one color pair are connected to the pins of a different color pair at the opposite end.

Split pairs   Split pairs occur when one wire on each of two pairs is reversed at both ends of the run. This is technically not a wire-mapping fault because all of the wires are connected to their equivalent pins at both ends. Because this type of fault essentially requires that the same mistake be made at both ends of the connection, accidental occurrence of split pairs is relatively rare.

The more likely reason is the use of the USOC connector pinouts, which are suitable for voice traffic but not data.

Figure 14.2 illustrates these faults.

FIGURE 14.2:

Common wire-mapping faults

Open Pairs

Shorted Pairs

Short between Pairs

Reversed Pairs

Crossed Pairs

Split Pairs

NOTE

Figures 14.1 and 14.2 show the T568A pinout configuration. If you are using the T568B pinout, pairs 2 and 3 switch positions from the T568A pinout.

Wire-mapping faults are usually caused by improper installation practices, although some problems like opens and shorts can result from faulty or damaged cable or connectors. The process of testing a connection's wire mapping is fairly straightforward and requires a remote unit that you attach at one end of the connection and a main unit for the other end. Wire-map testing is usually included in multifunction cable testers, but you can also purchase dedicated wire-map testers that are far less expensive.

The main unit simply transmits a signal over each wire and detects which pin at the remote unit receives the signal. The problem of split pairs (two wires in different pairs transposed at both ends of the connection) is the only one not immediately detectable using this method. Because each pin is connected to the correct pin at the other end of the connection, the wire map may appear to be correct and the connection may appear to function properly when it is first put into service. However, the transposition causes two different signals to run over the wires in a single twisted pair. This can result in an excess of near-end crosstalk that will cause the performance of the cable to degrade at high data rates. Although the occurrence of split pairs is relatively unlikely compared to the other possible wire-mapping faults, the ability to detect split pairs is a feature that you may want to check for when evaluating cable-testing products.

Cable Length

All LAN technologies are based on specifications that dictate the physical layer for the network, including the type of cable you can use and the maximum length of a cable segment. Cable length should be an important consideration from the very beginning of network planning. You must situate the components of your network so that the cables connecting them do not exceed the specified maximums.

You may therefore question why it is necessary to test the length of your cables if you have a plan that already accounts for their length. You may also deduce (correctly) that the maximum cable-length specifications are based, at least in part, on the need to avoid the signal degradation that can be caused by attenuation and crosstalk. If you are going to perform separate tests for these factors, why test the cable lengths, too?

You have several reasons. One is that if your network doesn't come close to exceeding the specifications for the protocol you plan to use, you may be able to double-check your cable lengths and omit other tests like those for crosstalk and attenuation. Another reason is that a cable-length test can also detect opens, shorts, and cable breaks in a connection. A third reason is that a length test measures the actual length of the wires inside the cable. Because the cable's wire pairs are twisted inside the casing, the actual length of the wires is longer than the length of the cable.

Time Domain Reflectometry   The length of a cable is typically tested in one of two ways: either by time domain reflectometry or by measuring the cable's resistance.

A time domain reflectometer (TDR) works much like radar, by transmitting a signal on a cable with the opposite end left open and measuring the amount of time that it takes for the signal's reflection to return to the transmitter, as shown in Figure 14.3. When you have this elapsed time measurement and you know the nominal velocity of propagation (NVP), you can calculate the length of the cable.

FIGURE 14.3:

Time domain reflectometry measures the time needed for a pulse to travel to the end of a cable and back.

The NVP for a particular cable is usually provided by its manufacturer and expressed in relation to the speed of light. Some manufacturers provide the NVP as a percentage, such as 72 percent, whereas others express it as a decimal value multiplied by the speed of light (c), such as 0.72c. Many cable testers compute the length internally, based on the results of the TDR test and an NVP value that is either preprogrammed or that you specify for the cable you're testing.

When testing cable length, it's critically important that your tester uses the correct NVP value. The NVP values for various cables can range from 60 percent (0.6c) to 90 percent (0.9c), which creates a potential for error in the cable-length results ranging from 30 to 50 percent if the tester is using the wrong value. Time domain reflectometry has other potential sources of inaccuracy as well. The NVP can vary as much as 4 to 6 percent between the different wire pairs in the same cable because of the deliberately varied twist intervals used to control crosstalk. The pulse generated by the TDR can be distorted from a square wave to one that is roughly sawtooth-shaped, causing a variance in the measured time delay of several nanoseconds, which converts to several feet of cable length.

Because of these possible sources of error, you should be careful when planning and constructing your network not to use cable lengths that closely approach or exceed the maximum recommended in your protocol specification.

Locating Cable Faults   Time domain reflectometry has other applications in cable testing as well, such as the detection and location of cable breaks, shorts, and terminators. The reflection of the test pulse back to the transmitter is caused by a change in impedance on the cable. On a properly functioning cable, the open circuit at the opposite end produces the only major change in impedance. But if an open or short exists at some point midway in the cable run, it too will cause a reflection back to the transmitter. The size of the pulse reflected back is in direct proportion to the magnitude of the change in impedance, so a severe open or short will cause a larger reflection than a relatively minor fault, such as a kink, a frayed cable, or a loose connection. If there is no reflection at all, the cable has been terminated at the opposite end, which causes the pulse signal to be nullified before it can reflect back.

Cable testers use TDR to locate breaks and faults in cable by distinguishing between these various types of reflections. For example, an open located at 25 feet in a cable run that should be at least 100 feet long indicates that a fault in the cable exists and gives an indication of its approximate location (see Figure 14.4). The problem may be caused by a cable that has been entirely severed or by faulty or damaged wires inside the cable sheath. Sometimes you can't tell that a cable is faulty by examining it from the outside. This is why a test of each cable run during the installation process is so important.

FIGURE 14.4:

TDRs are also used to locate breaks and other faults in a cable.

Resistance Measuring   The second method for determining the length of a cable is to measure its resistance using a digital multimeter (DMM). All conductors have a resistance specification, expressed in ohms per meter (or sometimes ohms per 100 meters or ohms per foot). If you know the resistance specification for the conductor per unit of length, you can measure the cable's resistance and divide the result by the manufacturer's specification to determine the cable's length. In the same way, if you already know the length of the cable from a TDR test, you can use the rating to determine the cable's total resistance.

Environmental factors can affect resistance as can the cable's design and improper installation. Resistance increases with temperature, so your length calculations will suffer accordingly if you are measuring in a high- or low-temperature environment too far from the 20° C (68° F) temperature the resistance specification is based on. The twist intervals of the pairs also will influence your resistance measurement. Because the twists increase the actual length of the conductors, the resistance reading will be higher and result in a longer-than-actual cable length. And, if the conductor was stretched during installation, high resistance readings will result, again producing longer-than-actual lengths for the cable.

Performance Testing

The tests we've discussed so far all relate to physical properties of the cable and ascertain if the cable has been terminated properly and is an acceptable length. They can be performed quickly and with relatively unsophisticated and inexpensive test devices. They are the basic, minimum levels of testing that should be performed to insure your network will work.

But to properly characterize your cabling's performance, a battery of transmission tests must be administered; they determine the data-carrying capability of your cables and connectors. The following characteristics were all defined in Chapter 1, so we won't explain them further here other than to note issues related to their testing.

All of the copper-cable tests discussed in the following sections, except for Propagation Delay and Delay Skew, have formula-based performance requirements along a continuous-frequency spectrum. In the case of Category 5 and 5e, this range is 1MHz through 100MHz. If at any point along the spectrum the cable exceeds the specification limits, the cable fails. This is called *sweep* testing because the entire frequency range is being scanned.

Testing for transmission performance requires much more sophisticated equipment than that used for wire mapping, opens, shorts, and crosses—equipment that can exceed $5,000 per test set. However, the testing is essential for qualifying your cabling installation to a particular level of performance, e.g., Category 5. If you can't afford such a set, either contract with an installation-and-testing company that has one, or rent an appropriate unit.

Impedance   As you learned earlier, variations in impedance cause signal reflections that a TDR uses to measure the length of a cable. However, these signal reflections can be caused by different factors, including variations in the cable manufacture, structural damage caused during installation, or connectors that are a poor match for the cable. The statistic that measures the uniformity of the cable's impedance is called its *structural return loss* (SRL), which is measured in decibels (dB), with higher values indicating a better cable. Even when the SRL of a particular cable is acceptable, it is still possible for an installation of that cable to suffer from variations in impedance that cause signal reflections. When you construct a network to conform to a particular cabling specification, such as Category 5 UTP, to maintain a consistent level of impedance throughout the entire length of the cable run you have to use connectors and other hardware that have the same rating as the cable.

If, for example, during a twisted-pair installation, you fail to maintain the twist of the wire pairs up to a point no more than 13mm from each connection, you run the risk of varying the impedance to the point at which a reflection occurs (as well as causing additional crosstalk). The cumulative amount of reflection caused by variations in impedance on a cable run is called its *return loss*, which, like imped-ance, is measured in ohms. If the return loss is too large, signal-transmission errors can occur at high transmission speeds. The worst-pair performance is reported at the frequency where the result came closest to the specified limits.

Attenuation   Attenuation is one of the most important specifications for high-speed networks; if it is too high, the signals can degrade prematurely and data can be lost. This is especially true if your network uses cable lengths that approach the maximum permitted by your networking protocol.

Testing the attenuation of a cable run requires a unit at both ends of the connec-tion: one to transmit a calibrated signal and another to receive the signal and cal-culate how much it has degraded during the trip. Attenuation is measured in decibels (dB), and most good-quality cable testers include the secondary module needed to perform the test. The worst-case result is reported.

Near-End Crosstalk (NEXT)   Along with attenuation, near-end crosstalk (NEXT) is one of the major impediments to successfully installing and running a high-speed data network on twisted-pair cabling. Figure 14.5 shows NEXT. Test-ing for NEXT is a relatively simple process with today's sophisticated test sets. After terminating the far end of the cable run to prevent any reflections from interfering with the test, a signal is transmitted over one pair, and the magnitude of the crosstalk signal is measured on the other pairs (in decibels). For a complete assessment, you must test each wire pair against each of the three other pairs, for a total of six tests, and you must perform the six tests from both ends of the cable. The worst-case combination is reported as the cable's performance result.

FIGURE 14.5:

Near-end crosstalk

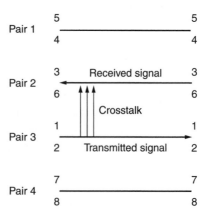

Power-Sum NEXT   Power-sum NEXT (sometimes called PS-NEXT) is a measurement of the cumulative effect of crosstalk on each wire pair when the other three pairs are transmitting data simultaneously. Figure 14.6 shows PS-NEXT. Each pair is tested separately, yielding four results. This test must also be performed at each end of the cable, and the worst-case result is reported.

FIGURE 14.6:

Some high-speed protocols can generate excessive crosstalk by transmitting over two wire pairs at once.

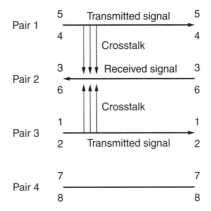

Attenuation to Crosstalk Ratio (ACR)   The attenuation to crosstalk ratio (ACR) is a calculation, not a separate test. ACR is the difference between the attenuation for the cable run and the amount of crosstalk it exhibits, both of which are measured in decibels. The ACR is one of the best measurements of a cable run's overall quality because it clearly indicates how robust the signal will appear in relation to the noise in the cable. Crosstalk varies at either end of the cable run, so you must run an ACR test at both ends. The worst of the ACR measurements is the rating for the cable run. You can also compare the PS-NEXT rating with the attenuation to determine the cable's power-sum ACR.

Far-End Crosstalk (FEXT)   Far-end crosstalk (FEXT) occurs when a signal crosses over to another wire pair as it approaches the far end of the cable, opposite the system that transmitted it. To equalize the FEXT measurement for the amount of attenuation present, you simply subtract the attenuation value from the FEXT value to achieve the equal-level FEXT (ELFEXT), which is the equivalent of the ACR for the far end of the cable. There is also a power-sum ELFEXT (PS-ELFNEXT) test, which is a combined measurement for all of the wire pairs in the cable, and a worst pair-to-pair ELFEXT test. In most cases, these measurements are not vital to an installation test, but some emerging technologies, such as Gigabit Ethernet, require them. Testing must be done from both ends of the cable (each end of the cable is attached to a transceiver, so at some point each end is the far end), and the worst-case combinations are reported.

Propagation Delay and Delay Skew The length of time required for a signal to travel from one end of a cable run to the other, usually measured in nanoseconds (ns), is its propagation delay. Because of the different twist rates used, the lengths of the wire pairs in a cable can vary. As a result, the propagation delay for each wire pair can be slightly different. When your network is running a protocol that uses only one pair of wires to transmit data, such as standard Ethernet, 100Base-TX Ethernet, and Token Ring, these variations are not a problem. However, protocols that transmit over multiple pairs simultaneously, such as 100Base-T4 and Gigabit Ethernet, can lose data when signals arrive too far apart over the different pairs.

To quantify this variation, some testers can measure a cable run's delay skew, which is the difference between the lowest and the highest propagation delay for the wire pairs within a cable. Propagation delay and delay skew are characteristics critical to some high-speed LAN applications, so they should be included in your battery of tests, especially for a network that will run one of the high-speed protocols that uses multiple pairs. For propagation delay, the worst pair is reported; for delay skew, it is the worst combination of any two pairs.

Noise Most cable tests attempt to detect and quantify problems that result from the effects of the installation on the cable's own characteristics. However, environmental factors can also affect the functionality of the cable installation, and you should be sure to test each cable run for noise that emanates from outside sources. Outside noise is usually generated either by EMI, which is low-frequency, high-amplitude noise generated by AC power lines, electric motors, and fluorescent lights, or *radio frequency interference* (RFI), which is high-frequency, low-amplitude noise created by radio and television sets and cellular phones. Once again, this type of noise is usually not a problem on lower-speed networks, but it can be on protocols that run the network at 100MHz or more.

Testing for outside noise is a matter of shutting off or detaching all devices on the LAN and testing the cable for electrical activity. One of the most important elements of this kind of test is to perform it when all of the equipment at the site is operating as it normally does during work hours. For example, performing a noise test on an office network during the weekend, when most of the lights, copiers, coffee machines, air conditioners, and other equipment are shut down, will not give you an accurate reading.

Fiber-Optic Tests

Just as installing fiber-optic cable is completely different from installing copper-cable, the testing processes also differ greatly. Much of the copper-cable testing revolves around the various types of interference that can affect the performance of a network. Fiber-optic cable is completely immune from interference caused by crosstalk, EMI, and RFI, however, so tests for these are not needed. What you do need for a fiber-optic installation is to ensure that the signals arrive at their destinations with sufficient strength to be read and that the installation process has not degraded that strength.

Because of its superior signal-carrying capabilities, fiber-optic cable installations can include various types of cable runs. The typical LAN arrangement consists of single-fiber links that connect a patch panel in a wiring closet or data center to wall plates or other individual equipment sites over relatively short distances, with patch cables at both ends to connect to a backbone network and to computers or other devices. Because of the limited number of connections they use, testing these types of links is fairly straightforward. However, fiber optic can also support extremely long cable runs that require splices every two to four kilometers, which introduces a greater potential for connection problems.

To completely test a fiber-optic installation, you should perform your battery of tests three times. The first series of tests should be on the spooled cable before the installation to ensure that no damage occurred during shipping. The installation costs for fiber-optic cable can be high—often higher than the cost of the cable and other hardware—so it's worthwhile to test the cable before investing in its installation. Because excessive signal loss is caused mostly by the connections, simply testing the continuity of the cable at this stage is usually sufficient. This continuity testing is sometimes referred to as a "flashlight" test because it amounts to shining light in one end of the fiber strand and seeing if there is light at the other end.

The second series of tests should be performed on each separate cable segment as you install it, to ensure that the cable is not damaged during the installation and that each individual connector is installed correctly. By testing at this stage, you can localize problems immediately, rather than trying to track them down after the entire installation is completed. Finally, you should test the entire end-to-end connection, including all patch cables and other hardware, to ensure that cumulative loss is within certified parameters.

For fiber-optic LAN installations, only two tests are generally required: optical power and signal loss. The following sections examine these tests and how you perform them. Other types of tests are used on long-distance fiber-optic links and in troubleshooting, which are much more complex and require more elaborate equipment. For more information on these, see the section "Cable-Testing Tools" later in this chapter.

Optical Power

The most fundamental test of any fiber-optic-cable plant is the *optical-power test*, as defined in the EIA's FOTP-95 standard, which determines the strength of the signal passing through a cable run and is the basis for a loss-measurement (attenuation) test. The testing process involves connecting a fiber-optic power meter to one end of the cable and a light source to the other. The power meter uses a solid-state detector to measure the average optical power emanating from the end of the cable, measured in decibels. For data networks using multimode cable, you should perform optical-power tests at 850 and 1,300nm wavelengths; many testers run their tests at both settings automatically. Single-mode cables require a 1,300nm test and sometimes 1,550nm, as well. The 1,550nm test determines whether the cable will support wavelength division multiplexing and can detect losses due to microbending, which are not apparent at 1,300nm.

WARNING   Some people claim that you can use an optical time domain reflectometer (OTDR) to test optical power and cable-plant loss but, generally speaking, these people are either mistaken or trying to sell you an OTDR. The combination of a fiber-optic power meter and light source is the industry-standard solution for measuring optical power and signal loss. These tools are also, by far, the more inexpensive solution.

Loss (Attenuation)

Loss testing, along with optical power, are the two most important tests for any fiber-optic cable installation. *Loss* is the term commonly used in the fiber-optic world for attenuation; it is the lessening of the signal as it travels through the cable. The physics of optical transmission make it less susceptible to attenuation than any copper cable, which is why fiber cable segments can usually be much longer than copper ones. However, even if your network does not have extremely long fiber cable runs, there can be a significant amount of loss, not because of the cable, but because of the connections created during the installation. Loss testing verifies that the cables and connectors were installed correctly.

Measuring the loss on a cable run is similar in practice to measuring its optical power, except that you use a calibrated light source to generate the signal and a fiber-optic power meter to measure how much of that signal makes it to the other end. The combination of the light source and the power meter into one unit is called an *optical loss test set* (OLTS). Because of the different applications that use fiber-optic cable, you should be sure to use test equipment that is designed for your particular type of network. For example, a light source might use either a laser or an LED to create the signal, and the wavelengths it uses may vary as well. For a fiber-optic LAN, you should choose a product that uses a light source at wavelengths the same as the ones your network equipment will use so that your tests generate the most accurate results possible.

The testing procedure begins with connecting the light source to one end of a *reference test cable* (also called the *launch cable*) and the power meter to the other end. The reference test cable functions as a baseline against which you measure the loss on your installed cable runs and should use the same type of cable as your network. After measuring the power of the light source over the reference test cable, you disconnect the power meter, connect the reference cable to the end of the cable you want to test, and connect the power meter to the other end. Some testers include a variety of adapters to accommodate various connector types. By taking another power reading and comparing it to the first one, you can calculate the loss for the cable run. As with the optical-power test, you should use both 850 and 1,300nm wavelengths for multimode fiber tests; you should also test the cable from the other direction in the same way. When you have the results, compare them to the *optical loss budget* (OLB), which is the maximum amount of signal loss permitted for your network and your application. (You may occasionally see *optical link budget*; though *optical loss budget* is preferred, the two terms are synonymous.)

WARNING   Be sure to protect your reference test cables from dirt and damage. A faulty reference cable can produce in your tests false readings of high loss.

This type of test effectively measures the loss in the cable and in the connector to which the reference test cable is attached. The connection to the power meter at the other end introduces virtually no additional signal loss. To test the connectors at both ends of the cable run, you can add a second reference test cable to the far end, which is called a *receive cable*, and connect the power meter to it. This is known as a *double-ended loss test*. The type of test you perform depends on the type of cable run you are testing and the Standard you're using as the model for your network.

The standard single-ended loss test is described in the FOTP-171 Standard, which was developed by the EIA in the 1980s and intended for testing patch cables. The double-ended loss test for multimode cables is defined in the OFSTP-14 Standard and is used to test an installed cable run. Another Standard, the OFSTP-7, defines testing specifications for single-mode cables. The document describes two testing methods: the double-ended source/meter test from OFSTP-14 and an OTDR test, but when the results differ (and they usually will), the source/meter test is designated as definitive.

WARNING   Some older manuals recommend that you calibrate your power meter using both launch and receive cables, connected by a splice bushing, when you perform double-ended loss tests. This practice introduces additional attenuation into your baseline and can obscure the fact that one of your reference test cables is dirty or damaged. Always establish your testing baseline using a launch cable only.

Depending on the capabilities of your equipment, the loss-testing process might be substantially easier. Some power meters have a *zero loss reference* capability, meaning that you can set the meter to read 0dB while measuring the reference test cable. Then, when you test the installed cable run, the meter displays only the loss in decibels; no calculation is necessary.

Cable-Plant Certification

So far in this chapter, you've learned about the types of tests you can perform on a cable installation but not about which tests you should perform for a particular type of network—or the results that you should expect from these tests. The tests you perform and the results you receive enable you to certify your cable installation as complying with a specific standard of performance. Many of the high-quality cable testers on the market perform their various tests automatically and provide you with a list of pass/fail results, but it is important to know not only what is being tested but also what results the tester is programmed to evaluate as passes and failures.

Changing standards and new technologies can affect the performance levels that you should expect and require from your network, and a tester that is only a year or two old may yield results that ostensibly pass muster but that are actually insufficient for the network protocol you plan to run. Always check to see what specifications a tester is using to evaluate your cable's performance. With some testers, the results that determine whether a cable passes or fails a test can be calibrated with whatever values you wish, whereas others are preprogrammed and cannot easily be changed. Obviously, the former is preferable, as it enables you to upgrade the tester to support changing standards.

The certification that you expect your network to achieve should be based not only on today's requirements but also on your expectation of future requirements. Professional consultants have been recommending that clients install Category 5 cable for many years, long before most of these clients even considered upgrading to Fast Ethernet or another technology that requires Category 5. This was because the additional investment for a Category 5 installation was then minimal compared to the cost of completely recabling the network later on.

For the same reason, it may be a good idea for the cabling you install today to conform to the requirements for technologies you're not yet considering using. A few years ago, Fast Ethernet was a new and untried technology, yet now it is commonplace. It makes sense to assume that Gigabit Ethernet will be just as common a few years from now. Installing Category 5e or 6 cable now and certifying it to conform to the highest standards currently available may not benefit you today, but in future years, you may be proud of your foresight. (Category 5e is actually now considered the minimum recommended performance level to install. Some consultants recommend Category 6, but it must be remembered that only draft requirements currently exist for Category 6 performance.)

Creating a Testing Regimen

The level of performance that you require from a cable installation should specify which tests you have to perform during the installation process and what test results are acceptable. For example, a UTP installation intended only for voice-telephone traffic requires nothing more than a wire-mapping test to ensure that the appropriate connections have been made. Other factors will probably not affect the performance of the network sufficiently to warrant testing them. A data network, on the other hand, requires additional testing, and as you increase the speed at which data will travel over the network and the number of wire pairs used, the need for more extensive testing increases as well. Table 14.1 lists the most common data link layer protocols used on copper cable networks and the corresponding tests you should perform on a new cable installation.

TABLE 14.1:   Minimum Cable Tests Required for Copper-Based Networking Protocols

Network Type	Tests Required
Voice telephone	Wire mapping
10Base-T Ethernet	Wire mapping, length, attenuation, NEXT
100Base-TX	Wire mapping, length, attenuation, NEXT, propagation delay, delay skew
100Base-T4	Wire mapping, length, attenuation, NEXT, propagation delay
100VG-AnyLAN	Wire mapping, length, attenuation, NEXT, delay skew
Token Ring	Wire mapping, length, attenuation, NEXT
TP-PMD FDDI	Wire mapping, length, attenuation, NEXT
155Mbps ATM	Wire mapping, length, attenuation, NEXT
Gigabit Ethernet	Wire mapping, length, attenuation, NEXT, propagation delay, delay skew, PS-NEXT, ELFNEXT, PS-ELFNEXT, return loss

For fiber-optic cable installations, optical-power and loss testing is sufficient for all multimode fiber LANs. For single-mode networks with long cable runs, OTDR testing is also recommended, as described in the section "Optical Time Domain Reflectometers" later in this chapter.

Copper-Cable Certification

While the ANSI/TIA/EIA-568-A Standard includes performance requirements for horizontal and backbone cabling, it provides no guidelines for the testing of Category 5 cable installations. As a result, the TIA/EIA PN-3287 Link Performance task group was formed, which in October 1995 published a document called "TIA/EIA Telecommunications Systems Bulletin 67: Transmission Performance Specifications for Field Testing of Unshielded Twisted-Pair Cabling Systems" or, more simply, TSB-67.

The TSB-67 document defines two types of horizontal links for the purposes of testing. The *basic link* (also called the *permanent link* by other specifications) refers to the permanently installed cable connection that typically runs from a wall plate at the equipment site to a patch panel in a wiring closet or data center. The *channel link* refers to the complete end-to-end cable run including the basic link and the patch cables used to connect the equipment to the wall plate and the patch-panel jack to the hub or other device.

Annex A to TSB-67 also defines Level I and Level II cable-performance requirements, the latter of which is more stringent. The two levels take into account the differences in hardware required to test basic links and channel links. When testing a channel, you nearly always have to use an RJ-45 jack on the tester to connect to the cable run, introducing (temporarily) a source of additional crosstalk that you don't want to include in the final results. Level I calls for lower performance standards to compensate for the presence of the additional connector. When testing a basic link, however, the tester can use an interface built into the unit that adds very little additional crosstalk, and the higher performance levels required by Level II provide an accurate test. If you plan to purchase an automated cable tester to certify your installation, look for one that is compliant with the TSB-67 Standard and be sure to find out which levels of performance the unit supports.

TSB-67 defines performance levels for only four tests: wire mapping, cable length, attenuation, and NEXT. However, more advanced networking protocols have appeared since TSB-67 was published, such as Gigabit Ethernet, which require specific performance levels for other tests, such as return loss and ELFEXT. In addition, Standards are also in the process of being established for new categories of UTP cable, specifically Category 6.

As a result of these new advances, several addenda to the ANSI/TIA/EIA-568-A have been published that take the additional cable requirements into account. These documents include "ANSI/TIA/EIA-568-A-1 Propagation Delay and Delay Skew Specifications for 100-Ohm Four-Pair Cable," "TIA 568-A-2 Correction and Additions to ANSI/TIA/EIA-568-A," and "ANSI/TIA/EIA-568-A-5 Additional Transmission Performance Specifications for Four-Pair 100-Ohm Enhanced Category 5 Cabling," among others. These documents define performance requirements for the following tests, which are in addition to the basic four tests defined in TSB-67:

- Power sum NEXT (PS-NEXT)
- Return loss
- Worst pair-to-pair ELFEXT

- Power-sum ELFEXT (PS-ELFEXT)
- Propagation delay
- Delay skew

Tables 14.2 and 14.3 summarize the performance levels required for copper cable testing, broken down by cable category and frequency, for basic link and channel link testing, respectively.

TABLE 14.2: TIA Basic-Link Testing Performance Standards

	Category 3	Category 5	Category 5e	Category 6
Wire mapping	All pins properly connected	All pins properly connected	All pins properly connected	All pins properly connected
Length (in meters, including tester cords)	≤ 94	≤ 94	≤ 94	≤ 94
Attenuation (dB)				
@ 1MHz	3.2	2.1	2.1	1.9
@ 10MHz	10.0	6.3	6.3	5.6
@ 100MHz	N/A	21.6	21.6	18.5
@ 250MHz	N/A	N/A	N/A	30.7
NEXT (dB)				
@ 1MHz	40.1	60.0	60.0	65.0
@ 10MHz	24.3	45.5	48.5	57.8
@ 100MHz	N/A	29.3	32.3	41.8
@ 250MHz	N/A	N/A	N/A	35.3
PS-NEXT (dB)				
@ 1MHz	N/A	N/A	57.0	62.0
@ 10MHz	N/A	N/A	45.6	55.5
@ 100MHz	N/A	N/A	29.3	39.3
@ 250MHz	N/A	N/A	N/A	32.7

Continued on next page

TABLE 14.2 CONTINUED: TIA Basic-Link Testing Performance Standards

	Category 3	Category 5	Category 5e	Category 6
ELFEXT (dB)				
@ 1MHz	N/A	N/A	58.0	64.2
@ 10MHz	N/A	N/A	40.0	44.2
@ 100MHz	N/A	N/A	20.0	24.2
@ 250MHz	N/A	N/A	N/A	16.2
PS-ELNEXT (dB)				
@ 1MHz	N/A	N/A	55.0	61.2
@ 10MHz	N/A	N/A	39.0	41.2
@ 100MHz	N/A	N/A	17.0	21.2
@ 250MHz	N/A	N/A	N/A	13.2
Propagation delay @ 10 MHz	N/A	< 518ns	< 518ns	< 498ns
Delay skew @ 10 MHz	N/A	< 45ns	< 45ns	< 44ns

TABLE 14.3: TIA Channel-Link Testing Performance Standards

	Category 3	Category 5	Category 5e	Category 6
Wire mapping	All pins properly connected	All pins properly connected	All pins properly connected	All pins properly connected
Length (in meters, including tester cords)	≤ 100	≤ 100	≤ 100	≤ 100
Attenuation (dB)				
@ 1MHz	4.2	2.5	2.5	2.1
@ 10MHz	11.5	7.0	7.0	6.3
@ 100MHz	N/A	24.0	24.0	21.3
@ 250MHz	N/A	N/A	N/A	36.0

Continued on next page

TABLE 14.3 CONTINUED: TIA Channel-Link Testing Performance Standards

	Category 3	Category 5	Category 5e	Category 6
NEXT (dB)				
@ 1MHz	39.1	60.0	60.0	65.0
@ 10MHz	22.7	44.0	47.0	56.6
@ 100MHz	N/A	27.1	30.1	39.9
@ 250MHz	N/A	N/A	N/A	33.1
PS-NEXT (dB)				
@ 1MHz	N/A	N/A	57.0	62.0
@ 10MHz	N/A	N/A	44.1	54.0
@ 100MHz	N/A	N/A	27.1	37.1
@ 250MHz	N/A	N/A	N/A	30.2
ELFEXT (dB)				
@ 1MHz	N/A	N/A	57.4	63.3
@ 10MHz	N/A	N/A	37.4	43.3
@ 100MHz	N/A	N/A	17.4	23.3
@ 250MHz	N/A	N/A	N/A	15.3
PS-ELFEXT (dB)				
@ 1MHz	N/A	N/A	54.4	60.3
@ 10MHz	N/A	N/A	34.4	40.3
@ 100MHz	N/A	N/A	14.4	20.3
@ 250MHz	N/A	N/A	N/A	12.3
Propagation delay @ 10 MHz	N/A	< 555ns	< 555ns	< 555ns
Delay skew @ 10 MHz	N/A	<50ns	<50ns	<50ns

NOTE   The values included in Tables 14.2 and 14.3 for Category 6 are derived from specifications still in various stages of development. The values in the final published Standard may vary slightly.

Fiber-Optic Certification

After testing the signal loss generated by a fiber-optic cable run, you compare the results to the optical loss budget (OLB) for the cable to determine if the installation is within performance parameters. The OLB is a calculation based on the number of connectors and splices in a cable run and the length of the cable. The basic formula for computing the OLB is as follows:

```
OLB = cable loss + connector loss + splice loss
```

Essentially, you add together the amount of acceptable loss for the length of the cable and for the number of splices and connectors. You do this by multiplying the actual cable length and the number of splices and connectors by predefined coefficients. These coefficients vary according to the type of fiber cable you're using, the wavelength of the network, the standard you adhere to, and the sources you consult. The values you opt to use for the coefficients determine how stringent your tests will be. Lower coefficients result in a lower OLB, meaning that you will tolerate a smaller amount of attenuation on your network.

For the connectors, coefficients range from 0.5 to a maximum of 0.75. For the splices, coefficients are 0.2 or 0.3. For the cable-length coefficient, use the values listed in Table 14.4.

TABLE 14.4: Cable Coefficients for Optical Loss Budget Calculations

	850nm	**1,300nm**	**1,550nm**
Multimode fiber	3 to 3.75dB/km	1 to 1.5dB/km	N/A
Single-mode fiber	N/A	0.4dB/km	0.3dB/km

Using these coefficient values, you construct an OLB formula like the following, which provides for the most stringent possible test standard on a multimode cable run at 850nm:

```
OLB = (number of connectors*0.5) + (number of splices*0.2) + (cable
length*3.0 dB/km)
```

Third-Party Certification

Testing your cable installation for compliance to a specific performance level is a great way to ensure that the cable plant will support the networking protocol you plan to run. If you have installed the cabling yourself, testing is needed to check your work, and if you have the cable installed by a third party, testing ensures that the job was done correctly. Hand-held testers can perform a comprehensive battery of tests and provide results in a simple pass/fail format, but these results depend on what standards the device is configured to use.

In most cases, it isn't difficult to modify the parameters of the tests performed by these devices (either accidentally or deliberately) so that they produce false positive results. Improper use of these devices can also introduce inaccuracies into the testing process. As a general rule, it isn't a good idea to have the same people check the work that they performed. This is not necessarily an accusation of duplicity. It's simply a fact of human nature that intimate familiarity with something can make it difficult to recognize faults in it.

For these reasons, you may want to consider engaging a third-party testing-and-certification company to test your network after the cable installation is completed and certify its compliance with published standards. If your own people are installing the cable, then this is a good way to test their work thoroughly without having to purchase expensive testing equipment. If your cable will be installed by an outside contractor, adding a clause into the contract that states acceptance of the work is contingent on the results of an independent test is a good way of ensuring that you get a quality job, even if you accept the lowest bid. What contractor would be willing to risk having to reinstall an entire network?

Cable-Testing Tools

The best method for addressing a faulty cable installation is to avoid the problems in the first place by purchasing high-quality components and installing them carefully. But no matter how careful you are, problems are bound to arise. This section covers the tools that you can use to test cables both at the time of their installation and afterwards, when you're troubleshooting cable problems. Cable-testing tools can range from simple, inexpensive, mechanical devices to elaborate electronic testers that automatically supply you with a litany of test results in an easy-to-read pass/fail format.

The following sections list the types of tools available for both copper and fiber-optic cable testing. This is not to say that you need all of the tools listed here. In fact, in some of the following sections, we attempt to steer you away from certain types of tools. In some cases, both high-tech and low-tech devices are available that perform roughly the same function, and you can choose which you prefer according to the requirements of your network, your operational budget, or your temperament. Some of the tools are extremely complicated and require extensive training to use effectively, where others are usable by anyone who can read.

You should select the types of tools you need based on the descriptions of cable tests given earlier in this chapter, the test results required by the standards you're using, and the capabilities of the workers—not to mention the amount of money you want to spend.

Wire-Map Testers

A *wire-map tester* transmits signals through each wire in a copper twisted-pair cable to determine if it is connected to the correct pin at each end. Wire mapping is the most basic test for twisted-pair cables because the eight separate wire connections involved in each cable run are a common source of installation errors. Wire-map testers detect transposed wires, opens (broken or unconnected wires), and shorts (wires or pins improperly connected to each other)—all problems that can render a cable run inoperable.

Wire-map testing is nearly always included in multifunction cable testers, but in some cases it may not be worth the expense to spend thousands of dollars on a comprehensive device. Dedicated wire-map testers are relatively inexpensive (from $200 to $300) and enable you to test your installation for the most common faults that occur during installation and afterward. If you are installing voice-grade cable, for example, a simple wire-mapping test may be all that's needed. Slightly more expensive (under $500) devices do wire-map testing in addition to other basic functions, such as TDR length testing.

A wire-map tester consists of a remote unit that you attach to the far end of a connection and the battery-operated, hand-held main unit that displays the results. Typically, the tester displays various codes to describe the type of faults it finds. In some cases, you can purchase a tester with multiple remote units that are numbered, so that one person can test several connections without constantly traveling back and forth from one end of the connections to the other to move the remote unit.

WARNING   The one wiring fault that is not detectable by a dedicated wire-map tester is split pairs, because even though the pinouts are incorrect, the cable is still wired straight through. To detect split pairs, you must use a device that tests the cable for the near-end crosstalk that split pairs cause.

Continuity Testers

A *continuity tester* is an even simpler and less expensive device than a wire-map tester. It is designed to check a copper-cable connection for basic installation problems, such as opens, shorts, and crossed pairs. At $50 to $200, these devices usually cannot detect more complicated twisted-pair wiring faults such as split pairs, but they are sufficient for basic cable testing, especially for coaxial cables, which have only two conductors that are not easily confused by the installer. Like a wire-map tester, a continuity tester consists of two separate units that you connect to each end of the cable to be tested. In many cases, the two units can snap together for storage and easy testing of patch cables.

Tone Generators

The simplest type of copper-cable tester is also a two-piece unit, a *tone generator and probe*, also sometimes called a *fox and hound* wire tracer. With a standard jack, you connect to the cable the unit that transmits a signal; or, with alligator clips, you connect the unit to an individual wire. The other unit is a penlike probe that emits an audible tone when touched to the other end of the cable or wire or even to its insulating sheath.

This type of device is most often used to locate a specific connection in a punch-down block. For example, some installers prefer to run all of the cables for a network to the central punch-down block without labeling them. Then they use a tone generator to identify which block is connected to which wall plate and label the punch-down block accordingly. You can also use the device to identify a particular cable at any point between the two ends. Because the probe can detect through the sheath the cable containing the tone signal, you can locate one specific cable out of a bundle in a ceiling conduit or other type of raceway. Connect the tone generator to one end and touch the probe to each cable in the bundle until you hear the tone.

In addition, by testing the continuity of individual wires using alligator clips, you can use a tone generator and probe to locate opens, shorts, and miswires. An open wire will produce no tone at the other end, a short will produce a tone on two or more wires at the other end, and an improperly connected wire will produce a tone on the wrong pin at the other end.

Using a tone generator is extremely time-consuming, however, and it's nearly as prone to errors as the cable installation. You either have to continually travel from one end of the cable to the other to move the tone generator unit or use a partner to test each connection, keeping in close contact using radios or some other means of communication. When you consider the time and effort involved, you will probably find that investing in a wire-map tester is a more practical solution.

Time Domain Reflectometers (TDR)

As described earlier in the section "Cable Length," a time domain reflectometer (TDR) is the primary tool used to determine the length of a copper cable and to locate the impedance variations that are caused by opens, shorts, damaged cables, and interference with other systems. Two basic types of TDRs are available: those that display their results as a waveform on an LCD or CRT screen and those that use a numeric readout to indicate the distance to a source of impedance. The latter type of TDR provides less detail but is easy to use and relatively inexpensive. Many of the automated copper-cable testers on the market have a TDR integrated into the unit. Waveform TDRs are not often used for field testing these days because they are much more expensive than the numeric type and require a great deal more expertise to use effectively.

You can use a TDR to test any kind of cable that uses metallic conductors, including the coaxial and twisted-pair cables used to construct LANs. A high-quality TDR can detect a large variety of cable faults, including open conductors; shorted conductors; loose connectors; sheath faults; water damage; crimped, cut, or smashed cables; and many other conditions. In addition, the TDR can measure the length of the cable and the distance to any of these faults. Many people also use the TDR as an inventory-management tool to ensure that a reel contains the length of cable advertised and to determine if a partially used reel contains enough cable for a particular job.

NOTE   A special kind of TDR, called an *optical time domain reflectometer (OTDR)*, is used to test fiber-optic cables. For more information, see the section "Optical Time Domain Reflectometers (OTDRs)" later in this chapter.

Fault Detection

When a TDR transmits its signal pulse onto a cable, any extraordinary imped-ance that the signal encounters causes it to reflect back to the unit, where it can be detected by a receiver. The amount of impedance determines the magnitude of the reflected signal. The TDR registers the magnitude of the reflection and uses it to determine the source of the impedance. The TDR also measures the elapsed time between the transmission of the signal and the receipt of the reflec-tion and, using the NVP that you supply for the cable, determines the location of the impedance. For example, on an unterminated cable with no faults, the only source of impedance is the end of the cable, which registers as an open, enabling the TDR to measure the overall length of the cable.

Faults in the cable return reflections of different magnitudes. A complete open caused by a broken cable prevents the signal from traveling any farther down the cable, so it appears as the last reflection. However, less serious faults enable the signal to continue on down the cable, possibly generating additional reflections. A waveform TDR displays the original test signal on an oscilloscopelike screen, as well as the individual reflections. An experienced operator can analyze the waveforms and determine what types of faults caused the reflections and where they are located.

Automated TDRs analyze the reflections internally and use a numerical display to show the results. Some of these devices are dedicated TDR units that can perform comprehensive cable-fault tests at a substantially lower price than a waveform TDR and are far easier to use. The unit displays the distance to the first fault located on the cable and may also display whether the reflection indicates a high impedance change (denoting an open) or a low impedance change (denoting a short). Some of these units even offer the ability to connect to a standard oscilloscope in order to display waveform results, if desired.

Blind Spots

Some TDRs enable you to select from a range of pulse widths. The *pulse width* speci-fies the amount of energy the unit transmits as its test pulse. The larger the pulse width, the longer the signal travels on the cable, enabling the TDR to detect faults at greater distances. However, signals with larger pulse widths also take longer to transmit, and the TDR is all but incapable of detecting a fault during the time that it is transmitting. For example, because the signal pulse travels at approximately 3ns per meter, a 20ns pulse means that the beginning of the pulse will be about 6.6 meters from the transmitter when the end of the pulse leaves the unit. This time interval during which the pulse transmission tales place is known as a *blind spot*, and it can be a significant problem because faults often occur in the patch cables, wall plates, and other connectors near to the end of the cable run.

When you have a TDR with a variable pulse-width control, you should always begin your tests with the lowest setting so that you can detect faults that occur close to the near end of the cable. If no faults are detected, you can increase the setting to test for faults at greater distances. Larger pulse widths can also aid in detecting small faults that are relatively close. If a cable fault is very subtle and you use a low pulse-width setting, the attenuation of the cable may prevent the small reflection from being detected by the receiver. Larger pulse widths may produce a reflection that is more easily detected.

If your TDR uses a fixed-pulse width, you may want to connect an extra jumper cable between the unit and the cable run to be tested. This jumper cable should be at least as long as the blind spot and should use cable of the same impedance as the cable to be tested. It should also have high-quality connections to both the tester and the cable run. If you choose to do this, however, be sure to subtract the length of the jumper cable from all distances given in the test results.

Integrated TDRs

Many of the combination cable testers on the market include TDR technology, primarily for determining the cable length, but they may not include the ability to detect subtle cable faults like the dedicated units can. Obviously, a severed cable is always detectable by the display of a shorter length than expected, but other faults may not appear. Some units are not even designed to display the cable length by default but instead simply present a pass/fail result based on a selected network type. If, for example, you configure the unit to test a 10Base-T cable, any length less than 100 meters may receive a pass rating. For the experienced installer, a unit that can easily display the raw data in which the pass/fail results are based is preferable.

Another concern when selecting a TDR is its ability to test all four of the wire pairs in a twisted-pair cable. Some devices use time domain reflectometry only to determine the length of the cable and are not intended for use as fault locators. So they might not test all the wire pairs, making it seem as though the cable is intact for its entire length when, in fact, opens or shorts could be on one or more pairs.

Fiber-Optic Power Meters

A *fiber-optic power meter* measures the intensity of the signal transmitted over a fiber-optic cable. The meter is similar in principle to a multimeter that measures electric current, except that it works with light instead of electricity. The meter uses a solid-state detector to measure the signal intensity and incorporates signal-conditioning circuitry and a digital display. Different meters are for different fiber-optic cables and applications. Meters for use on short-wavelength systems, up to 850nm, use a *silicon* detector, whereas long-wavelength systems need a meter with a germanium or InGaAs detector that can support 850 to 1,550nm. In many cases, optical power meters are marketed as models intended for specific applications, such as CATV (cable television), telephone systems, and LANs.

Other, more expensive units can measure both long- and short-wavelength signals. Given that the cost of fiber-optic test equipment can be quite high, you should generally try to find products specifically suited for your network and application so that you're not paying for features you'll never use. Low-end power meters that provide the basic features for a specific network type run from $300 to $500. Higher-end devices can run from $500 to over $1,000.

A good optical power meter enables you to display results in various units of measure and signal resolutions, can be calibrated to different wavelengths, and measures power in the range of at least 0dBm to -50dBm. Some meters intended for special applications can measure signals as high as +20dBm to -70dBm. An optical power meter registers the average optical power over time, not the peak power, so it is sensitive to a signal source with a pulsed output. If you know the pulse cycle of the signal source, you can compute the peak power from the average power reading.

A fiber-optic power meter that has been properly calibrated to NIST (the United States' National Institute of Standards and Technology) standards typically has a +/- 5 percent margin for error, due primarily to variances introduced by the connection to the cable being tested, low-level noise generated by the detector, and the meter's signal conditioning circuitry. These variances are typical for all optical power meters, regardless of their cost and sophistication.

The ability to connect the power meter to the cables you want to test is obviously important. Most units use modular adapters that enable you to connect to any of the dozens of connector styles used in the fiber-optic industry, although ST and SC connectors are most commonly used on LANs. The adapters may or may not be included with the unit, however, and reference test cables usually are not, so be sure to get all of the accessories you need to perform your tests.

Fiber-Optic Test Sources

To measure the strength of an optical signal, a signal source must be at the other end of the cable. Although you can use a fiber-optic power meter to measure the signal generated by your network equipment, accurately measuring the signal loss of a cable requires a consistent signal generated by a fiber-optic test source. A companion to the power meter in a fiber-optic tool kit, the test source is also designed for use with a particular type of network. Sources typically use LEDs (for multimode fiber) or lasers (for single-mode fiber) to generate a signal at a specific wavelength, and you should choose a unit that simulates the type of signals used by your network equipment.

Like power meters, test sources must be able to connect to the cable being tested. Some sources use modular adapters like those on power meters, but others, especially laser sources, use a fixed connector that requires you to supply a hybrid jumper cable that connects the light source to the test cable.

Like optical power meters, light sources are available in a wide range of models. LED sources can range from $300 to $1,500, whereas laser sources can run to well over $2,000. Beware, however, of extremely inexpensive (under $100) light sources, because some are intended only for identifying a particular cable in a bundle, using visible light. These devices are not suitable for testing signal loss in combination with a power meter.

Optical Loss Test Sets and Test Kits

In most cases, you need both an optical power meter and a light source in order to properly install and troubleshoot a fiber-optic network, and you can usually save a good deal of money and effort by purchasing the two together. You will thus be sure to purchase units that both support the wavelengths and power levels you need and that are calibrated for use together. You can purchase the devices together as a single combination unit called an optical loss test set (OLTS) or as separate units in a fiber-optic test kit.

An OLTS is generally not recommended for field testing, because it is a single unit. While useful in a lab or for testing patch cables, two separate devices would be needed to test a permanently installed link because you have to connect the light source to one end of the cable and the power meter to the other. However, for fiber-optic contractors involved in large installations, it may be practical to give workers their own OLTS set so that they can work with a partner and easily test each cable run in both directions.

Fiber-optic test kits are the preferable alternative for most fiber-optic technicians because they include a power meter and light source that are designed to work together, usually at a price that is lower than the cost of two separate products. Many test kits also include an assortment of accessories needed to test a particular type of network, such as adapters for various types of connectors, reference test cables, and a carrying case. Prices for test kits can range from $500 to $600 for basic functionality to as much as $5,000 for a comprehensive kit that can test virtually every type of fiber-optic cable.

TIP

Communications can be a vital element of any cable installation in which two or more people are working together, especially when the two ends of the permanent cable runs can be a long distance apart, as on a fiber-optic network. Some test sets address this problem by incorporating voice communication devices into the power meter and light source, using the tested cable to carry the signals.

Optical Time Domain Reflectometers (OTDRs)

An *optical time domain reflectometer (OTDR)* is the fiber-optic equivalent of the TDR used to test copper cables. The OTDR transmits a calibrated signal pulse over the cable to be tested and monitors the signal that returns back to the unit. Instead of measuring signal reflections caused by electrical impedance as a TDR does, however, the OTDR measures the signal returned by *backscatter*, a phenomenon that affects all fiber-optic cables. Backscatter is caused by photons bouncing off of the inside walls of the cable in every direction, as shown in Figure 14.7. The scattered signal returned to the OTDR is much weaker than the original pulse, due to the attenuation of the outgoing pulse, the relatively small amount of signal that is scattered (called the *backscatter coefficient* of the cable), and the attenuation of the scattered signal on its way back to the source.

FIGURE 14.7:

OTDRs detect the scattered photons on a fiber optic cable that return to the transmitter.

As with a TDR, the condition of the cable causes variances in the amount of backscatter returned to the OTDR, which is displayed on an LCD or CRT screen as a waveform. By interpreting the signal returned, it's possible to identify cable faults of specific types and other conditions. An OTDR can locate splices and connectors and measure their performance, identify stress problems caused by improper cable installation, and locate cable breaks, manufacturing faults, and other weaknesses. Knowing the speed of the pulse as it travels down the cable, the OTDR can also use the elapsed time between the pulse's transmission and reception to pinpoint the location of specific conditions on the cable.

The two primary tasks that OTDRs should *not* be used for are measuring a cable's signal loss and locating faults on LANs. Measuring loss is the job of the power meter and light source, which are designed to simulate the conditions of the network. Using an OTDR, it is possible to compute a cable's length based on the backscatter returned to the unit. The advantage to using an OTDR for this purpose is that you can test the cable from one end, whereas the traditional method requires that the light source be connected to one end and the power meter to the other.

OTDRs also have limited distance-resolution capabilities over short distances, making them quite difficult to use effectively in a LAN environment where the cables are only a few hundred feet long. OTDRs are used primarily on long-distance connections, such as those used by telephone and cable-television networks. As a result, you might find people who are experts at fiber-optic LAN applications that have never seen or used an OTDR. Other reasons could also account for why they may not have used an OTDR. One is that, as with TDRs, interpreting the waveforms generated by an OTDR takes a good deal of training and experience. Another reason is their jaw-dropping price. Full-featured OTDR units can cost anywhere from $17,000 to $30,000. Smaller units (sometimes called mini-OTDRs) with fewer features can run from $7,000 to $15,000.

Fiber-Optic Inspection Microscopes

Splicing and attaching connectors to fiber-optic cables are tasks that require great precision, and the best way to inspect cleaved fiber ends and polished connection ferrules is with a microscope. Fiber-optic inspection microscopes are designed to hold cables and connectors in precisely the correct position for examination, enabling you to detect dirty, scratched, or cracked connectors and ensure that cables are cleaved properly in preparation for splicing. Good microscopes typically provide approximately 100-power magnification (although products range from 30 to 800 power), have a built-in light source (for illuminating the object under the scope), and are able to support various types of connectors using additional stages (platforms on which the specimen is placed), which may or may not be included. A cost of $100 to $200 is typical.

Visual Fault Locators

The light that transmits data over fiber-optic cable is invisible to the naked eye, making it difficult to ensure without a formal test that installers have made the proper connections. A *visual fault locator* (sometimes called a *cable tracer*) is a quick and dirty way to test the continuity of a fiber-cable connection by sending visible light over a fiber-optic cable. A typical fault locator is essentially a flashlight that applies its LED or incandescent light source to one end of a cable, which is visible from the other end. A fault locator enables you to find a specific cable out of a bundle and ensure that a connection has been established.

More powerful units that use laser light sources can actually make points of high loss—such as breaks, kinks, and bad splices—visible to the naked eye, as long as the cable sheath is not completely opaque. For example, the yellow- or orange-colored sheaths commonly used on single-mode and multimode cables (respectively) usually admit enough of the light energy lost by major cable faults to make them detectable from outside. In a world of complex and costly testing tools, fault locators are one of the simplest and most inexpensive items in a fiber-optic toolkit, usually costing well under $100. Their utility is limited when compared to some of the other tools described here, but they are a convenient means of finding a particular cable and locating major installation faults.

Multifunction Cable Scanners

The most heavily marketed cable-testing tools available today are the *multifunction cable scanners*, sometimes called *certification tools*. These devices are available for both copper and fiber-optic networks and perform a series of tests on a cable run, compare the results against either preprogrammed standards or parameters that you supply, and display the outcome as a series of pass or fail ratings. Most of these units perform the basic tests called for by the most commonly used standards, such as wire mapping, length, attenuation, and NEXT for copper cables, and optical power and signal loss for fiber optic. Many of the copper-cable scanners also go beyond the basics to perform a comprehensive battery of tests, including propagation delay, delay skew, PS-NEXT, ELFNEXT, PS-ELFNEXT, and return loss.

The primary advantage of a multifunction cable scanner is that anyone can use it. You simply connect the unit to a cable, press a button, and read off the results after a few seconds. Many units can store the results of many individual tests in memory, download them to a PC, or output them directly to a printer. This primary advantage, however, is also the primary disadvantage. The implication behind these products is that you don't really have to understand the tests being performed, the results of those tests, or the cabling standards used to evaluate them. The interface insulates you from the raw data, and you are supposed to trust the manufacturer implicitly and believe that a series of pass ratings means that your cables are installed correctly and functioning properly.

The fundamental problem with this process, however, is that the user must have sufficient knowledge of applicable specifications to insure that appropriate parameters are being used by the test set. Some units claim to certify Category 6 and Category 7 cables, for example, when standards for these cables have not yet been ratified. One should even check the specification parameters loaded in testers that claim to certify Category 5e cables, because this standard was ratified only recently. When evaluating products like these, it's important to choose units that are able to be upgraded or manually configurable so that you can keep up with the constantly evolving requirements.

This configurability can lead to another problem, however. In many cases, it isn't difficult to modify the testing parameters of these units to make it easier for a cable to pass muster. For example, simply changing the NVP for a copper cable can make a faulty cable pass the unit's tests. An unscrupulous contractor can conceivably perform a shoddy installation using inferior cable and use his own carefully prepared tester to show the client a list of perfect "pass" test results. This should not preclude the use of these testers for certifying your cabling installation. Rather, you need to be vigilant in hiring reliable contractors.

As another example, some of the more elaborate (and more expensive) fiber-optic cable testers attempt to simplify the testing process by supplying main and remote units that both contain an integrated light source and semiconductor detector and by testing at the 850nm and 1,300nm wavelengths simultaneously. This type of device enables you to test the cable in both directions and at both wavelengths simply by connecting the two units to either end of a cable run. You needn't use reference test cables to swap the units to test the run from each direction or run a separate test for each wavelength.

However, these devices, apart from costing several times as much as a standard power meter/light source combination ($4,000 or more, in some cases), do not compare the test results to a baseline established with that equipment. Instead, they compare them to preprogrammed standards, which, when it comes to fiber-optic cables, can be defined as somewhat loose. So the device is designed primarily for people who really don't understand what they are testing and who will trust the device's pass-or-fail judgment without question—even when the standards used to gauge the test results are loose enough to permit faulty installations to receive a pass rating.

Multifunction test units are an extremely efficient means of testing and troubleshooting your network. But understand what they are testing and either examine the raw data gathered by the unit or verify that the requirements loaded to evaluate the results are valid. The prices of these products can be shocking, however. Both copper and fiber-optic units can easily run to several thousand dollars, with top-of-the-line models exceeding $5,000.

Troubleshooting Cabling Problems

Cabling problems account for a substantial number of network-support calls; some authorities say as many as 40 to 50 percent. Whether or not the figure is accurate, any network administrator will nevertheless experience network-communication problems that can be attributed to no other cause than the network cabling. The type of cable your network uses and how it is installed will have a big effect on the frequency and severity of cabling problems.

For example, a coaxial thin Ethernet network allowed to run wild on floors and behind furniture is far more likely to experience problems than a 10Base-T network installed inside the walls and ceilings. This is true not only because the coaxial cables are exposed and more liable to be damaged but also because the bus topology is more sensitive to faults and the BNC connectors are more easily loosened. This goes to show that you can take steps toward minimizing the potential for cable problems by selecting the right products and installing them properly.

Establishing a Baseline

The symptoms of many cable problems are similar to symptoms of software problems, so it can often be difficult to determine when the cable causes a problem. The first step in simplifying the isolation of the source of network problems is to make sure that all of your cables are functioning properly at the outset. You do this by testing all of your cable runs as you install them, as described earlier in this chapter, and by documenting your network installation.

If you use a multifunction cable tester, you can usually store the results of your tests by retaining them in the tester's memory, copying them to a PC, or printing them out. You thus establish a performance baseline against which you can compare future test results. For example, by recording the lengths of all your cable runs at the time of the installation, you can tell if a cable break has occurred later by retesting and seeing if the length results are different than before. In the same way, you can compare the levels of crosstalk, outside noise, and other characteristics that may have changed since the cable was installed. Even if your tester does not have these data-storage features, you should manually record the results for future reference.

Another good idea is to create and maintain a map of all your cable runs on a floor plan of your site. Sometimes cable problems can be the result of outside factors, such as interference from electrical equipment in the building. A problem that affects multiple cable runs might be traced to a particular location where new equipment was installed or existing equipment modified. When you install your cables inside walls and ceilings (and especially when outside contractors do it for you), it can be difficult to pinpoint the routes that individual cables take. A map serves as a permanent record of your installation, both for yourself and any future people working on the network.

Locating the Problem

Troubleshooting your network's cable plant requires many of the same common-sense skills as other troubleshooting. You try to isolate the cause of the problem by asking questions like the following:

- Has the cable ever worked properly?

- When did the malfunctions start?

- Do the malfunctions occur at specific times?

- What has changed since the cable functioned properly?

Once you've gathered all the answers to such questions, the troubleshooting consists of steps like the following:

1. Split the system into its logical elements.

2. Locate the element that is most likely the cause of the problem.

3. Test the element or install a substitute to verify it as the cause of the problem.

4. If the suspected element is not the cause, move on to the next likely element.

5. After locating the cause of the problem, repair or replace it.

You might begin troubleshooting by determining for sure that the cable run is the source of the problem. You can do this by connecting different devices to both ends of the cable to see if the problem continues to occur. Once you verify that the cable is at fault, you can logically break it down into its component elements. For example, a typical cable run might consist of two patch cables (one at each end), a wall plate, a punch-down block, and the permanently installed cable.

In this type of installation, it is easiest to test the patch cables, either by replacing them or testing them with a cable scanner. Replacing components can be a good troubleshooting method, as long as you know that the replacements are good. If, for example, you purchase a box of 100 cheap patch cables that are labeled Category 5 when they actually are Category 3 cable, replacing one with another won't do any good.

The most accurate method is to test the individual components with a cable scanner. If the patch cables pass, then proceed to test the permanent link. If you don't have a scanner available, you can examine the connectors at either end of the cable run and even reconnect or replace them to verify that they were installed correctly. However, there's little you can do if the problem is inside a wall or in some other inaccessible place. If you do have a scanner, the results of the tests should provide you with the information you need to proceed.

Resolving Specific Problems

Cable testers, no matter how elaborate, can't tell you what to do to resolve the problems they disclose. The following sections examine some of the courses of action you can take to address the most common cabling problems.

Wire-Map Faults

Wire-map faults are the result of an improper installation. When the wires within a twisted-pair cable are attached to the wrong pins, the cable is no longer wired straight through. If the pairs used to carry network data are involved, then signals won't reach their destination. In most cases, this fault occurs on a permanent link, although it is possible for a patch cable to be miswired.

The possible causes of wire-map faults are simple errors made during the installation or the use of different pinouts (T568A and T568B) at each end of the cable. Whatever the cause, however, the remedy is to rewire the connectors on one or both ends so that each pin at one end is connected to its equivalent pin at the other end.

Excessive Length

Cable lengths should be carefully planned before network installation and tested immediately after installation to make sure that the cables are not longer than the recommended maximum according to the ANSI/TIA/EIA-568-A Standard. Cable runs that are too long can cause problems like late collisions on an Ethernet network or excessive retransmissions due to attenuated signals. Don't be overly concerned, however, if the maximum allowable length for a cable segment is 95 meters and you have a run that is 96 meters long. Most protocols have some leeway built into them that permit a little excess.

TIP It's possible for a cable tester to generate incorrect length readings if the tester is improperly calibrated. If the cable length seems wrong, check to make sure that the nominal velocity of propagation (NVP) setting for the cable is correct. Also, some testers include the patch cable between the tester and the connection point in the calculated cable length.

To address the problem, you can start by using shorter patch cables, if possible. In some cases, you may find that an installer has left extra cable coiled in a ceiling or wall space that can be removed, and the end can be reconnected to the wall plate or punch-down block. Sometimes a more efficient cable route can enable you to rewire the run using less cable. If, however, you find that bad planning caused the problem and the wall plate is too far away from the punch-down block, you can still take actions.

The first and easiest action is to test the attenuation and NEXT on the cable run to see if they exceed the requirements for the protocol. These characteristics are the primary reasons for these maximum-length specifications. If you have installed cable that is of a higher quality than is required, you may be able to get away with the additional length, but if you are having network problems, chances are this isn't the answer. The other alternative is to use a repeater to amplify the signal at some point along the run. Stand-alone repeaters for coaxial cables and mini-hubs for twisted-pair cables can provide the additional boost needed to avoid signal degradation caused by attenuation and crosstalk on an excessively long cable.

Opens and Shorts

Opens and shorts can be caused by improper installation, or they can occur later if a cable is damaged or severed. If the cable's length is correct but one or more wires are open or shorted, then a connector is likely faulty or has come loose and needs repairing or replacing. If all of the wires in a cable are reported as open in the same place or if the length of all the wires is suddenly shorter than it should be, the cable may have been accidentally cut by nearby equipment or by someone working in the area. Cables damaged but not completely severed may show up with drastically different lengths for the wire pairs or as shorts at some interim point.

Cable scanners usually display the distance to the open or short so that you can more easily locate and repair it. For cables installed in walls and ceilings, the cable map you (we hope) created during the installation can come in handy. If you don't know the cable's route, you can use a tone generator and probe to trace the cable to the point of the break.

It is tempting to try to splice the ends of the severed wires. *Don't do it*. You'll create a nexus for all sorts of potential transmission problems, including SRL (structural return loss) reflections, higher attenuation, and increased crosstalk. You must completely replace the permanent cable run. Broken or damaged patch cables should always be discarded.

Excessive Attenuation

A cable run can exhibit excessive attenuation for several different reasons, most of which are attributable to improper installation practices. The most obvious cause is excessive length. The longer the cable, the more the signals attenuate. Address this problem as you would any other excessive-length condition.

Another possible cause is that the cable used in the run is not suitable for the rate at which data will be transmitted. If, for example, you try to run a 100Base-TX network using Category 3 cable, one of the reasons it will fail is that the specified attenuation level for Category 3 allows the signal to decay more than 100Base-TX can handle. In this case, there is no other alternative than to replace the cable with the proper grade. Inferior or untwisted patch cables are a frequent cause of this type of problem. These are easily replaced, but if your permanent links are not of an appropriate performance grade, the only alternatives are to replace them or use another protocol. In the example just given, you could conceivably switch to 100Base-T4, which uses all four pairs of Category 3 cable, instead of using 100Base-TX, which requires two pairs of Category 5. The change would require different network-interface cards, but the relatively minor inconvenience and expense may be preferable to completely reinstalling the cable plant.

Excessive attenuation can also be caused by other components that are of an inferior grade, such as connectors or punch-down blocks. Fortunately, these are generally easier to replace than the entire cable.

Environmental factors, such as a conductor stretched during installation or a high-heat environment, also cause excessive attenuation.

Excessive NEXT

Near-end crosstalk is a major problem that can have many different causes, including the following:

Inferior cable   Cables not of the grade required for a protocol can produce excessive crosstalk levels. The only solution is to replace the cable with the appropriate grade.

Inferior components   All the components of a cable run should be rated at the same grade, including all connectors. Using Category 3 connectors on a Category 5 network can introduce excessive crosstalk and other problems. Replace inferior components with those of the correct grade.

Improper patch cables   Replace inappropriate cables with twisted-pair patch cables that are rated the same as your permanent links. Silver-satin patch cables used for telephone systems may appear at first to work with data connections, but the wire pairs in these cables are not twisted, and the main reason for twisting them is to minimize crosstalk.

Split pairs   Incorrect pinouts that cause data-carrying wires to be twisted together result in additional crosstalk, even when both ends are wired in the same way. Split pairs can be the result of mistakes during the installation or the use of the USOC pinouts. The solution is to reattach the connectors at both ends using either the T568A or T568B pinouts.

Couplers   Using couplers to join short lengths of cable generates more NEXT than using a single cable segment of the appropriate length. Use one

12-foot patch cable (for example) instead of two 6-foot cables joined with a coupler. When repairing broken permanent links, pull a new length of cable rather than using couplers to join the broken ends together.

Twisting   The individual wire pairs of every Category 5 cable must be twisted up to a point no further than 0.5 inches (13mm) from any connector. If the wires are too loosely twisted, reattach the connectors, making sure that all of the wire pairs are twisted tightly.

Sharing cables   Many network protocols use only two of the four wire pairs in a standard twisted-pair cable, so some people believe they can utilize the other two pairs for voice traffic or some other application. They shouldn't, however, because other signals running over the same cable can cause additional NEXT. The problem may be difficult to diagnose in these cases because the crosstalk only occurs when the other application is using the other wire pairs, such as when the user is talking on the phone. If two pairs in a wire are used for another application, you must install new cabling for one application or the other so that they will no longer share a cable.

Excessive Noise

The potential for noise generated by outside sources should be considered during the planning phase of a network installation. Cables should be routed away from AC power lines, light fixtures, electric motors, and other sources of EMI and RFI. Sometimes outside noise sources can be difficult to detect. You may, for example, test your cables immediately after you install them and detect no excess noise from outside sources and then find during later testing that your network performance is severely degraded by noise. It is entirely possible that a new source of interference has been introduced into the environment, but you also have to consider that your original tests may not have been valid.

If you installed and tested the cable plant during nights and weekends, your tests for outside noise may have generated all pass ratings because some sources of noise were not operating. When lights and machinery are turned on Monday morning, noise levels could be excessive. Always test your cable runs in the actual environmental conditions in which they'll be used.

If, after cable installation, a new source generates excessive noise levels, you must either move the cables and source away from each other or replace the UTP cables with STP or fiber-optic cables.

Creating a Request for Proposal (RFP)

All journeys begin with a single step. In the case of a telecommunications infrastructure and/or hardware project that is not performed in-house, that first step is the creation of the *Request for Proposal* (RFP). The RFP is essential to the success of your telecommunications-infrastructure project.

Anyone who rushes into a project without a clear view of what he or she needs to accomplish is foolish. A vendor who accepts a job without a clear definition of the work to be performed is also a fool. The RFP is essential for setting the pace of a project that is going to involve both a client and an outside vendor. You may choose to write your own RFP, or you may choose to hand the entire cabling design project and RFP generation over to a specialized consulting company. Another option is to work with the consulting company but do much of the groundwork beforehand. Any of these three choices still requires that you have a good knowledge of generating an RFP.

The consulting companies that can perform the steps documented in this chapter are made up of experts in their field and can save you time and money. However, for installations smaller than a few hundred locations, you may not need a consulting company to prepare an RFP.

What Is a Request for Proposal?

The Request for Proposal (RFP) is essential for defining what you want designed and built for the physical layer of your voice and data networks. An improperly constructed physical layer will contribute to poor reliability and poor performance.

NOTE   Though certainly medium- and large-scale projects will require an RFP, smaller projects (a few dozen cabling runs) on which you're working with a trusted vendor do not require one.

The RFP sets the tone for the entire cabling-infrastructure project. The best way to think of an RFP is as a combination of a guidebook, map, and rulebook. It clearly articulates the project, goals, expectations, and terms of engagement between the parties. In addition, for it to serve your best interests, it must be designed to be fair to all parties involved. A well-thought-out and well-written RFP goes a very long way toward ensuring the success of the project. On the other hand, a poorly thought out and badly written RFP can make your project a nightmare.

Having been on both sides of the fence, we have seen the influence that the RFP has on both parties and upon the overall success of an effort. One of the mistakes that we have seen made is that the buyer and vendor often see the RFP as a tool with which to take advantage of the other party. This is most unfortunate because it sets the stage for an adversarial relationship right from the beginning.

WARNING   The RFP can ensure a successful relationship with your vendor and the successful completion of your cabling project. Unfortunately, some see it as a tool for taking advantage of the other party. We do *not* recommend using an RFP in this way!

The best way to prevent such a scenario from occurring is by making sure that the RFP clearly describes the scope of the project, the buyer's requirements and expectations of the vendor, and the responsibilities of all parties involved. Because it is to be used as a rule book, it must be designed to promote fairness.

To create that type of RFP, you or your consulting company must do much legwork to ensure that many of the issues associated with the effort are identified, defined, addressed, and properly articulated in the RFP document. That preplanning often involves many people.

It is important to remember that although the project involves the installation of technology, it involves many departments outside of the technology group, perhaps including management, finance, facility management, and legal departments as well as the departments getting the new network.

Before we get into some of the nuts-and-bolts aspects of creating the RFP, we'll talk about what the goal of the project should be.

What Do We Want in Life?

The goal of every RFP should be the creation of an infrastructure that satisfies the needs of the organization today while being flexible enough to handle the emerging technologies of tomorrow. Everyone wants a system that they do not have to upgrade every time they need to install a faster piece of hardware or advanced application. In addition, no one wants to spend megabucks on their infrastructure, upgrading it every $1\frac{1}{2}$ years to keep pace with industry advancements.

The goal of every RFP should also be to create an infrastructure that appears to be invisible. Wouldn't it be nice if an IT cabling infrastructure could be as invisible as electrical wiring? Think about your electrical wiring for just a second; when was the last time you had to upgrade it because you upgraded your LAN hardware?

Or when did you have to add additional breakers to your electrical panel because you wanted to plug in another lamp or another computer? And did you have to put in new electrical wiring when you upgraded from 10Base-T to 100Base-TX?

Well, the good news is that with the proper planning and design, your communication infrastructure can become virtually invisible—thanks to the many advances within the infrastructure segment of the telecommunications and information industries within the last five years. It is also now possible to create customized cabling configurations that can and should become standard throughout every type of office in every site within your organization.

Perhaps the best part is that the potential system will not limit the types of data-communications hardware purchased or the pool of infrastructure contractors from which you can invite to bid on the installation. It can also be flexible enough to satisfy everyone's needs. Sounds like a pipe dream, doesn't it? Well, it isn't. A well-designed, well-engineered, and well-installed infrastructure becomes the "enabler" for the rest of your applications and future technology requirements.

Developing a Request for Proposal

Developing the RFP involves quite a bit of work, depending on the size of both the project and your organization. The first part of the development process involves analyzing exactly what your current and future needs are. Along with this, you must determine any restrictions and constraints that may be placed upon the system you will install.

Once you know what your needs are and the factors that will constrain you, the next phase is to design the system and determine the components you will need. Once you have the system design and know what components will be necessary, you can proceed with putting together the RFP.

The Needs Analysis

Many people will be involved in the needs analysis, the most important step in creating an RFP, and you must be thorough. One of the reasons this step is important is because you can use this opportunity to establish "buy-in" from others in your organization.

For the sake of this discussion, we must assume that the infrastructure project being planned is at least of medium-sized scope. As one who is in charge of such things, your task may be to handle a simple 20-network node expansion. Then again, perhaps you have been given the task of overseeing and implementing an organization-wide infrastructure installation or upgrade involving hundreds of users located in multiple sites. In either scenario, the same basic approaches should be taken.

The objective of the needs analysis is to define the specific project. The needs analysis should involve anyone who will be affected by the installation of the system. Depending on the size of your organization, some of the people you will want to solicit advice from include the following:

- Those who are responsible for any type of information technology that will be affected by your project

- The people in facilities and/or facilities management

- The electrician or electrical contractor

- Managers who can help you gain a better understanding of the long-term goals of the organization as they relate to information technology and facilities

Getting Input from Key Players

It is important to get input from upper management and the strategic planners within your organization so you can understand the types of technology-dependent services, applications, and efficiencies that they may require or need to have deployed in order to realize the company's goals.

Through these meetings, those who are responsible will define the scope of the project, the intent, deadlines, payment terms, bonding, and insurance issues.

All the solicitations of input may sound like overkill, but we can assure you they are not. You may be saying to yourself, "Why would I want to make my life even more miserable than it already is by inviting all of these people's opinions into my project?" You may be surprised, but by doing so you will, in fact, be making your life much easier. Plus, you will save yourself a great deal of time, money, and aggravation in the not-too-distant future. Trust us on this one: A little bit of self-induced insanity today will save you from stark-raving madness tomorrow.

All the people from whom you will solicit opinions are going to have an opinion anyway. Furthermore, it is safe to assume that these opinions will be communicated to you about two hours after it is too late to do anything reasonable about them. In addition, think of all the new friends you will make (just what you were looking for, we're sure)! Most of these people are just dying to tell you what to do and how to do it. By asking them for their opinion up-front, you are taking away their right to give you another one later. "Speak now or forever hold your peace" strictly applies here.

NOTE   One IT director we know held "town hall" meetings with her company's managers when she began planning the infrastructure for their new location. The meetings often demonstrated how quickly the managers rushed to protect their own fiefdoms, but the combination of all the managers discussing the infrastructure needs also generated new ideas and requirements that she had not previously thought of.

Most important, though, is that scheduling meetings with these folks will help you understand the organization's overall needs from a variety of vantage points. The information and the understanding you receive will help you to get through the process. For instance, perhaps the facilities folks have information that, once conveyed to you and the wiring contractors, will lower the project cost and/or eliminate change orders and cost overruns. Or perhaps the in-house electrician or telephone department is planning an installation in the same buildings during the same time frame, which would allow you to combine efforts and create efficiencies that would save time, money, and work. And finally, getting feedback from upper management about their long-range plans could prevent you from being hit with a new imaging-application rollout that will require "only" one more UTP circuit to be installed to every outlet location you just paid to have cabled!

You'd be surprised at some of details that we have unearthed from employers and clients during the initial cabling-system planning meetings. Some of these details would have caused time, money, and effort to be wasted if they had not been revealed, including:

- An entire wing of a building was to be renovated three months after the new cable was to have been installed.

- Major expansion was planned in six months, and an area that currently had only a few workstation locations would be accommodating several dozen additional sales people.

- A departmental restructuring was taking place, and an entire group of people was going to be moved to a new location.

- The local building codes did not allow any data, voice, or electrical cabling in the plenum unless it was in conduit.

- Telecommunications infrastructure designs had to be approved by a registered, professional engineer, as required by the state in which the customer was located.

- A new phone-switch and voicemail system was being purchased and would also have to be cabled shortly after the data-cabling project. Management mistakenly viewed this as a separate project.

- In a law firm, all the attorneys were going to be given a notebook computer in addition to their desktop computers. These notebook computers would require network access while the attorneys were in their offices. So each attorney's office would require two network connections.

- A new photocopier tracking system was to be installed that would require cabling to a tracking computer located in the computer room. In addition, these new photocopiers were going to function as network devices and would require their own Ethernet connections.

- Management wanted all offices of managers and senior project personnel, as well as conference rooms, to have cable-TV hookups.

In each of these cases, prior to the initial meetings, we thought we had a pretty good idea of what the company was planning to do. The additional information was helpful (and sometimes vital) to the successful installation of the new cabling installation.

The Bonus: Getting Buy-In   In addition to gaining pertinent information, your wisely inclusive communication will get you "buy-in" on your project. In other words, if you show respect to the people involved by bringing them into the loop, many of them will feel a part of what is going on and (you hope) won't fight against it.

We must issue a warning here, however! You are the boss of the project and must remain so. If you let others control what you are responsible for, you have a recipe for disaster. No one gets a vote in Cableland. They need to know that they are involved in at best a benevolent dictatorship, and you are the dictator.

NOTE   Responsibility for a project and the authority to make the final decision on a project need to go hand-in-hand.

If the one who has authority over the project is not held responsible for the outcome, be prepared for disaster. For any project to have a chance of succeeding, authority and responsibility must be welded together.

Cabling @ Work: Questions to Ask When Gathering Information

You have the key players in a room, and you have outlined what your cabling project will entail. They may look at you with a "So what am I doing here?" expression on their faces. What are some of the key questions that you may want to ask them? Here is a list of our favorites:

- How long is the company planning to occupy the space we are cabling?

- Will new technologies be implemented in the near or long term? These may include voice, data, video, network-attached PDAs, notebook computers, remote-controlled devices, security systems, and new photocopier technology.

- Will any new voice and data applications require fiber-optic cabling? What type of fiber-optic cable do these applications require?

- What electrical-code requirements and building requirements will influence the data-communications cabling?

- Are the telecommunications closets properly grounded?

- Are there installation time requirements? Will the areas that need to be worked in be accessible only during certain hours? Are they accessible on weekends and at night? Will the installation personnel have to work around existing office furniture and/or employees?

- Do building-security requirements exist for contract personnel working in the areas in question? Are there places that contractors must be escorted?

- Does the contractor have to be unionized? Will any areas of the installation be affected by union rules, such as the loading dock and elevators?

- Are there plans to move to faster networking technologies, such as 100Base-TX, 155Mbps ATM, 622Mbps ATM, or Gigabit Ethernet?

- How many work area outlets should be installed? (You may have your own opinions on this, but it is a good idea to hear others' thoughts on the matter.)

Continued on next page

- If they are not already, should the voice and data cabling infrastructures be combined?

- What insurance should the contractor carry? Should he or she be bonded? Licensed? Certified?

- Will construction or rewiring affect any deadlines?

- Will the contractor have to access any areas of the building that are not part of your leased space (e.g., entrance facilities and telecommunications closets)?

- Will the company be providing parking and working space (e.g., storage space, office, telephone, fax, etc.) for the contractor and his or her employees?

- If the organization spans multiple floors of a single building, is space available in the risers (conduits between floors) to accommodate additional cables? If not, who will have to give approval for new risers to be drilled?

- If the organization spans multiple buildings, how will the cable (usually fiber) be connected between buildings?

These are all questions that you would want to know the answers to if you were writing an RFP or if you were a contractor responding to an RFP. Your newfound friends may answer some of these questions, and you may have to answer others.

Designing the Project for the RFP

Once you have completed the needs analysis of your project, you should be prepared to enter into the design phase. Although much of the design may be left up to the contractor whom you choose to install your system, many of the design-related questions should be answered in the RFP. This may seem a bit intimidating to the uninitiated, but we assure you that if you divide the project into small bite-sized (or "byte-sized," if you don't mind the pun) pieces, you will conquer the task. Even the largest and most intimidating projects become manageable when broken into small tasks.

Components of a Cabling Infrastructure

The first step in dividing the project is to identify the four major subsystems of a cabling infrastructure. These are the telecommunications closets, the backbone cabling, the horizontal cabling, and the work-area components. These and other subsystems are described by the ANSI/TIAEIA-568-A Standard and are discussed in more detail in Chapter 2. Within each of these categories are several components.

NOTE

When designing cabling systems, you should conform to a known standard. In the United States, the standard you should use is the ANSI/TIAEIA-568-A Commercial Building Telecommunications Cabling Standard. (This Standard is expected to be updated as ANSI/TIAEIA-568-B.) In Europe and other parts of the world, the ISO/IEC 11801 Generic Cabling for Customer Premises standard is the one to use. Most other countries in the world have adopted one of these Standards as their own, but they may call it something different.

Backbone Cabling The backbone (a.k.a. vertical, trunking, or riser) cabling connects the telecommunications closets (TC) with the equipment room; the equipment room is where the central phone and data equipment is located. Although the ANSI/TIAEIA-568 Standard allows for an intermediate telecommunications closet, we don't recommend these for data applications. Telecommunications closets should be connected to the equipment room via backbone cabling in hub-and-spoke manner.

Many RFPs will leave the determination of the number of cables and pairs up to the company that responds to the RFP; the responding company will figure out the number of pairs and feeder cables based on requirements you supply for voice and data applications. Other RFP authors will specify exactly how many cables and multipair cables must be used. The decision is up to you, but if you have little experience specifying backbone capacity, you may want to leave the decision to a professional. Some decisions that you may have to make with respect to backbone cable include the following:

- The number of multipair copper cables that must be used for voice applications.

- How many strands of fiber must be used between closets for data and voice applications.

- Whether single-mode or multimode fiber-optic cable will be used. Most data applications use multimode fiber, though some newer voice and applications use single-mode fiber.

- Whether any four-pair UTP cable (Category 5, 5e, or 6) will be installed as backbone cabling.

NOTE

Backbone sizing can be tricky. If you are not careful, you will incorrectly calculate the backbone capacity you need. If you are not sure of the exact capacity you require, leave it to the contractor to specify the right amount.

Telecommunications Closets   Still more decisions must be made about the telecommunications closet. Some of these decisions will be yours to make, and someone else in your organization will make other decisions. Here are some points about telecommunications closets that you may need to think about:

- If the telecommunications closet is to house electrical equipment, the room should be environmentally conditioned (temperature and humidity need to be maintained at acceptable levels).

- Appropriate grounding for racks and equipment has to exist. This is often the responsibility of the electrician. Don't ignore good grounding rules. Consult ANSI/TIAEIA-607 and the NEC for more information. If the closets are not grounded properly, you need to know who will be responsible for installing grounding.

- Sufficient space and lighting need to be provided so that all necessary equipment can be installed and people can be in the closet working on it.

- Backup power or uninterruptible power supplies (UPSs) should be installed in the telecommunications closets.

- Proper access should be given to information-technology personnel. However, the closets should be secure to prevent unwanted tampering or data theft.

  The typical telecommunications closet is going to include components such as the following:

- Punch-down blocks for voice. Some punch-down blocks can be used to cross-connect data circuits, but they are generally not recommended.

- Wall space, if you are going to use punch-down blocks (they are usually mounted on plywood that is mounted to the wall).

- Patch panels for copper and fiber circuits. It is a good practice to separate the patch panels used for data applications from the patch panels used for voice applications.

- Racks, cabinets, and enclosures for patch panels, telecommunication gear, UPSs, LAN hubs, etc. Shelves for the racks and cabinets are often forgotten on RFPs and in the initial design. Don't forget extra mounting hardware for the racks, cabinets, and enclosures.

- Wire-management equipment used on the walls and on the racks. These are also often forgotten during the initial design phase. Good wire-management practice means that the telecommunications closets will be cleaner and easier to troubleshoot.

- Patch cables for the copper and fiber-optic patch panels and hubs. These are the most commonly forgotten components on RFPs. Make sure that the patch cables match the category of cable that you use. ANSI/TIAEIA-568-A allows for patch cables up to six meters (20 feet) in the telecommunications closet; however, if you don't need cables that long, you should use only the length necessary. You may want to order varying lengths of patch cables to keep things neat and untangled.

Horizontal Cabling   The horizontal cabling, sometimes called the distribution cabling, runs from the telecommunications closet to the work area. The horizontal cabling is a component most often planned incorrectly. Cabling contractors know this and will often bid extremely low on the overall cost of a job so that they can get the follow-on work of adds, moves, and changes. This is because running single runs of horizontal cable is far more costly than installing many runs of cable at once. To save yourself future unnecessary costs, make sure that you plan for a sufficient amount of horizontal cable.

Some of the components you will have to think about when planning your horizontal cable include:

- How much cable should run between each work area and a telecommunications closet? ANSI/TIAEIA-568-A recommends either a minimum of one UTP and one fiber cable or two UTP cables. In an all-UTP environment, we recommend running four UTP cables to each work area.

- What category of UTP cable should be run? Most telephone applications today will use Category 3 cabling; 10Base-T Ethernet will also run on Category 3 cable. Faster Ethernet and other twisted-pair technologies require at least Category 5 cabling. A minimum of Category 5e is recommended.

- If using fiber-optic cable, what type of fiber cable should you use and how many pairs should you run to each work area? Typically, two pairs of multimode fiber-optic cable are used for horizontal cable, but this will depend on the applications in use and the number of data connections to be installed at each location. Care should be taken to ensure that no applications require single-mode fiber-optic cable.

- Per ANSI/TIAEIA-568-A, the maximum distance that horizontal cable can extend (not including patch cables and cross-connects) is 90 meters (285 feet).

- Should you use some type of "shared-sheath" cabling for horizontal cabling? For example, since 10Base-T only uses two pairs of a four-pair cable, some network managers decide to use the other two pairs for an additional 10Base-T connection or a telephone connection. We *strongly discourage* the use of a shared sheath for data applications. All four pairs should be terminated in a single eight-position outlet for future applications.

Work Area   The final major area is the work area, which includes the wall plates, user patch cables, and user equipment. The work area can also include adapters such as baluns that modify the cable impedance. Many design issues relating to the work area will revolve around the choice of wall plates. Here are some points to think about relating to the work area:

- Know what type of wall plates you will use. The wall plate must have sufficient information outlets to accommodate the number of horizontal cables you use. Many varieties of modular wall plates on the market will accommodate fiber, copper, video, audio, and coaxial modules in the same plates. See Chapter 8 for more information.

- For UTP cabling, the connecting hardware must also match the category of UTP cable you use.

- For fiber-optic cable, the wall plate and connector types must match the cable type you use and the requirements for the station cables (station patch cables) and fiber-optic connector types.

- Don't forget to estimate the number of patch cables you will need, and include this in the RFP. ANSI/TIAEIA-568-A specifies a maximum length for patch cables of three meters (10 feet). UTP patch cables should be stranded copper cable and should match the category of cable used throughout the installation.

- Though not as common now as they were a few years ago, impedance-changing devices such as baluns might be necessary. Make sure that you have specified these in your cabling RFP if they are not being provided elsewhere.

How Much Is Enough?

Now that the categories and their components have been identified, the next order of business is to determine how much of these items will be needed. This is when you will begin to realize the benefits of the needs analysis that you performed. The size and components of your infrastructure are always based upon the immediate needs of your organization coupled with a factoring in of "realistic" future needs.

Wall Plates and Information Outlets   When designing a cabling infrastructure, always start from the desktop and work backward. For instance, an accurate
count of the number of people and their physical locations will determine the
minimum number of information outlets that will be needed and where they will
be installed.

KEY TERMS   **Wall Plates and Information Outlets**   Depending on the design of the wall
plate, a single wall plate can accommodate multiple *information outlets*. An information outlet can accommodate voice, data, or video applications.

Some IT and cabling professionals will automatically double this minimum
number in order to give themselves room to grow. Our experience with information outlets is that, once you have your cabling system in place, you never seem
to have enough. With wall plates in particular, there never seems to be one close to
where you want to put phones and data equipment. Here are some ideas that
may help you to plan information outlets:

- Don't forget locations such as network-printer locations and photocopier
  locations.

- In some larger offices, it may be helpful to install two wall plates at each
  location on opposite walls. This keeps the station patch-cable lengths to a
  minimum and also helps keep cable clutter to a minimum, as cables would
  not have to cross the entire length of a large office.

- Special-use rooms, such as conference rooms and war rooms, should be cabled
  with at least one wall plate identical to one in a typical workstation area.

- Training rooms should have at least four more information outlets than you
  anticipate needing.

- Use extreme caution when cabling to locations outside of your organization's
  office space, such as to a shared conference room; it may allow outsiders to
  access your data and voice systems. Although it may seem unlikely, we have
  seen it happen.

Backbone and Horizontal Cabling   The number of information outlets
required and their wall-plate locations will determine the sizing of your horizontal cables (fiber strands and copper pairs) as well as the size and placement of
your main distribution frame (MDF) and any required intermediate distribution

frames (IDFs). The applications to be run and accessed at the desktop determine the types of cables to be installed and the number of circuits needed at each wall-plate location.

Some RFPs merely provide the numbers of wall plates and information outlets per wall plate and leave the rest of the calculations up to the cabling contractor. Other RFPs don't even get this detailed and expect the contractor to gather this information during his or her walk-through. Our preference is to have this information readily available to the contractor prior to the walk-through and site survey. The less ambiguous you are and the more you put into writing, the easier your job and your contractor's job will be. Information about wall plates and information outlets has to be gathered and documented by someone; you are the person who has to live with the results. Always remain open-minded to contractor's suggestions for additional locations, though.

Cabling @ Work: Putting Data Cables in Places You Would Never Imagine

A few years ago during a hotel's remodeling project, the hotel wired only the minimum locations required to install its new local area network. Later that year during a phone-system upgrade, the hotel had to rewire each room.

Shortly after that, this hotel decided to offer in-room fax machines and additional telephones on additional lines. Each room had to have additional cabling installed. Now the hotel is again succumbing to the pressures of the traveling businessperson and is installing 10Base-T Internet connections. At the same time, it is wiring its restaurants and retail locations for Category 5e cabling because its new cash-register system uses 10Base-T network connections.

Though no precise figures have been calculated to see exactly how much would have saved by doing the entire job at one time, estimates indicate that the 400-room hotel could have saved as much $80,000 by performing all the cabling infrastructure work at the same time.

Rules for Designing Your Infrastructure

As you gather information and start planning the specifics of your cabling infrastructure, keep in mind our rules outlined here. Some of these result from our own experiences, and cabling and information-technology professionals have contributed others to us:

- Think "flexibility" and design accordingly. You will always find more uses and have more requirements of your infrastructure than you are seeing today. Technology changes and organizations change; be prepared.

- Create organizational standards and stick to them. Define the different outlet types that exist in your facility. For instance, those in the accounting department may need fewer circuits than those in operations, and operations may need a different configuration than those in sales. Once you determine the various types of configurations required, standardize them and commit to installing the same configuration throughout the particular department. On the other hand, you may decide that it makes sense to give *everyone* the same configuration. Some companies shift employees and departments around frequently, so this approach may be better suited to such an environment. Whatever you do, standardize one option or another and stick to it. Doing so will make troubleshooting, ordering of parts, and moves, adds, and changes (MACs) much less confusing.

- Use modular wall plates. Buy a wall plate that has more "openings" than circuits installed at the location. If you install two cables, buy wall plates that have three or four ports. The cost difference is minimal, and you will preserve your investment in the event extra cables are installed or activated.

- Never install any UTP cable that is not at least Category 5–rated. For data applications, Category 3 is dead. You should even strongly consider installing an enhanced cable such as Category 5e, if your budget will allow. Three things in life never change: death, taxes, and the need for more bandwidth.

- Always install one more cable at each location than is going to be immediately used. If your budget is tight, you may choose not to terminate or test the circuit or not to add the necessary patch-panel ports, but do try to install the extra "pipe." Invariably, organizations find a use for that extra circuit. That cable will also enable you to quickly respond to any late special-connectivity needs with minimal cost and disruption.

- Use wire management above and below each patch panel. A neat patch panel begets a neat patch field. A messy patch field begets trouble.

- Make sure your connectors, patch cables, patch panels, and wall jacks are rated the same as your cable. Category 5 for Category 5. Category 5e for Category 5e. The same should hold true for installation practices.

- If you venture into the world of Category 6 cabling systems, remember that they are not standardized as of this writing. Further, vendor claims about the performance of these cables may be true only if you use all components from the same vendor or from a vendor alliance that includes cable and connectivity components.

- Label the circuits at the wall plate and at the patch panel. Although some people feel it is important to label the cable itself, do so only if it does not increase the cost of the cabling installation.

- Never underinstall fiber strands. *Never, ever, ever* install only two strands of fiber-optic cable between telecommunications closets and the equipment room! Install only four strands if you have no money at all. You must try to install a minimum of six or eight strands. Much convergence is occurring in the low-voltage industries—alarm systems, HVAC systems, and CCTV (Closed Circuit Television), CATV, and satellite video systems are all using digital information and running on fiber backbones. The installation of additional fiber beyond your current data needs could make you a hero the next time an alarm system or HVAC system is upgraded. Remember *Field of Dreams*: Build it, and they will come.

- Include a few strands (four or eight strands) of single-mode fiber with your multimode fiber backbone. Even if you do not see the need for it today, put it in. To save money, you may choose not to terminate or test it, but it should be part of your backbone. Video applications and multimode's inability to handle some of the emerging higher bandwidth and faster-moving data applications makes this a very smart bet.

- Oversize your voice/copper backbone by a minimum of 10 to 25 percent if you can afford it. A safe way to size your voice copper trunk is to determine the maximum number of telephone stations you anticipate you will need. Determine the number of voice locations that will be fed from each closet and then size your voice backbone to reflect 2.5 pairs per station fed. For example, in the case of a closet that will feed a maximum of 100 telephone stations, you should install 250 pairs.

- Test and document all copper distribution. If you install Category 5e cable and components, insist upon 100 percent Category 5e compliance on all copper distribution circuits. All conductors of all circuits must pass. More sophisticated UTP cable testers provide printed test results; you should obtain and keep the test results from each location. Some testing software packages will allow you to keep these in a database. Tests should be reviewed prior to acceptance of the work. Note, though, that if you ask for Category 5e cable testing for each circuit, it may increase the cost of the overall installation.

- Test and document all fiber backbone cable. Bidirectional attenuation testing using a power meter is sufficient for LAN applications. (*Bidirectional* refers to testing each strand by shooting the fiber from the MDF to the IDF and then shooting the fiber from the IDF to the MDF.) Testing should be done at both 850nm and 1300nm on multimode fiber. Much has been made of the need to use an OTDR (optical time domain reflectometer) to test fiber; however, this is overkill. The key factor in the functionality of the fiber backbone is attenuation. The use of an OTDR increases the cost of testing significantly while providing nonessential additional information.

- Document the infrastructure on floor plans. Once this is done, maintain the documentation and keep it current. Accurate documentation is an invaluable troubleshooting and planning tool. Show the outlet location and use a legend to identify the outlet types. Differentiate between these:

  - Data only, voice only, and voice/data locations

  - Each circuit at that location (by number)

  - All MDF and IDF locations

  - Backbone cable routings

Although there is more to designing a telecommunications infrastructure system, the information in this section provides some basic guidelines that should help to remove some of the mystery.

Writing the RFP

If you have been successful at gathering information and asking the right questions, you are ready to start writing your RFP. Although no *exact* guideline exists for writing an RFP, this section provides a list of suggested guidelines. (We have also included a sample RFP at the end of this chapter.) By following these steps, you will be able to avoid many mistakes that could become very costly during the course of the project and/or the relationship.

Remember, though, regardless of how much ink is used to spell out expectations, the spirit of the agreement under which everyone operates really works to make a project successful.

Including the Right Content in the RFP

Will the RFP accurately specify what you want? To ensure that it does, take the following steps:

- Educate yourself about the components of the system to be specified and some of the options available to you.

- Evaluate specific desired features and functionality of the proposed system, required peripherals, interfaces, and expectations for life cycle and warranty period.

- Solicit departmental/organizational input for desired features, requirements, and financial considerations.

- Determine the most cost-efficient solution for one-year, three-year, and even perhaps five-year projections.

- Evaluate unique applications (wireless, voice messaging, fiber, etc.) and their transmission requirements, and departmental or operational requirements and restraints that could impact those applications.

- Analyze perceived versus actual needs for features and functionality, future applications, system upgradability, etc.

- Define contractor qualifications. Strongly consider requirements that call for vendors to be certified by the infrastructure component manufacturer whose products they are proposing to install. The same holds true for hardware bids. It is important that any vendor selling hardware be an authorized reseller for the hardware manufacturer. Call for proof of each certification and authorization as part of the initial bid submittal.

- Prepare a draft outline of selected requirements and acceptable timelines (which is subject to minor changes by mutual agreement).

- Define project milestones and completion dates. Milestones include bid conference dates, walk-through dates, dates to submit clarifications, final bid due, acceptance dates, project-start dates, installation milestones, etc.

- Include in the RFP sections on scope of work, testing acceptance, proposed payment schedules, liquidated damages (damages to be paid in the event of default), restoration, licensing, permits fees, milestone dates, etc.

- Call for all pricing to be in an itemized format, listing components and quantities to be installed and unit and extended prices.

- Request that costs to add or delete circuits—on a per circuit basis—be included in the response to the RFP.

- Include detailed language addressing the "intent" of the bid. Such language should articulate that the intent is to have a system installed that contains all of the components necessary to create a fully functional system. Language should be included that calls for the contractors to address at time of contract completion any omissions in the bid that would prohibit the system from being fully functional.

- Ask for references from similar jobs.

- Make sure to allow for adequate time for detailed site survey/estimating.

- Upon receipt of bids, narrow field to three finalists and do the following:

  - Correlate information and prioritize or rank the three remaining bids on cost versus performance. Don't get hung up on costs. If a bid seems too good to be true, it may be. Examine the vendor's qualifications and the materials they are specifying.

  - Schedule meetings and/or additional surveys for best-and-final bids from remaining vendors.

  - Specify that the RFP is the intellectual property of the client and should not be distributed. Though this won't stop an unscrupulous vendor from passing around information about your infrastructure, you have instructed them not to. One consulting company we know of actually assigns each vendor's copy of the RFP a separate number that appears on the footer of each page.

What Makes a Good RFP?

Does a good RFP have many pages (did you do in a few trees printing it)? Can you take advantage of the contractor? These are *not* good benchmarks for determining if your RFP will help to create a good working relationship between yourself and the company that you contract. You may want to ask yourself the following questions about the RFP you are generating:

- Is it fair?

- Does it ensure that only competent bidders will meet the contractor qualifications?

- Is it nondiscriminatory?

- Does it communicate the objectives and the wishes of the client clearly and accurately?

- Does it provide protection to both the client and the service provider?

- Does it provide opportunities for dialog between the parties (e.g., mandatory site walk-throughs, regular progress meetings, etc.)?

- Does it clearly state all deadlines?

- Does it define payment terms?

- Does it define the relationship of the parties?

- Does it address change-order procedures?

Distributing the RFP and Managing the Vendor-Selection Process

Once the RFP has been written, you may think you are home free. However, the next step is just as important as the creation of the RFP: You will then be ready to distribute the RFP to prospective vendors and begin the vendor-selection process.

Distributing RFPs to Prospective Vendors

If you worked with an infrastructure consultant on your RFP, that person may already have a list of contractors and vendors that you can use to fulfill your vendor needs. Many of these vendors may have already been tried and tested by your consultant. However, if you have developed your own RFP, you will need to find prospective vendors to whom you can distribute your RFP for bids.

How do you find the vendors? We suggest the following ways:

- Ask IT professionals from companies similar to yours for a list of vendors they have used for cabling.

- If you are a member of a users group or any type of professional organization, ask for vendor suggestions at your next group meeting.

- If you work with a systems-integration company, ask your contact at that company for one or more vendor recommendations. Chances are good that the contact has worked with vendors in the past that can respond to your RFP.

- Consult your phone-system (PBX) vendor. Many phone-system companies have a division that does cabling.

- If you have a contact at the telephone company, consult that person for suggestions.

As you distribute RFPs to potential vendors, be prepared to schedule vendor meetings and site inspections. For a cabling installation that involves approximately 500 to 2,000 nodes, you can expect to spend at least one full day in meetings and on-site inspections for each vendor to whom you submit the cabling RFP.

Vendor Selection

When reviewing the proposals you get, you may be tempted to simply pick the lowest-cost proposal. However, we recommend that you select a vendor based upon criteria that include, but are not limited to, the following:

- Balance between cost and performance

- Engineering design and innovative solutions

- Proven expertise in projects of similar scope, size, and complexity

- Quality craftsmanship

- Conformance with all appropriate codes, ordinances, articles, and regulations

Check references. Ask not only about the quality of work but about the quality of a relationship the reference had with the specific vendor and whether the vendor completed all tasks on time.

Insist on a detailed warranty of a system's life cycle. Consider the ability to perform and any other requirements deemed necessary to execute the intent of contract.

Present a detailed description of work to be performed, payment agreements, and compliance with items contained in the RFP. Include this in the contract.

Identify key project personnel from both sides of the agreement, including the staff associated with accountability/responsibility for making decisions.

> **NOTE**   Once you have selected a vendor, promptly send letters or place phone calls to the rejected vendors. We agree that it is hard to tell vendors they have not been accepted, but it is worse if they hear about it through the grapevine or if they have to call you to find out.

Project Administration

After accepting the RFP, you are ready for the next phase of your installation challenge, the project-administration phase. This phase is no less critical than the others are. Here are some tips we have found to be helpful during an infrastructure deployment:

- Schedule regular progress meetings. Progress reports should be submitted and compared to project milestones. Accountability should be assigned, with scheduled follow-up and resolution dates.

- Make sure that the contractor supervises 100 percent of the quality inspections of work performed. Cable-certification reports should be maintained and then submitted at progress meetings.

- Make sure that the contractor maintains and provides as-built documentation, the progress of which should be inspected at the regular progress meetings. The as-built documentation may include outlet locations, circuit numbers, telecommunications-closet locations, and backbone and distribution routing. Particular care should be taken to make sure this documentation is done properly, as it tends to slip through the cracks.

Cutover

If you install cabling in a location that you do not yet occupy, you do not have to be aware of cutover from an existing system. As long as the new cabling system is properly designed, it is relatively easy to move to the new system as you occupy the new location.

However, if you are supervising the installation for a location you do occupy, you will need to consider interoperability and the task of switching over to the new system. In a small system (less than 200 horizontal runs), the cutover may occur very quickly, but in medium to large systems, cutover can take days or weeks. Follow these guidelines:

- Cutover preparation should begin 5 to 15 days prior to the scheduled date, unless otherwise mutually agreed upon.

- Cutover personnel and backups should be designated and scheduled well in advance.

- Cutover personnel should have access to all records, diagrams, drawings, or other documentation prepared during the course of the project.

- Acceptance should begin at the completion of the cutover and could continue for a period of 5 to 10 working days prior to signing. The warranty should begin immediately upon signing of acceptance.

- Acceptance criteria should include 100 percent of all circuits installed. All circuits should pass specified performance tests, and that should be recorded in the project-history file and cable-management systems.

By following the guidelines, as appropriate to your particular situation, you can greatly reduce the chances of any aspect of your project spiraling out of control.

The final part of this chapter provides a sample of an RFP that has been successfully used in several projects in which we have been involved. Although we caution anyone from adopting an existing RFP without first doing a thorough analysis of his or her own specific needs, the following document can be a guide.

Technology Network Infrastructure Request for Proposal (A Sample RFP)

The following sample RFP, used for a school, may help you generate your own. It is suitable for small installations (fewer than 500 circuits). For larger installations, consider working with an infrastructure consultant. Remember, this document will probably not fit anyone's needs exactly.

General

The general section of this RFP includes contractor's requirements and defines the purpose of the RFP, the work that the RFP covers, and the RFP intent.

Contractor's Requirements

(a) The successful contractor must be a certified installer of the infrastructure components being provided and show proof thereof.

(b) The contractor must be an authorized reseller of the networking and infrastructure components quoted and show proof thereof.

(c) Work will be supervised by a registered communications distribution designer (RCDD) during all phases of the installation. An RCDD must be on-site and available to technicians and installers any time work is being performed.

Purpose of This RFP

(a) The purpose of the "Technology Network Infrastructure RFP" is to provide a functional specification for a comprehensive technology network system, including required network cabling and components and required network devices. The purpose of this is also to provide adequate details and criteria for the design of this technology network system.

(b) The contractor shall provide cables, network equipment, and components necessary to construct an integrated Local Area Networking infrastructure.

(c) The contractor shall be responsible for the installation of the technology network systems as defined in the "Cable Plant."

This document provides specifications to be used to design the installation of a networking infrastructure and associated equipment. The contractor shall furnish all labor, materials, tools, equipment, and reasonable incidental services necessary to complete an acceptable installation of the horizontal and riser data communications cabling plant. This is to include, but is not necessarily limited to, faceplates, modular jacks, connectors, data patch panels, equipment racks, cable, and fiber optics.

Work Included

Work shall include all components for both a horizontal and riser data cable plant from workstation outlet termination to wire-closet terminations. All cable-plant components, such as outlets, wiring-termination blocks, racks, patch cables, intelligent-hub equipment, etc., will be furnished, installed, and tested by this contractor. The data cable plant is designed to support a 100Mbps Ethernet computer network. The data cabling plant and components shall carry a manufacturer-supported 10-year performance warranty for data rates up to 100Mbps. The bidder must provide such manufacturer guarantee for the above requirements as part of the bid submission.

The scope of work includes all activities needed to complete the wiring described in this document and the drawings that will be made available during the mandatory walk-through.

Any and all overtime or off-hours work required to complete the scope of work within the time frame specified is to be included in the contractor's bid. No additional overtime will be paid.

The awarded contractor must instruct the owner's representative in all the necessary procedures for satisfactory operation and maintenance of the plant relating to the work described in their specifications and provide complete maintenance manuals for all systems, components, and equipment specified. Maintenance manuals shall include complete wiring diagrams, parts lists, etc. to enable the owner's representative to perform any and all servicing, maintenance, troubleshooting, inspection, testing, etc. as may be necessary and/or requested.

The contractor shall respond to trouble calls within twenty-four (24) hours after receipt of such a call considered not in need of critical service. Critical-service calls must be responded to on-site, within four hours of receipt of a trouble call. Bidder must acknowledge their agreement to this requirement as part of the RFP response.

All basic electronic equipment shall be listed by Underwriters Laboratories, Inc. The contractor shall have supplied similar apparatuses to comparable installations, rendering satisfactory service for at least three years where applicable.

The installation shall be in accordance with the requirements of the National Electrical Code, state and local ordinances, and regulations of any other governing body having jurisdiction.

The cable-system design is to be based on the ANSI/TIAEIA-568-A Commercial Building Telecommunications Cabling Standard and Bulletins TSB-36 and TSB-40. No deviation from the Standards and recommendations is permitted unless authorized in writing.

Intent

This network cable-system design will provide the connectivity of multiple microcomputers, printers, and/or terminals through a local area Network environment. Each designated network interface outlet will have a capacity to support the available protocols, asynchronous 10- and 100Mbps Ethernet, 4- and 16Mbps Token Ring, FDDI, etc., through the network cabling and topology specified. The school may select one or any combination of the aforementioned media and access protocol methods; therefore, the design and installation shall have the versatility required to allow such combinations.

It is the intent of this document to describe the functional requirements of the computer network and components that comprise the "Technology Network System." Bid responses must include all of the above, materials, appliances, and services of every kind necessary to properly execute the work and to cover the terms and conditions of payment thereof and to establish minimum acceptable requirements for equipment design and construction and contract performance to assure fulfillment of the educational purpose.

Cable Plant

The following section covers the installation of horizontal cabling, backbone cabling, cable pathways, fire-code compliance, wire identification, and distribution frames.

Horizontal Cable

The following requirements apply for horizontal cabling:

(a) Each classroom shall have two quad-outlet wall plates installed. Each of the four information outlets shall be terminated with eight-pin modular jacks (RJ-45). The wall plates will be placed on opposite walls. There are a total of 37 classrooms.

(b) The computer-skills classroom shall have 15 quad-outlet wall plates installed. Each will have four information outlets terminated using eight-pin modular jacks. Each wall plate will be located to correspond to a computer desk housing two computers. These locations will be marked on the blueprints supplied during the walk-through.

(c) Each administration office shall have one quad-outlet wall plate with four information outlets, each terminated using eight-pin modular jacks. There are 23 such office locations.

(d) Common administrative areas shall have one quad-outlet wall plate with four information outlets terminated with eight-pin modular jacks. There are 17 such common administrative areas.

(e) The school library shall have quad-outlet plates placed in each of the librarian work areas, the periodical desk, and the circulation desk. The student research area shall have two quad-outlet plates. Eight work areas total require quad outlets. The exact locations of where these are to be installed will be specified on the blueprints supplied during the walk-through.

(f) The school computer lab shall have 20 quad-outlet wall plates installed. The locations of these will be specified on the blueprints to be supplied during the walk-through.

(g) Horizontal cable shall never be open but rather will run through walls or be installed in the raceway if the cable cannot be installed in walls.

(h) The contractor is responsible for pulling, terminating, and testing all circuits being installed.

(i) The horizontal cable for the data network shall be twisted-pair wire specified as Category 5e by the ANSI/TIAEIA-568-A Standard and addenda and shall be UL-listed and verified. If required by fire codes, cable shall have fire-retardant and smoke-producing requirements of the National Electrical Code (NEC), Section 800-3(d) and Section 800-3(b), according to UL.

(j) Testing for the distribution components will comply with ANSI/TIAEIA-568-A Category 5e specifications and will certify 100 percent functionality of all conductors. All circuits must be tested and found to be in compliance with TSB-95. All testing results will be provided to customer in a hard copy and electronic Excel format.

(k) The data-cable specifications are intended to describe the minimum standard for use in the "Technology Network System." The use of higher-grade data cabling is recommended if such can be provided in a cost-effective manner.

(l) Each cable shall be assigned a unique cable number.

(m) In the telecommunications closet, the contractor shall install four separate color-coded patch panels. Each wall plate's information outlet shall use a different patch panel, and the wall-plate information outlets will be documented using the patch panel's color code and the patch-panel number.

(n) Wire management shall be employed in all telecommunications closets and the equipment room.

Data Backbone Cabling

The following specifications apply to the data backbone cabling:

(a) An ANSI/TIAEIA-568-A–compliant 62.5/125-micron multimode fiber-optic cable network is to be the backbone between the equipment room (the MDF) and any telecommunications (wiring) closets.

(b) All telecommunications closets shall have 12 strands of multimode fiber-optic cable between the telecommunications closet and the equipment room.

(c) All fiber must be FDDI- and 100Base-FX–compatible.

(d) All fibers are to be terminated using SC-type connectors.

(e) All fiber is to be installed in an innerduct from rack to rack. A 15-foot coil of fiber is to be safely and securely coiled at each rack. The contractor will be responsible for any drilling or core holes and sleeving necessitated by national, state, and/or local codes.

(f) The fiber-optic patch panels are to be configured to the amount of strands terminated at each location. Fiber-optic panels shall be metallic, are to have a lockable slack storage drawer that can pull out, and shall occupy one rack position.

(g) Testing of fibers will be done using a power meter. The tests will be conducted at 850nm and 1300nm, bidirectionally. All test results will be provided to the customer in hard-copy format.

Fire-Code Compliance

All cabling installed in the riser and horizontal distribution shall meet or exceed all local fire codes.

Wiring Pathways

The following are related to the installation of cable in plenum and other cable pathways:

(a) Cable pathway design should follow the ANSI/TIAEIA-569 (Commercial Buildings Standards for Telecommunications Pathways and Spaces) Standard.

(b) The methods used to run cable through walls, ceilings, and floor shall be subject to all state and local safety code and fire regulations. The contractor assumes all responsibility for ensuring that these regulations are observed.

(c) Cables shall be routed behind walls wherever possible. Surface-mount raceway shall be used where necessary.

(d) New cables shall be independently supported using horizontal ladders or other wire-suspension techniques. Cables shall not be allowed to lie on ceiling tiles or attached to electrical conduits.

(e) System layout shall restrict excessive cable lengths; therefore, routing of cables shall be in a manner as not to exceed 90 meters from device plate to patch panel located in MDF/IDF distribution rack in the assigned wiring closet. Each cable shall be home-run directly from the main distribution frame (MDF) or intermediate distribution frame (IDF) to the wall plate.

(f) Cables shall be terminated at the rear of the patch panel within the MDF or IDF and at the wall plates only. There shall be no splicing of any of the cables installed. Intermediate cross-connects and transition points are not allowed.

(g) The following are the minimum distances that Category 5e UTP shall be run from common sources of EMI.

EMI Source	Minimum Cable Separation
Fluorescent lighting	12 inches
Neon lighting	12 inches
Power cable 2 KVA or less	5 inches
Unshielded power cable over 2 KVA	39 inches
Transformers and motors	39 inches

Wiring Identification

All cables, wall jacks, and patch-panel ports shall be properly tagged in a manner to be determined at a later date. Each cable end must be identified within six inches from the termination point.

Telecommunications Closets

The following are related to the installation of the telecommunications (wiring) closets:

(a) The wiring closets to be used as the originating points for network cables that home-run to the room outlets are referred to as wire closets or telecommunications closets. They may also be referred to as main distribution frames (MDF) and intermediate distribution frames (IDF). All racks and their exact locations will be confirmed during the mandatory walk-through; their locations are specified on the blueprints that will be provided during the initial walk-through.

(b) Rack layout should provide enough space to accommodate the cabling, equipment racks, patch panels, and network-control equipment, as required. Additionally, the locations should provide for convenient access by operational personnel.

(c) All racks are to be configured as shown on the attached diagram, with all the fiber-optic cables at the top of the rack, the distribution below the fiber, and the hardware components mounted below the distribution patch panels.

(d) All racks, panels, and enclosures for mounting equipment shall meet 19-inch EIA mounting-width specifications. Each equipment rack should include two 19-inch rack shelves that can support the weight of a 50-pound uninterruptible power supply.

(e) Equipment racks shall be properly grounded to nearest building ground and must be properly attached to the floor and supporting wall by means of horizontal-rack bracket mount. All equipment racks must have a six-outlet 20-amp power strip with surge protection installed inside.

MDF/IDF Cable Management

The following relates to cable management for the main distribution frame (MDF) and intermediate distribution frame (IDF) in the equipment room and telecommunications closets:

(a) The contractor is required to install cable management on all racks installed. Cable management is to consist of horizontal management between each panel and vertical management on the sides of the rack.

(b) All cable management is to be of the "base-and-cover" style. Cable management is to be provided for the front of the rack only.

As-Built Diagrams

Contractor will provide as-built documentation within 15 days of completion of the project. These prints will include outlet locations, outlet numbers, MDF/IDF locations, trunk-cable routing, and legends for all symbols.

Network Hardware Specifications

The networking hardware should be provided, installed, and serviced through a certified reseller/integrator or direct from the manufacturer.

Bidding Process

All work is to be completed based on the dates from the attached schedule. Dates on the attached schedule include walk-through dates, bid-submission dates, and expected project-start and completion dates. Questions and comments are welcomed; prospective contractors are encouraged to submit these questions in writing.

Bid Submittals

The following are related to submittal of bids:

(a)   All bids are to be submitted in triplicate.

(b)   Each bid is to list all labor, material, and hardware costs in an itemized fashion. The detail is to include itemized unit pricing, cost per unit, and extended prices for each of the material and hardware components as well as the specific labor functions.

(c)   A cost, per outlet, to add or delete outlet locations is to be included in the pricing format. This cost is not to include any changes in hardware or patch-panel quantities.

(d)   There is also to be a scope of work provided that details all of the functions to be provided by the contractor for the project.

(e)   Quote optional Category 5e patch cables and station cables on a per-unit cost basis. List pricing for 3-foot, 5-foot, 7-foot, 9-foot, and 14-foot patch cables.

(f)   Quote optional network cutover assistance on a per-hour basis per technician.

Miscellaneous

All data found in this RFP and associated documents is considered to be confidential information. Further, data gathered as a result of meetings and walk-through visits is considered to be confidential information. This confidential information shall not be distributed outside of organizations directly related to the contractor without expressed, written approval.

Further, all data submitted by prospected contractors will be treated as confidential and proprietary; it will not be shared outside of the vendor-evaluation committee.

Cabling @ Work:
Experience from the Field

■ Hints and Guidelines

■ Case Studies

Throughout the research phase for this book, cabling installers related to us their experiences, hints, tips, and stories from the field. There is no substitute for advice and stories from people who have been in the trenches. Though some of the topics mentioned in this chapter are also mentioned elsewhere in the book, we felt it was important to reiterate them through people's experiences.

Much of this chapter is targeted toward the professional cable installer, but anyone installing cabling will find some helpful information here. First, we'll give you some guidelines about the business of cable installation, and then we'll include a handful of case studies drawn from our experience in the industry.

Hints and Guidelines

After a few years in the cabling business, you'll learn skills and approaches not specifically related to cabling technology, which will mark your work as professional. These skills and approaches will help you even if you're simply evaluating the work of others. They are described in the following sections.

Know What You Are Doing

Purchasing (and reading!) this book is a step in the right direction. You need to know more than just how to install cable, however. To design and implement a good cable plant for yourself or for a customer, you also need to know how networks are used and how they grow. Consider the following:

Understand current technology.   You need to understand which technologies are appropriate for a given situation. UTP (Category 5 or greater) is the king of desktop cabling, for example, although optical-fiber cabling has become the rule for campus backbones. Wireless works great in mobile environments but over long distances introduces licensing issues. Read this book for information on cabling technologies and check other networking magazines and books for details on competing technologies.

Understand the standards that apply to your work.   The TIA/EIA publishes the ANSI/TIA/EIA-568-A Standard, and the ISO/IEC publishes the ISO/IEC 11801 Standard. Both are discussed in Chapter 2. Professionals will be intimately familiar with one or the other of these Standards (in the United States, it will be the ANSI/TIA/EIA-568-A Standard).

Know the limitations of the technology you use.   Don't try to run Category 5 twisted-pair cable for 500 meters, for example. Point-to-point lasers don't cope well with snow. Single-mode fiber can carry a signal farther than multimode fiber. You can pull only so many twisted-pair cables through a conduit. Outside plant cable is not the same as inside plant cable, which can be divided into plenum and nonplenum. (You do know the difference, don't you? Your fire marshal and building inspector certainly do.) This book tells you what you need to know about current network-cable technology.

Keep an eye on new developments.   Watch for changes in technology. Which advances in networking will make your cabling setup obsolete, and which will enhance it? We know people who were putting in 10Base-2 and 10Base-5 coaxial cable for networking in 1995, cable that was used for a year or two and then never used again because all local area networking moved to Category 5 twisted-pair cable. One of the interesting developments occurring as this book is being written is high-density fiber-optic connectors that allow the simultaneous connection of several fibers at once, much like the way RJ-45 jacks connect four pairs of cable at the same time. We suggest you subscribe to the cabling industry's trade magazines to keep abreast of the field; information about these magazines can be found in Appendix B.

Understand the business of cabling.   Even if you are just installing a network for your own company's use, you should strive to perform a professional job. After all, you are the customer in that instance, and you want to be pleased with the results. You should know how to plan the job, acquire materials, assemble a team, train and supervise the crew, oversee the installation, test, document, and sign off the job. Read the rest of this chapter for some hints on the business of cabling. Numerous industry periodicals can keep you up-to-date on the latest in cabling business. Again, see Appendix B for more information.

Understand the business of business.   Though not related specifically to networks, if you are installing networks for others, you need to need to know how to run a business (or you need to hire people who will do it for you). That includes knowing about attracting work, bidding, developing and negotiating contracts, hiring, scheduling, billing, accounting, and so on. For more detailed information on the business of business, check out your local college's or university's business school.

Plan the Installation

Every well-executed job was at one point merely a well-planned job with realistic appraisals of the time, equipment, materials, and labor required. The following steps will help you develop that realistic plan:

Get the complete specification.   Obtain in writing, with detailed and accurate blueprints, exactly what sort of network the customer wants. Often it is up to you to plan the cable paths, but the customer usually has a good idea of where the network drops and patch panels should be located. Don't forget to confirm that the blueprints are accurate and up-to-date.

Perform a job walk.   Go to the site and walk through the job. Peer up into ceilings and look at conduits. Examine any walls that you'll have to penetrate. Make sure that the wiring closet has room for your own racks and patch panels. Some areas are much easier to network than others—an office building that uses ceiling tiles and is still under construction, for example, is much easier to wire than an old brick building with plastered ceilings or an aircraft carrier with watertight bulkheads and convoluted cable paths.

Clarify inconsistencies and ambiguities.   If you don't see a way to get a cable from one location to another, point it out. Ask why the front desk doesn't have a drop planned. Doesn't the receptionist have a computer? Will a computer be placed there in the future? Questions you ask at this stage can save you from change orders later.

Calculate the lengths of network runs.   With an accurate blueprint, you can calculate lengths away from the site. Otherwise, you'll have to break out the measuring wheel and walk the path of the cables. You will have to use the measuring wheel for any outside cable runs (from one building to another, for example).

Plan for service loops and waste.   The last bit of cable you pull from the spool is always too short. Runs often have to go around unexpected obstacles. When you pull a group of cables to the same general area, some will need more length to get to their destination than others will. But you'll still have to pull the same amount of cable in the bundle for all the runs in an area and trim each cable to fit. You should trim the cable a little too long and push the extra back up into the wall or ceiling so that, if necessary, the jack location can be moved later without requiring the whole run to be pulled through again. That adds up to 10 to 30 percent more cable than a naïve plan would indicate.

Evaluate your manpower and skill level.   How many feet of cable can your installers pull in an hour? Do you have enough teams to pull groups of cable in different directions—and do you have supervisors for the teams? How many faceplates can each installer punch down in an hour? After you've gained some experience, you will be able to look at a job and know how long it will take your team. In the meantime, calculate it out.

Have the Right Equipment

The right tools indicate your commitment to doing the job right. Some tools are designed for the do-it-yourselfer, whereas others are designed for professionals that install cable every day. All experienced cable installers should carry punch-down tools, screwdrivers, snips, twine and fish tape, electrical tape, a measuring wheel, a cable tester, and patch-panel lights. See Chapter 6 for more information about tools.

Test and Document

Many cable installers view testing and documentation as a convenience to the customer and an annoyance to be avoided. We view the lack of testing and documentation as a threat to everyone's sanity.

We can't count the number of times a customer has come to one of us and said, "This cable that you installed is bad. None of us can get any work done, and it is all your fault." If you kept the test documents (and you should *always* keep a copy of them for your own records), you can point to them and say, "But it passed with flying colors then, and you signed here. Of course, we stand by our work and we'll come out and fix it if it's broken, but you just might want to check your network-adapter settings [or jumper cable or network hub] before someone drives all the way out there…"

NOTE   Don't discount the fact that damage can occur to a cable, jack, or patch-panel connection after the cabling system is installed.

Another common problem professional cable installers report is being called in to fix cabling problems left by another installer who didn't bother to test. Honest mistakes can be made in any cabling installation; the following are examples:

- Copper cables were routed past RF-noisy power lines.

- Cables had their jackets scraped off when pulled through narrow places or around corners.

- Installed cables, jacks, and/or patch panels were labeled incorrectly.

- Fiber optics were bent in too tight a radius.

- Category 5 copper cables had their wires punched down in the wrong order.

- Cable was installed that exceeded the maximum length specified by the standards.

Testing your cable plant after you install it will pinpoint any of these problems. We are amazed that some installers simply assume that they've made no mistakes. Nobody's perfect—but you don't have to remind your customers of that.

Train Your Crew

You can get any group of enthusiastic guys together and pull cable through a ceiling. Punching down the little colored strands of wire at the end of the cable into the faceplate is a different matter—show them how to do it first, give them some cable scraps, and have them punch down both ends. Then test those short cables. Until your crew gets a feel for punching down the cables correctly, you'll find crossed wires, marginal connections, and strands cut too short and too long. It takes practice to do it right, but the time you spend training your crew will be well worth the absence of problems to fix on the job site.

Terminating fiber-optic cable requires a different order of training altogether. Unless your installers have spent hours cutting, stripping, polishing, and terminating fiber-optic cable and then examining what they've done wrong in a microscope, they'll never get it done right. Have your installers make all their mistakes on your own property rather than on your customers' property.

Work Safely

Train your crew in safety as well as proper cabling methodology. In most areas of the United States, the cabling business is booming, and you need every able-bodied and trained installer you can get your hands on. Also, if you take some basic steps to reduce the likelihood of accidents and your liability, you will sleep better at night.

Make sure that the safety lectures you give are themselves done safely, too. Once we had a contract to install fiber-optic cable in military hospitals. This was a retrofit situation, so we did not have precut holes in the drop locations; we had to cut the holes ourselves. A supervisor was showing how to properly wield a drill with a hole-saw bit installed and said, "And never chock the bit with your hand, like this—,"whereupon he grabbed the hole-saw bit with one hand and touched the trigger of the drill with the other to tighten the bit. Naturally, the drill whined, the bit spun, and blood dripped on the floor from the new gouge in the supervisor's hand. Fortunately, he did not drill a new hole through his hand. Because the incident happened in a wing of a hospital, a nurse took him away and bandaged his hand. He returned shortly thereafter and resumed his safety lecture. "And in the case of an on-the-job accident," he continued after looking at his watch, "you can take 15 minutes off." He was kidding, of course, but his unintentional example made an impression on the crew.

Network installers work quite a bit in ceilings, tight places, new-construction areas, dusty areas, and around all sorts of construction equipment. Make sure your employees know proper safety methods for handling ladders, wearing safety helmets, using dust masks, and so on.

Make It Pretty

The cable we install looks good. We are proud of our work, and so is the customer when we're done. Our network closets look like something important happens there—huge bundles of cable swoop out of conduits and separate into neatly dressed branches that flow across to their requisite rack locations. The customer appreciates a wiring closet that looks orderly, and an orderly wiring closet is easier to diagnose and fix network problems in. We needn't jiggle and pull cables to figure out which direction a bad line is running—when we look at it we know just by where it is. This saves a tremendous amount of time, both for us and for the customer, long after we're gone.

You can feel real pride when cabling systems you have installed are printed up in magazines. In one case, a cabling company was installing a fiber-to-the desk network for a local biotech company. This was when fiber was new and expensive (as opposed to fiber-network equipment now, which is simply expensive), and the supervisor was nervous about its installation and anxious to test it to make sure it all worked properly. Once the far ends of the cables had all been terminated, he terminated the fiber patch panels (which involves much cutting, polishing, gluing, and so forth and isn't something you just redo without a lot of expense). Unfortunately, he neglected to dress the cables first. Now, you can't untangle a knot once you've glued the ends together, which is essentially what he'd done. Fortunately, he'd left enough cable for a service loop (see the section "Plan for Contingencies"), and he used the extra length to push his new and permanent knot up into the ceiling where it couldn't be seen. With a junction box around the knot (look—cables go in, cables come out—never mind what's inside!) the plant was neat and ready for the photographers.

Look Good Yourself

It is important that you and your installation crew look appropriate for the job. The customer forms an impression about you and your company by how you walk, talk, and dress. The customer is reassured and happy when he sees professionals behaving in a professional manner; he is dismayed and apprehensive when he sees yokels yokeling. Even if you are installing cable for your own company, the way you and your crew carry yourselves will carry over into the work you do. Of course, this doesn't mean you and your installers should be running around in three-piece suits pulling cables through walls, but neither should you look like you've been dragged out of the nearest alley.

Every cabling company we have worked with has had a dress code of jeans and a T-shirt for their installers, and the company provides the T-shirts (with a company logo on the back, of course.) The T-shirts identify the work crew on the site and provide free off-site advertisement as well (if the logo is not too terribly designed and the installers aren't embarrassed to wear them at home!).

Plan for Contingencies

No job ever goes exactly as planned. If you have only enough time, materials, and manpower for the job as planned, you will inevitably come up short. Make sure to keep the following in mind as you plan:

> **Service loops**   If you've read this far, you've already seen one reason for leaving service loops in installed cable (a service loop is an extra length of cable coiled up and left in the ceiling or wall). Another reason to leave service loops comes from a basic rule of cable—you can always cut it shorter,

but you can't cut it longer. Inevitably, racks need to be moved, desks are reoriented, and partitions are shifted—often even before you're done with the job. If the cable is a bit longer than you originally needed, you can just pull it over to the new location and re-terminate rather than pulling a whole new cable to the new location. Also, if you determine while you're testing the plant (you *are* testing, aren't you?) that the cable has been punched down incorrectly, you will need an extra couple of inches to punch it down correctly.

Additional drops   Customers are always forgetting locations that they need network connectivity in ("Oh, you mean the printer requires a LAN connection too?"), so you should be prepared with additional cable, faceplates, and jacks for the inevitable change order. You can charge for the extra time and material required to install the extra drops, of course. Some companies bid low and expect to make their profit on exorbitant change-order costs, but we prefer to plan ahead and pleasantly surprise the customer with reasonable change-order prices. Jim estimates that at least 75 percent of all cabling installations he has worked on required additional drops within the first month after installation.

Extra time required   What do you do when the installers punch down your entire network using Token Ring faceplates instead of Ethernet faceplates? (This actually happened to someone we know once, and although Ethernet and Token Ring use the same jack form factor, they connect different pins to the cable and the faceplates are not interchangeable. However, if the four-pair cable and either the T568A or T568B wiring patterns are used, the jack will support either type of connection.) What you do is tear out all the incorrect faceplates and reterminate your network. If you haven't budgeted extra time for mix-ups like this, you risk serious disruption of your (and your customer's) schedule.

Manpower shortages   People get sick. They drill holes in their hands with drills. Competitors steal your best employees. The customer wants all four phases rolled out at once instead of week-by-week as you'd originally planned. Either you need to budget extra time for shortages in manpower or you need to bring more installers on the job. Customers are always delighted when you beat your schedule, so it pays to pad the time budget a little bit (as long as you don't pad it so much you lose the bid).

Equipment and material shortages   When you plan a network installation, the amount of cable you allow for is always an estimate. Short of pulling a large amount of string from one location to another, you can't determine beforehand exactly how much cable an installation will require. The cable paths deviate from the planned ones due to interposed air ducts, inconvenient patch panels, already-full conduits, and so on. Typically, the amount of cable used exceeds the planned amount by 10 to 30 percent. Professionals are pretty good at estimating cable usage and will subconsciously add the "fudge factor" to their own calculations so that they are seldom more than 10 percent off (to the installers' chagrin—see the section "Waste Not, Want Not").

But cable isn't the only supply you can run short of. Depending on the job, you may need innerduct tubing, racks, panels, faceplates, jacks, jumpers, rack screws, raceways, zip ties, string, T-shirts, and Coca-Cola. It helps to have some spares on hand for when material is shipped to the wrong site, is held up in manufacturing, mysteriously disappears, gets used up too quickly, or gets stripped, scraped, burnt, painted, flooded, or stepped on. It pays especially to be sure of the arrival of any specialized equipment or peculiar material—for one job in particular, we were held up waiting for a manufacturer to actually *manufacture* the fiber-optic cable we needed.

Match Your Work to the Job

No two potential networks have exactly the same requirements. At first glance, two network jobs may appear to be identical—each may specify the same type of cable and indicate the same number of network drops to be installed in the same office environment with the same number of rack locations and so on. However, one job may take twice as long to execute as the other job. When a customer relaxes a constraint on how you install cable or if special considerations exist for a particular job, you should take advantage of the specific circumstances of that job.

When we install network cable, we find that some of our customers care about the order in which drop locations show up on the wiring closet patch panels. Other customers do not care, so long as the patch panels are clearly labeled. This simple distinction has a huge impact on how long it takes to install the network cables.

One typical customer of ours (who, refreshingly, had a complete and comprehensive requirement for us to work from) specified the rack layout and cable arrangement all the way down to which location on each patch panel should correspond to which faceplate location in the building. To get the right cable to the right location to satisfy this requirement, we had to start in the wiring closet, label one of each cable, pull them in groups to the general location of their destinations, and then cut and label the other ends. About 40 or 50 cable drops were in each general area, so we had to sort out the cables and pull them to their destinations from the general location that all the cables were originally pulled to. (We were lucky that none of the cable numbering had been rubbed off during the cable pulling!) We then cut them to the correct length and punched them down at the drop end. At the wiring-closet end of the cables the network technician also had the unwelcome job of sorting all those cables and punching them into the rack in correct order. All that writing and searching and sorting takes much time because you must not pull the wrong cable to the wrong location.

The other job we ran at the same time went far more quickly because the network administrator didn't care which patch-panel location went to which drop location—he was just going to plug them into a hub anyway. We just pulled cable from the closets to the drop locations, trimmed them, and terminated them in the wall sockets. The network technician in the wiring closet simply punched that end of the cables down one by one, regardless of where the other end of the cable went.

Of course, we then had to determine which cable went where for testing purposes (*always* test, document, and label your work). However, we have some nifty jacks that we plug into the patch panels that light up when a technician sticks a probe in the drop end of the cable. The technician calls out over the radio where that drop is, the patch-panel technician writes down the patch-panel location, they remove the LEDs and insert the test modules, and they move on to the next location. (If you are looking for these handy little gadgets, you can find them on the Internet at `www.idealindustries.com`.)

A job done this second way can take half the time (and therefore can be performed at a lower cost) of one done the hard way. But, of course, the easier method should only be done if the customer doesn't mind that the drop locations show up in random order in the patch panels.

Waste Not, Want Not

One cabling-company owner found a good method for solving the tedious chore of cleaning up after a job. (As a crew installs cable, a good 10 to 30 percent of the cable ends up as trash. About half of the waste piles up next to the wiring closets, and the rest lies scattered throughout the drop locations.) He observed that the scrap cable ends contained quite a bit of high-quality copper. Although his primary concern was to make sure the client had the best possible experience working with his company so that he'd get referrals, he was nevertheless bothered by the amount of trash he was generating.

He instituted a policy that all the leftover copper the installation technicians could scavenge from the cable belonged to them, and proceeds from the recycling of it would go toward a company party. All they had to do was gather it up, bag it, and place it in the back of his truck—one of the supervisors took it to the recycling plant for processing. The technicians were then meticulous about cleaning up—even the inch or two of a trimmed cable was picked up and stuck in the back pocket of a technician to go toward the fund. Of course, they had strict instructions not to pick up any of the other contractors' cable.

Customers were amazed at how clean this owner's job sites were at the final walk-through. He now has an excellent reputation in the industry because of his company's cleanliness and the way he handles other details of his business. And, finally, his employees enjoy working for him, have a reason to clean up their work, and have really cool parties.

Case Studies

To give you a better idea of what it is like to install network cable, here are a handful of case studies that are drawn from the experiences of real cabling installers and contractors in the field. The names have been changed to protect the innocent.

A Small Job

Recently, a medical Web-site-development company we'll call Quasicom decided to replace all the cables strewn through their hallways with a real network. They contacted a cabling contractor to whom they had been referred. The referring party said the company wouldn't have to worry about the quality of the contractor's work. A Quasicom representative asked the contractor to look at the company's problem and quote a price for installing the network.

That contractor took a hands-on approach, so he came down himself to perform the job walk. He talked with Quasicom's IS (Information Services) staff to determine the company's needs and got a written document that detailed where it wanted the network locations and the rack. With such a small network, the contractor didn't have much calculation to do, so he presented Quasicom with an offer that was accepted.

Two days later, after a contract was signed and exchanged, the contractor dispatched a team of two installers to the job site. Neither installer was a supervisor, but the senior member of the crew had enough experience to see that the job was done right. The contractor gave the plans to the crew at the job site, showing them where to put the rack and to run the cables and the wiring configuration to use when punching down the faceplates. He then left them to do the work (he had another job walk-through to do for a much larger customer).

Quasicom's premises were of typical modern office construction—a removable tile drop ceiling provided an easy way to run the cables from one location to another. (It is easy to drop network cables behind the drywall once you know how.) The crew expected no difficulties in installing the cable.

The two installers set up several boxes of spooled cable in the location where the rack was to be (in this case, it was not in a wiring closet but in a server room where all the company's Web hosts were hooked up to the Internet). The plan indicated that the biggest run they had was of eight cables to the eight drops in the front-office area, so they set up all eight boxes of cable. Quasicom's IS staff wanted the patch-panel terminations of the wire to be in room-number order, so the installers marked the ends of the cable and the boxes they came in with indelible black marker.

The crew then pulled out the requisite number of feet of cable. (Normally, they would measure it, but in this case they just pulled it down the hall to its approximate drop point and made allowance for going up into the wall and down behind the drywall and added some service-loop extra.) They then used their snips to cut the cable off and marked the other end according to which box it came from.

They did the same with four boxes of cable for the quad run back to the back offices. That left two locations, each with a double-jack faceplate, which did not share a run with any other locations. They picked the two boxes that looked like they had just enough cable left in them to pull those runs from, and they drew those cable runs out as well.

Now it was time to put the cable up in the ceiling. The crew started by removing a few ceiling tiles so that they had access to the ceiling space. Then they tied the bundle of eight cables to the free end of a ball of twine and tossed the twine through the ceiling to a reasonably central area for all of the front-office drops.

They used the twine to pull the cables through and down to that point. They performed the same operation for the other bundles of cables.

They had all the cables almost where they needed to be—just 20 feet shy of the goal. They removed the ceiling tiles directly above the drop locations to determine that there would be no inconvenient obstacles (such as power conduits) and used drywall saws to cut holes in the wall for the faceplates. For each location, one member of the installation team found the corresponding cable and fed it across the ceiling to the other installer. That installer dropped it down the wall for the first installer to pull out of the hole.

Now all the cable was in place and merely needed to be terminated. Although pulling cable is a team process, terminating it is a solitary one. One member of the team began installing the boxes for the faceplates, stripping and punching down the faceplates (leaving enough cable length pushed up in the wall for a service loop), and screwing the faceplates into the box on the wall. The other team member went back to the server room to set up the rack and dress the cable for punching down on the rack.

This contractor always has his best installers perform the important job of punching down the racks. A small margin for error exists when terminating cable on a rack because so many cables feed into the same space-constrained location. If someone makes a mistake punching the cable down, he or she has to draw more cable out of the service loop (see the importance of a service loop?) to reterminate. Doing so messes up the pretty swooping lines of cable tie-strapped to the rack and to the raceways. Installers can't terminate first and dress the cable later because they would end up with an ugly knot of cable in the ceiling.

That afternoon, the cabling contractor came back with his test equipment, and he and his crew verified that all of the drop locations passed a full Category 5 scan. They used a label gun to identify all of the drops and their corresponding rack locations and then had Quasicom's IS manager accompany them in a final walk-through. They provided Quasicom's manager with the documentation (the same plans he'd given them along with a printout of the test results), got his signature on an acceptance document, and it was all over but for the billing.

Job Summary: Quasicom

Type of network: Interior Category 5

Number of drops: 16

Number of wiring closets: 1

Total cable length: 800 feet

Crew required: 2

Duration: 6 hours

A Large Job

The job walk-through that the contractor of the small job left to perform was for a defense contractor we'll call TechnoStuff, which had a new building under construction. For this job, the contractor was a subcontractor for another firm that had bid for all of the premises wiring for the new location. The Category 5 cable plant was to provide network access to a maze of cubicles and a handful of offices on two floors of the building. All but two of the wiring closets were on the first floor.

Wiring cubicles is different from wiring offices because you have no walls to fish cable down. Also, interior-design consultants have an alarming tendency to move cubicles around. So instead of coming down the walls to faceplate locations, the runs to cubicle locations come up from locations in the floor. Sometimes the cables are terminated there (using *very* tough receptacles in the floor), and sometimes the customer wants the cables drawn up from the floor and along raceways in the cubicle walls to faceplates in the cubicles. In TechnoStuff's case, they wanted the cables terminated in the cubicles.

The contractor walked the site and examined the network plan. He talked with the foreman about construction schedules, when his crew would have access to the area (because he wanted to get in after the framing was done but before the drywall went up), who would be putting in the conduit and boxes, and so on. He emphasized that the conduit had to have string left in it (it's a pain to get cable through it otherwise). He also asked if he had to drill his own holes in the floor (typically the answer to this question is yes).

The next week, the contractor took his crew out and showed the supervisors what had to be done. At that point, they had the left wing of the first floor of TechnoStuff available to them, along with all of the wiring closets. An office-furniture contractor was setting up the cubicles in the right wing. The cabling contractor assigned one crew to set up the racks and pull the fiber-optic backbone from the periphery wiring closets to the central one. He directed the other two crews to pull the cable for that wing from the closets to the cubicle locations. He then left the supervisors in charge because he had a meeting with TechnoStuff regarding materials-delivery timetables and the pay schedule.

As soon as the supervisors had cable to the cubicle locations, one team began terminating the cable while the other continued pulling cable. TechnoStuff had no preference about which patch-panel location ended in what cubicle, so, to terminate for each location, the teams simply grabbed the next available cable in the area where they came up out of the floor. The cables were pulled in bundles of 25 (any thicker bunches become unwieldy).

The contractor had evaluated the timetable and his available manpower correctly. The crew just finished punching down the cable in the left wing when the right wing cubicles were all set up (the cable pullers had drawn their cables into the space and let the cubicles be set up around them). The first team had finished pulling and terminating the fiber-optic backbone and began terminating the Category 5 patch panels for the first floor.

The contractor came back at the end of the week to deal with some miscommunication about who was to provide the wall plates for the offices; he found to his disgust that the answer was he. The drywall had already gone up, and his crew would have to punch holes in it and dangle the cable down behind it instead of putting the cable in when the walls were open and easy to work with. In addition, TechnoStuff had decided at the last minute that it really did need network connections in its conference rooms, so extra cable had to be pulled to those locations as well. The contractor gave his supervisors the revised plans and additional instructions. He left to make sure that the additional cable and supplies would arrive in time.

With so much work in the open basement pulling cable from one place to another along the ceiling, one of the installers decided to "walk" his ladder from one hole to another while he was still on it instead of getting down and carrying it. Naturally, he overbalanced and fell, spraining his ankle. The supervisor sent him to get it checked, and the cable-pulling crew was down one member. He replaced him by pulling an installer off the punch-down crew, which was getting ahead of the cable pullers anyway.

At the end of two weeks, all of the cables were in place and terminated, and it was time to test and document. The contracting company discovered where each cable ended up by putting indicator lights in the patch panels and having an installer walk from location to location with a radio and a tool that would light up the indicator for that location when he plugged it in the faceplate. When the patch-panel location was found, they swapped the locator for the tester and measured the performance of that cable.

After all of the cables had been tested, labeled, and documented (and a handful of mistakes fixed) the supervisor took TechnoStuff's representative on a final walk-through and had him sign off to accept the job.

Job Summary: TechnoStuff

Type of network: Interior Category 5 with fiber-optic backbone

Number of drops: 500 (times 4 jacks per location)

Number of wiring closets: 6

Total cable length: 300,000 feet

Crew required: 12

Duration: 2 weeks

A Peculiar Job

One interesting job another contractor did a number of years ago required a great deal of ingenuity and adaptive thinking. A marine-research institute had contracted with a local shipbuilding firm to construct from scratch a vessel designed for deep-sea exploration that we'll call (naturally) Cool Marine Institute Research Vessel—or CMIRV, for short. CMIRV Institute wanted a ship designed for science, not just a fishing boat crudely adapted with generators, probes, computers, and insufficient living space for a bunch of scientists. The shipbuilding firm took the job but found itself at sea when it came to putting in a completely fiber-optic network with over 200 drops in a boat that was just 140 feet long.

The cabling contracting company had put networks in ships before (for the U.S. Navy) and felt comfortable putting in a bid for this job. It was awarded the job. The customer then asked the contractor if his company could put in a telephone system, an alarm system, and a video system while it was at it! Of course, the contractor said yes.

The contracting company learned quickly that putting systems into a vessel under construction is a far different matter than retrofitting 10- and 20-year-old ships with a new network. First, it could not perform a job walk-through at the beginning because the boat hadn't even been built yet. Second, the pace for installing cable and equipment is slow but strict—the company would have to be prepared to run a cable when a path is accessible, and no holes could be drilled in bulkheads later. Also, CMIRV Institute's main contractor required that the cabling contractor maintain a presence on the job site to resolve conflicts and ambiguities about cable and device placement, access requirements, and so on, regardless of whether any cabling work was planned.

The cabling contractor placed a reliable and steady employee at the job site and had him put in a portion of the network whenever it was possible. The company occasionally sent out additional crew when, for example, it was time to terminate a bunch of fiber-optic cable that had been pulled, to install and calibrate the cameras for the video system, or to hook up and program the telephone system.

Job Summary: CMIRV Institute

Type of network: Interior fiber optic

Number of drops: 200

Number of wiring closets: 1

Total cable length: 10,000 feet

Crew required: 1+

Duration: 1 year

An Inside Job

Don't think that good contractors and installers have always done cabling the right way. For many, the introduction to the art of network-cabling installation came while performing a completely unrelated job. One person we know got her introduction to cabling while working for a university, managing the computer department for one of the colleges, which we'll call Budget Nets College. It was finally time for Budget Nets to upgrade the campus network from ARCnet to Ethernet, and it had raised enough funds to upgrade internally rather than going through the traditional university appropriations channels. (Quite a bit of fuss was made about Budget Nets going outside the usual channels, but after the school got its LAN upgraded, the University's main Information Services group was more attentive to the other colleges' needs—probably because those in the group were afraid their jobs would become obsolete!)

Because Budget Nets had gone its own way to upgrade its network instead of waiting in queue for the university's dedicated networking crews to come in, it had to find someone else to pull the cable. The campus physical-plant department was happy to do that—all Budget Nets had to do was provide a requirement. The physical-plant department would make a proposal and, if Budget Nets agreed to the cost, the plant would pull the cable.

The physical plant's electrical workers knew everything about pulling wires through walls. They were even aware of the problems of RF interference and cable-length issues. They were not, however, experts in all the different kinds of jacks and jumpers that computer networking uses. Before Budget Nets knew it, the entire first floor of its building was wired with Token Ring instead of Ethernet faceplates.

Being a new administrator, our friend did not know what to do about the situation. The proper course of action would have been to call the electrical workers back in, make them take out the wrong faceplates, and have them put in the right ones. But meanwhile, the faculty and school staff needed to get back to work.

When used over twisted-pair cabling, both Ethernet and Token Ring use two pairs of the cable—one pair to receive and another pair to transmit. Unfortunately, Ethernet and Token Ring do not use the same pairs, so Token Ring faceplates can't be used in an Ethernet network—unless, of course, custom cables switch the pairs being used. So she made custom cables.

NOTE   If the network had been wired to the ANSI/TIA/EIA-568-A recommended wiring pattern (T568A or T568B), the situation would not have occurred. If only the needed pin positions are wired, the cabling infrastructure will only support applications that use those particular pins.

Although the plan worked as a necessary quick fix for our administrator, we do not suggest you take this course of action in a similar situation, because it confuses people terribly when they find out that one cable will work in their outlets but another almost identical one will not. Eventually, she had to pull all those faceplates out and replace them. Those custom cables still show up on occasion and cause problems.

Job Summary: Budget Nets College

Type of network: Interior Category 5

Number of drops: 160

Number of wiring closets: 2

Total cable length: 32,000 feet

Crew required: 4

Duration: 1 week

appendices

appendix **A**

Dictionary of Cabling and Telecommunications Terms and Concepts

1Base-5 StarLAN network with a 1Mbps data transfer rate. Developed by AT&T, this network has not been common since the late 1980s.

2B+D Shortcut for describing basic ISDN service (2B+D = two bearer channels and one data channel, which indicates two 64Kbps channels and one 16Kbps channel used for link management).

4B/5B Signal encoding method used in 100Base-TX/FX Fast Ethernet and FDDI standards. Four-bit binary values are encoded into five-bit symbols.

8B/10B Signal encoding method used by the 1000Base-X Gigabit Ethernet standards.

8B6T Signal encoding method used in 100Base-T4 Fast Ethernet standard.

10Base-2 Ethernet (10Mbps) based on Manchester signal encoding over thin coaxial cable. Commonly called *thinnet* or *cheapernet*. This implementation of Ethernet uses a 10Mbps signaling rate, baseband signaling, and coaxial cable with a maximum segment length of 185 meters.

10Base-5 Ethernet (10Mbps) based on Manchester signal encoding over thick coaxial cable. Also called *thicknet*. This was the original Ethernet medium.

10Base-F Ethernet (10Mbps) based on Manchester signal encoding over fiber-optic cable.

10Base-T Ethernet (10Mbps) based on Manchester signal encoding over Category 3 or better twisted-pair cable. This IEEE specification defines the requirement for sending information at 10Mbps on unshielded twisted-pair cabling and defines various aspects of running Ethernet on this cabling.

10Broad-36 Ethernet (10Mbps) on broadband cable. Not very common.

50-pin connector Commonly referred to as a *telco*, *CHAMP*, or *blue ribbon connector*. Commonly found on telephone switches, 66-blocks, 110-blocks, and 10Base-T Ethernet hubs and used as an alternate twisted-pair segment connection method. The 50-pin connector connects to 25-pair cables, which are frequently used in telephone wiring systems and typically meet Category 3. Some manufacturers also make Category 5–rated cables and connectors.

66-type connecting block Connecting block used by voice-grade telephone installations to terminate twisted pairs. Not recommended for LAN use.

100Base-FX Fast Ethernet (100Mbps) based on 4B/5B signal encoding over fiber-optic cable.

100Base-T2 Fast Ethernet (100Mbps) based on PAM5 signal encoding and using two pairs of Category 3 or better unshielded twisted-pair cable. This implementation of Ethernet is not very common.

100Base-T4 Fast Ethernet (100Mbps) based on 8B6T signal encoding and using four pairs of Category 3 or better unshielded twisted-pair cable. This implementation of Ethernet is not very common.

100Base-TX Fast Ethernet (100Mbps) based on 4B/5B signal encoding and using two pairs of Category 5 or better unshielded twisted-pair cable.

100Base-X Defines any 100Mbps Fast Ethernet system based on 4B/5B signal encoding, including 100Base-TX and 100Base-FX. IEEE 802.3 shorthand term for entire 100Mbps Fast Ethernet system.

110-block A connecting block that is designed to accommodate higher densities of connectors and to support higher-frequency applications. The 110-blocks are found on patch panels and cross-connect blocks for data applications. See Chapter 7 for more information.

1000Base-CX Gigabit Ethernet (1000Mbps) based on 8B/10B signaling over shielded copper cable; used over short distances.

1000Base-LX Gigabit Ethernet (1000Mbps) based on 8B/10B signaling using long-wavelength (1300nm) laser transmitters over fiber-optic cable. Designed to be used over long distances.

1000Base-SX Gigabit Ethernet (1000Mbps) based on 8B/10B signaling using short-wavelength (850nm) laser transmitters over fiber-optic cable. Designed for optical fiber that is used as horizontal cabling.

1000Base-T Gigabit Ethernet (1000Mbps) based on PAM5 signal encoding over unshielded twisted-pair cable (Category 5 or better) that has passed all performance tests specified by TSB-95.

1000Base-X Any Gigabit Ethernet, including 1000Base-T, 1000Base-CX, 1000Base-LX, and 1000Base-SX.

A

abrasion mark A flaw on an optical surface usually caused by an improperly polished termination end.

absorption The loss of power (signal) in an optical fiber resulting from conversion of optical power into heat and caused principally by impurities, such as transition metals and hydroxyl ions, and by exposure to nuclear radiation. Expressed in dB/km (decibels per kilometer). Absorption and scattering are the main causes of attenuation (loss of signal) of an optical waveguide.

abstract syntax notation (ASN) 1 Used to describe the language interface standards for interconnection of operating systems, network elements, workstations, and alarm functions.

AC See *alternating current*.

acceptance angle With respect to optical-fiber cable, the angle over which light entering the fiber core will be guided along the core rather than reflected off of the surface or lost through the cladding. Often expressed as the half angle of the cone and measured from the axis. Generally measured as numerical aperture (NA); it is equal to the arcsine. See also *numerical aperture*.

acceptance cone The cross section of an optical fiber is circular; the light waves accepted by the core are expressed as a cone. The larger the acceptance cone, the larger the numerical aperture (NA); this means that the fiber is able to accept and propagate more light.

acceptance pattern The amount of power transmitted represented as a curve over a range of launch angles. The actual fiber angle can be characterized as geometry of core terminations to find the optimal angle of entry.

access coupler An optical device to insert or withdraw a signal from a fiber from between two ends. Many couplers require connectors on either end, and for many applications they must be APC (angled physical contact) connectors. The most popular access coupler is made by the fused biconic taper process, wherein two fibers are heated to the softening point and stretched so that the mode fields are brought into intimate contact, thus allowing a controlled portion of light to move from one core to the other.

access method Rules by which a network peripheral accesses the network medium to transmit data on the network. All network technologies use some type of access method; common approaches include carrier sense multiple access/collision detection (CSMD/CD), token passing, and demand priority.

ACK See *acknowledgment*.

acknowledgment (ACK) A message confirming that a data packet was received.

ACR See *attenuation crosstalk ratio*.

active branching device Converts an optical input into two or more optical outputs without gain or regeneration.

active coupler A device similar to a repeater that includes a receiver and one or more transmitters. The idea is to regenerate the input signal and then send them on. These are used in optical-fiber networks.

active laser medium Lasers are defined by their medium; laser mediums such as gas, (CO_2, helium, neon) crystal (ruby) semiconductors, and liquids are used. Almost all lasers create coherent light on the basis of a medium being activated electronically. The stimulation can be electronic or even more vigorous, such as exciting molecular transitions from higher to lower energy states, which results in the emissions of coherent light.

active monitor In Token Ring networks, the active monitor is a process that prevents data frames from roaming the ring unchecked. If a Token Ring frame passes the active monitor too many times, it is removed from the ring. The active monitor also ensures that a token is always circulating the ring.

active splicing   A process performed with an alignment device, using the light in the core of one fiber to measure the transmittance to the other. Ensures optimal alignment before splicing is completed. The active splicing device allows fusion splicing to perform much better with respect to insertion losses when compared to most connectors and splicing methods. A splicing technician skilled at the use of an active splicing device can reliably splice with an upper limit of 0.03dB of loss.

A/D   Analog to digital.

AD or ADC   See *analog-to-digital converter*.

adapter   With respect to optical fiber, a passive device used to join two connectors and fiber cores together. The adapter is defined by connector type, such as SC, FC, ST, LC, MT-RJ, FDDI, etc. Hybrid adapters can be used to join dissimilar connectors together, such as SC to FC. The adapter's key element is a "split sleeve," preferably made from zirconia and having a specific resistance force to insertion and withdrawal of a ferrule. This resistance, typically between 4 and 7 grams, ensures axial alignment of the cores.

address   An identifier that uniquely identifies nodes on a network.

adjustable attenuator   An attenuator in which the level of attenuation is varied with an internal adjustment. Also known as variable attenuator.

administration   With respect to structured cabling, the functions needed in the wire center to accurately maintain records and identification of circuit-related records. The ANSI/-TIA/EIA-606 Administration Standard for Telecommunications Infrastructure of Commercial Buildings defines specifications for this purpose.

ADSL   See *Asymmetric Digital Subscriber Line*.

Advanced Intelligent Network (AIN)
Developed by Bell Communications Research, a telephone network architecture that separates the service logic from the switching equipment. This allows the rapid deployment of new services with major equipment upgrades.

aerial cable   Telecommunications cable installed on aerial supporting structures such as poles, towers, sides of buildings, and other structures.

AGC   Automatic gain control.

AI   Amplitude imbalance.

alternating current (AC)   An electric current that cyclically reverses the direction of flow. Frequency is the rate at which a full cycle occurs in one second.

AM   See *amplitude modulation*.

American Standard Code for Information Interchange (ASCII)
A means of encoding information.

American Wire Gauge (AWG)   Standard measuring gauge for nonferrous conductors (i.e., noniron and nonsteel). Gauge is a measure of the diameter of the conductor (the thickness of the cable). The higher the AWG number, the smaller the diameter of the wire. See Chapter 1 for more information.

ampere   A unit of measure of electrical current.

amplifier   Any device that intensifies a signal without distorting the shape of the wave.

amplitude   The difference between high and low points of a wavelength cycle. The greater the amplitude, the stronger the signal.

amplitude modulation (AM)   A method of signal transmission technique in which the amplitude of the carrier is varied in accordance with the signal. With respect to optical-fiber cabling, the modulation is done by varying the amplitude of a light wave, common in analog/RF applications.

analog   A continuously variable signal. A mercury thermometer, which gives a variable range of temperature readings and sound waves, is an example of an analog instrument. Analog signals are measured in hertz (Hz). Analog is the opposite of *digital*.

analog signal   An electrical signal that varies continuously without having discrete values (as opposed to a digital signal).

analog-to-digital converter   A device used to convert analog signals to digital signals.

angle of incidence   With respect to fiber optics, the angle formed between a beam of light striking a surface and the normal angle to that surface.

angle of reflection   With respect to fiber optics, the angle formed between the normal and a reflected beam. The angle of reflection equals the angle of incidence.

angle of refraction   With respect to fiber optics, the angle formed between the normal and a refracted beam.

angled end   An optical fiber whose end is polished with purpose to an angle to reduce reflectance.

angled physical contact (APC) connector   A single-mode optical-fiber connector whose angled end-face helps to ensure low mated reflectance and low unmated reflectance.

angular misalignment   The loss of optical power caused by deviation from optimum alignment of fiber-to-fiber or fiber-to-waveguide. Loss at a connector due to fiber angles being misaligned. Also known as angular misalignment loss.

ANSI   American National Standards Institute.

antireflection (AR)   Coating used on optical-fiber cable to reduce light reflection.

APC connector   See *angled physical contact (APC) connector*.

APL   See *average picture level*.

AppleTalk   Apple Computer's networking protocol and networking scheme, integrated into most Apple system software, that allows Apple computing systems to participate in peer-to-peer computer networks and to access the services of AppleTalk servers. AppleTalk operates over Ethernet (EtherTalk), Token Ring (TokenTalk), and FDDI (FDDITalk) networks. See also *LocalTalk*.

application   (1) A program running on a computer. (2) A system, the transmission method of which is supported by telecommunications cabling, such as 10Base-T Ethernet, 622Mbps ATM, digital voice, etc.

AR   See *antireflection*.

aramid   See *aramid strength member*.

aramid strength member   The generic name for Kevlar. A yarn used in fiber-optic cable that provides additional tensile strength, resistance to bending, and support to the fiber bundle. It is not used for data transmission.

aramid yarn   See *aramid strength member*.

ARCnet (Attached Resource Computer network)   Developed by Datapoint, a relatively low speed form of LAN data link technology (2.5Mbps, in which all systems are attached to a common coaxial cable or an active or passive hub). ARCnet uses a token-bus form of medium access control; only the system that has the token can transmit.

armoring   Provides additional protection for cables. Usually consists of plastic coated steel and may be corrugated for flexibility to provide protection against severe outdoor environments.

ARP table   A table used by the ARP protocol on TCP/IP-based network nodes that contains known TCP/IP addresses and their associated MAC (media access control) addresses. The table is cached in memory so that ARP lookups do not have to be performed for frequently accessed TCP/IP and MAC addresses. See also *address resolution protocol*.

ASCII   See *American Standard Code for Information Interchange*.

ASTM   American Society for Testing and Materials.

Asymmetric Digital Subscriber Line (ADSL)   One of the most exciting developments in telephone technology over the past few years, also sometimes called *Universal ADSL* or *G.Lite*. ADSL makes it possible to use ordinary phone lines to transmit up to 8Mbps downstream and up to 640Kbps upstream. (Downstream is from the service provider to the user. Upstream is from the user to the service provider.) An ADSL modem replaces your regular modem and you subscribe to the ADSL service from your local phone-service provider.

asynchronous   Transmission where sending and receiving devices are not synchronized (without a clock signal). Data must carry signals to indicate data division.

asynchronous transfer mode (ATM)

In networking terms, asynchronous transfer mode is a relatively new connection-oriented networking technology that uses a form of very fast packet switching in which data is carried in fixed-length units. These fixed-length units are called *cells*; each cell is 53 bytes in length, with 5 bytes used as a header in each cell. Because the cell size does not change, the cells can be switched very quickly. ATM networks can transfer data at extremely high speeds. ATM employs mechanisms that can be used to set up virtual circuits between users, in which a pair of users appear to have a dedicated circuit between them. ATM is defined in specifications from the ITU and ATM Forum. For more information, see the ATM Forum's Web site at www.atmforum.com.

ATM   See *asynchronous transfer mode*.

attachment unit interface (AUI) port

A 15-pin connector found on older network-interface cards (NIC). This port allowed connecting the NIC to different media types by using an external transceiver. The cable that connected to this port was known as a transceiver cable or a drop cable.

attenuation   A general term indicating a decrease in power (loss of signal) from one point to another. This loss can be a loss of electrical signal or light strength. In optical fibers, it is measured in decibels per kilometer (dB/km) at a specified wavelength. The loss is measured as a ratio of input power to output power. Attenuation is caused by poor quality connections, defects in the cable, and loss due to heat. The lower the attenuation value, the better. Opposite of *gain*. See Chapter 1 for additional information on attenuation and the use of decibels.

attenuation to crosstalk ratio (ACR)

A copper cabling measurement, the difference between attenuation and crosstalk (NEXT), measured in dB, at a given frequency. A quality factor for cabling to assure that the signal sent down a twisted pair is stronger at the receiving end of the cable than any interference imposed on the same pair by crosstalk from other pairs. ACR measurements are not used with optical-fiber cabling since crosstalk is not an issue. See Chapter 1 for more information.

attenuation-limited operation   In a fiber-optic link, the condition when operation is limited by the power of the received signal (rather than by bandwidth or distortion).

attenuator   A passive device that intentionally reduces a signal by inducing loss.

audio   Used to describe the range of frequencies within range of human hearing; approximately 20 to 20,000Hz.

AUI   See *attachment unit interface port*.

auxiliary AC power   Typically an AC 110V supply of power to equipment area for operation of some equipment such as computer equipment but primarily used for appliance outlets for portable test equipment.

avalanche photodiode (APD)   With respect to optical-fiber equipment, a photodiode that is designed to take advantage of avalanche multiplication of photocurrent. As the reverse-bias voltage approaches the breakdown voltage, hole-electron pairs created by absorbed photons acquire sufficient energy to create additional hole-electron pairs when they collide with ions; thus a multiplication or signal gain is achieved.

average picture level (APL)   A video parameter.

average power   The energy per pulse, measured in joules, times the pulse repetition rate, measured in hertz (Hz). This product is expressed as watts.

average wavelength (l)   The average of the two wavelengths for which the peak optical power has dropped to half.

AWG   See *American Wire Gauge.*

axial ray   A light ray that travels along the axis of an optical fiber.

B

back reflection   See *backscatter.*

backbone   A cable connection between telecommunications or wiring closets, floor distribution terminals, entrance facilities, and equipment rooms either within or between buildings. This cable can service voice communications or data communications. In star-topology data networks, the backbone cable interconnects hubs and similar devices, as opposed to cables running between hub and station. In a bus topology data network, it is the bus cable. Backbone is also called *riser cable, vertical cable,* or *trunk cable.*

backbone subsystem   The main feeder cable running from the cable entrance point to the distribution frame near the equipment area.

backbone wiring   The physical/electrical interconnections between telecommunications closets and equipment rooms. See *backbone.*

backscatter   Usually a very small portion of an overall optical signal, occurs when a portion of scattered light returns to the input end of the fiber; the scattering of light in the direction opposite to its original propagation. Light that propagates back towards the transmitter. Also known as *back reflection* or *backscattering.*

balance   An indication of signal voltage equality and phase polarity on a conductor pair. Perfect balance occurs when the signals across a twisted-pair cable are equal in magnitude and opposite in phase with respect to ground.

balanced cable   A twisted-pair cable that has two identical conductors that carry voltages of opposite polarities and equal magnitude with respect to ground. The conductors are twisted to maintain balance over a distance.

balanced coupler   A coupler whose output has balanced splits; for example, one by two is 50/50, or one by four is 25/25/25/25.

balanced line   See *balanced cable.*

balanced signal transmission   Two voltages, commonly referred to as *tip and ring,* equal and opposite in phase with respect to each other across the conductors of a twisted-pair cable. Balanced signal transmission occurs when you dedicate one wire to transmitting and one to receiving.

balun A device that is generally used to connect balanced twisted-pair cabling with unbalanced coaxial cabling. The balun is an impedance-matching transformer that converts the impedance of one interface to the impedance of another interface. Balun is short for balanced/unbalanced.

bandpass A range of wavelengths over which a component will meet specifications.

bandwidth Indicates the information-carrying capacity of a cable (fiber or copper). A range of frequencies between the highest and the lowest frequencies of a transmission channel (path for information transmission). Identifies the amount of data that can be sent through a given channel. Measured in hertz (Hz); higher bandwidth numbers mean higher data capacity. With copper cable, using higher frequencies than the recommended bandwidth causes excessive signal loss (attenuation) and crosstalk. With fiber-optic cable, using high frequencies causes modal dispersion, which distorts the signal and makes it unreadable.

bandwidth-limited operation Systems can be limited by power output or bandwidth; bandwidth-limited operation is the prevailing condition when the system bandwidth, rather than the amplitude of the signal, limits performance. The condition is reached when modal dispersion distorts the shape of the waveform beyond specified limits.

barrier layer A layer of glass deposited on the optical core to prevent diffusion of impurities into the core.

baseband A method of communication in which the entire bandwidth of the transmission medium is used to transmit a single digital signal. The signal is driven directly onto the transmission medium without modulation of any kind. Baseband uses the entire bandwidth of the carrier, whereas broadband only uses part of the bandwidth. Baseband is simpler, cheaper, and less sophisticated than broadband.

basic rate interface (BRI) As defined by ISDN, consists of two 64Kbps B-channels used for data and one 16Kbps D-channel. Thus, a basic rate user can have up to 128Kbps service.

battery distribution fuse bay (BDFB) An intermediate cabling interface that serves as a distribution point for converting from power feeder cables to distribution cables that, in turn, are distributed to transmission equipment.

baud The number of changes in signal level transitions per second. Commonly confused with bits per second, the baud rate does not necessarily transmit an equal number of bits/sec. In some encoding schemes, baud will equal bits per second, but in others it will not. For example, a signal with four voltage levels may be used to transfer two bits of information for every baud.

B-channel See *bearer channel*.

beacon A special frame in Token Ring systems indicating a serious problem with the ring such as a break. Any station on the ring can detect a problem and begin beaconing.

beamsplitter   An optical device, such as a partially reflecting mirror, that splits a beam of light into two or more beams. Used in fiber optics for directional couplers.

beamwidth   The distance between two diametrically opposed points at which the irradiance is a specified fraction of the beam's peak irradiance; most often applied to beams that are circular in cross section.

bearer channel (B-channel)   On an ISDN network, carries the data. Each bearer channel typically has a bandwidth of 64Kbps.

bel   Named for Alexander Graham Bell, this unit represents the logarithm of the ratio of two levels. See Chapter 1 for an explanation of *bel* and *decibels*.

bend loss   A form of increased attenuation in a fiber where light is escaping from bent fiber. Bend loss is caused by bending a fiber around a restrictive curvature (a macrobend) or from minute distortions in the fiber (microbend). The attenuation may be permanent if fractures caused by the bend continue to affect transmission of the light signal.

bend radius (minimum)   The smallest bend a cable can withstand before the transmission is affected. UTP copper cabling usually has a bend radius that is four times the diameter of the cable; optical fiber is usually 10 times the diameter of the cable. Bending a cable any more than this can cause transmission problems or cable damage. Also referred to as *cable bend radius*.

BER   See *bit error rate*.

BERT   See *bit error rate tester*.

biconic connector   Optical connector with a conical shape for highly repeatable optical connections. The biconic connector was developed by AT&T but is not commonly used.

BICSI   See *Building Industry Consulting Service International*.

bidirectional couplers   Couplers that operate in both directions and function in the same way in both directions.

binder   A tape or thread used to hold assembled cable components in place.

binder group   A group of 25 pairs of wires in a cable with more than 25 pairs. The binder group has a strip of colored plastic around it to differentiate it from other binder groups in the cable.

BISDN   See *broadband ISDN*.

bistable optics   Optical devices with two stable transmission states.

bit   A binary digit, the smallest element of information in binary system. A 1 or 0 of binary data.

bit error rate (BER)   In digital applications, a measure of data integrity. It is the ratio of bits received in error to bits sent. The ratio of incorrectly transmitted bits to correctly transmitted bits. BERs of one error per billion bits sent are typical.

bit error rate tester (BERT)   A device that tests the bit error rate across a circuit. One common device that does is this is called a T-BERT because it is designed to test T-1 and leased line error rates.

bit stream   A continuous transfer of bits over some medium.

bit stuffing   A method of breaking up continuous strings of 1 bits by inserting a 0 bit. The 0 bit is removed at the receiver.

bit time   The length of time required to transmit one bit of information.

bits per second (bps)   The number of energy pulses (bits) passing a given point in a transmission medium in one second.

BL   Blue. Refers to blue cable pair color in UTP twisted-pair cabling.

black body   A body or material that, in equilibrium, will absorb 100 percent of the energy incident upon it, meaning it will not reflect the energy in the same form. It will radiate nearly 100 percent of this energy, usually as heat and/or IR (infrared).

blown fiber   A method for installing fiber in which fibers are blown through a conduit or tube using air.

BNC   Bayonet-Neill-Concelman (Neill and Concelman were the inventors), sometimes called British Naval Connector. A coaxial connector that uses a "bayonet"-style turn-and-lock mating method. Used with RG-58 or smaller coaxial cable. Used with 10Base-2 Ethernet thin coaxial cable.

BNO   Broadband network operator.

bonding   (1) The method of permanently joining metallic parts to form an electrical contact that will ensure electrical continuity and the capacity to safely conduct any current likely to be imposed on it. (2) Grounding bars and straps used to bond equipment to the building ground. (3) Combining more than one ISDN B-channel using ISDN hardware.

bounded medium   A network medium that is used at the physical layer where the signal travels over a cable of some kind, as opposed to an unbounded medium such as wireless networking.

BPON   Broadband passive optical network.

bps   See *bits per second*.

BR   Brown. Refers to brown cable pair color in UTP twisted-pair cabling.

braid   A group of textile or metallic filaments interwoven to form a tubular flexible structure that may be applied over one or more wires or flattened to form a strap. Designed to give a cable more flexibility or to provide shielding from EMI or grounding.

break-out cable   Multifiber cables where each fiber has additional protection by using additional jackets and strength elements such as aramid yarn.

break-out kit   Used to build up the outer diameter of fiber cable when connectors are being installed.

BRI   see *basic rate interface.*

bridge   A network device, operating at the data link layer of the OSI model, that logically separates a single network into segments but lets the two segments appear to be one network to higher layer protocols.

bridged tap   Multiple appearances of the same cable pair at several distribution points. Bridged taps are allowed in coaxial cable but not in optical-fiber or twisted-pair cables. Also known as *parallel connections.*

broadband   A transmission facility, typically referring to copper, that has the ability to handle a wide range of frequencies simultaneously. Broadband transmission medium has a bandwidth sufficient to carry multiple voice, video, or data channels simultaneously. Each channel occupies (is modulated to) a different frequency bandwidth on the transmission medium and is demodulated to its original frequency at the receiving end. Channels are separated by "guard bands" (empty spaces) to ensure that each channel will not interfere with its neighboring channels. This technique is used to provide many CATV channels on one coaxial cable.

broadband ISDN   New ISDN technology that can expand the capabilities of ISDN. Emerging because digital systems such as ISDN will not be able to completely replace analog-based systems in the foreseeable future.

broadcast   Sending data simultaneously to more than one receiving device at a time.

B-router   A device that combines the functionality of a bridge and a router but can't be distinctly classified as either. Most routers on the market incorporate features of bridges into their feature set. Also called a *hybrid router.*

buffer (buffer coating)   A protective layer or tube applied to a fiber-optic strand. This layer of material, usually thermoplastic or acrylic polymer, is applied in addition to the optical-fiber coating, which provides protection from stress and handling. Fabrication techniques include tight or loose-tube buffering as well as multiple buffer layers. In tight-buffer constructions, the thermoplastic is extruded directly over the coated fiber. In loose-tube buffer constructions, the coated fiber "floats" within a buffer tube that is usually filled with a nonhygroscopic gel. See Chapter 10 for more information.

buffer tube   Used to provide protection and isolation for optical-fiber cable. Usually hard plastic tubes, with an inside diameter several times that of a fiber, which holds one or more fibers.

buffered fiber   See *buffer.*

buffering   See *buffer.*

building cable   In-building plant cable, as opposed to outside plant (OSP) cable. Building cable typically will not protect the transmission media from moisture or other environmental factors found in the outside plant, and it is constructed from nonflammable-grade materials. Also referred to as *premises cable.*

building distributor (BD)   An ISO/IEC 11801 term that describes a location where the building backbone cable terminates and where connections to the campus backbone cable may be made.

building entrance   The location in a building where a trunk cable between buildings is typically terminated and service is distributed through the building. Also the location where services enter the building from the phone company and antennas.

Building Industry Consulting Service International (BICSI)   A nonprofit association concerned with promoting correct methods for all aspects of the installation of communications wiring. More information can be found on their Web site at www.bicsi.org.

bundle (fiber)   A group of individual fibers packaged or manufactured together within a single jacket or tube. Also a group of buffered fibers distinguished from another group in the same cable core.

bundled cable   An assembly of two or more cables continuously bound together to form a single unit prior to installation.

bus topology   In general, a physical layout of network devices in which all devices must share a common medium to transfer data.

bypass   The ability of a station to isolate itself optically from a network while maintaining the continuity of the cable plant.

byte   A group of eight bits.

(

c   The symbol for the speed of light in a vacuum.

C   The symbol for both capacitance and Celsius.

cable   (1) Copper: A group of insulated conductors enclosed within a common jacket. (2) Fiber: One or more optical fibers enclosed within a protective covering and material to provide strength.

cable-access fireproofing   Procedure and materials required to apply firestopping to openings where cables pass through floors or walls.

cable assembly   With respect to optical-fiber cables, cable that has connectors installed on one or both ends. If connectors are attached to only one end of the cable, it is known as a *pigtail*. If its connectors are attached to both ends, it is known as a *jumper*. General use of these cable assemblies includes the interconnection of multimode and single-mode fiber-optical cable systems and optical electronic equipment.

cable bend radius   See *bend radius*.

cable duct   A single pipe, tube, or conduit that holds cabling.

cable entrance conduits   Typically, holes in the wire center foundation where cable conduits enter into the cable entrance facility (CEF).

cable entrance facility (CEF)   Primary entrance point for cables into a building, typically where conduits from the street end. The CEF usually has a framing structure (such as 19-inch racks or plywood on the wall) for the organization of splices, cables, cross-connects, and network equipment.

cable management system   A total cable pathway system from point-to-point within the wire center designed so that cable placement will be clear and growth will be easy to accomplish.

cable modem   Connects to your CATV connection (usually with coaxial cable) and provides you with a 10Base-T connection for your computer. All of the cable modems attached to a cable TV company line communicate with a cable modem termination system (CMTS) at the local CATV office. Cable modems can receive and send signals only to and from the CMTS and not to other cable modems on the line. Some services have the upstream signals returned by telephone rather than cable, in which case the cable modem is known as a *telco-return* cable modem; these require the use of a phone line. The theoretical data rate of a CATV line is up to 27Mbps on the download path and about 2.5Mbps of bandwidth for upload. The overall speed of the Internet and the fact that the cable provider may not have a line faster than a T-1 (1.544Mbps) to the Internet restricts the actual amount throughput. However, even at the lower end of the possible data rates, the throughput is many times faster than traditional modem connections to the Internet.

cable plant   Consists of all the copper and optical elements including patch panels, patch cables, fiber connectors, splices, etc., between a transmitter and a receiver.

cable rearrangement facility (CRF)   A splice cabinet that can be used in place of a splice closure, especially in the vertical splice arrangement.

cable sheath   A covering over the core assembly that may include one or more metallic members, strength members, or jackets.

cable TV   See *community antenna television*.

campus   The buildings and grounds of a complex, such as a university, college, industrial park, or military establishment.

campus backbone   Cabling between buildings that share data and telecommunications facilities.

campus distributor (CD)   The ISO/IEC 11801 term for the main cross-connect; this is the distributor from which the campus backbone cable emanates.

CAN   Cable area network.

capacitance   The ability of a dielectric material between conductors to store electricity when a difference of potential exists between the conductors. The unit of measurement is the *farad*, which is the capacitance value that will store a charge of a one coulomb when a one-volt potential difference exists between the conductors. In AC, one farad is the capacitance value, which will permit one ampere of current when the voltage across the capacitor changes at a rate of one volt per second.

carrier   An electrical signal of a set frequency that can be modulated in order to carry voice, video, and/or data.

carrier detect (CD)   Equipment or a circuit that detects the presence of a carrier signal on a digital or analog network.

carrier sense   With Ethernet, a method of detecting the presence of signal activity on a common channel.

carrier sense multiple access/collision avoidance (CSMA/CA)   A network media access method that sends a request to send (RTS) packet and waits to receive a clear to send (CTS) packet before sending. Once the CTS is received, the sender sends the packet of information. This method is in contrast to CSMA/CD, which merely checks to see if any is currently using the media.

carrier sense multiple access/collision detect (CSMA/CD)   A network media access method employed by Ethernet. CSMA/CD network stations listen for traffic before transmitting. If two stations transmit simultaneously, a collision is detected and both stations wait a brief (and random) amount of time before attempting to transmit again.

Category 1   Also called *CAT 1*. Unshielded twisted pair used for transmission of audio frequencies up to 1MHz. Used as speaker wire, doorbell wire, alarm cable, etc. Category 1 cable is not suitable for networking applications or digital voice applications. See Chapters 1 or 7 for more information.

Category 2   Also called *CAT 2*. Unshielded twisted pair used for transmission at frequencies up to 4MHz. Used in analog and digital telephone applications. Category 2 cable is not suitable for networking applications. See Chapters 1 or 7 for more information.

Category 3   Also called *CAT 3*. Unshielded twisted pair with 100-ohm impedance and electrical characteristics supporting transmission at frequencies up to 16MHz. Used for 10Base-T Ethernet and digital voice applications. Defined by the ANSI/TIA/EIA-568-A specification. See Chapters 1 or 7 for more information.

Category 4   Also called *CAT 4*. Unshielded twisted pair with 100-ohm impedance and electrical characteristics supporting transmission at frequencies up to 20MHz. Not commonly used. Defined by the ANSI/TIA/EIA-568-A specification. See Chapters 1 or 7 for more information.

Category 5   Also called *CAT 5*. Unshielded twisted pair with 100-ohm impedance and electrical characteristics supporting transmission at frequencies up to 100MHz. This is currently the most common cable installed. Defined by the ANSI/TIA/EIA-568-A specification. See Chapters 1 or 7 for more information.

Category 5e   Also called *CAT 5e* or *Enhanced CAT 5*. Defined in ANSI/TIA/EIA-568-A-5. CAT 5e has improved specifications for NEXT, PS-ELFEXT, and attenuation. Like Category 5, it consists of unshielded twisted pair with 100-ohm impedance and electrical characteristics supporting transmission at frequencies up to 100MHz. See Chapters 1 or 7 for more information.

Category 6   Also called *CAT 6*. A proposed Standard, still in draft form, that aims to support transmission at frequencies up to 250MHz over 100-ohm twisted pair. See Chapters 1 or 7 for more information.

Category 7   Also called *CAT 7*. A proposed ISO/IEC Standard that aims to support transmission at frequencies up to 600MHz over 100-ohm twisted pair. See Chapters 1 or 7 for more information.

CATV   See *community antenna television*.

CBX   Computerized branch exchange.

CCD   Change-coupled devices.

CCIR   Consultative Committee on Radio.

CCIT   See *International Telephone and Telegraph Consultative Committee*.

CCTV   Closed-circuit television.

CD   See *carrier detect*.

CDDI   See *Copper Distributed Data Interface*.

CDMA   See *code division multiple access*.

CEF   See *cable entrance facility*.

center wavelength (laser)   The nominal value central operating wavelength defined by a peak mode measurement where the effective optical power resides.

center wavelength (LED)   The average of two wavelengths measured at the half amplitude points of the power spectrum.

central member   The center component of a cable, which serves as an antibuckling element to resist temperature-induced stresses. Sometimes serves as a strength element. The central member is composed of steel, fiberglass, or glass-reinforced plastic.

central office (CO)   The telephone company building where subscriber's lines are joined to telephone company switching equipment that serves to interconnect those lines. Also known as an exchange center or head end. Some places call this a public exchange.

central office ground bus   A ground bar that is connected into the central office ground system to provide for multiple connections on a particular floor.

CEPT   See *Conference of European Postal and Telecommunications Administrations*.

CEV   See *controlled environmental vault*.

channel   The end-to-end transmission or communications path at which application specific equipment is connected. Through multiplexing several channels, voice channels can be transmitted over an optical channel.

channel bank   Equipment that combines a number of voice channels into a digital signal; in the case of a T-1 channel bank, it converts 24 separate voice channels into a single digital signal.

channel insertion loss   With respect to fiber-optic links, the static loss of a link between a transmitter and receiver. It includes the loss of the fiber, connectors, and splices.

channel service unit/digital service unit (CSU/DSU)   A hardware device that is similar to a modem that connects routers' or bridges' WAN interfaces (V.35, RS-232, etc.) to wide area network connections (Fractional-T1, T-1, Frame Relay, etc.). The device converts the data from the router or bridge to frames that can be used by the WAN. Some routers will have the CSU/DSU built directly into the router hardware, while other arrangements require a separate unit.

characteristic impedance   The impedance that an infinitely long transmission line would have at its input terminal. If a transmission line is terminated in its characteristic impedance, it will appear (electrically) to be infinitely long, thus minimizing signal reflections from the end of the line.

cheapernet   A nickname for thin Ethernet (thinnet) or 10Base-2 Ethernet systems.

chromatic dispersion   The spreading of a light pulse caused by the difference in refractive indices at different wavelengths. Different wavelengths travel along an optical medium at different speeds. Wavelengths reach the end of the medium at different times, causing the light pulse to spread. This chromatic dispersion is expressed in picoseconds per kilometer per nanometer (of bandwidth). It is the sum of material and waveguide dispersions.

churn   Cabling slang for the connection, disconnection, and rearrangement activity of cross-connections of a frame. Office environments where network equipment and phones are frequently moved will experience a high churn rate.

CIR   See *committed information rate*.

circuit   A communications path between two pieces of associated equipment.

cladding   The layer of material (usually glass) that surrounds the core of an optical fiber. The cladding has a lower index of refraction that causes the transmitted light to travel down the core. The interface between the core and the cladding creates the mode field diameter, wherein the light is actually held reflectively captive within the core.

cladding mode   A mode of light that propagates through and is confined to the cladding.

Class A   (1) ISO/IEC 11801 designation for twisted-pair cabling rated to 100KHz. Used in voice and low-frequency applications. Comparable to Category 1 cabling; not suitable for networking applications. (2) IP addresses that have a range of numbers from 1 through 127 in the first octet.

Class B   (1) ISO/IEC 11801 designation for twisted-pair cabling rated to 1MHz. Used in medium bit-rate applications. Comparable to Category 2 cabling; not suitable for networking applications. (2) IP addresses that have a range of numbers from 128 through 191 in the first octet.

Class C   (1) ISO/IEC 11801 designation for twisted-pair cabling rated to 16MHz. Used in high bit-rate applications. Corresponds to TIA/EIA Category 3 cabling. (2) IP addresses that have a range of numbers from 192 through 223 in the first octet.

Class D (1) ISO/IEC 11801 designation for twisted-pair cabling rated to 100MHz. Used in very high bit-rate applications. Corresponds to TIA/EIA Category 5 cabling. (2) IP addresses used for multicast applications that have a range of numbers from 224 through 239 in the first octet.

Class E (1) ISO/IEC proposal for twisted-pair cabling rated to 250MHz. Corresponds to the proposed TIA/EIA Category 6 cabling Standard. (2) IP addresses used for experimental purposes that have a range of numbers from 240 through 255 in the first octet.

cleave The process of separating an unbuffered optical fiber by a controlled fracture of the glass for the purpose of obtaining a fiber end that is flat, smooth, and perpendicular to the fiber axis. This is done prior to splicing or terminating the fiber.

closet An enclosed space for housing telecommunications and networking equipment, cable terminations, and cross-connect cabling. It contains the horizontal cross-connect where the backbone cable cross-connects with the horizontal cable. Called a *telecommunications closet* by the TIA/EIA Standards; sometimes referred to as a *wiring closet*.

cm Centimeter. Approximately 0.4 inches.

CO See central office.

coating A material surrounding the cladding of a fiber and put on a fiber during the drawing process to protect it from the environment. Do not confuse the coating with the buffer.

coaxial cable Also called *coax*. Coaxial cable was invented in 1929 and was in common use by the phone company by the 1940s. Today it is commonly used for cable TV and by older Ethernet; twisted-pair cabling has become the desirable way to install Ethernet networks. It is called *coaxial* because it has a single conductor surrounded by insulation and then a layer of shielding. The outer shielding serves a ground and to reduce the effects of EMI. Can be used at high bandwidths over long distances.

code division multiple access (CDMA) In time division multiplexing (TDM), one pulse at a time is taken from several signals and combined into a single bit stream.

coherence In light forms, characterized as a consistent, fixed relationship between points on the wave. In each case, there is an area perpendicular to the direction of the light's propagation in which the light may be highly coherent.

coherence length or time The distance time over which a light form may be considered coherent. Influenced by a number of factors, including medium, interfaces, launch condition, etc. Time, all things being equal, is calculated by the coherence length divided by the phase velocity of light in the medium.

coherent communications Where the light from a laser oscillator is mixed with the received signal, and the difference frequency is detected and amplified.

coherent light   Light in which all parameters are predictable and correlated at any point in time or space, particularly over an area in a lane perpendicular to the direction of propagation or over time at a particular point in space.

collision   The network error condition that occurs when electrical signals from two or more devices sharing a common data transfer medium crash into one another. This commonly happens on Ethernet-type systems.

committed information rate (CIR)   A commitment from your service provider stating the minimum bandwidth you will get on a frame relay network.

common mode transmission   A transmission scheme where voltages appear equal in magnitude and phase across a conductor pair with respect to ground. May also be referred to as *longitudinal mode*.

communication panel   A piece of auxiliary communication equipment that provides various voice communication circuits that are used in system maintenance operations. The panel may provide access to an order wire, which provides maintenance communications between the central office and any repeater location along a span.

community antenna television (CATV)   More commonly known as *cable TV*, a broadband transmission facility that generally uses a 75-ohm coaxial cable to carry numerous frequency-divided TV channels simultaneously. CATV is now carrying high-speed Internet service in many parts of the world.

compliance   A wiring device that meets all characteristics of a standard is said to be in compliance with that standard. For example, a data jack that meets all of the physical, electrical, and transmission Standards for TIA/EIA-568 Category 5 is compliant with that Standard.

concatenation   The process of joining several fibers together end to end.

concatenation gamma   The coefficient used to scale bandwidth when several fibers are joined together.

concentrator   A multiport repeater or hub.

conductivity   The ability of a material to allow the flow of electrical current; the reciprocal of resistivity. Measured in "mhos" (the word *ohm* spelled backward).

conductor   A material or substance (usually copper wire) that offers low resistance (opposition) to the flow of electrical current.

conduit   A rigid or flexible metallic or nonmetallic raceway of circular cross section in which cables are housed for protection and to prevent burning cable from spreading flames or smoke in the event of a fire.

Conference of European Postal and Telecommunications Administrations (CEPT)   A set of Standards adopted by European and other countries, particularly defining interface Standards for digital signals.

connecting block   A basic component of a distribution frame. Also called a *terminal* block, a *punch-down* block, a *quick-connect* block, and a *cross-connect* block, a connecting block is a plastic block containing metal wiring terminals to establish connections from one group of wires to another. Usually each wire can be connected to several other wires in a bus or common arrangement. There are several types of connecting blocks: 66 clip, BIX, Krone, 110, etc. A connecting block has insulation displacement connections (IDCs), which means you don't have to remove insulation from around the wire conductor before you punch it down or terminate it.

connectionless protocol   A transport protocol that does not create a virtual connection between sending and receiving stations.

connection-oriented protocol   A transport protocol that uses acknowledgments and responses to establish a virtual connection between sending and receiving stations.

connector   With respect to fiber optics, a device attached to the end of a fiber-optic cable, receiver, or light source that joins it with another device or fiber. A connector is a mechanical device used to align and join two fibers together to provide a means for attaching and decoupling it to a transmitter, receiver, or another fiber. Commonly used connectors include the FC, ST, LC, MT-RJ, FDDI, Biconic, and SMA connectors.

connector-induced optical-fiber loss   With respect to fiber optics, the part of connector insertion loss due to impurities or structural changes to the optical fiber caused by the termination within the connector.

connector plug   With respect to fiber optics, a device used to terminate an optical fiber.

connector receptacle   With respect to fiber optics, the fixed or stationary half of a connection that is mounted on a patch panel or bulkhead.

connector variation   With respect to fiber optics, the maximum value in decibels of the difference in insertion loss between mating optical connectors (e.g., with remating, temperature cycling, etc.). Also known as *optical connector variation*.

consolidation point (CP)   A location defined by the TIA/EIA-568-A Standard for interconnection between horizontal cables that extends from building pathways and horizontal cables that extend into work area pathways. Often an entry point into modular furniture for voice and data cables. The ISO/IEC 11801 defines this as a *transition point (TP)*.

consumables kit   Resupply material for splicing or terminating fiber optics.

continuity   An uninterrupted pathway for electrical signals.

controlled environmental vault (CEV)   A cable termination point in a below-ground vault whose humidity and temperature are controlled.

Copper Distributed Data Interface (CDDI)   A version of FDDI that uses copper wire media instead of fiber-optic cable and operates at 100Mbps. See also *twisted-pair physical media dependent (TP-PMD)*.

core   The central region of an optical fiber through which light is transmitted. Common core sizes are 8.3 microns, 50 microns, and 62.5 microns. The core is surrounded by a cladding that has a higher refractive index that keeps the light inside the core.

core eccentricity   A measure of the displacement of the center of the core relative to the cladding center.

counter-rotating   An arrangement whereby two signal paths, one in each direction, exist in a ring topology.

coupler   With respect to optical fiber, a passive, multiport device that connects three or more fiber ends, dividing the input between several outputs or combining several inputs into one output.

coupling   The transfer of energy between two or more cables or components of a circuit. With respect to copper wire coupling, see also *crosstalk*.

coupling efficiency   The efficiency of optical power transfer between two components.

coupling loss   The power loss suffered when coupling light from one optical device to another.

coupling ratio/loss   The ratio/loss of optical power from one output port to the total output power, expressed as a percent. This percentage represents the percentage of light transferred to a receiving output port with respect to the total power of all output ports.

CPC   Customer premises communication.

CPE   Customer premises equipment.

CRC   See *cyclic redundancy check*.

critical angle   The smallest angle of incidence at which total internal reflection occurs. At lower angles, the light is refracted through the cladding and lost. Due to the fact that the angle of reflection equals the angle of incidence, total internal reflection assures that the wave will be propagated down the length of the fiber.

cross-connect   A facility enabling the termination of cables as well as their interconnection or cross-connection with other cabling or equipment. Also known as a *punch-down* or *distributor*. In a copper-based system, jumper wires or patch cables are used to make connections. In a fiber-optic system, fiber-optic jumper cables are used.

cross-connection   A connection scheme between cabling runs, subsystems, and equipment using patch cords or jumpers that attach to connecting hardware at each end.

crossover   A conductor that connects to a different pin number at each end. See also *crossover cable*.

crossover cable   A twisted-pair patch cable wired in such a way as to route the transmit signals from one piece of equipment to the receive signals of another piece of equipment, and vice versa. Crossover cables are often used with 10Base-T or 100Base-T Ethernet cards to connect two Ethernet cards together "back-to-back" or to connect two hubs together if the hubs do not have crossover or uplink ports. See Chapter 9 for more information on Ethernet crossover cables.

crosstalk   The coupling or transfer of unwanted signals from one pair within a cable to another pair. Crosstalk can be measured at the same (near) end or far end with respect to the signal source. Crosstalk is considered noise or interference and is expressed in decibels. Chapter 1 has an in-depth discussion of crosstalk.

crush impact   A test is typically conducted using a press that is fitted with compression plates of a specified cross sectional area. The test sample is placed between the press plates and a specified force is applied to the test specimen. Cable performance is evaluated while the cable is under compression and/or after removal of load depending on the test standard specifications.

CSA   Canadian Standards Association.

CSMA/CA   See *carrier sense multiple access/collision avoidance.*

CSMA/CD   See *carrier sense multiple access/collision detect.*

CSU   Channel service unit. See *channel service unit/digital service unit.*

CSU/DSU   See *channel service unit/digital service unit.*

current   The flow of electrons in a conductor. See also *alternating current* and *direct current.*

curvature loss   The macro-bending loss of signal in an optical fiber.

customer premises   The buildings, offices, and other structures under the control of an end-user or customer.

cutback   A technique or method for measuring the optical attenuation or bandwidth in a fiber by measuring first from the end and then from a shorter length and comparing the difference. Usually one is at the full length of the fiber-optic cable and the other is within a few meters of the input.

cutoff wavelength   For a single-mode fiber, the wavelength above which the operation switches from multimode to single-mode propagation. This is the longest wavelength at which a single-mode fiber can transmit two modes. At shorter wavelengths the fiber fails to function as a single-mode fiber.

cut-through resistance   A material's ability to withstand mechanical pressure (such as a cutting blade or physical pressure) without damage.

cycles per second   The count of oscillations in a wave. Once cycle per second equals a hertz.

cyclic redundancy check (CRC)   An error-checking technique used to ensure the accuracy of transmitting digital code over a communications channel before and after the data is transmitted. Transmitted messages are divided into predetermined lengths that are divided by a fixed divisor. The result of this calculation is appended onto the message and sent with it. At the receiving end, the computer performs this calculation again. If the value that arrived with the data does not match the value the receiver calculated, an error has occurred during transmission.

D

D/A   Digital to analog.

DAC   See *dual attachment concentrator*.

daisy chain   In telecommunications, a wiring method where each telephone jack in a building is wired in series from the previous jack. Daisy chaining is *not* the preferred wiring method, since a break in the wiring would disable all jacks "downstream" from the break. Attenuation and crosstalk are also higher in a daisy-chained cable. See also *home run cable*.

dark current   The external current that, under specified biasing conditions, flows in a photo detector when there is no incident radiation.

dark fiber   An unused fiber; a fiber carrying no light. Common when extra fiber capacity is installed.

DAS   See *dual attachment station*.

data communication equipment (DCE)   With respect to data transmission, the RS-232 interface that is used by a modem to communicate with a computer.

data connector   See *IBM data connector*.

data-grade   A term used for twisted-pair cable that is used in networks to carry data signals. Data-grade media has a higher frequency rating than voice-grade media used in telephone wiring does. Data-grade cable is considered Category 3 or higher cable.

data packet   The smallest unit of data sent over a network. A packet includes a header, addressing information, and the data itself.

data rate   The maximum number of bits of information that can be transmitted per second, as in a data-transmission link. Typically expressed as megabits per second (Mbps) for LANs, but often expressed as kilobits per second (kbps) in WANs. The data rate may or may not be equal to the baud rate.

data-terminal equipment (DTE)   (1) The interface that electronic equipment uses to communicate with a modem or other serial device. This port is often called the computer's RS-232 port or the serial port. (2) Any piece of equipment at which a communications path begins or ends.

datagram   A unit of data smaller than a packet.

dB   See *decibel*.

DB-9   Standard 9-pin connector used with Token Ring and serial connections.

DB-15   Standard 15-pin connector used with Ethernet transceiver cables.

DB-25   Standard 25-pin connector used with serial and parallel ports.

dBm   Decibels below 1mW.

DC   See *direct current*.

DC loop resistance   The total resistance of a conductor from the near end to the far end and back. For a single conductor, it is just the one-way measurement doubled. For a pair of conductors, it is the resistance from the near end to the far end on one conductor and from the far end to the near end on the other.

DC resistance   See *resistance*.

DCE   See *data communication equipment*.

D-channel   Delta channel. On ISDN networks, the channel that carries control and signaling formation at 16Kbps for BRI ISDN services or 64Kbps for PRI ISDN services.

D-connector   See *subminiature D-connector*.

decibel (dB)   A measurement of gain or loss in optical or electrical power. A unit of measure of signal strength, usually the relation between a transmitted signal and a standard signal source. Expressed as the logarithmic ratio of the strength of a received signal to the strength of the originally transmitted signal. For example, every 3dB equals 50 percent of signal strength, so therefore a 6dB loss equals a loss of 75 percent of total signal strength. See Chapter 1 for more information.

degenerate waveguides   A set of waveguides having the same propagation constant for all specified frequencies.

delay skew   The difference in propagation delay between the fastest and slowest pair in a cable or cabling system. See Chapter 1 for more information on delay skew.

delta   In fiber optics, equal to the difference between the indices of refraction of the core and the cladding divided by the index of the core.

delta channel   See *D-channel*.

demand priority   A network access method used by Hewlett Packard's 100VG-AnyLAN. The hub arbitrates requests for network access received from stations and assigns access based on priority and traffic loads.

demarc   See *demarcation point*.

demarcation point   A point where the operational control or ownership changes, such as the point of interconnection between telephone company facilities and a user's building or residence.

demultiplex   The process of separating channels that were previously joined using a multiplexer.

detector   (1) A transducer that provides an electrical output signal in response to an incident optical signal. The current is dependent on the amount of light received and the type of device. (2) An optoelectric transducer used in fiber optics to convert optical power to electrical current. In fiber optics, the detector is usually a photodiode.

detector noise limited operations
Occur when the detector is unable to make an intelligent decision on the presence or absence of a pulse due to the losses that render the amplitude of the pulse too small to be detected.

DGM Data-grade media. See also *data-grade*.

diameter mismatch loss The loss of power that occurs when one fiber transmits to another and the transmitting fiber has a diameter greater than the receiving fiber. It can occur at any type of coupling where the fiber/coupling sizes are mismatched: fiber-to-fiber, fiber-to-device, fiber-to-detector, or source-to-fiber. Fiber-optic cables and connectors should closely match the size of fiber required by the equipment.

dichromatic filter Selectively transmits or reflects light according to selected wavelengths. Also referred to as *dichromatic mirror*.

dichromatic mirror See *dichromatic filter*.

dielectric Material that does not conduct electricity; such as nonmetallic materials that are used for cable insulation and jackets. Optical-fiber cables are made of dielectric material.

dielectric constant The property of a dielectric material that determines the amount of electrostatic energy that can be stored by the material when a given voltage is applied to it. The ratio of the capacitance of a capacitor using the dielectric to the capacitance of an identical capacitor using a vacuum as a dielectric. Also called *permittivity*.

dielectric loss The power dissipated in a dielectric material as the result of the friction produced by molecular motion when an alternating electric field is applied.

dielectric nonmetallic Refers to materials used within a fiber-optic cable.

differential mode attenuation A variation in attenuation in and among modes carried in an optical fiber.

differential mode transmission A transmission scheme where voltages appear equal in magnitude and opposite in phase across a twisted-pair cable with respect to ground. Differential mode transmission may also be referred to as *balanced mode*. Twisted-pair cable used for Category 1 and above is considered differential mode transmission media or balanced mode cable.

diffraction The deviation of a wavefront from the path predicted by geometric optics when a wavefront is restricted by an edge or an opening of an object. Diffraction is most significant when the aperture is equal to the order of the wavelength.

diffraction grating An array of fine, parallel, equally spaced reflecting or transmitting lines that mutually enhance the effects of defraction to concentrate the diffracted light in a few directions determined by the spacing of the lines and by the wavelength of the light.

digital Refers to transmission, processing, and storage of data by representing the data in two states: on or off. On is represented by the number 1 and off by the number 0. Data transmitted or stored with digital technology is expressed as a string of 0s and 1s.

digital loop carrier A carrier system used for pair gain in loop applications.

digital signal (DS)   Transmission rates and coding schemes in the time-division multiplex hierarchy. In North American digital hierarchy, a DS-1 operates at 1.544Mbps per second, a DS-1C at 3.152Mbps, and a DS-3 at 44.736Mbps. The term DS-0 generally applies to the 64Kbps component of a DS-1 signal that represents the equivalent of a voice channel. A DS-1 circuit consists of 24 individual DS-0 circuits. Digital signal rates are documented by industry standards organizations such as the American National Standards Institute (ANSI), the Conference of European Postal and Telecommunications Administrations (CEPT), and the International Telephone Union (ITU).

digital signal cross-connect (DSX)   A centralized termination, interconnection, and test point for digital equipment at a particular digital signal bit rate. DSXs are identified by the transmission rate of the signals terminated on them. The DSX-1 is for DS-1 signals; the DSX-3 is for DS-3 signals. These capabilities enable a DSX frame to provide several operational functions, including equipment interconnection, test access, and patching. All equipment terminated on a DSX must conform to the industry standards for the DS transmission rate.

digital subscriber line (DSL)   A relatively new technology for delivering high bandwidth to homes and business using standard telephone lines. Though many experts believed that standard copper phone cabling would never be able to support high data rates, local phone companies are deploying equipment that is capable of supporting up to theoretical rates of 8.4Mbps. Typical throughput downstream (from the provider to the customer) are rates from 256Kbps to 1.544Mbps. DSL lines are capable of supporting voice and data simultaneously. There are many types, including HDSL (high bit-rate DSL) and VDSL (very high bit-rate DSL).

DIL   Dual in-line.

diode   A device that allows a current to move in only one direction. Some examples of diodes are light emitting diodes (LEDs), laser diodes, and photodiodes.

direct current (DC)   An electric current that flows in one direction and does not reverse direction, unlike alternating current (AC). Direct current also means a current whose polarity never changes.

direct inside wire (DIW)   Twisted-pair wire used inside a building, usually two- or four-pair AWG 26.

dispersion   A general term for the phenomena that cause a broadening or spreading of light as it propagates through an optical fiber. There are three major types of dispersion: modal, material, and waveguide. Modal dispersion is caused by differential optical path lengths in a multimode fiber. Material dispersion is caused by a differential delay of various wavelengths of light in a waveguide material. Waveguide dispersion is caused by light traveling in both the core and cladding materials in single-mode fibers. Dispersion is one of the limits on bandwidth on fiber-optic cables. It is also called *pulse spreading* because dispersion causes a broadening of the input pulses along the length of the fiber.

dispersion flattened fiber A single-mode optical fiber that has a low chromatic dispersion throughout the range between 1300nm and 1600nm.

dispersion limited operation Describes cases where the dispersion of a pulse rather than loss of amplitude limits the distance an optical signal can be carried in the fiber. If this is the case, the receiving system may not be able to receive the signal.

dispersion shifted fiber A single-mode fiber that has zero dispersion wavelength at 1550nm. Dispersion shifted fibers are made so that optimum attenuation and bandwidth are at 1550nm.

dispersion unshifted fiber A single-mode optical-fiber cable that has zero dispersion wavelength at 1300nm. Often called *conventional* or *unshifted fiber*.

distortion Any undesired change in a waveform or signal.

distortion-limited operation In fiber-optic cable, synonymous with bandwidth limited operation.

distribution subsystem A basic element of a structured distribution system. The distribution subsystem is useful for terminating and distributing cables to equipment. Typical functions include electrical protection, interconnection, gauge-size conversion, and cross-connection or interconnection. Other subsystems include the cable entrance facility, backbone or riser, distribution frame, and equipment cabling. Also called *distribution frame subsystem*.

distributor See *cross-connect*.

DIW See *direct inside wire*.

DLC Digital loop carrier.

DNP See *dry nonpolish connector*.

DoD Networking Model The Department of Defense's four-layer conceptual model describing how communications should take place between computer systems. From the bottom up, the four layers are network access, Internet, transport (host-to-host), and application.

drain wire An uninsulated wire in contact with a shielded cable's shield throughout its length. It is used for terminating the shield. If a drain wire is present, it should be terminated.

dry nonpolish connector (DNP) Optical-fiber connector used for POF (plastic optical fiber).

DS See *digital signal*.

DS-1 See *T-1*.

DS-3 See *T-3*.

DSL See *digital subscriber line*.

DSU See *channel service unit/digital service unit*.

DSX See *digital signal cross-connect*.

DSX bay A supporting structure called a frame and all the DSX apparatus mounted on it.

DSX complexes One or more DSX lineups that are interlinked with tie circuits to provide the DSX functions.

DSX lineup   One or more contiguous DSX bays that are equipped with the necessary jumper pathways to provide the ability to perform all required DSX functions.

DTE   See *data terminal equipment*.

DTMF   See *dual tone multifrequency* or *tone dial*.

D-type connector   A type of network connector that connects computer peripherals. It contains rows of pins or sockets shaped in a sideways D. Common connectors are the DB-9 and DB-25.

DU connector   A fiber-optic connector developed by the Nippon Electric Group in Japan.

dual attachment concentrator (DAC)   An FDDI concentrator that offers two attachments to the FDDI network that are capable of accommodating a dual (counter-rotating) ring.

dual attachment station (DAS)   A term used with FDDI networks to denote a station that attaches to both the primary and secondary rings; this makes it capable of serving the dual (counter-rotating) ring. A dual attachment station has two separate FDDI connectors.

dual ring   A pair of counter-rotating logical rings.

dual tone multifrequency (DTMF)   The signal that a touch-tone phone generates when you press a key on it. Each key generates two separate tones, one in a high frequency group of tones and one from a low frequency group of tones.

dual window fiber   An optical-fiber cable manufactured to be used at two different wavelengths. Single-mode fiber cable that is usable at 1300nm and 1550nm is dual window fiber. Multimode fiber cable is optimized for 850nm and 1300nm operations and is also dual window fiber.

duct   (1) A single enclosed raceway for wires or cable. (2) An enclosure in which air is moved.

duplex   With respect to data communications, a circuit used to transmit signals simultaneously in both directions.

duplex cable   A two-fiber cable suitable for duplex transmission. Usually two fiber strands surrounded by a common jacket.

duplex transmission   Data transmission in both directions, either one direction at a time (*half duplex*) or both directions simultaneously (*full duplex*).

duty cycle   With respect to a digital transmission, the ratio of high levels to low levels.

E

E-1   The European version of T-1 data circuits. Runs at 2.048Mbps.

E-3   The European version of T-3 data circuits. Runs at 34.368Mbps.

earth   A term for zero reference ground (not to mention the planet most of us live on).

ECMA   See *European Computer Manufacturer's Association*.

EIA See *Electronic Industries Association*.

electromagnetic compatibility (EMC)
The ability of a system to minimize radiated emissions and maximize immunity from external noise sources.

electromagnetic field The combined electric and magnetic field caused by electron motion in conductors.

electromagnetic interference (EMI)
Electrical noise generated in copper conductors when electromagnetic fields induce currents. Copper cables, motors, machinery, and other equipment that uses electricity may generate EMI. Copper-based network cabling and equipment are susceptible to EMI and also emit EMI, which results in degradation of the signal. Fiber-optic cables are desirable in environments that have high EMI because they are not susceptible to the effects of EMI.

Electronic Industries Association (EIA)
An association of manufacturers and users that establishes Standards and publishes test methodologies. The EIA (with the TIA and ANSI) helped to publish the TIA/EIA-568-A cabling Standard.

electrostatic coupling The transfer of energy by means of a varying electrostatic field. Also referred to as *capacitive coupling*.

electrostatic discharge (ESD) A problem that exists when two items with dissimilar static electrical charges are brought together. The static electrical charges jump to the item with fewer electrical charges, which causes ESD; ESD can damage electrical and computer components.

ELFEXT See *equal level far-end crosstalk*.

EMD Equilibrium mode distribution.

EMI See *electromagnetic interference*.

emitter A source of optical power.

encoding A method of combining timing and data information into a synchronized stream of signals. Encoding is accomplished by representing digital 1s and 0s through combining high and low signal voltage or light states.

end finish The quality of a fiber's end surface.

end separation The distance between the ends of two joined fibers. The end separation is important because the degree of separation causes an extrinsic loss, depending on the configuration of the connection.

end–to-end loss The optical signal loss experienced between the transmitter and the detector due to fiber quality, splices, connectors, and bends.

energy density Expressed in joules per square meter. Sometimes called *irradiance*.

entrance facility (EF) A room within a building where antenna, public, and private network service cables can enter the building and be consolidated. Should be located as close as possible to the entrance point. Entrance facilities are often used to house electrical protection equipment and connecting hardware for the transition between outdoor and indoor cable. Also called *entrance room*.

entrance point The location where telecommunications enter a building through an exterior wall, a concrete floor slab, a rigid metal conduit, or an intermediate metal conduit.

entrance room See *entrance facility*.

E/O Electronic to optical.

EPR See *ethylene-propylene copolymer rubber*.

equal level far-end crosstalk (ELFEXT) Crosstalk that is measured at the opposite end from which the disturbing signal is transmitted and normalized by the attenuation of the cable.

equipment cable Cable or cable assembly used to connect telecommunications equipment to horizontal or backbone cabling systems in the telecommunications closet and equipment room. Equipment cables are considered to be outside the scope of cabling standards.

equipment cabling subsystem Part of the cabling structure, typically between the distribution frame and the equipment.

equipment room (ER) A centralized space for telecommunications equipment that serves the occupants of the building or multiple buildings in a campus environment. Usually considered distinct from a telecommunications closet because it is considered to serve a building or campus; the telecommunications closet serves only a single floor. The equipment room is also considered distinct because of the nature of complexity of the equipment that is contained in it.

error detection The checking of a signal for line-code violations, such as bipolar violations.

error rate The frequency of errors detected in a data service line, usually expressed as a decimal.

ESD See *electrostatic discharge*.

Ethernet A local area network (LAN) architecture developed by Xerox that is defined in the IEEE 802.3 Standard. Ethernet nodes access the network using the carrier sense multiple access/collision detect (CSMA/CD) access method.

ethylene-propylene copolymer rubber (EPR) A material with good insulating properties.

European Computer Manufacturer's Association (ECMA) A European trade organization that issues its own specifications and is a member of the ISO.

excess loss (1) In a fiber-optic coupler, the optical loss from that portion of light that does not emerge from the nominally operational pods of the device. (2) The ratio of the total output power of a passive component with respect to the input power.

exchange center A local telephone exchange building where switching systems are located. Also called *exchange office* or *central office*.

extrinsic loss In a fiber interconnection, the portion of loss that is not intrinsic to the fiber but is related to imperfect joining, which may be caused by the connector or splice. These are losses caused by defects and imperfections that cause the loss to exceed the theoretical minimum loss that is intrinsic (called *intrinsic loss*).

f

f   Frequency.

fan-out cable   A multifiber cable that is designed for easy connectorization. These cables are sometimes sold with installed connectors or as part of a splice pigtail, with one end carrying many connectors and the other installed in a splice cabinet or panel ready for splicing or patching.

fan-out kit   Used to build up the outer diameter of fiber cable for connectorization.

farad   A unit of capacitance that stores one coulomb of electrical charge when one volt of electrical pressure is applied.

faraday effect   A phenomenon that causes some materials to rotate the polarization of light in the presence of a magnetic field.

far-end crosstalk (FEXT)   Crosstalk that is measured on the wires that are not being used for transmission at the opposite end from the source (the transmitter) of energy on the active line. See Chapter 1 for more information on various types of crosstalk.

fast Ethernet   Ethernet standard supporting 100Mbps operation.

FC connector   A threaded optical-fiber connector that was developed by Nippon Telephone and Telegraph in Japan. The FC connector is good for single-mode or multimode fiber and applications requiring low back reflection. The FC is a screw type and is prone to vibration loosening.

FCC   Federal Communications Commission.

FCS   See *frame check sequence*.

FDDI   See *fiber distributed data interface*.

FDM   See *frequency division multiplexing*.

FDMA   Frequency division multiplex access.

feeder cable   A voice backbone cable that runs from the equipment room cross-connect to the telecommunications cross-connect. A feeder cable may also be the cable running from a central office to a remote terminal, hub, head end, or node.

FEP   See *fluorinated ethylene propylene*.

FER   Forward error correction.

ferrule   A small alignment tube attached to the end of the fiber and used in connectors. These are made of stainless steel, aluminum, or zirconia. The ferrule is used to confine and align the stripped end of a fiber.

fiber   A single, separate optical transmission element characterized by core and cladding. The fiber is the dielectric material that guides light or waveguides.

fiber building cable   A nonflammable cable containing one or multiple fibers.

fiber channel   A gigabit interconnect technology that, through the 8B/10B encoding method, allows concurrent communications among workstations, mainframes, servers, data-storage systems, and other peripherals using SCSI and IP protocols.

fiber curl   Occurs when there is misalignment in a mass or ribbon splicing joint. The fiber or fibers curl away from the joint to take up the slack or stress caused by misalignment of fiber lengths at the joint.

fiber distributed data interface (FDDI)
ANSI Standard X3.166-1990, Fiber Distributed Data Interface (FDDI)—Token Ring Physical Layer Medium Dependent (PMD). This Standard details the requirements for all attachment devices concerning the 100Mbps fiber-optic network interface. It uses a counter-rotating ring topology. FDDI is typically known as a backbone LAN because it is used for joining file servers together and for joining other LANs together.

fiber distribution frame (FDF)   A cross-connect or interconnect system using fiber-optic jumpers and cables. See also *horizontal distribution frame.*

fiber illumination kit   Used to visually inspect continuity in fiber systems and to inspect fiber connector end-face for cleanliness and light quality.

fiber-in-the-loop (FITL)   Indicates deployment of fiber-optic feeder and distribution facilities.

fiber loss   The attenuation of light in an optical-fiber transmission.

fiber-optic attenuator   An active component that is installed in a fiber-optic transmission system that is designed to reduce the power in the optical signal. It is used to limit the optical power received by the photodetector to within the limits of the optical receiver.

fiber-optic cable   Cable containing one or more optical fibers.

fiber-optic communication system
Involves the transfer of modulated or unmodulated optical energy (light) through optical-fiber media.

fiber-optic interrepeater link (FOIRL)
An Ethernet fiber-optic connection method intended for connection of repeaters.

fiber-optic pigtail   Used to splice outside plant cable to the backside of a fiber-optic patch panel.

fiber-optic test procedures (FOTP)
Test procedures outlined in the EIA-RS-455 Standards.

fiber-optic transmission   A communications scheme whereby electrical data is converted to light energy and transmitted through optical fibers.

fiber-optic transmission system (FOTS)
A set of transmission equipment and facilities used for optical communications.

fiber-optic waveguide   A long, thin strand of transparent material (glass or plastic), which can convey electromagnetic energy in the optical waveform longitudinally by means of internal reflection.

fiber optics   The optical technology in which communication signals in the form of modulated light beams are transmitted over a glass or plastic fiber transmission medium. Fiber optics offers high bandwidth and protection from electromagnetic interference and radioactivity; it also has small space needs.

fiber protection system (FPS)   A system of ducts and supports that includes guides and transition pieces that are used for organizing and protecting fiber building cables and individual fiber interconnection cables. The fiber protection system is used to protect installed fiber-optic cabling as well as to ensure fiber minimum bend radius criteria.

fiber test equipment   Diagnostic equipment used for the testing, maintenance, restoration, and inspection of fiber systems. This equipment includes optical attenuation meters and optical time domain reflectometers (OTDRs).

fibre   The British spelling of fiber.

fillers   Nonconducting components cabled with insulated conductors or optical fibers to impart flexibility, tensile strength, roundness, or a combination of all three.

FIR   Finite impulse response.

firestop   Material, device, or collection of parts installed in a cable pathway (such as a conduit or riser) at a fire-rated wall or floor to prevent passage of flame, smoke, or gases through the rated barrier.

firestopping material   Nonflammable material specifically designed to block cable holes and ducts, thereby limiting the propagation of a fire. See also *firestop*.

FITL   See *fiber-in-the-loop*.

flex life   The ability of a cable to bend many times before breaking.

floating   A floating circuit is one that has no ground connection.

floor distributor (FD)   The ISO/IEC 11801 term for horizontal cross-connect. The floor distributor is used to connect between the horizontal cable and other cabling subsystems or equipment.

fluorinated ethylene propylene (FEP)   A thermoplastic with excellent dielectric properties that is often used as insulation in plenum-rated cables. FEP has good electrical-insulating properties and chemical and heat resistance. FEP is the most common material used for wire insulation in Category 5 and better cables that are rated for use in plenums.

FM   See *frequency modulation*.

FOIRL   See *fiber-optic interrepeater link*.

FOTP   See *fiber-optic test procedures*.

FOTS   Fiber-optic transmission system.

FOX   Fiber-optic extension.

FOXI   Fiber-optic transparent synchronous transmitter-receiver interface.

frame check sequence (FCS)   The error detection field.

frame relay   A wide area networking (WAN) technology that allows switched digital channels (such as 1.5 Mbps) to be offered to customers upon demand.

frequency   The number of cycles per second at which a waveform alternates. Frequency is expressed in hertz (Hz); one hertz equals one cycle per second.

frequency division multiplexing (FDM)
A technique for combining many signals onto a single circuit by dividing the available transmission bandwidth by frequency into narrower bands; each band is used for a separate communication channel. FDM can be used with any and all of the sources created by wavelength division multiplexing (WDM).

frequency modulation (FM)   A method of adding information to a sine wave signal in which its frequency is varied to impose information on it. Information is sent by varying the frequency of an optical or electrical carrier. Other methods include *amplitude modulation (AM)* and *phase modulation (PM)*.

frequency response   The range of frequencies over which a device operates as expected.

Fresnel diffraction pattern   The near-field diffraction pattern.

Fresnel loss   The loss at a joint due to a portion of the light being reflected.

Fresnel reflection   The reflection of light from an optical discontinuity; it occurs at the air/glass interfaces at entrance and exit ends of an optical fiber.

Fresnel reflection method   A method for measuring the index profile of an optical fiber by measuring reflectance as a function of position on the end-face.

FTF   Fiber trunk feeder.

FTM   Fiber telecommunications module.

FTMB   Fiber to major business.

FTP   (1) Foil twisted-pair cable. See also *screened twisted-pair (ScTP) cable*. (2) Abbreviation for *file transfer protocol*.

FTTB   Fiber to the business.

FTTC   Fiber to the curb.

FTTD   Fiber to the desk.

FTTH   Fiber to the home.

FTTS   Fiber to the school.

full duplex transmission   Data transmission over a circuit capable of transmitting in both directions simultaneously.

fundamental mode   The lowest order mode of a waveguide.

fusion splicing   A splicing method accomplished by the application of localized heat sufficient to fuse or melt the ends of the optical fiber, forming continuous single strand of fiber. As the glass is heated it becomes softer, and it is possible to use the glass's "liquid" properties to bond glass surfaces permanently.

FUT   Fiber under test.

G

G   Green. Used when referring to color-coding of cables.

gamma   The coefficient used to scale bandwidth with fiber length.

gap loss   The loss that results when two axially aligned fibers are separated by an air gap. This loss is often most significant in reflectance. The light must launch from one medium to another (glass to air to glass) through the waveguide capabilities of the fiber.

Gbps   Gigabits per second.

GHz   See *gigahertz*.

gigahertz (GHz)   A billion hertz or cycles per second.

GIPOF   Graded index plastic optical fiber.

GOSIP   Government open system interconnect protocol.

graded-index fiber   An optical-fiber cable design in which the index of refraction of the core is lower toward the outside of the core and progressively increases toward the center of the core, thereby reducing modal dispersion of the signal. Light rays are refracted within the core rather than reflected as they are in step index fibers. Graded index fibers were developed to lessen the modal dispersion effects found in multimode fibers with the intent of increasing bandwidth.

ground   A common point of zero potential such as a metal chassis or ground rod that grounds a building to the earth. The ANSI/TIA/EIA-607 Commercial Building Grounding and Bonding Requirements for Telecommunications Standard is the Standard that should be followed for grounding requirements for telecommunications. Grounding should never be undertaken without consulting with a professional licensed electrician.

ground loop   A condition where an unintended connection to ground is made through an interfering electrical conductor that causes electromagnetic interference. See also *ground loop noise*.

ground loop noise   Electromagnetic interference that is created when equipment is grounded at ground points having different potentials, thereby creating an unintended current path. Equipment should always be grounded to a single ground point.

ground window   A single point used to isolate the sensitive electronics associated with the electronic switching system.

guided ray   A ray that is completely confined to the fiber core.

H

half-duplex transmission   Data transmission over a circuit capable of transmitting in either direction. Transmission can be bidirectional but not simultaneous.

halogen   One of the following elements: chlorine, fluorine, bromine, or iodine.

hard-clad silica fiber   An optical fiber with a hard plastic cladding surrounding a step index silica core.

hardware address   The address is represented by six sections of two hexadecimal addresses; for example, 00-03-fe-e7-18-54. This number is hard coded into networking hardware by manufacturers. Also called the *physical address*; see also *MAC address*.

hardware loopback Connects the transmission pins directly to the receiving pins, allowing diagnostic software to test whether a network-interface card can successfully transmit and receive.

HC See *horizontal cross-connect*.

HDSL High bit-rate digital subscriber line. See *digital subscriber line*.

head end (1) The central facility where signals are combined and distributed in a cable television system or a public telephone system. See *central office*. (2) That position in the ring where the signals are captured, often by microwave or by from the backbone, and entered into the system.

header The section of a packet (usually the first part of the packet) where the source and destination addresses reside.

headroom The number of decibels by which a system exceeds the minimum defined requirements. The benefit of more headroom is that it reduces the bit-error rate (BER) and provides a performance safety net to help ensure that current and future high-speed applications will run at peak accuracy, efficiency, and throughput. Also called *overhead* or *margin*.

Hertz (Hz) A measurement of frequency as defined as cycles per second.

HF High frequency.

hicap service A high-capacity communications circuit service such as a private line T-1 or T-3.

home-run cable A cable run that connects a user outlet directly with the telecommunications or wiring closet. This cable has no intermediate splices, bridges, taps, or other connections. Every cable radiates out from the central equipment or wiring closet. This configuration is also known as *star topology* and is the opposite of a daisy-chained cable that may have taps or splices along its length. Home-run cable is the recommended installation method for horizontal cabling in a structured cabling system.

hop A packet passing though a router is counted as a hop.

horizontal cabling The cabling between and including the telecommunications outlet and the horizontal cross-connect. Horizontal cabling is considered the permanent portion of a link; may also be called *horizontal wiring*.

horizontal cross-connect (HC) A cross-connect of horizontal cabling (cable that runs to the work area outlets) to other cabling, such as voice backbone cable and LAN equipment.

horizontal distribution frame A physical structure, usually constructed of steel and lying on the floor, that contains the components that provide interconnection between inter- and intrabuilding cabling. There are many names for this; see also *fiber distribution frame*.

HRC Hybrid ring control.

hub A physical layer hardware device that contains multiple independent but connected modules of network and internetworking equipment. Hubs that repeat the signals that are sent to them are called *active hubs*. Hubs that do not repeat the signal and merely split the signal sent to them are called *passive hubs*. In some cases, *hub* may also refer to a repeater, bridge, switch, or any combination of these.

HVAC Heating, ventilation, and air conditioning.

hybrid cable A cable that contains fiber, coaxial, and/or twisted-pair conductors bundled in a common jacket. May also refer to a fiber-optic cable that has strands of both single-mode and multimode optical fiber.

hybrid connector A connector containing both fiber and electrical connectivity.

hydrogen loss Optical signal loss (attenuation) resulting from hydrogen found in the optical fiber. Hydrogen in glass absorbs light and turns it into heat and thus attenuates the light. For this reason, glass manufacturers serving the fiber-optic industry must keep water and hydrogen out of the glass and deliver it to guaranteed specifications in this regard. In addition, they must protect the glass with a cladding that will preclude the absorption of water and hydrogen into the glass.

Hypalon A DuPont trade name for a synthetic rubber (chlorosulfonated polyethylene) that is used as insulating and jacketing material for cabling.

I

I Symbol used to designate current.

IBM data connector Used to connect IBM Token Ring stations using Type 1 shielded twisted-pair 150-ohm cable. This connector has both male and female components, so every IBM data connector can connect to any other IBM data connector

IC See *intermediate cross-connect*.

ICEA Insulated Cable Engineers Association.

ICS IBM cabling system.

IDC See *insulation displacement connector*.

IDF See *intermediate distribution frame*.

IDP Integrated detector/preamplifier.

IEC International Electrotechnical Commission.

IEEE 802.1 LAN/MAN Management The IEEE Standard that specifies network management, internetworking, and other issues that are common across networking technologies.

IEEE 802.2 Logical Link Control The IEEE Standard that provides specifications for the operation of the logical link control (LLC) sublayer of the OSI data link layer. The LLC sublayer provides an interface between the MAC sublayer and the network layer.

IEEE 802.3 CSMA/CD Networking   The IEEE Standard that specifies a network that uses a logical bus topology, baseband signaling, and a CSMA/CD network access method. This is the Standard that defines Ethernet networks. See also *carrier sense multiple access/collision detect*.

IEEE 802.4 Token Bus   The IEEE Standard that specifies a physical and logical bus topology that uses coaxial or fiber-optic cable and the token-passing media access method.

IEEE 802.5 Token Ring   The IEEE Standard that specifies a logical ring, physical star, and token-passing media access method based on IBM's Token Ring.

IEEE 802.6 Distributed Queue Dual Bus (DQDB) Metropolitan Area Network
The IEEE Standard that provides a definition and criteria for a Metropolitan Area Network (MAN), also known as a Distributed Queue Dual Bus (DQDB).

IEEE 802.7 Broadband Local Area Networks   The IEEE Standard for developing local area networks (LANs) using broadband cabling technology.

IEEE 802.8 Fiber-Optic LANs and MANs
The IEEE Standard that contains guidelines for the use of fiber optics on networks, including FDDI and Ethernet over fiber-optic cable.

IEEE 802.9 Integrated Services (IS) LAN Interface   The IEEE Standard that contains guidelines for the integration of voice and data over the same cable.

IEEE 802.10 LAN/MAN Security   The IEEE Standard that provides a series of guidelines dealing with various aspects of network security.

IEEE 802.11 Wireless LAN   The IEEE Standard that provides guidelines for implementing wireless technologies such as infrared and spread-spectrum radio.

IEEE 802.12 Demand Priority Access Method   The IEEE Standard that defines the concepts of a demand priority network such as HP's 100VG-AnyLAN network architecture.

IF   Intermediate frequency.

ILD   See *injection laser diode*.

impact test   Used to determine a cable's susceptibility to damage when subjected to short-duration crushing forces. Rate of impact, the shape of the striking device, and the force of the impact all are used to define the impact test procedures.

impedance   The total opposition (resistance and reactance) a circuit offers to the flow of alternating current. It is measured in ohms and designated by the symbol Z.

impedance match   A condition where the impedance of a particular cable or component is the same as the impedance of the circuit, cable, or device to which it is connected.

impedance matching transformer   A transformer designed to match the impedance of one circuit to another.

incident angle   The angle between the subject light wave and a plane perpendicular to the subject optical surface.

index matching gel   A fluid with a refractive index close to glass that reduces refractive-index discontinuities that can cause reflective loss.

index matching material   A material in liquid, paste, gel, film, or cement form whose refractive index is nearly equal to the core index; it is used to reduce Fresnel reflections from a fiber end-face. Liquid forms of this are also called *index matching gel*.

index of refraction   The ratio of light velocity in a vacuum to its velocity in a given transmission medium. This is usually abbreviated *n*.

index profile   The curve of the refractive index over the cross section of an optical waveguide.

infrared   The infrared spectrum consists of wavelengths that are longer than 700nm but shorter than 1mm. Humans cannot see infrared radiation, but we feel it as heat. The commonly used wavelengths for transmission through optical fibers are in the infrared at wavelengths between 1100nm and 1600nm.

injection laser   Another name for a semiconductor or laser diode.

injection laser diode (ILD)   A laser diode in which the lasing takes place within the actual semiconductor junction and the light is emitted from the edge of the diode.

insertion loss   A critical measurement for optical-fiber connections, insertion loss measures the attenuation of a device by determining the output of a system before and after the device is inserted into the system. Loss in an optical fiber can be due to absorption, dispersion, scattering, microbending, diffusion, and the methods of coupling the fiber to the power. Usually measured in dB per incident; for example, a coupler, connector, splice, or fiber is measured in dB per km. Most commonly used to describe the power lost at the entrance to a waveguide (an optical fiber is a waveguide) due to axial misalignment, lateral displacement, or reflection that is most applicable to connectors.

inside plant (IP)   Cables that are the portion of the cable network that is inside buildings, where cable lengths are usually shorter than 100 meters. This is the opposite of outside-the-plant (OP or OTP) cables.

Institute of Electrical and Electronic Engineers (IEEE)   A publishing and Standards-making body responsible for many Standards used in LANs, including the 802 series of Standards.

insulation   A material with good dielectric properties that is used to separate electrical components close to one another, such as cable conductors and circuit components. *Good dielectric properties* means that the material is nonconductive to the flow of electrical current. In the case of copper communication cables, *good dielectric properties* also refers to enhanced signal-transfer properties.

insulation displacement connection (IDC)   A type of wire termination in which the wire is punched down into a metal holder that cuts into the insulation wire and makes contact with the conductor, thus causing the electrical connection to be made. These connectors are found on 66-blocks, 110-blocks, and telecommunications outlets.

integrated optical circuit   An optical circuit that is used for coupling between optoelectronic devices and providing signal processing functions. It is composed of both active and passive components.

integrated optics   Optical devices that perform two or more functions and are integrated on a single substrate; analogous to integrated electronic circuits.

integrated optoelectronics   Similar in concept to *integrated optics* except that one of the integrated devices on the semiconductor chip is optical and the other electronic.

Integrated Services Digital Network (ISDN)   A telecommunications standard that is used to digitally send voice, data, and video signals over the same lines. This is a network in which a single digital bit stream can carry a great variety of services. For the Internet it serves much better than analog systems on POTS (plain old telephone service), which is limited to 53Kbps. See also *basic rate interface* and *primary rate interface*.

intelligent hub   A hub that performs bridging, routing, or switching functions. Intelligent hubs are found in collapsed backbone environments.

intelligent network (iN)   A network that is capable of carrying overhead signaling information and services.

intensity   The square of the electric field amplitude of a light wave. Intensity is proportional to irradiance and may be used in place of that term if relative values are considered.

interbuilding backbone   A telecommunications cable that is part of the campus subsystem that connects one building to another.

interconnect   A circuit administration point, other than a cross-connect or an information outlet, that provides capability for routing and rerouting circuits. It does not use patch cords or jumper wires and is typically a jack-and-plug device that is used in smaller distribution arrangements or connects circuits in large cables to those in smaller cables.

interconnect cabinet   Cabinets containing connector panels, patch panels, connectors, and patch cords to interface from inside the plant to outside the plant. The interconnect cabinet is used as an access point for testing and rearranging routs and connections.

interconnection   A connection scheme that provides direct access to the cabling infrastructure and the capability to make cabling system changes using patch cords.

interference   (1) Fiber optic: the interaction of two or more beams of coherent or partially coherent light. (2) Electromagnetic: interaction that produces undesirable signals that interfere with the normal operation of electronic equipment or electronic transmission.

intermediate cross-connect (ICC)   A cross-connect between first-level and second-level backbone cabling. This secondary cross-connect in the backbone cabling is used to mechanically terminate and administer backbone cabling between the main cross-connect and horizontal cross-connect (station cables).

intermediate distribution frame (IDF)
A metal rack (or frame) designed to connect cables that is located in an equipment room or telecommunications (wiring) closet. Consists of components that provide the connection between interbuilding cabling and the intra-building cabling, for instance between the equipment room (where the MDFs are located) and the telecommunications closets (where the IDFs are located). There's usually a permanent, large cable running between the MDF and IDF. Changes to the wiring are usually performed at the IDF and sometimes at the MDF.

International Organization for Standardization (ISO)   The Standards organization that developed the OSI model. This model provides a guideline for how communications occur between computers. See www.iso.ch for more information.

International Telecommunications Union (ITU)   The branch of the United Nations that develops communications specifications.

International Telephone and Telegraph Consultative Committee (CCiTT)
International Standards committee that develops Standards for interface and signal formats.

Internet Architecture Board (IAB)   The committee that oversees management of the Internet, which is made up of several subcommittees including the Internet Engineering Task Force (IETF), the Internet Assigned Numbers Authority (IANA), and the Internet Research Task Force (IRTF). See www.iab.org for more information.

Internet Engineering Task Force (IETF)
An international organization that works under the Internet Architecture Board to establish specifications and protocols relating to the Internet. See www.ietf.org for more information.

Internet Research Task Force (IRTF)   An international organization that works under the Internet Architecture Board to research new Internet technologies. See www.irtf.org for more information.

interoffice trunks (IOF)   A communication channel, of copper or fiber media, between two points. Typically, IOF refers to telephone channels that can transport voice and/or data.

intrabuilding backbone   Telecommunications cables that are part of the building subsystem that connect one telecommunications closet to another or a telecommunications closet to the equipment room.

intrinsic joint loss   The theoretical minimum loss that a given joint or device will have as a function of its nature. Intrinsic joint loss may also be used to describe the given theoretical minimum loss that a splice joint, coupler, or splitter may achieve.

intrinsic loss splice   The optical signal loss arising from differences in the fibers being spliced.

intrinsic performance factor (IPF)
Performance specification whereby total optical channel performance is specified, rather than performance of individual components.

I/O   Input and output.

IOC   See *integrated optical circuit.*

IOF   See *interoffice trunks.*

ion exchange techniques   A method for making and doping glass by ion exchange.

IPF   See *intrinsic performance factor.*

IR   See *infrared.*

irradiance   The power density at a surface through which radiation passes at the radiating surface of a light source or at the cross section of an optical waveguide. The normal unit is watts per centimeters squared.

ISDN   See *Integrated Services Digital Network.*

ISDN terminal adapter   The device used on ISDN networks to connect a local network or single machine to an ISDN network. The ISDN terminal adapter provides line power and translates data from the LAN or individual computer for transmission on the ISDN line.

ISO   See *International Organization for Standardization.*

isochronous   Signals that are dependent on some uniform timing or carry their own timing information imbedded as part of the signal.

isolated ground   A separate ground conductor that is insulated from the equipment or building ground.

isolation   The ability of a circuit or component to reject interference.

ITU   See *International Telecommunications Union.*

J

jabber   A term used with Ethernet to describe the act of continuously sending data. When a station is jabbering, its network adapter circuitry or logic has failed, and it has locked up a network channel with its nonstop transmission.

jack   A receptacle used in conjunction with a plug to make electrical contact between communication circuits. A variety of jacks and their associated plugs are used to connect hardware applications, including cross-connects, interconnects, information outlets, and equipment connections. Jacks are also used to connect cords or lines to telephone systems. A jack is the female component of a plug/jack connector system and may be standard, modified, or keyed.

jacket   The outer protective covering of a cable, usually made of some type of plastic or polymer.

jitter A slight movement of a transmission signal in time or phase that can introduce errors and loss of synchronization. More jitter is introduced when cable runs are longer than the network-topology specification recommends. Other causes of jitter include cables with high attenuation and signals at high frequencies. Also called *phase jitter*, *timing distortion*, or *intersymbol interference*.

joint Any joining or mating of a fiber by splicing (by fusion splicing or physical contact of fibers) or connecting.

jumper (1) A manually placed wire, cable, or fiber connection between two terminations, usually on some form of distributing frame. The connection may be single or multiconductor. A jumper is also called a *cross-connection*. (2) A small connector (cap or plug) that connects pins. This creates a circuit that indicates a setting to a device.

jumper wire An assembly of twisted pairs without connectors on either end used to join telecommunications links at a cross-connect.

junction laser A semiconductor diode laser.

K

Kevlar A strong, synthetic material developed and trademarked by DuPont; the preferred strength element in cable. Also used as a material in body armor and parts for military equipment. Also known by the generic name *aramid*; see also *aramid yarn*.

keying A mechanical feature of a connector system that guarantees correct orientation of a connection. The key prevents the connection to a jack or an optical-fiber adapter of the same type that was intended for another purpose.

kHz Kilohertz; 1,000 hertz.

kilometer One thousand meters; 3,281 feet. The kilometer is a unit of measurement for fiber optics.

KPSI A unit of tensile strength expressed in thousands of pounds per square inch.

L

L Symbol used to designate inductance.

LAN See *local area network*.

LAN adapter See *network-interface card*.

large core fiber Usually a fiber with a core of 200 microns or more. This type of fiber is not common in structured cabling systems.

laser Acronym for *light amplification by stimulated emission radiation*. The laser produces a coherent source of light with a narrow beam and a narrow spectral bandwidth (about 2cm). Lasers in fiber optics are usually solid-state semiconductor types.

laser diode (LD)   A semiconductor diode that emits coherent light above a threshold current. Laser diodes are usually used in higher speed applications (622Mbps to 10Gbps) such as ATM, 1000Base-LX, and SONET. The mode is usually ellipse shaped and therefore requires a lens to make the light symmetrical with the mode of the fiber, which is usually round.

lasing threshold   The lowest excitation level at which a laser's output is dominated by stimulated emission rather than spontaneous emission.

LATA   Local access and transport area.

lateral displacement loss   The loss of signal power that results from lateral displacement from optimum alignment between two fibers or between a fiber and an active device.

launch angle   The angle between the propagation direction of the incident light and the optical axis of an optical waveguide.

launch cable   Used to connect fiber-optic test equipment to the fiber system.

launch fiber   An optical fiber used to couple and condition light from an optical source into another optical fiber. Launch fibers are most often used in test systems to improve the precision of measurements. Also referred to as *launching fiber*.

launching fiber   See *launch fiber*.

lay   The axial distance required for one cabled conductor or conductor strand to complete one revolution around the axis around which it is cabled.

lay direction   The direction of the progressing spiral twist of twisted-pair wires while looking along the axis of the cable away from the observer. The lay direction can be either left or right.

Layer 2 switch   A network device that operates at the data link layer. The switch builds a table of MAC addresses of all connected stations and uses the table to intelligently forward data to the intended recipients.

Layer 3 switch   A network device that can route LAN traffic (layer 3) at a speed that is nearly as quick as a layer 2 switch device. Layer 3 switches typically perform multiport, virtual-LAN, and data-pipelining functions of a standard Layer 2 switch and can also perform routing functions between virtual LANs.

lbf   Abbreviation for pounds force.

leakage   An undesirable passage of current over the surface of or through a connector.

leaky modes   In the boundary region between the guided modes of an optical waveguide, light waves are not capable of propagation so they are called *leaky modes*; they are not guided but are capable of limited propagation with increased attenuation. Leaky modes may be a possible source of error in the measurement of fiber loss, but the effect of leaky modes can be reduced by mode strippers.

leased line   A private telephone line (usually a digital line) rented for the exclusive use of a leasing customer without interchange switching arrangements.

LED See *light emitting diode*.

LF Low frequency.

light The electromagnetic radiation visible to the human eye between 400nm and 700nm. The term is also applied to electromagnetic radiation with properties similar to visible light; this includes the invisible near-infrared radiation in most fiber-optic communication systems.

light emitting diode (LED) A semiconductor device used in a transmitter to convert information from electric to optical form. The LED typically has a large spectral width; LED devices are usually used on low-speed applications (100–256Mbps) such as 100Base-F and FDDI.

light waves Electromagnetic waves in the region of optical frequencies. The term *light* was originally restricted to light that is visible to the human eye with wavelengths between 400nm and 700nm. Referring to light waves that are in the adjacent spectral regions to visible light (infrared from 700nm to about 2000nm) as *light* emphasizes the physical and technical characteristics they have in common with visible light.

lightguide cable An optical fiber, multiple fiber, or fiber bundle that includes a cable jacket and strength members and is fabricated to meet optical, mechanical, and environmental specifications.

line build-out (LBO) An attenuator inserted into the signal path to ensure that the received power level is within the manufacturer's specification.

line conditioner A device used to protect against power surges and spikes. Line conditioners use several electronic methods to clean all power coming into the line conditioner so that clean, steady power is put out by the line conditioner.

link An end-to-end transmission path provided by the cabling infrastructure. Cabling links include all cables and connecting hardware that compose the horizontal or backbone subsystems. Equipment and work-area cables are not included as part of a link.

link light A small light emitting diode (LED) that is found on both the NIC and the hub and is usually green and labeled "Link." A link light indicates that the NIC and the hub are making a data link layer connection.

listed Equipment included on a list published by an organization, acceptable to the authority having jurisdiction, that maintains periodic inspection of production of listed equipment, and whose listing states either that the equipment or material meets appropriate standards, or that it has been tested and found suitable for use in a specified manner. In the United States, electrical and data communications equipment is typically listed with Underwriters Laboratories (UL).

LLDPE Linear low-density polyethylene jacketing.

lobe An arm of a Token Ring that extends from a multistation access unit (MSAU) to a workstation adapter.

local area network (LAN) A network connecting multiple nodes within a defined area, usually within a building. The linking can be done by cable that carries optical fiber or copper. These are usually high bandwidth (4Mbps or greater) and connect many nodes within a few thousand meters. LANs can, however, operate at lower data rates (less than 1Mbps) and connect nodes over only a few meters.

local exchange carrier (LEC) The local regulated provider of public switched telecommunications services. The LEC is regulated by the local Public Utilities Commission.

local loop The loop or circuit between receivers (and, in two-way systems, receivers and senders), who are normally the customers or subscribers to the systems products, and the terminating equipment at the central office.

LocalTalk A low-speed form of LAN data link technology developed by Apple Computer. It was designed to transport Apple's AppleTalk networking scheme; it uses a carrier sense multiple access/collision avoidance (CSMA/CA) form of medium access control. Supports transmission at 230Kbps.

logical network addressing The addressing scheme used by protocols at the OSI network layer.

logical ring topology A network topology in which all network signals travel from one station to another, being read and forwarded by each station. A Token Ring network is an example of a logical ring topology.

ogical topology Describes the way the information flows. The types of logical topologies are the same as the physical topologies, except that the information flow specifies the type of topology.

long wavelength Light whose wavelength is greater than 1000nm (longer than one micron).

longitudinal conversion loss (LCL) A measurement (in decibels) of the differential voltage induced on a conductor pair as a result of subjecting that pair to longitudinal voltage. This is considered to be a measurement of circuit balance.

longitudinal conversion transfer loss (LCTL) Measures cable balance by the comparison of the signal appearing across the pair to the signal between ground and the pair, where the applied signal is at the opposite end of the cable from the location at which the across-pair signal is measured. LCTL is also called *far-end unbalance attenuation*.

longitudinal modes Oscillation modes of a laser along the length of its cavity. Each longitudinal mode contains only a very narrow range of wavelengths; a laser emitting a single longitudinal mode has a very narrow bandwidth. The oscillation of light along the length of the laser's cavity is normally such that two times the length of the cavity will equal an integral number of wavelengths. Longitudinal modes are distinct from transverse modes.

loop (1) A complete electrical circuit. (2) The pair of wires that winds its way from the central office to the telephone set or system at the customer's office, home, or factory.

loopback   A type of diagnostic test in which a transmitted signal is returned to the sending device after passing through a data communications link or network. This test allows the comparison of a returned signal with the transmitted signal to determine if the signal is making its way through the communications link and how much signal it is losing upon its return.

loose tube   A protective tube loosely surrounding an optical fiber, often filled with gel used as a protective coating. Loose-tube cable designs are usually found in outdoor cables, not inside buildings.

loss   The attenuation of optical or electrical signal, normally measured in decibels. With respect to fiber-optic cables, there are two key measurements of loss: insertion loss and return loss; both of these are measured in decibels. The higher the decibel number, the more loss there is. Some copper-based and optical fiber–based materials are lossy and absorb electromagnetic radiation in one form and emit it in another; for example, heat. Some optical-fiber materials are reflective and return electromagnetic radiation in the same form as it is received, usually with little or no power loss. Still others are transparent or translucent, meaning they are "window" materials; loss is the portion of energy applied to a system that is dissipated and performs no useful work. See also *attenuation*.

loss budget   A calculation and allowance for total attenuation in a system that is required in order to ensure that the detectors and receivers can make intelligent decisions about the pulses they receive.

lossy   Describes a connection having poor efficiency with respect to loss of signal.

M

mA   Milliampere (one thousandth of an ampere).

MAC   (1) See *media access control*. (2) Abbreviation for *moves, adds, and changes*.

macrobending   Macroscopic axial deviations (visible bends) of a fiber from a straight line, in contrast to microbending.

macrobending loss   Optical power loss due to large bends in the fiber.

main cross-connect   A cross-connect for first-level backbone cables, entrance cables, and equipment cables. The main cross-connect is at the top level of the premises cabling tree.

main distribution frame (MDF)   A wiring arrangement that connects the telephone lines coming from outside on one side and the internal lines on the other. The MDF may be a central connection point for data communications equipment in addition to voice communications. An MDF may also carry protective devices or function as a central testing point.

MAN   See *metropolitan area network*.

Manchester coding   A method of encoding a LAN in which each bit time that represents a data bit has a transition in the middle of the bit time. Manchester coding is used with 10Mbps Ethernet (10Base-2, 10Base-5, 10Base-F, and 10Base-T) and Token Ring LANs.

margin   The allowance for attenuation in addition to that explicitly accounted for in system design.

mass splicing   The concurrent and simultaneous splicing of multiple fibers at one time. Currently mass splicing is done on ribbon cable, and the standard seems to be ribbon cable with 12 fibers. Special splice protectors are made for this purpose, as well as special equipment for splicing.

material dispersion   A pulse dispersion that results from each wavelength traveling at a speed different from other wavelengths through an optical fiber. See also *chromatic dispersion*.

MBE   Molecular beam epitaxy.

Mbps (megabits per second)   A data rate of one million bits per second.

MC   See *main cross-connect*.

MCVD   Modified chemical vapor deposition.

MDF   See *main distribution frame*.

MDI   See *media dependent interface*.

MDPE   Medium-density polyethylene jacketing.

MDU   Multiple dwelling unit.

meantime between failures (MTBF)
A measurement of how reliable a hardware component is. Usually measured in thousands of hours.

mechanical splice   With respect to fiber-optic cables, a splice in which fibers are joined mechanically (e.g., glued, crimped, or otherwise held in place) but not fused together using heat. Mechanical splice is the opposite of a fusion splice in which the two fiber ends are butted and then joined by permanently bonding the glass end-faces through the softening of the glass, which is fused together.

media   Wire, cable, or conductors used for transmission of signals.

media access   The process of vying for transmission time on the network media.

media access control (MAC)   A sublayer of the OSI data link layer (Layer 2) that controls the way multiple devices use the same media channel. It controls which devices can transmit and when they can transmit. For most network architectures, each device has a unique address that is sometimes referred to as the MAC address. See also *media access control (MAC) address*.

media access control (MAC) address
Network-adapter cards such as Ethernet, Token Ring, and FDDI cards are assigned addresses when MAC addresses are built. A MAC address is 48 bits separated by six sections of two hexadecimal addresses. No two cards have the same hardware address. The IEEE helps to achieve the unique addresses by assigning three-byte prefixes to manufacturers so that no two manufacturers have the same first three bytes in their MAC address. The MAC address is also called the *hardware address*.

medium attachment unit (MAU)   When referring to Ethernet LANs, the transceiver in Ethernet networks.

media filter   An impedance-matching device used to change the impedance of the cable to the expected impedance of the connected device. For example, media filters can be used in Token Ring networks to transform the 100-ohm impedance of UTP cabling to the 150-ohm impedance of media interface connections.

media interface connector (MIC connector)   A pair of fiber-optic connectors that links the fiber media to the FDDI network card or concentrator. The MIC consists of both the MIC plug termination of an optical cable and the MIC receptacle that is joined with the FDDI node.

medium dependent interface (MDI)   Used with Ethernet systems; it is the connector used to make the mechanical and electrical interface between a transceiver and a media segment. An 8-pin RJ-45 connector is the MDI for the 10Base-T, 100Base-TX, 100Base-T2, 100Base-T4, and 1000Base-T media systems.

medium independent interface (MII)   Used with 100Mbps Ethernet systems to attach MAC-level hardware to a variety of physical media systems. Similar to the AUI interface used with 10Mbps Ethernet systems. The MII is a 40-pin connection to outboard transceivers or PHY devices.

mega   Prefix meaning one million.

megahertz (Mhz)   A unit of frequency that is equal to one million hertz.

meridian plane   Any plane that includes or contains the optical axis.

meridianal ray   A light ray that passes through the axis of an optical fiber.

metropolitan area network (MAN)   A network that encompasses an entire city or metropolitan area.

MFD   See *mode field diameter*.

MHz   See *megahertz*.

MIC connector   See *media interface connector*.

micro   Prefix meaning one millionth.

microbending   Minute but severe bends in fiber cable that involve axial displacements of a few micrometers and spatial wavelengths of a few millimeters. Microbends cause loss of light and consequently increase the attenuation of the fiber. Most microbending can be avoided by selecting proper buffer materials and proper cabling, handling, and installation techniques.

microbending loss   The optical power loss due to microscopic bends in the fiber.

microfarad   One millionth of a farad. Abbreviated *μF* and, less commonly, *μfd*, *mf*, or *mfd*.

micrometer   Also referred to as a *micron*; one millionth of a meter, often abbreviated as um or with the symbol μ. A micrometer is equal to 10^{-6} meters. Fiber optics can only be understood in these dimensions; optical wavelengths are measured in nanometers. Fiber that carries these optical wavelengths is measured in microns.

micron (μ)   See *micrometer*.

midsplit broadband   A broadcast network configuration in which the cable is divided into two channels, each using a different range of frequencies. One channel is used to transmit signals and the other is used to receive.

MII   See *medium independent interface*.

milli   Prefix meaning one thousandth.

misalignment loss   The loss of optical power resulting from angular misalignment, lateral displacement, or end separation.

mixing segment   An Ethernet term that is used in IEEE 802.3 Standards to describe a segment that may have more than two MDI connections.

MLM   Multilongitudinal mode.

MMF   See *multimode fiber*.

MMJ   See *modified modular jack*.

modal bandwidth   The bandwidth-limiting characteristic of multimode fiber systems caused by the variable arrival times of various modes.

modal dispersion   The spreading that arises from differences in the times that different modes take to travel through multimode fibers.

modal noise   The disturbance in multimode fibers fed by laser diodes. This occurs when fibers contain elements with mode-dependent attenuation, such as imperfect splices; the better the coherence of the laser light, the more severe the modal noise is.

mode   A single wave traveling in an optical fiber or in a light path through a fiber. Light has modes in optical-fiber cable. In a single-mode fiber, only one mode (the fundamental mode) can propagate through the fiber. Multimode fiber has several hundred modes that differ in field pattern and propagation velocity. The upper limit to the number of modes is determined by the core diameter and the numerical aperture of the waveguide.

mode field diameter (MFD)   The diameter of optical energy in a single-mode fiber-optic cable. Since the mode field diameter is greater than the core diameter, mode field diameter replaces the core diameter as a practical parameter.

mode filter   A device that can select, attenuate, or reject a specific mode. Mode filters are used to remove high-order modes from a fiber and thereby simulate EMD.

mode mixing   The numerous modes of a multimode fiber differ in their propagation velocities. As long as they propagate independently of each other, the fiber bandwidth varies inversely with the fiber length due to multimode distortion. As a result of irregularities in the geometry of the optical-fiber cable and of the index profile, a gradual energy exchange occurs between modes with differing velocities. Due to this mode mixing, the bandwidth of long multimode fibers is greater than the value obtained by linear extrapolation from measurements on short fibers.

mode scrambler   A device composed of one or more optical fibers in which strong mode coupling occurs. Mode scramblers are frequently used to provide a mode distribution that is independent of source characteristics.

mode stripper A device that removes high-order modes in a multimode fiber to give standard measurement conditions.

modem A device that implements modulator-demodulator functions to convert between digital data and analog signals.

modified modular jack (MMJ) A six-wire modular jack used by the DEC wiring system. The MMJ has a locking tab that is shifted to the right-hand side.

modular Equipment is said to be modular when it is made of plug-in units that can be added together to make the system larger, improve the capabilities, or expand its size. Faceplates made for use with structured cabling systems are often modular and permit the use of multiple types of telecommunications outlets or modular jacks such as RJ-45, coaxial, audio, fiber, etc.

modular jack A female telecommunications interface connector. Modular jacks are typically mounted in a fixed location and may have four, six, or eight contact positions; though most typical standards-based cabling systems will have an eight-position jack. Not all positions need be equipped with contacts. The modular jack may be keyed or unkeyed so as to permit only certain types of plugs to be inserted into the jack.

modulation (1) Coding of information onto the carrier frequency. Types of modulation include Amplitude Modulation, Frequency Modulation, and Phase Modulation. (2) When light is emitted by a medium, it is coherent, meaning that it is in a fixed phase relationship within fixed points of the light wave. The light is used because it is a continuous, or sinusoidal, wave (a white or blank form) upon which a signal can be superimposed by modulation of that form. The modulation is a variation imposed upon this white form, a variation of amplitude, frequency, or phase of the light. There are two basic forms of this modulation: one by an analog form, another by a digital signal. This signal is created in the form of the "intelligence" and superimposed upon the light wave. It is then recovered by a photodetector and converted into electrical energy.

monitor level signal A digital signal that is 20dB below the standard DS-1 or DS-3 signal level.

monochromatic Light consisting of a single wavelength. In practice, radiation is never perfectly monochromatic but at best displays a narrow band of wavelengths.

Motion Pictures Experts Group (MPEG) A standards group operating under the ISO that develops standards for digital video and audio compression.

MOVPE Metal organic vapor phase epitaxy.

MPEG See *Motion Pictures Experts Group*.

MRN See *multiple reflection noise*.

MSAU See *multistation access unit*.

MTBF See *meantime between failures*.

MT-RJ connector A proposed duplex fiber-optic connector standard from AMP/-Siecor that looks similar to the RJ-45-type connector.

multifiber jumpers   Used to interconnect fiber-optic patch panels from point to point.

multimedia   (1) An application that communicates to more than one of the human sensory receptors such as audio and video components. (2) Applications that communicate information by more than one means or cabling media.

multimode   Transmission of multiple modes of light. See also *mode*.

multimode distortion   The signal distortion in an optical waveguide resulting from the superposition of modes with differing delays.

multimode fiber   Optical-fiber cable whose core is between 8 and 200 microns with a refractive index that is graded or stepped; multimode fiber supports the propagation of multiple modes (several beams of light). It allows the use of inexpensive LED light sources, and connector alignment and coupling is less critical than with single-mode fiber. Distances of transmission and transmission bandwidth are less than with single-mode fiber due to dispersion. The ANSI/TIA/EIA-568-A Standard recommends the use of 62.5/125-micron multimode fiber for horizontal cabling.

multimode laser   A laser that produces emissions in two or more longitudinal modes.

multiple reflection noise (MRN)   The noise at the receiver caused by the interface of delayed signals from two or more reflection points in an optical-fiber span.

multiplex   The combination of two or more signals to be transmitted along a single communications channel.

multiplexer   A device that combines two or more discrete signals into a single output. Many types of multiplexing exist, including time-division multiplexing and wavelength-division multiplexing.

multistation access unit (MAU or MSAU)   Used in Token Ring LANs, a wiring concentrator that allows terminals, PCs, printers, and other devices to be connected in a star-based configuration to Token Ring LANs. MAU hardware can be either active or passive and is not considered to be part of the cabling infrastructure.

multiuser telecommunications outlet assembly (MuTOA)   A connector that has several telecommunications/outlet connectors in it. These are often used in a single area that will have several computers and telephones.

mutual capacitance   The capacitance between two conductors when all other conductors are connected together.

MUX   See *multiplexer*.

Mylar   The DuPont trademark for polyethylene terephtalate (polyester) film.

MZI   Mach Zehnder Interferometer.

N

NA   See *numerical aperture*.

nanometer   A unit of measurement equal to one billionth of a meter; abbreviated *nm*.

nanosecond   One billionth of a second; abbreviated *ns*.

National Electrical Code (NEC)   The U.S. electrical wiring code that specifies safety standards for copper and fiber-optic cable used inside buildings. See Chapter 4 for more information.

National Security Agency (NSA)   The U.S. government agency responsible for protecting U.S. communications and producing foreign intelligence information. It was established by presidential directive in 1952 as a separately organized agency within the Department of Defense.

N-connector   A coaxial cable connector used for Ethernet 10Base-5 thick coaxial segments.

NDFA   Neodymium doped fiber amplifier.

near-end crosstalk (NEXT)   Crosstalk between two twisted pairs measured at the near end of the cable. *Near* is defined as the end of the cable where the original transmission originated. See Chapter 1 for more information.

near-field radiation pattern   The distribution of the irradiance over an emitting surface (over the cross section of an optical waveguide).

near infrared   The part of the infrared spectrum near the visible spectrum, typically 700nm to 1500nm or 2000nm; it is not rigidly defined.

NEC   See *National Electrical Code*.

NEMA   National Electrical Manufacturers Association.

NEP (noise equivalent power)   The radiant power that provides a noise-to-signal ratio of one at the output of a given detector within defined parameters for modulation, frequency, wavelength, and a given effective noise bandwidth.

network   Ties things together. Computer networks connect all types of computers and computer-related peripherals—terminals, printers, modems, door entry sensors, temperature monitors, etc. The networks we're most familiar with are long-distance ones, such as phone or train networks. Local area networks (LANs) connect computer equipment within a building or campus.

network-interface card (NIC)   A circuit board installed in a computing device that is used to attach the device to a network. An NIC performs the hardware functions that are required to provide a computing device physical communications capabilities with a network.

network media   The physical cables that link computers in a network; also known as physical media.

NEXT   See *near-end crosstalk*.

NFPA   National Fire Protection Association. See Chapter 4 for more information.

nibble   One-half byte.

NIC   See *network-interface card*.

NIC diagnostics   Software utilities that verify that the NIC is functioning correctly and that test every aspect of NIC operation, including connectivity to other nodes on the network.

Nippon Telephone and Telegraph (NTT)
The Japanese equivalent of AT&T.

NIR   Near-end crosstalk-to-insertion loss ratio.

Node   End point of a network connection. Nodes include any device connected to a network such as file servers, printers, or workstations.

noise   In a cable or circuit, any extraneous signal that interferes with the desired signal normally present in or passing through the system.

noise equivalent power (NEP)   The optical input power to a detector needed to generate an electrical signal equal to the inherent electrical noise.

Nomex   A DuPont trademark for a temperature resistant, flame retardant nylon.

nominal velocity of propagation (NVP)
The speed that a signal propagates through a cable expressed as a decimal fraction of the speed of light in a vacuum. Typical copper cables have an NVP value of between 0.6 and 0.9.

non-return to zero (NRZ)   A digital code in which the signal level is low for a 0 bit and high for a 1 bit and which does not return to 0 between successive 1 bits.

normal angle   The angle that is perpendicular to a surface.

NRZ   See *non-return to zero*.

NRZI   Non-return to zero inverted.

NT-1   An NT1 is used to terminate ISDN at the customer premises. It converts a two-wire ISDN U interface to a four-wire S/T interface.

NTSC   National Television Standards Code.

NTT   See *Nippon Telephone and Telegraph*.

numerical aperture (NA)   The light gathering ability of a fiber, defining the maximum angle to the fiber axis at which light will be accepted and propagated through the fiber.

NVOD   Near video on demand.

NVP   See *nominal velocity of propagation*.

O

O   Orange, when used in conjunction with color-coding for twisted-pair cabling.

OC-1   Optical carrier level one, equal to 51.84Mbps. This is a SONET channel, whose format measures 90 bytes and is composed of the transport overhead and the synchronous payload envelope.

OC-2   SONET channel of 622.08Mbps.

OC-48   SONET channel of 2.4Gbps.

OC-192   SONET channel of 13Gbps, currently the highest level now available.

octet   Eight bits (also called a *byte*).

ODC   See *optical directional coupler*.

O/E   Optical to electronic.

OEIC   Optoelectronic-integrated chip.

OEM   Original equipment manufacturer.

OFDM   Orthogonal frequency division multiplexing.

off-hook   The handset's state of being lifted from its cradle. The term originated from when the early handsets were actually suspended from a metal hook on the phone. With modern telephones, when the handset is removed from its hook or cradle, it completes the electrical loop, thus signaling the central office to provide dial tone. Opposite of *on-hook*.

office principle ground point (OPGP)
The principle ground point/bus that is directly connected to the office ground array or water pipe.

OFSTP   Optical-fiber standard test procedure.

ohm   A unit of electrical resistance. The value of resistance through which a potential of one volt will maintain a current of one ampere.

OIU   Optical interface unit.

OLTS   Optical loss test set.

on-hook   The telephone handset's state of resting in its cradle. The phone is not connected to any particular line. Only the bell is active—i.e., it will ring if a call comes in. Opposite of *off-hook*.

ONU   Optical network unit.

open circuit   A break in a cable.

open fault   A break in the continuity of a circuit. This means that the circuit is not complete or the cable/fiber is broken. This condition is also called *unmated, open,* or *unterminated.*

open systems interconnect (OSI)
A model defined by the ISO to categorize the process of communication between computers in terms of seven layers. See also *International Organization for Standardization.*

operations, administration, maintenance, and provisioning (OAM&P)   A common industry term given to the functions performed in support of the telecommunications network.

OPM   Open power meter.

optical amplifier   Increases the power of an optical signal without converting any of the signals from optical to electrical energy and then back to optical so that the amplification processes the optical signal wholly within optical amplification equipemnt. The two most common optical amplifiers are semiconductor laser amplifiers and those made from doped fiber, such as the EDFA (erbium doped fiber amplifier), which amplifies with a laser pump diode and a section of erbium doped fiber.

optical attenuator   Reduces the intensity of light waves, usually so that the power is within the capacity of the detector. There are three basic forms of attenuators: fixed optical attenuators, stepwise variable optical attenuators, and continuous variable optical attenuators. Attenuation is normally achieved either by a doped fiber or an offset or core misalignment. See also *attenuator.*

optical bandpass   The range of optical wavelengths that can be transmitted through a component.

optical cable entrance facility (OCEF) An area providing space for splicing fibers connecting equipment to outside plant.

optical carrier *n*   Optical signal standards. The *n* indicates the level where the respective data rate is exactly *n* times the first level OC-1. OC-1 has a data rate of 51.84Mbps. OC-3 is three times that rate, or 155.52Mbps, etc. Associated with SONET.

optical detector   A transducer that generates an electronic signal when excited by an optical power source.

optical directional coupler (ODC)   A directional coupler used to combine or separate optical power.

optical-fiber cable   An assembly consisting of one or more optical fibers. These optical fibers are thin glass or plastic filaments used for the transmission of information via light signals. This is the signal carrying part of a fiber-optic cable. See also *single-mode fiber* and *multimode fiber*.

optical-fiber duplex adapter   A mechanical media termination device designed to align and join two duplex connectors.

optical-fiber duplex connector   A mechanical media termination device designed to transfer optical power between two pairs of optical fibers.

optical isolator   A component used to block out reflected and other unwanted light.

optical loss test set   An optical power meter and a light source calibrated for use together to detect and measure loss of signal on an optical cable.

optical polarization   A term used to describe the orientation in space of time varying field vector of an optical signal.

optical receiver   An optoelectronic circuit that converts an incoming signal to an electronic signal. The optical receiver will include a transducer in the form of a detector, which might be a photodiode or other device. When irradiated by an optical power device, it will be able to translate the optical signal into an electronic signal.

optical reference plane   Defines the optical boundary between the MIC (media interface connector) plug and the MIC receptacle.

optical repeater   An optoelectronic device, which could include an amplifier, that receives a signal and amplifies it, especially in the case of analog signals. In the case of a digital signal, the optical repeater reshapes or retimes the signal and then retransmits it.

optical return loss (ORL)   The ratio (expressed in decibels) of optical power reflected by a component or an assembly to the optical power incident on a component port when that component or assembly is introduced into a link or system.

optical spectrum   Starts with red, then orange, yellow, green, blue, indigo, and finally violet. Each color represents a wavelength or frequency of electromagnetic energy; the spectrum is between 400nm and 700nm. 400nm is the ultraviolet portion of the spectrum and 700nm is the infrared portion of the spectrum. Lasers are often used to create light of very precise and pure color.

optical time domain reflectometer (OTDR)   A device and method for characterizing a fiber wherein an optical pulse is transmitted through the fiber, and the resulting backscatter and reflections to the input are measured as a function of time. Useful in estimating attenuation coefficient as a function of distance and identifying defects and other localized losses.

optical transmitter   An optoelectronic circuit that converts an electronic signal into an optical signal.

optical waveguide   Any structure that can guide light; the optical waveguide is a dielectric waveguide with a core consisting of optically transparent material of low attenuation (usually silica glass) and with cladding consisting of optically transparent material of lower refractive index than that of the core. It is used for the transmission of signals with light waves and is frequently referred to as *fiber*.

optoelectronic   Pertains to a device that responds to optical power, emits or modifies optical radiation, or utilizes optical radiation for its internal operation. Any device that functions as an electrical-to-optical or optical-to-electrical transducer.

OSI   Open systems interconnection.

OTDR   See *optical time domain reflectometer*.

outlet   See *telecommunications outlet*.

outlet box   A metallic or nonmetallic box mounted within a wall, floor, or ceiling used to hold outlet, connector, or transition devices.

output   The useful signal or power delivered by a circuit or device.

outside plant (OSP) cables   Typically used outside of the wire center but also may be routed into the CEF. Since OSP cables are more flammable than plenum-grade cables, the distance of penetration into the building must be limited.

oversampling   A method of synchronous bit synchronization. The receiver samples the signal at a much faster rate than the data rate. This permits the use of an encoding method that does not add clocking transitions.

over-voltage threshold   The level of over-voltage that will trip the circuit breaker in a surge protector.

P

P region   The area in a semiconductor that is doped to have an abundance of electron acceptors in which vacancies in the valence electron level are the dominant current carriers.

PABX   See *private branch exchange*.

packet   Bits grouped serially in a defined format containing a command or data message sent over a network. The packet is the basic division of data sent over a network.

packet switching   The process of breaking messages into packets. Each packet is then routed optimally across the network. Packet sequence numbers are used at the destination node to reassemble packets.

packing fraction   The fraction of the surface area of a fiber-optic bundle that is fiber core.

PAD   Packet assembler/dissembler.

PAM5x5   The signal-encoding technique used in the Ethernet 100Base-T2 and 1000Base-T media systems.

panel   See *patch panel*.

Part 68 requirements   Specifications established by the FCC as the minimum acceptable protection that communications equipment must provide to the telephone network.

PAS   See *profile alignment system*.

passive branching device   A device that divides an optical input into two or more optical outputs.

passive coupler   Divides light without generating new light.

patch cable   Any flexible piece of cable that connects one network device to the main cable run or to a patch panel that in turn connects to the main cable run; also called *patch cord*. Used for interconnecting circuits on a patch panel or cross-connect. Patch cables are short distance, usually have connectors preinstalled on both ends, are used to connect equipment, and are generally between three and six meters long.

patch panel   A connecting hardware that typically provides means to connect horizontal or backbone cables to an arrangement of fixed connectors that may be accessed using patch cords or equipment cords to form cross-connections or interconnections. Patch panels may connect either copper or optical-fiber cables.

patching   A means of connecting circuits via cords and connectors that can be easily disconnected and reconnected at another point. May be accomplished by using modular patch cords connected between jack fields or by patch cord assemblies that plug onto connecting blocks.

pathway   A facility (e.g., conduit, cable tray, raceway, ducting, or plenum) for the placement and protection of telecommunications cables.

PBS   Polarizing beam splitter.

PBX   See *private branch exchange*.

PCC   Premises communication cable (a CSA cable designation).

PCM   Pulse code modulation.

PCS fiber   See *plastic-clad silica fiber.*

PDN   Public data network.

PE   See *polyethylene.*

peak   The maximum instantaneous value of a varying current or voltage.

peak wavelength   The wavelength at which the optical power of a source is at a maximum.

pedestal   A device, usually mounted on the floor, which is used to house voice/data jacks or power outlets at the point of use. Also commonly referred to as a *monument, tombstone, above-floor fitting,* or *doghouse.*

periodicity   Uniformly spaced variations in the insulation diameter of a transmission cable that result in reflections of a signal.

permanent virtual circuit (PVC)
Technology used by frame relay that allows virtual data communications (circuits) to be set up between the sender and receiver over a packet-switched network.

permittivity   See *dielectric constant.*

phase   An angular relationship between waves or the position of a wave in its oscillation cycle.

phase modulation (PM)   One of three basic methods of adding information to a sine wave signal in which its phase is varied to impose information on it. See also *amplitude* and *frequency modulation.*

phase shift   A change in the phase relationship between two alternating quantities.

photo-bleaching   A reduction in added loss that occurs when a fiber is exposed to light. Ionizing radiation causes added loss. This loss can be reduced by transmitting light through the fiber during normal operation or by exposing the fiber to sunlight.

photocurrent   The current that flows through a photosensitive device, such as a photodiode, as the result of exposure to radiant power (light).

photodetector   An optoelectronic transducer, such as a pin photodiode or avalanche photodiode, that acts a light detector.

photodiode   A diode designed to produce photocurrent by absorbing light. Photodiodes are used for the detection of optical power and for the conversion of optical power into electrical power.

photon   A quantum of electromagnetic energy.

photonic   A term coined to describe devices using photons, analogous to *electronic,* describing devices working with electrons.

PHY   Physical layer device.

physical bus topology   A network that uses one network cable that runs from one end of the network to the other. Workstations connect at various points along this cable. These networks are easy to run cable for, but they are typically not as reliable as a star topology. 10Base-2 Ethernet is a good example of a network architecture that uses a physical bus topology.

physical mesh topology   A network configuration that specifies a link between each and every device in the network. A physical mesh topology requires a lot of cabling and is very difficult to reconfigure.

physical ring topology   A network topology that is set up in a circular fashion. Data travels around the ring in one direction, and each device on the ring acts as a repeater to keep the signal strong as it travels. Each device incorporates a receiver for the incoming signal and a transmitter to send the data on to the next device in the ring. The network is dependent on the ability of the signal to travel around the ring. Cabling a physical ring topology is difficult because of the amount of cable that must be run. FDDI is an example of a network that can be wired to use a physical ring topology.

physical star topology   A network in which a cable runs from each network device to a central device called a hub. The hub allows all devices to communicate as if they were directly connected. The network may electrically follow another type of topology such as bus or ring topology, but the wiring is still a star topology.

physical topology   The physical layout of a network, such as bus, star, ring, or mesh.

PIC   (1) Photo-optic integrated circuit. (2) Plastic Insulated Conductors.

pico   Prefix meaning one millionth of one millionth.

picofarad   One millionth of one millionth of a farad. Abbreviated *pf*.

picosecond (PS)   One trillionth of a second.

pigtail   (1) A short length of fiber with a permanently attached device, usually a connector, on one end. (2) A fiber-optic cable assembly consisting of a connector and an unterminated fiber at the other end. Normally found in applications wherein a splice is convenient for terminating a device with a connector. Also used when the loss characteristics of the connector must be known precisely. For instance, a splice of .03dB might be reliably predicted and controlled, but the variability of most commercially available terminations is unacceptable so a precharacterized cable assembly is cut into a pigtail and attached to the device through splicing.

PIN device   Positive intrinsic negative device.

plain old telephone service (POTS)   The basic service that supplies standard single line telephones, telephone lines, and access to the public switched network; it only receives and places calls and has no added features like call waiting or call forwarding.

planar waveguide   A waveguide fabricated in a flat material such as a thin film.

plastic-clad silica (PCS) fiber   A step index multimode fiber that has a silica core and is surrounded by a lower index plastic cladding.

plastic fiber   Optical fiber having a plastic core and plastic cladding rather than using glass.

plasticizer   A chemical added to plastics to make them softer and more flexible.

plenum   The air-handling space between the walls, under structural floors, and above drop ceilings when used to circulate and otherwise handle air in a building. Plenum-grade cable can be run through these spaces if local building codes permit it.

plenum cable   Cable whose flammability and smoke characteristics allow it to be routed in plenum spaces without being enclosed in a conduit.

plug   The male component of a plug/jack connector system. In premises cabling, a plug provides the means for a user to connect communications equipment to the communications outlet.

PMD   Physical media dependent.

POF   Plastic optical fiber.

POFDI   Plastic optical-fiber distributed interface.

point-to-point transmission   Carrying a signal between two endpoints without branching to other points.

polarity   Identifies which side of an electrical circuit is positive and which is negative.

polarization   (1) Alignment of the electric and magnetic fields that make up an electromagnetic wave. Normally refers to the electric field. If all light waves have the same alignment, the light is polarized. (2) The direction of the electric field in the light wave.

polarization maintaining fiber   Optical fiber that maintains the polarization of light that enters it.

polarization stability   The variation in insertion loss as the polarization state of the input light is varied.

polling   A media access control method that uses a central device called a controller, which polls each device in turn and asks if it has data to transmit. 100VG-AnyLAN hubs poll nodes to see if they have data to transmit.

POLSK   Polarization shift keying.

polybutadene   A type of synthetic rubber often blended with other synthetic rubbers to improve their dielectric properties.

polyethylene (PE)   A thermoplastic material with excellent electrical properties. PE is used as an insulating material and as jacket material where flame-resistance requirements allow.

polymer   A substance made of repeating chemical units or molecules. The term is often used as a synonym for plastic, rubber, or elastomer.

polypropylene   A thermoplastic material that is similar to polyethylene but is somewhat stiffer and has a higher softening point (temperature).

polyurethane (PUR)   A broad class of polymers that are noted for good abrasion and solvent resistance. Not as common as PVC (polyvinyl chloride).

polyvinyl chloride (PVC)   A general-purpose thermoplastic used for wire and cable insulation and jackets.

PON   Passive optical network.

POTS   See *plain old telephone service*.

potting   The process of sealing by filling with a substance to exclude moisture.

power brownout   Occurs when power drops below normal levels for several seconds or longer.

power distribution system   The system of cables, connectors, and distribution frames required to efficiently deliver power from the power plant to the network elements.

power level   The difference between the total power delivered to a circuit, cable, or device and the power delivered by that device to a load.

power overage   Occurs when too much power is coming into a piece of equipment. See also *power spike* and *power surge*.

power ratio   The ratio of power appearing at the load to the input power. Expressed in decibels.

power sag   Occurs when the power level drops below normal and rises to normal in less than one second.

power spike   Occurs when the power level rises above normal and drops back to normal for less than a second. See also *power overage* and *power surge*.

power sum   A test method for cables with multiple pairs of wire whereby the mathematical sum of pair-to-pair crosstalk from a reference wire pair is measured while all other wire pairs are carrying signals. Power-sum tests are necessary on cables that will be carrying bidirectional signals on more than two pairs. Most commonly measured on four-pair cables.

power surge   Occurs when the power level rises above normal and stays there for longer than a second or two. See also *power overage* and *power spike*.

power underage   Occurs when the power level drops below the standard level. Opposite of *power overage*.

prefusing   Fusing the end of a fiber-optic cable with a low current to clean the end; it precedes fusion splicing.

premises   A telecommunications term for the space occupied by a customer or an authorized/joint user in a building on continuous or contiguous property that is not separated by a public road or highway.

premises wiring system   The entire wiring system on a user's premises, especially the supporting wiring that connects the communications outlets to the network-interface jack.

prewiring   Wiring that is installed before walls and ceilings are enclosed. Prewiring is often easier than waiting until the walls are built to install wire.

PRI   See *primary rate interface*.

primary coating   The plastic coating applied directly to the cladding surface of the fiber during manufacture to preserve the integrity of the cladding surface.

primary rate interface (PRI)   As defined by the ISDN standard, consists of 23 B-channels (64Kbps each) and one 64Kpbs D-channel (delta channel) in the United States, or 30 B-channels and one D-channel in Europe.

private branch exchange (PBX)   A private telephone switching system usually serving an organization, such as a business, located on the customer's premises. It switches calls both inside a building and outside to the telephone network, and it can sometimes provide access to a computer from a data terminal. Now used interchangeably with *PABX (private automatic branch exchange)*.

profile alignment system (PAS)   A fiber splicing technique for using nonelectro-optical linked access technology for aligning fibers for splicing.

propagation delay   The amount of time that passes between when a signal is transmitted and when it is received at the opposite end of a copper or optical-fiber cable.

protector   A device that limits damaging voltages on metallic conductors by protecting them against surges and transients.

protocol   A set of predefined, agreed-upon rules and message formats for exchanging information among devices on a network.

protocol analyzer   A software and hardware troubleshooting tool used to decode protocol information to try to determine the source of a network problem and to establish baselines.

PS   See *picosecond*.

PS-ELFEXT   Power-sum equal-level far-end crosstalk.

PS-NEXT   Power sum near-end crosstalk.

PSTN   See *public switched network*.

public data network   A network established and operated for the specific purpose of providing data transmission services to the public. See also *public switched network*.

public switched network   A network provided by a common carrier that provides circuit switching between public users, such as the public telephone network, telex, Sprint's TELENET, or MCI's Execunet.

public switched telephone network (PSTN)   The basic phone service provided by the phone company. See also *plain old telephone service*.

pull strength   The pulling force that can be applied to a cable without damaging a cable or affecting the specified characteristics of the cable. Also called *pull tension*.

pull tension   See *pull strength*.

pulse   A current or voltage that changes abruptly from one value to another and back to the original value in a finite length of time.

pulse code modulation (PCM)   The most common method of representing an analog signal, such as speech, by sampling at a regular rate and converting each sample to an equivalent digital code.

pulse dispersion   The dispersion of pulses as they travel along an optical fiber.

pulse spreading   The dispersion of an optical signal with time as it propagates through an optical fiber.

punch-down   A method for securing copper wire to a quick clip in which the insulated wire is placed in the terminal groove and pushed down with a special tool. As the wire is seated, the terminal displaces the wire insulation to make an electrical connection. The punch-down operation may also trim the wire as it terminates. Punch-downs are performed on telecommunications outlets, 66-blocks, and 110-blocks. Also called *cut down*.

PUR   See *polyurethane*.

PVC   See *polyvinyl chloride* and *permanent virtual circuit*.

PVDF   Polyvinylidene fluoride.

Q

QAM   See *quadtrature amplitude modulation*.

QoS   See *quality of service*.

QPSK   Quadrature phase shift key.

quadtrature amplitude modulation (QAM)   The modulation of two separate signals onto carriers at a single frequency and kept separate by having the two signals 90 degrees out of phase.

quality of service (QoS)   Data prioritization at the network layer of the OSI model. QoS results in guaranteed throughput rates.

quartet signaling   The encoding method used by 100VG-AnyLAN, in which the 100Mbps signal is divided into four 25Mbps channels and then transmitted over different pairs of a cable. Category 3 cable transmits one channel on each of four pairs.

quick clip   An electrical contact used to provide an insulation displacement connection (IDC) to telecommunications cables.

R

R   Symbol for *resistance*.

raceway   Any channel designated for holding wires or cables. Raceways may be metallic or nonmetallic and may totally or partially enclose the wiring (e.g., conduit, cable trough, cellular floor, electrical metallic tubing, sleeves, slots, under-floor raceways, surface raceways, lighting fixture raceways, wireways, busways, auxiliary gutters, and ventilated flexible cableways). See also *pathway*.

radial refractive index profile   The refractive index measured in a fiber as a function of the distance from the axial core or center.

radian flux   The time rate in watts of flow of radiant energy.

radiation (rad) hardened   Used to describe material that is not sensitive to the effects of nuclear radiation; such material is usually used for military applications.

radio frequency (RF)   The frequencies in the electromagnetic spectrum that are used for radio communications.

radio frequency interference (RFI)   The interference on copper cabling systems caused by radio frequencies.

Raleigh scattering   A loss due to scattering of the light wave due to the atomic and molecular structure of the wave guide (optical fiber), which is dependent upon the material and the distance considered. The Raleigh scattering is named after the English physicist who used it to explain the apparent blueness of the sky.

ray   A geometric representation of a light path through an optical medium; a line normal to the wave front indicating the direction of radiant energy flow.

RBOC (Regional Bell Operating Company)   The RBOCs were the result of the AT&T/Bell System divestiture in 1984.

RCDD   See *Registered Communications Distribution Designer*.

reactance   A measure of the combined effects of capacitance and inductance on an alternating current. The amount of such opposition varies with the frequency of the current. The reactance of a capacitor decreases with an increase in frequency. The opposite occurs with an inductance.

receiver   A device whose purpose is to capture transmitted signal energy and convert that energy for useful functions. In fiber-optic systems, an electronic component that converts light energy to electrical energy.

receiver sensitivity   The optical power required by a receiver for low error signal transmission. In the case of digital signal transmission, the mean optical power is usually quoted in watts or dBm (decibels referred to 1 milliwatt).

reflectance   Light that is reflected back along the path of transmission from the coupling region, the connector, or a terminated fiber.

reflection   (1) A return of electromagnetic energy that occurs at an impedance mismatch in a transmission line, such as a LAN cable. See also *return loss*. (2) In fiber optics, the abrupt change in direction of a light beam at an interface between two dissimilar media so that the light beam returns into the media from which it originated. Reflection causes several spectral problems including high optical distortion and enhanced intensity noise.

refraction   The bending of a beam of light at an interface between two dissimilar media (such as the core and cladding of an optical-fiber cable) or a medium whose refractive index is a continuous function of position (graded index medium).

refractive index   The ratio of the speed of light in a vacuum to the speed of light in a given material; it is abbreviated n. See also *index of refraction*.

refractive index gradient   The change in refractive index with respect to the distance from the axis of an optical fiber.

regenerative repeater   A repeater designed for digital operations that both amplifies and reshapes the signal.

regenerator A receiver-transmitter pair that detects a weak signal, cleans it up, then sends the regenerated signal through another length of fiber.

Registered Communications Distribution Designer (RCDD) A professional title, the rating of which is granted by BICSI (the Building Industry Consulting Service International). RCDDs have demonstrated a superior level of knowledge of the telecommunications wiring industry and associated disciplines.

registered jack (RJ) Telephone and data jacks/applications that are registered with the FCC. Numbers such as RJ-11 and RJ-45 are widely misused in the telecommunications industry—the *RJ* abbreviation was used to identify a type of service and wiring pattern to be installed, not a specific jack type. A much more precise way to identify a jack is to specify the number of positions (width of opening) and number of conductors. Examples include the eight-position, eight-conductor jack and the six-position, four-conductor jack.

REM Remote electronic maintenance.

repeater (1) A device that receives, amplifies (and sometimes reshapes), and retransmits a signal. It is used to boost signal levels and extend the distance over which a signal can be transmitted. It can physically extend the distance of a LAN or connect two LAN segments. (2) In an optical system, an optoelectronic device or module that receives an optical signal, converts it to electrical form, amplifies or reconstructs it, and retransmits it in optical form.

rerouting Changing the route or spans that the system traverses.

resistance In DC (direct current) circuits, the opposition a material offers to current flow, measured in ohms. In AC (alternating current) circuits, resistance is the real component of impedance and may be higher than the value measured at DC.

responsivity The ratio of a detector's output to input, usually measured in units of amperes per watt (or microamperes per microwatt).

retermination The process of moving cable terminations from one location to another, usually by Y-splicing old cables.

retractile cord A cord with a specially treated insulation or jacket that causes it to retract like a spring. Retractile cords are commonly used between a telephone and a telephone handset.

return loss The ratio of reflected power to inserted power. Return loss is a measure of the signal reflections occurring along a channel or basic link and is related to various electrical mismatches along the cabling. This ratio, expressed in decibels, describes the ratio of optical power reflected by a component, for instance a connector, to the optical power introduced to that component.

return to zero A digital coding scheme where the signal level is low for a 0 bit and high for a 1 bit during the first half of a bit interval; in either case, the bit returns to zero (0) for the second half of the interval.

reversed pair   A wiring error in twisted-pair cabling where the conductors of a pair are reversed between connector pins at each end of a cable. A cabling tester can detect a reversed pair.

RF   See *radio frequency*.

RFI   See *radio frequency interference*.

RFITL   Rural fiber in the loop.

RFP   Request for Proposal.

RFQ   Request for Quote or Quotation.

RG-58   The type designation for the coaxial cable used in thin Ethernet (10Base-2). It has a 50-ohm impedance rating and uses BNC connectors.

RG-62   The type designation for the coaxial cable used in ARCNet networks. It has a 93-ohm impedance and uses BNC connectors

RG/U   Radio grade/universal. RG is the common military designation for coaxial cable.

ribbon   Up to 12 fibers clad in a single optical-fiber cable.

ribbon cable   A cable in which many fibers are embedded in a plastic material in parallel, forming a flat, ribbonlike structure.

ring   (1) A polarity designation of one wire of a pair indicating that the wire is that of the secondary color of a five-pair cable (which is not commonly used anymore) group (e.g., the blue wire of the blue/white pair). (2) A wiring contact to which the ring wire is attached. (3) The negative wiring polarity

(see also *tip*). (4) Two or more stations in which data is passed sequentially between active stations, each in turn examining or copying the information before finally returning it to the source. See also *ring network*.

ring architecture   A network scheme in which a transmission line forms a complete ring. If the ring is broken, signals can still be sent among the terminals.

ring conductor   A telephony term used to describe one of the two conductors that is in a cable pair used to provide telephone service. This term was originally coined from its position as the second (ring) conductor of a tip-ring-sleeve switchboard plug. See also *ring*.

ring network   A network topology in which terminals are connected in a point-to-point serial fashion in an unbroken circular configuration. Many logical ring topologies such as Token Ring are wired as a star for greater reliability.

riser   (1) A cable typically used in vertical cabling runs between floors. Fire-code rating for indoor cable that is certified to pass through the vertical shaft from floor to floor. (2) A space for indoor cables that allow cables to pass between floors, normally a vertical shaft or space.

riser cable   A type of cable used in vertical building shafts, such as telecommunications and utility shafts. Riser cable typically has more mechanical strength than general use cable and has an intermediate fire protection rating.

RJ   See *registered jack*.

RJ-45 A USOC code identifying an eight-pin modular plug or jack used with unshielded twisted-pair cable. Officially, a RJ-45 connector is a telephone connector designed for voice-grade circuits only. RJ-45-type connectors with better signal handling characteristics are called eight-pin connectors in most standards documents, though most people continue to use the RJ-45 name for all eight-pin connectors.

RJ-connector A modular connection mechanism that allows for as many as eight copper wires (four pairs). Commonly found in phone (RJ-11) or 10Base-T (RJ-45) connections.

RMS Root mean square.

rolling Usually a telephone company term for reassigning part of a circuit from one piece of digital equipment to another with minimum effect on the digital transmission. Patching and rolling are used in a variety of operations, including retermination and rerouting.

rope strand A conductor composed of groups of twisted strands.

router A device that connects two networks and allows packets to be transmitted and received between them. A router may also determine the best path for data packets from source to destination. Routers usually operate on Layer 3 (the network layer) of the OSI model.

routing A function of the network layer that involves moving data throughout a network. Data passes through several network segments using routers that can select the path the data takes.

RS-232C The EIA's registered standard that defines the interface that computers use to talk to modems and other serial devices such as printers or plotters.

RSU Remote service unit.

Rx Receive.

RZ See *return to zero*.

S

SAS See *single attachment station*.

SC connector An optical-fiber connector made from molded plastic using push-pull mechanics for joining to a fiber adapter. The SC connector has a 2.5mm ferrule push-pull latching mechanism and can be snapped together to form duplex and multifiber connectors. SC connectors are the preferred fiber-optic cable for premises cabling and are recommended by the TIA/EIA-568-A Standard for structured cabling. Used with Ethernet 100Base-FX and 1000Base-LX/SX fiber-optic media systems.

scanner A cable-testing device that uses TDR methods to detect cable transmission anomalies and error conditions.

scattering A property of glass that causes light to deflect from the fiber and contributes to losses.

SCM Subcarrier multiplex.

screen See *shield*.

screened twisted-pair (ScTP) cable   A balanced four-pair UTP with a single foil or braided screen surrounding all four pairs in order to minimize EMI radiation or susceptibility. Screened twisted-pair is also sometimes called *foil twisted-pair (FTP)*. ScTP is a shielded version of Category 3, 4, and 5 UTP cables; they are less susceptible to electromagnetic interference than UTP cables but are more susceptible than STP cables.

ScTP   See *screened twisted-pair cable*.

segment   A portion of a network that uses the same length of cable (electrically contiguous). Also the portion of a network that shares a common hub or set of interconnected hubs.

Selfoc Lens   A trade name used by the Nippon Sheet Glass Company for a graded index fiber lens. A segment of graded index fiber made to serve as a lens.

semiconductor   In wire industry terminology, a material possessing electrical conductivity that falls somewhere between that of conductors and insulators. Usually made by adding carbon particles to an insulator. This is not necessarily the same as semiconductor materials such as silicon, germanium, etc.

semiconductor laser   A laser in which the injection of current into a semiconductor diode produces light by recombination of holes and electrons at the junction between p- and n-doped regions. Also called a *semiconductor diode laser*.

sensitivity   For a fiber-optic receiver, the minimum optical power required to achieve a specified level of performance, such as BER.

separator   Pertaining to wire and cable, a layer of insulating material such as textile, paper, Mylar, etc., which is placed between a conductor and its dielectric, between a cable jacket and the components it covers, or between various components of a multiple conductor cable. It can be utilized to improve stripping qualities or flexibility, or it can offer additional mechanical or electrical protection to the components it separates.

series wiring   See *daisy chain*.

service loop   A loop or slack left in a cable when the cable is installed and terminated. This loop allows future trimming of the cable or movement of equipment if necessary.

service profile identification (SPID)
The ISDN telephone number issued by the phone company that identifies the ISDN terminal equipment attached to an ISDN line.

SFF connector   See *small form factor connector*.

sheath   An outer protective layer of a fiber-optic or copper cable that includes the cable jacket, strength members, and shielding.

shield   A metallic foil or multiwire screen mesh that is used to prevent electromagnetic fields from penetrating or exiting a transmission cable. Also referred to as a *screen*.

shield coverage   The physical area of a cable that is actually covered by shielding material, often expressed as a percentage.

shield effectiveness   The relative ability of a shield to screen out undesirable interference. Frequently confused with the term *shield coverage*.

shielded twisted pair (STP)   A type of twisted-pair cable in which the pairs are enclosed in an outer braided shield, although individual pairs may also be shielded. STP most often refers to the 150-ohm IBM Type 1, 2, 6, 8, and 9 cables used with Token Ring networks. Unlike UTP cabling, the pairs in STP cable have an individual shield, and the individual shielded cables are wrapped in an overall shield. The primary advantages of STP cable are that it has less attenuation at higher frequencies and is less susceptible to electromagnetic interference. STP cable is becoming less popular as UTP cable capabilities become better and as optical fiber becomes more affordable.

short wavelength   In reference to light, a wavelength shorter than 1000nm.

SI units   The standard international system of metric units.

signal   The information conveyed through a communication system.

signal encoding   The process whereby a protocol at the physical layer receives information from the upper layers and translates all the data into signals that can be transmitted on a transmission medium.

signaling   The process of transmitting data across the medium. Two types of signaling are digital and analog.

signal-to-noise ratio (SNR or S/N)   The ratio of received signal level to received noise level, expressed in decibels and abbreviated *SNR* or *S/N*. A higher SNR ratio indicates better channel performance. The relationship

between the usable intended signal and extraneously present noise present. If the SNR limit is exceeded, the signal transmitted will be unusable.

silica glass   Glass made mostly of silicon dioxide used in conventional optical glass that is used commonly in optical-fiber cables.

Silicone   A General Electric trademark for a material made from silicon and oxygen. Can be in thermosetting elastomer or liquid form. The thermosetting elastomer form is noted for high heat resistance.

silver satin cable   The silver-gray voice-grade patch cable used to connect a telephone to a wall jacket such as is used by home telephones. Silver satin cables are unsuitable for use in LAN applications because they do not have twisted pairs, and this results in high levels of crosstalk.

simplex cable   A term sometimes used to describe a single-fiber cable.

simplex transmission   Data transmission over a circuit capable of transmitting in only one direction.

single attachment station (SAS)   With FDDI networks, denotes a station that attaches to only one of two rings in a dual ring environment.

single-ended line   An unbalanced circuit or transmission line, such as a coaxial cable (see also *balanced line* and *unbalanced line*).

single-frequency laser   A laser that emits a range of wavelengths small enough to be considered a single frequency.

single-mode fiber (SMF)   Optical-fiber cable with a small core, usually between two and nine microns, which can support only one wavelength. It requires a laser source for the input because the acceptance cone is so small. The small core radius approaches the wavelength of the source. Single-mode optical-fiber cable is typically used for backbones and to transmit data over long distances.

single polarization fibers   Optical fibers capable of carrying light in only one polarization.

sinusoidal   A signal that varies over time in proportion to the sine of an angle. Alternating current (AC) is sinusoidal.

skew ray   A light ray that does not intersect the fiber axis and generally enters the fiber at a very high angle.

skin effect   The tendency of alternating current to travel on the surface of a conductor as the frequency increases.

SLA   Semiconductor laser amplifier.

SLED   Surface emitting light emitting diode.

SLM   Single longitudinal mode.

SMA connector   See *surface mount assembly connector*.

small form factor (SFF) connector   A type of optical-fiber connector that provides support for two strands of optical fiber in a connector enclosure that is similar to an RJ-45. There is currently no standard for SFF connectors; types include the LC and the MT-RJ connectors.

SMDS   Switched multimegabit data service.

SMF   See *single-mode fiber*.

SMOLTS   Single-mode optical lost test set.

SMSR   Side-mode suppression ratio.

S/N   See *signal-to-noise ratio*.

sneak current   A low level current that is of insufficient strength to trigger electrical surge protectors and thus may be able to pass between these protectors undetected. The sneak current may result from contact between communications lines and AC power circuits or from power induction. This current can cause equipment damage unless secondary protection is used.

SNR   See *signal-to-noise ratio*.

solid-state laser   A laser whose active medium is a glass or crystal.

soliton   A device used in fiber-optic communications in combination with optical amplifiers to help carry a signal longer distances.

SONET   See *Synchronous Optical Network*.

source   In fiber optics, the device that converts the electrical information carrying a signal to an optical signal for transmission over an optical fiber. A fiber-optic source may be a light emitting diode or laser diode.

source address   The address of the station that sent a packet, usually found in the source area of a packet header. In the case of LAN technologies such as Ethernet and Token Ring, the source address is the MAC (media access control) address of the sending host.

spectral bandwidth (1) The difference between wavelengths at which the radiant intensity of illumination is half its peak intensity. (2) Radiance per unit wavelength interval.

spectral width A measure of the extent of a spectrum. For a source, the width of wavelengths contained in the output at one half of the wavelength of peak power. Typical spectral widths are between 20nm and 60nm for an LED and between 2nm and 5nm for a laser diode.

spectrum Frequencies that exist in a continuous range and have a common characteristic. A spectrum may be inclusive of many spectrums; the electromagnetic radiation spectrum includes the light spectrum, the radio spectrum, and the infrared spectrum.

speed of light (c) In a vacuum, light travels 299,800,000 meters per second. This is used as a reference for calculating the index of refraction.

SPID See *service profile identification*.

splice (1) A permanent joint between two optical waveguides. (2) Means for joining two fiber ends.

splice closure A container used to organize and protect splice trays.

splice tray A container used to organize and protect spliced fibers.

splicing The permanent joining of fiber ends to identical or similar fibers without the use of a connector. See also *fusion splicing* and *mechanical splice*.

split pair A wiring error in twisted-pair cabling where one of a pair's wires is interchanged with one of another pair's wires. Split pair conditions may be determined with simple cable testing tools (simple continuity tests will not reveal the error because the correct pin-to-pin continuity exists between ends). The error may result in impedance mismatch, excessive crosstalk, susceptibility to interference, and signal radiation.

splitting loss See *coupling ratio/loss*.

splitting ratio The ratio of power emerging from two output ports of a coupler.

spontaneous emission Occurs when there are too many electrons in the conduction band of a semiconductor. These electrons drop spontaneously into vacant locations in the valence band, a photon being emitted for each electron. The emitted light is incoherent.

ScTP See *screened twisted-pair cable*.

S/T interface The four-wire interface of an ISDN terminal adapter. The S/T interface is a reference point in ISDN.

ST connector A fiber-optic connector with a bayonet housing; it was developed by AT&T but is not in favor as much as SC or FC connectors. It is used with older Ethernet 10Base-FL and FIORL links.

stabilized light source An LED or laser diode that emits light with a controlled and constant spectral width, central wavelength, and peak power with respect to time and temperature.

standards   Mutually agreed-upon principles of protocol or procedure. Standards are set by committees working under various trade and international organizations.

star coupler   A fiber-optic coupler in which power at any input port is distributed to all output ports.

star network   A network in which all stations are connected through a single point such as a hub in an ArcNet network.

star topology   (1) A method of cabling each telecommunications outlet/connector directly to a cross-connect in a horizontal cabling subsystem. (2) A method of cabling each cross-connect to the main cross-connect in a backbone cabling subsystem. (3) A topology in which each outlet/connector is wired directly to the hub or distribution device.

star wiring   See *home-run cable*.

static charge   An electrical charge that is bound to an object.

station   A unique, addressable device on a network.

stay cord   A component of a cable, usually of high tensile strength, used to anchor the cable ends at their points of termination and keep any pull on the cable from being transferred to the electrical conductors.

step index fiber   An optical-fiber cable, usually multimode, having a uniform refractive index within the core; at the core/cladding interface there is a sharp decrease in refractive index. The light is reflected down the path of the fiber rather than refracted as in graded index fibers. Step index multimode fibers generally have lower bandwidths than graded index multimode fibers.

step index single-mode fiber   A fiber with a small core that is capable of carrying light in only one mode. Sometimes referred to as *single-mode optical-fiber cable*.

step insulated   A process of applying insulation to a cable in two layers. Typically used in shielded networking cables so that the outer layer of insulation can be removed and the remaining conductor and insulation can be terminated in a connector.

stimulated emission   Occurs when the photons in a semiconductor stimulate available excess charge carriers to the emission of photons. The emitted light is identical in wavelength and phase with the incident coherent light.

stitching   The process of terminating multiconductor cables on a punch-down block such as a 66-block or 110-block.

STP   See *shielded twisted pair*.

STP-A   Refers to the enhanced IBM Cabling System specifications with the Type A suffix. The enhanced Type 1A, 2A, 6A, and 9A cable specifications were designed to support operation of 100Mbps FDDI signals over copper. See *Type 1A*, *Type 2A*, *Type 6A*, or *Type 9A*.

strength member   The part of a fiber-optic cable composed of Kevlar aramid yarn, steel strands, or fiberglass filaments that increases the tensile strength of the cable.

structural return loss (SRL) A measurement of the impedance uniformity of a cable. It measures energy reflected due to structural variations in the cable. The higher the SRL number, the better the performance; this means more uniformity and lower reflections.

structured cabling Telecommunications cabling that is organized into a hierarchy of wiring termination and interconnection structures. The concept of structured wiring is used in the common Standards from the TIA and EIA. See Chapter 1 for more information on structured cabling and Chapter 2 for more information on structured cabling Standards.

submarine cable A cable designed to be laid underwater.

subminiature D-connector The subminiature D-connector is a family of multipin data connectors available in 9-, 15-, 25- and 37-pin configurations. Sometimes referred to as DB9, DB15, DB25, and DB37 connectors respectively.

subnetwork A network that is part of another network. The connection is made through a gateway, bridge, or router.

supertrunk A cable that carries several video channels between the facilities of a cable television company.

surface emitting diode A light emitting diode (LED) that emits light from its flat surface rather than its side. These are simple and inexpensive and provide emission spread over a wide range.

surface mount assembly (SMA) connector An optical-fiber cable connector that is a threaded type connector. The SMA 905 version is a straight ferrule design, whereas the SMA 906 is a stepped ferrule design.

surge A rapid rise in current or voltage, usually followed by a fall back to a normal level. Also referred to as a *transient*.

surge protector A device that contains a special electronic circuit that monitors the incoming voltage level and then trips a circuit breaker when an over-voltage reaches a certain level, called the *over-voltage threshold*.

surge suppression The process by which transient voltage surges are prevented from reaching sensitive electronic equipment. See also *surge protector*.

switched network A network that routes signals to their destinations by switching circuits. Two different packets of information may not take the same route to get to the same destination in a switched network.

synchronous Transmission in which the data and bits are transmitted at a fixed rate with the transmitter and receiver being synchronized.

Synchronous Optical Network (SONET)
The underlying architecture in most systems, which uses cells of fixed length. Until recently it was thought that ATM and SONET would be in conflict, but new developments show that ATM will be superimposed upon the embedded SONET architecture. Issues of survivability have or are in the process of being solved.

T

T-1   A standard for digital transmission in North America. A digital transmission link with a capacity of 1.544Mbps (1,544,000 bits per second), T-1 lines are used for connecting networks across remote distances. Bridges and routers are used to connect LANs over T-1 networks. Also referred to as *DS-1* (data services).

T-3   A 44.736Mbps multichannel digital transmission system for voice or data provided by long-distance carriers. T-3C operates at 90Mbps. Also referred to as *DS-3* (data services).

tap   (1) A device for extracting a portion of the optical fiber. (2) On Ethernet 10Base-5 thick coaxial cable, a method of connecting a transceiver to the cable by drilling a hole in the cable, inserting a contact to the center conductor, and clamping the transceiver onto the cable at the tap. These taps are referred to as *vampire taps*.

tap loss   In a fiber-optic coupler, the ratio of power at the tap port to the power at the input port. This represents the loss of signal as a result of tapping.

tapered fiber   An optical fiber whose transverse dimensions vary monotonically with length.

TC   See *telecommunications closet*.

T-carrier   A carrier or provider that is operating at one of the standard levels in the North American digital hierarchy, such as T-1 (1.544Mbps) or T-3 (44.736Mbps).

T-coupler   A coupler having three ports.

TDM   See *time division multiplexing*.

TDR   See *time domain reflectometry*.

Teflon   DuPont Company trademark for fluorocarbon resins. See also *fluorinated ethylene propylene* and *tetrafluoroethylene*.

telco   An abbreviation for *telephone company*.

telecommunications   Any transmission, emission, or reception of signs, signals, writings, images, sounds, or information of any nature by cable, radio, visual, optical, or other electromagnetic systems.

telecommunications closet (TC)   An enclosed space for housing telecommunications equipment, cable terminations, and cross-connect cabling used to serve work areas located on the same floor. The telecommunications closet is the typical location of the horizontal cross-connect and is considered distinct from an equipment room because it is considered to be a floor serving (as opposed to building or campus serving) facility. Also known as a *wiring closet*.

telecommunications equipment room   See *equipment room*.

Telecommunications Industry Association (TIA)   The Standards body that helped to author the ANSI/TIA/EIA-568-A Commercial Building Telecommunications Cabling Standard in conjunction with EIA and that continues to update it, along with Standards for pathways spaces, grounding, bonding, administration, field testing, and other aspects of the telecommunications industry. See Chapter 2 for more information.

telecommunications infrastructure
A collection of telecommunications components that together provide the basic support
for the distribution of all information within
a building or campus. This excludes equipment such as PCs, hubs, switches, routers,
phones, PBXs, and other devices attached to
the telecommunications infrastructure.

telecommunications outlet   A fixed connecting device where the horizontal cable terminates that provides the interface to the work
area cabling. Typically found on the floor or in
the wall. Sometimes referred to as a *telecommunications outlet/connector* or a *wall plate*.

**Telecommunications Systems Bulletin
(TSB)**   A document released by the TIA to
provide guidance or recommendations for a
specific TIA Standard.

terminal   (1) A point at which information
may enter or leave a communications network. (2) A device by means of which wires
may be connected to each other.

terminal adapters   ISDN customer-
premise equipment that is used to connect
non-ISDN equipment (computers and
phones) to an ISDN interface.

terminate   To connect a wire conductor to
something, typically a piece of patch panel,
cross-connect, or telecommunications outlet.

terminator   A device used on coaxial cable
networks that prevents a signal from bouncing off the end of the network cable, which
would cause interference with other signals.

Its function is to absorb signals on the line,
thereby keeping them from bouncing back
and being received again by the network or
colliding with other signals.

tetrafluoroethylene (TFE)   A thermoplastic material with good electrical insulating
properties and chemical and heat resistance.

TFE   See *tetrafluoroethylene*.

theoretical cutoff wavelength   The
shortest wavelength at which a single light
mode can be propagated in a single-mode
fiber. Below the cutoff several modes will
propagate; in this case, the fiber is no longer
single-mode but multimode.

thermal rating   The temperature range
in which a material will perform its function without undue degradation such as
signal loss.

thermoplastic   A material that will soften,
flow, or distort appreciably when subjected to
sufficient heat and pressure. Examples are
polyvinyl chloride and polyethylene, which
are commonly used in telecommunications
cable jackets.

thicknet   Denotes a coaxial cable type
(RG-8) that is commonly used with Ethernet
(10Base-5) backbones. Originally, thicknet
cabling was the only cabling type used with
Ethernet, but it is now being replaced as backbone cabling by optical-fiber cabling. Thicknet cable has an impedance of 50 ohms and is
commonly about 0.4 inches in diameter.

thinnet   Denotes a coaxial cable type (RG-58) that is commonly used with Ethernet (10Base-2) local area networks. This coaxial cable has an impedance of 50 ohms and is 0.2 inches in diameter. It is also called *cheapernet* due to the fact that it was cheaper to purchase and install than the bulkier (and larger) thicknet Ethernet cabling. The maximum distance for a thinnet segment is 180 meters.

TIA   See *Telecommunications Industry Association*.

tight buffer   A type of optical-fiber cable construction where each glass fiber is buffered tightly by a protective thermoplastic coating to a diameter of 900 microns. High tensile strength rating is achieved, providing durability and ease of handling and connectorization.

time division multiple access (TDMA)
A method used to divide individual channels in broadband communications into separate time slots, allowing more data to be carried at the same time.

time division multiplexing (TDM)
Digital multiplexing that takes one pulse at a time from separate signals and combines them in a single stream of bits.

time domain reflectometry   A technique for measuring cable lengths by timing the period between a test pulse and the reflection of the pulse from an impedance discontinuity on the cable. The returned waveform reveals undesired cable conditions, including shorts, opens, and transmission anomalies due to excessive bends or crushing. The length to any anomaly, including the unterminated cable end or cable break, may be computed from the relative time of the wave return and

nominal velocity of propagation of the pulse through the cable. For optical-fiber cables, see also *optical time domain reflectometry*.

tinsel   A type of electrical conductor composed of a number of tiny threads, each having a fine, flat ribbon of copper or other metal closely spiraled about it. Used for small size cables requiring limpness and extra-long flex life.

tip   (1) A polarity designation of one wire of a pair indicating that the wire is that of the primary (common) color of a five-pair cable (which is not commonly used anymore) group (e.g., the white/blue wire of the blue pair). (2) A wiring contact to which the tip wire is connected. (3) The positive wiring polarity. See also *ring*.

tip conductor   A telephony term used to describe the conductor of a pair that is grounded at the central office when the line is idle. This term was originally coined from its position as the first (tip) conductor of a tip-ring-sleeve switchboard plug. See also *tip*.

TNC   A threaded connector used to terminate coaxial cables. TNC is an acronym for Threaded Neill-Concelman (Neill and Concelman invented the connector).

token passing   A media access method in which a token (data packet) is passed around the ring in an orderly fashion from one device to the next. A station can transmit only when it has the token. The token continues around the network until the original sender receives the token again. If the host has more data to send, the process repeats. If not, the original sender modifies the token to indicate that the token is free for anyone else to use.

Token Ring   A ring topology for a local area network (LAN) in which a supervisory frame, or token, must be received by an attached terminal or workstation before that terminal or workstation can start transmitting. The workstation with the token then transmits and uses the entire bandwidth of whatever communications media the token ring network is using. The most common wiring scheme is called a star-wired ring. Only one data packet can be passed along the ring at a time. If the data packet goes around the ring without being claimed, it eventually makes its way back to the sender. The IEEE Standard for Token Ring is 802.5.

tone dial   A push-button telephone dial that makes a different sound (in fact, a combination of two tones) for each number pushed. The technically correct name for tone dial is *dual-tone multifrequency* (DTMF) since there are two tones generated for each button pressed.

tone generator   A small electronic device used to test network cables for breaks and other problems that sends an electronic signal down one set of UTP wires. Used with a tone locator or probe.

tone locator   A testing device or probe used to test network cables for breaks and other problems; designed to sense the signal sent by the tone generator and emit a tone when the signal is detected in a particular set of wires.

topology   The geometric physical or electrical configuration describing a local communication network, as in network topology; the shape or arrangement of a system. The most common topologies are bus, ring, and star.

total internal reflection   The reflection of light back into a material after reaching an interface with a material of a lower refractive index at an angle at or above the critical angle. Total internal reflection occurs at the core/cladding interface within an optical-fiber cable.

TP   See *transition point*.

TPON   Telephone passive optical network.

TP-PMD   See *twisted pair–physical media dependent*.

tracer   The contrasting color-coding stripe along an insulated conductor of a wire pair.

transceiver   The set of electronics that sends and receives signals on the Ethernet media system. Transceivers may be small outboard devices or they may be built into an Ethernet port. Transceiver is a combination of the words transmitter and receiver.

transducer   A device for converting energy from one form to another, such as optical energy to electrical energy.

transfer impedance   For a specified cable length, relates to a current on one surface of a shield to the voltage drop generated by this current on the opposite surface of the shield. The transfer impedance is used to determine shield effectiveness against both ingress and egress of interfering signals. Shields with lower transfer impedance are more effective than shields with higher transfer impedance.

transient   A high-voltage burst of electrical current. If the transient is powerful enough, it can damage data transmission equipment and devices that are connected to the transmission equipment.

transition point (TP)   ISO/IEC 11801 term that defines a location in the horizontal cabling subsystem where flat under-carpet cabling connects to round cabling or where cable is distributed to modular furniture. The TIA/EIA-568-A equivalent of this term is *consolidation point*.

transmission line   An arrangement of two or more conductors or an optical waveguide used to transfer a signal from one location to another.

transmission loss   The total signal loss encountered in transmission through a system.

transmission media   Anything such as wire, coaxial cable, fiber optics, air, or vacuum that is used to carry a signal.

transmitter   With respect to optical-fiber cabling, a device that changes electrical signals to optical signals using a laser and associated electronic equipment such as modulators. Among various types of light transmitters are light emitting diodes (LEDs), which are used in lower speed (100 to 256Mbps) applications such as FDDI, and laser diodes, which are used in higher speed applications (622Mbps to 10Gbps) such as ATM and SONET.

transverse modes   In the case of optical-fiber cable, light modes across the width of the waveguide.

tree coupler   A passive fiber-optic component in which power from one input is distributed to more than two output fibers.

tree topology   A LAN topology similar to linear bus topology, except that tree networks can contain branches with multiple nodes.

triaxial cable   Coaxial cable with an additional outer copper braid insulated from signal carrying conductors. It has a core conductor and two concentric conductive shields. Also called *triax*.

triboelectric noise   Electromagnetic noise generated in a shielded cable due to variations in capacitance between the shield and conductor as the cable is flexed.

trunk   (1) A phone carrier facility such as phone lines between two switches. (2) A telephone communication path or channel between two points, one of them usually being a telephone company facility.

trunk cable   The main cable used in thicknet Ethernet (10Base-5) implementations.

trunk line   A transmission line running between telephone switching offices.

TSB   See *Telecommunications Systems Bulletin*.

T-series connections   A type of digital connection leased from the telephone company or other communications provider. Each T-series connection is rated with a number based on speed. T-1 and T-3 are the most popular. The phone company refers to these as DS-1 and DS-3 circuits, respectively.

TSI   Time slot interchanger.

turn-key agreement   A contractual arrangement in which one party designs and installs a system and "turns over the keys" to another party who will operate the system. A system may also be called a turn-key system if the system is self-contained or simple enough that all the customer has to do is "turn the key."

turnoff time   See *fall time*.

twinaxial cable   A type of communications cable consisting of two center conductors surrounded by an insulating spacer, which is in turn surrounded by a tubular outer conductor (usually a braid, foil, or both). The entire assembly is then covered with an insulating and protective outer layer. Twinaxial is often thought of as dual coaxial cable. Twinaxial cable was commonly used with Wang VS terminals, IBM 5250 terminals on System/3x, and AS/400 minicomputers. Also called *twinax*.

twin lead   A transmission line used for television receiving antennas having two parallel conductors separated by insulating material. Line impedance is determined by the diameter and spacing of the conductors and the insulating material. The conductors are usually 300 ohms.

twisted pair   Two insulated copper wires twisted around each other to reduce induction (thus interference) from one wire to the other. The twists, or lays, are varied in length to reduce the potential for signal interference between pairs. Several sets of twisted-pair wires may be enclosed in a single cable. In cables greater than 25 pairs, the twisted pairs are grouped and bound together in groups of 25 pairs. Twisted pair comes in two varieties: shielded twisted pair (STP) and unshielded twisted pair (UTP). A third variety of twisted-pair cabling, screened twisted-pair (ScTP) cabling, is also becoming popular.

twisted-pair–physical media dependent (TP-PMD)   Technology developed by the ANSI X3T9.5 working group that allows 100Mbps transmission over twisted-pair cable. Also called *CDDI* or *copper distributed data interface*.

Tx   Transmit.

Type 1   150-ohm shielded twisted-pair (STP) cabling conforming to the IBM Cabling System specifications. Two twisted pairs of 22 AWG solid conductors for data communications are enclosed in a braided shield covered with a sheath. Type 1 cable has been tested for operation up to 16MHz. Available in plenum, non-plenum, riser, and outdoor versions.

Type 1A   An enhanced version of IBM Type 1 cable rated for transmission speeds up to 300Mhz. Meets electrical specifications for 150-ohm STP-A cable as documented in the TIA/EIA-568-A Standard.

Type 2   150-ohm shielded twisted-pair (STP) cabling conforming to the IBM Cabling System specifications. Type 2 cable is popular with those who insist on following the IBM Cabling System because there are two twisted pairs of 22 AWG solid conductors for data communications that are enclosed in a braided shield. In addition to the shielded pairs, there are four pairs of 22 AWG solid conductors for telephones that are included in the cable jacket but outside the braided shield. Tested for transmission speeds up to 16MHz. Available in plenum and nonplenum versions.

Type 2A   An enhanced version of IBM Type 2 cable rated for transmission speeds up to 300Mhz. Meets electrical specifications for 150-ohm STP-A cable as documented in the TIA/EIA-568-A Standard.

Type 3   100-ohm unshielded twisted-pair (UTP) cabling similar to TIA/EIA Category 3 cabling. 22 AWG or 24 AWG conductors with a minimum of two twists per linear foot. Typically four twisted pairs enclosed within cable jacket.

Type 5   100/140-micron optical-fiber cable conforming to the IBM Cabling System speci-fications. Type 5 cable has two optical fibers that are surrounded by strength members and a polyurethane jacket. There is also an IBM Type 5J that is a 50/125-micron version defined for use in Japan.

Type 6   150-ohm shielded twisted-pair (STP) cabling that conforms to the IBM Cabling System specifications. Two twisted pairs of 26 AWG stranded conductors for data communi-cations. Flexible for use in making patch cables. Tested for operation up to 16MHz. Available in nonplenum version only.

Type 6A   An enhanced version of IBM Type 6 cable rated for transmission speeds up to 300Mhz. Meets electrical specifications for 150-ohm STP-A cable as documented in the TIA/EIA-568-A Standard.

Type 8   150-ohm under-carpet cable con-forming to the IBM Cabling System specifica-tions. Two individually shielded parallel pairs of 26 AWG solid conductors for data communications. The cable includes "ramped wings" to make it less visible when installed under carpeting. Tested for transmission speeds up to 16MHz. Type 8 cable is not very commonly used.

Type 9   150-ohm shielded twisted-pair (STP) cabling that conforms to the IBM Cabling System specifications. A plenum-rated cable with two twisted pairs of 26 AWG solid or stranded conductors for data communications enclosed in a braided shield covered with a sheath. Tested for transmission speeds up to 16MHz.

Type 9A   An enhanced version of IBM Type 9 cable rated for transmission speeds up to 300MHz. Meets electrical specifications for 150-ohm STP-A cable documented in the TIA/EIA-568-A Standard.

U

UL   See *Underwriters Laboratories, Inc.*

ultraviolet   The electromagnetic waves invisible to the human eye with wavelengths between 10nm and 400nm.

unbalanced line   A transmission line in which voltages on the two conductors are unequal with respect to ground; one of the conductors is generally connected to a ground point. An example of an unbalanced line is a coaxial cable. This is the opposite of a bal-anced line or balanced cable.

underground cable   Cable that is designed to be placed beneath the surface of the ground in ducts or conduit. Underground cable is not necessarily intended for direct burial in the ground.

Underwriters Laboratories, Inc. (UL)   A privately owned company that tests to make sure that products meet safety standards. UL also administers a program for the certification of Category-rated cable with respect to flame ratings. See Chapter 4 for more information on Underwriters Laboratories.

uniformity   The maximum insertion loss difference between ports of a coupler.

uninterruptible power supply (UPS)
A natural line conditioner that uses a battery and power inverter to run the computer equipment that plugs into it. The battery charger continuously charges the battery. The battery charger is the only thing that runs off line voltage. During a power problem, the battery charger stops operating, and the equipment continues to run off of the battery.

Universal Service Order Code (USOC)
Developed by AT&T/the Bell System, the Universal Service Order Code (pronounced "U-sock") identifies a particular service, device, or connector wiring pattern. Often used to refer to an old cable color-coding scheme that was current when USOC codes were in use. USOC is not used in wiring LAN connections and is not supported by current standards due to the fact that high crosstalk is exhibited at higher frequencies. See Chapter 9 for more information.

unmated   Optical-fiber connectors in a system whose end-faces are not in contact with another connector, resulting in a fiber that is launching light from the surface of the glass into air. Also called *unterminated* or *open*.

unshielded twisted pair (UTP)
Unshielded twisted-pair (UTP) cable consists of multiple pairs of copper wire where each wire pair is twisted around one another between two or more times per foot (higher grade UTP cable can have more than 20 twists per foot). The twists serve to cancel out electromagnetic interference that the transmission of electrical signal through the pairs generates. An overall jacket made of some type of plastic then surrounds the individual twisted pairs. Twisted-pair cabling includes no shielding. UTP most often refers to the 100-ohm Categories 3, 4, and 5 cables specified in the TIA/EIA 568-A Standard.

UPS   See *uninterruptible power supply*.

USOC   See *Universal Service Order Code*.

UTP   See *unshielded twisted pair*.

V

V   Symbol for *volt*.

VA   See *volt ampere*.

vampire tap   See *tap*.

VCSE   Vertical cavity emitting surface.

VCTV   Viewer-controlled TV.

velocity of propagation   The transmission speed of electrical energy in a length of cable compared to speed in free space. Usually expressed as a percentage. Test devices use velocity of propagation to measure a signal's transit time and thereby calculate the cable's length. See also *nominal velocity of propagation (NVP)*.

vertical equalizer   A part of the telephone company's central office grounding system that equalizes the electrical potential from one floor to the next.

vertical trough   A jumper pathway that is provided between adjacent bays or modules in a frame, which allows jumpers to run vertically on the frame from one panel location to another or between a panel and the upper or lower express trough.

very high frequency (VHF)   Frequency band extending from 30MHz to 300MHz.

very low frequency (VLF)   Frequency band extending from 10KHz to 30KHz.

VGM   Voice-grade media. See *voice-grade*.

VHDSL   Very high digital subscriber line.

VHF   See *very high frequency*.

video   A signal that contains visual information, such as a picture in a television system.

videoconferencing   The act of conducting conferences via a video telecommunications system, local area network, or wide area network.

videophone   A telephonelike device that provides a picture as well as sound.

visible light   Electromagnetic radiation visible to the human eye at wavelengths between 400nm and 700nm.

VLF   See *very low frequency*.

VOD   Video on demand.

voice circuit   A telephone company circuit capable of carrying one telephone conversation. The voice circuit is the standard unit in which telecommunications capacity is counted. The U.S. analog equivalent is 4KHz. The digital equivalent is 56Kbps in the U.S. and 64Kbps in Europe. In the U.S., the Federal Communications Commission restricts the maximum data rate on a voice circuit to 53Kbps.

voice-grade   A term used for twisted-pair cable used in telephone systems to carry voice signals. Usually Category 3 or lower cable, though voice signals can be carried on cables that are higher than Category 3.

volt   A unit of expression for electrical potential or potential difference. Abbreviated as *V*.

voltage drop   The voltage developed across a component by the current flow through the resistance of the component.

volt ampere (VA)   A designation of power in terms of voltage and current.

VSB   Vestigial sideband.

W

W   (1) Symbol for *watt* or *wattage*. (2) Abbreviation for *white* when used in conjunction with twisted-pair cable color codes; may also be "Wh."

WAN   See *wide area network*.

watt   A unit of electrical power.

waveform   A graphical representation of the amplitude of a signal over time.

waveguide   A structure that guides electromagnetic waves along their length. The core fiber in an optical-fiber cable is an optical waveguide.

waveguide couplers   A connection in which light is transferred between planar waveguides.

waveguide dispersion   That part of the chromatic dispersion resulting from the different speeds at which light travels in the core and cladding of a single-mode fiber. For the most part, this deals with the fiber as a waveguide structure.

waveguide scattering   The variations caused by subtle differences in the geometry and fiber index profile of an optical fiber.

wavelength   With respect to optical-fiber communications, the distance an electromagnetic wave travels in the time it takes to oscillate through a complete cycle. This distance is the distance between successive peaks or nodes of a wave; wavelengths of light are measured in nanometers or micrometers.

wavelength division multiplexers   A multiplexing transmission technique in which separate optical channels that are distinguished by their wavelength are multiplexed onto a single optical fiber for transmission.

wavelength division multiplexing (WDM)   Multiplexing technique whereby signals are multiplexed by transmitting them at different wavelengths through the same optical-fiber cable. See also *frequency division multiplexing*.

wavelength isolation   A wave division multiplexer's isolation of a light signal from the unwanted optical channels in the desired optical channel.

wavelength variance   The variation in an optical parameter caused by a change in the operating wavelength.

webbed conductors   A manufacturing process that binds the conductor insulation of the wire pairs of an unshielded twisted-pair cable.

WIC   Wavelength independent coupler.

wide area network (WAN)   A network that crosses local, regional, and international boundaries. Some types of WAN technology such as a leased-line, ATM, or frame relay connect local area networks (LANs) together to form WANs.

wire center   (1) Another name for a wiring or telecommunications closet. (2) A telephone company building where all local telephone cables converge for service by telephone switching systems. Also called *central office* or *exchange center*.

wire cross-connect A piece of equipment or location at which twisted-pair cabling is terminated to permit reconnection, testing, and rearrangement. Cross-connects are usually located in equipment rooms and telecommunications closets and are used to connect horizontal cable to backbone cable. Wire cross-connects typically use a 66- or 110-block. These blocks use jumpers to connect the horizontal portion of the block to the backbone portion of the block.

wire fault A break in a segment or cable that causes an error. A wire fault might also be caused by a break in the cable's shield.

wiring closet See *telecommunications closet*.

work area The area where horizontal cabling is connected to the work area equipment by means of a telecommunications outlet. A telecommunications outlet serves a station or desk. See also *work area telecommunications outlet*.

work area cable A cable used to connect equipment to the telecommunications outlet in the user work area. Sometimes called a *patch cable* or *patch cord*, work area cables are considered to be outside the scope of structured cabling standards.

work area telecommunications outlet Sometimes called a *wall plate*, a connecting device located in a work or user area where the horizontal cabling is terminated. A work-area telecommunications outlet provides connectivity for work area patch cables, which in turn connect to end-user equipment such as computers or telephones. The telecommunications outlet can be recessed in the wall, mounted on the wall or floorboard, or recessed in the floor or a floor monument.

workgroup A collection of workstations and servers on a LAN that are designated to communicate and exchange data with one another.

workstation A computer connected to a network at which users interact with software stored on the network. Also called a *PC (personal computer)*, *network node*, or *host*.

X

X (1) Symbol for reactance. (2) Symbol often used on wiring diagrams to represent a cross-connect.

xDSL A generic description for the different DSL technologies such as ADSL, HDSL, RADSL. See also *digital subscriber line*.

XTC An optical-fiber connector developed by OFTI; not in general use.

Y

Y-coupler In fiber optics, a variation on the T-coupler, where input light is split between two channels that branch out like a "Y" from the input

Y-splice   Used to bridge a circuit or connection to another location. The Y-splice is a direct tap of a pair of wires onto another pair of wires.

Z

Z   Symbol for impedance.

zero dispersion slope   In single-mode fiber, the chromatic dispersion slope at the fiber's zero dispersion wavelength.

zero dispersion wavelength   In single-mode fiber, the wavelength where waveguide dispersion cancels out material dispersion and total chromatic dispersion is zero. This arises when waveguide dispersion cancels out material dispersion.

Cabling Resources

This appendix contains information about vendor resources, Internet sites, books, publications, and other tools that may be useful for learning more about cabling. The resources are generally listed in order of what we find most useful.

Informational Internet Resources

The Internet is wonderful because it enables speedy communication and access to valuable information. Without the Internet, the time required to complete projects such as this book would be much longer. With that said, we should also issue a caution: Just because information is on the Internet does not mean it is true. We found the sites listed here to be trustworthy sources of information.

wiring.com

Our favorite cabling site on the Internet is www.wiring.com. From here you can link to information on network, electrical, home, cable-TV, and alarm wiring. Janice Boothe, RCCD, maintains the Web site, which has technical information, links to white papers, product reviews, current cabling news, and common pinouts. Best of all, a cabling Q&A lets you post questions, read other people's questions, and offer your own answers to others' queries. This site should be bookmarked in every cable professional's Web browser.

Engineering Notebook for Communication Cables

David Barnett, RCDD, has 18 years of experience in the engineering and marketing of communication cables and wires. As a hobby, he maintains the Engineering Notebook for Communication Cables site at http://home1.gte.net/res025bi/index .htm. The site is geared toward wiring for the home and the SOHO (small office, home office), but even professional cable installers will find useful information here. This site has information on color coding, NEC flame ratings, cabling categories, codes, and residential-wiring basics.

comp.dcom.cabling

If you have newsreader software (such as Outlook Express), point your newsreader to the Usenet newsgroup comp.dcom.cabling. This interactive forum has a plethora of information. You can post your own questions, respond to others' questions, or just read the existing postings and learn from them. This particular forum has a number of dedicated and knowledgeable individuals who monitor it and try to assist everyone who posts queries. A word to the wise: Because this forum is not moderated, any self-proclaimed expert can post responses to questions. Use common sense, and if an answer doesn't seem right, get a second opinion.

The Cabling News Group FAQ

If you frequent the `comp.dcom.cabling` newsgroup, you will see references to "the FAQ," the group's list of frequently asked questions. Before posting to this newsgroup, it is considered good forum etiquette to read the FAQ to make sure your question has not been previously asked. The FAQ can be found on the Internet at `http://netman.cit.buffalo.edu/FAQs/cabling.faq`.

Whatis

Whatis is one of our favorite reference sites on the Internet; its URL is `www.whatis.com`. It contains more than 2,000 commonly used computer and telecommunications terms and seems to grow every day. Also included at this reference site is the word of the day, information for the beginner, concepts, and book recommendations.

TIA Online

The Telecommunication Industry Association's Web site is found at `www.tiaonline.org`. This Web site is the place to go for updated information on the TIA committee meetings, current proposals and Standards, and current events; it also includes a tremendous glossary.

TechFest

Is everything you ever wanted to know about networking here? Well, not quite, but it is pretty close. A huge amount of information is available on LANs, WANs, cabling, protocols, switching, networking standards, ATM, and more at `www.techfest.com/networking/`.

TechEncyclopedia

CMP's TechWeb sponsors the TechEncyclopedia. This thorough listing of more than 13,000 computer- and technology-related terms can be found at `www.techweb .com/encyclopedia`.

Global Technologies, Inc.

Global Technologies has a technical-information section to its Web site (`www .globaltec.com/tech.htm`) that includes pinout diagrams, standards information, networking basics, organization information, wiring diagrams, and more.

Cabletesting.Com

If you want to learn more about cable testing, the progress of the standards committees, and more, visit `www.cabletesting.com`. Microtest (`www.microtest.com`) sponsors the site; the company is one of the leading manufacturers of cable-testing and certification tools.

National Electrical Code Internet Connection

This site is operated by Mike Holt (better known among electrical and data cabling professionals as Mr. Code). Mike Holt is *the* expert on the National Electrical Code, and he gives excellent seminars around the world. Visit his site for more information on the National Electrical Code, some really interesting stories from people in the field, his free e-mail newsletter, and more. Mr. Holt has also written a number of books on how to interpret and work with the National Electrical Code; professional electricians and data-communications designers should own his book on the 1999 NEC. The site can be found at `www.mikeholt.com`.

Charles Spurgeon's Ethernet Web Site

This site, at `www.ots.utexas.edu/ethernet/ethernet.html`, is the first place on the Internet we go for information on Ethernet, Fast Ethernet, and Gigabit Ethernet. Extensive information is here about various Ethernet technologies, planning cabling for Ethernet, and Ethernet analyzing software, as well as FAQs, technical papers, a history of Ethernet, and troubleshooting information. On the home page is a neat drawing of Ethernet done by Bob Metcalfe, the original designer of Ethernet.

Federal Standard 1037C: Glossary of Telecommunications Terms

Federal Standard 1037C is one of the most thorough Internet sites you can use for finding technology-related terms. This site is sponsored by the U.S. National Communications System Technology and Standards Division and can be found at http://ntia.its.bldrdoc.gov/fs-1037.

Twisted-Pair Ethernet

This site, at www.wown.com/j_helmig/thisted.htm, has a comprehensive overview for cabling an Ethernet network; much of the information on this site also applies to 100Base-T networks.

Networking-Hardware Course Notes

While researching material for this book, we stumbled across this neat assemblage of notes for a networking course at Del Mar College. It includes good information on network architectures, cabling, and data transfers. The site can be found at www.delmar.edu/Courses/ITNW2313.

Directory for WAN, LAN, and ATM Protocols

Though not specifically related to cabling, we found a site for learning more about WAN, LAN, and ATM protocols. The site, found at www.protocols.com, includes protocol references and physical-network interfaces; of particular interest were pinouts for different WAN-interface technologies.

Webopedia: Online Computer Dictionary for Internet Terms and Technical Support

Another valuable site for finding technology-related terms is Webopedia. This online dictionary, http://Webopedia.internet.com, has a thorough computer dictionary, technology-related news, and a listing of the top terms.

Books, Publications, and Videos

You may wish to own a number of the following books and videos for your professional library. In addition, two publications that we highly recommend are listed in this section.

Cabling Business Magazine

Cabling Business Magazine covers copper and fiber-optic cabling for voice, data, and imaging. The monthly has features written by some of the leaders in the industry, a stock-market watch, how-to columns, and more. *Cabling Business Magazine* also offers seminars and classes on a variety of telecommunications topics. For more information on the magazine or information on a free subscription to qualified subscribers, check out the publication on the Web at www.cablingbusiness.com.

Cabling Installation and Maintenance

Cabling Installation and Maintenance is a monthly magazine, published by Pennwell, that has columns (including Q&A), Standards Watch, and more. Its Web site, at www.cable-install.com, has links to contractors, a buyers' guide, a calendar of events, and an article archive. Online subscriptions are free to qualified print subscribers.

Cabling Installation and Maintenance Tips and Videos

Cable Installation and Maintenance (CI&M) magazine publishes a book of installation tips and best practices, contributed by cabling professionals, that all professional installers should own and read. Two more must-haves for cabling professionals are *CI&M*'s *Cable Pulling* video series and its *Installer Tips* video. These may be purchased through *CI&M*'s Web site at www.cable-install.com (click on the Training Resources link).

Newton's Telecom Dictionary by Harry Newton

This 900-page book is a guide to the world of modern data and voice telecommunications terms. It's not easy to keep up with all the terms, acronyms, and concepts today, but this book is a great start. Anyone who owns one will tell you it is indispensable. It is available through most bookstores.

Premises Network Online

This virtual community is designed for people who work with premises cabling. It includes a buyers' guide and allows you to submit an RFQ/RFP, respond to an RFQ/RFP, search for jobs, and purchase used equipment and products in its online marketplace. The site can be found at www.premisesnetworks.com.

Building Your Own High-Tech Small Office by Robert Richardson

This book is a wonderful resource for those wanting to run their business in an efficient and high-tech manner. The author discusses everything from Internet connections to office design. The book is available through most bookstores. The author has developed a Web site to provide ongoing assistance to readers: www.smallofficetech.com.

BICSI's *Telecommunications Distribution Methods* and *Cabling Installation Manuals*

The Building Industry Consulting Services International's *Telecommunications Distribution Methods* (TDM) and *Cabling Installation* manuals are great study guides for the RCDD certification and excellent resources for professional cable installers. BICSI members can get discounts to these publications on the BICSI Web site (www.bicsi.org).

Understanding the National Electrical Code (3rd Edition) by Mike Holt and Charles Michael Holt

Electricians, engineers, and telecommunications designers need to have a good understanding of the National Electrical Code, and this book explains the NEC's sections in easy-to-understand language. Mike Holt also has a new book called *Technology Wiring—Holt's Illustrated Guide* that explains wiring from the perspective of the NEC. These books are available from almost any bookstore.

ANSI/TIA/EIA-568-A Commercial Building Telecommunication Cabling Standard

The ANSI/TIA/EIA-568-A Standard is the definitive guide to commercial building cabling. All professional cable designers and installers should own or have access to this standards document. It can be purchased online through Global Engineering Documents at `http://global.ihs.com`. The company has a great deal on a CD containing the entire structured wiring collection of Standards, which includes free updates for a year.

Vendors and Manufacturers

To say that many manufacturers and vendors handle telecommunications and cabling products would be a bit of an understatement. The following is a list of vendors and manufacturers that we have found to provide not only good products but also good service and information.

The Siemon Company

Telecommunications vendor The Siemon Company has an informative Web site, at `www.siemon.com`, which includes technical references, standards information, an online catalog, white papers, and frequently-asked questions. If you visit the site, order the company's catalog—it is one of the best telecommunications catalogs in the industry.

MilesTek, Inc.

MilesTek has one of the neatest sites and is one of the easiest companies on the Internet to work with for purchasing cabling supplies and tools. It also has a good catalog and helpful people on the ordering side if you are not quite ready for online commerce. The company sells cabling supplies, tools, cable, components, connectors, and more. Its site, at `www.milestek.com`, also has good information on standards, cabling, and telecommunications.

IDEAL DataComm

IDEAL DataComm is a leading supplier of cabling and wiring tools and supplies. If you have handled any cabling tools, you have probably used one of IDEAL Datacomm's tools. Its Web site, at `www.idealindustries.com`, has much useful information about the tools that it sells, as well as tips and tricks for premises cabling and electrical wiring. The company's customer service is good.

Ortronics

Manufacturer Ortronics maintains one of our favorite Web sites and catalogs. Ortronics also offers training and a certified installer program. Its catalog is easy to understand and follow. You can find the company on the Internet at www .ortronics.com.

Superior Essex

Superior Essex is one of the largest manufacturers of premises, outside plant, and fiber-optic cable in the world. Its Web site, at www.superioressex.com, has excellent technical information pertaining to copper and fiber cabling as well as performance specifications for its products.

Jensen Tools

Jensen Tools has a huge variety of tools, tool kits, and other products for the computer and telecommunications professional. Visit its Web site at www.jensentools .com and order its catalog.

Labor Saving Devices, Inc.

This company has one of the best selections we've found of cabling-installation tools for those who need to retrofit existing structures. In addition to its impressive product offering, Labor Saving Devices, Inc. offers online instructions and an interactive Q&A forum. You can find LSD Inc.'s Web site at www.lsdinc.com.

Avaya (formerly Lucent) SYSTIMAX SCS

Lucent recently sold its SYSIMAX business to Avaya. To learn more about the Avaya SYSTIMAX SCS (Structured Cabling System), the best place to start is with the source. Avaya designs and installs the SYSTIMAX SCS system to meet and exceed current cabling performance standards; the system continues to remain compatible with existing technologies. You can find the SYSTIMAX home page at http://connectivity.avaya.com/commerce/systimax.

Erico

Erico is a leading manufacturer of electrical products, including the CADDY system of fastening and fixing solutions. These products help you to better organize and run cabling. Visit Erico on the Internet at www.erico.com and check out the Fastening and Fixing section of its Web site.

Berk-Tek

Cable manufacturer and supplier Berk-Tek has a great Web site that includes a technical section with standards information, white papers, and industry standards. You can find it at www.berktek.com.

Microtest

Microtest is one of the world's leading manufacturers of cabling-testing equipment. Its products include the immensely popular (and easy to use!) PentaScanner. Visit the company on the Internet at www.microtest.com.

Fluke

Fluke is a premier manufacturer of electronic test equipment. Its DSP series of LAN testers are widely used by the professional installer community. Fluke's Web site address is www.fluke.com.

Amp

Amp is the world leader in construction of connectors. Its online catalog has over 100,000 items. The company makes connectors for many industries, including the networking and telecommunications industry. You can find it on the Internet at www.amp.com.

Panduit

Panduit is a leading supplier of telecommunications products and tools. Its Web site, at www.panduit.com, offers online ordering and information about its products.

Anixter

Telecommunications-product vendor Anixter has a Web site that includes one of the most extensive technical libraries about cabling and standards found on the Net. It can be found on the Internet at www.anixter.com.

Registered Communications and Distribution Designer (RCDD) Certification

Certification programs are all the rage in the technology industry. The cabling business is no exception. As with all industry certifications, an organization has to be responsible for the certification program, manage the testing, and set the quality requirements. BICSI (Building Industry Consulting Services International) is a professional organization devoted to promoting standards for the design and installation of communications systems and is instrumental in the provision of guidelines, training, and professional certification of knowledge and experience related to the communication infrastructure.

The breakup and divestiture of the Bell system in 1984 created a void of expertise where communication system design and deployment was concerned. Not only was a single national entity no longer governing standard practices, but also many of the old-timers (the ones who really knew what worked—*and why*) left the baby Bells during, and shortly following, the divestiture period.

BICSI recognized the need to acknowledge and certify cabling professionals; it filled the void with a two-pronged effort. First, BICSI developed and published the *TDMM* (*Telecommunications Distribution Methods Manual*), a compendium of guidelines, standards, and best practices for the engineering of a communications system. Second, it initiated the RCDD (Registered Communications Distribution Designer) accreditation program to establish a benchmark of expertise for the industry.

At year-end 2001, BICSI expects to have membership exceeding 20,000 worldwide. More than 5,500 members have achieved the professional accreditation of Registered Communications Distribution Designer. The designation of RCDD is not awarded lightly. It takes knowledge, experience, and much hard work to qualify for those four letters that follow your name on your business card and stationery.

Today, the RCDD is a recognized standard of excellence and professionalism within the communications industry. Increasingly, architects and building-management consortia specify that an RCDD must perform the design of a building project's low-voltage systems: video, security, and communications. Often, the contractor awarded the installation work is required to have an RCDD either on staff or as a direct supervisor of the work performed. In some companies, obtaining your RCDD is a condition of employment if you are in technical sales or technical support. As a result, RCDDs are very much in demand in the job market. These reasons are pretty compelling ones to become an RCDD if you are serious about working in the field of communications infrastructure.

How do you get there? You will go through three stages:

1. Apply and be accepted as a candidate for the designation of RCDD.
2. Successfully pass the stringent RCDD exam.
3. Maintain your accreditation through continuing membership and education.

Apply and Be Accepted as a Candidate for the Designation of RCDD

You must be a member of BICSI before you can apply to become an RCDD. Membership requires a nominal annual fee, currently $100 for an individual. (BICSI is a nonprofit organization, and all its fees are very reasonable compared to other professional organizations of the same caliber.)

NOTE   You can find out more about membership in BICSI by visiting its Web site at www.bicsi.org.

Next, you must submit your qualifications to become an RCDD. BICSI doesn't let just anyone sit for the exam; you must be a bona fide member of the industry. The requirement is part of the quality control that elevates the RCDD designation in the industry. BICSI requires that you have a minimum of two years of system-design experience. You show your experience by doing the following:

*   Filling out an application, much as if you were applying for employment. You list work experience, educational background, and any awards, accomplishments, or other professional credentials you may have. The application includes a Communications Distribution Design Experience list that you must complete by ranking your experience in a number of different distribution-design areas.

*   Supplying three letters of reference:

    *   One letter from your current employer detailing your involvement in design activities

- One from a client for whom you have performed design work
- One personal reference touting you as an all-around swell person
- Sending a nonrefundable application fee of $100 and waiting a couple of weeks to see if you are accepted as a candidate to sit for the exam.

> **NOTE** BICSI members, RCDD candidates, and those who have written letters of reference for colleagues and employees will attest to the fact that BICSI diligently follows up these letters of reference to establish their legitimacy.

Successfully Pass the Stringent RCDD Exam

Okay, you've been accepted, now what? Well, next is the hard (some would say *grueling*) part. You have to study for and take the RCDD examination, which consists of 280 multiple-choice questions selected randomly from a bank of more than 2,500 questions. Each copy of the exam is unique. It is given during a strictly proctored 3½-hour session. To be admitted to the test room, you must show a photo ID.

The testing procedure includes using sealed envelopes and a personal test-code number that's assigned to you. The exam is a closed-book test, and no calculators or reference materials are permitted in the test room. You won't be told your score— only that you either passed or failed. These procedures may sound hokey and unnecessary, but, in fact, they ensure the integrity of the RCDD title by eliminating the possibility of cheating or favoritism and putting all RCDDs on level ground.

The exam is difficult. It takes a grade of 78 percent to pass, meaning you can miss only 61 of the 280 questions. Only 30 to 40 percent of those who take the test pass the first time. BICSI allows you to retake the test up to three times within one year. If, after that third attempt, you still don't pass, you must wait a full year and then begin the application process again.

The potential test questions all come directly from the *TDMM* (*Telecommunications Distribution Methods Manual*). This is a very important point, and you will fail if you don't take it to heart. *Do not* answer questions from your own experience or based on reference material other than the *TDMM*. The *TDMM* is the bible as far as the RCDD exam is concerned, and you should *only* respond to test questions with answers from the *TDMM*, *regardless of whether or not you agree*. RCDDs are convinced that two reasons account for the 60 to 70 percent first-time failure rate. The first is that people come to the test believing their own experience and know-how should supersede what BICSI teaches in the *TDMM*; the second is that they simply don't study the *TDMM* enough.

For an RCDD candidate with two years of experience and heavy specialization in a few areas of communication-system distribution design, BICSI recommends the following study regimen prior to sitting for the exam:

- Study the *TDMM* for 50 hours.

- Attend the five-day BICSI DD102 distribution-system design course.

- Attend the 2½-day BICSI DD101 distribution-system review course immediately prior to the exam.

NOTE   More information on the BICSI classes can be found on BICSI's Web site at www.bicsi.org.

More extensive experience over a broader range of subjects reduces the number of hours required in study and can eliminate the need for the distribution design courses. However, we recommend the courses to anyone that even slightly doubts his or her ability to pass the exam. Who knows, even skilled professionals may learn something in the process.

Here's the regimen successful candidates have used in the past. Almost everyone who followed this course of study passed the RCDD test on the first try, which is a pretty good endorsement:

- Study the *TDMM* as much as possible prior to any course work.

- Attend the BICSI DD102 class. (Note: In general, first-time test takers who attend this class as administered by BICSI raise their chances of passing significantly. Some instructor teams have 70 percent or better first-time pass rates for students in their classes.)

- Participate in study groups in the evenings during the DD102 class. Studying and quizzing each other using the *TDMM* or flash cards greatly reinforces the learning and memorization required to pass the exam.

- Purchase and use one of the RCDD practice test packages available from third-party vendors. One such third-party practice exam is from NET CBT (formerly Clark Technology Group); it is computerized test software. You can find the company on the Internet at www.netcbt.com. Purchase at least two practice tests. Then, begin testing yourself with one version. Use it over and over, interweaving it with study periods. When you are consistently achieving above 90 percent correct on the first practice test, switch to the other and follow the same procedure. These tests are also a great adjunct to the study group if you use them interactively and answer by panel instead of by individual. Discuss your answers with the group until you all agree why the answer is right or wrong.

- Take the RCDD exam immediately following the DD102 course. There is some controversy over this approach. Some think it is better to wait, let the course material sink in, then take the DD101 as a refresher. Many successful candidates have gone full steam ahead right into the exam and been successful.

TIP
Assuming you're going for broke directly from DD102 into the exam, your brain will be packed to bursting with information from the *TDMM*. The most fragile items are the numerous tables that you've memorized, on information like the number and size of conduits required to service a building of *x* square feet. These tables don't lend themselves to logical sequence or mnemonic clues. The morning of the exam, you won't want to talk with anyone for fear that you'll lose concentration and these delicate matrices will collapse like a house of cards. Get your test packet, tear it open, and dump your brain onto the back of the test. Then, start the exam.

The exam is offered at each BICSI conference. Three of these are held each year in the United States, with several others held in other parts of the world. The exam is also offered immediately following BICSI courses such as the DD101 and DD102. In addition, the exam is scheduled periodically in varying locations across the United States. Finally, special proctoring of the exam can be scheduled for a special-purpose group, such as when a company processes a large number of RCDD candidates at the same time. Usually, such exams are held in conjunction with specially scheduled design courses.

One interesting fact about the exam: BICSI recognizes that neither the *TDMM* nor the exam is absolutely infallible. The *TDMM* has different sections written by different individuals. In a few cases, contradictory information is given. A few buggy questions are also in the question bank (although BICSI works hard to weed them out).

If you think you've encountered one of these contradictory or erroneous questions, answer it as best you're able but make a note by the question to refer to the back of the test. There, you are allowed to challenge the question by providing an explanation of why you believe the question to be faulty. It's best if you can quote chapter and paragraph numbers for the conflicting or bad information (doing so is not far-fetched, considering the preparation you'll have done). If you really know your stuff, you will probably catch a buggy question. Though one question probably won't make a difference if you are ready to take the test, it could swing the balance if your score is marginal.

The test costs $100 each time you take it. This is in addition to the membership fee and RCDD application fee you will have already paid.

> **TIP**   Don't rely completely on the practice tests to memorize potential types of questions. Learn the material and concepts and then use the tests to ensure that you are ready. Memorizing test-type questions will only be a disservice to you and the industry.

Maintain Your Accreditation through Continuing Membership and Education

When you've passed (congratulations!), you can't just sit back and coast. The world of communications changes very rapidly. BICSI recognizes that for RCDDs to be effective in servicing clients, they must keep up with ever-changing standards and best practices.

Your RCDD designation is awarded for a three-year period. During those three years, you must maintain your BICSI membership. *Don't let your membership lapse, or you'll have to sit for the exam again.* (Yikes!)

You must also accumulate a minimum of 45 Continuing Education Credits (CECs). You can accomplish that by attending more BICSI or third-party education courses (check with the BICSI office to see if the third-party courses are sanctioned for CECs) or by attending BICSI's scheduled technical conferences.

A BICSI conference is worth 15 CECs. You must attend at least one during your three-year period as an RCDD. By attending one each year, you accumulate all the CECs you need for renewal of your RCDD accreditation.

A BICSI conference is packed with presentations, workshops, or seminars that will keep you up-to-date on what's happening in your industry. Virtually everyone will have an update on what's happening in the industry-standard development committees, such as the committee that works on TIA/EIA 568-A. New developments in areas such as cable performance, connectors, electronics, fiber versus twisted pair, and changes to the NEC are all topics of regular discussion. In addition, information on how to better serve your customers and run your business is often provided. In addition, nightly receptions allow you to network with other industry professionals and review the offerings of vendors that are mainstays of the communications market.

Check Out BICSI and the RCDD Program for Yourself

Visit the BICSI Web site at www.bicsi.org for additional information on the organization and the RCDD program. You can download applications, view membership lists, review presentations made at prior BICSI conferences, read status reports from the TIA working groups involved in cabling standards, and much more.

Home Cabling:
Wiring Your Home for
Now and the Future

In case you haven't noticed, you're standing knee-deep in the future of data interchange. High-speed, inexpensive computers, high-bandwidth network technologies, and the usefulness of the Internet are advancing faster than most can assimilate and react to. Corporations, to a large degree, are keeping up when it comes to providing LAN and Internet functionality for their employees.

The home, however, is the last bastion of low-end technology for data exchange. Even the home you just built may only have voice-grade wiring in it—and it may not even support more than one phone line. Category 5 wiring may be the buzz in new houses above a certain price point, but few contractors know how to properly install and terminate it.

If cable is improperly pulled or terminated, it will be useless for data communications. You can quickly convert Category 5 to Category 1 by stretching it, crimping it, daisy-chaining it, bridge tapping, or using low-quality connectors.

Many homes constructed today simply do not have enough outlets to meet the demands of a modern family. If your home builder wired your home for a typical number of outlets, i.e., one in the master bedroom, one in the kitchen, maybe one in the family room, you won't have enough connection points to take advantage of a number of in-home systems that are rapidly being adopted.

In the past few years, the concept of the "smart home" has begun to emerge. Increasingly more people run businesses out of the home or simply work there, requiring them to install multiple personal computers as well as home-automation appliances. A home that is wired to support voice, video, and data networking is becoming a valuable asset. The Multiple Listing Service is considering a technology rating for homes. One that is properly wired will score well on this rating. Realtors estimate that future-wiring a home can increase value by 5 to 10 percent.

KEY TERM   **SOHO (small office, home office)**   A *SOHO* is a small office or home office. The trend toward having offices at home is driving a need for more sophisticated cabling.

Home-Cabling Facts and Trends

The growth of the home computer over the past few years is staggering. The growth of the Internet and the use of home computers have far outpaced similar growth patterns of telephone or VCR usage. Consider too the explosive growth of other "connected" devices and services. Pagers, cell phones, e-mail, and PDAs are almost ubiquitous now but were relatively rare five years ago.

Here are some other facts relating to the need for more advanced communication wiring in the home:

- More than 50 percent of single-family households own PCs.

- Approximately 20 percent of single-family households contain two or more PCs. The number is expected to double by the year 2005.

- More than 30 percent of single-family households have access to the Internet.

- About 30 percent of the workforce works at home at least part time.

- The number of homes with fast Internet access (DSL or cable modem) will increase *10 times*, to over 20 million households, by the year 2005.

- Windows 95 and subsequent releases of the Windows operating system make networking multiple computers simple. When used with an inexpensive hub or router, multiple home computers or devices can easily share access to the Internet.

- Your TV and refrigerator can now connect directly to the Internet for programming guides, VCR control, and automated shopping.

- MP3 and other audio and video compression technology will soon make an Internet or home-network connection to your PC an integral part of your home-entertainment system. At very affordable prices, MP3 devices already exist that will download and play music files through your stereo system. Inexpensive and efficient video technology is not far behind.

These trends are just at the beginning of their growth curves, and home networks and smart appliances will be common within five years (probably less, if the rapid adoption of the Internet is any indicator).

NOTE Parks Associates conducts extensive market research in the area of communications. Read about trends for residential structured cabling at www.parksassociates.com.

In-home networks? Smart appliances? Connection points located conveniently throughout the house? Bah, humbug! Ridiculous frivolities! Oh, yeah? Well, so were electricity, the telephone, indoor plumbing, home air conditioning, dishwashers, color TV, and cable or satellite TV when they were introduced. Now they are almost necessities for most people in the United States.

Imagine buying a house and then discovering that you can't install an air conditioner or that the wiring isn't adequate for running a dishwasher. A similar situation exists for the communication wiring in many homes in the United States today when it comes to having a network, multiple phone lines, or even connecting to the Internet at decent speeds via a modem. A home is expected to last years—at least as long as the term of its mortgage. Based on the aforementioned trends, many new homes have communication wiring that will be obsolete in fewer months than the loan term for a new car.

Structured Residential Cabling

The FCC has recognized some of the problems associated with residential cabling and, on February 15, 2000, put into effect a requirement that voice and data wiring in new residential structures should be a minimum of Category 3 UTP. Enforcement of this ruling began in July 2000. (Note that because the requirement is not a safety-related issue, enforcement by most local code authorities is minimal.) The FCC ruling only addresses part of the problem and doesn't address the need for flexible, centrally controlled access to the wiring in your home.

What's the rest of the answer for residences? Just as in the commercial, corporate world, the answer is structured cabling. A cabling system distributed throughout the building, with every connection point leading back to a central location where systems and outside services are connected, is what works.

Enter ANSI/TIA/EIA-570-A, or the Residential Telecommunications Cabling Standard. The latest revision was published in October 1999, and it details the requirements for low-voltage cabling systems in single and multi-tenant residences. Included in the TIA/EIA-570-A Standard are definitions for the two grades of residential cabling installations, which are shown in Table D.1.

TABLE D.1:   Grades of Residential Cabling

TIA 570-A Grades	Cable Types		
	Four-pair UTP	75 Ohm coax	Fiber optic
1	Category 3[1]	RG-6	Not included
2	Category 5[2]	RG-6[3]	Two-fiber MM[4]

[1]Category 5 recommended
[2]Category 5e recommended
[3]Quad shield recommended
[4]Optional for future upgrades

For both grades of installation, the following guidelines shall apply to cabling and communication-services providers:

- Providers, such as a phone company or CATV company, bring service to the exterior of the house. This is the demarcation point, or the location at which ownership of the infrastructure (wiring and connections) transfers to you, the homeowner.

- From the demarcation point, a cable brings the service into a central distribution device installed inside the residence. The distribution device consists of a cross-connect device of some sort so that incoming service can be transferred to the horizontal wiring that runs to wall outlets. The distribution device provides a flexible method of distributing service to desired locations throughout the house.

- From the distribution device, cables are run to each wall outlet on a one-to-one basis. Outlets are never connected in series (daisy-chained). The one-to-one method is referred to as *star*, or *home-run*, wiring.

- At a minimum, one outlet is required in the kitchen, each bedroom, family/-living room, and den/study. In addition, one outlet is required in any wall with an unbroken space of 12 feet or more. Additional outlets should be added so that no point on the floor of the room is more than 25 feet from an outlet. Note that these minimum-outlet requirements refer to UTP, coax, and fiber-optic cables (if installed).

- Connecting hardware (plugs, jacks, patch panels, cross-connects, patch cords) shall be at least the same grade as the cable to which they connect, for example, Category 5 cable requires Category 5 or better connectors.

- UTP plugs and jacks shall be eight-position (RJ-45 type), configured to the 568A wiring scheme. Coaxial plugs and jacks shall be F-type connectors, properly sized for the grade and shielding of the coaxial cable used. Fiber-optic connectors shall be SC-type in either simplex or duplex configuration.

- Proper labeling of the cables is required, along with documentation that decodes the labeling.

For a Grade 1 installation, you should populate each wall plate with just one cable of each type. For a Grade 2 installation, two cables of each type should be run to each wall plate. We recognize that Grade 2 may seem like overkill *at the present*. But again, break your old ways of thinking. One coax with signals going *to* your entertainment center and one coax with signals *from* your entertainment center means that you can watch a movie in a completely different room from the one in which your VCR or DVD player is playing (from your computer monitor, for instance). Or, you could use a centrally located video switch to route satellite, VCR, CATV, or antenna inbound signals around your house to wherever a TV is located. Likewise, say you've got ADSL coming to your computer via UTP for direct access to the Internet, but you still want to use the modem in your computer for faxing. You need two UTP outlets right there.

Following installation, the cabling system should be tested. At a minimum, continuity tests for opens, shorts, and crosses should be performed. You may want to insist on the UTP and optical-fiber cable (if terminated) being tested to transmission performance requirements; further, you may want to assure yourself that your Category 5 or better components will actually deliver Category 5 or better performance.

This appendix is just a short summary of what is contained in the TIA 570-A Standard. The Standard specifies a great deal of additional detail about cables, installation techniques, electrical grounding and bonding, etc. If you want to read about these details (perhaps you're an insomniac), a copy may be purchased from Global Engineering Documents at `http://global.ihs.com` and is currently priced at $65.

Picking Cabling Equipment for Home Cabling

So you're going to move forward with your home-cabling project. One of the decisions you will need to make is what type of equipment you will have to purchase and install. Although you can use any commercial structured cabling components in your home, many vendors are now building cabinets, panels, and wall plates that are specifically designed for home use. Manufacturer Ortronics (www.ortronics.com) builds a line of cabling products called In House that is designed with the small or home office in mind. Figures D.1 and D.2 show two cabinets that can hold specially designed Category 5 patch panels, a hub, and a video patch panel.

FIGURE D.1:

Ortronics' compact-sized In House cabinet

(Photo courtesy of Ortronics)

FIGURE D.2:

Ortronics' large-sized In House cabinet

(Photo courtesy of Ortronics)

Pick a centrally located but out-of-the-way location for your residential cabling cabinet; you probably don't want it on the wall in your living room. Common locations for residential wiring cabinets include the utility room, laundry room, and mechanical room in the basement. The cabinet should ideally be placed close to the termination point of the telephone service, cable-TV service, and a power source.

In addition to the cabinets, Ortronics also makes a specially designed series of modular faceplates for the In House product family. The faceplates (pictured in Figure D.3) offer a variety of modular outlets for RJ-45 connectors, coaxial video, RCA audio/video, S-video, and RJ-25C for voice.

NOTE   More hints, wiring patterns, and information about residential cabling can be found on David Barnett's Engineering Notebook for Communications Cables at `http://home1.gte.net/res025bi/index.htm` and at the Web site for his residential structured-cabling installation company at `www.pnpnetworks.com`.

FIGURE D.3:

Different configurations of Ortronics' In House modular faceplate

(Photo courtesy of Ortronics)

Thinking Forward

Maybe you have looked at the TIA/EIA-570-A Standard and are now asking why you may need to put coaxial cable and data cable in every room in the house. After all, you may only have one TV in the family room. But think about other possible services, such as Internet service via cable modem. What about networking using coax? What about delivering VCR output from your entertainment center in the family room to your computer in the study or home office?

It's time to break your old habits of thinking about wiring only being used in traditional ways. The modern idea is to put a universal wiring infrastructure in place so that you can reconfigure at will.

Builders, as a rule, don't add costs willingly, unless it will clearly allow differentiation or some additional premium to be added to the price of the home. Smart, forward-thinking builders are beginning to install higher-grade wiring, and some are installing structured cabling systems as well. However, of the 1.125 million new homes that will be built in 2001, only 20 percent of the builders plan to install structured cabling. It will be up to the consumer to take the trend into the mainstream.

Overview of IEEE 1394 and USB Networking

In 1986, Apple Computer conceived and developed a computer-to-computer and computer-to-peripheral interface system to transmit large volumes of data between devices very, very quickly. Apple turned the interface over to IEEE (the Institute of Electrical and Electronics Engineers) in 1990 to develop as a multimedia serial-bus standard. Now correctly called IEEE 1394, or just 1394, the system is also marketed under the trade names FireWire by Apple and i.LINK by Sony. All the names are often used interchangeably because the technology and functionality are identical. IEEE 1394 can be either a small network or a connecting interface for peripheral devices, or a combination of both.

USB, which stands for Universal Serial Bus, is a complementary technology to IEEE 1394. It shares a number of characteristics with 1394 but is more limited in bandwidth and distance. Its niche is the connection of peripheral devices such as mice, printers, keyboards, scanners, etc.

Both technologies are specifically designed to allow consumer electronics, such as entertainment devices (TVs, VCRs, CD players, DVD players), video cameras, digital cameras, etc., to connect and interact with computers.

NOTE

The 1394 Trade Association, found on the Web at www.1394ta.com, was formed to advance the technology behind IEEE 1394 and to promote its acceptance by the marketplace. Apple is a staunch supporter of IEEE 1394, as is Sony, Intel, Microsoft, JVC, IBM, Matsushita, Compaq, NEC, Philips, Samsung, and a host of other companies in the computer and consumer-electronics market.

USB-IF (IF stands for Implementers Forum) is an organization that supports USB and is similar to the 1394 Trade Association. A consortium of computing industry giants formed and supports this organization—Compaq, Hewlett-Packard, Intel, Lucent Technologies, Microsoft, NEC, and Philips all share positions on the board of directors of the USB-IF. USB-IF has a Web site at www.usb.org.

Both IEEE 1394 and USB interfaces are growing rapidly in popularity and deployment. According to the Cahners In-Stat Group research firm, 112 million 1394-equiped PCs and peripherals will be in use by 2004, with 33 million of those being printers and mass-storage devices. USB is growing at an even faster rate. By 2004, 750 million PCs and peripherals will incorporate USB connectivity. USB technology is already built into 99 percent of PCs, 54 percent of video cameras, and 38 percent of scanners sold, and it is well on its way to wholesale replacement of serial- and parallel-port interfaces for printers.

NOTE   The Web sites of 1394 Trade Association and USB-IF are chock-full of technical and marketing information on their respective technologies, and both were relied on heavily to research this appendix.

Although neither IEEE 1394 nor USB are networking technologies on the scale of Ethernet, they are still important in the overall scheme of networking PCs and peripherals. In addition, revisions to the IEEE specification currently being drafted will allow IEEE 1394 to compete with Ethernet over the structured wiring installations described in this book.

Among the features shared by IEEE 1394 and USB technologies are the following:

- High data throughput compared to most network technologies.

- Short distances between devices and for the network overall.

- Hot-swap technology. Devices can be plugged in and unplugged without taking down the PC or network.

- Self-configuring devices.

- Similar cable constructions.

- Robust jacks and plugs with small footprints.

- Daisy-chain or "tree" network topology. No loops are allowed.

NOTE   IEEE-1394a-2000 and USB 2.0 are documents defining the respective interfaces. They are specifications written by experts in the field, but they have not been sanctioned by ANSI as National Standards. They have become, however, de facto standards.

IEEE 1394

After Apple turned the technology over to IEEE to develop as a specification, IEEE published IEEE 1394-1995, a specification defining the technology. The original specification defined data-transfer rates of 100-, 200-, and 400Mbps. It also defined the cables, plugs, and jacks required for connecting devices. Cable-length limits were set to 4.5 meters (about 15 feet) from node to node. Network architectures, signaling protocols, and electrical requirements were all defined as well.

Since then, the specification has been revised and published as IEEE-1394a-2000, which enhances parts of the specification but does not alter the original cable, plug, and distance requirements. IEEE-1394b is being worked on and will allow throughput speeds of up to 3.2Gbps and distances of up to 100 meters using fiber-optic cables. (Specifically, 1394 will support 100 meters with glass fiber-optic cables and 50 meters with plastic fiber-optic cables.) It will also allow the interface to transmit 100Mbps over Category 5 cabling at up to 100 meters distance between nodes. This sets the stage for IEEE 1394 to compete directly with Ethernet in the commercial environment and, because of the ability to interface with consumer electronics, gives it a substantial leg up in the residential-networking market.

NOTE   The current version of the IEEE 1394 specification may be purchased from Global Engineering Documents at `http://global.ihs.com/index.cfm`.

Up to 63 network nodes (devices) can be daisy-chained on an IEEE 1394 network bus. Cable-length limitations (4.5 meters) confine such networks to relatively small areas. But each node acts as a signal repeater (booster), so you can concatenate nodes for greater distances. Besides the 4.5-meter node-to-node limit, a maximum of 16 hops (links) between nodes is allowed, so a 72-meter (236-foot) distance is the maximum between the nodes farthest apart. The future implementations of the specification for fiber-optic cables or the installed base of Category 5 will remove the length limitations (or at least expand them), and so IEEE 1394 will be a powerfully viable competitor to Ethernet.

Under the current version of the specification, the cable for 1394 is shielded twisted pair (STP). It contains two 28 AWG twisted pairs for data transmission, each enclosed in a metallic foil/braid combination shield. It also contains one unshielded, 22 AWG, twisted pair for carrying power to devices. These components make up the core of the cable. A metallic foil/braid combination shield is applied over the core. Finally, the shielded core is enclosed in a plastic jacket. Conductors must be stranded for flexibility.

NOTE   IEEE 1394 cables can be purchased with (six position) and without (four position) the power-carrying pair, depending on the device being connected. The four-position cables are usually for manufacturer-specific configurations, as the IEEE 1394 cable specifies a power pair. Check your device before buying a cable.

As discussed in Chapter 1, conductor resistance is a major factor in signal attenuation, or decay of the signal. The smaller the conductor, the greater the resistance and the more decay of the signal. The 28 AWG conductors in an IEEE 1394 cable have much greater resistance, and therefore much greater attenuation, than does a 24 AWG Category 5 UTP cable. Although all the shielding helps protect the signal from noise, the conductor size limits how far the signal can travel before a receiver can't detect it. That is the primary reason why the 4.5-meter length limitation exists for the 1394-type cables, although electronics and protocol have built-in limitations as well. Larger conductor sizes in the data pairs, such as the 24 AWG pairs in Category 5, are what will allow distances between nodes to increase in future revisions of the IEEE 1394 specification.

IEEE 1394 plugs and connectors are simple male/female designs, keyed so that they can only be plugged in the proper way. The devices have the female socket, so most cables are male-to-male, as shown in Figure E.1.

FIGURE E.1:

Male-end plugs on a six-position IEEE 1394 cable

(Photo from Milestek.com)

Most cable/plug assemblies are purchased. Although you could make your own IEEE 1394 cables and terminate the plugs on the ends, the complexity of the plug design, combined with the necessity for correctly tying in the shielding components, make this ill advised. You should buy ready-made cables, with molded-on plugs, for your 1394 connections.

IEEE 1394 transmits data in both *isochronous* and *asynchronous* modes. Isochronous data transfer is a real-time, constant delivery technique. It is perfect for delivery of multimedia from device to device; audio and video streams utilize isochronous transfer. Asynchronous transfer is typically used for data in a networking environment. Instead of a steady stream of information being delivered, data is sent in packets and acknowledged by the receiver before more is transmitted.

In its current implementation, IEEE 1394 peripheral and networking abilities make it extremely well suited for storage-device connections, multimedia, and small networks. As its popularity grows, we envision it making major inroads in the residential networking arena. What a perfect place for this technology to be implemented! Home networking, tied directly to the entertainment devices of the home using IEEE 1394 technology, will facilitate the convergence of traditional computing, the Internet, and home entertainment. It will be especially effective when the IEEE 1394b specification is ratified. Those homeowners with the foresight to install Category 5 structured wiring systems will then be positioned to take advantage of 1394 connectivity immediately—without needing room-to-room cabling installed.

USB

The USB interface can be thought of as a younger sibling of IEEE 1394. It uses similar cable and connectors and shares the ability to transfer large chunks of data in a small amount of time.

The current specification defining USB interfacing is USB 2.0. Like the IEEE 1394 specification, USB 2.0 defines the architecture, signaling protocol, electrical requirements, cable types, and connector configuration for the technology.

NOTE   USB 2.0 is available for free download at www.usb.org.

USB, as currently defined by the specification, allows data-transfer speeds of 1.5Mbps and 12Mbps, for low-speed and full-speed devices, respectively. Some high-speed implementations can transmit at 480Mbps.

USB is not a networking technology in the same sense as is IEEE 1394. Peripheral devices, such as printers, must be connected directly to a PC or to a PC through a USB hub. The PC must then connect to a traditional network such as Ethernet or even an IEEE 1394 network, for the peripheral to be a shared network device.

Up to 127 devices can be connected to a single PC using USB hubs. USB devices, from digital cameras to pocket-watch-sized hard drives, are sprouting like toadstools. USB is supported by Windows 98, 2000, and ME versions and by Macintosh OS 8.5 and higher. Its true Plug-and-Play capabilities make it a dream for PC users who are inexperienced at adding equipment to their computers.

The cable construction specified for USB is screened twisted pair (ScTP). The cable contains one 28 AWG unshielded data pair and a power-conducting pair that can range from 28 AWG to 20 AWG in size (depending on the power requirements of the device for which the cable is designed). Conductors must be stranded for flexibility. These core components are enclosed in an overall metallic foil/braid combination shield. A plastic jacket covers this outer shield. This construction is mandated for the full speed (25Mbps) and high-speed (480Mbps) implementations. For low-speed devices (1.5Mbps), the specification does not require that the data pair be twisted.

As with IEEE 1394, the 28 AWG data conductors necessitate short distances between devices if the data rates are to be maintained. For low-speed devices, a 3-meter (10-foot) cable-length limit is imposed. Full-speed and high-speed devices can be connected using a 5-meter (16-foot) cable. The specification allows up to five hubs between devices, so from PC to the farthest device, a 30-meter (98-foot) distance can be achieved. PC-to-PC connections are possible using a USB bridge.

Connectors for USB cables have *A* ends and *B* ends. The A end goes upstream to the host (PC or hub), and the B end goes downstream to the device.

WARNING   The USB-IF is adamant that only A-to-B cables be used. Some cable vendors are selling A-to-A cables in the mistaken idea that two PCs or devices can be connected together directly. Doing so will short the power supplies and/or create a shock hazard. Beware.

An ECN (Engineering Change Notice) has been published for USB 2.0; it specifies the requirements for a "mini-B" connector. The mini-B is for PDAs and other small devices where the footprint of the regular B connector is too big for the device. Figure E.2 shows various USB male and female connectors.

FIGURE E.2:

USB connector configurations

(Graphics from the USB 2.0 specification published by USB-IF, Inc.)

You should purchase ready-made cables with molded-on connectors.

USB is a virtually ubiquitous technology on all new PCs, and more devices will utilize this interface. Conceivably, USB could replace all other PC interfaces except for ultra-fast IDE or 1394 transfer for mass-storage devices. Increasingly more consumer electronics will be shipped with USB ports. In conjunction with IEEE 1394, USB technology may help drive the convergence of information and entertainment technologies.

References

IEEE 1394 Trade Association (www.1394ta.org)

USB-IF (www.usb.org)

Fire on the Wire: The IEEE 1394 High Performance Serial Bus (http://www.chumpchange.com/parkplace/Video/DVPapers/FireWire.htm)

Will USB or FireWire Connect with Consumers? (http://news.cnet.com/news/0-1003-200-3701430.html)

FireWire-1394.com (www.firewire-1394.com)

ChipCenter (www.chipcenter.com/networking/ieee1394)

Texas Instruments (www.ti.com/sc/docs/products/msp/intrface/1394/)

The Electronics Technicians Association, International (ETA) Data-Cabling Installer Certification (DCIC) Program

The Electronics Technicians Association, International (ETA) is a nonprofit professional trade association established in 1978 "by technicians, for technicians" to promote the electronics-service industry and to better benchmark the knowledge and skills of individual electronics technicians. The ETA currently has a membership of more than 3,000 individuals, primarily from the electronics-installation, maintenance, and repair occupations. It provides 20 different certifications in various electronics areas.

Data-Cabling Installer Certification Program (DCIC)

One of the ETA's top certifications is its Data-Cabling Installer Certification (DCIC). The program was designed to test the knowledge and technical skills of technicians working with fiber- and copper-cabling media.

DCIC Categories and Competencies

A list of basic competencies tested by the DCIC program follows.

1. 0: Basic Electricity

- Voltage and current in an electric circuit
- Resistance in wiring circuits
- Power and power loss
- Signal-to-noise ratio
- Inductance, inductive reactance, capacitance, and impedance in wiring circuits
- Ground and grounding
- Conductor insulation

2.0: Data-Communications Basics

- Analog and digital communication, applications, and principles

3.0: Definitions, Symbols, and Abbreviations

- Frequency
- Bandwidth
- Baud
- Decibel
- Attenuation
- Crosstalk

4.0: Cable Construction

- Basic twisted-pair cabling construction
- Basic coaxial cabling construction

5.0: Cable Performance Characteristics

- Electrical characteristics of twisted-pair cabling
- Electrical characteristics of coaxial cabling
- Performance characteristics of twisted-pair cabling
- Performance characteristics of coaxial cabling

6.0: Cabling Standards

- ANSI/TIA/EIA-568A
- ANSI/TIA/EIA-569A
- ANSI/TIA/EIA-607
- ANSI/TIA/EIA-570-A
- ISO/IEC 11801

7.0: Basic Network Topologies

- Star topology
- Bus topology
- Ring topology

8.0: Basic Network Architectures

- Ethernet
- Token ring
- ATM
- 100VG-AnyLAN

9.0: National Electric Code

- NEC Chapter 1: "General Requirements"
- NEC Chapter 2: "Wiring and Protection"
- NEC Chapter 3: "Wiring Methods and Materials"
- NEC Chapter 5: "Special Occupancy"
- NEC Chapter 7: "Special Conditions"
- NEC Chapter 8: "Communication Systems"

10.0: Cabling-System Components

- Horizontal and backbone cables
- Patch cords
- Cabling pathways
- Wiring closets

11.0: DCIC Installation Tools

- Wire strippers
- Wire cutters
- Cable crimpers
- Punch-down tools
- Fish tapes

12.0: Connectors and Outlets

- Twisted-pair connectors
- Coaxial connectors
- Fixed-design wall plates
- Modular wall plates
- Biscuit jacks

13.0: Cabling-System Design

- Cabling topologies
- Telecommunications closets
- Cabling management

14.0: Cabling Installation

- Cabling-installation process

15.0: Connector Installation

- Twisted-pair cable-connector installation
- Coaxial cable-connector installation

16.0: Cabling Testing and Certification

- Installation testing
- Cable-plant certification
- Cable testing tools

17.0: Cabling Troubleshooting

- Establishing a baseline
- Locating the problem
- Resolving specific problems

18.0: Documentation

- Documentation

ETA Contact Information

For more information about the ETA and its certification program, see the following information:

Contact People

Richard Glass, president, ETA

Teresa Maher, certification director, ETA

Address and Contact Numbers

ETA, International

502 N. Jackson Street

Greencastle, Indiana 46135

Phone: (800) 288-3824 or (765) 653-4301

Fax: (765) 653-4287

Mail and Web

eta@tds.net

www.eta-sda.com

INDEX

Note to the Reader: Throughout this index **boldfaced** page numbers indicate primary discussions of a topic. *Italicized* page numbers indicate illustrations.

NUMBERS

B

I

M

P

S

T

U

X

How do I...